INDUSTRIAL RELATIONS IN CANADA

INDUSTRIAL RELATIONS IN CANADA

FIONA A. E. MCQUARRIE
University College of the Fraser Valley

WILEY
wiley.com

Permission Acknowledgements

Statistics Canada information is used with the permission of the Minister of Industry, as Minister responsible for Statistics Canada. Information on the availability of the wide range of data from Statistics Canada can be obtained from Statistics Canada's Regional Offices, its World Wide Website at http://www.statcan.ca, and its toll-free access number, 1-800-263-1136.

Tables 4-1, 5-5, 5-6, 6-1, 6-2, 6-3, 6-4, 7-4, 9-2, 9-3, 9-4, 10-1, 10-3, 10-5, 12-1 and 12-2 are reproduced with the permission of the Minister of Public Works and Government Services Canada, 2002.

National Library of Canada Cataloguing in Publication

McQuarrie, Fiona Anne Elizabeth, 1958-
 Industrial Relations in Canada / Fiona McQuarrie.—1st ed.

Includes bibliographical references and index.
ISBN 0-470-83155-3

 1. Industrial relations—Canada. I. Title

HD8106.5.M29 2002   331'.0971   C2002-903909-6

Production Credits

Publisher: John Horne
Publishing Services Director: Karen Bryan
Editorial Manager: Karen Staudinger
Developmental Editor: Leanne Rancourt
Marketing Manager: Janine Daoust and Carolyn Wells
New Media Editor: Elsa Passera
Publishing Services/Permissions Co-ordinator: Michelle Marchetti
Interior Design & Typesetting: Interrobang Graphic Design Inc.
Cover Design: Ian Koo, Senior Graphic Designer
Photo Research: Jane Affleck
Cover Image: Harris, Lawren S, Canadian 1885–1970, Miners' Houses, Glace Bay c. 1925. Oil on canvas 107.3 x 127.0 cm, Art Gallery of Ontario, Toronto, Bequest of Charles S. Band, Toronto, 1970
Printing and Binding: Tri-Graphic Printing Limited

Printed and Bound in Canada
10 9 8 7 6 5 4 3 2 1

John Wiley and Sons Canada Ltd.
22 Worcester Road
Etobicoke, Ontario M9W 1L1

Visit our website at www.wiley.ca

ABOUT THE AUTHOR

Fiona A. E. McQuarrie is a Professor of Human Resources and Organizational Studies and Program Co-Chair in the Business Administration Department at the University College of the Fraser Valley (UCFV). She received her Ph.D. in organizational analysis from the University of Alberta, and also has a bachelor's degree in business administration and an MBA from Simon Fraser University. She has taught industrial relations at Simon Fraser University, the University of Prince Edward Island, and UCFV, and has experience in industrial relations processes in both union and management roles.

Her current research interests include an examination of the effects of organizational support for employee leisure and the role of gender equity in leisure participation and provision. Her articles on these and other topics have appeared in such journals as the *Academy of Management Executive*, *Business Horizons*, *Leisure/Loisir*, the *Journal of Management Education*, and the *Journal of Career Development*.

In addition to her academic interests, she is also a competitive figure skater and enjoys reading all types of books and listening to all kinds of music.

PREFACE

Introduction

Industrial Relations in Canada is a comprehensive introduction to the theories, issues, and processes that characterize contemporary Canadian industrial relations. In this it is significantly different from other Canadian industrial relations texts. The intent of this book is to introduce students who have generally had little or no industrial relations experience to the subject. Since only 11% of Canadians age 15–24—the age group including most college and university students—belong to a union, it is not uncommon for industrial relations classes to include students who have no prior union experience because they have never belonged to a union themselves or known anyone who has. These students' experiences with a union may therefore be limited to being inconvenienced by a strike or lockout or to hearing second-hand information (usually negative) about what unions do in a workplace.

This book is intended to introduce these students to the main features of the Canadian industrial relations system, the processes that operate within that system, and the forces that shape it. After finishing this book, students should be able to continue on to further studies in industrial relations or human resource management, and will have the information they need to function more effectively in a unionized workplace as a union member, a management representative, or a business partner.

Features of the Book and Supplemental Materials

For the Student

Industrial Relations in Canada is intended to be as reader-friendly and accessible as possible. Achieving this goal is something of a challenge when dealing with material that can be quite complex and legalistic. Thus, this book has several features intended to help students gain a complete understanding of the material more easily.

Chapter Opening Stories   Each chapter opens with a news article that illustrates one of the issues discussed in that chapter. These stories have been chosen to represent all regions in Canada and to demonstrate contemporary, real-life applications of industrial relations principles.

Chapter Objectives   A set of chapter objectives are included to indicate what students should know after completing each chapter.

Key Terms   Throughout each chapter, important terms are identified with boldface type and explained in the text. The key terms are also listed at the end of each chapter with page numbers indicating where they can be found within the text.

Chapter Summary   Each chapter concludes with a summary of the major points covered. Students can read the summary prior to reading the chapter to get a sense of what lies ahead, or can read the summary after reading the chapter to enhance their understanding of the material they have just covered.

Discussion Questions   A set of discussion questions are included at the end of each chapter that can be used for review to ensure that the student is familiar with the concepts discussed. The discussion questions also challenge students to explain the material in their own terms and present their own opinion on an issue based on their interpretation of the chapter material.

Cases and Exercises   Each chapter also includes exercises or cases that build on the concepts discussed. The exercises challenge students to learn more about industrial relations in their own area or region. The cases are adapted from actual labour relations boards cases from across Canada and put the student in the position of a labour relations board member who must assess the evidence and render a decision. The book also includes a collective bargaining simulation exercise and a grievance arbitration simulation exercise.

Glossary   A full glossary of key terms, cross-referenced by chapter, is included at the end of the text.

Website   The text website, www.wiley.com/canada/mcquarrie, contains several features designed specifically for students:

- on-line quizzes and question material for each chapter
- hyperlinks to useful websites
- news updates regarding industrial relations issues

For the Instructor

PowerPoint Slides and Lecture Notes   The instructor's manual for *Industrial Relations in Canada* includes a full set of PowerPoint slides for each chapter with accompanying lecture notes. A thumbnail picture of each slide is presented alongside summary notes for the material covered by that slide. Instructors can use the PowerPoint slides directly or print them to use as transparency masters for overhead projectors.

Teaching Notes for Cases and Exercises   The instructor's manual includes teaching notes to facilitate the use of the cases or exercises in class.

Suggested Answers to Discussion Questions   The instructor's manual also contains suggested answers to the discussion questions found at the end of each chapter.

List of Websites   Each chapter in the instructor's manual contains a list of websites related to the material in that chapter for further reference.

Test Bank   A comprehensive test bank contains questions in four formats: true-false, multiple choice, short essay, and critical thinking.

Website   The website for the text, www.wiley.com/canada/mcquarrie, also contains material for instructors using the textbook, including:

- hyperlinks to websites listed in the instructor's manual
- regular updates and information regarding industrial relations issues, including changes to industrial relations legislation and significant court and arbitration decisions

Acknowledgements

A book such as this could not be created singlehandedly. It is a pleasure to acknowledge the contributions of the many individuals whose work has helped create the final product.

Suzan Beattie, B.A., LL.B., co-wrote the original proposal for the book and co-authored the first two versions of the manuscript. The material in the book is much richer thanks to her extensive practical knowledge and experience, and the book would not be as comprehensive as it is without her input.

The reviewers who read the manuscript gave extensive, detailed, and very thoughtful comments that greatly improved the final text. The reviewers are:

Jean-Louis Castonguay, McGill University

Timothy DeGroot, McMaster University

Claude Dupuis, Athabasca University

Geoffrey England, University of Lethbridge

Edward G. Fisher, University of Alberta

Linda M. Gaudet, University of Prince Edward Island

Richard Guerin, McGill University

Larry Haiven, University of Saskatchewan

Terry Hercus, University of Manitoba

Thomas R. Knight, University of British Columbia

Maurice Mazerolle, Ryerson Polytechnic University

Joseph B. Rose, McMaster University

Basu Sharma, University of New Brunswick

A. Tarik Timur, University of Calgary

Mark Thompson, University of British Columbia

J. David Whitehead, Brock University

Dr. Robert Rogow, now sadly deceased, taught industrial relations for many years in the Faculty of Business Administration at Simon Fraser University. Both Suzan and I were students in his classes and also worked for him as teaching and research assistants.

His passionate commitment to the study, teaching, and practice of industrial relations strongly influenced us both, and his perspectives shaped the presentation of the material in this book in numerous places.

Our own students in BUS 305 at the University College of the Fraser Valley and BUEC 384 at Simon Fraser University willingly offered honest feedback on what a student-friendly industrial relations text should look like. They also served as guinea pigs for test runs of cases and exercises. We appreciate their input and their generous participation.

Another source of very useful information came from Steve McShane, formerly of Simon Fraser University and now at the University of Western Australia. Steve, a textbook author himself, was always willing to draw on his own experience for suggestions to guide us along the path of the textbook production process. We are extremely grateful for his help.

Halldor Bjarnson, LL.B., and Joseph Blessin both provided valuable research assistance during the preparation of the manuscript. The textbook and supplemental materials also benefited from the work of Jane Affleck (photo researcher), Tom Barrett (PowerPoint slides and website research), Ron Edwards (proofreader), Richard Guerin (test bank), Audrey McClellan (indexer), Christine Rae (designer), and Judith Turnbull (copy editor).

Thanks are also due to Margaret H. Knox, daughter of Lawren S. Harris, for graciously granting permission to reproduce *Miners' Houses*, *Glace Bay* on the cover of this book. In addition to being a powerful work of art, the painting represents an important time in Canadian industrial relations history, and I am honoured that the Harris estate has permitted its reproduction here.

The staff at John Wiley and Sons Canada Ltd. deserve special recognition for their commitment to every part of this project. As Acquisitions Editor, John Horne started the work on this book, and as Publisher, guided its progress through the production process and its eventual publication. Karen Staudinger, Editorial Manager, was a welcome constant presence throughout the various phases of development, and both she and John were very helpful in answering questions and providing direction, even on the most simple matters that often seemed quite challenging for novice authors. Elsa Passera, New Media Editor, designed the website and the PowerPoint slides that accompany the text and did a wonderful job with both. Janine Daoust and Carolyn Wells oversaw the marketing for the book at various phases; particular thanks to Carolyn for her thoughtful and strategic efforts, and to the Wiley Sales Representatives for getting the book "out there." Developmental Editors Karen Leishman, Hal Harder, and Leanne Rancourt all contributed to the development of the material and were extremely diligent in managing the many tasks that had to be completed at each stage. Leanne joined the project at a relatively late stage and did a very impressive job of catching up while learning a new job at the same time.

I also extend my personal thanks to a number of individuals who contributed to this project in both direct and indirect ways. My colleagues in the Department of Business Administration at the University College of the Fraser Valley have been a source of motivation and inspiration. In particular, D.J. Sandhu, Program Co-Chair, and Grace Gould, Departmental Assistant, have been very flexible and generous in helping me meet the time demands of this project. Karen Evans, Dean of Community Access, Business, and Information Technology at UCFV, has also been very accommodating. I am also grateful to the UCFV Joint Professional Development Committee for giving me educational leave to work on this project.

Thanks also to Stanley and Sylvia Ho at MailBoxes Etc. in Port Coquitlam, British Columbia, for their practical assistance in getting things to the right place at the right time.

I could not have accomplished my work on this book without the enthusiastic support of my family. Thanks to my mother, Carol; my father, Michael; and my brother, Mike.

Tom Barrett, my husband, was a constant source of encouragement throughout this entire project, and sometimes his belief made all the difference. My appreciation for his patience and love is boundless. OK, Tom, now I'll get excited!

Finally, suggestions and comments from users of this book are encouraged. Feedback from users will help improve future editions and ensure that the material remains user-friendly, contemporary, and relevant. We have done our best to produce an error-free text, but if any mistakes have slipped through, please let us know so that corrections can be made to subsequent printings.

Fiona A.E. McQuarrie
September, 2002

BRIEF TABLE OF CONTENTS

CONTENTS

Chapter 9   Strikes and Lockouts   316

Chapter 10   Third-Party Intervention During Negotiations   364

Labour union concept irrelevant?

Author says huge demand for high-tech workers puts them in the driver's seat

MONTREAL—High-tech workers are in the driver's seat today and don't need unions, says Sherry Cooper, chief economist at investment dealer Nesbitt Burns.

"There is huge demand for labour worldwide and particularly highly skilled workers—knowledge workers, as they're called," Cooper said in a recent interview. "These people aren't unionized and neither do they need to be. In fact, it's a seller's market for their skills."

But couldn't such employees become a generation of overworked "microserfs"?

"They don't need to be unionized—they have stock options," Cooper said. "Yeah,

the days are long, but that's their choice. It's not like they can't demand better working conditions—they can get 10 jobs for every one that they've got."

Cooper conceded labour unions had an important role "in the first Industrial Revolution" a century ago, as "the sweatshops of the inner cities were notoriously bad to their workers." Do they have a constructive future role? "I don't think so, frankly," she said.

(*Gazette* [Montreal], September 7, 1999, p. E2)

Solidarity and the silicon set:

Tech giants will be a test for unions

OTTAWA—The problem with unionizing high-tech assembly workers is twofold. First, they are a plentiful resource, even at a comparatively low industry average of $10 per hour for unskilled workers. Second, the term "assembler" applies to such a broad spectrum of labour—from relatively routine tasks such as monitoring machines to complex work like building and testing the printed circuit boards that run computers—that comparing and standardizing wages from one plant to another is a meaningless exercise.

In other words, assemblers with little or no background in technology and who are performing basic tasks are likely to earn little more than minimum wage—union or no union. The way to improve wages, analysts say, is to improve skills.

That argument cuts little ice with Rick Adams, though. The 28-year-old JDS Fitel assembler is blunt when explaining why he wants a union at the company. "I live paycheque to paycheque. I see figures saying that the company is making millions of dollars, and I'm still making $10 an hour. It's depressing."

In all, Adams figures he has about $100 a month left over each month after bills are paid. That, he said, leaves no money to invest in RRSPs or prepare for the future he and his fiancée are planning.

Adams said workers at other local high-tech assembly plants make $18 an hour, or close to double his $10 an hour rate. "I want wages comparable to other high-tech companies."

(*Ottawa Citizen*, July 22, 1998, p. H1)

chapter 1

AN INTRODUCTION TO INDUSTRIAL RELATIONS IN CANADA

objectives

In this chapter, we will introduce the subject of industrial relations, describe the legislative framework that Canadian industrial relations operate within, give a brief overview of various Canadian industrial relations facts, and provide an overview of the structure and content of this book. By the end of the chapter, you should be able to:

- identify the various terms used to describe union-management relationships

- describe how other academic subjects might address industrial relations issues

- identify the major pieces of legislation that regulate Canadian industrial relations and explain the common elements among these laws

- understand how other kinds of Canadian legislation affect industrial relations

- explain some of the major demographic and statistical features of Canadian union membership

INTRODUCTION

The two news stories that open this chapter illustrate some of the interactions that make industrial relations such an interesting topic of study. In the first story, an economist speculates that unions have outlived their usefulness, while in the second, a worker says that his salary is barely enough to live on and that a union would correct the problem. A number of different forces affect the situations leading to these conflicting views: internal forces, such as job classification and worker training, and external forces, such as competition and the labour market. A complex interaction of internal and external elements affects the situation of both the individual and the organization; gaining an understanding of this interaction and its effects is one of the major aims of the study of industrial relations.

The term "industrial relations" generally conjures up an image of greedy union members continually on strike for excessive salary rates. Throughout this text, we will show that industrial relations encompass much more than that. The scope of industrial relations as a topic of study includes fundamental issues of work control, the structure of work, the value of work, and the balance between the conflicting goals of workers and management. Understanding how industrial relations work is very important to anyone who participates in a workplace, whether as a worker or manager, or whether the workplace is unionized or non-unionized.

WHAT DOES THE TERM "INDUSTRIAL RELATIONS" MEAN?

The term "industrial relations" is generally used to refer to the relationship between a **union** (an organization run by and for workers) and the **employer** (the organization or organizations the workers in the union work for). The employer is also referred to as management, the company, or the organization, although "employer" is the more commonly used term, since it reflects the employer-employee relationship that is the basis of the connection between the union and the organization. As we will see in subsequent chapters, the union's primary role in the workplace is to represent the workers or employees in interactions with the employer. The union is able to carry out this role because Canadian provincial and federal law gives it the formal power to negotiate mutually acceptable workplace rules and working conditions with the employer.

Both of these employees belong to unions, though "blue collar" workers were the first ones to seek collective bargaining in the 19th century.

The term "labour relations" is sometimes used to describe the union-employer relationship. This term is derived from the definition of unions as organized labour (that is, as workers who have formally joined together to advocate for work-related issues), and legislation governing industrial relations is usually referred to as labour law or labour legislation. However, "industrial relations" is the preferred term for union-employer interactions in the Canadian context; it has been used by the Canadian federal government since 1919, when the Royal Commission to Enquire into Industrial Relations in Canada issued its report. In our opinion, "industrial relations" is a more appropriate descriptive of the union-employer relationship than "labour relations," since it emphasizes that there are two parties in the relationship and does not focus only on "labour." It also indicates that the relationship exists within the context of an industry or workplace. Hence, we have chosen to use "industrial relations" as the primary descriptive term in this book.

One part of the debate over the appropriate usage of the term "industrial relations" questions whether the term should also be used to describe workplace relationships between employers and non-unionized workers. According to one widely used definition, "industrial relations" is "a broad, interdisciplinary field of study and practice that encompasses all aspects of the employment relationship."[1] This definition clearly implies that the study of industrial relations includes both non-unionized and union-ized workplaces, and, in fact, in recent years the scope of industrial relations research has expanded to include studies of non-unionized workplaces. We would argue, how-ever, that the term "industrial relations" is more appropriate as a descriptor of union-employer relationships than of non-union-employer relations. We offer three reasons for this contention:

1. The term occurs in general usage as a reference to unionized workplaces as opposed to non-unionized workplaces.

2. The field of study of non-unionized workplaces is already clearly defined as "employ-ment relations" or "human resource management" (although the latter field of study can, and does, include overviews of the main characteristics of unionized workplaces).

3. A considerable amount of industrial relations research on non-unionized workplaces focuses on how non-unionized organizations replicate or adopt structures found in unionized workplaces; therefore, non-union industrial relations research is still closely related to the study of unionized organizations.

Throughout this book, the focus will be on union-employer relationships, although where appropriate reference will be made to how employer-worker relationships are conducted in non-unionized workplaces.

Before proceeding, we should take a moment to examine how industrial relations differs from human resource management. This is an important issue because many post-secondary institutions do not have courses devoted solely to the study of industri-al relations, and instead address the subject only in the context of human resource man-agement courses or courses dealing with employment relationships. The simplest way to explain the difference between the terms "human resource management" and "indus-trial relations" is to say that the former has a broader range and is generally applied to employment-related issues of importance to all organizations. One Canadian human resource management textbook defines human resource management as "the activities, policies, and practices involved in obtaining, developing, utilizing, evaluating, main-taining, and retaining the appropriate number and skill mix of employees to accomplish the organization's objectives."[2] This definition is applicable to both unionized and non-unionized workplaces, since these human resource management functions occur in any organization that has employees, whether those employees are unionized or not. This definition could even be applied to organizations whose "workers" may not be in an employment relationship with the organization (e.g., volunteers donating their time or labour to not-for-profit organizations).

Thus, the distinction between human resource management and industrial relations can be summed up as follows: "industrial relations," as we have defined the term, deals primarily with employee-employer relationships in unionized organizations, while "human resource management" deals with employer-employee or organization-worker relationships in all types of organizations. The two fields certainly have issues in common, but the focus of industrial relations is more specific and less generalized than that of human resource management.

INDUSTRIAL RELATIONS AS AN ACADEMIC SUBJECT

In most academic settings, as elsewhere, "industrial relations" is the term used to refer to the study of union-employer relationships. As an academic subject, industrial relations draws on a number of different academic fields;[3] this is because many of the topics of interest to current industrial relations researchers have been addressed in the context of other disciplines of study. Union-management relationships and, more broadly, conflict between workers and employers are not new topics of interest. A quick examination of any database of academic publications will show that industrial relations topics were and are addressed in many other academic fields. Here are some examples of how researchers in other academic areas could address industrial relations issues:

- A historian might be interested in the events that led to the formation of a union or to a particular industrial relations conflict.

- A psychologist might be interested in how individual attitudes toward unions or employers develop or change.

- An economist might be interested in how negotiated wage rates in a unionized organization affect wage rates in non-unionized organizations or the cost of living in a particular geographic area.

- A political scientist might be interested in how or why a governing political party changes labour legislation.

- A lawyer might be interested in how the language and conditions in labour legislation affect unions' ability to represent their membership effectively.

- A sociologist might be interested in how group or cultural dynamics affect the actions of a union or an employer.

It is clear from reviewing this list of the approaches of different academic disciplines to union-employer issues that the field of industrial relations draws its ideas and theories from a broad spectrum of subjects. While industrial relations courses at colleges and universities are most commonly found in economics or business administration departments, this list demonstrates why they might also be found in several other academic areas.

It can be frustrating for new students of industrial relations to find that there is no single unifying theory or perspective underlying their field of study. How do we know what is "right" when various disciplines offer multiple and sometimes conflicting theories to explain a single event? However, as is true in many other areas of study, it is unrealistic to expect to find one industrial relations theory that explains everything. Union-employer relationships involve complex human interactions, and these occur within many different types of work, work structures, and workplaces.[4] Therefore, no single theory or solution could explain every possible situation. A more realistic approach is to recognize the rich contributions that different perspectives make toward an understanding of the union-employer relationship, and to appreciate how these contributions create a broader, rather than narrower, understanding of that relationship.

WHY STUDY INDUSTRIAL RELATIONS?

As we have mentioned, many post-secondary institutions in Canada do not offer courses devoted specifically to industrial relations, but instead address industrial relations only as a secondary topic in another course, such as one on human resource management. Students enrolled in industrial relations courses or in broader courses that touch on the subject often argue that the study of industrial relations is irrelevant. This argument can take a number of different forms:

- "Unions have achieved everything they set out to do because workers are now treated fairly, so there is no reason for unions to exist any more and no reason to study them."

- "Only part of the workforce in Canada is unionized, so it is quite possible to go through an entire career working in non-unionized firms; there's no point to learning about unions if I'm never going to have to join one."

- "I personally don't believe in unions and would never vote to join one, so I'm not interested in learning about them because I'm never going to be a union member."

Many instructors of industrial relations have encountered these arguments from students of all ages and backgrounds. We acknowledge that there is a great deal of validity to each of these arguments. As we show in Chapter 2, unions emerged in response to working conditions that are almost unknown today, at least in most industrialized First World countries. In several chapters, we address the fact that only about 30 percent of the Canadian workforce is unionized, and much of that unionization is concentrated in a few sectors of the labour market. And we certainly would not argue against an individual's right to hold the beliefs or attitudes he or she personally considers meaningful. However, let us present our arguments in favour of industrial relations as a relevant topic worthy of in-depth study.

First, in many unionized workplaces or occupations, union membership is a prerequisite to employment. Therefore, attaining a desired job or career may require joining a union, regardless of one's own feelings about unions. If one has to belong to an organization, surely it is better to be informed about the organization's purpose and operations than to run the risk of making mistakes out of ignorance or misunderstanding.

Second, even if only part of the Canadian workforce is unionized, people who are not union members sometimes have to interact with a unionized organization or with unionized workers. For example, on the day these paragraphs are being written, federal public sector workers in several provinces are engaging in a "workless Wednesday" and are picketing airports to make their case for higher wages in a new collective agreement. Not everyone passing through those airports is a union member, but most of the travellers are being affected by the union's actions. Because of the likelihood of this sort of interaction occurring, it is important to have some understanding of unions and the activities unions might undertake, even if one is never personally involved in a union.

Third, in every jurisdiction in Canada, legislation makes unionization an option for workers who are dissatisfied with their treatment and want to have their concerns formally addressed by the employer. While the horrific working conditions described in Chapter 2 that motivated the formation of the first unions are relatively uncommon in modern Canada, not every workplace in Canada is a model of perfect employer-employee relationships. It is important to know about unions because Canadian law makes unionization an option for nearly every kind of worker and because unions have the potential to influence employee satisfaction and working conditions.

Fourth, learning about the history of unionization in Canada helps one understand how the modern Canadian workplace, both unionized and non-unionized, has reached its current form. The influence of unions is apparent in the passage of legislation that affects every Canadian worker and workplace. Minimum wage legislation and occupational health and safety regulations are two obvious examples.

Fifth, for people considering human resource management as a career, a working knowledge of industrial relations is a definite asset. Aspiring human resource managers who are familiar with industrial relations issues are much more employable than those who are only experienced in non-unionized workplaces. In many organizations, human resource functions are no longer the sole responsibility of the human resource management department. Managers of all kinds and at all organizational levels may be expected to participate in human resource management activities such as maintaining discipline, determining wage levels, appraising performance, and interviewing job candidates.[5] Anyone considering managerial work of any sort should be familiar with how these and other human resource management activities are conducted in both unionized and non-unionized firms.

Finally, an individual may be so opposed to unions that he or she wishes to actively resist their presence, either as an unwilling potential union member or as a manager or employer. Opposing a union is much easier if one has some knowledge about what a union is, what legal requirements underlie a union's existence, and what an employer or employee can or cannot legally do to counteract unionization.

By writing this textbook, we are not attempting to change the attitudes of individuals who are fundamentally opposed to unions. We also do not intend to try to convince people to join or support unions. And we do not want to present unions as perfect organizations that act appropriately in every situation. A union, like any organization, is the product of the individuals who belong to it, and individuals in unions, as in any organization, can make poor decisions or act unfairly. Unions are no more perfect and no less flawed than other organizations. They do, however, influence the lives of most Canadians, directly or indirectly, and Canadian legislation enshrines the right of unions to exist and the right of employees to join unions if they so desire. Thus, we believe it is important to learn about union-employer relationships in order to be a better-informed worker or manager and, more generally, a better-informed member of Canadian society.

INDUSTRIAL RELATIONS LEGISLATION IN CANADA

To begin our introduction to the topic of industrial relations in Canada, we will review the legal framework that regulates the union-employer relationship. We will introduce the legal framework first in order to give students a general understanding of what laws in Canada affect industrial relations and to provide some context for our subsequent discussions of the activities that these laws regulate. At this point, we will provide a general overview of the relevant legislation; the detailed provisions of many of these pieces of legislation will be discussed in subsequent chapters in relation to particular topics.

The Question of Jurisdiction

In Canada, legislation relating to labour relations is found in every province and territory as well as at the federal level. The conflict over the division of **jurisdiction**, or legal responsibility for an issue, between federal and provincial legislatures has been ongoing throughout Canadian history. The question of jurisdiction over industrial relations arises because of the question of whether a union-employer relationship should be governed by federal or provincial labour relations legislation.

As Chapter 3 describes, up until the mid-1920s, all Canadian industrial relations issues fell under federal labour relations legislation and industrial relations was considered to be solely within the federal jurisdiction. This concentration of labour legislation in the federal jurisdiction reflected the strong federal focus of other Canadian legislation at the time. The concentration of Canadian legislative power at the federal level was a deliberate choice of the authors of the 1867 *British North America Act* (the act that established the first federal Canadian government); they had seen how the United States' system of decentralized "states' rights" had contributed to the American Civil War.[6] However, the outcome of a 1925 legal case, *Snider v. Toronto Electrical Commission*, established that jurisdiction over industrial relations in Canada was mostly, but not completely, a provincial responsibility. As a result of this ruling, each province eventually developed its own labour relations legislation; however, there is still also a federal labour relations act to govern employer-union relationships that are deemed to be under federal jurisdiction.

CN is an interprovincial company, and its union-employer relationships are federally regulated.

How, then, do we know whether a union-employer relationship is regulated by federal or provincial law? The answer is quite simple. If an employer's business has an **interprovincial component**—that is, if the employer's activities regularly cross provincial boundaries—then the union-employer relationship is federally regulated. This means that industries such as banking, telecommunications, broadcasting, and interprovincial transport, which all involve business transactions across provincial boundaries, are governed by federal labour relations legislation. Federal labour relations legislation also applies to employees of the federal government and some Crown corporations. If an employer's activities take place within the boundaries of a single province or territory, the union-employer relationship is governed by the labour relations legislation of that province or territory. In practice, this means that approximately 90 percent of union-employer relationships in Canada are under provincial jurisdiction and approximately 10 percent are federally regulated.

In both federal and provincial jurisdictions, there are a number of pieces of legislation that affect industrial relations. The most obvious are the labour relations laws, but other laws also affect the union-employer relationship. We will outline each of these types of legislation in turn.

Labour Relations Laws

Table 1-1 lists the names of the major provincial and federal labour relations acts. These are the primary pieces of legislation that govern industrial relations in each Canadian jurisdiction. Although, as we will see, there are variations in the terms and conditions of the acts, common characteristics can be found in all of them.[7] Every one of these pieces of legislation includes the following:

- The establishment of procedures to legally recognize the union as the workplace representative for the employees. This procedure is called "certification" and is discussed in detail in Chapter 5.

- A requirement that collective agreements between the union and the employer have a minimum term. In most Canadian jurisdictions, this term is one year.

- The establishment of procedures that must be followed for a legal strike or lockout to take place. Most jurisdictions also have some regulations governing activity that might take place during a strike or lockout, such as picketing or the use of replacement workers. These procedures are discussed in detail in Chapter 9.

- The establishment of procedures that must be followed to resolve disputes while the collective agreement is in effect. These procedures are usually referred to as grievance-resolution procedures. Some jurisdictions simply require that collective agreements contain a grievance-resolution procedure, while others detail the terms that must be contained in these procedures. These procedures are discussed in detail in Chapter 11.

- The definition of legal behaviour by union and management in situations such as a campaign for certification. Usually, these definitions take the form of identifying so-called unfair labour practices. These practices are discussed in more detail in Chapter 6.

- The establishment of a **labour relations board** to administer and enforce labour relations legislation. The specific name of the board varies by jurisdiction (in Quebec, it is called the Labour Court), but its purpose is similar in all jurisdictions. It resolves disputes relating to the application of the legislation and also provides specific services, such as assistance in resolving grievances. The labour relations board has a **quasi-judicial** status; like a civil or criminal court, it rules on cases brought before it and issues interpretations of the law. In addition, as with a civil or criminal court, the government funds the costs of running a labour relations board, but the board's operations are independent of government influence or control. However, a labour relations board does not have the same legal status as a civil or criminal court, since it has the option of suggesting remedies as well as imposing solutions. It also has slightly broader guidelines than civil or criminal courts regarding what evidence can be submitted when a case is heard.

In most jurisdictions, the labour relations board is composed of an equal number of union and employer representatives. These appointed representatives are then selected to sit on panels to adjudicate specific cases. One exception is Quebec, where the members of the Labour Court are judges of the Court of Quebec who have been appointed to serve on the Labour Court. Usually, a panel consists of one union representative, one employer representative, and a third party chosen by the first two parties, although in most jurisdictions a panel can also consist of a single member. Most labour relations boards have a chair and a number of vice-chairs who are appointed by the government, as well as staff members who assist the board members in their work and provide other services to unions, employers, and the public.

TABLE 1-1 Labour Relations Laws in Canadian Jurisdictions[i]

Jurisdiction	Name of Primary Labour Relations Law
Federal	Canada Labour Code
Alberta	Labour Relations Code
British Columbia	Labour Relations Code
Manitoba	Labour Relations Act
Ontario	Labour Relations Act
Newfoundland	Labour Relations Act
New Brunswick	Industrial Relations Act
Nova Scotia	Trade Union Act
Prince Edward Island	Labour Act
Quebec	Labour Code/Code du travail
Saskatchewan	Trade Union Act

[i] The Northwest Territories does not have a specific law dealing with industrial relations; union-employer relationships are governed under the Fair Practices Act. The Yukon and Nunavut do not have a specific private sector industrial relations law.

Public Sector Labour Relations Legislation

Most Canadian jurisdictions have separate labour relations acts to govern **public sector** employees—employees of the government itself or of organizations affiliated with the government, such as Crown corporations. Some jurisdictions also have separate labour legislation for **para-public** or **quasi-public sector** employees—employees who work for organizations funded by the government but who are not directly employed by the government. Examples of para-public sector employees are court workers, health-care workers, and employees of colleges, technical institutes, and universities.

There are several reasons for having separate labour legislation for these types of employees. One is that the government and its employees have a unique employment relationship. The government is the employer, but it is also the body that sets the rules under which all employees and employers operate. Separate public sector labour legislation is intended to recognize that the government holds considerably more power than an ordinary employer, and thus public sector labour legislation may contain terms and conditions designed to recognize this larger-than-usual power imbalance between employer and employee. Another reason for separate public sector labour legislation is that public and para-public sector employees often provide services that are needed for communities and provinces to function effectively, such as fire protection, social services, and health care. Public sector labour legislation recognizes this reality by stipulating different conditions under which public sector employees may strike or otherwise withdraw their services, or by implementing dispute-resolution procedures that minimize or avoid any service disruption.

In some Canadian jurisdictions, disputes over the interpretation or application of public sector labour relations legislation are taken to the labour relations board that administers other labour legislation. In other Canadian jurisdictions, the public sector labour relations legislation provides for the establishment of a public sector labour relations board. While this board is similar in structure and function to the "regular" labour relations board, its mandate is limited to the administration and enforcement of public sector labour laws.

Occupation-Specific Labour Relations Legislation

Some Canadian jurisdictions have additional labour relations legislation that applies only to particular occupations or industries. This type of legislation usually exists to address specific conditions in an occupation or industry that would not be adequately covered under the regular labour relations legislation. Examples of public sector, para-public sector, and occupation-specific labour relations legislation in Canada can be found in Table 1-2.

The legislation that will be discussed next is not usually identified as labour relations legislation, but it is included in this section because its contents can directly or indirectly affect workplace conditions or the relationship between unions and employers.

TABLE 1-2	Examples of Public Sector, Para-Public Sector, and Occupation–Specific Labour Relations Laws in Canadian Jurisdictions[i]
Jurisdiction	**Names of Laws**
Federal	Public Sector Staff Relations Act
Alberta	Public Service Employee Relations Act, Police Officers Collective Bargaining Act
British Columbia	Public Sector Labour Relations Act, Fire and Police Services Collective Bargaining Act
Manitoba	Civil Service Act
Ontario	Public Sector Act, Hospital Labour Disputes Arbitration Act, Colleges Collective Bargaining Act
Newfoundland	Public Service Collective Bargaining Act, Fishing Industry Collective Bargaining Act, Teachers' Collective Bargaining Act
New Brunswick	Public Service Labour Relations Act
Nova Scotia	Public Service Act, Teachers' Collective Bargaining Act
Prince Edward Island	Civil Service Act, Health and Community Services Act
Quebec	Public Service Act/Loi de la fonction publique, An act respecting the process of negotiation of the collective agreements in the public and para-public sectors
Saskatchewan	Public Service Act, Construction Industry Labour Relations Act
Yukon	Public Service Staff Relations Act

[i] The Northwest Territories does not have a specific law dealing with industrial relations; union-employer relationships are governed under the Fair Practices Act. Nunavut does not have a specific public sector industrial relations law.

Employment Standards Legislation

In every Canadian jurisdiction, there is an employment standards act or code that establishes minimum standards for working conditions in all workplaces. Employment standards legislation usually covers such matters as working hours, minimum wage rates, holiday time, and the minimum time needed for notice of termination or layoff.

Employment standards legislation applies to all workplaces, whether unionized or non-unionized. Its terms and conditions are important to unions and management because their mutually negotiated collective agreements must not contain terms that are inferior to those outlined in employment standards legislation. It would, for example, usually be illegal for a collective agreement to outline wage rates that are less than those in the relevant employment standards law, even if the union and management had agreed to those terms.

Human Rights Legislation

Every Canadian jurisdiction has some form of human rights legislation that forbids discrimination against individuals on the basis of personal attributes such as gender, ethnic origin, or sexual orientation. Discrimination in the context of these laws is defined as the refusal to grant someone access to accommodation, contracts, goods and services, or employment opportunity because they possess one of the identified personal attributes (called **protected grounds** in the legislation).[8] It would be illegal, for example, for a landlord to refuse to rent an apartment to anyone who is black or for an employer to deny a woman a job promotion because the employer believes that all women eventually quit work to take care of their children. However, if there is an important part of the job that requires the exclusion of members of a particular group, refusing to hire members of that group would not be considered discrimination. For example, it might be inappropriate to hire male prison guards for a women's prison, since body searches of the prisoners are among the guards' duties. Thus, it would likely be considered acceptable for a job advertisement or hiring committee to recruit only female candidates for prison guard jobs in women's prisons.

It is important to note that Canadian human rights legislation identifies two kinds of discrimination. One is **intentional discrimination**; this type of discrimination involves direct and deliberate refusal based on the prohibited grounds. The other is **systemic discrimination** (also called unintentional or constructive discrimination); this form of discrimination occurs when an organization or individual uses policies or practices that have the effect of discriminating against groups of individuals. Systemic discrimination can be identified even if the individual or organization, when adopting the policy or practices, did not intend to discriminate. An example of systemic discrimination would be a policy that required applicants for a job to be a certain height. If it were not essential for the individual to be a certain height to perform the job successfully, such a requirement would be systemic discrimination because it would exclude many women and also individuals from ethnic groups whose average heights are shorter than the Canadian norm.

Human rights legislation has two major implications for unions and employers. The first is that collective agreements must not contain any terms that intentionally or systematically discriminate (unless, as noted above, certain restrictions are imposed because of legitimate job requirements). The second is that unions and employers, as organizations in and of themselves, must not act in a discriminatory fashion. A union, for example, could not refuse to support an employee in a complaint against the employer simply because the employee was of Asian origin.

If an individual feels that he or she has been discriminated against on the basis of one or more of the protected grounds, he or she can file a complaint with the relevant human rights commission. A human rights commission is similar to a labour relations board in structure and function; however, its mandate is to administer and enforce only human rights legislation. The human rights commission will investigate the complaint and suggest or impose a remedy if the complaint is substantiated. In addition, employees who feel their union has discriminated against them can file a complaint with a labour relations board, alleging that the union has breached its "duty of fair representation." The concept of duty of fair representation is discussed in more detail in Chapter 11.

The Charter of Rights and Freedoms

The *Charter of Rights and Freedoms* is contained in the federal *Constitution Act*, which became law in 1982. It guarantees certain basic rights and freedoms to all Canadians and is considered to take precedence over all other laws, with two exceptions. The first are laws that "can be demonstrably justified as reasonable limits in a 'free and democratic society.'"[9] An example of the use of these limits is when the Supreme Court of Canada decided to uphold mandatory retirement laws in several provinces. The reasoning behind the Court's decision was that while mandatory retirement was clearly discrimination on the basis of age (individuals were forced to retire when they reached a certain age, regardless of whether they were still capable of performing their job satisfactorily or not), the objectives of mandatory retirement were "of sufficient significance" to justify such discrimination.[10] The second kind of laws that can override the superior status of the Charter are those that provincial legislatures pass by invoking the so-called "notwithstanding" provision. This provision prevents the challenge of a law passed by a provincial legislature if the basis for the challenge is the law's perceived infringement of Charter rights. The purpose of this provision is to permit individual provinces some flexibility in applying the Charter to conditions in their particular jurisdiction.

Queen Elizabeth signs the *Constitution Act*, the document that officially severed Canada's last ties to Britain and contains the *Charter of Rights and Freedoms*, Ottawa, April 17, 1982.

The *Charter of Rights and Freedoms* defines a number of fundamental rights. Because these rights are broadly defined, without much specific guidance on their practical application, numerous court cases have tested the applicability of these rights in certain situations. To date, these are the rights that have been the subject of major cases involving industrial relations issues:

• freedom of association

• freedom of peaceful assembly

• freedom of thought, belief, opinion, and expression

Three particular "Charter cases" involving these issues have important implications for industrial relations, and each will be briefly described here.[11] In the first, the 1982 *Dolphin Delivery* case,[12] employees involved in a dispute with their employer wanted to set up a picket line at a company that did business with the employer but was not directly involved in the dispute. The company successfully applied for a court injunction to stop the picket line, and the union appealed the injunction on the grounds that the inability to picket restricted the union members' freedoms of expression, association, and assembly. The Supreme Court of Canada ruled in this case that a court order like an injunction could not be considered "the type of government action that would attract the application of the Charter."[13] In other words, the Charter provisions were not considered applicable to court orders resolving common-law-based disputes between private parties.

The second set of cases occurred in 1987 and is referred to as the "labour trilogy."[14] A decision in a subsequent case in 1990 reinforced the general direction of the judgements in the previous cases.[15] The basic question in each of these cases was whether the Charter provisions outlining the rights to freedom of association also protected the right to bargain collectively and strike. The Supreme Court of Canada ruled in these cases that the rights to establish, belong to, and maintain an association, along with the right to participate in the association's lawful activities, were protected under the Charter. However, the rights to strike and to participate in collective bargaining were, in the court's view, rights created by law and not fundamental freedoms protected by the Charter.

The third Charter case is the 1991 *Lavigne* case.[16] A college instructor claimed that the mandatory union dues he had to pay as part of his employment contract violated his freedom of association. His complaint was not primarily about the mandatory dues payment, but about his union spending part of his dues to support organizations that he personally objected to and would not voluntarily donate money to. The question in this case, then, was whether freedom of association also implied the freedom not to associate. The Supreme Court of Canada narrowly ruled that mandatory dues payment did not violate the provisions of the Charter, since all individuals in the workplace benefited from the union's representation of their interests and that unions had the right to spend dues in support of political and social causes. The reasoning behind this decision was that distribution of funding raised through dues payment would be determined by the wishes of the membership, and that each member of the union had the opportunity to influence the distribution of those funds through voting or other participation in union activities.

A further case, only recently resolved, may also have important implications for workers' ability to unionize in Canada. In many Canadian jurisdictions, specific groups of workers are not permitted to unionize for a variety of reasons. In Ontario in 1995, the provincial government repealed a law that permitted agricultural workers to unionize. The government excluded farmworkers from the jurisdiction of labour law by arguing that unionization of these workers would cause excessive labour costs for small family farms, many of which were already in financial difficulty. This decision was appealed in a series of court cases, and the issue eventually reached the Supreme Court of Canada in the case of *Dunmore v. Ontario (Attorney-General)*.[17] The Supreme Court ruled that the right to freedom of association was violated if an entire class of workers was excluded from protection under labour legislation. Steven Barrett, a lawyer who represented labour organizations in the case, predicted that this ruling would encourage other groups currently excluded from collective bargaining (such as domestic workers, professionals, and some classifications of public servants) to undertake similar challenges to the laws excluding them from participating in this activity.[18]

Though union membership has traditionally been higher among men than women, many women are joining non-traditional trades and becoming involved in unions.

The rulings in these cases give some idea of how the general principles expressed in the Charter may have practical applications in the workplace. However, it is still difficult to specify the implications of the Charter provisions for union-employer relationships at the workplace level, since many issues remain untested by court challenges. The identified fundamental freedoms have the potential for very broad application, but the extent of many practical applications of those freedoms will not be clarified until cases involving particular situations are addressed by the Supreme Court of Canada. In the meantime, unions and employers should be aware of the Charter's provisions and keep in mind the applications that the Supreme Court has outlined to date.

THE UNIONIZED WORKPLACE IN CANADA

To conclude our introductory overview of Canadian industrial relations, we will provide in Tables 1-3, 1-4, and 1-5 some statistics that outline the characteristics of the unionized workplace in Canada. From these statistics, we can observe a number of distinctive characteristics of unionized workplaces in Canada. Unionized workplaces are more likely to be in the public sector and to be relatively large in size. The rates of unionization are quite similar across broad industrial categories, but there are wide variations in unionization rates across different occupations. Certain demographic characteristics also distinguish Canadian union members. Union membership is slightly higher among men than among women and higher among older workers than among younger workers. Union members are relatively well educated, and they usually hold full-time rather than part-time jobs.

TABLE 1-3   Unionization Rates by Province, 2000

Province	Number of Unionized Workers	Number of Unionized Workers as Percentage of Total Provincial Workforce[i]
Alberta	270,080	21.3
British Columbia	544,600	35.0
Manitoba	156,408	34.3
New Brunswick	78,680	28.0
Newfoundland	66,640	39.2
Nova Scotia	101,952	28.8
Ontario	1,329,237	27.3
Prince Edward Island	14,382	28.2
Quebec	1,037,875	36.1
Saskatchewan	120,085	35.0

Source: Labour Force Survey data, quoted in "Unionization: an update," *Perspectives on Labour and Income* (Statistics Canada catalogue number 75-001-XPE), Autumn 2000.

[i] This figure does not include workers who are not union members but who are covered by the terms of a collective agreement (the "coverage-only" group of workers as defined by Statistics Canada). There were 287,000 of these workers in Canada in 1999.

TABLE 1-4 Demographic Indicators of Union Membership in Canada, 2000

Gender	Total Number of Union Members	Union Membership as a Percentage of Total National Workforce in This Category*
Male	1,970,185	31.1
Female	1,752,320	29.6

Work Status	Total Number of Union Members	Union Membership as a Percentage of Total National Workforce in This Category*
Full time	3,228,694	32.2
Part time	490,160	22.0

Age	Total Number of Union Members	Union Membership as a Percentage of Total National Workforce in This Category*
15 to 24	260,064	12.6
25 to 44	2,001,026	34.0
45 to 54	1,113,545	42.1
55 and over	348,492	33.9

TABLE 1-4 Continued

Education	Total Number of Union Members	Union Membership as a Percentage of Total National Workforce in This Category*
Less than Grade 9	124,527	30.9
Some high school	384,877	24.1
High school graduation	742,788	28.2
Some post-secondary education	284,885	22.7
Post-secondary certificate or diploma	1,361,360	36.3
University degree	819,614	37.9

Source: Labour Force Survey data, quoted in "Unionization: an update," *Perspectives on Labour and Income* (Statistics Canada catalogue number 75-001-XPE), Autumn 2000.

* These percentages do not include workers who are not union members but who are covered by the terms of a collective agreement (the "coverage-only" group as defined by Statistics Canada). In 1999 there were 287,000 Canadian workers in this group.

TABLE 1-5 Sectoral, Industrial, Occupational, and Workplace Union Membership in Canada, 2000

Sector	Number of Union Members	Union Membership as a Percentage of Total National Workforce in This Category*
Public	1,939,056	69.9
Private	1,775,752	18.7

Industry	Number of Union Members	Union Membership as a Percentage of Total National Workforce in This Category*
Goods producing	994,560	32.0
Service producing	2,725,806	29.8

Occupation	Number of Union Members	Union Membership as a Percentage of Total National Workforce in This Category*
Management	85,904	9.1
Business, finance, and administrative	595,122	25.4
Natural and applied sciences	196,826	23.8
Health	411,203	61.1
Social and public service	566,712	61.2
Culture and recreation	67,080	26.0
Sales and service	664,263	20.7
Trades, transport, and equipment	644,352	38.4
Unique to primary industries	35,485	15.1
Unique to production industries	453,180	39.0

Workplace Size	Number of Union Members	Union Membership as a Percentage of Total National Workforce in This Category*
Under 20 employees	505,176	12.4
20 to 99 employees	1,229,984	30.4
100 to 500 employees	1,171,587	44.7
Over 500 employees	815,507	53.9

Source: Labour Force Survey data, quoted in "Unionization: an update," *Perspectives on Labour and Income* (Statistics Canada catalogue number 75-001-XPE), Autumn 2000.

* This percentage does not include workers who are not union members but who are covered by a collective agreement (the "coverage-only" group as defined by Statistics Canada). In 1999 there were 287,000 workers in this group.

We will revisit these statistics throughout the book and discuss in more depth some of the reasons behind the characteristics of Canadian unionization. In Chapter 13, we will assess what these statistics indicate for future workplace trends in Canada.

AN OVERVIEW OF THE BOOK

After surveying the legislation that forms the framework for Canadian industrial relations and outlining some of the statistics that describe unionization in Canada, we now turn to a description of the framework of this book. We have ordered the material to replicate as closely as possible the process that a union and employer would go through in starting a relationship, carrying out their mandated duties and roles once the relationship is established, and altering that relationship in response to internal or external forces.

In this first chapter, we have introduced some theoretical and historical background to explain how modern Canadian workplaces and legislation have evolved into their present form. In Chapter 2, we explain the reasons for the creation of unions and how unions' purposes have changed over time. The emergence of craft guilds, the significant shifts in work and production that occurred with the Industrial Revolution, and the development of the first modern trade unions are described. We then examine the origins of the modern trade union, the functions of unions, and the future challenges unions may face.

In Chapter 3, we focus on the events and forces that have created the unique circumstances of Canadian labour relations. We begin with an overview of some of the characteristics of Canada that have affected the history of unions. We then discuss the early years of the Canadian union movement in the 1800s, the industrial age in the early 1900s, and the advent of the First World War. We describe the forces that led to increased unionization before and during the Second World War and the start of modern-day federal and provincial labour legislation. We outline the growth of unionization in the public sector, the effects of unemployment and inflation in the 1970s, and more recent events such as the passage of free trade legislation.

In Chapter 4, we describe the structure of Canadian unions, which roughly parallels the three levels of government in Canada. At the federal level, the Canadian Labour Congress (CLC) and several other bodies represent organized labour nationally. In each of the provinces and territories, the federations of labour are the coordinating bodies for the labour movement. At the municipal level, the labour movement operates through labour councils. Finally, the local union is the base level for the regional, national, or international unions. We describe the structure of local unions and the activities that they engage in.

After examining the structure of unions, we turn in Chapter 5 to a discussion of why employees may (or may not) wish to join a union. After looking at the personal, workplace, economic, and societal factors that explain why employees do (or do not) support a union, we consider the dynamics of an organizing campaign itself. To succeed, an organizing campaign requires the support of a specific number of employees. We explore the definitions of "employee," "trade union," and "employer," and describe the criteria that are used to determine the bargaining unit that the union wishes to represent. The outcome of a successful organizing campaign is the establishment of the union's status as the employee's exclusive bargaining agent.

In Chapter 6, we explain how a labour relations board assesses a certification application. This explanation includes a description of a representation vote and the circumstances under which a labour relations board may hold a hearing into a certification application. We also explore special circumstances of certification, such as a certification application for a previously unionized workplace and a certification application for a workplace whose parties to the original certification have changed. As a final consideration in the certification process, we discuss various "bars" to certification—these determine when and under what circumstances an application for certification may be filed. We then outline unfair labour practices and the legislative provisions used to balance the rights of the various parties involved in the certification process. We end this chapter with a description of the remedies for unfair labour practices.

Once a certification order is issued, the union and the employer are compelled to commence collective bargaining. In Chapter 7, we discuss the effects of a certification order. As well as directing the parties to start bargaining, the certification order also implements provisions requiring all union members to pay union dues, provisions for union dues check-off, and an exemption from paying union dues on religious grounds. We also examine the concept of a "union shop." We then discuss the actual structure of collective bargaining. The simplest bargaining structure is a single union negotiating with a single employer at a single location. We also review more complex structures, including structures in which groups of unions or groups of employers bargain as a single unit. Next, we discuss the individuals who participate in collective bargaining on behalf of the union and of the employer. We conclude by outlining what the parties can bargain for and what is implied by the expectation of bargaining in good faith.

In Chapter 8, we outline the stages in union-management negotiations, subprocesses, strategies, and tactics in collective bargaining. We discuss the four stages that can be observed in the bargaining process and identify the subprocesses within each stage that influence the parties' behaviour. We also outline the strategies and tactics used in each subprocess and discuss the factors that affect how much power each side might hold or be perceived to hold at any time. Finally, we explore two alternative models of union-management negotiations.

If the parties are unable to reach a collective agreement or if collective bargaining breaks down, a strike or lockout may occur. In Chapter 9, we define strikes and lockouts and describe their use as part of the collective bargaining process. We also review some of the factors and motivators that would lead unions or employers to consider striking or locking out.

Canadian labour legislation specifies several conditions that must exist before a strike or lockout can be considered legal, and we examine these preconditions in this chapter. If a strike or lockout occurs, two major factors will affect how it will proceed: picketing and the use of replacement workers. We explore the major functions of picketing and whether the employer should be permitted to use or hire replacement workers. Finally, we examine the ways a lockout or strike can end and, if a collective agreement results, the ratification process. We conclude Chapter 9 with a comparison of Canada's strike record to that of other industrialized countries.

In Chapter 10, we examine the use of third-party intervention in collective bargaining. These interventions can help the parties to resolve their differences without having to resort to a strike or lockout. The main types of third-party intervention are conciliation, mediation, and arbitration. To conclude Chapter 10, we discuss the advantages and disadvantages of using mediation/arbitration as a form of third-party dispute resolution, differences between disputes in the private sector and public sector, and other methods of resolving bargaining disputes.

Once a collective agreement is achieved, Canadian labour legislation provides for a method of settling disputes between the employer and the union during the term of a collective agreement. In Chapter 11, we discuss the grievance arbitration process. The term "grievance" is defined and the various types of grievances are explained. We describe the steps in the grievance procedure as well as procedural issues such as timelines, and we also provide an explanation of who is involved at the various steps in the procedure. A union's duty of fair representation is defined and explained.

The remainder of Chapter 11 focuses on the arbitration process. We begin by discussing the appointment of an arbitrator and how an arbitration hearing is arranged. We then discuss the arbitration procedure itself, including issues such as preliminary steps, procedural onus, standard of proof, order of proceeding, and issuing of the award. We then turn to alternatives to the traditional arbitration process, first examining the complaints about the arbitration process and then exploring the processes of expedited arbitration, grievance mediation, and mediation/arbitration.

In Chapter 12, we discuss the changes that may take place during the life of the collective agreement and that can affect the status of the union-employer relationship. Successorship usually involves some form of change of employer, while raiding and union mergers may change the union that represents the employees. Decertification significantly changes the union-employer relationship by removing the union from the workplace. Finally, both technological change and workplace restructuring may cause changes to work structure or content that need to be addressed by the union, the employer, or both.

In Chapter 13, we address some recent trends that are changing the Canadian workplace and look at their implications for unions and employers. Changes in workplace demographics have caused unions to examine their certification and representation strategies in order to maintain membership levels. Changes in work arrangements, such as telecommuting, involve new structures of work that do not always lend themselves to the standard model of union-employer relationships; the same issue arises with organizational changes that are characterized by flatter hierarchies and fewer distinctions between workers and employers. We discuss some of the actions that unions and employers have taken in response to these trends. We also outline some of the recent Canadian industrial relations trends and discuss their implications for the future of union-employer relationships.

SUMMARY

In this chapter, we have presented some reasons why industrial relations is an exciting and relevant subject. Understanding industrial relations is essential to understanding how the Canadian workplace has evolved and how it currently operates. To begin that process of understanding, we have outlined the major components of Canadian labour legislation and presented some statistics on Canadian union-employer relationships. Finally, we have presented an overview of the rest of the textbook to convey some sense of the discussion that is yet to come.

KEY TERMS FOR CHAPTER 1

employer (p. 4)

intentional discrimination (p. 18)

interprovincial component (p. 12)

jurisdiction (p. 11)

labour relations board (p. 13)

para-public/quasi-public sector (p. 14)

protected grounds (p. 17)

public sector (p. 14)

quasi-judicial (p. 13)

systemic discrimination (p. 18)

union (p. 4)

DISCUSSION QUESTIONS FOR CHAPTER 1

1. What are some of the arguments for and against using the term "industrial relations" to describe union-management relationships?
2. Why could the field of industrial relations be characterized as multidisciplinary? Do you see this as a positive or a negative attribute?
3. Distinguish between industrial relations and human resource management.
4. Outline the common features of the different pieces of Canadian labour legislation.
5. What is the importance of the "interprovincial component"?
6. Describe some of the characteristics of Canadian union members and unionized workplaces. Choose at least one of these characteristics and explain how or why you think it has evolved (e.g., why more men than women are union members).

CHAPTER EXERCISES FOR CHAPTER 1

1. Describe your experiences with unions, either as a member or as a non-member. Have your experiences been positive or negative? How have your experiences affected your attitudes toward unions and toward industrial relations in general? Compare your experiences and your attitudes with those of other students in your class to see if there are similarities or differences. If differences exist, try to identify the reasons why.
2. Explain what you, at this point in the course, see as the benefits and drawbacks of a unionized workplace, both for the workers and for the employer. As in the previous exercise, compare your explanation with those of other students in the class to see if there are similarities or differences. If differences exist, try to identify the reasons why.

References

[1] Kochan, T., & Katz, H. (1988). *Collective bargaining and industrial relations: from theory to policy and practice* (2nd edition). New Homewood, IL: Richard D. Irwin.

[2] Dessler, G., Cole, N.D., & Sutherland, V.L. (1998). *Human resources management in Canada* (7th Canadian edition). Scarborough, ON: Prentice-Hall Canada.

[3] Dunlop, J. (1958). *Industrial relations systems*. New York: Holt.

[4] Dabscheck, B. (1989). A survey of theories of industrial relations. In Barbash, J., & Barbash, K. (Eds.), *Theories and concepts in comparative industrial relations*. Columbia, SC: University of South Carolina Press.

[5] Dessler, Cole & Sutherland, *op. cit.*

[6] Creighton, D. (1970). *Canada's first century, 1867-1967*. Toronto, ON: Macmillan.

[7] This summary is based on the discussion in Dessler, Cole, & Sutherland, *op. cit.*

[8] Dessler, Cole, & Sutherland, *op. cit.*

[9] Dessler, Cole, & Sutherland, p. 75.

[10] Dessler, Cole, & Sutherland, p. 76.

[11] The summaries of these cases are based on Alter, S. (1993). *The courts, the Charter, and labour relations*. Ottawa, ON: Research Branch, Library of Parliament. Background paper BP-305E.

[12] *Retail, Wholesale and Department Store Union, Local 580* v. *Dolphin Delivery Ltd.* [1986] 2 S.C.R. 573 at 583.

[13] Alter, *op. cit.*, p. 6.

[14] *Reference Re Public Service Employee Relations Act* [Alberta] [1987] 1 S.C.R. 313; *Public Service Alliance of Canada* v. *R.* [1987] 1 S.C.R. 424; *Government of Saskatchewan* v. *Retail, Wholesale and Department Store Union, Local 544 et al.* [1987] 1 S.C.R. 460.

[15] *Professional Institute of the Public Service of Canada* v. *Northwest Territories* [1990] 2 S.C.R. 367.

[16] *Lavigne* v. *Ontario Public Service Employees Union* [1991] 2 S.C.R. 211.

[17] Makin, K. (2001). Farm workers win right to unionize. *The Globe and Mail*, December 21, 2001, A6.

[18] Quoted in Makin, *op. cit*.

UBC's non-tenure teaching staff launches union drive:

The sessionals receive low pay and no benefits, despite a heavier teaching load than many tenured academics

VANCOUVER—Exploited part-time workers at Starbucks and McDonald's have been making headlines as they unionize to get better wages. The University of British Columbia is now facing the charge of exploiting members of its non-tenure-track teaching staff.

A union organizing drive will be launched today by the so-called sessionals, who are the lowest in UBC's economic hierarchy. The 83-year-old school has 1,820 full-time faculty, an $800-million budget, and a $4.5-million accumulated operating deficit this year.

Graduate students or recent PhDs used to teach as sessionals to gain experience and improve their CVs while seeking tenure-track jobs. With that apprenticeship mindset, they worked for low pay and no benefits. Today, many face dramatically different futures. Tenure-track positions are scarce due to cutbacks. Several years of poorly paid part-time teaching are the best many can hope for.

"I teach the same course load as a full professor—he makes $80,000, I make $20,000," says one single mom. "I can be teaching a course and have a teaching assistant who will earn significantly more than me," adds Donna Vogel, one of the union organizers. UBC's 1,612 teaching assistants are members of the Canadian Union of Public Employees.

For teaching a one-term course, sessionals at UBC initially earn less than $4,000. At Simon Fraser University, sessionals earn $4,837 if the course requires three hours of classroom time per week, $5,975 if the course requires four hours a week.

By comparison, York University in Toronto pays sessionals between $7,000 and $10,000 for a similar workload. Sessionals at York and at the universities of Saskatchewan, Manitoba, Carleton, Toronto, Trent, Guelph, Quebec (Trois-Rivières), Dalhousie, St. Mary's, and Mount St. Vincent belong to the Canadian Union of Public Employees.

Most UBC sessionals have no union representation because about 70 percent of them teach only one course and are therefore excluded from the union representing faculty members.

"We have a great deal of sympathy, obviously," says Mary Russell, president of the faculty association. "We can understand their dilemma and their feelings of not having a voice in the university. We haven't been able to persuade the administration to let all the sessionals be part of the faculty association. But we're also concerned that [if sessionals unionize] the administration could use divide-and-conquer tactics." Russell said the sessionals' hope of winning big salary increases is unlikely even with a union because current public sector wage guidelines restrict salary increases to zero, zero, and two percent over three years.

"There is a problem with wage disparity, but we have to keep chipping away at it," Russell says. "It's unlikely to be hugely or dramatically changed until we get out from under these guidelines, and who knows when that will be."

As for the administration, it's waiting to see. "We have a collective agreement [with the faculty association] we're happy with," said Dennis Pavlich, associate vice-president of academic and legal affairs. "The organizing drive has just begun and we don't want to be seen interfering in any way."

(*Vancouver Sun*, December 2, 1998)

chapter **2**

THEORIES OF INDUSTRIAL RELATIONS

objectives

In this chapter, we will introduce and discuss the ideas of some of the theorists who have attempted to explain the reasons for the creation of unions and the purposes that unions serve in the workplace and for their members. By the end of the chapter, you should be able to:

- describe how the structure of work changed from the 15th to the 19th century
- identify the functions of early forms of unionism
- outline the conditions that gave rise to the modern trade union
- describe the theories of authors who discuss trade union origins, functions, and futures

INTRODUCTION

As unions have emerged and developed as a force in the workplace, a number of authors and researchers have attempted to explain the reasons for unions' continued existence and to identify the purposes unions serve. A review of the work of these individuals is important for two reasons. First, such a review demonstrates how, over time, opinion about unions has evolved alongside the evolution of unions themselves. Second, the different perspectives that these authors and researchers bring to the study of unions illustrate that unions have not served just one function throughout their history, but instead have played multiple roles for their members, responding to changes in work and the workplace.

To create a context within which we can assess the work of these authors, we will begin our discussion with a brief outline of the general historical origins of unions. (We will discuss the specific history of the Canadian union movement in Chapter 3.) We will then present the works of the authors in roughly chronological order, to show how theories about unionism have evolved over time.

THE ORIGIN OF UNIONS

The earliest organizations that can be identified as similar to the modern trade union are the craft guilds that emerged in Europe during the 14th century and in North America during the 17th century. The membership of craft guilds usually consisted of workers involved in a single trade, such as weaving, woodworking, metalwork, or pottery. In order to understand the reasons for the existence of craft guilds, we must understand how work and production were structured during those pre-industrial times.[1] Most craftspeople worked at home or in a small, shared workshop located in the community where they lived. Craftspeople usually owned their business and in effect worked for themselves (much like the self-employed do today). Production of goods was on a custom

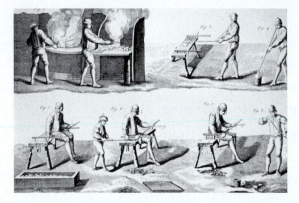

Pre-industrial craftspeople, such as this glassblower, completed an entire product from start to finish.

basis; work would be generated by an order from a customer and each unit would be produced to the requirements of the customer. The craftsperson was usually responsible for the production of an entire unit from start to finish, although parts of some jobs might be given to apprentices, who learned their craft by working alongside an experienced practitioner. If part of the job required a skill that the craftsperson did not have (for example, a leatherworker might not have the skills or equipment to produce the metal parts of a horse's bridle), the craftsperson would commission the needed materials from another craftsperson. If the skills of a different craftsperson were required on a regular basis, the two craftspeople could arrange to work cooperatively.

The lack of mass transportation and the poor quality of most roads in that era meant that the process of transporting goods was lengthy and expensive, and hence the market served by individual craftspeople did not usually extend far beyond their own community. There was no intermediary such as a distributor or wholesaler between the producer and the consumer. Furthermore, craftspeople had to do their own marketing; they were responsible for identifying the markets and customers they might serve.

This method of structuring work offered some degree of freedom and independence to craftspeople, since they worked at their own pace on projects of their own choosing. They were also responsible for deciding how the work was to be carried out and how their business would be administered. However, success within this structure required good health, the ability to work, and skills sufficiently up to date to meet the market's demands. Since craftspeople were in effect self-employed, there was usually no backup or support if they were injured, ill, or otherwise unable to work. As well, little opportunity existed for craftspeople to develop or expand their skills because of the demands of maintaining the business. It was because of these weaknesses in the craft system that craft guilds emerged.

The craft guild served several important functions for the craftsperson. One function was to supply insurance. Many guilds had schemes similar to modern unemployment insurance or workers' compensation plans. Craftspeople would pay a regular fee to the guild, and if they were injured or otherwise unable to work, the guild would make payments to offset their lack of income. Some guilds provided the services of another craftsperson to keep the business in operation during the owners' absence, so that the owner would not lose customers while they were inactive. Another function of the guild was to ensure an adequate supply of trained practitioners of the craft. This function was possible in occupations where the guild had exclusive control over apprenticeships and other forms of education. A person wanting to become, for example, a goldsmith or a carpenter would contact the appropriate craft guild, which would then arrange for the individual to serve as an apprentice with various craftspeople so that he or she could learn all aspects of the craft from experienced practitioners. At the end of the apprenticeship, usually after completing a test intended to demonstrate mastery of the craft, the individual would be declared a full member of the craft guild and was permitted to operate a business on his or her own.

The apprenticeship and training function of the craft guild provided a form of quality control for products. To maintain the guild's control over the labour market, guild members would usually refuse to work, or to share skills, with craftspeople who were not affiliated with a guild. This ensured a shared body of knowledge among guild members that was not accessible to non-guild members. Thus, a customer purchasing a product from a member of the guild could be assured that the craftsperson had been adequately trained in making an acceptable product. Guilds were also able to maintain something of a monopoly over the price of goods by encouraging guild members to charge similar prices for their products and to refrain from undermining other members' businesses by undercharging for goods.

In providing a forum for the exchange of information and knowledge among the craft's practitioners, guilds also served an educational function for their members. Guild members could share information about new techniques, expanding markets, or new products. Some guilds in more populated and accessible areas reduced production costs for their members by purchasing supplies or raw materials in bulk.

The initial challenges to the craft guild system came in Italy during the 14th century, when merchants created the Wool Guild to displace the clothmakers' guild. The Wool Guild acted much like an employers' association, combining the collective knowledge and influence of the producers and sellers to counteract the power of the craft guild. It succeeded in reducing the power of the clothmakers' guild by controlling the supply of raw materials and distribution of finished products. This permitted the Wool Guild to change the predominant method of production from a single craftsperson creating a product from start to finish to a method in which different steps in the production were divided among different craftspeople. Instead of a single craftsperson spinning fleece into wool, weaving the wool into fabric, and then dying the fabric, for example, one craftsperson would spin the wool, the next would weave, and the next would dye. The Wool Guild was able to enforce this division of labour because it controlled the supply of raw materials and was thus able to ensure that each craftsperson received only the materials needed for his or her part of the production process.

This division of labour allowed for faster production, since individual craftspeople became specialists in their part of the production process and thereby developed more efficient methods of carrying out their task. However, a more significant change instigated by the Wool Guild was in the way that the craftspeople were paid. Rather than being paid directly by the customer for the completed product—a price that would cover the costs of the worker's labour, the raw materials, and the production tools—the craftspeople were instead paid a standard piecework rate by the producer who coordinated their work. The producer would then sell the completed product to the market or consumer.

This method of compensation reduced wage and production costs for the producer, since the producer was not obligated to compensate the craftspeople for their time or skill. Rather, the producer simply paid a set rate depending on how many finished pieces the craftspeople were able to produce, regardless of how long it took them to generate those pieces or what skills were needed to carry out the work. The producer also did not have to carry the costs of purchasing the tools for production, since the craftspeople were expected to provide their own tools. Since craftspeople usually worked at home, the producer did not have to carry the overhead costs associated with operating a production facility or workplace. The popularity of this system of production soon expanded beyond Italy; by the 18th century, the so-called putting-out system was prevalent throughout Europe.[2]

The next major shift in the structure of work and production occurred with the Industrial Revolution in the mid-18th century. The degree of change that mechanization and industrialization brought to the work of craftspeople was immense; in England, nearly 1,000 patents for new inventions were issued in one 30-year period.[3] These new inventions, such as the flying shuttle (for weaving) and the spinning jenny (for spinning wool), meant great increases in production capacity, since the people working them could produce output more quickly and in greater quantities than craftspeople could. This mechanization also reduced

The Toronto Rolling Mills is typical of many 19th-century factories. Centralized production brought new concerns about working conditions and safety.

the demand for skilled workers, since machines rather than human workers could now carry out many of the complex steps in the production process. Relatively low prices for land facilitated the establishment of large-scale factories. Improvements in transportation and communication meant that raw materials and finished goods could easily be marketed in areas far from their place of origin.

These changes, however, meant substantial changes in the structure of work and of workplaces. These are summarized in Table 2-1. Because factories were centralized places of production, workers were required to travel to the workplace rather than working from home as before. In addition, because factories were generally located in urban areas, many workers had to leave their rural communities to find employment in cities. And, as mentioned, the work itself had substantially changed due to mechanization. Where previously a worker would participate from start to finish in producing an item, industrialization resulted in production being broken down into distinct stages, some or most of

TABLE 2-1　Pre- and Post-Industrial Revolution Work Structure

	Pre-Industrial Revolution	Post-Industrial Revolution
Work location	Home or workshop in home community	Factory in urbanized centre
Work division	Responsible for entire production process	Specialized part of production process
Work training	Apprenticeship with established craftsperson or worker	Minimal because tasks are specialized and simplified
Ownership of business	Craftsperson owns own business	Employer
Market for goods	Local/Regional	National/International
Type of goods	Custom	Mass produced
Design/Control of work	By individual craftsperson/ worker	By employer

which were handled by machinery. A worker would perform only one or a few of the steps in production. The production process was divided so these steps usually required minimal skill and, if necessary, workers could easily be replaced without any significant loss of production time to training.

More importantly, however, control over work had also changed. In the pre-Industrial Revolution economy, the individual craftsperson was both worker and business owner. The craftsperson designed his or her product, produced it, sold it, and received the financial rewards directly. In the factories of the Industrial Revolution, control of the workplace and ownership of the business rested solely with the factory owner. The owner decided what the factory would produce, designed the production process, and purchased the necessary machinery and raw materials. The owner also controlled how labour was used in the process, decided who would or would not work in the factory and how they would do their work, and paid the workers whatever wage rates he or she deemed appropriate.

These major changes in work and production initially resulted in generally horrific working conditions. The focus in the new economy was on increased production and consumption, which meant that factories operated continuously in order to produce sufficient goods for expanding consumer markets. Because of the pressure to maintain competitive retail prices, goods were produced at the lowest cost possible, the result being little consideration for the safety or job satisfaction of workers. Women and children worked alongside men in the factories—the "dark Satanic Mills"[4]—since the high cost of living in an urban centre usually meant that the labour of more than one family member was needed to provide sufficient household income. Another factor compelling as many family members as possible to earn an income was the decline in wage rates caused by industrialization. One writer visiting a major British cloth-manufacturing region in 1830 reported that weavers who formerly earned 20 to 30 shillings a week as craftspeople earned 5 shillings or less per week working in clothmaking factories.[5]

The use of child labour was commonplace in factories. In fact, for tasks requiring delicate manual work, such as stripping tobacco leaves from plants, children were preferred because their small fingers allowed them to work more neatly and with less waste than adults. Not all children worked alongside their parents in factories; some were sent to work alone in factories by impoverished parents who could not afford the fees for trade apprenticeships in their home communities.[6] Children living away from their parents were often housed in sheds near the factory and forced to work shifts that lasted for as long as they could stay awake. In Britain, it was not until 1819 that laws were passed forbidding the employment of children younger than nine years old and prohibiting older children from working more than 12 hours per day. Although this legislation protected child labourers, there was almost no legal protection for adult workers, and the few laws that did exist were rarely enforced because of a lack of factory inspectors. If workers were injured on the job or became ill after prolonged exposure to unsafe working conditions, the usual remedy was to fire them and hire new workers; new workers could easily replace the injured (or deceased) workers because factory jobs were standardized and simplified.

The negative impact that these working conditions had on workers was the major reason that the first modern trade unions developed. Our discussion of trade union theories will begin with authors who addressed the origins of the modern trade union, and will then proceed to authors who analyse the historical evolution of unions' functions. We will conclude with a review of more recent authors who address the role that unions might play in the future.

THEORIES OF UNION ORIGINS

The Webbs: The Effects of Industrialization

Sidney and Beatrice Webb were English authors whose interest in trade unions developed through their co-founding of the Fabian Society, a socialist group dedicated to large-scale social reform. The Webbs and their colleagues advocated the reform of working conditions like those found in the industrialized factories; however, they believed that these conditions were not simply problems in the workplace but also manifestations of larger societal problems, such as the division between rich and poor. In their opinion, the immediate problems could only be addressed in a meaningful way if the larger long-term problems were also solved. The Webbs were interested in how trade unions emerged in response to industrialized work structures. They researched the origins of trade unions and published their results in two important books.[7]

The results of the Webbs' research identified that the primary purpose of trade unions was to improve the conditions of their members' working lives. The Webbs suggested that unions emerged primarily because of the separation between capital and labour caused by industrialization. In the pre-Industrial Revolution economy, labour and capital were both controlled by the worker, who invested in his or her own work and subsequently gained all the financial benefits from the sale of that work. In the factory-based economy, the worker provided labour but the factory owner provided capital. The factory owner also controlled how labour would be used in the production process.

In the Webbs' analysis, this division between capital and labour would lead owners and businesspeople to exploit labour for their own gain, since owners and businesspeople would want to maximize return on their investment. One method of maximizing return was to minimize production costs such as wages; owners and businesspeople would therefore attempt to keep wages as low as possible regardless of the financial needs of the

A child coal miner in 1912. The effects of industrialization, as documented by the Webbs and their colleagues, eventually led to reforms such as compulsory schooling.

workers. The pressures to maximize return and minimize cost would be even greater in competitive markets, where the owner or businessperson would have less freedom to adjust selling prices if costs changed in other areas of the business. Thus, according to the Webbs, one important objective of unions was to "regulate the conditions of employment" to protect workers' interests against pressures caused by the owner or businessperson's financial situation. Unions also served the larger purpose of representing workers' interests at a level beyond that of the individual workplace or particular trade; for example, they would lobby governments or regulatory authorities for legislation that would serve the interests of working people.

The Webbs identified three instruments, or "methods," that unions employed to achieve these purposes and objectives. The first was the **method of mutual insurance**. This method involved unions accumulating funds from union membership fees and then using those funds to make payments to workers unable to work. These payments took two forms: (1) "benevolent" or "friendly" payments for workers who were sick, injured, or laid off, and (2) "out-of-work" payments for workers whose tools were lost or whose factories were temporarily or permanently closed. This method helped achieve the objective of improving union members' working lives by providing an alternative form of support for workers who were sick or hurt or whose source of income had disappeared through no fault of their own. The second was the **method of collective bargaining**. This method involved unions acting as the workers' representative in negotiating terms and conditions of work with the employer. By ensuring fair and consistent rules in the workplace and adequate wage rates, this method also helped achieve the objective of improving union members' working lives. The third was the **method of legal enactment**, whereby unions lobbied governments to enact laws guaranteeing basic minimum employment standards. This method helped achieve the goal of representing workers' interests at a higher level, since it ensured that the interests of all workers, not just union members, were brought to the attention of decision makers and other influential individuals.

The Webbs described two internal mechanisms, or "devices," that unions used to ensure that the unions themselves were democratic and were truly representative of their members' interests. The first of these was the **device of the common rule**, whereby unions would ensure their survival by fighting for better conditions for all workers (not just their own membership). The use of this device would increase the support for unions, since non-union members would be impressed by the work that unions had done on their behalf and would thus be interested in joining a union themselves. The second device was the **device of restriction of numbers**, whereby unions limited their membership through qualifying requirements like apprenticeships. Unions argued that the device of restriction of numbers allowed them some control over conditions in the labour market. Employers would have to depend on unions for a supply of workers guaranteed to have a certain level of training, and unions would have more power to negotiate wages and working conditions with employers, since they could threaten to cease supplying skilled labour if their demands were not met. However, the Webbs felt that the system of restriction of numbers caused injustice and exploitation in the labour market; under this system, access to certain kinds of work was limited, for only those who were approved or accepted by the union would have access to the training needed for particular jobs.

Selig Perlman: Unions and the Class System

Born and raised in Poland, Perlman immigrated to the United States where he joined the University of Wisconsin-Madison. The university would subsequently become a renowned centre for teaching and research on unionism. The contrasts Perlman observed between the Marxist system of labour and the North American system were at the centre of his major work, *A Theory of the Labor Movement*.[8]

Like the Webbs, Perlman identified the emergence of capitalism as one of the catalysts for the emergence of unions, his reasoning being that the capitalist system was based on a separation between capital and labour that did not exist in the pre-Industrial Revolution economy. However, he also argued that if unions' support came solely from the working class, they would not be successful in representing workers' concerns to capitalists, since the working class was only one part of society and a part that historically had less power and influence. He suggested that unions needed the support of the middle class and that they had to respect some of the basic tenets of capitalism (like the institution of private property) in order to represent the interests of workers effectively. If unions had a broader base of support in society, their concerns would be more widely circulated and noticed. Also, if they supported some of the principles of capitalism and did not reject it outright, they would appear to be cooperative rather than radical and thus be more acceptable to parts of society beyond the working class.

That did not mean, though, that unions should be dominated or controlled by the middle class or by capitalists. Perlman stated that unions would be most effective if they were motivated by what he called the **psychology of the labourer**. Labourers, unlike middle- or upper-class individuals, had the experience of scarcity of work, of not being able to find work at all or of having difficulty obtaining jobs in a highly competitive labour market. This experience would affect their unions' goals and objectives, because the issue of employment security would be uppermost in the minds of the members. In addition, because their views would be shaped by practical realities, labourers would not be distracted by socialist or intellectual idealism. Perlman's concern was that while middle- or upper-class individuals might be sympathetic to the goals of unionism, their personal experience would not be the same as that of the labourer and they would thus not be as sensitive to workers' concerns. Allowing those individuals to dominate unions would ultimately mean that unions would not reflect the needs or concerns of the labourers they were intended to support. Also, because middle- or upper-class individuals' actual experience with unions would tend to be limited to intellectual or theoretical discussions of unionism, these individuals would have more theoretical than practical ideas of how a union should function. The problem Perlman anticipated was that these ideas might not reflect the needs or concerns of the working-class union members and that, again, unions would not function in a way that would serve the members they were intended to support.

While the Webbs proposed that one of the purposes of unions was to promote large-scale social change, Perlman suggested that the primary purpose of unions was to provide "collective mastery" over employment opportunities and standards. He did not believe that unions should be concerned with gaining ownership of businesses, but instead proposed that they should focus on creating economic security and opportunity for their members. This strategy, he felt—in contrast to one that entailed entering the volatile area of business ownership—would create a stable, long-term basis for union existence.

John Commons: The Effects of the Market

Like Perlman, Commons was a professor at the University of Wisconsin-Madison. In much of his work on unions, he investigated the emergence of unions as a response to changes in the economic system and the subsequent changes in the structure of work.[9] However, unlike Perlman and the Webbs, Commons focused his research on unions in the United States, seeing them as part of a larger economic, industrial, and political framework.

In his article on shoemakers, Commons identified the development of competitive markets as a force driving the emergence of unions. In competitive capitalist markets, workers were separated from the distribution and sale of their work; workers created a product but were not responsible for transporting it to buyers or for determining a competitive selling price. Unions, Commons believed, would serve as a means to ensure that competition in markets was based on product quality and not on wages paid to workers. A competitive product would not be the product that was sold at the lowest price (a condition that would exert downward pressure on wages); rather, it would be the product that was the best made and would thus give the greatest value to the consumer. If unions were able to organize workers in a majority of organizations in a single industry, or if they could organize significant numbers of workers with the same occupation, they would influence competitiveness by ensuring that skilled workers received wages that represented their contribution to the making of a quality product. Commons called this perspective "taking [wages] out of competition."

Commons also noted that the broadening of markets through improved transportation and communication provided opportunities for unions as well as for capitalists. No longer would unions be confined to representing workers in a restricted geographic area; instead, workers could organize workers in other areas who were engaged in the same trade or occupation. By allowing workers in different areas to share common concerns more easily, communication and travel improvements, he suggested, led to the development of national and even international unions.

A summary of the theories dealing with the origins of unions can be found in Table 2-2.

TABLE 2-2   Theories of the Origins of Unions

Sidney and Beatrice Webb	– separation between capital and labour
	– method of mutual insurance
	– method of collective bargaining
	– method of legal enactment
	– device of common rule
	– device of restriction of numbers
Selig Perlman	– unions needing support of middle class
	– emphasis on "psychology of the labourer"
John Commons	– influence of competitive markets
	– influence of expanding markets

THE FUNCTIONS OF UNIONS

Robert Hoxie: Union Types

Hoxie, an economist, was interested in identifying the actions that unions undertook to serve their members' interests. He had a somewhat different perspective on the emergence of unions than the authors previously discussed. While those authors focused on the role of unions as unifiers of the working class, Hoxie believed that unions would not be confined to the working class but could emerge in any workplace where the workers had a "class consciousness."[10] In other words, a union could be created by any group of individuals in a workplace or organization who recognized shared interests and common goals.

Hoxie's major contribution to theories of unionism was his identification of four "functional types" of unionism. He stated that unions were established to serve different purposes for their members and that the structure and actions of any individual union would be shaped by the function the union was established to fulfill. Thus, in order to understand why a union acted as it did, it was important to understand what type of union it was.

The first type of unionism Hoxie identified was **business unionism**. The role of a business union was to protect workers in a particular occupation or trade. Business unions would achieve their goals primarily through collective bargaining and would be less concerned with larger social issues or with alternative means of resolving workplace issues.

The second type of unionism was **friendly or uplifting unionism**. This type of union acted as a mechanism to improve standards of living for workers and thereby improve society at large. Friendly unions, like business unions, engaged in collective bargaining, but they also used the Webbs' mechanism of mutual insurance and political action to gain desired outcomes. Friendly unions provided a means for workers to interact socially and develop a sense of membership or belonging that might not have been developed in other workplace situations.

The third type of unionism that Hoxie identified was **revolutionary unionism**. Unions of this kind would attempt change either through large-scale political action or through direct action such as sabotage or violence. Hoxie noted that revolutionary unions were extremely class-conscious; they were concerned with the long-term objective of changing the class structure of society as well as with the short-term goal of gaining power for workers.

Finally, Hoxie identified **predatory unionism**. Here, unions were mainly concerned with increasing their own power by whatever means possible—sometimes through unethical or illegal activity. Hoxie noted that predatory unionism was distinct from business unionism in that predatory unions often operated in partnership with employers. Predatory unions would, for example, take bribes from employers to agree to collective agreements with little value for workers (so-called sweetheart agreements). Business unions, on the other hand, would maintain an arm's-length relationship with the employer and not agree to anything that would compromise the workers' interests.

It is important to note that Hoxie did not present these four functional types of unionism as mutually exclusive. He argued that one union could serve more than one of these functions at the same time and that, in fact, many unions simultaneously engaged in, for example, business and friendly unionism. Hoxie also suggested that a union might move from one form of unionism to another as the union developed or as the workplace or the attitude of employers changed. A union that was newly certified might be more concerned with business unionism as a means to establish favourable workplace conditions, but as the union became more skilled in that role, it might acknowledge larger social issues and develop the ability to engage in friendly or even revolutionary unionism.

E. Wight Bakke: Choosing to Join a Union

Like Hoxie, Bakke, a professor at Yale, was also interested in how unions served the interests of their members. His primary interest, however, was why workers chose to join or to reject unions and how the role a union played for its members affected this decision. Bakke researched this question through extensive interviews with workers and presented his results in a series of articles and books.[11]

Bakke stated that workers' main reasons for joining unions were to reduce their frustration and anxiety in the workplace and to improve their opportunity to achieve specific "standards of successful living." If workers perceived that joining a union would be a means to attain these goals, they would join; if workers did not see that a union would assist them in reaching these outcomes, they would not join.

Bakke elaborated on these findings by identifying five factors that constituted the standards of successful living, and he explained how workers perceived that unions might help them attain these standards. The first factor is **social status**. Union membership—more specifically, holding a designated position in a union (e.g., being an executive member or shop steward)—may provide a means for a worker to gain the respect of others in the workplace or in society. Such respect may not be attainable through other means if the worker is perceived to belong to a lower-ranked social or economic class.

The second factor is **creature comforts**. Union membership may allow a worker to enjoy a similar standard of living to that of his or her peers, because the union negotiates on behalf of the workers for competitive wages and benefits. Non-unionized workers may not have enough formal influence in the workplace to obtain these conditions.

The third factor is **control**. The presence of a union in a workplace gives workers a formal voice in operations through negotiation, the presence of a collective agreement, and the opportunity to file grievances. These mechanisms guarantee that the individual worker will have influence over his or her working conditions; a non-unionized worker may or may not have this influence, depending on the attitude of the employer.

The fourth factor is **information**. Unions serve as a source of information on companies, the economy, and society at large; they also run programs to educate workers on labour-related matters. This means that unionized workers may be better informed and better educated than non-unionized workers.

The final factor is **integrity**, which, according to Bakke, would include self-respect and fairness. A worker's decision to join a union would be partly based on whether union membership would enhance his or her sense of integrity.

Bakke concluded that a worker's decision whether or not to join a union would be based on their perception of whether the union was able to provide the factor or factors of importance to him or her. If, for example, a worker perceived creature comforts to be a high priority, he or she would only join a union that seemed to promise a means through which creature comforts could be obtained.

John Dunlop: The Industrial Relations System

Dunlop, a professor at Harvard, created one of the most influential theories of union functions with his "systems theory" of industrial relations.[12] Dunlop attempted to explain how unions functioned by looking at how unions fit into larger social systems. He analysed how unions interacted with other organizations and what guidelines existed to regulate or shape those interactions.

In its general form, systems theory explains why an organization functions as it does by depicting it as a system with three interdependent components: inputs, processes, and outputs. At the simplest level, the processes are the means by which inputs (e.g., resources and raw materials) are converted into outputs (e.g., products and services). The type of input affects the choice of processes, and the choice of processes affects the output. To illustrate this idea, think of a manufacturing plant that produces cars. The model of car being produced will determine which inputs are needed. A plant producing minivans, for example, would not need materials to make convertible tops or workers with the skills to produce convertible tops. Similarly, the production process would be organized to produce minivans in the most efficient manner. If the plant changes its product to two-door economy sedans, the production process has to be altered. However, the outputs may also be affected or constrained by the components used in the production process. The manufacturer may want to offer minivans in four different colours, but the painting machinery may only allow three colours of paint to be available at any given time. Either the manufacturer will have to revise its expectations or the production process will have to be redesigned to permit four paint colours to be used during production.

We can see from this example that systems theory emphasizes not only the existence of distinct parts of the organization but also the interrelationships between those parts. What happens in one part of the organization may directly or indirectly affect other parts of the organization because of these linkages. Because systems theory explores the effect of interrelationships, it can be used to analyse social and cultural activity in the organization in addition to the more tangible processes. Understanding the social and cultural interrelationships between individuals, groups, or departments can be crucial to understanding how an organization really functions. Systems theory can also be used to analyse the interactions of the organization with the external environment and thus help us to understand how events or forces in the external environment affect events within the organization.

Dunlop took the principles of systems theory and used them to explain how industrial relations systems operate on two levels: within the framework of the individual organization and with other organizations in the external environment. His "framework" is depicted in Figure 2-1.

Actors	Contexts	Web of Rules
Unions	Technologies	Procedures for determining substantive rules
Management/Employer	Markets	Substantive rules
Government and other third parties	Budgets Power	Procedures for applying substantive rules

Figure 2-1
Dunlop's Industrial Relations System

In Dunlop's framework, unions are one of three actors in the industrial relations system. The other two actors are management (the employer) and government and/or private agencies. The definition of "actors" may be expanded to include external stakeholders, such as customers or other businesses. Dunlop argued that each of these actors has a distinct ideology—a set of values and beliefs that determines how they will act within the system. For example, management may believe that it is their right to control the workplace because they represent the individuals who have made financial investments to create and sustain the organization. Holding this belief would lead managers to undertake actions consistent with maintaining or increasing that control. On the other hand, unions may believe that they have a right to "have a say" in the workplace because they represent the workers whose labour makes it possible for management to earn profits. This belief would lead them to undertake actions intended to counteract or balance the control exerted by management.

It is apparent that the ideologies of the actors within the industrial relations system are often in conflict over fundamental issues. What, then, keeps the system functioning? Dunlop proposed that, despite their different beliefs on certain issues, the actors also have a shared ideology about the system itself and each actor's role. It is this shared ideology that maintains stability within the system, even if the representatives of the actors or the actors themselves change. While the actors may have ideological disagreements over particular issues, they are committed to participation in the system as a method of interaction and conflict resolution. This commitment allows the system to function even when there are disputes between the actors because they share a belief in the system.

The interactions that occur among the actors include, for example, collective bargaining and grievance resolution procedures. These are processes to which the actors bring their inputs (general ideologies and positions on specific issues), and it is through these interactions that the inputs are converted into outputs (generally, the collective agreement and the resolution of grievances). The actors also have guidelines, either informal or legislated, for how the interactions will occur (e.g., a mutually agreed upon series of steps the parties will follow in resolving a grievance after a collective agreement is in effect).

Dunlop's framework identifies the contexts within which the interactions occur. These contexts both shape the interactions and influence the eventual outputs: the collective agreement, which can include outputs related to the negotiation of the agreement (e.g., strikes or lockouts), and the general quality of the ongoing relationships between the parties. Dunlop identified four contexts: the technological context (such as the skill level of the workers, degree of flexibility within the workplace, and job content), the market context (labour, product, geographical), the budgetary context, and the power context (the amount of power the actors have or are able to generate). An example of contexts influencing outputs would be a situation where an employer wants to negotiate lower wage rates as a means of lowering prices to stay competitive. In this situation, the market context influences the employer's desired output because the perceived basis of competition in the market is pricing. However, the union could argue that the workers are highly skilled and that reducing wages would cause workers to seek better-paying employment elsewhere and thus lead to a shortage of trained labour for the employer. This argument would reflect the influence of the technological context. The power context would come into play if the government, as another actor in the system, then passes legislation forbidding employers to cut wage rates below a certain level; in our example, the employer will lose negotiating power, since it can no longer threaten to lower wages beyond that level.

Finally, Dunlop's framework recognized "a web of rules" that governs the interactions between the parties within the system. There are three general types of rules in this "web." The first type includes the rules in the workplace that are created through negotiation; these are usually contained in the collective agreement. The second type of rules determine how disputes such as grievances will be governed; these rules are also contained in the collective agreement but they may be influenced by other actors or contexts, such as government legislation. The rules of the third type govern the processes underlying how rules themselves will be determined; these are usually legislative guidelines determining such matters as when management and unions must meet to commence collective bargaining or when a strike or lockout can legally be used as a bargaining tactic. Dunlop speculated that the web of rules and the processes the rules govern are themselves influenced by feedback. Once a process or a rule is in place, the actors monitor its success or failure and, depending on the result, can alter subsequent processes or rules to reinforce future successes or avoid repeating failures.

Dunlop also contributed to industrial relations theory through his research with Clark Kerr, Frederick Harbison, and Charles Myers. The work of these four authors focused on similarities and differences between industrial relations systems in different countries.[13] They contended that the emergence of unions was not a response to capitalism but a response to industrialization. The process of industrialization was consistent across different countries, while the markets and economies in different parts of the world differed substantially. The consistency in the process of industrialization, they argued, explained the similarity of union functions and actions in many countries, even if economic structures and markets were different.

They noted that the major exception to this theory existed in Communist countries, where unions were controlled by the ruling Communist Party and were thus not as independent in representing workers' interests as were unions in non-Communist countries. They argued, however, that as industrialization spread throughout the world and as workers and managers grappled over universal issues like job security and technological change, there would be a "convergence" of industrial relations systems among developed nations. Industrial relations systems around the world would gradually come to resemble each other, rather than remain distinct.

A summary of the theories of the functions of unions can be found in Table 2-3.

TABLE 2-3   Theories of Functions of Unions

Robert Hoxie	– class consciousness as cause of union formation
	– business unionism
	– friendly/uplifting unionism
	– revolutionary unionism
	– predatory unionism
E. Wight Bakke	Factors affecting decision to join a union:
	– social status
	– creature comforts
	– control
	– information
	– integrity
John Dunlop	– systems theory of industrial relations
	– parties as actors
	– actors operating within contexts
	– web of rules
	– eventual convergence of industrial relations systems in industrial countries

THE FUTURE OF UNIONS

Karl Marx and Friedrich Engels: Unions and the Class Struggle

If strict chronological order had been followed, Marx and Engels would have been placed earlier in our discussion, and in fact their writings did deal with many of the issues relating to the origins of unions. However, these authors also discussed how unions would develop and function after their establishment, and hence we have placed them at the start of our discussion about the future of unions.

In a number of different works, Marx and Engels identified the emergence of unions as one symptom of an ongoing class struggle. Like some of the other authors we have discussed, Marx and Engels saw unions as a means by which the working class could avoid exploitation by the upper classes. Unions would serve as a countervailing force to the power exerted by the upper classes because they would unite the members of the working class in a single body that would be powerful simply because of its great size. Unions would also enlighten the working class about the injustice of their position in society, and this knowledge would inspire workers to take action to improve their circumstances.

However, Marx and Engels also believed that unions in and of themselves would not be sufficient to offset the ongoing exploitation of workers, which they viewed as an inherent part of the capitalist system. They proposed that the continued operation of the capitalist system was dependent on maintaining a large class of workers who would work (willingly or otherwise) for substandard wages. Keeping wages low created greater profits for the upper classes, and those profits gave the members of the upper class a continued source of wealth that could be reinvested or retained to maintain their economic dominance. Marx and Engels argued that unions would need to have a larger purpose beyond gaining increased control of the workplace if they were to continue to survive, given the inherent oppression that workers faced in the capitalist system. Once unions had satisfied the work-related demands of their members, there would then be no reason for them to exist if their only focus was the workplace.

Thus, Marx and Engels argued, unions had to have a larger political purpose as well. In the future, unions would be a vehicle of class discontent, and that discontent would eventually contribute to the overturning of capitalism and the development of a "classless

A cartoon from the height of the "Red Scare" in 1919. Unions were linked with the communist ideology espoused by Marx, though most worked hard to quell their radical wings.

society." This process would, ironically, be aided by means developed by the upper classes: "[T]he ever-expanding union of the workers … is helped on by the improved means of communication that are created by modern industry…. [T]his contact was needed to centralize the numerous local struggles, all of the same character, into one national struggle between classes."[14] Their contention was that once workers recognized the power that they could exert through a collective mechanism such as a union, they would turn their attention to using collective power as a way to break down larger structures in society. Eventually, classes in society would disappear because all individuals would be equally represented and have equal amounts of power in decision making.

Harry Braverman: The Effect of Deskilling

While Harry Braverman's theories do not always deal directly with unionism, his work is included in this section because of its ongoing implications for union-related issues like wages and workplace control.

In his book *Labor and Monopoly Capital*,[15] Braverman discusses the enduring popularity of management techniques such as industrial engineering and scientific management, despite the demoralizing effect these techniques have on workers. While industrial engineering and scientific management were developed in the early 1900s, their principles are still used in the design of production processes involving, for example, assembly lines and fast-food restaurants. Work is broken down into small, simple, repetitive components that are designed to maximize production and minimize the skill requirements of the workers. Rather than praising these techniques as innovative and efficient, Braverman identifies them as part of the ongoing attempt by management to increase control over workers and workplaces.

Braverman distinguishes two general methods of achieving the goal of increased management control. The first method is **deskilling**, where tasks are specialized or subdivided to such a degree that dependence on highly skilled labour is reduced or eliminated. Deskilling means that management can reduce the use of skilled labour and instead use unskilled and semi-skilled workers, who are in greater supply and who can be paid less. For example, rather than using a highly trained chef to produce a burger from start to finish, a restaurant could employ workers who only know how to operate a grill or a toaster or a chopping knife, and collectively use all of their limited skills to produce the burger. The second method of increasing management control entails controlling the methods by which work is done and the pace at which work is conducted. In the restaurant example, management could increase its control over burger production by producing guidelines for how each step in the burger production process is to be performed and/or by setting a maximum time that can elapse between an order being submitted and the customer receiving the burger. Implementing this method of control has the effect of increasing output since the predetermined steps in the production process are designed for efficiency, and decreasing worker resistance since the worker has little or no say in determining how work will be conducted. The combined use of these two methods of control has resulted, Braverman argues, in more production for less pay.

Braverman suggests that the effect of this managerial orientation has been, and will continue to be, to encourage managers to select workplace technologies not on the basis of quality of service or output, or even of overall technical efficiency. Instead, managers will make their selections based on which technologies permit them to continue to exercise the greatest amount of control over their workers and the workplace, even if the technologies are more costly or inefficient in other regards. For example, management might have to choose between a machine whose price exceeds the organization's capital budget but which allows standardization of a significant part of the production process, and a machine whose price is within budgetary guidelines but whose operation gives more autonomy to the workers. Braverman's argument suggests that management will select the more expensive machine because of its greater capacity for control, even though its purchase will result in inefficiencies in other parts of the organization, since budgets will have to be altered to compensate for the excessive cost of the machine. Braverman suggests that a managerial orientation favouring this kind of choice will result in continuous downward pressure on wages and reduced opportunity for workers to develop advanced or varied skills. Although he does not explicitly address the role of unions in this process, it is logical to assume that unions would likely attempt to counteract these restrictions.

Thomas Kochan, Robert McKersie, and Peter Cappelli: New Union and Employer Roles

Kochan, McKersie, and Cappelli, all professors at American universities,[16] built on Dunlop's systems theory of industrial relations. They believe that Dunlop's proposed industrial relations system would be a more accurate reflection of industrial relations reality if it included the larger societal and international framework that the employer operates within. They contend that this larger framework ultimately affects the relationship between the employer and the union at the level of the individual workplace, since events in this larger framework, such as international trade agreements, may have an impact on the terms of individual workplace-level collective agreements.

Kochan, McKersie, and Cappelli also point out that earlier industrial relations theory portrayed the employer's role in industrial relations as that of a reactor to the union. In earlier conceptualizations of the union-employer relationship, the employer did not actively attempt to manage the relationship with the union, but instead simply responded to whatever the union brought to its attention. In their view, the employer's role is no longer passive; employers are now more sophisticated and active, rather than reactive, participants in industrial relations. Kochan, McKersie, and Cappelli support this assertion by pointing to a number of events in the United States. American employers have lobbied for legislative changes to reduce the power of unions or even outlaw them entirely. Professional strikebreaking firms can legally provide labour to organizations whose regular workers are on strike; there are also cases of non-union firms harassing or intimidating individuals attempting to organize unions. These events are all evidence that employers are actively trying to manage their relationship with unions and the framework that guides that relationship.

Kochan, McKersie, and Cappelli argue that if unions are to continue to be effective as worker representatives, they need to recognize this fundamental change in the nature of employer participation in industrial relations. The authors do not suggest that all employers would undertake actions as extreme as the examples they cite, but they do note that it is essential for unions to realize the change of the employer's role from passive responder to active intervenor because of the implications this change has for the quality of the union-employer relationship. More importantly, Kochan, McKersie, and Cappelli suggest that industrial relations and the entire human resource management function of a firm are now, more than ever, integrated into the overall strategy of an organization. The effect of this integration is that decisions made at the organizational strategic level could ultimately affect the workplace union-employer relationship. For example, if an organization decides to outsource part of its production process to another country or another organization, this decision will have a direct impact on the number of workers on the payroll and will, quite possibly, exert downward pressure on wage levels because of the cost savings generated by the outsourcing. These are outcomes that would clearly be of concern to the union as well as the employer.

Thus, Kochan, McKersie, and Cappelli argue, for unions to continue to survive and be effective worker representatives, they must attempt to be included in decisions at the highest strategic levels of the organization and not to be narrowly focused on workplace rules and regulations. This inclusion could take many forms, ranging from informal consultations with management to a worker representative having a formal role on the board of directors or the executive planning committee. This change in direction may mean that unions will have to rethink their traditionally adversarial attitudes toward management and instead attempt a more cooperative relationship focused on positive outcomes for all parties involved. It is unlikely that unions would be considered for participation in strategic planning if they were perceived as hostile or opposed to management's intentions, so unions must emphasize common goals like the long-term survival and health of the organization, which both unions and management have an interest in supporting. The authors suggest that cooperative high-level union-management relationships, rather than the traditional adversarial bargaining-level relationships, are more suitable for addressing the potentially wide-ranging impact of strategic-level issues.

Richard Chaykowski and Anil Verma: The Distinctive Canadian Context

Chaykowski and Verma, both Canadian industrial relations professors, address some of the same issues as Kochan, McKersie, and Cappelli, but do so in the context of the Canadian industrial relations system.[17] Chaykowski and Verma acknowledge the shortcomings of the workplace-level, short-term focus of most industrial relations interactions. However, their findings differ from those of the American authors in that they do not see as extensive changes in Canadian management practices or attitudes as the American authors see in the American counterparts. While Canadian employers have experimented with different innovative forms of human resource management practices, any resulting changes have not been as lasting or as wide-ranging as in the United States. Furthermore, Canadian employers have not engaged in the kind of extreme anti-union activity practised by some American employers, although this may be because Canadian labour legislation places stronger restrictions than American legislation does on employer activity. For example, many Canadian jurisdictions prohibit or restrict the use of replacement workers during legal strikes or lockouts, while such regulations are rare in the United States.

Chaykowski and Verma thus characterize the Canadian industrial relations system as relatively stable in comparison to the American system. They attribute this stability in large part to higher levels of unionization in Canada; since Canadian unions represent a greater proportion of the workforce, they have more power than American unions to resist changes they see as detrimental to their members' interests. While Chaykowski and Verma generally support Kochan, McKersie, and Cappelli's opinion on the need for a cooperative rather than confrontational union-management relationship, they note that Canadian unions are likely to resist cooperative relationships with management for fear that cooperation will weaken their ability to oppose unwanted change in the future. If unions compromise on smaller issues, the expectation on the part of management may be that they will then compromise on larger issues later on. In other words, unions could find it difficult to maintain an adversarial position if they have cooperated on earlier issues. Union members may also perceive union-management cooperation as a form of "selling out" to management and an indication that their interests are not being represented strongly enough.

More recently, Verma and Chaykowski[18] have identified several unique trends in the Canadian context that they speculate will affect the Canadian industrial relations system. The most prominent is a technologically driven shift in economic activity away from traditional production industries and toward service provision. This shift has reduced workforces because of flatter organizational structures and more efficient operations, and has threatened union membership in Canada because of unions' past focus on membership in production rather than service industries. Verma and Chaykowski note that Canadian unions have been more successful than American unions in organizing workers in service-based organizations. Another important trend relates to the implementation of the North American Free Trade Agreement, which may have two effects on the Canadian industrial relations system. First, if organizations use the provisions of the agreement to transfer work to other countries, there may be further job loss in Canada and further declines in union membership. Second, Canadian unions may see their influence reduced because it might seem excessive in contrast to the relatively weak power of American unions.

The theories of the future of unions are summarized in Table 2-4.

TABLE 2-4   Theories of the Future of Unions

Marx and Engels	– unions as means of worker resistance to exploitation by upper classes – unions serving larger political purpose – unions as method of achieving classless society
Harry Braverman	– management theories promoting control by management in workplace rather than efficiency or job satisfaction – deskilling – control of work methods and control of pace of work
Kochan, McKersie, and Cappelli	– societal and international framework in industrial relations system – employers changing from passive to active participants in industrial relations system – industrial relations part of overall organizational strategy
Chaykowski and Verma	– distinct features of Canadian industrial relations system – stability of Canadian managerial practices and attitudes in comparison to United States – Canadian unions resisting cooperation with employers

SUMMARY

As unions have developed over time, so have the perspectives on unions offered by the authors and researchers reviewed in this chapter. Significant changes in the structure, content, and control of work occurred with the Industrial Revolution, and early writers on unions suggested that unions began as a response to these changes and the poor working conditions they caused. However, as workplaces further evolved and some of the early concerns of unions were addressed, such as safety and pay rates, the functions of unions expanded to include more comprehensive attention to workers' concerns and to social issues outside the workplace. More recent authors have addressed the question of whether the historically adversarial union-management relationship is still viable in a changing workplace and economy, and have suggested issues that unions need to address in the future to remain viable.

KEY TERMS FOR CHAPTER 2

business unionism (p. 48)

control (p. 50)

creature comforts (p. 49)

deskilling (p. 56)

device of restriction of numbers (p. 44)

device of the common rule (p. 44)

friendly or uplifting unionism (p. 48)

information (p. 50)

integrity (p. 50)

method of collective bargaining (p. 44)

method of legal enactment (p .44)

method of mutual insurance (p. 43)

predatory unionism (p. 48)

psychology of the labourer (p. 45)

revolutionary unionism (p. 48)

social status (p. 49)

DISCUSSION QUESTIONS FOR CHAPTER 2

1. Describe the functions of craft guilds and identify how these are similar to the functions of modern unions.

2. How did industrialization change workers' personal and workplace conditions?

3. Identify common themes among the writers who discuss the origin of unions. Are these themes still applicable to unions being formed in the 21st century?

4. Which of the functions of unions do you see as being most relevant to current unions? Why?

5. Use Dunlop's theory of industrial relations systems to describe the relationship between a specific union and employer that you are familiar with.

6. Provide arguments for and against the validity of Braverman's theories of management control.

7. Do you agree with the assertion that unions and management need to be cooperative, not confrontational, in the modern economic system? Why or why not?

CHAPTER EXERCISES FOR CHAPTER 2

1. Read the news story at the beginning of this chapter. Which of the theories discussed in this chapter do you think best explain(s) this situation? Choose the theories that you think are most relevant, and use them to analyse the situation and to suggest what the outcomes of this conflict might be.

2. Choose a union that you are personally familiar with or one that you can research. From the information available to you, can you see evidence that supports a theory or theories in this chapter? You can look at the reasons for the origin of the union, the functions the union currently serves, its future plans, its relationship with employers, or any other area that you think is relevant. Explain how the theories you have chosen are illustrated or explained by the information you have collected. Also identify where or how the theories do not address or explain your information, and suggest why these apparent discrepancies might exist.

References

[1] This discussion is based on Commons, J. (1909). American shoemakers, 1648–1895: a sketch of industrial evolution. *The Quarterly Journal of Economics*, Vol. 24, Nov. 1909.

[2] Marsden, R. (2000). Labour history and the development of modern capitalism. In Gunderson, M., Ponak, A., & Taras, D.G. (Eds.), *Union-management relations in Canada* (4th edition). Toronto, ON: Addison-Wesley Longman.

[3] Hibbert, C. (1988). *The English: a social history, 1066–1945*. London, UK: Paladin Books.

[4] Blake, W. (ca. 1804). Jerusalem. Anthologized in Palgrave, F.T. (1861), & Williams, O. (1961), *The golden treasury of the best songs and lyrical poems*. New York, NY: Mentor Books.

[5] Thompson, E.P. (1963). *The making of the English working class*. London, UK: Victor Gollancz/Penguin Books.

[6] Hibbert, *op. cit.*

[7] Webb, S. & B. (1894). *The history of trade unionism*. New York, NY: Longmans Green and Co.; Webb, S. & B. (1897) *Industrial democracy*. New York, NY: Longmans Green and Co.

[8] Perlman, S. (1928). *A theory of the labor movement*. New York, NY: reprinted in 1949 by Augustus M. Kelley.

[9] Commons, *op. cit.*

[10] Hoxie, R.F. (1919). *Trade unionism in the United States*. New York, NY: D. Appleton and Co.

[11] Among others, Bakke, E.W. (1945). Why workers join unions. *Personnel*, 22(1), 2–11.

[12] Dunlop, J. (1958). *Industrial relations systems*. New York, NY: Holt.

[13] Dunlop, J.T., Harbison, F.H., Kerr, C., & Myers, C.A. (1975). *Industrialism and industrial man reconsidered: some perspectives on a study over two decades of the problems of labor and management in economic growth*. Princeton: Inter-University Study of Human Resources in National Development.

[14] Marx, K., & Engels, F. (1888; reprinted 1985). *The Communist manifesto* [translation by Samuel Moore]. London, UK: Penguin Books.

[15] Braverman, H. (1974). *Labor and monopoly capital*. New York: Monthly Review Press.

[16] Kochan, T., McKersie, R., & Cappelli, P. (1984). Strategic choice and industrial relations theory. *Industrial Relations, 23(1)*.

[17] Chaykowski, R., & Verma, A. (Eds.) (1992). *Industrial relations in Canadian industry*. Toronto: Dryden Press.

[18] Verma, A., & Chaykowski, R.P. (Eds.) (1999). *Contract and commitment: employment relations in the new economy*. Kingston, ON: IRC Press, Industrial Relations Centre, Queen's University.

The miners' meeting:

The Colonel makes a scene

(The following is taken from an anonymous account of the August 18, 1913 meeting at the Nanaimo, British Columbia Athletic Club at which members of the United Mine Workers of America considered an employers' proposal to end a coal miners' strike on Vancouver Island.)

Colonel Hall [Vancouver Island militia leader] recorded some splendid tricks in Nanaimo and district. He seemed to be invariably under the inspiration of some brilliant stroke of generalship. Anyhow, something had him going. This was most marked at a public meeting held by the miners to consider the Jingle Pot Mine proposal, when he appeared to think a good time had arrived for the display of some nice stage effects. When the meeting was in progress, he rushed his troops to the scene under cover of the night and surrounded the hall and placed his machine guns at the back door.

Some of his trustees peeped through the cracks and alleged that they saw the miners with guns and knives and every conceivable weapon. He thereupon sent an officer into the hall, who told the chairman that he had two minutes in which to clear the place. There were probably 14 or 15 hundred men in the hall and you can imagine what effect an order like that would have. I can conceive of many cases wherein a similar blunder might have led to a terrible tragedy in the struggle for exits.

The Colonel then said they could have one hour in which to finish their business. Later, he desired to address the meeting, and on this being granted, said they could go ahead and finish their business, but that he was tired and was going to bed. Strong suspicion is entertained that the gallant gentleman had been gazing on the wine that was red.

When the meeting had closed, the miners having voted to accept an agreement with the Vancouver and Nanaimo Coal Company, they were marched out in groups of 10, single file, in charge of special police, a guard of soldiers with bayonets fixed on either side, and marched to the courthouse. There, each man was searched, his name taken, and if he was desired, placed in detention. The remainder were then marched out on to the ground at the front of the courthouse and kept there under guard. Forty-three were detained, the remainder being kept under guard until 2 a.m. until they were allowed to disperse.

The Colonel came along the next morning and tore up the floor of the building. Perhaps he was looking for the provincial prosperity of which we have heard so much, but certain it is that he did not find any ammunition such as was alleged to have been deposited there.

(Quoted in P. Wejr and H. Smith. "Fighting for Labour: Four Decades of Work in British Columbia, 1910–1950, *Sound Heritage* 7, no. 4 [1978], pp. 18–19.)

HISTORY OF THE CANADIAN UNION MOVEMENT

objectives

In this chapter, we will discuss the origins and historical development of the Canadian union movement. By the end of the chapter, you should be able to:

- describe the geographic, cultural, economic, and political factors that are relevant to Canada
- identify the major events in Canadian labour history
- understand the role of craft and industrial unionism in shaping Canadian union structure
- discuss how American unions have influenced Canadian unions
- identify some of the regional differences in Canadian labour history

INTRODUCTION

In Chapter 2, we reviewed some of the general history and theories of unions. Our focus in this chapter will be specifically on events and forces that have affected union history in Canada. As the opening vignette shows, union history in Canada has been marked by conflict between different cultures, classes, and regions. Many of the conflicts of earlier years would be almost unknown in most 21st-century workplaces.

We will begin with an overview of some of the characteristics of this country that have affected the history of unions, and then turn to a chronologically organized discussion of significant events in the history of organized labour in Canada.

CANADA AS A COUNTRY: DISTINCT CHARACTERISTICS

Before embarking on our discussion of Canadian union history, we will first identify some distinct characteristics that have formed the framework within which this history has occurred. While some of these characteristics may seem, at first glance, rather obvious or simplistic, they are nevertheless important because of their effect on the development of industrial relations in Canada.

The first characteristic is the physical geography of this country. Canada is a large country, and it has expanded greatly since its beginnings in the 1867 merger of modern-day Ontario and Quebec with Nova Scotia and New Brunswick.[1] It currently encompasses 10 provinces and three territories within a total area of almost 10 million square kilometres.[2] Its borders reach from the Atlantic Ocean in the east to the Pacific Ocean in the west, and from the United States in the south to the Arctic Circle in the north. This vast expanse of land contains climates and physical landscapes ranging from desert to tundra, but the fact that Canada is located in the earth's northern hemisphere means that most regions in Canada have distinct seasons and severe weather conditions in at least one of those seasons. The extreme conditions in the northern part of the country make much of the land within Canada unsuitable for agricultural and other primarily resource-based activities; as a consequence, the majority of Canadians live in the southern part of the country, close to the U.S. border.

The physical characteristics of Canada have affected the history of Canadian industrial relations in several ways. As we will see, most early Canadian unions were local or regional because of the difficulty of communicating with or travelling to other parts of such a large country. Canadian climate and land conditions have forced much of Canadian industry to be either seasonal or resource based; these circumstances have made successful union organizing difficult because of the isolation and lack of permanence in employment in these industries. Proximity to the United States has also meant, at various times in Canadian union history, that American workers have competed with Canadian workers in the Canadian labour market and that American unions have exerted an influence on Canadian workers.

Another distinct characteristic of Canada is its cultural mix. The history of Canada as a whole has been influenced by immigration from other parts of the world. First Nations inhabitants were joined by British and French settlers at the time the country was formed, and much of Canada's early history was shaped by struggles between these founding groups for authority and dominance. The early influence of the French settlers is still strongly apparent in the distinct identity of Quebec and in the existence of francophone communities throughout Canada; many of these communities were influenced not only by settlement from Quebec but also by French-speaking immigrants from other countries. Immigrants from Europe, Asia, Central America, South America, and other regions around the world have also been attracted to Canada. These immigrants have settled throughout the country and brought the influence of their own cultures to their new homes. Canada's proximity to the United States has also allowed the pervasive influence of American culture.

This mix of multiple cultural influences has had both positive and negative effects on Canadian union history. The development of some early Canadian unions was assisted by immigrants who had had experience with union or union-like organizations in their countries of origin. On the other hand, Canadian unions have not always been successful in addressing the challenges of organizing or representing a culturally diverse workforce; in fact, some Canadian unions have a sad history of racial or cultural discrimination. And, as noted above, Canadian unions and workers have been affected by American unions and workers' easy access to this country.

Canada's economic system is the third characteristic we will discuss. Because of Canada's vast land mass and the rich stores of resources that can be taken from the land, the Canadian economy was historically based on activity in what are referred to as **primary** and **secondary industries**. Primary industries are resource-based industries such as forestry, fishing, and mining, and secondary industries are those industries that process or use the products of resource-based industries, such as construction and steel production. Agriculture has also been an important industry in Canada in those parts of the country where the land is suitable for farming. Toward the end of the 20th century, however, the importance of these industries has declined and **tertiary industries** (service industries) have increased their role in the Canadian economy. Another important sector of the Canadian economy is international trade, particularly with the United States. This reliance on trade with other countries means that Canada's economy is more susceptible to the influence of external events than the economy of a country less dependent on external trading relationships. Canadian unions have historically focused on workers in resource-based industries and have only been partly successful in organizing workers in tertiary industries. International trade has also challenged Canadian unions by providing employers with the opportunity to move jobs outside the country and by pressuring Canadian unions and employers to establish work conditions that are competitive internationally. In Canada, the latter has often implied a reduction in existing standards.

Our fourth and final characteristic is Canada's political structure. Canada's historical relationship with Britain is still recognized by the presence of a ceremonial federal head of state, the governor-general, and a lieutenant-governor in each province and territory. These individuals act as the British monarch's representatives and must give "royal assent" to legislation passed by provincial and federal governments. In practice, however, Canada is formally governed by a federal Parliament and by provincial or territorial legislative assemblies. Canadians elect both federal and provincial representatives; unlike other countries, such as the United States, Canadians do not vote directly for a prime minister or premier. Instead, the prime minister or premier is the leader of the political party that has the most elected members in the House of Commons or regional legislative assembly.

The importance of this division between federal and provincial jurisdictions will become more apparent as we discuss how Canadian labour legislation has developed. We will note at this point that while there are both federal and provincial labour codes, labour relations is considered to be primarily a provincial responsibility, as outlined in Chapter 1. In contrast, labour relations in the United States is considered a federal responsibility. The basis of this decision in the United States was the desire to provide a single law that would create identical frameworks for union-employer relationships across the country and ensure the same basic rights for all workers.[3] However, some evidence suggests that this decision has seriously hindered the growth of the American union movement, since a single piece of legislation cannot fully address different regional conditions. The Canadian structure of different jurisdictions in each province, while causing difficulties for employers and unions that operate in more than one province, has allowed for experimentation and reform to meet the particular needs of each jurisdiction.[4]

EARLY CANADIAN UNIONISM: THE 1800s

The early years of the Canadian union movement have been called the "period of local unionism."[5] The earliest attempts to organize trade unions were limited to specific geographic areas and small groups of workers, usually those in a particular trade or occupation. This model of organizing is known as the **craft union** model. The popularity of this organizing model in Canada in the 1800s can be attributed to two main factors. One factor was the size of Canada. The consequent difficulties of transportation and communication over long distances made organizing at the local level much more practical than attempting to organize a regional or national union. In fact, as we will see, different unions representing the same types of workers emerged at roughly the same time in different parts of Canada. The focus on organizing workers in a specific geographic area also meant that issues specific to that group could be the main focus of the union's activity; the union did not have to attempt to balance the varied concerns that would have emerged in a union encompassing workers in different regions.

The second main factor contributing to the popularity of the craft union model of organizing was the need to protect wage rates for workers in skilled trades. This factor was particularly important in areas where tradespeople's expertise could not easily be replaced by the work of unskilled immigrant labourers.[6] Forming a union was a means for tradespeople to control the market for their skills and thus to control wage rates.

Canada's economic role as an exporter, rather than importer, of goods has been identified as another factor in the predominance of the craft union model of organizing. Many of the skilled craftspeople involved in Canada's first unions were employed in trades like shipbuilding and carpentry that "benefited from the economic strategy of export-led growth."[7] The international market for exported Canadian-made goods created domestic production demand, which in turn increased the demand for skilled tradespeople's work and gave those tradespeople increased bargaining power with employers.

Informal workers' groups that undertook collective action such as strikes were formed in Canada as early as 1827. These groups protested poor wages and working conditions on large public works projects, and their structure may have been modelled on the social or fraternal societies to which many of the workers already belonged.[8] Their experiences with social and fraternal societies gave the workers the skills and knowledge needed to create informal workers' groups, and these informal alliances quite naturally operated on democratic and structural principles similar to those of the societies.

The first formal unions emerged at roughly the same time as the informal alliances. One historian identifies the first union in Canada as being either a printers' union in Quebec City in 1827 or a shoemakers' or tailors' union in Montreal in 1830.[9] Other authors point out that the Nova Scotia government of 1816 was sufficiently concerned about groups of "journeymen workmen" in Halifax who had joined together to regulate wages for their work that it attempted to outlaw such groups.[10] Still others claim that the earliest unions emerged in Saint John, New Brunswick, which in the early 1800s was a major port and shipbuilding centre. By 1840, Saint John had 10 different trades associations with a total of 1,200 members.[11]

The emergence of regionally based craft unions is understandable given the geographic and occupational difficulties that would have occurred if other forms of organizing had been used, but the prevalence of craft unionism initially inhibited any wider growth of unions in Canada. While craft unions were able to control the regional labour market for the particular skills of their members, as well as ensure consistent quality of work by controlling training, their membership was restricted to practitioners of the craft. This model of organizing did not encourage unionization of larger numbers of less-skilled workers or workers in non-trade occupations[12]—the alternative organizing model of **industrial unionism**. This form of unionism focuses on "strength in numbers" and maximizing power by recruiting as many members as possible, regardless of occupation, rather than on concentrating solely on representation of a particular elite group. In contrast, several early Canadian craft unions, such as the early miners' unions in British Columbia, were deliberately established along craft lines to exclude workers who were seen as threats to their members' living standards (e.g., immigrant Chinese labourers were perceived to be undercutting miners' wage rates in British Columbia). As we will

see, conflicts between different regional interests and conflicts between craft and industrial unionism have reoccurred throughout Canadian labour history.

Because of the dominance of craft unions, the next major expansion of the Canadian
labour movement came through affiliation with **international unions**—"international"
in this case usually meaning based in the United States. International influences were
informally present in many of the early Canadian unions. Immigrant workers from
Britain brought their experience in the British trade union movement to Canadian workplaces, and there is evidence that the first international unions in Canada were British
unions of engineers and carpenters that established affiliated locals in southern Ontario
in the mid-1800s.[13] However, because of the easy mobility of skilled workers between
Canada and the United States, it made sense for Canadian craft unions to affiliate with
American unions representing workers in similar occupations. The mid- and late 1800s
saw the **continental movement**[14] of American-based international unions entering central Canada. These unions either formally affiliated with existing Canadian unions or
recruited members into new Canadian locals of the American unions. However, the continental movement was restricted primarily to Ontario and other regions with trade
links to the United States. Few Quebec unions saw any commonalities with the
American unions, and thus most chose to remain independent to preserve their distinct
regional culture. Most of the Maritime unions also continued to be regional and craft
based. The first regional unions in British Columbia—representing typographers, ship-
wrights, and miners—emerged at approximately the same time.[15]

In the late 1800s, several events further solidified the existence of Canadian unions.
During this period, unions began to realize that it was better to work together for common
issues rather than simply to concentrate on their own concerns and activities. They thus
began to cooperate in campaigns and joint action. One example of this sort of cooperation
was the **Nine-Hour Movement** in 1872. The standard working day in most trades at this
time was 10 to 12 hours, and in Britain and the United States a movement was under way
to pass legislation restricting the working day to nine hours. It was argued that a shorter
working day would produce better quality work because workers would not be exhausted,
and it would benefit society as a whole by freeing up time that workers could spend with
their families and communities. A Nine-Hour Movement similar to the American and
British movements emerged in Hamilton and spread across southern Ontario and
Quebec.[16] "Nine-Hour Leagues" held public meetings to promote the benefits of a shorter
working day. Employers, however, resisted the idea, and this resistance eventually resulted

in a major strike in the spring of 1872 involving typesetters and printers in Toronto. Even though a rally of 10,000 workers and citizens expressed their support for the strikers, 24 union executive members were arrested and charged with conspiracy.[17]

It is important to note that at this point there was almost no Canadian legislation specifically addressing industrial relations issues. Around the time unions started to emerge in Canada, British legislators, attempting to stop the growth of unions in Britain, used existing "criminal conspiracy" or **monopoly laws** against union organizers. These laws were originally designed to stop merchants or traders from colluding with each other for the purpose of controlling or dominating a product market. British legislators expanded the application of the laws, defining unions as a method of monopolizing the labour market. Thus, under the monopoly laws, unions could be considered a means to restrain trade and "criminal conspiracy" charges could be laid against union organizers. This use of the British law was eliminated by the passage of a new *Trades Union Act* in 1871, which established the right of workers to organize a union (although there were still severe penalties against striking and picketing). Even though the Canadian legal system was dominated by the British legal system at this time, the Canadian Parliament did not choose to adopt its own version of the British *Trades Union Act*. Canadian employers could therefore still use monopoly laws to resist organizing attempts. It was under the Canadian version of the monopoly laws that the Toronto union organizers were charged in the 1872 Toronto strike.

A rather unusual set of circumstances led to the repeal of the Canadian monopoly laws. The person who laid the charges against the leaders of the Toronto strikers was George Brown, the publisher of the *Globe* newspaper. The *Globe* had been a persistent and vocal critic of the federal government led by Prime Minister Sir John A. Macdonald. Macdonald identified the "criminal conspiracy" charges against the Toronto strikers as providing an excellent opportunity to strike back against Brown and his newspaper. He promptly presented Canadian versions of the British legislation to the Canadian Parliament, and these proposals were adopted as law.[18] The charges against the Toronto strikers were dropped, but the incident had had the effect of "[breaking] the momentum" of the Nine-Hour Movement[19] and the desired reforms to the length of the working day were not gained.

The Nine-Hour Movement did, however, have one lasting effect. The inter-union networks that participation in the movement had helped to establish inspired the formation of the first federations of trade unions. The Canadian Labour Union was established in 1873, although the "Canadian" part of the name was somewhat misleading, since the first non-Ontario delegate did not attend an annual meeting until 1878.[20] A more representative group, the **Trades and Labour Congress** (TLC), formed in 1883. Although at this point only about 2 percent of the Canadian workforce was unionized,[21] the TLC was effective in lobbying for reforms to labour legislation that would benefit all workers. As we will see, the TLC remained a national force in the Canadian labour movement for the next 70 years.

Another event that significantly expanded the scope of the Canadian union movement was the entry of the first international industrial union into Canada in 1881. Several unions in the United States, recognizing the limitations of organizing on the craft-based model, were promoting the idea that all workers, regardless of occupation or employer, should belong to unions. The first union to bring this idea to Canada was the **Knights of Labor**, which had successfully organized railway workers in the United States. The Knights' entry into the Canadian union movement began with the organization of a small group of workers in Hamilton. Eventually, the Knights had 400 "local assemblies" in Canada and over one million members worldwide.[22] The Knights of Labor had a significant impact on the Canadian labour movement because they organized workers in occupations that existing Canadian unions considered too challenging to organize, such as railway work, mining, and employment in the resources sector. They even succeeded in organizing workers in "company towns,"

The Knights of Labor march down the main street of Hamilton, 1881. Such processions were seen as a symbol of order and respectability rather than militancy.

where simple matters like getting access to the town itself were challenging, since the employer who controlled the town would usually forbid even a preliminary visit from a union organizer. The Knights of Labor also organized workers—such as women and minorities—who had previously been excluded, intentionally or otherwise, from other unions' organizing efforts.[23]

The Knights' influence in Quebec was such that the province's "hierarchy" (the elite members of churches and government) obtained a letter from the Vatican that was read aloud in all Roman Catholic Churches in the province in June 1886. The papal letter

declared membership in the Knights of Labor a "grievous sin," because the organization supposedly required "unswerved obedience to occult chiefs" and thus allegedly required members to renounce their religious beliefs and loyalty to the church. Members of the Knights of
Labor who belonged to the Roman Catholic Church were banned from taking communion
and had to file declarations with their parish priest that they had left the Knights if they
wished to regain the privilege.[24] The letter caused some decline in the Knights' membership
in Quebec, but it also caused a controversy in the province because of its perceived interference with union organizing and membership. The "General Master Workman" of the
Knights, a position roughly parallel to president, met with American and Canadian Roman
Catholic bishops to lobby against the letter's pronouncements. The bishops intervened with
the church authorities on the Knights' behalf, and the letter was rescinded in mid-1887. After
the letter was withdrawn, Quebec membership in the Knights promptly increased.

A timeline of events in the 1800s is presented in Table 3-1.

TABLE 3-1	Canadian Industrial Relations Events in the 1800s
Early 1800s	Some evidence of craft unions in Saint John, New Brunswick
1816	Nova Scotia legislation involving "journeymen workmen" groups
1827	Informal worker groups formed in several regions
1827/1830	First recorded Canadian unions formed
Mid-1800s	Some British craft unions create international affiliates in Southern Ontario
Mid/late 1800s	Continental movement
1872	Nine-Hour Movement
1872	Toronto typesetters' strike and use of monopoly laws to arrest strikers
1872	First federal industrial relations legislation passed
1873	First labour federation formed (Canadian Labour Union)
1881	First international industrial unions formed
1883	Trades and Labour Congress formed
1886	Papal letter in Quebec denouncing Knights of Labor

THE INDUSTRIAL AGE: THE EARLY 1900s

In the late 1800s and early 1900s, the structure of work in Canada continued to undergo the process of transformation outlined in Chapter 2, evolving from rural-based individually controlled work to urban factory-based work. An additional complication in the Canadian scenario was American ownership of Canadian organizations and industries. While foreign investment brought new industries to Canada, such as nickel mining and pulp and paper processing, many companies in these and other Canadian industries were controlled or owned outright by American financial interests.[25] Thus, the owners were not only separate from the workers in the factory but also located in another country, exacerbating the effects of the separation between capital and labour described in Chapter 2. While Canadian workers appreciated the employment that the new industries created, particularly since many of these industries' operations were in rural or remote areas with otherwise limited job opportunities, they resented the American management that too often seemed to favour options that would maximize profits that flowed to the United States and too rarely took into consideration the circumstances of the workers or the communities where the industries were located.

A somewhat more positive form of American influence was evident in the Canadian union movement as more American union organizers arrived in Canada to recruit new members. While there were concerns about American unions being unsympathetic to Canadian workers' issues, it was also felt that the greater goal of increasing unionization in Canada was more important than the issue of which country the union was based in. Generally, the American organizers were welcomed. In 1898, the American Federation of Labor (AFL), the federation of craft unions headed by the influential leader Samuel Gompers, sent its first "fraternal delegate" to Canada to organize workers. By 1900, the AFL had over 10,000 members in its Canadian locals. Another significant event in 1900 was the passage of the federal **Conciliation Act**. This legislation created a federal department of labour and gave it the ability to appoint third-party intervenors or commissions of inquiry to assist in resolving labour disputes.[26]

The AFL's most active organizer in Canada, a carpenter from Hamilton named John Flett, was elected president of the TLC at its 1902 convention. The election of a craft union member as the president of the largest Canadian labour federation further reinforced craft unionism as the dominant model of organizing in Canada.[27] The influence of the American union movement in Canada was further solidified at the same convention by a motion restricting TLC membership. The delegates voted to forbid any national Canadian union from joining the TLC if an international union represented workers in the same occupation or with the same employer. The TLC delegates also decided to accept membership from only one central labour organization or federation in any given region of Canada. As a result of these decisions, the Knights of Labor locals and several national unions—totalling about one-fifth of the TLC's membership—were expelled.[28]

Much union organizing, however, took place independent of American or international unions in the early 1900s. An active economy created a high demand for workers, giving them greater power to advocate for better wages and working conditions. Workers often perceived unionization as necessary to ensure that wage rates matched the cost of living.[29] Economists who have studied wage levels during this period have noted that while the dollar amounts of wages increased, there was no increase in real wages (purchasing power) and that during some periods real wages actually decreased. Achieving a steady income was also important to the ever-increasing number of immigrants arriving in Canada to seek a better life, although many of these "cheap labour" immigrants were brought to the country specifically to work for substandard wages.[30]

One major industry that saw a good deal of union activity was the railway. Railways were expanding rapidly across Canada during this time and carrying increasing amounts of goods and passengers. Several major railway strikes took place, either to gain union recognition or to support demands for wage increases in light of hefty government subsidies to the industry. Workers felt that the government should subsidize not only expanded service but also better wages, since the expansion of service was only possible because of the workers' efforts. Several of the major unions representing Canadian railway workers were international unions based in the United States, however, and the American unions were not totally sympathetic to the Canadian cause. In some of the strikes, the American-based railway unions, attempting to avoid conflict with American employers, sided with the railway owners and insisted that the Canadian workers accept less than desirable contract terms.[31] These events may be seen as some of the first indications that the continental movement might have negative, rather than positive, implications for Canadian workers.

As a result of the railway strikes, the federal government, with the encouragement of Deputy Minister of Labour William Lyon Mackenzie King, passed the **Industrial Disputes Investigation Act** in 1907. This legislation required that industrial disputes under federal jurisdiction be submitted to a neutral third party, who then would either make recommendations or, by prior agreement of the parties, impose a binding decision to solve the dispute. This act was later supplemented and replaced by other legislation, but it introduced principles that are still present in many current Canadian labour laws, such as the prohibition of strikes and lockouts during the time of a third-party intervention in a dispute and requirements for conciliation before a strike or lockout takes place.[32] (Conciliation and other forms of third-party intervention in collective bargaining disputes are described in detail in Chapter 10.)

During the early 1900s, significant strike activity took place in Atlantic Canada, where unions had been much more active in organizing less-skilled and non-craft workers than unions in central Canada. The majority of these strikes were undertaken by coal miners, who were represented mainly by the regionally based and locally controlled Provincial Workmen's Association.[33] But coal miners were not the only eastern workers going on strike. A total of 411 strikes were recorded in Atlantic Canada in the period between 1901 and 1914, and 140 of these strikes were attributed to associations of unskilled labourers.[34] This statistic indicates that organizing and collective action in this region was not restricted to tradespeople and that it was much more broadly based than in the rest of the country.

The period of economic growth that began in the early 1900s lasted until about 1914, when American-based unions accounted for approximately 80 percent of total Canadian union membership.[35] Part of this American domination in the union movement was due to extensive organizing in western Canada by the **Industrial Workers of the World** (IWW), nicknamed the "Wobblies." (The origin of the nickname is unclear, although the most common explanation is that it resulted from a mispronunciation of the "IWW" acronym by an IWW organizer who had emigrated from China.) The American-based IWW was similar in philosophy and strategy to the Knights of Labor, although the Wobblies were more explicitly socialist in orientation, advocating general strikes as a means not only of achieving workers' demands, but of bringing about a new egalitarian society.[36]

A timeline of events in the early 1900s is presented in Table 3-2.

TABLE 3-2	Canadian Industrial Relations Events in the Early 1900s
Early 1900s	American investment in Canadian industries
Early 1900s	Extensive organizing in Canada by American unions
Early 1900s	Strike activity in many regions and industries
1900	Federal *Conciliation Act* passed
1901	Knights of Labor and several national Canadian unions expelled from Trades and Labour Congress
1907	*Industrial Disputes Investigation Act* passed
1910s	International Workers of the World organize extensively in western provinces.

THE FIRST WORLD WAR ERA

The advent of the First World War, following a short economic depression, had a dramatic effect on the growth of Canadian unions. Three simultaneously occurring factors made unionization more attractive to Canadian workers. The first factor was the increased production needed to supply the war effort. Dissatisfaction in the workplace grew as workers were pressured to improve their rate of production without any corresponding improvement in wages. The second factor was the continuing mechanization of production that further reduced the market value of skilled craftspeople, as tasks formerly performed by workers were taken over by machines. And, finally, the federal government expanded the jurisdiction of the *Industrial Disputes Investigation Act* to include munitions industries. This expanded jurisdiction limited the ability of workers in those industries to strike in support of their demands. As one historian states, "Resentments began to coalesce into a conviction that the whole system was stacked against workers."[37]

Many workers felt that the unions that were already established in Canada, both international and domestic, were not adequately addressing workers' concerns. A central focus for this discontent was the issue of conscription, or forced enrolment in the military.

The federal government, led by Prime Minister Robert Borden, brought in conscription to meet the government's commitment to Britain to supply a certain number of troops for its war effort. Many Canadians were upset that individuals opposed to the war were being forced through conscription to go to war and to endanger their lives; they also objected to the fact that the conscription process was structured so that workers, rather than the businesspeople profiting from the war, were being sent to the battlefields of Europe.

Despite these protests against conscription, the large Canadian unions and labour federations did not formally oppose it. The response of the TLC to the implementation of conscription was "one of inaction and compromise,"[38] and at the 1918 TLC convention, motions opposing conscription were defeated. This rejection may have occurred because of the perception in some parts of Canadian society that opposition to conscription was either outright treason or a failure to support the Canadian troops already at war. Nevertheless, the refusal of the majority of TLC delegates to take action on this significant issue caused dissent within the federation's ranks. Many of those frustrated with the inaction of established labour unions on conscription and other issues turned to more radical unions, which they felt could better represent their interests. One of the larger unions these dissenters joined was the American-based **One Big Union** (OBU), an industrial union that by 1919 had nearly 30,000 members in British Columbia.[39]

Two major events in this period illustrate how extreme the divisions between workers, government, and employers had become. The first was the death of Albert "Ginger" Goodwin, a labour organizer in British Columbia. Goodwin worked in the province's coal mines, mills, and smelters and organized unions in several of those industries. (As a union organizer, he was involved in the strike that is described at the beginning of this chapter.) Goodwin also ran for the British Columbia legislature in 1916 as a Socialist Party of Canada candidate.

When the First World War began, Goodwin actively opposed conscription. He hid in the woods of Vancouver Island to avoid being forced into military service, and when his hiding place was discovered, he was shot and killed. The Dominion Police officer who shot him claimed that Goodwin had pointed a rifle at him. The officer's version of events did not completely match some interpretations of physical evidence from the incident, and as a consequence, many union supporters believed that the officer was under special military orders to shoot Goodwin because of his union organizing activity. (One account of these events refutes the physical evidence that supposedly supports the "government conspiracy" theory, but notes: "Government and business rarely need to operate in the shadows or illegally to suppress workers' resistance to capital.... [Goodwin] was the victim of a particular set of social relations and the institutions created to protect them.")[40] Goodwin's death caused a one-day general strike of protest in Vancouver, and he is still considered a martyr by many in the union movement.

Workers topple a streetcar at the height of the Winnipeg General Strike, June 21, 1919. At the end of "Bloody Sunday," two lay dead and thirty injured.

The other major event that illustrated the widening of social divisions is the **Winnipeg General Strike**. The strike, which occurred in May 1919, is particularly significant in Canadian labour history because it was the first extended, large-scale general strike involving workers from different occupations and unions. Previous large strikes either had been short in duration or had involved workers from a single union, occupation, or employer. In the months prior to the strike, many unions across Canada had gone on strike for increased wages and the regulation of working hours, and many had been unsuccessful in reaching their demands. This general frustration boiled over in Winnipeg, where some workers, primarily in the metal and building trades, were being denied the right to collective bargaining because employers were refusing to respond to contract demands.[41]

On May 15, between 30,000 and 35,000 unionized and non-unionized workers walked off their jobs.[42] The resulting shutdown had a major impact on a city of 200,000 residents, and the reaction of the establishment was swift. A Citizens' Committee of 1000, representing most of the businessmen and employers in the city and all three levels of government, attempted to force the workers to return to work. Sympathy strikes in support of the Winnipeg strikers took place in Edmonton, Saskatoon, Toronto, and Vancouver, as well as in many smaller Canadian cities.[43]

As the strike continued, tensions increased. The mayor of Winnipeg fired the entire city police force, which had supported the strikers but had agreed to remain on duty, and replaced them with volunteer "special constables." The special constables clearly had more commitment to the orders of the civic government than to respecting the civil rights of the strikers, and their presence was denounced and resented. At the same time, the federal government took action in response to the lobbying efforts of the Citizens' Committee of 1000. Parliament passed an emergency motion that altered the *Immigration Act* to allow for immediate deportation of any immigrant and broadened the Criminal Code to allow police to make arrests on suspicion rather than evidence, and to place the burden of proof of innocence on any accused who were arrested. These were highly exceptional alterations to some very basic principles of Canadian law, and it soon became clear what the purpose of the changes was.

In mid-June, eight of the strike leaders were arrested in a single night and charged with various offences relating to conspiracy. As it happened, seven of the eight arrested were immigrants and thus were eligible for deportation under the newly altered *Immigration Act*. The acting minister of justice, Arthur Meighen, suggested that all of those arrested who were immigrants should be deported. This statement made it apparent that opposition to the Winnipeg strike was becoming entrenched at the highest levels of power in Canadian society. In response to the arrests, the strikers organized a protest march in Winnipeg on June 21. The Royal Northwest Mounted Police forcefully interrupted the relatively peaceful march, and at the end of the subsequent violence, two people were dead and 30 seriously injured.

The strike leaders gradually recognized that the objectives of the strike would not be accomplished in the face of organized opposition from such powerful forces as the government, businesses, and employers. The strike ended on June 25 with an agreement establishing limited collective bargaining rights for the metal and building trades workers. However, the divisions and resentments caused by the strike did not quickly dissipate, even after the strikers returned to work.

Many Canadian labour historians identify the Winnipeg General Strike as a turning point in the Canadian union movement. Even with extensive organizing and widespread worker support, the union movement was unable to achieve its demands when faced with the power of the state and the capitalist system. The workers involved in the strike were also disadvantaged by the dominance of international craft unions in the union movement. As had previously happened in strikes involving the Canadian railway industry, the international craft unions were willing to compromise their members' demands in order to maintain their own exclusivity and control over groups of workers and their close relationship with employers.

The OBU had been involved in events leading up to the Winnipeg General Strike, but soon after the strike, its influence in Canada decreased dramatically. This was because many members, although enthusiastic supporters of the OBU in principle, were unable to pay their union dues. Infighting between various regions and industries represented within the membership distracted attention from more significant issues, such as the financial problems facing the union.[44] The departure of lumber industry members, who intended to establish their own union, severely threatened the OBU's survival, since these members constituted about one-fourth of the total OBU membership in Canada. (The lumber workers were not completely successful in establishing an independent union of their own.) The OBU was also hurt by its participation in the 1919 Crowsnest Pass coal miners' strike, which failed to achieve the workers' demands. Consequently, the OBU's reputation as an effective worker representative was damaged. Although the OBU continued to exist, it was never able to regain the influence it once exerted.[45]

The end of the decade saw a somewhat more positive trend with new levels of unification in the Quebec labour movement. The development of unions in Quebec followed a somewhat different pattern than in the rest of Canada because of the involvement of the Catholic Church, which played a highly influential role in Quebec society at the time. Initially, many unions in Quebec were founded with the encouragement of Catholic leaders, who saw involvement in unionization as one way to re-establish the church's influence over the "labouring poor."[46] Unionization by Quebec-based and -controlled unions was also perceived as a way to resist the influence of international unions, which might not be sensitive to issues of Quebec independence and autonomy.[47] In 1921, the so-called Catholic unions formed the Confédération des travailleurs catholiques du Canada (CTCC). This federation became extensively involved in organizing workers in Quebec, and although its formal links with the Catholic Church gradually dissipated, it was increasingly militant in defending workers against the "practised ethnocentrism" of American-owned firms.[48] The CTCC was also involved in several high-profile strikes, such as the 1949 dispute involving mineworkers in the Quebec community of Asbestos. The outcome of this dispute—the achievement of most of the workers' demands—was seen as a victory both against American-based corporations and the "autocratic" government of Premier Maurice Duplessis.[49] In 1961, the CTCC became the Confédération des syndicats nationaux (CSN), or, in English, the **Confederation of National Trade Unions** (CNTU), which continues to exist today.

A timeline of events during the First World War era is presented in Table 3-3.

TABLE 3-3	Canadian Industrial Relations Events during the First World War Era
1918	War effort increases pressure for production without wage increases
1918	*Industrial Disputes Investigation Act* expanded to include munitions industries
1918	Trades and Labour Congress convention refuses to oppose conscription
1918	One Big Union organizes extensively in western provinces
1918	"Ginger" Goodwin killed on Vancouver Island
1919	Winnipeg General Strike
1919	Crowsnest Pass miners' strike
1921	Formation of Confédération des travailleurs catholiques du Canada (CTCC)

AFTER THE WAR

The conclusion of the Winnipeg General Strike was followed by the economic consequences of the end of the First World War: widespread unemployment and wage cuts. Promoting unionization was difficult when most workers were grateful just to have a job and did not want to threaten that status by antagonizing their employers. There was also disunity in the Canadian labour movement, with fighting between Canadian and international unions, craft and industrial unions, and unions with different regional concerns; such disharmony did not help to make unionization attractive to workers.[50] A poor agricultural market, the crash of the American stock market in 1929, and the subsequent Depression made life difficult for most Canadian workers and even more difficult for those who were unable to find or keep work that paid enough to live on.

There was, however, some positive activity for Canadian unions during this period of gloom.[51] First, skilled workers were still needed for many production functions in factories and workplaces, and many of these groups of workers were able to maintain their unity as craftspeople. Their ability to organize powerful unions was limited by their relatively small numbers in the workforce, but they at least were able to maintain unions that represented their own interests. Second, in some occupations (such as steelworking and longshoring), workers formed "industrial councils" (these included the less-skilled workers in the same organization) to support demands made to employers. Third, communities of ethnic immigrants within many occupations, such as Ukrainians in mining and Jews in the clothing and fabric industries, created support and information networks that could then be built upon for unionization efforts.

Unemployed workers in many parts of Canada banded together in associations to lobby for better "relief payments" (similar to modern-day employment insurance). These associations also demanded better conditions in the government-created "relief camps," where many individuals—mostly young single men—were forced to reside if they could not find employment. The relief camps were run by the federal Department of Defence, and were very strictly governed. Inmates were forced to perform manual labour for minimal wages and live in primitive conditions; moreover, they were not permitted to undertake any actions that would publicize their plight, such as making speeches, circulating petitions, or writing letters.

Two major events demonstrated the extent of the resistance to the relief camps. In 1935, a group of unemployed workers undertook the "On to Ottawa Trek," a protest that was intended to mobilize opposition to relief camps and culminate in a massive demonstration at the Parliament Buildings. The trek originated in Vancouver and swelled in size as supporters joined it in its journey across the country, but it was violently halted by the Royal Canadian Mounted Police when it reached Regina. In May 1938, protestors occupied several government buildings in downtown Vancouver to attempt to force an end to the relief camp system. The RCMP forcibly evicted the protestors on "Bloody Sunday," June 19, an event which came to be known as the "post office riots." Though neither of these events succeeded in persuading governments to dismantle the relief camps, the experience that participants gained in planning and generating support proved useful in subsequent union organizing campaigns.

Though government relief projects provided work for unemployed men in the 1930s, many objected to the harsh working conditions, which culminated in the "On to Ottawa Trek" in 1935.

Radical politics entered Canadian unionism during this period, most notably through the influence of the Communist Party.[52] The Communist Party was distrusted by many Canadians, particularly those who had immigrated to Canada to escape countries under the oppressive rule of Communist governments. Despite this distrust, the Canadian Communist Party became an attractive political alternative for workers disillusioned by the way that established parties dominated the federal and provincial governments. The Communist Party promoted unionism as one way through which the economic and capitalist systems would be transformed—a prospect that appealed to workers suffering through the Depression and events like the Winnipeg General Strike. Communist Party members became active in a number of union organizing efforts across Canada. The party also launched the All-Canadian Congress of Labour, the first major alternative to the TLC as a national federation for Canadian unions. The Congress was formed in 1927 with a membership composed primarily of industrial unions.

A significant legal event during this time was the resolution of the question of federal and provincial jurisdiction over labour relations. The case of *Snider v. Toronto Electrical Commission* raised the question of whether federal labour relations legislation—specifically, the *Industrial Disputes Investigation Act*—applied to provincially owned industries. The case went to the highest court of Canadian jurisdiction at the time, the British Privy Council. The Privy Council's ruling in 1925 determined that the federal government's jurisdiction over labour relations only extended to federally regulated industries and that all other labour relations matters were the responsibility of provincial governments. While this ruling was welcomed because it cleared up an area of long-standing confusion, it also hampered the development of Canadian unions by establishing, not a single (federal) jurisdiction, but separate provincial and federal jurisdictions for labour relations law. Organizing was thus more difficult because of the necessity to comply with multiple, and possibly varied, provincial and federal labour laws.

Although it was clear from the *Snider* ruling that provincial governments were responsible for regulation of most industrial relations in Canada, not every provincial government had labour legislation at this point. The next major development in Canadian labour legislation occurred, like several other innovations in Canadian labour relations, as a result of legislative changes in the United States. One of the ways in which American president Franklin Roosevelt attempted to counteract the effects of the Depression was by promoting legislation that encouraged worker-driven initiatives, including legislation that would protect workers' rights to unionize. Roosevelt believed that such legislation would increase productivity by reducing strikes and other time-consuming conflicts caused by American employers' refusal to recognize or to bargain with unions (such refusal was legal at that time).

Roosevelt introduced several pieces of legislation that improved conditions for American workers, including a social security plan guaranteeing pensions for retired workers and a set of basic employment standards. For the Canadian labour movement, however, the **Wagner Act** of 1935 was the most important of these laws. It guaranteed three basic rights to American workers: the right to organize, the right to collective bargaining, and the right to strike without employer harassment. Under the *Wagner Act*, employers could not refuse to acknowledge a union as the workers' representative if a vote indicated majority support among the workers for a union. Once a union was recognized, the employer was compelled to bargain with the union and could not refuse to meet with it or simply ignore its demands. Under certain conditions, the union also had the right to undertake strike action to pressure the employer to agree to its bargaining demands. While the *Wagner Act* was criticized for being too biased in favour of unions and workers, there was also recognition that formal legislation of these rights would do much to reduce union-employer conflict in the United States, some of which had resulted in very bloody and violent clashes.

The effect of enshrining these rights in legislation was powerful, and union membership in the United States increased substantially after the *Wagner Act* was passed. The *Wagner Act*'s influence on Canadian law was not immediate, but within the space of a few years after its passage, several provinces adopted provincial labour codes that included the same basic principles as the *Wagner Act*, although in a form that was somewhat less binding on the employer. Thus, the *Wagner Act* is very important in Canadian labour legislation. It was the model on which many Canadian labour codes were based, and it contains principles that are still present in most Canadian labour law.

Another influential event in the United States in 1935 was the founding of the **Congress of Industrial Organizations** (CIO). This federation was founded for two reasons: to represent workers in mass-production industries (these were becoming increasingly important in the American economy) and to organize unorganized workers. The CIO immediately ran into jurisdictional conflict with the existing American Federation of Labor (AFL), whose member unions already represented workers in some of the industries targeted for membership by the CIO. The AFL did not want to see its own membership base weakened by CIO member unions taking away AFL members, and its response to this perceived infringement was to expel CIO-affiliated unions from its own membership. The TLC in Canada, which was the AFL's Canadian affiliate, was instructed by the AFL to expel the same unions that had been expelled from the AFL in the United States. The TLC was reluctant to do so, recognizing the loss this would mean to its own membership base, but under pressure from the AFL it expelled its member unions that were CIO affiliates. In so doing, the TLC lost about 22,000 members and a considerable amount of power.[53] The CIO opened a Canadian office in 1937 and was successful in organizing Canadian steelworkers, autoworkers, and other production workers. The newly formed Canadian affiliate of the International Woodworkers of America, representing forestry workers, also joined the CIO.

The year 1935 saw the election of the first federal members of Parliament from the Co-operative Commonwealth Federation (CCF). This party was the forerunner of the present-day New Democratic Party, the Canadian political party that has been most strongly identified with the interests of the labour movement.

A timeline of events in the post–First World War period is presented in Table 3-4.

TABLE 3-4	Canadian Industrial Relations Events After the First World War
1920s	Communist Party involved in union organizing
1925	*Snider v. Toronto Electrical Commission* ruling
1929–early 1940s	Depression
1930s	Formation of associations for unemployed workers
1935	*Wagner Act* passed in United States
1935	On to Ottawa Trek
1935	Congress of Industrial Organizations (CIO) formed in United States; CIO-affiliated unions in Canada expelled from Trades and Labour Congress
1935	First Canadian Co-operative Commonwealth Federation members elected to Parliament
1938	"Post office riots" in Vancouver

THE SECOND WORLD WAR

The start of the Second World War gave the same stimulus to the Canadian economy as the start of the First World War had done. Employment dramatically increased because of increased production in support of the war effort. However, governments feared that war-related production would be disrupted by political radicals and militant workers, such as Communists involved in the Canadian union movement and workers who had been politicized by the relief camp experience. Thus, the federal government was much more interventionist in regulating the economy than it had been during the First World War.[54] One indication of this increased desire for governmental control was the 1939 expansion of the jurisdiction of the *Industrial Disputes Investigation Act*. The act's jurisdiction now included all "essential" war-related industries, and the act itself was changed to require strike votes (a vote among the membership on whether to undertake strike action or not) for a strike to be legal. As something of a balance to these controls on unionized workplaces, wage and price controls were introduced to quell workers' fear that businesses and entrepreneurs would "profiteer" from wartime shortages of goods.

Unionization rates increased significantly after the start of the war, and the divisions between industrial and craft unions became more formal at the national levels of the Canadian union movement. In 1940, the All-Canadian Congress of Labour and the CIO joined to form the **Canadian Congress of Labour** (CCL). This gave Canada two national labour federations: the CCL, which maintained its affiliation with the American industrial union-based CIO, and the Trades and Labour Congress (TLC), which as we have seen was historically affiliated with the American craft union-based American Federation of Labour. The CCL's affiliation with the CIO was less rigid than the TLC's affiliation with the AFL. Most notably, the CIO did not try to direct the business of its Canadian affiliates, which was something that the TLC had actively done in the past.[55]

Despite the restrictions imposed by the newly expanded jurisdiction of the *Industrial Disputes Investigation Act*, strike activity increased in the first few years of the war. By 1943, one of every three union members was on strike, a number that exceeded the previous peak of strike activity in 1919.[56] This level of strike activity was attributable to the expertise and resources that were now available to Canadian unions through their international affiliations. The international unions provided guidance and leadership based on experience gained elsewhere, and offered financial support so that striking workers could continue their actions after other resources were exhausted. The high level of strike activity was also attributable to the organizing and political experience that many union members had gained in the pre-war years. The federal government, headed by William Lyon Mackenzie King, did not recognize this new reality. It was only after a long and bitter gold miners' strike in northern Ontario in 1941–42, during which the government was criticized for ineffectiveness, that the government took action and reworked the federal labour legislation to acknowledge the increased skills and resources that union members possessed. The government was also encouraged to be more supportive of workers by some significant provincial and federal electoral wins by the CCF, indications that workers were prepared to vote for political parties friendly to labour and to vote against governments that did not support workers' interests.

In early 1944, the federal government passed **P.C. 1003**, a wartime order-in-council (similar in effect to a law passed by Parliament in peacetime) modelled on the American *Wagner Act*. The provisions of P.C. 1003 included compulsory collective bargaining and the right of "employee representatives" to be certified as bargaining agents by a labour relations board if the representatives could prove that they had sufficient support among employees in a workplace. The passage of P.C. 1003 led to further union organizing because of the legislative recognition of employee and union rights, and Quebec and British Columbia passed similar acts at the provincial level.

A timeline of events during the Second World War is presented in Table 3-5.

TABLE 3-5	Canadian Industrial Relations Events During the Second World War
1939	*Industrial Disputes Investigation Act* expanded to cover "essential" war-related industries and to require strike votes
1940	Canadian Congress of Labour formed
1941-42	Gold miners' strike in Ontario
1943	Highest level of strike activity to that point in Canadian history
1944	P.C. 1003 passed

AFTER THE SECOND WORLD WAR

When the Second World War ended in 1945, there were fears that the experience of post-war economic depression that had followed the First World War would be repeated.[57] The return of soldiers from the war and the gradual reduction of the war industry led to unemployment in large cities, especially among women workers who had worked in factories while male workers were serving in the armed forces. The Mackenzie King government attempted to offset this economic decline by giving gratuities and tax credits to the returning veterans. The government also subsidized retraining and education programs to keep the veterans temporarily out of the labour market and thus avoid massive increases in unemployment rates.

An important event for union-management relations during this time was the settlement of the first major Canadian post-war strike. In late 1945, workers at the Ford motor plant in Windsor struck over the issue of job security, motivated by concerns about post-war downsizing, and demanded a "closed shop," where union membership was a condition of employment—that is, workers would have to join the union if they wanted to work in the plant. The dispute over the issue of the closed shop went to arbitration, and Justice Ivan Rand was chosen to make a decision. According to Rand's settlement, union dues would be automatically deducted from every worker's paycheque. In exchange, the union would allow individuals to formally opt out of union membership if they so desired. The automatic deduction of union dues was awarded in recognition of the union's activities in representing the interests of all workers to management. The so-called **Rand Formula** was being used by 90 percent of Canadian unions by 1950.[58]

Other unions, however, were less concerned with the closed shop and job security issues and more concerned with immediate issues, such as ensuring that wage rates kept pace with inflation. Post-war price increases led unionized workers to demand matching wage increases. Despite the existence of legislation ensuring workers' rights to organize and bargain collectively, many employers were not responsive to these demands. Employers had assumed that the passage of P.C. 1003 had been a temporary necessity to keep operations going during the war and that they would not be compelled to recognize or to bargain with unions once the war was over.[59] This conflict led to a series of large, extended strikes in 1946 involving the lumber industry in British Columbia, the shipping industry on the Great Lakes, and the textile industry in Quebec.

Further large-scale strikes occurred regularly across the country for the next four years. It was clear that the Canadian industrial relations system needed the same sort of permanent regulation as the *Wagner Act* had brought to the American system. Thus, the federal government enshrined the principles of P.C. 1003 in the *Industrial Relations and Disputes Investigation Act* of 1948 (the precursor to the current *Canada Labour Code*), and by 1950 nearly every province had a provincial labour code with similar guidelines.[60]

Another significant event in this period was the previously mentioned strike in the Quebec community of Asbestos in 1949. This strike was notable both because of the level of conflict it generated and because of its repercussions for the Quebec union movement. The cause of the strike was a breakdown in negotiations between the asbestos workers' union and the management of the American-owned plant in the community. The workers chose to undertake an illegal strike, which was promptly declared as such by the Quebec government. However, the union had support from the local Catholic churches and also from the powerful archbishop of Montreal, Joseph Charbonneau.[61] The archbishop had spent several years working in impoverished communities in northern Ontario and was well aware of the problems faced by workers in isolated towns controlled by American-based companies. He ordered that collections of money to support the strikers be taken at every Catholic church in Quebec. The provincial government of Premier Maurice Duplessis responded to the strike by sending armed police to Asbestos; strikers retaliated against the police presence by beating company officials and dynamiting company property. In early May, strikers, incensed that the company had hired replacement workers to operate the mines, attacked the mines and their police guards. More police arrived and arrested over 200 strikers.

The strike lasted until late June, when a settlement was negotiated with the help of the archbishop of Quebec. The initial agreement was that the union would be re-certified and the striking workers would receive a small raise and be reinstated (except for those who had been convicted of violent activity during the strike). Other issues would be sent to arbitration. However, after production resumed, approximately 100 strikers were not reinstated, and the arbitration did not produce many gains. Nevertheless, the continued existence of the union was considered a victory both against the employer and against the Duplessis government, which had not been supportive of the strikers or the strike.

The Asbestos strike "served notice to the world that the Catholic unions were no less militant than their secular counterparts."[62] It also marked the end of the formal relationship between the Catholic Church and the union movement in Quebec. Under pressure from more conservative elements in Quebec society, the church sent Archbishop Charbonneau to a new posting in British Columbia. A "pastoral letter" in early 1950 formally removed the church from involvement in Quebec's trade unions.

A timeline of post-Second World War events is presented in Table 3-6.

TABLE 3-6	Canadian Industrial Relations Events After the Second World War
1945	Post-war unemployment
1945	Ford strike in Windsor; resolution creates Rand Formula
1946	Major strikes in lumber, shipping, and textile industries
1947	*Industrial Relations and Disputes Investigation Act* passed
1950	Provincial labour codes in place in nearly every province
1949–50	Asbestos strike in Quebec

THE 1950s AND 1960s

Most Canadian labour historians view the 1950s and 1960s as a period of relatively strife-free growth and development for unions.[63] Many basic issues, like the ability of workers to organize and to bargain collectively, had been resolved by the passage of federal and provincial labour legislation. And by this time the post-war effects on the economy and unemployment had dissipated. Even the inter-union disputes within Canada were reduced somewhat when, in 1956, the TLC and the CCL followed the lead of their American affiliates and merged to form a single national Canadian labour federation, the **Canadian Labour Congress** (CLC). The CLC in turn affiliated with a Quebec counterpart, the Quebec Federation of Labour (QFL). (The QFL operates under a different affiliation agreement with the CLC than do other CLC components, one significant difference being that local unions in Quebec whose parent union is a CLC member can choose to be affiliated with either the CLC or the QFL. This relationship is outlined in more detail in Chapter 4.)

One issue of concern to many people in the labour movement during this period was the increasing bureaucratization and centralization of the predominantly international unions.[64] Most large unions had a centralized office and paid staff, usually located in Ottawa or in a provincial capital to facilitate interactions with government. But there was concern, particularly in unions that had membership across the country, that this form of bureaucratic structure did not facilitate operations in a country with strong regional differences. The centralization of major operations and paid staff in a single location was thought to make union bureaucrats less sensitive to regional issues. There was also concern that those at the top of the centralized union structures were more focused on formalizing and strengthening their own power than on addressing the needs of the membership.

The influence of "parent" American unions was another problematic issue. The American branches of international unions were much larger than most Canadian branches; Canadian membership in international unions was usually a relatively small percentage of the union's total membership. Some Canadian union members felt that American union leaders did not care about Canadian concerns, since there were not usually enough Canadian members to make Canadian issues a priority in the international union. There was also a perception that American union leaders simply expected Canadian union members to follow what American members were doing, without taking into consideration the distinct characteristics of the Canadian economy and Canadian working conditions. And the concerns about centralization of Canadian union operations were heightened in the international unions, whose offices were usually located in American cities.

Despite the general climate of relative peace, there were some bitter industrial disputes during this time. In 1957, a disagreement over the legality of a denied certification led to a lengthy and violent strike in Murdochville, Quebec, involving the United Steelworkers and a copper mining firm.[65] A striker

Jean Marchand (right) pitches in during the Murdochville Copper Strike in Quebec, 1957. It helped pave the way for the "Quiet Revolution" reforms of the 1960s.

was killed in a dynamite explosion, and strikebreakers rolled boulders onto the cars of demonstrators who supported the union. The strike, which lasted nearly seven months and involved 1,100 workers, ended with the union conceding defeat. The company sued the union for damages in a court case that dragged on for nearly 13 years. Although the union ended up having to pay over $2 million in damages, it later succeeded in certifying the mine.

Another major dispute occurred in 1958 and 1959, when a local of the International Woodworkers of America (IWA) succeeded in obtaining a certification for lumber industry workers in Newfoundland after a lengthy organizing campaign. The employer rejected a conciliator's suggestions for terms of a first collective agreement, and the union went on strike on the last day of 1958.[66] Violence soon erupted on the picket lines when replacement workers were brought in, and many strikers and union leaders were arrested and jailed. The premier of Newfoundland, Joey Smallwood, was opposed to the presence of the IWA because he considered it a "foreign union." It has been suggested he was more concerned about the possibility of having a strong union in the Newfoundland lumber industry as opposed to the existing weak unions in the province that generally conceded to employers' demands.[67] Smallwood announced the formation of a new union to replace the IWA. He also pushed a bill through the Newfoundland legislature that gave the government the authority to dissolve any union whose leaders "have been convicted of any heinous crime such as trafficking in narcotics, manslaughter, extortion, embezzlement, or perjury."[68] Under this bill, the IWA was decertified, as were the Teamsters, even though the latter had no direct involvement in the lumber industry dispute.

Although Smallwood's actions were denounced across the country, the IWA's reputation was severely damaged by a March 11, 1959, fight between strikers, RCMP, and Royal Newfoundland Constabulary police in which a policeman, William Moss, was fatally injured. This turned the tide of public opinion in Newfoundland against the IWA, and Smallwood's union, the Brotherhood of Woods Workers, was taken over by the carpenters' union and became part of the CLC. Eventually, the carpenters' union was given the certification that the IWA had originally been granted, and Smallwood's controversial amendments to the province's labour code were rescinded.

The start of the 1960s saw the beginning of an extended period of growth in the Canadian union movement, mostly due to extensive organizing in the public sector. Public sector unionization had been relatively minor up to this point because of the perception that employment in the public service was, as the name suggests, a form of service to the community or the country that implicitly required a long-term commitment. The concept of "service" included the intrinsic satisfaction of contributing to the successful functioning of a democratic society. Because of the intrinsic satisfaction and service orientation of the work, public sector workers were usually prepared to accept a lower standard of compensation than they would earn for similar work in the private sector.[69] However, public servants were not unaware that private sector wages and working conditions were increasingly becoming superior to those in the public sector. Although federal and most provincial public servants had previously been explicitly denied collective bargaining rights, public servants in some provinces, such as Saskatchewan and Quebec, were granted full bargaining rights by the early 1960s. This innovation led to demands from other public servants—federal, provincial, regional, and municipal—for the same conditions.

In 1965, two circumstances made public sector unionization more of a priority for the federal government. Drawing lessons from a national postal strike, the government realized that ignoring public sector bargaining issues would have negative consequences. A federal election around the same time as the postal strike resulted in the election of a Liberal minority government. The Liberals in Parliament were dependent on the parliamentary support of the New Democratic Party—labour's friend—to maintain their power to govern.[70] Since the minority government would thus benefit in several ways from satisfying labour's demands, the federal government passed the *Public Service Staff Relations Act*, which gave federal public servants the right to arbitration or strike action to settle bargaining disputes. This act served as the model for most provincial public service legislation, and by 1975 every province and territory had some form of labour relations legislation governing public service employees.

During the same period, when federal public service labour issues were prominent, extensive organizing took place in the **para-public sector**. This sector, as noted earlier, consists of municipal or regional governments and organizations that receive funding from governments but whose employees are not directly employed by the government; hospitals and schools, for example, are in the para-public sector. There was dissatisfaction among workers in this sector because of threatened funding cutbacks, which would likely result in job losses. There was also frustration, particularly among professionals, that the bureaucratic structures of para-public organizations did not respect or value employees' skills and judgement.[71] Disputes over pay equity for public servants eventually led to extensive public sector strikes in Quebec, some involving as many as

200,000 workers.[72] The pattern of unionization in the para-public sector was somewhat different from that in the public sector, where most workers joined a public sector union rather than a union specific to their occupation. Some para-public sector workers joined existing public sector unions; others joined the Canadian Union of Public Employees (CUPE), a newer public sector union that conducted extensive organizing campaigns among municipal and regional government workers. Other public and para-public sector workers, such as teachers and social workers, already belonged to professional associations representing their occupation. They obtained certification by remaining in the same association but applying to have the association recognized as a union.

It was apparent during this period that changes in technology were having an impact on Canadian workplaces, as they had begun to reduce or eliminate entire occupations. As early as 1957, railway workers had gone on strike (and lost) over the issue of the replacement of coal-burning locomotives with diesel-powered locomotives. The introduction of diesel locomotives meant the loss of jobs for workers who handled coal for the railways. In 1964, typesetters at Toronto-area newspapers went on strike because technological changes in printing had eliminated the need for jobs such as theirs. Management was able to continue production of the newspapers, and the strike did not formally end until 1972, "although the union had lost long before then."[73]

A timeline of events in the 1950s and 1960s is presented in Table 3-7.

TABLE 3-7	Canadian Industrial Relations Events in the 1950s and 1960s
1956	Canadian Labour Congress (CLC) forms and affiliates with Quebec Federation of Labour (QFL)
1957	Murdochville copper miners' strike
1957	Railway workers' strike over introduction of diesel locomotives
1958	International Woodworkers' strike in Newfoundland
1960s	Extensive public and para-public sector organizing
1964–72	Toronto typesetters' strike
1965	*Federal Public Service Staff Relations Act* passed

THE 1970s AND 1980s

By the early 1970s, several different factors were at work to cause disruption in the Canadian economy.[74] Unemployment and inflation were both on the rise, and growth in North American markets was being overshadowed by the emergence of new economic powers in other parts of the world. Much discussion about this disruption focused on unions, especially the relatively new public sector unions. Unions' emphasis on wages in collective bargaining contributed to the perception that unions caused price inflation; the cost of higher wages, it was argued, led to higher prices. Unions were also blamed for lower productivity, since the workplace rules imposed by collective agreements supposedly reduced employers' ability to use workers in the most efficient fashion. In sum, union demands for better wages and working conditions were seen as a widespread cause of rising prices and, more simply, as "greed and selfishness."[75]

As a result of these perceptions, the federal government began to explore the possibility of imposing wage controls. The CLC and other labour organizations mounted strong opposition to this idea, believing that it would be unfair to restrict wages if there were no parallel controls on prices. Despite these concerns, in October 1975, the government implemented a three-year program of wage and price controls. The entire public sector workforce, workers in large private sector companies, and self-employed professionals were restricted to predetermined limits for annual wage increases. Collective agreements falling under the program had to be submitted to an Anti-Inflation Board in Ottawa, which would determine whether the agreements followed the guidelines and recommend or impose revisions if not. The board was also expected to regulate price increases, which were to match increases in costs, but "this stipulation was a good deal more flexible than the explicitly defined wage targets."[76]

Opposition to the wage and price controls was immediate and strong. The CLC pulled its representatives from all federal consultative committees and promoted the idea of a one-day national strike to protest the program. Strike activity rose significantly after the program was introduced, and the one-day national strike proposed by the CLC took place on October 15, 1976. More than one million workers across the country participated, although levels of participation were uneven across regions.[77] However, overall participation was high enough to set records for amounts of time lost due to industrial conflict.[78] The wage and price controls program ended as planned in 1978, but its effects were unclear. Prices increased sharply after the program ended, but, as several historians point out, controlling domestic prices and wages is a difficult task in an economy as dependent on international trade as Canada's. Thus, the fact that prices increased after the program was no longer in effect does not indicate that the program was a success.

By the start of the 1980s, Canadian government economic policy was much more interventionist than it had been in the years immediately preceding.[79] Interest rates were deliberately increased to combat high inflation, but the side effect was a recession that saw the worst unemployment levels since the 1930s. At the same time, eligibility for the established "safety net" of social programs was tightened, which meant that many Canadians who formerly relied on various forms of social assistance to carry them through periods of unemployment or underemployment were no longer eligible for such support. In addition, the amount of funding directed to social assistance programs was reduced in many Canadian jurisdictions, further restricting the support available for Canadians unable to find work.

Because the unionization of the public sector was still perceived as a cause of Canada's economic problems, both federal and provincial governments took action to reduce the bargaining power of public sector unions. Stricter penalties against public sector strikes were instituted in many jurisdictions, and back-to-work legislation was frequently used to end strikes. These deterrents, however, did not slow down strike activity in the public sector. In fact, there were numerous private and public sector strikes in the 1970s and 1980s, some resulting in jail terms for union leaders and financial penalties for unions that refused to obey back-to-work orders. These high-profile strikes included the 1972 Quebec public sector strike, which resulted in the jailing of several union leaders who defied a back-to-work order, and the 1978 nationwide postal worker strike, during which union leaders were arrested after refusing to honour Parliament's law forcing a return to work. There was also an eight-and-a-half-month-long strike by Ontario steelworkers in 1978, followed by another lengthy strike by the same workers in 1981.

The 1980s saw cutbacks in public service employment in many provinces owing to reduced government funding and the "contracting out" of functions previously performed by unionized public sector workers. Changes in legislation in several Canadian jurisdictions made organizing and bargaining more difficult than in the past; one such change was the federal government's 1982 suspension of public servants' bargaining rights for two years.

The passage of the federal **Charter of Rights and Freedoms** in 1982 provided a new set of guidelines for Canadian industrial relations, as the Charter included guarantees of such rights as the freedom of association. As outlined in Chapter 1, several cases tested the applicability of Charter provisions to such questions as whether the choice to belong to a union or the right to picket were protected, and the decisions in most of these cases did not strengthen or protect unions' powers. The election of a federal Conservative government in 1984 and the emergence of major business alliances such as the Business Council on National Issues also created a hostile atmosphere for Canadian unions. The period saw several major private sector strikes, such as the lengthy and occasionally violent 1984 strike at the Gainer's meatpacking plant in Edmonton, a conflict that indicated that unionized workers were not prepared to give up the standards they had previously achieved.

During this period, a fair amount of internal dissent within the union movement threatened solidarity on larger issues. In 1973, the **Confederation of Canadian Unions** (CCU) was formed as an alternative to the Canadian Labour Congress. The CCU was meant to be a national federation for Canadian-based unions that felt that the CLC's domination by American-controlled international unions did not serve Canadian interests. However, the CCU had difficulty challenging the established power and control of the CLC. Their position received some support from the construction workers' unions in the CLC, which shared the resentment of American dominance in the CLC. This resentment was intensified when the CLC did not support the construction unions in a dispute between local and international unions in Quebec. (These unions broke away to form a new Canadian Federation of Labour in 1982, which lasted until 1997.) However, the American dominance of the CLC was most severely challenged in 1985, when one of the largest constituencies within the CLC, the Canadian locals of the United Auto Workers, split with their American parent and formed the Canadian Auto Workers. This union has since merged with other unions and organized new locals to become one of the largest private sector unions in Canada.

The trend that developed in this period toward Canadian control of Canadian unions has continued to the present day. The demise of the CFL and CCU has left the CLC and the Quebec-based QFL and CNTU, as the major national labour federations in Canada.

A timeline of events in the 1970s and 1980s is presented in Table 3-8.

TABLE 3-8	Canadian Industrial Relations Events in the 1970s and 1980s
1973	Confederation of Canadian Unions (CCU) formed
1974	Federal wage and price controls program begins
1976	National one-day strike on October 15
1978	Postal workers' strike
1978	Federal wage and price controls program ends
1982	Canadian Federation of Labour (CFL) formed
1982	*Charter of Rights and Freedoms* becomes law
1984	Gainer's meatpacking plant strike in Edmonton begins
1985	Canadian Auto Workers formed

THE 1990s AND BEYOND

The major event affecting Canadian industrial relations in the 1990s has been the advent of liberalized international trade.[80] This has included the signing of the **North American Free Trade Agreement** (NAFTA) in 1992, Canada's participation in world-wide tariff reductions under the 1994 General Agreement on Tariffs and Trade, and the 1995 creation of the World Trade Organization. A side agreement to NAFTA protects basic standards in each member country, such as minimum wages and the right to bargain collectively. However, NAFTA does not provide for the creation of common social and labour standards among participating countries, as do similar trade agreements such as the European Union agreement.

The effects of NAFTA and other agreements have been varied. Some employers have used NAFTA provisions to move formerly unionized jobs to regions where labour costs are lower and workers are not unionized. These movements have caused job losses in Canada and brought pressure on unions to agree to lower wage rates so products can remain cost-competitive. As will be outlined in chapters 12 and 13, Canadian unions have been more reluctant to agree to such concessions than their American counterparts and have proposed increases in productivity and workplace structuring rather than wage reductions to keep product costs competitive.

Unionization rates in Canada did not drop significantly in the 1990s, although there has been a slow gradual decline since the 1970s. Chapter 13 outlines how unions are attempting to reverse this trend by targeting organizing campaigns at groups of workers traditionally under-represented in union membership: women, minorities, and workers in service industries, where the majority of new jobs in Canada are created. Unions in Quebec have tried other strategies to maintain their viability, including signing "social contracts" wherein unions guarantee labour peace in exchange for employment security and a formal role in administration of the collective agreement. This strategy has, at least initially, resulted in a dramatic drop in strike rates in Quebec, formerly one of the most strike-prone jurisdictions in Canada.[81]

A final trend of note in the 1990s, and one that is still playing itself out, is the reduced political influence of the New Democratic Party (NDP), historically, as noted previously, the Canadian political party most closely allied with union interests. The NDP has not had the same formal links with organized labour as the Labour Party in Britain has had with the Trades Union Congress (TUC), the British equivalent of the CLC (the TUC, for example, enjoys elected representation on the national Labour Party executive), but the NDP has still been the political party considered most sympathetic to workers' and unions' concerns. Although the NDP has never formed a federal government in Canada, in the 1960s and 1970s it had a sizeable number of members in the House of Commons and NDP majorities were achieved in several provincial legislative assemblies. At present, however, the NDP has barely enough Members of Parliament to maintain official party status in the House of Commons, and it is the majority party in only two provincial or territorial governments (Saskatchewan and Manitoba). No feasible political alternative to the NDP has yet presented itself to the labour movement; it remains to be seen what this reduction in union-friendly political representation will imply for future legislation and policy.

SUMMARY

The history of industrial relations in Canada is long and varied. It contains manifestations of many of the forces that have shaped Canada as a whole: conflict between regions, conflict between economic and social classes, and conflict between different ideals. At the conclusion of this intricate story, and with the lessons of the past kept in mind, the future can be viewed negatively or positively. The negative perspective would include the power of internationalization, perhaps greater now than at any time in Canada's past, and the pressures it may exert on Canada's industrial relations system. The negative perspective might also view the slow decline in unionization rates and the weakening representation of unions' interests in the political arena as forces that will further erode the power of unions in Canada. On the other hand, the positive perspective would compare the Canadian industrial relations experience to the American industrial relations experience and note that Canada's unionization rates have remained steady while American rates have declined sharply and show little signs of recovery to previous levels. The positive perspective, after considering the history that this chapter has reviewed, would note how the actors in the Canadian industrial relations system have continually been successful in shaping the system to adapt to whatever challenges have developed. The positive perspective would suggest that the Canadian industrial relations system has continued to exist and function for well over a century and that there is no reason to expect that its adaptability will not continue. As with all histories, the story will continue to be written one way or the other.

KEY TERMS FOR CHAPTER 3

Canadian Congress of Labour (p. 90)

Canadian Labour Congress (p. 94)

Charter of Rights and Freedoms (p. 101)

Conciliation Act (p. 77)

Confederation of Canadian Unions (p. 101)

Confederation of National Trade Unions (p. 84)

Congress of Industrial Organizations (p. 88)

continental movement (p. 73)

craft union (p. 71)
Industrial Disputes Investigation Act (p. 79)
industrial unionism (p. 72)
Industrial Workers of the World (p. 79)
international union (p. 73)
Knights of Labor (p. 75)
monopoly laws (p. 74)
Nine-Hour Movement (p. 73)
North American Free Trade Agreement (p. 102)
One Big Union (p. 81)
para-public sector (p. 97)
P.C. 1003 (p. 91)
primary industry (p. 70)
Rand Formula (p. 92)
secondary industry (p. 70)
tertiary industry (p. 70)
Trades and Labour Congress (p. 75)
Wagner Act (p. 88)
Winnipeg General Strike (p. 82)

DISCUSSION QUESTIONS FOR CHAPTER 3

1. Explain why the craft union model of organization was dominant in the early Canadian union movement.

2. What are the negative aspects of the craft union model?

3. How does a craft union differ from an industrial union?

4. What were the advantages and disadvantages for Canadians joining an international union rather than a Canadian-based union?

5. Describe and contrast the effects that the two world wars had on the Canadian economy and on the union movement.

6. Describe the relationship between the *Wagner Act* and *P.C. 1003*.

7. How has the history of the union movement in Quebec differed from that in the rest of Canada?

8. Outline the reasons why union organizing occurred in the public and para-public sectors.

9. How have Canada's international trade linkages affected conditions for workers in Canada?

10. Do you agree with the negative or the positive perspectives outlined at the end of the chapter? Explain why.

CHAPTER EXERCISES FOR CHAPTER 3

1. Choose a union that you are familiar with or that you can research. (You can select either a local of a union or a union as a whole, although this exercise may be easier to conduct if you select a local.) Using the information available to you, describe the history of this union. You may want to answer such questions as:

   - When was the union formed?

   - What were the reasons for its formation?

   - How has the union evolved or changed since its formation, and why?

   - What would you see as the most significant events in the history of this union?

   - Can you identify events or trends described in this chapter that have had an impact on the history of this union?

   - What do you think will be important issues in the future for this union?

2. Using the information in this chapter and whatever additional material you can acquire, describe the history of industrial relations in your province or geographic area. You may want to address questions such as:

   - What was the first union (or worker group) organized in your area, and how did it come into existence?

   - How has labour legislation in your province or area evolved and changed?

   - Who are some of the more significant individuals or groups in your province's or area's industrial relations history, and why are they important?

- Have any of the events or trends described in this chapter affected your province's or area's industrial relations history?

- What do you see as being important future issues for industrial relations in your province or area?

R e f e r e n c e s

[1] Creighton, D. (1970). *Canada's First Century, 1867–1967*. Toronto, ON: Macmillan.

[2] The National Atlas of Canada, <http://atlas.gc.ca/english/facts/faq.htm>.

[3] Downie, B.M. (1992). Industrial relations in elementary and secondary education: a system transformed? In Chaykowski, R.P., and Verma, A. (Eds.), *Industrial relations in Canadian industry*. Toronto, ON: Dryden.

[4] Craig, A.W.J., and Solomon, N.A. (1996). *The system of industrial relations in Canada*. Toronto, ON: Prentice-Hall Canada.

[5] Forsey, E. (1982). *Trade unions in Canada*. Toronto, ON: University of Toronto Press.

[6] Morton, D., and Copp, T. (1984). *Working people: an illustrated history of the Canadian labour movement*. Ottawa, ON: Deneau Publishers.

[7] Drache, D. (1994). The Canadian working class, 1820–1920. In Bercuson, D.J., and Bright, D. (Eds.), *Canadian labour history: selected readings* (2nd edition). Toronto, ON: Copp Clark Longman.

[8] Russell, B. (1990). *Back to work? Labour, state, and industrial relations in Canada*. Toronto, ON: Nelson.

[9] Lipton, C. (1978). *The trade union movement in Canada, 1827–1959*. Toronto, ON: NC Press.

[10] For example, Williams, J. (1975). *The story of unions in Canada*. Toronto, ON: J.M. Dent and Sons (Canada); Morton and Copp, *op. cit.*

[11] Forsey, *op. cit.*

[12] Heron, *op. cit.*

13 Logan, H. (1928). *The history of trade-union organization in Canada*. Chicago, IL: University of Chicago Press.

14 Heron, *op. cit.*

15 Forsey, *op. cit.*

16 Heron, *op. cit.*

17 Forsey *op. cit*; Logan, *op. cit.*

18 Morton and Copp, *op. cit.*

19 Heron, *op. cit.*

20 Heron, *op. cit.*

21 Drache, *op. cit.*

22 Heron, *op. cit.*

23 Forsey, *op. cit.*

24 Forsey, *op. cit.*

25 Heron, *op. cit.*

26 Russell, *op. cit.*

27 Morton and Copp, *op. cit.*

28 Drache, *op. cit.*

29 Lipton, *op. cit.*

30 Creese, G. (1988). Exclusion or solidarity? Vancouver workers confront the "Oriental problem." In MacDowell, L.S., and Radforth, I.W. (Eds.) (2000), *Canadian working class history* (2nd edition). Toronto, ON: Canadian Scholars' Press.

31 Lipton, *op. cit.*

32 Williams, *op. cit.*

[33] Logan, *op. cit.*

[34] McKay, I. (1983). Strikes in the Maritimes, 1901–1914. In Bercuson and Bright, *op. cit.*

[35] Palmer, B.D. (1983). *Working-class experience: the rise and reconstitution of Canadian labour, 1800–1980.* Toronto, ON: Butterworth and Co.

[36] Leier, M. (1999). *Rebel life: the life and times of Robert Gosden, revolutionary, mystic, labour spy.* Vancouver, BC: New Star Books.

[37] Heron, *op. cit.*, p. 52.

[38] Leier, *op. cit.*

[39] Leier, *op. cit.*

[40] Leier, *op. cit.*, p. 84.

[41] Palmer, *op. cit.*

[42] Lipton, *op. cit.*

[43] Palmer, *op. cit.*

[44] Bercuson, D. (1978). Labour's civil war. In Bercuson and Bright, *op. cit.*

[45] Bercuson, *op. cit.*

[46] Palmer, *op. cit.*

[47] Rouillard, J. (1987). Major changes in the Confédération des travailleurs catholiques du Canada. In MacDowell and Radforth, *op. cit.*

[48] Palmer, *op. cit.*

[49] Williams, *op. cit.*

[50] Wejr and Smith, *op. cit.*

[51] Heron, *op. cit.*

[52] Heron, *op. cit.*

[53] Williams, *op. cit.*

[54] Heron, *op. cit.*

[55] Williams, *op. cit.*

[56] Heron, *op. cit.*

[57] Morton and Copp, *op. cit.*

[58] Roberts, W., and Bullen, J. (1985). A heritage of hope and struggle: workers, unions, and politics in Canada, 1932–1982. In Bercuson and Bright, *op. cit.*

[59] Morton and Copp, *op. cit.*

[60] Heron, *op. cit.*

[61] Morton and Copp, *op. cit.*

[62] Morton and Copp, *op. cit.*, p. 200.

[63] Godard, J. (1990). *Industrial relations, the economy and society.* Toronto, ON: McGraw-Hill Ryerson.

[64] Heron, *op. cit.*

[65] Williams, *op. cit.*

[66] Williams, *op. cit.*

[67] Morton and Copp, *op. cit.*

[68] Bill amending *Labour Relations Act*, Newfoundland House of Assembly, 6 March 1959, quoted in Williams, *op. cit.*

[69] Godard, *op. cit.*

[70] Heron, *op. cit.*

[71] Heron, *op. cit.*

[72] Williams, *op. cit.*

[73] Williams, *op. cit.*, p. 213.

[74] Heron, *op. cit.*

[75] Heron, *op. cit.*, p. 121.

[76] Russell, *op. cit.*

[77] Heron, *op. cit.*

[78] Russell, *op. cit.*

[79] Heron, *op. cit.*

[80] Lipsig-Mummé, C. (2000). Trade union and labour relations systems in comparative perspective. In Gunderson, M., Ponak, A., and Taras, D.G. (Eds.), *Union-management relations in Canada* (4th edition). Toronto, ON: Addison Wesley Longman.

[81] Déom, E. and Boivin, J, (2000). Labour-management relations in Quebec. In Gunderson, Ponak, and Taras, *op. cit.*

Renegade CAW sets sights on disgruntled public servants:

Union no longer welcome in "House of Labour"

OTTAWA—The footloose Canadian Auto Workers (CAW) union, which has been booted out of the mainstream labour movement, is setting its sights on organizing disgruntled workers in the federal public service.

The renegade CAW is about to swallow a former federal union that includes 350 marine radio operators in Canada's coast guard, a merger that gives the union its first breakthrough in the highly unionized federal public service.

Federal unions have been braced for an all-out and costly assault on their members since the CAW and its controversial president, Buzz Hargrove, were effectively cast out of the Canadian Labour Congress (CLC).

"I think Buzz Hargrove's gloves have been off for some time—he has decided to go alone and play his way," said Steve Hindle, president of the Professional Institute of the Public Service of Canada, the second largest union in the federal government.

The deal with the public service workers would defy Hargrove's written promise to the Public Service Alliance of Canada (PSAC), the country's largest federal union, that the CAW would stop recruiting those workers. But Hargrove signed that promise when the CAW was under the CLC umbrella. CLC forbids its member unions from raiding each other, says CAW official Gary Fane. He said that deals made under CLC rules no longer apply now that the "House of Labour" has effectively ousted his union.

The CLC imposed full sanctions against the CAW for raiding a rival union, the U.S.-based Service Employees International Union. The sanctions stripped the CAW of any voice and clout within the CLC. The CAW denied the raiding charge and argued that workers have the right to belong to any union they want.

The exile of the CAW is the most explosive and damaging rift the "House of Labour" has faced in years. Left unchecked, it's a rift many say could change the face of labour in Canada.

"I believe labour is at the most important crossroads I've seen in my 40 years in the labour movement, and it's certainly a bad situation when the CAW is outside the CLC," said Daryl Bean, the recently retired PSAC president who filed the raiding complaint against the CAW. "Workers aren't chattels and should be able to pick their union, but that doesn't mean another union should be spending money to get workers to leave their union and join them. Unions should be organizing the unorganized."

(*Ottawa Citizen*, September 4, 2000)

chapter 4

THE STRUCTURE OF CANADIAN UNIONS

objectives

In this chapter, we discuss the structure of unions in Canada. We begin by examining the function, structure, and role of the local union. Then we will turn our attention to labour councils. Finally, we will discuss the provincial, national, and international organizations of labour. At the end of the chapter, you should be able to:

- describe the formation and operation of a local union
- understand the relationship between a local union and its regional, national, or international union
- outline the function of labour councils
- describe how a labour federation is structured
- identify the role played by provincial, territorial, national, and international labour federations

INTRODUCTION

As the newspaper story at the beginning of this chapter indicates, the labour movement in Canada consists of a large and complex network of direct and indirect relationships. The structure of the Canadian labour movement contains three levels that roughly parallel the three levels of Canadian government. The Canadian Labour Congress (CLC) is the largest national labour federation, and several smaller, Quebec-based national labour federations also represent specific groups within the Canadian labour movement. At the provincial or territorial level, provincial or territorial labour federations act as the coordinating bodies for the labour movement in each area. At the municipal or regional level, labour councils are the coordinating body for joint union activity. And at the workplace level, we find the local union. The local union is the smallest unit of regional, national, and international unions, but it is considered the cornerstone of the union structure, as it is the basis for all other parts of the structure.

Figure 4-1 outlines the relationships between the various union structures in Canada. To facilitate our discussion of this complex structure, we will start our examination of union structures at the local level and then move upwards through the larger levels of union structures.

THE LOCAL UNION

The first level of the structure of the Canadian labour movement is the **local union**, often referred to simply as the local. The term "local" is used to indicate the fact that most workplace-level unions in Canada are smaller units of a larger union. The local union's name will reflect this relationship with the larger union. For example, the local union representing telephone operators at one Vancouver-area office of Telus, the telecommunications company, is Local 52 of the Telecommunication Workers' Union.[1]

A local union is created when workers at one or more work sites, often having the same occupation or working at different locations for the same employer or type of employer, come together to form a union. At the point of formation, the workers have the choice of forming an independent union or joining an existing one. Usually, workers choose to join an established union because of the expertise and resources that an exist-

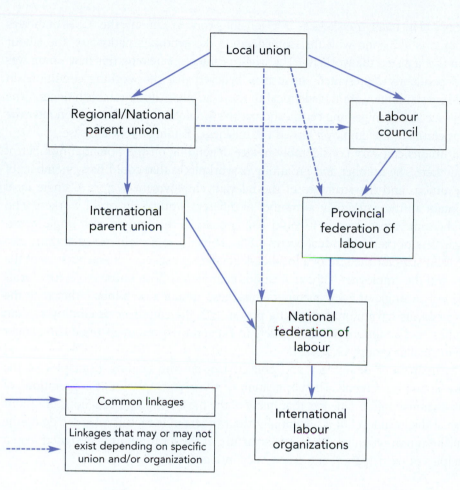

Figure 4-1
*Relationships
Between the Parts
of the Canadian
Labour Movement*

ing union can offer new members who may be relatively inexperienced in such skills as negotiating collective agreements. However, new unions do occasionally decide to establish an independent union. One recent Canadian example of a new independent union is the one formed by workers at a McDonald's restaurant in downtown Montreal. A Quebec labour federation assisted the restaurant workers in their organizing, but the workers chose to create a new union: le syndicat des travailleuses et travailleurs du

McDo-CSN.[2] (The name translates as "McDonald's Workers' Union"; the "CSN" indicates the new union's affiliation with the Confédération des syndicats nationaux, the labour federation that assisted the workers.) The workers' intent in creating this new union was to be independently represented, since they believed that the working conditions in McDonald's restaurants were not identical to those at other eating establishments. (The union was successful in gaining certification at the Montreal location, but soon after the union was certified, the employer closed the business, blaming a rent increase.)[3]

Local unions can vary considerably in size depending on the potential number of union members, the number and proximity of workplaces that could have members of the same union, and the structure of the relevant employment sector. A single local could contain all the workers at a number of different workplaces or all workers who perform the same type of work; it could also contain all the workers at a single workplace regardless of their individual occupations. Thus, there is really no such thing as a "typical" local size, for the size of a local is dependent on specific characteristics of the employer and the employees. Labour relations boards have been known to certify locals that have only a single or a few members, but these are rare exceptions rather than the rule. Larger locals have more bargaining power with the employer or employers than smaller ones, and so unions are more likely to expend their resources organizing larger rather than smaller groups of workers.

The principles of democracy and collectivism are the guiding principles of the Canadian labour movement. The application of these principles in the operations of unions is demonstrated by the fact that many of the most important functions of unions take place at the local level. It is, essentially, the workers in the locals who decide on the direction the union will take. Thus, the structure of the local union is designed to put the principles of participation and democracy into action.

Structure of the Local Union

The "administrative apparatus" of Canadian unions is "only lightly regulated" by Canadian labour law.[4] Most Canadian labour legislation only requires unions to file their constitutions with the appropriate labour relations board and to make regular financial reports to the membership; beyond those minimal requirements, the union membership is generally free to structure the union as it sees fit. However, as we will see, the union is also expected to operate in a manner that is free from discrimination and that allows democractic participation by the membership.

At the initial meeting of a new local and at regular intervals thereafter, the members of the local union elect the members they wish to run their local union. This group of elected individuals is known as the **union executive**. Most unions are governed by an executive consisting of a president, one or more vice-presidents, a secretary, and a treasurer. There may be other positions on the executive depending on the size of the local and the strategic interests of the membership. For example, if a local includes workers from different work sites, the executive may include an elected position for a representative from each location where the local has members. Other unions have executive positions to represent particular constituencies within the membership, such as an executive member representing female or First Nations workers. Some unions have executive positions to represent specific issues such as health and safety or human rights. These types of positions are more common in larger locals, where issues of concern to constituent groups or individual workplaces might not otherwise come to the executive members' attention.

Depending on the size of the local, the executive positions can be full- or part-time, paid or volunteer positions. Some unions negotiate clauses in their collective agreements to allow for paid time off work for those members who are elected to union executive positions. Workers who take time away from their jobs to serve on the union executive usually retain the seniority, benefits, and other conditions associated with their jobs. In other words, their status when they return to their job is the same as it would be if they had not taken any time off, and they must be permitted to return to the same job they had before taking time off for union activities. Most union constitutions also allow executive members to be appointed rather than elected if there are no candidates for an elected position or if other circumstances preclude holding an election (for example, if an executive member resigns and the vacated position needs to be filled immediately).

There are two other positions in the structure of many local unions: shop stewards and paid staff. **Shop stewards** are union members who investigate individual workers' complaints or grievances and act as the workers' advocate to management. The shop steward is the union's first-line representative in the workplace, the person whom workers will approach if a situation requiring immediate assistance arises in the workplace. One of the several functions shop stewards serve is to attend disciplinary meetings where a worker meets with management to discuss his or her behaviour. Shop stewards attend such meetings in order to ensure that correct disciplinary procedures are followed and also to act as a witness to the events in case there are subsequent disputes over what was discussed or agreed to. Distributing union literature and welcoming new union members are other functions that shop stewards perform in the workplace. Shop stewards may be elected or they may be volunteers.

Larger local unions will often have a paid staff to assist in the administration of the union's operations. Some locals, particularly those that are part of craft unions, will have a **business agent**. This individual is responsible for handling day-to-day union functions and assisting the executive members in their jobs.[5] In some industries and occupations, one business agent may serve more than one local, especially if there are many small locals of the union in the same geographic area.

In addition to providing support to the union executive members, the business agent usually plays a significant role in important union activities such as contract negotiations and grievance handling. Both of these activities are outlined in greater detail in subsequent chapters, but at this point we will note that the business agent is usually a member of or an advisor to the union negotiating team during collective bargaining. The business agent also may be responsible for presenting grievances to the employer and achieving a resolution of the conflict, or for presenting grievance cases to a third party for resolution.

In many unions, the business agent has a great deal of responsibility and power. The business agent has the advantage of remaining in his or her job on a permanent basis, while union executive members serve for a limited term. This situation means that the business agent acquires the kind of in-depth knowledge of the union and its operations that executive members do not have the time to develop. Consequently, executive members often must rely on the business agent for guidance and direction, rather than the other way around. In some unions, the business agent is not hired by the local union itself, but is appointed by the regional, national, or international union, which means that the business agent may also serve as the messenger who tells the local union what direction the larger union wishes it to follow.

Locals also may employ administrative or secretarial support staff. It is interesting to note that these paid staff members may be unionized, but they generally belong to a different union than the one they are employed by.

The members of a local union pay monthly dues; these are either calculated as a flat fee or as a percentage of salary or wages. The amount of dues and the method of calculation are outlined in the local's constitution and bylaws. The funds generated by the monthly dues pay for the services and support required by the members of the local union: staff salaries, operating costs, and fixed expenses such as office rent or equipment maintenance. Some of the revenue from dues may be directed to special causes such as building funds or cash reserves to be used for strike pay in the event of a strike or lock-out. As we will see, a portion of the dues revenue is given to the larger regional, national, or international union, and some of those funds are directed to the operations of the Canadian Labour Congress.

Functions of the Local Union

The local union carries out several important functions on behalf of its members. As noted, the direction of each of these functions is determined by collective and democratic action, usually through a vote of the membership. Unions usually have regular membership meetings to vote on issues, although most union executives are empowered to call for votes to be held independent of regular meetings if an issue warrants immediate attention.

The local union carries out three major functions: dealing with workplace problems or grievances, collective bargaining, and political or social activity. As we saw in the discussion of the shop steward's role, the local union represents its membership in day-to-day interactions in the workplace, and this extends to representing workers if there are problems or complaints. The union also represents its members in the process of collective bargaining. In this process, which is discussed in more detail in chapters 7 and 8, the union is responsible for three types of bargaining-related activity: it determines what outcomes the membership wants to achieve from the bargaining process, it prioritizes the desired outcomes and

Buzz Hargrove supports Marc Hall (right) in his bid to take his boyfriend to the school prom. The CAW participates in many social issues through its local unions.

determines bargaining strategy, and it participates in bargaining sessions with the employer. And finally, the local union usually participates in political or social activities outside the workplace. Examples of this sort of activity include making presentations to local government bodies such as city councils, participating in events to support other unions or social organizations that are facing difficulties, and participating in charitable or fundraising activities.

Decisions on how these functions are carried out are, as previously indicated, made by the membership, usually through votes or through discussion at membership meetings. In reality, however, two factors determine whether the actions of the union are actually those that the majority of the membership desires.

The first factor is the influence of the union's business agent. If the business agent has more experience than the union members or executive in dealing with a particular issue, the agent may advise (or pressure) the membership into following his or her preferred course of action. This situation may be particularly noticeable when the business agent has several years of experience in the job and the union executive has undergone turnover on a regular basis, thus giving the business agent far greater expertise than the elected officials. The business agent, furthermore, is sometimes encouraged by the local's regional or national affiliate union to advise (or pressure) the membership into following the regional or national union's preferred direction.

The second factor affecting whether union activities truly reflect the membership's wishes is the proportion of union members who actually participate in votes or discussions. Historically, there are varied levels of participation in local union activities in Canada. Member participation tends to be high for important events, such as votes to ratify collective agreements after the conclusion of negotiations, but low for unexceptional though regular events, such as monthly meetings.[6] The numbers of members willing to undertake such activities as running for executive positions or serving on committees also varies considerably.[7]

The effects of varying member participation in local unions have been addressed by a number of researchers. Some have argued that low levels of participation in regular union activities are not a problem because low participation indicates that the membership is satisfied with the executive's work and the direction that the union as a whole is taking. According to this perspective, unions should only be concerned about participation levels if participation is low for important events like contract ratification votes.[8]

Others argue that continuously low participation levels are a problem because they cause excessive amounts of work for those who do participate, which can ultimately lead to burnout, stress, and frustration for those individuals.[9] Low levels of general participation can make it difficult for union leaders to determine what the membership's true needs or wishes are, since the majority of the membership have not taken part in activities like meetings or voting, thereby demonstrating their opinions.

Another problem caused by low membership participation in union activities is suggested by the so-called **iron law of oligarchy**.[10] This "law" states that if the majority of the membership of any organization does not consistently participate in the organization's operations, leadership of the organization eventually becomes concentrated in the hands of an elite who are not easily removed from their positions of power. In the case of a union, the iron law of oligarchy explains the possible effect of actions such as union executive members serving multiple terms. If union members do not regularly volunteer for election or appointment to the executive, the same small group of individuals will continue to form the union executive. These individuals' extensive executive experience allows them to acquire even more experience and power, making it difficult for other, non-executive union members to oppose them.

Researchers point out that union participation can take many different forms.[11] Informal participation may simply involve talking about union issues with other union members, while formal participation may entail serving on the union executive. If members participate in both informal and formal ways, then their degree of participation is not reflected in the numbers attending meetings or standing as candidates in union elections. There are varied reasons for participation, and different forms of participation are driven by distinct motivations. Members may participate because they want a voice in the organization or because they feel obligated to serve the organization that works to represent them—that is, their motivation is similar to the motivations that result in "organizational citizenship" behaviour.[12] The willingness to participate may also be driven by the individual's perception of how successful the union is in serving its members. If that perception is negative—that is, if the union is seen as not adequately serving its members—the individual may participate in a negative way, such as by complaining about the union's activities to co-workers or to the union leadership.[13]

To conclude our discussion of local union functions, we should mention that some research suggests that while Canadians are generally satisfied with the common functions that unions carry out, some feel that the range of union activities could be broadened. A survey of 341 employed Canadians indicated that they are generally satisfied with unions' performance in so-called **business union** activities such as bargaining.[14] However, a significant number of respondents felt that local unions placed a relatively low level of importance on "integrative" activities such as conflict resolution and representing workers to management, activities that they felt should also be considered important union functions. Respondents also thought that unions should put more effort into informing workers about political issues, advocating laws to help working people, and fighting for the interests and values of working Canadians.

REGIONAL, NATIONAL, AND INTERNATIONAL UNIONS

As noted in the previous section, most, although not all, local unions belong to a larger regional, national, or international union. As we know from the history outlined in Chapter 3, an "international" union in Canada is usually one based in the United States, a "national" union is based in Canada, and a "regional" union is one that, for practical reasons, has a specific attachment to a region. In British Columbia, for example, the College and Institute Educators Association is a regional union representing instructors at community colleges and technical institutes in that province only. Because of differences in how post-secondary education is structured and administered across provinces, college instructors in British Columbia have chosen to belong to a regional union existing only in their province. (In contrast, however, college instructors in some other provinces have decided to join national unions [e.g., the National Union of Public and Government Employees or the Canadian Union of Public Employees] because of the increased power associated with membership in a larger union.)

The generic term for regional, national, and international unions is **parent unions**. For the sake of brevity, we will use this term in our subsequent discussion, although we will use the specific terms when appropriate in order to identify differences in how regional, national, and international unions are structured.

To give some perspective on the size of parent unions, Table 4-1 presents membership figures for the largest regional, national, and international unions in Canada.

TABLE 4-1   Largest Regional, National, and International Unions in Canada

Name of Union	Number of Members	Affiliation with National or Centralized Labour Federation	Number of Canadian Locals
Canadian Union of Public Employees (CUPE)	485,000	CLC	2,252
National Union of Professional and Government Employees (NUPGE)	325,000	CLC	1,235
Canadian Auto Workers (CAW)	220,000	CLC	326
United Food and Commercial Workers (UFCW)	210,390	AFL-CIO/CLC	102
United Steelworkers of America (USA)	190,000	AFL-CIO/CLC	548
Communications, Energy and Paperworks Union (CEP)	144,320	CLC	765
International Brotherhood of Teamsters (IBT)	100,170	CLC	35
Fédération du personnel de la santé et des services sociaux (FPSSS)	96,970	CSQ	897
Service Employees International Union (SEIU)	90,000	AFL-CIO/CLC	22
Fédération des syndicats de l'enseignement (FSE)	80,920	CSQ	45
Labourers' International Union of North America (LIUNA)	60,000	AFL-CIO/CLC	34
International Brotherhood of Electrical Workers (IBEW)	59,590	AFL-CIO/CLC	97
United Brotherhood of Carpenters and Joiners (UBC)	56,000	AFL-CIO/CLC	100
Ontario Secondary School Teachers' Federation (OSSTF)	51,400	CLC	135
International Association of Machinists and Aerospace Workers (IAMAW)	45,000	AFL-CIO/CLC	107
Ontario Nurses' Association (ONA)	45,000	Independent	63

Source: Information from Human Resources Development Canada, *Directory of Labour Organizations in Canada* (available at <http://www.hrdc-drhc.gc.ca>).

Key to affiliations:
CLC – Canadian Labour Congress
AFL-CIO – American Federation of Labor-Congress of Industrial Organizations
CSQ – Centrale des syndicats du Québec

Structure of Parent Unions

Like local unions, parent unions are governed by an elected executive. The executive of a parent union usually consists of the same main positions as the executive of a local union (e.g., president, vice-president(s), secretary, and treasurer). Parent union executives usually also contain representation from constituencies within the union. For example, a regional union executive often has representation from each local in its membership. A national union executive usually has representation from each region where it has members (e.g., by province or by area, such as Western Canada or Atlantic Canada). International unions operating in Canada usually have a designated executive position for a Canadian representative. The individuals in these positions are, depending on the individual union, either elected directly by the entire membership or elected by delegates who are expected to represent the views of the members at the local level. As at the local level, under certain circumstances executive members can be appointed rather than elected.

The affairs of the parent union are governed by a democratic decision-making process that is based on membership participation. However, parent unions do not usually rely on a decision-making mechanism involving every individual member at the local level. The main decision-making mechanism for a parent union is the **convention, or congress**, a meeting that is usually held on an annual basis. Each local union is entitled to send delegates to the convention; delegates are elected by the local members, appointed by the executive, or chosen by some combination of these two methods. The number of delegates that each local is allowed to send to the convention is usually based on the size of the local union, and thus larger locals are permitted to send more delegates. In some parent unions, however, each local is allocated the same number of delegates regardless of local size, the principle being that one member's vote should not carry more weight than another's simply because that member happens to belong to a larger local.

New president Ken Georgetti (left) celebrates with outgoing president Bob White at the CLC convention in 1999.

At the convention, delegates usually hear reports on the union's business since the previous convention, such as financial and activity reports. They may also vote on such issues as whether to alter the terms of the parent union's constitution or adjust the amount of dues that members of local unions should be required to pay. Policies of a more general nature may also be brought forward with a request for a formal motion of support from the parent union: for example, a human rights organization may request that the convention pass a motion condemning the actions of a certain government or country. The delegates also decide upon the policies and directions that will guide the parent union in its operations. Some parent unions hold executive elections at their conventions as well.

Decisions and votes at conventions are usually taken in general plenary sessions that all delegates attend; however, committees or caucuses of delegates often discuss issues before they are presented to the plenary and make recommendations on whether the plenary should support a particular motion. As in any large organization, the parent union's convention is characterized by a great deal of political activity, as individuals or delegations lobby others in attempts to sway the direction of votes on a motion. Sometimes a motion is passed or defeated not because that choice represents the preferences of the union members, but because the motion's supporters or opponents have been the most persuasive lobbyists.

Like the local union, the parent union also has a paid staff, but because the parent union is larger and performs more functions than the local union, its staff is larger and fulfills a wider range of functions. Most large unions have a number of specially trained staff members who provide assistance in negotiations with employers or in organizing new locals. Parent unions may also employ economists, lawyers, and research specialists to assist locals or the parent union itself in gathering and analysing information. National or international unions may also employ, directly or on contract, government lobbyists to present the union's views to government members. And, of course, the parent union will employ administrative staff to oversee day-to-day operations.

Functions of Parent Unions

Parent unions serve a variety of functions designed both to support the locals and to maintain the overall health of the union as a whole. Parent unions help in the creation of local unions by providing support, often in the form of a trained organizer who will guide potential union members through the process of gaining legal recognition for the new local. Once a local is established, the parent union supports the local's ongoing activities. This support includes assisting the local union with workplace issues. For example, the parent union can help a local to resolve a conflict with an employer by informing the local of solutions reached by other locals facing the same problem. It is also common for the parent union to offer advice to locals involved in collective bargaining, even to the point of having parent union representatives observe bargaining sessions and suggest strategy to the local union negotiators. If the parent union includes locals that represent workers in similar occupations, the parent union can help those working in the same occupation achieve comparable gains in collective bargaining or assist them in promoting changes to legislation governing their occupation. The parent union may conduct educational programs for its members. These are delivered by trained union educators and cover issues such as labour law or conflict-resolution techniques. Member education can also be conducted through regular publications or website updates that keep the entire parent union membership informed on union activities and issues.

The parent union's operations are financed through the union dues paid by individual union members. A percentage of the fees paid to the local union is sent to the parent union to finance its operations. A parent union usually designates a percentage of the fees it receives for a strike fund, which is used to pay union members during strikes or lockouts. This fund may be channelled directly to local members as soon as a strike or lockout begins if the local does not have its own strike fund, or it may be used as a supplement if the individual local has insufficient funds in its own strike fund.

The parent union may also perform the important function of representing its membership on labour councils, provincial labour federations, or national labour federations. This is a somewhat difficult function to describe in structural terms because a parent union or a local union may belong to these organizations either directly or through another affiliation. For example, if a regional union is also part of a national union, it may belong to a provincial or national labour federation directly or it may be represented in the federation by the national union. Local unions that are not affiliated with a parent union may also be affiliated with these organizations either directly or through an intermediary organization. For example, a local union that belongs to a labour council may be represented in a provincial or national labour federation through the labour council or it may be directly affiliated on its own. The form this affiliation takes depends on the individual union, its own affiliations, and the membership policies of the labour council or labour federation.

Rather than attempting to untangle these potentially complex structural relationships, we will instead focus on explaining the structure and functions of labour councils and labour federations in order to provide a general understanding of how these organizations operate.

LABOUR COUNCILS

A **labour council** is an organization comprised of delegates from many different local unions. It is distinct from a labour federation in that it usually represents unions in a region within a province or territory, whereas labour federations in Canada are provincial or national in scope. Examples of labour councils in some Canadian provinces are shown in Table 4-2.

TABLE 4-2 Examples of Labour Councils in Canada

Alberta	Bow Valley Labour Council
	Lethbridge and District Labour Council
British Columbia	North Okanagan and District Labour Council
	Vancouver District Labour Council
Manitoba	Winnipeg Labour Council
	Southeast Manitoba Labour Council
Newfoundland	Labrador West District Labour Council
	St. John's and District Labour Council
Nova Scotia	Truro and District Labour Council
Ontario	Guelph District Labour Council
	Sarnia and District Labour Council
Saskatchewan	Saskatoon and District Labour Council

Structure of the Labour Council

Each local union that is a member of the labour council appoints or elects a delegate to represent the local on the labour council. These delegates then democratically elect officers to form an executive of the labour council. Each officer of the labour council must be a member **in good standing** of an affiliated union. To be a member in good standing, a member must be eligible for membership in his or her local union and must comply with the constitution and bylaws of the local union. This provision is in place to ensure that delegates to labour councils, rather than acting on their personal beliefs, act as much as possible in accordance with the wishes of the local union members they represent.

As most labour councils across Canada have limited funds and no full-time staff, unpaid elected officers, together with volunteers from among the delegates and other union members, carry on the labour council's work. This work is financed through dues from local union affiliates, usually calculated on a per capita basis (each union affiliate is charged a membership rate based on how many members the affiliate has).

Affiliation with a labour council is voluntary for a local union, but all local unions are encouraged to join a labour council. The constitution of the Canadian Labour Congress (CLC), the largest national labour federation in Canada, requires that local unions affiliated with the CLC also be affiliated with a labour council in their region to maintain their standing as CLC members.

Functions of Labour Councils

Labour councils represent workers' interests to local government, municipal councils, boards, and commissions. They bring together local unions in a community and help these unions actively participate in their community. Labour councils are also responsible for carrying out the policies of the labour movement at the regional level.

A labour council involves itself in a diverse range of activities. It is often involved in providing strike support for local unions, and it works toward broader social goals such as available and affordable child care, accessible education, and maintenance of health-care and social services systems. Labour councils are also involved in regional community campaigns and fundraising for charitable organizations. Those labour councils that are affiliated with the Canadian Labour Congress also take on the task of hosting local CLC education programs.

Recently, labour councils have sought alliances among women's, anti-poverty, and seniors' groups, churches, and non-affiliated unions to build consensus and support for legislation and other actions to benefit all Canadians. Working within the community and with other organizations keeps labour councils active in efforts to achieve changes benefiting all workers in Canada.

Labour councils are also active in their provincial or territorial federations of labour. They often serve as the mechanism through which information from the provincial or territorial federation is distributed to unions in their region. We will now outline the structure and functions of provincial labour federations.

PROVINCIAL LABOUR FEDERATIONS

A **provincial labour federation** is, like a labour council, an organization composed of unions. However, as the name suggests, the federation is comprised of unions from an entire province or territory. Local unions without a regional, national, or international affiliation may join a provincial labour federation directly; local unions that are affiliated with parent unions are usually represented in the provincial labour federation by the parent union. Table 4-3 outlines the size of each Canadian provincial labour federation.

TABLE 4-3   Provincial Labour Federations in Canada

Name	Number of Members
Alberta Federation of Labour	107,000
British Columbia Federation of Labour	450,000
Manitoba Federation of Labour	90,000
New Brunswick Federation of Labour	32,000
Newfoundland Federation of Labour	50,000
Nova Scotia Federation of Labour	70,000
Ontario Federation of Labour	650,000
Prince Edward Island Federation of Labour	9,000
Quebec Federation of Labour (Fédération des travailleurs et travailleuses du Québec)	500,000
Saskatchewan Federation of Labour	80,000

Note: Membership figues as of September 2001.

Structure of Provincial Labour Federations

The structure of provincial labour federations is similar to the structure of regional, national, and international unions. The members of the federation elect executive officers who are in charge of carrying out the federation's business; this election usually takes place at an annual or biannual convention that is attended by delegates from member unions. At the conventions, policies and action plans are developed and voted on. As well, delegates decide upon the directions and issues that the federation will pursue in the coming year. The labour federation executive also meets with memberships and constituencies throughout the year to deal with issues of immediate concern.

Participation issues and the effect of the "iron law of oligarchy" are apparent within provincial federations of labour as they are within local or regional unions. Small unions or unions with limited resources may belong to a provincial federation of labour, but they may not have sufficient membership or resources to participate fully in the federation's operations. Other unions may put a higher priority on managing their own internal operations and serving their membership's immediate needs than on participating in external organizations. Thus, the direction and control of provincial federations may fall primarily to larger unions or unions with the time or inclination to devote resources to participation in the federation.

Per capita dues from union members finance the operations of provincial federations of labour. Because of the size of these organizations, as shown in Table 4-3, most employ a number of full-time paid staff, and most executive members take a leave from their regular jobs to devote their full attention to the federation's affairs.

Functions of the Provincial Labour Federation

As we have seen, labour legislation in most employment sectors is a provincial responsibility. Therefore, one of the most important roles played by provincial labour federations is dealing with issues affecting the labour legislation within their respective jurisdictions. Provincial labour federations pressure and lobby provincial or regional governments in order to promote their point of view, especially if the government appears likely to change labour legislation in ways that do not favour union interests. The federations also coordinate the activities of their member unions to support federation lobbying efforts.

Provincial federations provide their local unions and affiliated labour councils with a range of services in the fields of communications, education, and research. In the same manner that a regional or national union supports individual locals, the provincial federations support their affiliates by acting as a source of information, a coordinator of joint action, and a provider of resources that may be beyond the reach of individual members.

NATIONAL AND CENTRALIZED LABOUR FEDERATIONS

The Canadian union movement includes several federations that have affiliates either across the country or within certain geographic areas. Table 4-4 identifies the major national and centralized federations and the size of their respective memberships. We will discuss each of these federations in detail.

TABLE 4-4 National and Centralized Labour Federations in Canada

Name	Number of Members
Canadian Labour Congress (including the membership of the Fédération des travailleurs et travailleuses du Québec/Quebec Labour Federation)	2,300,000 (500,000)
Centrale des syndicats du Québec	232,000
Confédération des syndicats nationaux	90,000

Note: Membership figues as of September 2001.

NATIONAL LABOUR FEDERATIONS

Canadian Labour Congress

The **Canadian Labour Congress (CLC)** is the largest central labour body in Canada. It is made up of 65 national and international unions that represent workers such as steelworkers, government workers, autoworkers, postal workers, retail and service workers, and resource sector workers. The CLC membership also includes provincial and territorial labour federations, and 137 community labour councils. A number of local unions are directly affiliated to the CLC without representation through a secondary body such as a regional or national union or a labour council. The CLC member organizations are referred to as **affiliates**.

Structure of the Canadian Labour Congress

As Chapter 3 outlined, the CLC's current structure has evolved over several decades through the amalgamation of several earlier national and regional labour federations. Perhaps because of this complex history and the desire to avoid some of the conflict that has doomed earlier national labour federations in Canada, the present-day CLC has a clear set of principles that guide its actions. These principles are outlined in the CLC constitution, which includes a code of union citizenship, a code of organizing practices, and a code of ethical practices.

The code of union citizenship acknowledges the distinctions in size, internal structure, and geographic location of the affiliates of the CLC. It also recognizes that each local union, as well as its regional, national, or international union, develops structures and functions that are appropriate for its industry and its collective bargaining situation. The code of union citizenship is presented in Table 4-5. Without unduly restricting the ability of individual unions to adapt to their unique circumstances, it outlines the objectives of CLC affiliates in providing service to union members.

TABLE 4-5   Canadian Labour Congress Code of Union Citizenship

Article V

Code of Union Citizenship

The affiliates of the Canadian Labour Congress vary substantially in their size, internal structures, and the geographic distribution of their membership. Every union develops in a way which is appropriate to the industries in which they operate, and the collective bargaining situations with which they have to deal. Taking into consideration the important differences of structure, circumstances and size, all affiliates recognize the following objectives in providing service to their membership and promoting the principles and practice of trade unionism according to the Constitution and policies of the Canadian Labour Congress:

1. To fully protect and ensure the application of all legislative rights which workers may have in the industrial and community environments.

2. To provide whatever assistance is necessary to ensure that their membership receive their full entitlement to social insurance benefits which may be available to them by reason of lay-off, unemployment, disability, retirement or any other legitimate cause.

3. To provide the best available information as to wage levels, fringe benefits and contract language, and such other negotiating services as are necessary to achieve the maximum and most suitable benefits through collective bargaining.

4. To press for such legislative changes as are necessary to protect and enhance the welfare and rights of their members.

5. To provide education to members in the duties and responsibilities of officers and representatives, structure, and important issues within their own union, the Canadian Labour Congress, and the movement as a whole, and in the principles and practices of trade unionism.

6. To ensure that all its members can exercise their fundamental trade union rights.

7. To co-ordinate collective bargaining or any other activities with other unions where such co-operation will be to the mutual aid of the members of each union involved.

8. To promote the active participation of their membership in local labour councils and federations of labour.

9. To encourage the full participation of their membership in the political life of this country.

10. To provide the means whereby all members will have an equal opportunity to participate actively and effectively in determining the policies of the affiliate and directing its affairs.

11. To provide all possible assistance necessary to members who are injured or disabled or suffer industrial disease in the workplace.

12. To conduct union business with and to provide services to all members without discrimination on the basis of race, colour, creed, sex, age or national origin in an environment free of sexual harassment.

The CLC code of ethical practices is presented in Table 4-6. It outlines the principles that should be followed to ensure a free and democratic union. As well, the CLC constitution has a code of organizing practices that governs the "orderly regulation of relationships" among affiliates. This code, presented in Table 4-7, outlines the desired relationships between unions that are involved in competitive organizing campaigns or other disputes resulting from jurisdictional conflicts. The CLC encourages affiliated unions or organizations to organize new locals primarily, if not exclusively, in the jurisdictions they have historically occupied. The CLC's constitution expresses the belief that the interests of non-unionized workers in a given industry are best served by joining a union that has developed resources and experience in the same industry.[15] If disputes occur between CLC-affiliated unions wanting to represent the same group of non-unionized workers, the CLC will act as a mediator to clarify the issue of jurisdiction.

TABLE 4-6   Canadian Labour Congress Code of Ethical Practices

Article VII

Code of Ethical Practices

The record of union democracy, like the record of our country's democracy, is not perfect. A few unions do not adequately, in their constitutions, provide for the basic elements of democratic practice. A few unions do not practice or implement the principles set forth in their constitutions. Finally, while the overwhelming majority of unions both preach and practice the principles of democracy, in all too many instances the membership, by apathy and indifference, have forfeited their rights of union citizenship.

All unions shall try to ensure maximum attendance and participation by the membership in union meetings and affairs. The real corrective in this area is not so much the establishment of new principles as the exercise of rights presently recognized and accorded. Just as eternal vigilance is the price of liberty, so is the constant exercise of the rights of union citizenship the price of union democracy.

It is valuable, nevertheless, to restate the principles which should govern all free and democratic unions, and to rededicate the labour movement to the preservation of these principles.

1. The Canadian Labour Congress and each of its affiliated unions shall undertake the obligation, through appropriate constitutional or administrative measures and orderly procedures, to ensure that any person who exercises a corrupt influence or who engages in corrupt practices shall not hold office of any kind in such trade unions or organizations.

2. No person shall hold or retain office or appointed position in the Canadian Labour Congress or any of its affiliated national or international unions or subordinate bodies thereof who has been proven guilty through union procedure or courts of law of preying on the labour movement and its good name for corrupt purposes.

3. Each member of a union shall have the right to full and free participation in union self-government. This shall include the right:

    (a) to vote periodically for local, national and/or international officers, either directly by referendum vote or through delegate bodies;

    (b) to honest elections;

    (c) to stand for and to hold office, subject only to fair qualifications uniformly imposed, and;

    (d) to voice views as to the method in which the union's affairs should be conducted.

4. Each member of a union shall have the right to fair treatment in the application of union rules and law. The general principle applicable to union disciplinary procedures is that such procedures shall contain all the elements of fair play. No particular formality is required. No lawyers need be used. The essential requirements of due process, however—notice, hearing, and judgment on the basis of evidence—shall be observed. A method of appeal to a higher body shall be provided to ensure that judgment at the local level is not the result of prejudice or bias.

5. Each member of a union has the responsibility to:

    (a) fully exercise the right of union citizenship; and

    (b) loyally support the union. The right of an individual member to criticize the policies and personalities of union officers does not include the right to undermine the union as an institution, to advocate dual unionism, to destroy or weaken the union as a collective bargaining agency, or to carry on slander and libel.

6. To safeguard the rights of the individual members and to safeguard its democratic character, each affiliated national or international union shall hold regular Conventions at stated intervals, which shall be not more than four years apart. The Convention shall be the supreme governing body of the unions.

7. Officers of the Canadian Labour Congress, and of each affiliated national or international union, should be elected, either by referendum vote or by the vote of delegate bodies. Whichever method is used, elections should be free, fair and honest, and adequate internal safeguards should be provided to ensure the achievement of that objective.

8. All general conventions of the Canadian Labour Congress and of affiliated national or international unions should be open to the public, except for necessary executive sessions. Convention proceedings or an accurate summary thereof shall be published and made available to the membership.

9. The appropriate officials of the union and such bodies which are given authority to govern a union's affairs between Conventions shall be elected, whether from the membership at large or by appropriate divisions, either by referendum vote or by the vote of delegate bodies. Such bodies shall abide by and enforce the provisions of the union's constitution and carry out the decisions of the Convention.

10. Membership meetings of local unions shall be held periodically with proper notice of time and place.

11. Elections of local union officers shall be democratic, conducted either by referendum or by vote of a delegate body which is itself elected by referendum or at union meetings.

12. The term of office of all union officials shall be stated in the organization's constitution or bylaws and shall be for a reasonable period.

13. To ensure democratic, responsible, and honest administration of its locals and other subordinate bodies, the Canadian Labour Congress and affiliated national and international unions shall have the power to institute disciplinary and corrective proceedings with respect to their own local unions and other subordinate bodies, including the power to establish trusteeships where necessary. Such powers should be exercised sparingly and only in accordance with the provisions of the union's constitution, and autonomy should be restored promptly upon correction of the abuses requiring trusteeship.

14. Where constitutional amendments or changes in internal administrative procedures are necessary to comply with the standards herein set forth, such amendments and changes shall be undertaken at the earliest practicable time.

TABLE 4-7   Canadian Labour Congress Code of Organizing Practices

Article VI

Code of Organizing Practices

The present Constitution of the Canadian Labour Congress provides for orderly regulation of relationships among its affiliates.

Public attacks by one affiliate upon another result in adverse publicity which causes grave injury to organized labour. More serious is the fact that jurisdictional disputes, boycotts, and the resulting unfavourable publicity give rise to regulatory legislation.

A code governing relations among unions engaged in competitive organizing campaigns or involved in disputes resulting from jurisdictional conflicts, has therefore been approved by the Executive Council for the guidance of affiliated unions, and the Congress calls upon the officers and members of all affiliated unions to enforce this code at all times and to instruct all representatives, business agents and local officers to adhere to its provisions:

1. Where two or more affiliates of the Congress are seeking to organize the same employees, each affiliate shall conduct its organizing campaign in such a manner as to increase the respect of the workers involved for the trade union movement, and will not impugn or attack the motives or character of any competing affiliate, its officers or subordinate units.

2. Affiliates or their representatives shall not, either directly or indirectly, issue or cause the issuance of any propaganda which:

   (a) alleges or implies that any other affiliate is guilty of undemocratic practices, corruption, or any other improper conduct;

   (b) attacks the principles of international, national, provincial and regional unionism. The Constitution recognizes all such types and such propaganda is therefore a public attack upon established Congress constitutional policy;

    (c) attacks the craft or industrial structure of other affiliates. Both structures are recognized by the Constitution of the Congress;

    (d) criticizes the benefits received from or the dues and initiation fees paid to another affiliate.

3. Affiliates or their representatives shall not organize or conduct boycotts against products or services produced under a bona fide collective bargaining relationship of another affiliate.

4. Any complaint of a violation of this code shall be forwarded by an affiliate to the ranking official of the other affiliate involved, requesting that the spirit and intent of this Code be observed.

5. If compliance is not promptly obtained, a complaint may be filed with the Canadian Labour Congress. The Congress shall, after investigation, endeavour to obtain compliance, and failing to do so, shall refer the complaint to the Executive Council of the Congress. The Executive Council shall make a report to the parties of its decision in the matter, and shall take such action as it deems advisable and appropriate to enforce compliance.

The CLC constitution sets out the premise that affiliates will not organize or attempt to represent employees who are already organized and have an established collective bargaining relationship with another affiliate.[16] This constitutional provision is intended to stop unions from expanding their influence by taking over the membership of other unions, a process that can consume excessive amounts of both parties' resources and result in long-lasting feelings of bitterness. This provision is also intended to reinforce the principle that unions should concentrate on organizing non-unionized workers as the preferred way to expand their membership. The situation described in the newspaper story at the beginning of this chapter involves an alleged violation of this part of the CLC constitution.

If an affiliate of the CLC undertakes an action that might be considered a violation of the provision against unionizing workers in an existing union, the affiliate can claim **justification** to the CLC president by outlining the reasons for the organizing action that is being contemplated. The provisions of the constitution outline the process of investigation for such a claim, which can result in a "justification hearing" before the executive committee of the CLC.[17] The executive committee has the ability to impose penalties if the affiliate's actions are found to be unjustified. As the story that opened this chapter describes, a dispute over the issue of unions organizing already unionized workers resulted in the Canadian Auto Workers union, one of the largest private sector unions in Canada, receiving "full sanctions" from the CLC. These full sanctions meant that CAW representatives were removed from all CLC and CLC affiliates' executive bodies and CAW members were restricted from participating in CLC activities.[18]

Another provision of the CLC constitution allows some unions to join the CLC directly, instead of through membership in a larger union, a provincial or territorial labour federation, or a labour council. These independent unions come into existence in a number of ways. For example, workers might want to belong to a union but might not want to join the existing union that would usually represent workers in their industry or occupation. This situation could occur, for example, if the workers are former members of the existing union who do not want to or cannot rejoin that union. The workers might then choose to start their own union within an industry or occupation traditionally represented by the existing union. Independent unions can also be formed by organizing workers into unions that do not have any regional, national, or international parent unions; an example is the Atomic Energy Workers of Canada.

In cases such as these, the Canadian Labour Congress will directly charter the independent union as an affiliate and provide this directly chartered union with the same type of services that a regional, national, or international union provides to its local union. If the independent affiliate decides to join a parent union, the independent affiliation ends and the union is then represented within the CLC by its new parent union.

The structure of the CLC is designed to ensure that, as with other democratic union structures, the organization is directed by the wishes of the membership. The CLC national convention, held every third year, is the major mechanism through which this direction is determined. The convention has been described as "the parliament of Canadian labour." Every local union, provincial federation of labour, and labour council is entitled to send at least one delegate to the convention and to submit motions to be voted on by the delegates. Some 2,500 delegates attend the convention, which lasts five days, and devote most of their time to discussing the motions that are presented for consideration. These motions usually cover a broad range of concerns: economic policy, regional economic development, health care, social legislation and equity programs, labour legislation, women's and human rights, technological change, pension issues, environmental concerns, immigration issues, consumer issues, and international issues. The motions are either adopted or rejected through a vote of the delegates, and their disposition decides the policies and activities to be followed by the CLC in the next three years. This direction by the vote of the convention delegates enables the CLC to act as the "voice of labour" at the national and international levels.

The delegates to the CLC convention elect four full-time salaried officers: the president, the secretary-treasurer, and two executive vice-presidents.[19] These individuals lead the Executive Council, which is the governing body of the CLC between conventions. The executive council also includes 42 representatives of CLC-affiliated unions. In order to encourage diversity within the executive council membership, six council seats are reserved for women, two are reserved for workers of colour, and one is reserved for an aboriginal worker. Many CLC executive council members have extensive experience in other labour organizations or federations. Bob White, CLC president from 1992 to 1999, was the national president of the Canadian Auto Workers before becoming CLC president; Ken Georgetti, the current CLC president, was previously the president of the British Columbia Federation of Labour.

Like the structure of other labour organizations in Canada, the CLC structure includes a number of paid staff members. These staff members work at the CLC's central office in Ottawa as well as at a number of regional offices throughout the country. Staff members may be professional employees, such as economists or statisticians; others may be union members who are on paid or unpaid leave from their regular jobs to work with the CLC.

Functions of the Canadian Labour Congress

One of the most important functions of the CLC is to provide services to its affiliates. The CLC assists its affiliates through union education and organization, communications, political education, research and legislation, and representation on international issues. These services are financed through per capita dues charged to each CLC affiliate. In addition, the CLC maintains service and education staff and organizers in all regions throughout Canada to assist existing unions and to assist workers who wish to form new unions. An example of one of the service and education programs that the CLC provides is "Labour College," a multi-day workshop that union executives or members can attend to acquire skills such as grievance handling or contract negotiating.

The CLC at the national level acts as the "voice of labour" and frequently speaks for

The CLC acts as the voice of labour at the national level, and has spearheaded many positive reforms through collective action.

workers as a whole, regardless of whether or not they are members of trade unions. This is particularly true in representations that are made to governments on issues such as unemployment insurance, health care, workers' compensation, and pension legislation.

CENTRALIZED LABOUR FEDERATIONS

One distinctive feature of the Canadian industrial system is the existence not only of a large national labour federation but also several large centralized labour federations located in Quebec. The complex history of industrial relations in Quebec, outlined in Chapter 3, explains why there are several centralized labour federations in Quebec rather than a single provincial labour federation as is the case in most Canadian provinces. The different labour federations in Quebec have developed to represent different sectors of the Quebec union movement and in response to the different forces that have shaped Quebec society. The influences of language, culture, religion, and outside ownership and control, and the desire to retain a distinctive character in the larger Canadian society, have all contributed to the development of centralized labour federations in Quebec. We will describe the three largest federations.

Quebec Federation of Labour

The **Quebec Federation of Labour** is generally referred to by its French acronym, **FTQ** (standing for "Fédération des travailleurs et travailleuses du Québec"). The FTQ is the largest centralized labour federation in Quebec. Its membership includes 25 unions, primarily from the private sector, which collectively have nearly half a million members.

The FTQ is affiliated with the CLC, but, as noted in Chapter 3, its relationship with the CLC is structured somewhat differently than the CLC's relationship with other labour federations. The president of the FTQ is guaranteed a vote on the CLC executive committee, and the FTQ has an assigned seat on the CLC Executive Council. The FTQ's relationship with the CLC has three distinct features that do not exist in other federations' terms of affiliation with the CLC. First, the FTQ has exclusive jurisdiction in Quebec over some functions, such as education, that the CLC carries out in other regions of Canada. Second, the per capita fees paid by FTQ members to the CLC are adjusted to compensate for the cost of CLC services that FTQ members do not benefit from, such as materials produced in English. Third, the FTQ has exclusive jurisdiction over the operation of local labour councils in Quebec, which means that the FTQ decides how funds and staffing are allocated to those organizations. The FTQ also has the right to create its own policies on such issues as internal jurisdictional disputes.

Thus, the FTQ functions as an affiliate of the CLC in some respects and as an independent federation in others. This arrangement has been called the "sovereignty-association" agreement.[20] It recognizes the FTQ's special role within the CLC as the representative of Quebec labour organizations but also the need for special membership provisions for the FTQ in light of the so-called plurality[21] of labour federations within Quebec. The FTQ is given more authority over its own operations than other provincial labour federations affiliated with the CLC, on the basis that such authority and the accompanying flexibility is needed to maintain the FTQ's status as Quebec's largest labour federation and the CLC's "voice" in Quebec.

The internal structure of the FTQ is very similar to the structure of the CLC. The congress of the FTQ, held every three years, is the supreme authority of the organization and sets direction and policy based on the votes of the delegates. Each union that is an FTQ member is entitled to send at least one delegate to the Congress, and each of the 14 regional councils within the FTQ can send a three-person delegation. The congress also elects a 19-person executive, that, with the FTQ general council, oversees the operations of the organization between congresses. The general council has approximately 150 members representing FTQ-affiliated unions.[22]

Functions of the FTQ

As noted, the FTQ plays a dual role as a regional labour federation and as a CLC-affiliated federation. Thus, it provides many of the functions that provincial labour federations provide in other parts of Canada and also provides services from the CLC. Its functions include lobbying several levels of government, providing assistance in organizing, providing assistance to member unions in grievances and collective bargaining, and supplying information and resources. As noted above, the FTQ is responsible for educational services for its members, whereas the CLC provides these services for its other regional affiliates.

One initiative that the FTQ and other Quebec-based labour federations have undertaken that has not been replicated in many other parts of Canada is the creation of labour-sponsored investment funds. The FTQ fund, the Solidarity Fund, was established in 1983. This fund was the first labour-sponsored investment fund in Canada and has since become the largest venture capital institution in Quebec.[23] Investors in the fund receive both provincial and federal tax credits for their contributions, and the fund's proceeds are used to create new job opportunities and to assist companies in preserving existing jobs.

Centrale des syndicats du Québec

The **Centrale des syndicats du Québec (CSQ)** is a "federation of federations." Its membership contains 13 federations that in turn contain more than 250 unions. There are also some organizations that are affiliated directly to the CSQ. Nearly two-thirds of the CSQ's members are employed in education, and the majority of CSQ members are public sector employees in Quebec.[24] The CSQ was known as the CEQ (Centrale de l'enseignement du Québec) until 2000, when the name was changed to reflect the broadening of its membership beyond unionized workers in education.

Structure of the CSQ

The CSQ, like the other federations described in this section, is directed by the votes of delegates at the general congress, which occurs every three years. Nearly 1,000 delegates attend each conference. A five-person executive is elected at each congress for a three-year term. An executive council with approximately 300 members oversees the CSQ's operations between general congresses. The CSQ also has an "intersectoral council" consisting of approximately 20 representatives from member federations and unions. This council deals with issues such as budgeting and integrating new affiliates.

Functions of the CSQ

Because the CSQ's membership base is located in the public sector, negotiation of collective agreements is a major concern. In order to ensure consistency in the different collective agreements in the Quebec public sector, the CSQ has established a number of "negotiation structures" to determine consistent negotiation strategies and to coordinate bargaining among its members. The CSQ has an intersectoral negotiation council, which coordinates the strategy for and content of all negotiations, and a general negotiation council, which defines bargaining objectives and establishes common bargaining demands and settlements.

Other services that the CSQ provides to its members are legal services, support for organizing efforts, insurance plans, union education and training, research, communications, administrative services, and representation in lobbying the Quebec and federal governments.

Confédération des syndicats nationaux

As described in Chapter 2, the Confédération des syndicats nationaux (CSN, or Confederation of National Trade Unions) was founded in Quebec in 1921 as the Confédération des travailleurs catholiques du Canada. As the original name suggests, this organization was founded as a federation for Catholic workers; at the time of its name change in 1960, individual members were no longer required to be Catholic and the federation's formal connection with the Catholic Church had ended. During the 1960s and 1970s, the CSN had a reputation as a "radical" federation, prompting several member union groups to leave in order to start their own federations.[25] In the 1980s, new leadership and a recognition that membership was declining led to the federation's gradual change from being "a hotbed of hardline Marxism riven with factional disputes over ideological purity"[26] to being a more "civilized" and less confrontational organization. The CSN membership currently includes 2,174 affiliated union locals.[27]

Structure of the CSN

The CSN membership includes federations of unions in commerce, construction, communications, education, mining, forestry and pulp and paper, the professions, health and social services, and the public service. There are 13 regional councils to represent unions in particular geographic areas. The CSN membership also includes a number of directly affiliated unions that are chartered as members, under a structure similar to that governing directly affiliated unions in the CLC. The CSN has a central office in Montreal and offices in 26 other locations throughout Quebec.

The supreme authority in the CSN is the congress, which meets annually and has approximately 2,000 delegates. The delegates at the congress vote on such matters as budgeting, dues, and action plans. Each member union has the right to present motions for consideration by the congress. Seven committees that meet during the congress also present recommendations. Between congresses, the CSN's direction and day-to-day activities are overseen by the Executive Committee, which consists of six executive members elected by the Congress, and a Council of 200 delegates representing the member federations and regional councils.

Functions of the CSN

The CSN provides services to its membership similar to those provided by the other federations described in this section. It offers its members, among other services, an information service that produces publications and audio-visual materials, a research service, a library, support services for unions on strike, organizing services for workers who wish to form a union, coordination for collective campaigns, assistance to union members dealing with workers' compensation claims, and legal services for unions involved in arbitrations and bargaining.

Two other major activities of the CSN should be mentioned. One is the CSN's involvement in several labour-management cooperation agreements that have explored alternative forms of workplace relationships between the parties, often as a way to preserve jobs that otherwise might disappear. The other activity is the establishment of a labour-sponsored investment fund, named Fondaction. Like the FTQ's Solidarity Fund, the monies from this capital investment fund operated by the CSN are used to encourage investment in creating new jobs or in maintaining existing ones. Some commentators point to the CSN's creation of this fund as evidence of the federation's ideological evolution, since the CSN leadership at the time the Solidarity Fund was created accused the FTQ of "co-opting the labour movement."[28]

INTERNATIONAL LABOUR FEDERATIONS

To this point, we have focused our discussion on the activities of the Canadian union movement within Canadian borders. Several Canadian unions and federations, however, have international affiliations. We will conclude our overview of the Canadian union movement with a look at the activities of Canadian unions outside Canada. International affiliations are becoming more important to many Canadian unions and labour federations because of globalization of businesses and employers, which puts greater pressure on Canadian unions to work in cooperation with other unions throughout the world.

The CLC and the CSN are both affiliated with the **International Confederation of Free Trade Unions (ICFTU)**, an "international union of unions" which assists union organizations throughout the world. The FTQ also has an affiliation with the ICFTU through the FTQ's affiliation with the CLC. The ICFTU is a worldwide organization representing some 125 million workers. One of its most important functions is delivering labour education programs to assist workers in such regions as Asia, Africa, and Latin America in forming their own unions, developing leadership, and engaging in collective bargaining.

Buzz Hargrove of the CAW meets with Nelson Mandela in 1998. Such international affiliations are becoming increasingly important to Canadian unions.

Another important international body is the **International Labour Organization (ILO)** which is based in Geneva, Switzerland. The ILO is not an international federation in the sense of having formal affiliates in member countries; it is an agency of the United Nations and has been in existence since 1919, when it was created as part of the League of Nations, the precursor to the United Nations. The ILO's main purposes are to formulate and promote international labour standards and to offer technical assistance in labour-related matters to countries around the world.[29] The ILO researches and publishes reports on international labour issues, such as women in the workplace and employment policies. It also collects comparative statistics from around the world on such issues as strike and lockout rates and unionization rates.

The CLC is an affiliate of two other international organizations. One is the **Trades Union Advisory Committee of the Organization for Economic Co-operation and Development (TUAC-OECD)**. The TUAC acts as an information conduit between its member organizations and the OECD on labour-related issues that come before the

OECD partners.[30] The TUAC also holds plenary sessions twice a year to guide the direction of the organization and has an elected nine-member administrative committee (which currently includes representation from the CLC) and a five-member executive committee. The other organization is the Commonwealth Trade Union Council, which represents unions in the Commonwealth countries. The council's membership includes unions representing a total of 30 million members, and its main purposes are to promote international labour standards and to exchange information among its member unions.[31]

SUMMARY

The structure of Canadian unions can be as simple as an independent union representing a single group of workers or as complicated as a union that has regional, national, and even international affiliations. We can see from this overview that the variations in Canadian union structure, although they may seem unnecessarily complex, are reflective of the variations in occupations, employers, and regions that characterize the Canadian industrial relations system. There is a common theme, however: unions and federations are democratic organizations that are guided by the direction of their members and by structures designed to facilitate the democratic process.

At the individual workplace level, local unions represent workers in collective bargaining and dispute resolution procedures. While there are some independent local unions, most locals belong to a larger parent union, which can be regional, national, or international in scope. Locals have an elected executive directed by votes of the membership and, depending on their size, may also have a business agent and other paid staff.

Most locals belong to a labour council, which is an organization representing unions in a particular geographic area. Labour councils provide networking and information sharing for their members and may also sponsor activities and participate in events within their communities and regions.

Parent unions, like locals, also have an elected executive and paid staff. Their directions are governed by delegate votes at a regular convention. Parent unions provide services to their members such as lobbying, education, and assistance in bargaining.

On a larger geographic level, each province and territory in Canada has a provincial or territorial labour federation. This organization's membership consists of independent locals, parent unions, and labour councils, and these members appoint delegates to a convention that sets the federation's direction by voting on motions. The provincial or territorial federation acts as the "voice of labour" in its area and represents organized labour's concerns to governments and the media. The federation also offers support services to its membership.

Provincial and terroritorial labour federations in Canada are affiliated with the Canadian Labour Congress, which is the largest centralized labour federation in the country. The CLC's membership also includes independent unions and locals. Other centralized labour federations include the Quebec Federation of Labour, the Confédération des syndicats nationaux, and the Centrale des syndicats du Québec. The CLC and the QFL have a number of international affiliations that connect them with other labour organizations throughout the world.

KEY TERMS FOR CHAPTER 4

affiliates (p. 132)

business agent (p. 118)

business union (p. 122)

Canadian Labour Congress (CLC) (p. 132)

Centrale des syndicats du Québec (CSQ) (p. 142)

Commonwealth Trade Union Council (p. 146)

Confédération des syndicats nationaux (CSN) (p. 143)

convention or congress (p. 124)

in good standing (p. 128)

International Confederation of Free Trade Unions (ICFTU) (p. 145)

International Labour Organization (ILO) (p. 145)

iron law of oligarchy (p. 121)

justification (p. 137)

labour council (p. 127)

local union (p. 114)

parent union (p. 122)

provincial labour federation (p. 129)

Quebec Federation of Labour (FTQ) (p. 140)
shop steward (p. 117)
Trades Union Advisory Committee of the Organization for Economic Co-Operation and
    Development (TUAC-OECD) (p. 145)
union executive (p. 117)

DISCUSSION QUESTIONS FOR CHAPTER 4

1. Explain how a local union is formed. What role can a regional, national, or international union play in forming a local union?

2. What distinguishes the structure of a labour council from the structure of a local union?

3. Give some examples of services that a federation of labour might provide for its affiliates.

4. Why is the CLC called the "union of unions"?

5. Discuss the role of democracy in the formation and operation of unions in Canada.

6. What is the role of the CLC in organizing disputes between affiliated members?

7. Explain why there are several centralized labour federations in Quebec.

8. Why are international affiliations becoming more important to Canadian unions?

CHAPTER EXERCISES FOR CHAPTER 4

1. Choose a union that you are familiar with or that you can research. Using Figure 4-1 as a guide, draw a diagram of the relationships that this union has with other organizations within the Canadian union structure. Explain how these relationships have come to exist and outline what the union gains from having these relationships.

2. Choose a labour organization or federation, such as a labour council or provincial or centralized labour federation, in your region of the country. Describe how that organization is structured, identify its membership, and describe how that membership has

evolved or developed. Also describe some of the functions that the organization carries out and identify what you think are the most important functions or activities of the organization.

R e f e r e n c e s

[1] Luke, P. (1999). Labour on youthful quest: B.C. unions hope to swell ranks from the service sector. *Province* (Vancouver), September 5, 1999, p. A47.

[2] Yakabuski, K. (2001). Arch enemy. *R.O.B. Magazine*, September 2001, 34–43.

[3] Yakabuski, *op. cit.*

[4] Lynk, M. (2000). Union democracy and the law in Canada. *Journal of Labor Research*, 21(1), 37–63.

[5] Godard, J. (1994). *Industrial relations, the economy, and society*. Toronto, ON: McGraw-Hill Ryerson.

[6] Godard, *op. cit.*

[7] Kelloway, E.K, Catano, V.M., and Carroll, A.C. (1995) The nature of member participation in local union activities. In Tetrick, L.E., and Barling, J. (Eds.), *Changing employment relations: behavioral and social perspectives*. Washington, DC: American Psychological Association.

[8] Strauss, G. (1991). Union democracy. In Strauss, G., Gallagher, D., and Fiorito, J. (Eds.), *The state of the unions*. Madison, WI: IRA.

[9] Kelloway, K., and Barling, J. (1994). Industrial relations stress and union activism: costs and benefits of participation. In *Proceedings of the 46th Annual Meeting of the Industrial Relations Research Association*. Boston, MA: Industrial Relations Research Association; Winch, G. (1993). The turnover of shop stewards. *Industrial Relations Journal, 14*, 84–86.

[10] Michels, R. (1962). *Political parties*. New York, NY: Collier Books.

[11] McShane, S. L. (1986). The multidimensionality of union participation. *Journal of Occupational Psychology, 59*, 177–187.

[12] Fullagar, C.J.A., Parks, J.M., Clark, P.F., and Gallagher, D.G. (1995). Organizational citizenship and union participation: measuring discretionary membership behaviors. In Tetrick, L.E., and Barling, J. (Eds.), *Changing employment relations: behavioral and social perspectives*. Washington, DC: American Psychological Association.

[13] Shore, L.M., and Newton, L.A. (1995). Union-member relations: loyalty, instrumentality, and alienation. In Tetrick and Barling, *op. cit.*

[14] Godard, J. (1997). Beliefs about unions and what they should do: a survey of employed Canadians. *Journal of Labor Research*, 18(4), 621–639.

[15] Constitution of the Canadian Labour Congress (CLC), revised June 1999. Article IV, section 1.

[16] CLC constitution, article IV, section 3.

[17] CLC constitution, article IV, section 9–18.

[18] Parsons, L. (2001). Canada: What lies behind the split in the union officialdom? At <http://www.wsws.org/articles/2001/mar2001/can-m05.shtml>.

[19] Information from the CLC website, <http://www.clc-ctc.ca>.

[20] Déom, E., and Boivin, J. (2001). Union-management relations in Quebec. In Gunderson, M., Ponak, A., and Taras, D.G. (Eds.), *Union-management relations in Canada* (4th edition). Toronto, ON: Addison Wesley Longman.

[21] Déom and Boivin, *op. cit.*

[22] Information from the FTQ website, <http://www.ftq.qc.ca>.

[23] Déom and Boivin, *op. cit.*

[24] Information from the CSQ website, <http://www.ceq.qc.ca>.

[25] Déom and Boivin, *op. cit.*

[26] Bauch, H. (1999). Larose tough act to follow: Labour scene will not be so colourful. *The Gazette* (Montreal), March 20, 1999, p. B1.

[27] Information from the CSN website, <http://www.csn.qc.ca>.

[28] Bauch, *op. cit.*

[29] Information from International Labour Organization website, <http://www.ilo.org>.

[30] Information from the Trades Union Advisory Committee website, <http://www.tuac.org>.

[31] Information from the Commonwealth Trade Union Council website, <http://www.commonwealthtuc.org>.

McDonald's union drive tough:

Restrictive legislation for certification in Ontario and Alberta will make for a difficult campaign, but even in B.C., organizers aren't expecting an easy time

TORONTO—A new union campaign aimed at organizing McDonald's restaurants across Canada will find it easier going in some provinces than in others.

Labour experts say tougher legislation for union certification in Ontario and Alberta will make organizing the fast-food outlets in those provinces more difficult than in other jurisdictions.

But even in relatively union-friendly B.C. and Quebec, organizers aren't expecting a cakewalk.

McDonald's workers tend to be young, part-time, transient, and in small operations, conditions which make it difficult to mount a successful union drive.

Ontario Federation of Labour president Wayne Samuelson said unions are needed to help service sector workers deal with problems such as irregular hours and lack of benefits.

McDonald's has about 1,000 restaurants in Canada employing 70,000 people. None of its North American outlets is unionized, although organized labour has had some success in Europe.

Charlotte Yates, a professor of labour studies at McMaster University in Hamilton, Ontario, said the campaign signals a new wave of unionization.

Earlier efforts concentrated on the skilled trades, the industrial sector, and public servants, she said. But unions today recognize they need to tackle the service sector, where most new jobs are being created.

Yates said organizing will be tougher in provinces such as Alberta and Ontario, where a formal vote must be held to determine if a majority of employees want a union.

(*Vancouver Sun*, March 20, 1998)

chapter 5

THE ORGANIZING CAMPAIGN

objectives

In this chapter, we discuss the reasons why employees decide to unionize and outline how an organizing campaign is conducted. We explain what is entailed in making and assessing an application for certification. At the end of the chapter, you should be able to:

- explain why a collective bargaining relationship would be considered
- describe the steps in an organizing campaign
- understand what is required to apply for certification
- identify what factors must be addressed in a certification application
- identify two special situations involving organizing campaigns and certification applications

INTRODUCTION

Canadian labour legislation in all jurisdictions recognizes the right of most kinds of employees to freely choose to be a member of a trade union and to participate in the union's lawful activities. In this chapter, we will focus on how employees exercise that right.

Many employees are first introduced to the idea of joining a union through an organizing campaign, which is the campaign that a union conducts in a workplace to persuade employees to choose the union as their legal representative. The organizing campaign is a very important part of the industrial relations system, because its success or failure ultimately determines whether employees will be represented by a union or not. Thus, it is important to understand what an organizing campaign is, how it is initiated, and what legislation governs how the campaign is conducted.

We will start by examining reasons why employees might support a union and will then describe how a union organizing campaign is initiated. We will conclude by looking at the means by which unions come to be recognized as the freely chosen workplace representative of the employees.

FACTORS AFFECTING EMPLOYEE SUPPORT FOR A UNION

There are many reasons why employees might want to establish a union in their workplace. A number of studies have attempted to identify these reasons and also to identify the reasons that are most influential in employees' decisions to actively support a union organizing campaign. In other words, what are the factors that ultimately determine whether employees will vote for or against having a union as their representative in the workplace? Identifying these factors is important because the difference between the number of votes for and against a union can be very small, even in a large workplace with many potential voters. Every single vote is important in determining whether an organizing campaign is ultimately successful.

It is important for unions to understand the reasons why workers would support a union, since such knowledge would allow unions to address those reasons in their organizing campaigns. If unions know what influences are at work in motivating employees to support a union, they can tailor their organizing campaigns to address and strengthen those influences. Conversely, an employer who wishes to resist a unionization drive would find it useful to understand why workers reject unions. The employer can then, within the guidelines of labour legislation, address those factors in communications with employees. Additionally, an employer who understands why workers are dissatisfied enough to consider joining a union has the opportunity to address the causes of dissatisfaction and to create a workplace where employees are treated fairly.

The research exploring why employees do or do not support unions is wide-ranging. Many different and potentially influential factors have been identified. It is important to note, however, that this research has not always distinguished between the different decision-making points that employees pass through in the organizing process. Workers first must decide whether or not a union would be an asset for them in the workplace. Then they must decide whether to invite a union to undertake an organizing campaign among the employees. Finally, each individual worker must decide whether or not to cast a formal vote in favour of union representation. Different factors may be more or less important in affecting choices at each of these three decision points.[1] Nevertheless, the research studies roughly fall into four categories based on the type of factors that have been examined: personal factors, workplace factors, economic factors, and societal factors. We will discuss each of these in turn.

Personal Factors

Interestingly, an employee's intention to support a union may be influenced by factors that were present long before the union entered the workplace or even before the employee joined the organization. One study showed that individuals whose parents held positive attitudes toward unions or were active participants in unions tended to have positive attitudes toward unions themselves.[2] This may be because they received positive rather than negative information about unions as they were growing up. Socio-economic status is another influential factor; members of ethnic minorities and low-income or low-status workers, for example, have more positive attitudes toward unions than do higher-status workers.[3] It is speculated that these favourable attitudes are a consequence of the fact that unions address issues related to race, gender, and other attributes that may result in low social status; they develop member loyalty by extending their focus beyond wage and benefit issues, which are corporations' main methods of developing worker loyalty.

Positive attitudes toward unions, however, whether these pre-existed or developed after employment at an organization, do not necessarily translate into active support for unions in the form of a vote in favour of union representation. Several intervening factors may determine whether an employee with a pro-union attitude will actually vote in favour of a union in the workplace. In order to support a union, an employee must feel that he or she lacks any individual ability to influence or change unsatisfactory working conditions and that a union is the mechanism by which that change can be achieved.[4] This perception—that a union is an effective means to achieve what individual employees want but cannot achieve on their own—is called the **instrumentality** of the union.[5] Even employees with pro-union attitudes will not support a union that, in their view, lacks the ability to make the desired changes in the workplace. The concept of instrumentality also implies that employees might not support a union, even one they feel positively toward, if they think that they can make desired changes without the union's assistance.

Workers express their views, both for and against union certification, at a CAW rally at the Sterling Truck plant in St. Thomas, Ontario.

An important implication of instrumentality, and one that is often very significant in the success or failure of a unionization vote, involves the employee's perception of a particular union. For example, the Teamsters union was historically perceived as being controlled by individuals with ties to organized crime.[6] This perception might have led an employee with generally pro-union attitudes to vote against being represented by the Teamsters. On the other hand, we should keep in mind that instrumentality can have a positive effect for a union in situations where the union is not capable of achieving what the employees desire. As long as the employees perceive that the union can cause the desired change, even if in reality it cannot, instrumentality may still motivate the employees to support the union.

The personal factors that may affect union support are summarized in Table 5-1.

TABLE 5-1   Personal Factors Affecting Union Support

Factor	Effect
Parental attitudes or union activity	If parents were active in unions or held positive attitudes toward unions, workers may be more likely to support a union.
Socio-economic status	Low socio-economic status, low income, or minority group membership may make workers more likely to support a union.
Instrumentality	If a specific union is perceived as being able to achieve changes that the worker cannot achieve alone, the worker is more likely to support the union.

Workplace Factors

Most studies that explore the reasons for unionization acknowledge that dissatisfaction with workplace conditions is the most common reason why employees consider joining a union.

Dissatisfaction with the workplace can be generated from a number of different sources. Compensation levels are an important factor in determining whether dissatisfaction exists or not. Compensation affects dissatisfaction not only in absolute terms (i.e., the actual amount of pay and benefits), but also in relative terms (how one's pay and benefits compare with those of other workers in the organization or workers in similar positions in other organizations).[7] Dissatisfaction may result if an employee perceives that he or she is being paid significantly less than other workers, and the prospect of unionization may become more attractive if unionization is seen as a way to remedy the perceived discrepancies.

A similar comparative effect arises with employees in industries that have already been unionized to some degree. One study indicated that the likelihood of unionization in a particular organization rises when the level of unionization in the organization's industry is 35 percent or higher.[8] This effect may occur because workers in non-unionized organizations within an industry perceive unionized workers in the same industry as having better working conditions and they thus want to gain the same outcomes for themselves. It has also been pointed out, however, that some non-unionized firms in highly unionized industries adopt the same levels of pay and benefits as those in union-ized firms in order to be competitive in the labour market and to remain non-unionized; this is known as the "union threat effect."[9] If the union threat effect comes into play, non-unionized workers will have the same workplace conditions as unionized workers; these non-unionized workers may be disinclined to support a union because they do not see any additional improvements that joining a union would provide.

Dissatisfaction within the workplace can also be generated by management's refusal to correct problems brought to its attention, problems with administration in general, inadequate benefits, lack of opportunity for promotion, and job security concerns.[10] Workers also identify the lack of opportunity for worker participation and cooperation with management in decision making as a major cause of dissatisfaction in the work-place.[11] However, the factor of instrumentality is again important in determining whether a worker's dissatisfaction will result in his or her actively supporting a union. As noted above, in order to gain the employees' support, the union must be perceived as being able to correct the conditions causing dissatisfaction.

One study suggested that the union-related attitudes of others in the workplace may be another workplace factor that affects whether an individual supports a union. If co-workers feel positively about the presence of a union, an individual is more likely to support a union.[12] A second study showed that a similar effect is apparent if an indi-vidual's family members want him or her to support the union.[13] The co-workers and family members of individual workers are both interested in the individuals' work-relat-ed activities, and thus both can influence the workers' decisions related to the work-place. These two studies demonstrated another interesting result of workplace atti-tudes.[14] While most of the subjects in these studies perceived that their management and supervisors did not want them to vote for the union, the supervisors' and managers' attitudes did not affect whether the individual employees supported the union or not.[15] In fact, if it was perceived that management might actually retaliate against employees if they supported a union (e.g., by demoting or firing union supporters), the subjects were more, not less, likely to support a union.[16]

Another study identified the structure of the workplace itself and the type of work engaged in by the organization as important factors in determining the level of support for a union.[17] This study, which investigated why the level of unionization was relatively low in the American high-tech industry as compared to other American industries, reported that the high-tech industry was characterized by "rule-bound, rigid and insecure" work climates. These conditions would usually suggest a workplace that would be favourable to unionization, but the study's authors observed that this was not so in the high-tech industry. They suggested that workers were anxious to hold on to their jobs and feared that actively pursuing unionization would threaten what little job security they had. The results of this study suggest that there may exist factors or conditions in specific organizations or industries that affect whether employees support unionization or not.

The workplace factors affecting support for a union are summarized in Table 5-2.

TABLE 5-2   Workplace Factors Affecting Union Support

Factor	Effect
Compensation	Absolute levels and comparative levels may increase support for union if levels are perceived as insufficient.
Level of unionization in industry	Support for union may increase if rest of industry is unionized; however, non-union firms may match unionized firms' conditions.
Dissatisfaction with management/administration	This dissatisfaction may increase support for union if union is perceived as being able to resolve dissatisfaction.
Dissatisfaction with workplace conditions	This dissatisfaction may increase support for union if union is perceived as being able to resolve dissatisfaction.
Union attitudes of co-workers and family	If attitudes are positive, workers may be more likely to support union.
Union attitudes of management	These have no influence on employees' intentions to support union; if management is perceived as being willing to act against union, intention to support union may increase.
Organizational structure	Factors unique to specific industry or organization may increase or decrease union support.

Economic Factors

Factors beyond the organization and the individual affect whether individuals support unionization of their workplace or not. An American study found that the level of unemployment in the individual's state had an effect on whether an individual would vote for a union or not.[18] As unemployment in a state increased, the likelihood of an individual voting for unionization increased and the overall probability of a union organizing campaign being successful also increased. The amount of change in the unemployment rate in the previous year was also important; the greater the amount of change, the more likely it was that individuals would support a union. These findings indicate that many workers feel that a union shields them from the effects of an unstable labour market by increasing job security. However, we should keep in mind contradictory findings that suggest that the fear of unemployment makes some individuals less likely to unionize.[19]

Another possible economic influence on the decision to unionize is the rate of inflation. Some evidence suggests that if the inflation rate increases, workers are more likely to want to join a union, since they believe that unions will help them to offset the decrease in real wages caused by price inflation.[20] However, analysis of economic data on union membership trends has not always demonstrated that inflation rates affect union membership rates; furthermore, the suggested relationship between these two variables has not been found in some countries outside North America.

The economic factors affecting support for a union are summarized in Table 5-3.

TABLE 5-3   Economic Factors Affecting Union Support

Factor	Effect
Unemployment rate in region	If rate increases, likelihood of worker joining union increases.
	If there is a significant change in rate, unionization is more likely.
Inflation	Price inflation can increase intent to unionize and actual rate of unionization.

Societal Factors

General societal attitudes about unions influence individuals' inclinations to support a union in their own workplace. One study investigated the union-related attitudes of people in two western Canadian cities in 1981 and 1987.[21] The time periods covered by this study included a recession in both cities and a very visible, prolonged, and violent strike in one of the cities; despite these events, approximately half the respondents in both surveys had generally positive attitudes toward unions. However, more than half of the respondents said that they themselves would not join a union. The researchers attributed these apparently contradictory findings to a variety of possible factors, including the following: some individuals may extol the positive effects of unions but personally distrust their power; a recession may cause residents with less positive union attitudes to seek opportunities elsewhere; the union-related experiences of an individual's friends and family members may have a negative effect; and individual demographic characteristics such as age and levels of education may discourage union participation.

A similar discrepancy between attitudes and intentions was discovered in a study of 622 American non-union workers.[22] Roughly three-quarters of the respondents thought that unions were effective in improving wages and working conditions, but only one-third stated that they themselves would join a union. The authors of this study suggested that specific beliefs about the effects of a union in one's own workplace are more influential than general beliefs about unions in determining whether an individual will support a union or not. The authors of the study involving western Canadian cities made a similar suggestion, noting that if individuals do not see a benefit for themselves in the presence of a union in their own workplace, they may not wish to join a union, even if they generally hold pro-union attitudes.[23]

Another societal factor affecting the decision to unionize that deserves mention at this point (one that will be discussed in subsequent chapters) is whether the relevant labour legislation facilitates or hinders the certification process. A comparative analysis of Canadian and American unionization rates between 1984 and 1998 indicated that a shift toward "anti-union" legislation in Canada may be one explanation for the decline in Canadian unionization rates during the period of analysis.[24] Anti-union legislation includes, for example, legislation requiring a mandatory vote in the workplace on every certification application.

The societal factors that may affect support for a union are summarized in Table 5-4.

TABLE 5-4   Societal Factors Affecting Union Support

Factor	Effect
General attitudes toward unions	These may not affect individual attitudes, even during labour-related events like strikes and recessions.
	Individual may support general concept of unions but not be personally willing to join one.
Labour legislation	Anti-union legislation may reduce likelihood of a successful organizing campaign.

STEPS IN THE ORGANIZING CAMPAIGN

If, for whatever reason, enough employees in a workplace feel that a union is needed to represent their interests, the employees may decide to initiate an organizing campaign. A successful organizing campaign results in the union's ability to request recognition of its status as the **bargaining agent** for the employees. Being the "bargaining agent" means that the union is legally recognized as the sole representative of employees in that particular workplace. As bargaining agent, the union acts on behalf of the employees in negotiating conditions and terms of work and in administering the resulting collective agreement.

An organizing campaign can be initiated either by a union or by the employees. If a union becomes aware of a group of dissatisfied employees, it may contact the employees to see if there is already sufficient interest in pursuing unionization or if there is a good chance that the union can persuade the employees to consider unionization. If the employees initiate the campaign, they must decide whether to start their own union or whether to contact an established union with the intention of joining that union. As described in Chapter 4, most employees who initiate an organizing campaign decide to contact an established union because of the organizing experience and campaign resources that the union can offer. Organizing campaigns in the Canadian private sector all follow the pattern outlined in Figure 5-1. We will now look at this pattern in detail.

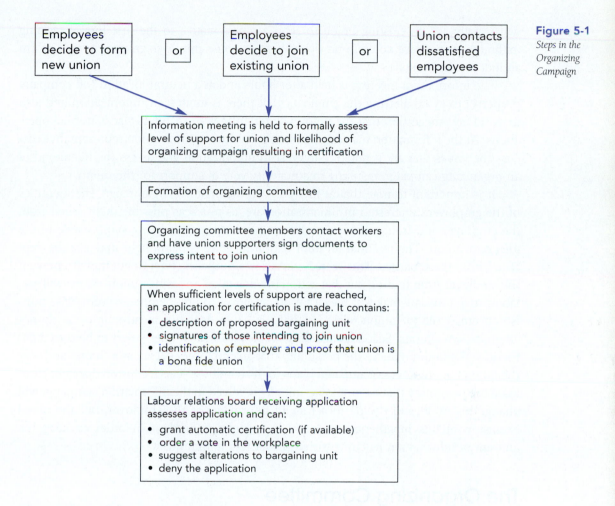

Figure 5-1
Steps in the Organizing Campaign

Employees decide to form new union

or

Employees decide to join existing union

or

Union contacts dissatisfied employees

Information meeting is held to formally assess level of support for union and likelihood of organizing campaign resulting in certification

Formation of organizing committee

Organizing committee members contact workers and have union supporters sign documents to express intent to join union

When sufficient levels of support are reached, an application for certification is made. It contains:
- description of proposed bargaining unit
- signatures of those intending to join union
- identification of employer and proof that union is a bona fide union

Labour relations board receiving application assesses application and can:
- grant automatic certification (if available)
- order a vote in the workplace
- suggest alterations to bargaining unit
- deny the application

The Information Meeting

The first formal step in the organizing campaign is to convene an information meeting, which is held after working hours and off company property. This meeting may be preceded by smaller informal gatherings during which those employees considering unionization attempt to determine whether there are enough co-workers interested in unionization to justify holding a formal meeting. If sufficient interest exists, one of the initiators will usually ask an existing union to send a representative to the first formal meeting (although, as we have noted in previous chapters, some employee groups choose to form an independent union).

The information meeting is held after hours and at a neutral location (off company property) to avoid alerting the employer that there is interest in unionization and also to avoid any suggestion that the union is interfering with the workplace's normal operations. At the information meeting, interested employees and a union representative discuss the issues that are generating interest in unionization and assess the likelihood of an organizing campaign resulting in a majority vote of support for the union.

It is important to note that at this point in the organizing campaign, the identities of the employees interested in unionization are, as much as possible, kept secret from the employer and from employees who are perceived as not being sympathetic to the idea of a union. The fact that an information meeting is being held may also be kept secret from these parties. This secrecy serves two purposes. First, it attempts to prevent the employer from finding out that action is being taken to form a union. As we will see, labour relations law makes it illegal for an employer to fire, demote, or otherwise punish an employee for union-related activity, but that does not mean employers do not attempt such actions. Second, excluding employees who are perceived to be unsympathetic to the union reduces the possibility that an employee will act as a "mole" and leak the union's or employees' campaign plans to the employer. This exclusion does not eliminate the possibility that an employee initially involved in the information campaign will change his mind and decide to act as an informant for the employer, but the initial exclusion of unsympathetic employees is considered prudent in order to keep the amount of information reaching the employer to a minimum.

The Organizing Committee

If sufficient interest in unionization is apparent at the information meeting and those present at the meeting perceive that an organizing campaign could be successful (that is, it might result in certification), an organizing committee will be created. The organizing committee usually consists of several employees in the workplace as well as, perhaps, an experienced organizer from the union on whom they can call for assistance. The reason that the organizing committee tends to consist of employees rather than professional organizers from the union is that employees are generally considered more credible than "outsiders" in discussions about workplace issues. Also, employees will already be familiar to the potential union members and will have better knowledge of workplace issues because of their first-hand experience.

The members of the organizing committee will contact other employees before or after work, on breaks, or at their homes to sound them out on their union sympathy. Under Canadian labour law, an employer is entitled to forbid individuals who are acting on behalf of the union from soliciting support at the workplace during working hours, for the simple reason that such activity could significantly disrupt the normal operations of the workplace. When the organizing committee members contact other employees, their goal is to obtain a formal indication of support for the union. This is accomplished by having employees sign a membership card or a petition indicating their intent to join the union. In some jurisdictions, employees may also be asked to pay a small sum of money, usually one or two dollars, to materially signify their support for the union. This money is held in trust until the results of the unionization vote are known. If the vote results in support for the union, the union retains the money; if the vote is against the union, the money is returned to those who paid it.

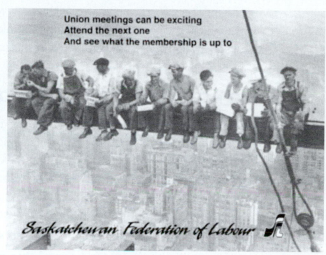

Posters and union publications are often used during an organizing campaign to introduce workers to unions and collective action.

A constant concern throughout the organizing campaign is the possibility of **unfair labour practices**. These will be discussed in more detail in Chapter 6, but essentially, unfair labour practices are any actions by the employer or the union that make potential union members act differently than they would have otherwise. Unfair labour practices are a concern during the organizing campaign because of their potential to influence the vote for or against the union in such a way that the outcome of the vote does not reflect the employees' actual desires. Canadian labour relations law contains guidelines describing what is and what is not an unfair labour practice. As we will see, however, it is sometimes very difficult to determine whether or not an action is an unfair labour practice or what impact the action had on the employees' attitudes or intentions. Notably, in many Canadian labour relations board decisions, the employer's intention in undertaking the action has been deemed less important than whether or not employees were intimidated by the action. In other cases, employer actions have been so blatantly intimidating that a labour relations board has certified the union even in the absence of sufficient levels of employee support.[25]

The Application for Certification

When the organizing committee believes it has sufficient membership support as defined in their jurisdiction's labour legislation, the union will file an **Application for Certification** form with the appropriate labour relations board. This application form indicates that a group of employees wish to be represented by a particular union in their dealings with the employer.

The application form has three major components:

- an indication of sufficient membership support for the application
- a description of the desired **bargaining unit** (the group of employees that will be represented in collective bargaining with the employer)
- an indication of the employer and the trade union covered by the application

We will discuss each of the components of the certification application in turn.

Sufficient Membership Support

The union filing a certification application must be able to show that it has sufficient support from the "employees" of the "employer" to make the application worthwhile. (The terms "employee" and "employer" have specific meanings in the context of labour relations legislation that will be outlined later.) The question of what constitutes sufficient support for certification is one of the more contentious issues that labour relations boards and legislators have to deal with. If not enough employees in a workplace support the union, serious problems with negotiating and administering the collective agreement will ensue because the union's position may not truly reflect the feelings of the employees. On the other hand, given that union membership is established as a basic legal right of employees, it might be unfair to turn away a group of employees who wanted to exercise their right to form a union simply because of the size of the group.

In most Canadian jurisdictions, a certification application must be accompanied by an indication of a sufficient level of support from the employees in the proposed bargaining unit. Table 5-5 shows how different Canadian jurisdictions define a "sufficient" level of membership support.

TABLE 5-5   Required Levels of Support for Certification Applications

	Level of Support Required for Certification Application to be Considered	Level of Support Required for Application for Automatic Certification
Federal	Majority of employees in proposed bargaining unit	Over 50% of employees in proposed bargaining unit
Alberta	40% of employees in proposed bargaining unit	No automatic certification
British Columbia	45% of employees in proposed bargaining unit	No automatic certification
Manitoba	40% of employees in proposed bargaining unit	At least 65% of employees in proposed bargaining unit
New Brunswick	40% of employees in proposed bargaining unit	At least 60% of employees in proposed bargaining unit
Newfoundland	Majority of employees in proposed bargaining unit	Majority of employees in proposed bargaining unit
Nova Scotia	40% of employees in proposed bargaining unit	No automatic certification
Ontario	40% of employees in proposed bargaining unit	No automatic certification
Prince Edward Island	Majority of employees in proposed bargaining unit	No automatic certification
Quebec	Absolute majority of employees of an employer	Not specified (see information on voluntary recognition)
Saskatchewan	Majority of employees in proposed bargaining unit	No automatic certification

Source: Human Resources Development Canada, Labour Program, Synoptic Charts on Legislation Pertaining to Certain Major Collective Bargaining Issues: Trade Union Application for Certification (available at <http://www.hrdc-drhc.gc.ca>).

As Table 5-5 shows, all Canadian jurisdictions set a minimum level of support that must be demonstrated for an application for certification to be considered. However, a labour relations board may consider applications with less than the required level of support if the union making the application can show that the employer committed an unfair labour practice that intimidated the employees into not expressing support for the union. In such situations, a labour relations board will attempt to assess the effect that the employer's behaviour has had and, depending on the result of the assessment, will allow the application to proceed, permit the union to attempt to collect further indications of support, or deny the application. As previously noted, a labour relations board also has the option of declaring a union's certification immediately if it believes that the employer's actions have had such an impact that the employees' intentions can no longer be discerned by a vote or by the number of signatures supporting the application. A labour relations board might also take this action if it believes that the employer may not cease its intimidating behaviour before a vote on the application is taken in the workplace.

If the percentage of bargaining unit employees expressing support for the union exceeds the minimum required percentage, the certification process may be faster in some jurisdictions. As Table 5-5 indicates, in some jurisdictions, if the level of support exceeds a specified amount, the union making the application may receive what is called **automatic certification**. Automatic certification means that the union is granted the right to represent the employees without any further tests of employee support. The reasoning behind this policy is that if a large number of employees support the application, any further polling of employee opinions would be redundant; further tests would also allow employers an opportunity to intimidate employees and pressure them to vote against their true feelings.

If the level of support for the certification exceeds the stated minimum but does not reach the level needed for automatic certification (in jurisdictions where automatic certification is allowed), the labour relations board will, after assessing the application criteria described below, require an employee vote before granting certification. This process is described in more detail in Chapter 6.

The level of support required for certification applications is a part of labour legislation that tends to fluctuate in accordance with the philosophy of the government in power. A political party with anti-union opinions is likely to raise the necessary level of support, with the justification that there must be support from a clear majority of the bargaining unit members. This point of view contends that it would be unjust for a relatively small group of employees to impose their feelings about unionization on the majority of the workers. This view was recently demonstrated by the new provincial government in British Columbia, which eliminated the legislation that previously permitted automatic certification, reasoning that certification without a formal secret-ballot vote did not truly allow employees to express their opinions on unionization.[26]

Ontario NDP leader Howard Hampton reiterates the NDP's traditional alliance with labour after a split with CAW president Buzz Hargrove over election tactics.

A pro-union political party is likely to lower the required level of support or to create mechanisms—such as automatic certification—that speed up the certification process. The justification for this position is that since the employer, by controlling how the workplace operates and what the organization does, always holds the balance of power in a workplace, legislation must give the benefit of the doubt to the workers and assist them in exercising their legal right to form a union. This argument also contends that the opportunity for employers to influence their employees' expression of opinion should be minimized and that procedures like automatic certification are appropriate because they reduce the opportunity for employer interference where a clear majority of workers support unionization.

The effect of changes in certification legislation on levels of unionization can be clearly seen in a study that compared numbers of certifications in Canadian provinces over time.[27] This analysis compared the numbers of certifications in Canadian jurisdictions over periods when the level of support for certification applications varied. The results of this analysis demonstrated that changes in the level of support required by provincial labour legislation were closely related to the success of certification applications. If the required level of support for certification applications was increased, both the number of applications for certification and the number of successful applications decreased. The same was true in reverse: when the required level of support was decreased, certification applications and successful certifications increased. These find-ings indicate that the level of support needed for certification applications to be made is extremely important in determining whether organizing campaigns succeed or not.

One other factor that may affect a labour relations board's assessment of sufficient membership support is the timeliness of the application. As Chapter 6 will show, every Canadian jurisdiction has guidelines restricting when an application for certification can be filed. However, we should also note here that in addition to counting the level of support accompanying an application for certification, a labour relations board also looks at how long it has taken the organizing committee to assemble the expressions of support. If, in the board's opinion, an excessively long period has passed between the start of the organizing campaign and the attainment of the required level of sup-port, there is the apprehension that the expressions of support obtained near the start of the campaign may no longer be valid; that is, given the amount of time that has passed between the expression of support and the filing of the certification application, some employees may have changed their minds about supporting the union or may have even left the organization altogether. As long as there is no evidence that unfair labour practices by the employer unduly extended the length of the organizing cam-paign, a labour relations board may decide to disallow an application for certification if, in the board's opinion, the campaign was long enough to cause concerns about the timeliness or accuracy of expressions of support.

Appropriate Bargaining Unit

Every certification application must contain a description of the bargaining unit that the proposed union is seeking to represent. Generally, this description consists of the job titles of the jobs that will or will not be represented by the union. For example, a pro-posed bargaining unit might be described as "all production, distribution, and support employees of Cardboard Box Manufacturers at the location of 1234 Jones Road, Industrytown, with the exception of supervisors, managers, payroll clerks, and human resources clerks."

The purpose of the bargaining unit description is twofold. First, there is sometimes con-cern about whether signatures in support of the certification application are valid—that is, whether the signatures are legitimate or whether they are the signatures of employees who are not included in the union. The labour relations board can cross-check the description of the proposed bargaining unit against the organization's list of employees and thus identify which specific employees are included in the proposed bargaining unit. It can then be determined whether individual signatures should or should not be included in calculating whether the required level of support exists.

Second, a description of the proposed bargaining unit allows a labour relations board to assess whether the proposed unit is appropriate or not. There are several considerations that a board will address in determining whether a bargaining unit is appropriate or not: size and location of the bargaining unit, managerial and non-managerial employees, and definition of an employee. The principle underlying each of these considerations is **community of interest**: that is, there should be enough relevant characteristics in common among the applicants to make the union a cohesive and representative unit, one structured in such a way as to sufficiently represent its members in interactions with the employer. We will now outline each of these considerations.

Size and Location   The determination of an appropriate bargaining unit is an important issue for both the union and the employer. The union would like to represent as many workers as possible. This is desirable for the union not only because it will gain more revenue from **union dues**—the membership fees paid to the union by its members—but also because representing more workers gives the union more power in dealing with the employer.

However, there are practical difficulties associated with administering a bargaining unit that is too large or too widely dispersed. Communicating with or getting agreement among a very large membership can be challenging. Also, members located in several different places or performing very different jobs may have issues particular to their job or location that are lost in more universal issues within a large bargaining unit. Thus, the union may not be able to represent its members competently if the bargaining unit is too large or too diverse.

A labour relations board must also consider the effect of the bargaining unit's size and location on the relationship with the employer. One of the goals that a labour relations board tries to achieve in establishing an appropriate bargaining unit is a relative balance of bargaining power between the employer and the union. A bargaining unit so large that it gives the union far more bargaining power than the employer might be as inappropriate as a bargaining unit so small that the union would have very little bargaining power against the employer.

Managerial and Non-Managerial Employees   Another consideration in determining what makes an appropriate bargaining unit is the question of who is eligible to be represented by the union. In other words, who is eligible to be in the bargaining unit? A general policy in labour legislation is that bargaining units should not include both managerial and non-managerial employees. This policy exists for several reasons. First, since managers are the workplace representatives of the owners of the company and the employer is entitled to rely on the loyalty of its representatives, management employees should not cause the employer concern by favouring other interests within the organization, such as the union or the employees. Second, a conflict of interest would seem to exist if a manager with the power to discipline another employee was in the same bargaining unit as that employee. A general principle of union democracy is that all members are equal; it is clear that a situation where one union member can discipline another would violate that principle. Third, as we know, a trade union by definition is legally entitled to be established and administered without employer interference. Placing managers in the same bargaining unit as non-managers would violate this principle, because the manager, as the employer's representative in the workplace, could influence issues like union bargaining proposals to favour the employer's interests. And fourth, managers often have access to confidential material, such as budgets and personnel records, and hence excluding them from a bargaining unit that represents non-managerial employees would protect the employer's interests (by not making this material available to bargaining unit members) and would also preserve the equality principle of union democracy.

While, there are clearly several very good reasons to exclude managers from the same bargaining unit as non-managers, to do so is not always easy in practice, as it is sometimes very difficult to determine who is a manager and who is not. The job title alone may not be sufficient. Consider, for example, a situation at a restaurant where someone fills a position with the title of "shift manager." This person may be in charge of operations during a particular period and may have managerial authority while the shift is in progress, but this same person, during the "managerial" shift, may fill in for regular workers who are absent or assist those workers who need help in their non-management tasks. This same person may also be scheduled to work as a regular employee at other times during the working week. Is this person a manager, and should he or she be excluded from the bargaining unit?

The question of who is or is not a manager has become even more difficult to answer in light of workplace trends like downsizing, flatter organizational hierarchies, teamwork, and flexible organizational structures. All of these trends have blurred the traditional boundaries between managerial and non-managerial work. Thus, it is no longer appropriate to exclude a position from a bargaining unit simply because the position is titled "manager." A labour relations board will usually look beyond the job title and consider the following criteria in determining whether a position should be included in the bargaining unit:

1. Does the job description of the position give the person in the position the authority to hire, fire, and discipline other persons in the organization?

2. Does the job description of the position indicate that the position is responsible for production or operations?

3. In the organizational structure and/or lines of authority, do other positions report to this position? Does this position involve direct supervision of the work performed in other positions?

4. Is the person in this position the immediate authority if a crisis or emergency occurs?

5. Does the person in this position have access to confidential information such as employee records or budgets?

6. If the position includes both managerial and non-managerial work, what is the division of working time between these two sets of duties?

If the answer to any of the first five questions is yes, a labour relations board will likely exclude the position from the bargaining unit, regardless of what the formal title of the position is. A labour relations board may go beyond the written job description and examine evidence of actual workplace practices if there appears to be a significant discrepancy between the job description and the actual operations of the organization. In assessing the answer to the sixth question about the proportion of time spent on managerial and non-managerial duties, a labour relations board will likely exclude a position from the bargaining unit if the majority of the employee's time is spent performing managerial duties, regardless of the formal job title the employee holds.

Some Canadian jurisdictions have attempted to deal with the issue of managerial exclusion from bargaining units by permitting managers to unionize in different bargaining units from those they supervise. This provision recognizes the right of workers to unionize but also maintains the separation between manager and employees that is considered fundamental to the democratic operation of a union.

Another consideration in this regard is whether to include employees whose work shares some of the characteristics (but not all) of managerial positions. These employees are usually referred to as **exempt employees**. Exempt employees perform work involving administrative support to top managers. In such a position, the employees may have access to confidential information such as employee records or employers' plans for collective bargaining. Although these employees do not possess other powers that managers traditionally have, such as authority over hiring, they are usually excluded from the bargaining unit because of their access to confidential information that could benefit the union or harm other bargaining unit members.

Defining an "Employee"

Another consideration in determining who should be included in the bargaining unit is deciding who is an employee. This may seem like a fairly straightforward question, but because of changing employment relationships, it is actually quite complex. New forms of employment such as contract work, temporary work, limited-term contracts, and job sharing make the employment relationship much more variable than in the past.

The labour codes in all Canadian jurisdictions clearly state that one must be an employee in order to be included in a bargaining unit. The definition of "employee" is included in each jurisdiction's labour code as well as in the relevant act governing employment standards, but generally these definitions recognize an "employee" as someone who works on a regular basis for an employer in a dependent relationship. In other words, the worker depends on the employer for the majority or all of his or her work, and the employer compensates the worker for performing the work. An employee is also someone who performs his or her work under the direction and control of the employer. The employer determines what the work will be and how it will be conducted, assigns the work to the employee, and determines when the work is completed and what level of performance or quality is needed for successful completion.

These criteria for defining an "employee" are broad enough to include most full-time and part-time employees and shift workers. However, it is questionable whether employees in less permanent forms of work, including some kinds of part-time work or some forms of contract work, would be defined as employees if these criteria were used. This issue of definitions is of particular concern to unions, since the size of the bargaining unit may be eroded if employers replace full-time permanent workers with temporary, part-time, or contract workers. Another concern is the possibility that the employer might eliminate positions entirely and instead have the work performed by workers employed by another (non-union) company, in the employment arrangement known as **outsourcing**.

In situations where it is unclear whether a worker is an "employee" or not, the position of labour relations boards has generally been that if a worker has an ongoing dependent relationship with the organization, the worker should be considered an employee and included in the bargaining unit. For example, if an employee is a limited-term contract employee whose only contract is with the employer (i.e., the employee does not perform contract work for any other employer), then he or she would likely be considered an employee. Likewise, if a worker is hired on a less-than-permanent basis but performs the same work as bargaining unit members, the worker might be considered part of the bargaining unit. Temporary workers who are rehired on successive contracts to perform the same work—in effect, who work as permanent workers but are not recognized as such because they are formally employed on a temporary basis—would likely also be considered part of the bargaining unit.

Labour relations boards and legislators are strict about enforcing the definition of "employee" in order to prevent employers from escaping their responsibilities under the collective agreement by decreasing the size of the bargaining unit. A smaller bargaining unit means a less powerful union, and thus employers who would prefer to deal with a less powerful union might be tempted to hire workers who do not meet the definition of an employee and thus would not be included in the bargaining unit. Often, too, there is a considerable cost incentive for employers to replace permanent full-time unionized employees with temporary, part-time, or contract employees, since these latter employees usually receive lower rates of pay and fewer benefits. Because of these factors, a labour relations board will generally insist that an employer demonstrate that the removal of work or workers from the jurisdiction of the bargaining unit was done for legitimate business reasons and was not motivated solely by a desire to weaken the union. "Legitimate business reasons" are usually ascertained by determining whether the employer would have undertaken the action regardless of whether the union was present or not. (This issue of employer motivation for actions will also be discussed in the sections on unfair labour practices and successorship in chapters 6 and 12.)

In concluding our discussion of issues related to the appropriate bargaining unit, we will note that a labour relations board will not reject an application for certification simply because the application contains a bargaining unit description that the board considers inappropriate. If such an application is received, the board will usually contact the union making the application and suggest alterations to the proposed bargaining unit that would make the unit appropriate in the board's opinion. The union then has the choice of proceeding with the application as it stands, taking the chance that it may be rejected because of the concerns over the proposed bargaining unit, or resubmitting the application with the suggested alterations.

Defining an "Employer"

Franchise operations are often difficult to unionize. This McDonald's restaurant outside of Montreal closed down due to declining profits while its workers were seeking union certification.

The application for certification requires the applicant to indicate which employer the application is intended to address. Not every Canadian labour code provides a definition of "employer." The codes that do (federal, British Columbia, Quebec, and Nova Scotia) state that an employer is someone who employs at least one or more employees. This lack of precision in definition has led to some practical difficulties that become apparent when one considers the many different forms of ownership that exist (e.g., sole proprietorship, partnership, franchise, branch office, subcontracting, one company owning another differently named company, etc.).

Generally, it is expected that the certification application will name the business entity that is the actual employer. Thus, a certification application may contain employer definitions such as "Company [name] doing business as [another company name]" or "[Corporation] franchise located at [franchise location]." If a certification application covers more than one geographical location of the same employer—for example, multiple locations of a chain store or restaurant—the certification application will specify which locations will be included in the proposed bargaining unit.

In situations where the structure or operations of a business make it difficult to determine the actual employer, a labour relations board will consider several criteria in identifying the employer. One question a labour relations board may ask is where the authority for hiring lies. The part of the business that actually hires employees or carries out other human resource management functions (e.g., keeping employee records) may be identified as the employer. A second question a board may ask is what part of the business is accountable for establishing and monitoring work conditions. This question can be particularly relevant in situations such as a franchise arrangement, where one part of the business may have to follow directions established by a central authority, such as a franchisor. If such directions are absolute and the business has little or no flexibility in applying them, the franchisor rather than the operator of the franchise may be considered the actual employer. A third question a board may ask is who exercises control over day-to-day work and production. Does one part of the business completely control another part, or does each part have individual autonomy and judgement in overseeing everyday functions? The answers to these questions assist a labour relations board in determining who the actual employer is.

In some organizational structures, an owner or corporation conducts business through multiple corporate entities that share resources such as workers, supplies, or work sites. In situations involving such a complex structure, a labour relations board has the option of declaring all of the entities to be a **single employer** or **common employer**, as long as all the entities are under the same control and direction. For example, if one individual operates several franchises of the same restaurant in different geographic locations, a labour relations board could declare that, despite the geographic dispersion, the restaurants are a single operation and thus workers at all the restaurants should be included in the same bargaining unit. Giving labour relations boards the power to make this declaration discourages employers from avoiding unionization by creating non-union subsidiary companies and shifting operations into those companies and away from unionized operations.

Defining a "Trade Union"

The final component in a certification application is an indication that the application comes from a bona fide trade union. Most labour codes state that a bona fide trade union is a union that was established free of employer interference and is run on democratic principles (i.e., every member is entitled to a vote and has an equal voice in running the union's business).

As previously mentioned, most certification applications come from established unions that are seeking to organize new locals. However, there is nothing to stop a group of workers from starting their own union, provided they can show that the employer did not assist them or force them to do so and that there is no employer interference in the ongoing operation of the union. If a certification application is submitted by a new union, a labour relations board will examine such documents as the new union's constitution and meeting minutes to ensure that there was and is no employer interference in the union's formation and operations. A labour relations board will also usually ensure that the union's constitution indicates that the union operates on democratic and non-discriminatory principles.

ORGANIZING IN THE CONSTRUCTION INDUSTRY AND VOLUNTARY RECOGNITION

Before closing our discussion of organizing campaigns and certification applications, we will describe two situations that do not completely fit the process of organizing and application for certification described above. The first situation involves organizing in the construction industry, which does not follow the same model as other Canadian industries. In the second situation, the employer voluntarily agrees to recognize the union as the employees' bargaining agent.

Before addressing these special situations, however, we will briefly discuss how labour legislation deals with the possibility that an employer, rather than the employees, might initiate an organizing campaign. Most Canadian labour legislation does not recognize as a union any organization or association of employees that is dominated or influenced by an employer. The common name for unions created or dominated by an employer is a **company union**. Historically, when employers have created or dominated unions, the result—known as a **sweetheart agreement**—is a union-management agreement that unduly favours management and/or does not consider the needs and wants of the employees. A company union is usually powerless or unwilling to negotiate a collective agreement that is not a sweetheart agreement because, in effect, it is controlled by the employer. Thus, the employer would insist that the union agree to contract clauses that favour the employer (e.g., clauses that give the employer unilateral power to set and change wage rates). Another problem with company unions is that normal union-management processes such as addressing employee grievances become essentially meaningless if the union cannot independently represent the employees' interests or concerns.

Because of the disadvantages of company unions, it is almost unknown for an employer to initiate an organizing campaign successfully. The employer's initiation of the campaign, even if it is done with the worthy intention of giving employees a formal voice in the workplace, could lead to an employer-dominated union. This would likely be the case if the union was financially dependent on the employer, since the employer could withdraw financial support if there was a disagreement with the union and thus leave the union unable to function. While a labour relations board would not reject outright an application for certification that was generated by an employer-initiated organizing campaign or that came from an employer-dominated union, it would certainly examine the application with much more care and precision than it would an application resulting from an employee-initiated organizing campaign or from a union free of employer domination.

The Construction Industry

Canadian labour legislation recognizes that conditions for organizing in the construction industry are somewhat different than in other Canadian industries because of the mobility of workers and employment. Most Canadian labour law thus has a separate section dealing with the construction industry. In effect, each project or work site is considered to be a workplace, and a separate certification must be obtained for each project and for each unionized trade working on the project. Timeliness is clearly an important consideration of certification for construction work sites because of the time schedules associated with completing the project in an efficient manner. It would be pointless to issue a certification order after the project had been completed.

Thus, most Canadian labour law permits the unions that represent workers on construction projects to dispense with the responsibility of conducting an organizing campaign and filing an application for certification. Instead, the process of obtaining unionized workers is initiated by the employer. A construction employer who bids on and secures a contract stipulating the use of unionized workers will contact the appropriate union and request that the union provide the appropriate unionized employees for the project. If, for example, a contractor secures a contract that requires that the project be completed with the use of unionized carpenters, the contractor will contact the carpenters' union and request that the union supply the required number of carpenters. This form of employer involvement in certification is accepted by labour relations boards because the union providing the workers is an independent union and not one created by the employer.

Voluntary Recognition

In some situations, a union may be able to satisfy an employer that it has organized employees in a unit appropriate for collective bargaining without going through the formality of making an application for certification to a labour relations board. If the employer accepts the union's proposed bargaining unit, most Canadian labour law permits the employer to recognize the union's right to act as the exclusive bargaining agent for those employees without official recognition from a labour relations board. This acceptance by the employer is called **voluntary recognition**. If voluntary recognition occurs, the appropriate provisions of the relevant labour legislation will govern the employer-union collective bargaining relationship.

Under voluntary recognition, the employer accepts the union as the employees' bargaining agent without any representation vote or other formalization of the union's existence. Labour law in several provinces allows a labour relations board to grant certification if a voluntary recognition agreement has been in effect for several years. Table 5-6 outlines which jurisdictions in Canada have provisions for voluntary recognition.

TABLE 5-6 Voluntary Recognition

	Voluntary Recognition Available
Federal	Yes
Alberta	Yes
British Columbia	Yes
Manitoba	Not specified
New Brunswick	Yes
Newfoundland	Not specified
Nova Scotia	Yes
Ontario	Yes
Prince Edward Island	Not specified
Quebec	Immediate certification available if employees and employer agree on composition of bargaining unit
Saskatchewan	Not specified

Source: Human Resources Development Canada, Labour Program, Summaries of General Private Sector Collective Bargaining Legislation (available at <http://www.hrdc-drhc.gc.ca>).

SUMMARY

The organizing campaign is important to understand because it is the start of the process through which a union enters a workplace. There are numerous reasons why employees may decide to join a union. The most common are dissatisfaction with workplace conditions or dissatisfaction with management. There are also several personal, economic, and societal factors that may affect whether employees decide to support a union in their workplace or not.

If there is sufficient interest among workers to justify pursuing the idea of unionization, an organizing campaign can be initiated. The purpose of the organizing campaign is to generate sufficient support to make an application for certification to a labour relations board. The labour relations board assesses several components of the application, including whether there is sufficient support for unionization, whether the composition of the proposed bargaining unit is appropriate, whether the members of the proposed bargaining unit meet the definition of "employee," and whether the proposed union meets the definition of a legitimate trade union. The labour relations board will also be concerned if there was employer or union activity that might have persuaded employees to act against their true wishes.

If a labour relations board is satisfied that the application for certification meets all these tests, the board will then proceed with the process of certification. This process is described in detail in Chapter 6.

KEY TERMS FOR CHAPTER 5

Application for Certification (p. 166)
automatic certification (p. 168)
bargaining agent (p. 162)
bargaining unit (p. 166)
community of interest (p. 171)
company union (p. 178)

DISCUSSION QUESTIONS FOR CHAPTER 5

1. Why would an employee's family background influence whether an employee would want a union in his or her workplace?

2. What factors in the workplace are likely to cause the kind of dissatisfaction that would lead to unionization?

3. Outline the steps in an organizing campaign.

4. Explain why most provincial labour codes require a minimum level of support among workers for a certification application to be filed.

5. A small group of clerical workers who are employed in the administrative office of a large manufacturing plant want to form a union. Identify and discuss the considerations that would be raised in deciding whether this group is an appropriate bargaining unit.

6. What are the factors to consider in determining who is an employee? What factors should be considered in deciding who is a manager?

7. If workers at a franchise operation want to unionize, who would be named as the employer and why?

CASE *5-1*

TOWN OF PINEWOOD AND GENERAL WORKERS UNION

(Based on *Tecumseh (Town) and Teamsters Local 880*, 1998)

The General Workers Union ("union") is applying for certification of a bargaining unit consisting of the volunteer firefighters for the Town of Pinewood ("Pinewood"). A certification vote was held, and the results indicate that a majority of employees wish to be unionized. However, Pinewood is arguing that the firefighters do not meet the definition of "employee" and that the union is therefore not entitled to be certified.

Background to the Case

The Town of Pinewood is in a rural area with little industry. Fire protection services for Pinewood are provided exclusively by a volunteer fire department. Such departments are called "volunteer" both colloquially and in legislation to differentiate them from fire departments staffed by full-time firefighters. Volunteer firefighters receive some remuneration for the work they perform.

The only full-time member of the Pinewood fire department is the chief, Kurt Blackman. Both parties agree that Blackman is an employee of the Town of Pinewood; he reports to the town council and is empowered to oversee the administration of the fire department and the discipline of its members. Blackman is also expected to attend major-alarm incidents and to perform fire inspections.

Volunteer firefighters in Pinewood are recruited through newspaper advertisements. Most respondents to the ads have regular full-time employment elsewhere. Chief Blackman reviews the applications and selects the most promising candidates. The candidates take an aptitude test, and those who achieve the highest test scores are then interviewed by a committee consisting of the mayor, a town councillor, the chief, and a deputy chief. The committee makes recommendations for hiring to the town council, which always accepts the recommendations and makes the formal appointments.

The firefighters are offered regular training twice a month in two-hour sessions. Attendance at these training sessions is voluntary, but those who attend are paid for their time. Firefighters are expected to attend two paid evenings a month to perform maintenance on the fire hall and equipment. Blackman said that there is no obligation for firefighters to undertake either of these activities, but regular non-attendance might result in a recommendation for removal. He has never had to remove a firefighter for non-attendance but recently suspended two firefighters for speaking directly to the media, thus breaching fire department policy and the chain of command.

Firefighters are not scheduled for regular shifts; they are instead issued with pagers and dispatched by the fire department of the city nearest Pinewood. Whoever is available when a page is issued is expected to respond. Firefighters are paid $20 an hour for time spent responding to a call. While firefighters are working on a call, the chief, the deputy chief, or the most senior captain present is responsible for directing their activities. In 1996 the fire department attended 120 calls, and in 1997 it attended 167 calls. These numbers include calls to assist at incidents in neighbouring areas covered by other fire departments.

The Pinewood firefighters are paid an honorarium of around $900 a year. Captains receive $1,500 and the deputy chief receives $2,350. No income tax or Canada Pension Plan payments are deducted from these amounts, although employees of the Town of Pinewood have these deductions made from their paycheques. However, Pinewood pays for a life insurance policy that covers the firefighters and will also reimburse costs associated with dental, vision, or hearing-aid damage that occurs in the course of duty. If a firefighter is injured in the course of duty and is unable to perform his regular full-time job, Pinewood will supplement any workers' compensation or Canada Pension disability payments to equal 70 percent of the firefighter's regular salary.

The Employer's Position

The lawyer representing the Town of Pinewood argued that the town and the firefighters never intended to create a relationship of employment, nor have they done so. He characterized the firefighters as volunteers who provide a valuable community service in the capacity of civic-minded citizens. He noted that all the firefighters have full-time jobs elsewhere and could not live only on the amounts of money they earn as firefighters. He argued that both parties have already acknowledged that the firefighters' real employment relationship exists elsewhere by agreeing that Pinewood will compensate for firefighters' regular salaries if they are injured while on duty.

Pinewood's lawyer noted that the firefighters are paid differently from other employees of Pinewood and that they do not enjoy benefits similar to those employees. He argued that Pinewood exercises little control over the firefighters, since it cannot compel them to attend training, maintenance sessions, or pager calls. Pinewood also does not schedule the firefighters or otherwise control their attendance.

The Union's Position

The union's representative argued that the relationship between Pinewood and the firefighters exhibits many of the characteristics of an employment relationship and that it is not unlike the relationships that exist between many casual workers and their employers. He acknowledged that the wages the firefighters are paid are not full-time wages, but noted that they are not insignificant for part-time work. He also pointed out that some components of the wages, like training and maintenance compensation, are related to the amount of work performed.

The union representative stated that the firefighters provide all of Pinewood's fire protection services, which are an important function of the town's operations. He suggested that Chief Blackman provides a high level of direction and control in the recruiting and operation of the fire department, and that makes the relationship between the town and the firefighters look like one of employment.

CASE 5-2

RECREATION WAREHOUSE INC. AND RETAIL WORKERS UNION

(Based on *Sports Experts Inc. and UCFW Local 175*, 1995)

In this case, the Retail Workers Union (the "union") has applied for certification of a bargaining unit at one retail store, and Recreation Warehouse (the "employer") has responded by proposing a bargaining unit that would include all six of its stores in a geographic region.

Background of the Case

Recreation Warehouse operates six retail stores in the Tri-Cities area that all sell sporting goods. The Simpson Mall store is the subject of the certification application. There are 18 full-time and 16 part-time employees in the bargaining unit that the union has proposed.

Employees at all six Tri-Cities stores exercise the same skills and perform the same kind of work under the same terms and conditions of employment. There is a standard payroll system, insurance program, and benefits plan. The six stores are a single establishment for pay equity purposes, and Recreation Warehouse has a single-firm number with the Workers' Compensation Board. Advertising for the stores is handled nationally, with ads frequently tailored to the requirements of regional stores or groups of stores.

Each of the Tri-Cities stores has a manager who has the authority to hire and fire employees. District supervisors oversee the work of the store managers, and these supervisors report to the director of operations.

Employees at all Tri-Cities stores are trained in-store by merchandise suppliers and off-site by employee coaches who work for Recreation Warehouse. Employees from a variety of stores attend these training sessions to ensure consistency among the stores in product knowledge and sales techniques. Some employees, including a few from the proposed bargaining unit, are also part of product buying teams that attend product shows and trade fairs and purchase products for all the stores. Because of the similarity of product in the six stores, it is common for stock to move from store to store. For example, if a particular product is out of stock in one store, the staff at that store will contact other stores to see if the product is available elsewhere and, if so, arrange for an inter-store transfer if the customer desires.

There is often an interchange of employees among the six stores in the Tri-Cities area. The interchange can happen in one of two ways. Employees can be temporarily reassigned to cover absent staff or to supplement staff during busy periods, or they can be permanently transferred (these can be lateral transfers or promotions). There were 17 permanent transfers among the Tri-Cities stores last year. Three employees transferred to the Simpson Mall store, but no employees transferred from the Simpson Mall store to other stores.

If an employee accepts a temporary reassignment, the store where the employee now works pays the wages for the time of the reassignment. However, the payment is issued through the regular paycheque that the employee receives from his or her permanent location.

Evidence presented to the Labour Relations Board indicated that the Simpson Mall store used employees on temporary reassignment during 19 of 26 pay periods last year, but none of the permanent Simpson Mall employees had temporary reassignments at any of the other Tri-Cities stores during that same period. Several individual employees testified before the board that it was a common practice for employees wishing to work additional hours to solicit shifts at other stores above and beyond their regularly scheduled shifts at their own stores.

The Employer's Position

The employer believed that, because of the interactions among the six stores, especially the employee interchange, a single-store bargaining unit would be inappropriate for collective bargaining purposes. The employer argued that if one store were unionized and the other five stores were not, the flow of employees in and out of the unionized store would be impeded. The current interchange of employees, in the employer's view, helps the stores meet customer demand and ensures that all stores are adequately staffed during busy periods. Because of this interchange, the employer suggested, it would be difficult to determine what constitutes bargaining unit work during a strike or lockout. The employer also argued that seniority provisions in unionized stores would be different from those in non-unionized stores and that this would cause difficulties in calculating seniority when selecting candidates for permanent transfers. Centralized training and buying teams might also be affected by a distinction between unionized and non-unionized employees.

The employer cited several previous cases in which the Labour Relations Board had expressed a preference for larger bargaining units over smaller bargaining units, as well as concerns about "fragmentation" caused by numerous small units.

The Union's Position

The union argued that the situation at Recreation Warehouse was similar to several previous cases where the Labour Relations Board had allowed a single unit of a retail operation to be unionized. It cited a particular case that it believed was similar to the Recreation Warehouse case. In this case, a retail business had two locations in the same geographic area; the two locations sold the same product; employees at the two locations performed the same work and were given joint training; there were single advertisements for the same sales and merchandise at the two stores; and products and staff were routinely moved from one location to another, particularly if one of the locations was experiencing a busy period.

R e f e r e n c e s

[1] Barling, J., Fullagar, C., and Kelloway, E.K. (1992). *The union and its members: a psychological approach*. Oxford, UK: Oxford University Press.

[2] Barling, J., Kelloway, E.K., and Bremermann, E.H. (1991). Preemployment predictors of union attitudes: the role of family socialization and work beliefs. *Journal of Applied Psychology*, 76(5), 725–731.

[3] Cornfield, D.B. and Kim, H. (1994). Socioeconomic status and unionization attitudes in the United States. *Social Forces*, 73(2), 521–532.

[4] Brett, J.M. (1980). Why employees want unions. *Organizational Dynamics*, Spring 1980, 47–59.

[5] Youngblood, S.A., DeNisi, A.S., Molleston, J.L., and Mobley, W.H. (1984). The impact of work environment, instrumentality beliefs, perceived labour union image, and subjective norms on union voting intentions. *Academy of Management Journal*, *27(3)*, 576–590.

[6] Cooke, W.N. (1983). Determinants of the outcomes of union certification elections. *Industrial and Labour Relations Review*, *36(3)*, 402–414.

[7] Premack, S.L., and Hunter, J.E. (1988). Individual unionization decisions. *Psychological Bulletin*, *103(2)*, 223–234.

[8] Cooke, *op. cit.*

[9] Cooke, *op. cit.*

[10] Premack and Hunter, *op. cit.*; Brett, *op. cit.*

[11] Freeman, R.B., and Rogers, J. (1999). *What workers want*. Ithaca, NY: ILR Press/Cornell University Press.

[12] Deshpande, S.P. (1995). Factors influencing employee association members' votes for unionization. *The Journal of Psychology*, *129(6)*, 621–628.

[13] Montgomery, B.R. (1989). The influence of attitudes and normative pressures on voting decisions in a union certification election. *Industrial and Labour Relations Review*, *42(4)*, 262–279.

[14] Deshpande, S., and Fiorito, J. (1989). Specific and general beliefs in union voting models. *Academy of Management Journal*, *32(4)*, 883–897; Montgomery, *op. cit.*

[15] Montgomery, *op. cit.*

[16] Deshpande and Fiorito, *op. cit.*

[17] Robinson, J.G., and McIlwee, J.S. (1989). Obstacles to unionization in high-tech industries. *Work and Occupations*, *16(2)*, 115–136.

[18] Cooke, *op. cit.*

[19] Robinson and McIlwee, *op. cit.*

[20] Chaison, G.N., and Rose, J.B. (1991). The macrodeterminants of union growth and decline. In Strauss, G., Gallagher, D.G., and Fiorito, J. (Eds.), *The state of the unions*. Madison, WI: Industrial Relations Research Association.

[21] Lowe, G.S., and Krahn, H. (1989). Recent trends in public support for unions in Canada. *Journal of Labour Research*, *10*(4), 391–410.

[22] Deshpande and Fiorito, *op. cit.*

[23] Lowe and Krahn, *op. cit.*

[24] Riddell, C., and Riddell, W.C. (2001). *Changing patterns of unionization: the North American experience, 1984–1998*. Vancouver, BC: University of British Columbia, Department of Economics, Discussion Paper No. 01-23.

[25] For example, *United Steelworkers of America and Radio Shack [1980]*, 1 CLRBR 281 (OLRBR).

[26] Beatty, J. (2001). An overhaul of labour law, in a single sweeping bill: Liberals fulfill promise to make education an essential service. *Vancouver Sun*, August 15, 2001, p. A1.

[27] Martinello, F. (1996). *Certification and decertification activity in Canadian jurisdictions*. Kingston, ON: Industrial Relations Centre, Queen's University.

Failed union drive leads to charges of unfair labour practices:

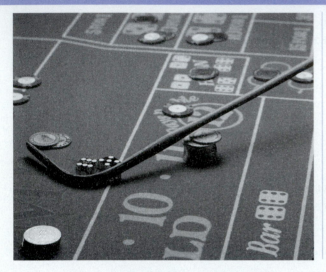

Union alleges casino operator fired employees

EDMONTON—Edmonton's largest casino operator has been charged with unfair labour practices in connection with the suspension of four employees after a failed union drive.

The Canadian Union of Public Employees applied Nov. 18 for certification of 354 employees at Alberta Bingo Supplies' downtown and Argyll Road casinos. While casinos in B.C., Saskatchewan, Manitoba, and Ontario have been organized in recent years, unions have failed in Alberta casinos.

An Alberta Labour Relations Board-supervised vote Dec. 4 and 5 failed by six votes to get the necessary 51 percent for union certification. It saw 145 or 49 percent of the 295 voters approve a union with 148 against, with two spoiled ballots.

At least four employees were dismissed after the vote, says Roxanne Wells, an organizer in the CUPE drive. "We'd like that to be reviewed as to whether there's any correlation between the terminations and the organizing drive," she said.

The labour board could hold a hearing in early January, a board official said Monday.

The four employees were suspended, not fired, said ABS vice-president Barry Pritchard. They're suspected of spray-painting obscenities on managers' garages and vandalizing other property, he said.

"They were the leaders of the union sign-up movement or whatever you want to call it. They are suspect until such time as we find out who is responsible for the vandalism and the obscene, harassing phone calls," he said.

"We didn't fire anyone and we're not disciplining them for being involved in union activities. They were suspended because they're under suspicion of vandalizing private property.

"I guess if you're a leader you have to take responsibility for your followers' actions." It's the third time in the past three years a union drive has failed at the two ABS casinos in Edmonton, Pritchard said. ABS casinos in Calgary and Lethbridge have not been targeted.

The United Food and Commercial Workers narrowly lost out on a drive at the two casinos in 1995–1996 while a Teamsters' drive lost by a wider margin last year.

The repeated attempts probably have more to do with Alberta Bingo Supplies' size than its management style, Pritchard said. "We are the largest casino operator in the province. So we're the biggest target. There are no casinos in the province that are unionized. I would think if we were unionized, the other casinos would fall into place rather quickly."

(*Edmonton Journal*, December 15, 1998)

chapter 6

ESTABLISHING UNION RECOGNITION

objectives

In this chapter, we discuss in more detail how a labour relations board deals with an application for certification. We also explore some of the problems that arise when there are special circumstances surrounding the application, and we discuss the issue of unfair labour practices. At the end of this chapter, you should be able to:

- explain how an application for certification is handled by a labour relations board
- understand the effect of certification
- explain some of the special circumstances that may arise in a certification application
- define and give examples of an unfair labour practice

INTRODUCTION

In Chapter 5, we outlined the process of organizing in the workplace and described how an application for certification is submitted to a labour relations board. In this chapter, we will describe in more detail how a labour relations board assesses an application for certification and how a vote on the application is conducted in the workplace. We will then discuss some of the special circumstances that can surround a certification application, such as time limits on when applications can be made and what happens to applications that represent workers who are already certified. We will then define unfair labour practices, outline the legislation that governs them, and explain how unfair labour practices can affect the certification process.

ASSESSING THE CERTIFICATION APPLICATION

The Workplace Notice

When an application for certification is received by a labour relations board, in most provinces the employer and the employees must be officially informed that a certification application has been received. An official notice is sent by registered mail (to ensure a record of receipt) to the employer, along with a similar notice to the employees. The employer is obligated to post the notice to the employees in the workplace. The notice will name the union that is applying for certification, describe the union's proposed bargaining unit, indicate that interested parties can make submissions about the application, and specify where such submissions should be directed. The reason for requiring this posting is to ensure that all employees are aware that the application for certification has been made and to give employees the opportunity to make written submissions supporting or opposing the application to the relevant labour relations board. Any submissions made to the board will be taken into consideration when the board assesses the application. (In some provinces, the notice posted by the employer also includes a **terminal date**, which is the date by which submissions must be received in order for the board to consider them along with the application.)

Determining Employee Support

After determining the appropriate bargaining unit (which is not always the exact unit the union has applied to represent, as described in Chapter 5), a labour relations board will assess the level of employee support for the application. This process usually requires that the employer provide a list of employees, which the board then compares with the union's list of signatures supporting the application and the list of positions included in the proposed bargaining unit. A labour relations board's intent in making this comparison is to verify that the certification application is supported by the required number of workers in the proposed bargaining unit.

The process of assessing levels of employee support becomes complicated if there has been a delay between the collection of signatures and the submission of the certification application. During that delay, employees may have left the organization or moved to different positions within the organization. The board must be able to verify that employees who support the application are currently employed by the organization in positions that will be part of the proposed bargaining unit. There may also be confusion over the readability of the signatures or whether a signature was actually written by the person whose name appears as a union supporter. If these types of questions arise, the board may require additional documentation such as copies of driver's licences or other identification to support the validity of the signatures.

The Representation Vote

As described in Chapter 5, the level of support for a certification application must be deemed sufficient for the application to proceed, as determined by the level of support identified in the relevant labour legislation. If the level of support is above the required minimum and automatic certification is not an option, a labour relations board will usually set a date for a **representation vote**. This is a vote held to determine whether employees wish to be represented by a union or not. Table 6-1 outlines the levels of support that must be present among workers in the proposed bargaining unit for a representation vote to take place.

TABLE 6-1   Canadian Legislation Governing Representation Votes

	Required Level of Support for Representation Vote to Occur	Required Level of Support for Representation Vote to Succeed
Federal	Between 35% and 50% of employees in the proposed bargaining unit	Majority of those voting
Alberta	At least 40% of employees in the proposed bargaining unit	Majority of those voting
British Columbia	More than 45% of employees in the proposed bargaining unit	Majority of those voting
Manitoba	Between 45% and 65% of employees in the proposed bargaining unit	Majority support among those employees in the proposed bargaining unit who vote
New Brunswick	Between 45% and 60% of employees in the proposed bargaining unit	More than 50% of those voting
Newfoundland	At least 40% of employees in proposed bargaining unit	Majority of voters, or at least 70% of employees in proposed bargaining unit have voted and the majority of voters support the union
Nova Scotia	40% of employees in proposed bargaining unit	Majority of votes cast
Ontario	40% of employees in proposed bargaining unit	More than 50% of voters in bargaining unit approved by labour relations board
Prince Edward Island	Majority of employees in proposed bargaining unit	Majority of voters in proposed bargaining unit
Quebec	Between 35% and 50% of employees in proposed bargaining unit	Absolute majority vote of employees in proposed bargaining unit
Saskatchewan	25% of employees in proposed bargaining unit if unit is already certified	Majority of voters in proposed bargaining unit

Source: Human Resources Development Canada, Labour Program, Synoptic Charts on Legislation Pertaining to Certain Major Collective Bargaining Issues: Trade Union Application for Certification (available at <http://www.hrdc-drhc.gc.ca>).

Labour relations boards generally attempt to minimize the time between the filing of a certification application and the holding of a representation vote because of the possibility that activities in the workplace in the time between the application and the vote may unduly influence the employees' voting intentions. Both unions and employers may take advantage of any excessive delays before the vote to attempt to persuade potential voters to support or oppose the union. Some jurisdictions have provisions to permit a representation vote to be conducted even if all the issues related to the certification have not been completely resolved; this affords the employer and the union less opportunity to influence employees prior to the vote.

"You're lucky with your timing…we're holding off our strike until we settle a moot point with the Labour Relations committee."

The representation vote itself consists of a vote by secret ballot conducted at the workplace by a labour relations board. In some provinces, only those employees included in the proposed bargaining unit are eligible to vote; in other provinces, all employees in the workplace are eligible. (See Table 6-1 for the provisions in specific jurisdictions determining who is considered eligible to participate in representation votes.) The question on the ballot, requiring a simple yes/no answer, asks the voters if they want the union to be their exclusive bargaining agent. For the representation vote to be successful—that is, for the union to be recognized as the employees' bargaining agent—in most jurisdictions a majority of 50 percent + 1 of voters must vote in favour of the union. For example, if there are 100 voters participating in the election, at least 51 must vote "yes" for the representation vote to be successful.

If a representation vote is successful and no other extraordinary circumstances arise (such as evidence of undue influence on the employees), a labour relations board will then issue the **certification order**. This document legally creates the bargaining relationship between the union and the employer, makes the union the exclusive bargaining agent for the employees in the bargaining unit, and compels the parties to commence bargaining for a collective agreement. Certification also compels the parties to bargain in good faith, which essentially means that the parties are expected to bargain honestly and with the intent of completing a collective agreement. (This concept will be discussed in more detail in Chapter 7.) The certification order applies to all employees in the bargaining unit, including employees hired into jobs in the bargaining unit after the certification order takes effect.

On average, the percentage of successful certification applications in Canadian jurisdictions is approximately 70 percent.[1] In other words, 70 percent of certification applications result in a union being legally recognized as the employees' bargaining agent. It should be noted that approximately 18 percent of all certification applications are withdrawn before the certification process is completed. Withdrawals are made for a variety of reasons. A labour relations board and a union may disagree over the determination of an appropriate bargaining unit. A labour relations board may impose a different definition of the bargaining unit than that proposed by the union. The union, perhaps feeling that it has little chance of winning a representation vote in the bargaining unit defined by the labour relations board, may decide that resources spent on the organizing campaign could be used more productively elsewhere. Another problem could be an unusually large number of questionable signatures supporting the certification application. Rather than having the application rejected outright, the union may choose to withdraw the application, re-examine its procedures for collecting signatures, and resubmit another application with more substantive indications of support.

If a representation vote fails, the labour legislation in most Canadian jurisdictions imposes a period after the failed vote during which other certification applications are banned. The rationale for this restriction is that the certification process is often time-consuming and divisive, and even though organizing activities are usually conducted outside the workplace and outside working hours, the issues involved in the individual decision to unionize are powerful and may spill over to affect productivity in the workplace and relationships between workers. If restrictions on the timing of certification applications were not in effect, the workplace could be seriously disrupted by a never-ending series of organizing campaigns. Thus, most Canadian labour codes set limits, known as **time bars**, that restrict the time within which such organizing efforts can take place.

The time bars that apply after a previous certification attempt has failed are outlined in Table 6-2. This particular type of time bar is known as an **application bar**, since it imposes a mandatory waiting period after an unsuccessful certification attempt before another certification application can be made. As Table 6-2 shows, some jurisdictions also impose application bars if a previous certification application is still under review or is the subject of court proceedings.

TABLE 6-2 Time Bars to Certification Applications After a Previous Failed Application

	Previous Unsuccessful Application for Certification	Previous Certification Being Reviewed by Court	Previous Certification Revoked or Cancelled
Federal	6 months unless board consents otherwise	No specifications	No specifications
Alberta	90 days unless board consents otherwise	10 months from date of final disposition	6 months
British Columbia	Bar imposed at board's discretion; if imposed, 90-day minimum	No specifications	10 months
Manitoba	At least 6 months	From date of termination of court proceedings	No specifications
New Brunswick	Board may prescribe a waiting period	No specifications	No specifications
Newfoundland	6 months unless board consents otherwise	No specifications	No specifications
Nova Scotia	At board's discretion	No specifications	No specifications
Ontario	Before the end of one year after dismissal	No specifications	No specifications
Prince Edward Island	Board may prescribe waiting period	No specifications	No specifications
Quebec	3 months	No specifications	No specifications
Saskatchewan	8 months; less with board's consent	12 months from termination of court proceedings	6 months

Source: Human Resources Development Canada, Labour Program, Summaries of General Private Sector Collective Bargaining Legislation (available at <http://www.hrdc-drhc.gc.ca>).

In most Canadian jurisdictions, a union cannot withdraw a certification application for non-technical reasons as a way of avoiding the application bar. This condition exists so that unions are not tempted to salvage an unsuccessful organizing campaign by terminating one certification application and immediately reapplying to represent the same group of workers. However, in most jurisdictions, a labour relations board has some ability to waive the application bar if the union made some inadvertent error in its application, such as miscalculating the size of the bargaining unit.

The Hearing

At any point during the assessment of the certification application, a labour relations board has the option of holding a hearing to collect more evidence relating to the application. This option is usually exercised if there is some dispute over the content of the application or its surrounding circumstances. For example, if an application is made for a very small bargaining unit within a very large company, the labour relations board may set a hearing to investigate why the union is applying for this particular bargaining unit and to determine the appropriateness of the proposed bargaining unit. A hearing can also be justified if there are allegations of unfair labour practices. A labour relations board may want to collect detailed information on the substance of the complaint and the effect of the alleged practices before issuing its decision and remedy. (See the discussion of unfair labour practices later in this chapter for more details on this issue.) If there is a dispute between the union and employer over the composition of the proposed bargaining unit, the labour relations board may want to investigate both parties' reasons for their positions.

A hearing is conducted in a similar manner to a court session. Labour relations board members assigned to the case will listen to submissions on the dispute from parties such as the union, the employer, and the employees. Each party will present their evidence and will be questioned by the board members. The parties who testify in front of the board members may also be cross-examined by other parties. When the hearing is over, the board members will consider the evidence and render a decision.

A labour relations board has several options after completing a hearing. If, for example, the board feels that a proposed bargaining unit is inappropriate, it can reject the application, giving written reasons for its decisions, or it can alter the bargaining unit composition to one it considers appropriate. If the board feels that actions taken on behalf of the union or employer have unduly influenced the employees, it may order a representation vote or reject the certification application entirely. The board can impose these remedies even if the level of support is such that a vote would not usually be required or the certification application would usually be considered. The board may also order a new representation vote if circumstances exist that call the results of an earlier vote into question. These circumstances could include evidence of tampering with sealed ballots or of individuals voting who should have been excluded from the process. The board can impose remedies such as requiring the employer to post notices or send letters apologizing for its actions. And, as mentioned in Chapter 5, the boards in most jurisdictions have the option of declaring a certification even when the required minimum level of support is not present. This option may be exercised when there is evidence that employer or union actions so intimidated the employees that the results of a vote would not indicate the employees' true wishes.

To this point, and in the previous chapter, we have described the certification process that would take place in a workplace where the employees are not already represented by a union and where no unusual events during the certification process have taken place. We will now turn to describing how labour legislation and labour relations boards deal with special circumstances that may occur during the certification process.

SPECIAL CIRCUMSTANCES DURING CERTIFICATION

Certification for a Previously Unionized Workplace

A certification is, in a sense, timeless. It remains in effect for as long as the parties involved wish it to and as long as the parties themselves do not change. Sometimes, however, a certification is sought for employees who are covered by an existing certification order and have a union in place as their exclusive bargaining agent. A union attempting to certify workers represented by another union is attempting what is known as a **raid**.

Some unions do not conduct raids on principle. These unions feel that if workers have freely chosen to be represented by a particular union, that choice should be respected; also, unions should not deliberately attempt to weaken other unions by taking away their membership. As we learned in Chapter 4, some Canadian labour federations—the Canadian Labour Congress, for example—require their member unions to declare that they will not undertake raids. This requirement is based on the position that while raids may increase the membership of individual unions, they damage the strength of the labour movement as a whole by causing dissent among unions and reducing the ability of smaller unions to effectively represent their membership. This position encompasses the view that union membership should be increased by recruiting unorganized workers rather than by persuading already unionized workers to switch their allegiances.

There are unions, however, that conduct raids regularly. Some unions raid because they feel they could do a better job of representing the workers in question than the currently certified union. Others prefer to recruit unionized workers, because these workers already have union experience and thus do not need as aggressive or as extensive an organizing campaign as workers with no union experience; there is consequently less cost and effort involved in the organizing effort. Raids are also undertaken by unions that see their traditional membership base eroding and want to bring in more members in order to survive. Some public sector unions and unions in the manufacturing and processing sectors of the economy raided quite vigorously in the 1980s and 1990s to replace decreasing membership caused by cutbacks in public sector and primary sector employment.

The ability of unions to conduct raids is facilitated by the fact that no Canadian labour legislation explicitly forbids raiding; such a restriction, after all, would interfere with the right of employees to freely choose their workplace representative. There is also no legal requirement for workers to be represented by a union directly associated with their type of employment, which means that unions that choose to conduct raids need not confine themselves to industries or occupations similar to those already represented. This leads to situations such as the British Columbia

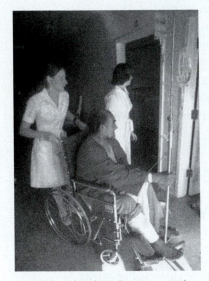

Hospital workers have been recruited by the CAW in their bid for new members, but charges of raiding have caused a rift between the CAW and the CLC.

Government Employees' Union including restaurant staff and cinema employees in its membership, the Canadian Auto Workers representing hospital workers, and the Communication, Energy and Paperworkers union representing workers in a chocolate factory.

Raids can also occur in situations where employees feel dissatisfied with the representation provided by their current union. If employees do not feel that their union is accurately or competently representing their interests, they may contact a union or unions that they think would be more appropriate representatives and encourage those unions to commence an organizing campaign. A raid, then, may begin on the initiative of either the employees or a union.

As previously noted, organizing campaigns, whether directed at unionized or non-unionized workers, can disrupt the workplace. For this reason, labour codes impose time bars that restrict when a raid can take place. Generally, labour codes ban organizing for a certain time after a certification order has been granted to a previously non-unionized workplace. The purpose of this restriction is to give newly certified unions a chance to represent their members without the threat of a larger or more experienced union poised to take over their interests. This protection is particularly important for new unions, which may be run by individuals with little experience in such matters as contract negotiation. The restriction on organizing of newly certified bargaining units allows the new union executives and members to gain the skills needed to run the union effectively, without having to immediately fend off an organizing campaign by another union.

Another time bar that exists in most jurisdictions involves the appropriate time to submit a certification application to represent workers already covered by a collective agreement. Such certification applications can only be made during certain times during the term of the existing collective agreement. The terms of these **open periods** vary by jurisdiction; Table 6-3 describes the conditions in each Canadian jurisdiction. Generally, a certification application can only be made during specified times during the term of a multi-year agreement or within a certain period toward the end of the term of a single-year agreement. The intent of these restrictions is to ensure stability in the collective bargaining process so that union and management representatives do not have to deal with a raiding attempt while trying to negotiate a new collective agreement. These terms are also intended to allow the negotiated agreement to run its course without the interference or distraction caused by a competing union's attempt to organize the workers.

TABLE 6-3 Time Bars to Certification Applications for Already Certified Bargaining Units

	No Collective Agreement and No Union Certified	No Collective Agreement and Union Certified	Collective Agreement (CA) in Force and Union Certified
Federal	At any time	12 months; earlier with consent of board	CA<3 years: after beginning of last three months CA>3 years: during 34th, 35th, and 36th months of agreement and during last 3 months of subsequent years of term
Alberta	At any time	10 months from date of certification	CA<2 years: within 2 months of end of CA term CA>2 years: in the 11th and 12th month of second term but 10 months prior to end of term
British Columbia	At any time	6 months from date of certification or earlier with board's consent	7th and 8th month in each year of CA term
Manitoba	At any time	12 months from certification	CA<18 months: 3 months immediately before last 3 months of term CA>18 months: 3 months before anniversary date or 3 months immediately before last 3 months of term

TABLE 6-3 Continued

	No Collective Agreement and No Union Certified	No Collective Agreement and Union Certified	Collective Agreement (CA) in Force and Union Certified
New Brunswick	At any time	12 months after certification	CA<3 years after beginning of last 2 months of term
			CA>3 years: during 35th and 36th months of agreement and during last 2 months of each subsequent year of term
Newfoundland	At any time	12 months after certification; earlier by consent of board	CA<2 years: within last 2 months of term
			CA>2 years: during 23rd and 24th months of agreement and during last 2 months of each subsequent year of term
Nova Scotia	At any time	12 months after certification	CA<3 years: after beginning of last 2 months of term
			CA>3 years: during 34th, 35th, and 36th months of agreement and during last 3 months of each subsequent year of term
Ontario	At any time	12 months after certification	CA<3 years: after beginning of last 2 months of term
			CA>3 years: during 35th and 36th months of term and during last 2 months of each subsequent year of term

TABLE 6-3 Continued

	No Collective Agreement and No Union Certified	No Collective Agreement and Union Certified	Collective Agreement (CA) in Force and Union Certified
Prince Edward Island	At any time	10 months after certification	CA<2 years: after beginning of last 2 months of term CA>2 years: during 23rd and 24th months of term and during last 2 months of each subsequent year of term
Quebec	At any time	12 months after certification or 9 months after expiration of previous agreement	CA<3 years: from 90 to 60 days before expiration of CA CA>3 years: from 180 to 150 days before expiration of CA
Saskatchewan	At any time	Between 30 and 60 days before anniversary date of certification	Between 30 and 60 days before anniversary of effective date of agreement

Source: Human Resources Development Canada, Labour Program, Summaries of General Private Sector Collective Bargaining Legislation (available at <http://www.hrdc-drhc.gc.ca>).

We should note that there are no legal restrictions on the number of unions that can simultaneously attempt to organize the same existing bargaining unit. Although there is usually only one union conducting a raid, it has happened in Canadian jurisdictions that more than one union has attempted to conduct a raid on the same group of workers at the same time.

A certification application covering a currently unionized workplace is assessed by a labour relations board on the same criteria that would be used to assess any other type of certification application. However, it is more likely that a representation vote will be ordered in such a situation, to ensure that the employees truly wish to change their representation to the new union. If the representation vote is successful or if a certification order is issued without a vote, a new certification order is issued to replace the previous certification. If the representation vote fails or if the certification application is rejected for other reasons, the time bars on subsequent applications are the same as those that would apply if the workers were previously non-unionized.

Certification If the Parties Change

A certification order, as noted, names the two parties (employer and union) that are covered by the order. However, sometimes there are changes involving the parties named. A union or an employer may merge with another union or employer, cease to exist, or otherwise be altered. If any of these events occur, then a form of re-certification may be required.

For example, if the union changes its status by merging with one or more other unions, the usual procedure is for the merged union to apply for certification under its new name to represent the same bargaining unit. If a labour relations board feels it is appropriate, a representation vote may be conducted to confirm that all the members of the former union wish to be represented by the merged union. This procedure is not required, however, and the board can alter the certification without a vote being held. If the union ceases to exist and the workers do not wish to be represented by another union, the usual procedure would be for the workers to file a request for decertification, which, when granted, cancels the existing certification and makes the workplace non-unionized. (See the section on decertification in Chapter 12 for a more detailed discussion of this process.)

Changes on the employer's side are slightly more complex. If the employer goes out of business, the certification is considered to have lapsed, as one of the parties named in the certification order no longer exists and the workers are no longer employees of the named employer. The union or the employer can apply for decertification if they wish to have a legally binding declaration that the union-employer relationship has ended. If, however, the employer merges with another business or expands its operations, there is a question as to whether the existing certification order should automatically include the new employees whose positions were not part of the bargaining unit before the expansion or merger. The labour relations board will have to decide whether to expand the existing certification order or require a new certification application before the new workers can be unionized. This circumstance is called "successorship" and is discussed more fully in Chapter 12.

Certification Applications during a Strike or Lockout

Another special circumstance that may arise in the certification process is the submission of a certification application while there is a strike or lockout in progress at the place of employment addressed by the application. In several Canadian jurisdictions, there are time bars restricting when or if applications can be made under these circumstances.

In some Canadian jurisdictions, an application for certification cannot be made if an illegal strike has taken place in support of the certification attempt. This provision, where it exists, embodies the philosophy that certification, not striking, is the process through which employees should attempt to promote change in the workplace. As we know from Chapter 3, one reason that legislation was created to formalize the certification process was to make certification a viable alternative to striking as a way for dissatisfied employees to express their concerns. The legislation in some jurisdictions makes it clear that if employees choose to engage in an illegal strike related to certification, their application for certification will not be accepted.

In some Canadian jurisdictions, a certification application cannot take place during a legal strike or lockout. Such an application would usually come from another union that is attempting to represent the workers who are on strike or locked out. An application during this time might be perceived as undue interference with the collective bargaining process or as an attempt by one union to exploit the weak status of another union. A strike or lockout is usually an emotionally charged event for employees and management alike, and if not all employees agree with the rationale for a strike or lockout, some of them may be particularly vulnerable to the suggestion of different union representation. It is for these reasons that some jurisdictions restrict certification applications during a legal strike or lockout.

Table 6-4 outlines the restrictions that exist in Canadian jurisdictions regarding certification applications during strikes or lockouts.

TABLE 6-4 Time Bars Relating to Certification Application during Strike or Lockout Activity

	Legal or Illegal Strike or Lockout in Progress
Federal	New application only with board's consent
Alberta	New application only with board's consent
British Columbia	New application only with board's consent
Manitoba	After 6 months with consent of the board
New Brunswick	Subject to delays
Newfoundland	No specifications
Nova Scotia	No specifications
Ontario	Subject to delays
Prince Edward Island	With board's consent
Quebec	No specifications
Saskatchewan	No specifications

Source: Human Resources Development Canada, Labour Program, Summaries of General Private Sector Collective Bargaining Legislation (available at <http://www.hrdc-drhc.gc.ca>).

A final special circumstance that may arise during the certification process is the occurrence of unfair labour practices, as noted in Chapter 5. We will discuss this circumstance in a separate section because of the large impact that an unfair labour practice can have on both the progress and the outcome of a certification attempt.

UNFAIR LABOUR PRACTICES
Definition and Legislative Philosophy

In the context of certification, an **unfair labour practice** is an action undertaken by an employer or, less commonly, a union that has the effect of unduly influencing the "private decisions" made by the employee in the certification process.[2]

Legislation dealing with unfair labour practices must incorporate several different considerations. One consideration is the inherent imbalance of power in the structure of most workplaces. The employer has extensive power over an employee's working life, to the extent of deciding whether the employee has a job at all. Therefore, it is important that there be legal restraints to prevent the employer from abusing this power during the certification process. As we have seen, the employee has the legal right to join a union without retaliation or interference from the employer.

The employer's legal rights must also be considered. Like any other Canadian, the employer has the right to free speech. As a result, a complete ban on employer-employee contact during the certification process is neither feasible nor fair. The fear that an employer might unduly influence employees during an organizing campaign should not result in extreme restrictions such as forbidding the employer to say anything at all about the campaign or to speak to employees. It would be nearly impossible for an organization to operate normally if the employer were banned from having any contact with employees.

There are indeed some challenging practical issues associated with balancing employer and employee rights in the workplace during an organizing campaign. It may, for example, be hard to establish whether an employer's actions during an organizing campaign are a legitimate part of running the business or are intended to intimidate employees into not supporting a union. If an employer says, "I do not support a union in this workplace," is that a justifiable expression of opinion or an implied threat? Another issue is the impossibility of ensuring that employers or unions do not engage in activity that could be labelled as unfair labour practices. A labour relations board representative cannot be continuously present in the workplace to monitor employer and employee behaviour and assess the impact of that behaviour. And even if a complaint about an unfair labour practice is upheld (i.e., if a labour relations board rules that the disputed behaviour is indeed an unfair labour practice), the effects of the behaviour can still influence the outcome of an organizing campaign, even after the behaviour has ceased.

Although unfair labour practices can occur at any point in the employer-employee relationship, they tend to occur more often during the certification process than at any other time. This is because employees are vulnerable prior to certification, since they are not yet protected by a collective agreement. After certification is granted and a collective agreement is signed, employees are protected by the terms of the agreement that govern such procedures as promotions, discipline, and dismissal. Before certification takes place, however, employers who wish to discourage unionization may exploit the absence of a collective agreement by demoting, disciplining, or firing employees who are known union supporters, the intent being to intimidate other employees, who would fear that the same thing could happen to them.

Bill Nicholson, leader of the Victoria Hunger Strike of 1933, lost his pension due to union activity. Today's labour codes prohibit such unfair labour practices.

Although unions can also be charged with committing unfair labour practices during certification, it is more common for complaints to be brought against employers. This is because the union has much less power than the employer does to intimidate employees. (It could be argued that the union is much more likely to exert undue influence in its attempt to persuade employees to support certification by promising rewards like better wages and working conditions if the employees join the union.) Unlike the employer, the union does not have the ability to fire or discipline employees for non-compliance with its suggestions; thus, a union's coercion of employees is a much less frequent and less compelling occurrence than an employer's coercion. Employer complaints about unions' unfair labour practices during certification attempts usually focus on union organizing activity that has taken place during prohibited times (working hours) or in prohibited locations (the employer's premises).

Legislation

In an attempt to balance the rights of employers and employees in the workplace and to restrict the occurrence of unfair labour practices, most labour codes in Canada contain a set of guidelines for employer and union behaviour. We will now look at the general terms of these guidelines.

The first guideline, as discussed in Chapter 5, states that an employer cannot participate in or interfere with the formation, selection, or administration of a trade union. An employer also cannot participate in the representation of employees by a trade union or contribute financial or other support to a trade union. This guideline implies that a manager cannot oppose an organizing campaign (opposition could be interpreted as interference), but also cannot support an organizing campaign (support could be interpreted as participation). This guideline addresses the concern that employer participation in the union or in union activities might compromise the independence of the union's role as representative of the employees, as outlined in Chapter 5.

The second guideline governing employer/union behaviour in most Canadian labour codes is that an employer is free to express views for or against the union so long as the employer does not use coercion, intimidation, threats, promises, or undue influence to pressure employees into acting against their personal beliefs. This language might appear to be very restrictive, but in reality it is often very difficult to apply. Comments that appear to be innocuous in one set of circumstances can seem threatening in a different set of circumstances. An employer's comment such as "I don't like the idea of a union" would seem quite harmless in a casual conversation with a first-level supervisor but would have a completely different impact in a formal meeting called by the management that employees were compelled to attend. Additionally, comments that one individual perceives as intimidation can be perceived as meaningless by another individual. An employer might say to one employee, "I personally would not vote for a union," and that employee would interpret the comment as the employer's personal opinion and as having nothing to do with the employee's own intentions. Another employee hearing the same comment might interpret it as an implicit threat that there would be negative consequences for anyone who did not agree with the employer's views and voted for the union. Thus, the context and perception of the expressed views, as well as the content of the views themselves, need to be considered when determining what constitutes an unfair labour practice.

The wording of this guideline in Canadian labour law attempts to capture the range of possible behaviour or statements that could be considered unfair labour practices. At the same time, the wording is also broad enough to not explicitly exclude any behaviour that could be an unfair labour practice.

The language in Canadian labour relations codes does not deny the employer's right to carry out actions such as employee discipline and termination of employment in the course of operating the business, but if such actions take place during a certification attempt, the employer may need to prove that they were justified or necessary. If a complaint of an unfair labour practice is filed, a labour relations board will examine both the motive behind the alleged unfair labour practice and the effect of the alleged practice. For example, if an employee active in an organizing campaign is demoted to a lower-paying position during the campaign, the labour relations board would look at a number of different types of evidence. The board would likely examine the employee's previous work record to see whether the employee was the subject of previous disciplinary action and, if so, whether the disciplinary action was carried out in accordance with established procedures, such as progressive discipline. This evidence would indicate whether the employee's performance problems existed before the organizing campaign or whether they had mysteriously emerged as soon as the employee had become active in the union. The board would also investigate whether or not demotion was a justifiable response to the employee's most recent actions and whether the demotion would have occurred regardless of whether the organizing campaign was in progress or not.

A labour relations board's concern in such a case is whether the employer's action resulted from an **anti-union animus**—that is, whether the employer's opposition to the union manifested itself in actions that harmed employees who were active in the union. In some Canadian jurisdictions, anti-union animus, even if it exists in combination with other reasons for employee discipline, is in itself sufficient to support a declaration of an unfair labour practice: that is, even if an employee's performance record justifies discipline, the employer might still be judged to have committed an unfair labour practice if the employee was disciplined because of an anti-union animus.

Note that a **reverse onus** applies in most Canadian jurisdictions. This means that the employer is the party that must prove that its actions were not motivated by anti-union animus. In discipline cases not adjudicated by labour relations boards—that is, in discipline cases adjudicated in civil court—the onus would be on the employee to prove that the employer's actions were not justified.

We should also note that an employer might be found to have committed an unfair labour practice if the employer's action had the effect of influencing employees' behaviour, even if that was not the employer's intent. For example, in distributing a handout containing information about union-related problems in other organizations, the employer may intend merely to ensure that the employees are making an informed decision when they participate in a representation vote. However, employees could perceive this action as an implied threat that similar problems will occur in this organization if the employees choose to unionize. Thus, employers need to be aware of both the content and the potential effect of their actions, since actions may be perceived differently than they are intended.

Dealing with an Unfair Labour Practice Complaint

If an employer, a union, or an employee believes that an unfair labour practice has occurred, they can file a complaint with the appropriate labour relations board. The standard of proof that is used to determine the outcome of a complaint in all cases before a labour relations board is the **balance of probabilities**. This standard is somewhat less rigorous than the "beyond a reasonable doubt" standard used in criminal court, but it still requires sufficient evidence showing the probability that the disputed action was justified. For example, if an employee who was active in an organizing campaign was fired, the employer would have to meet the balance of probabilities standard by showing such evidence as a poor work record and prior sufficient warnings of poor performance. The warnings would have had to be given prior to the certification application to show that they were related to the employee's performance rather than his or her involvement in the organizing campaign. To reinforce the relationship of the warnings to the employee's performance rather than to his or her union activity, the employer might need to show additional evidence. This could include evidence that the employee was offered assistance in dealing with the performance problem, such as additional training, and that the employee was given sufficient time to correct the problem.

An Example of an Unfair Labour Practice Complaint

In order to understand how difficult it can be to regulate unfair labour practices, we will give an example of an unfair labour practice complaint related to an employer's actions during a certification attempt. We will briefly describe the case (*American Airlines Inc. v. Brotherhood of Railway, Airline and Steamship Clerks, Freight Handlers, Express and Station Employees* [1981] 3 CLRBR 90 at 91-109)[3] and then examine the labour relations board's decision in the case.

A company operated a reservations call centre where employees worked both staggered and rotating shifts. Because of the complicated work scheduling, the employees each had a mailbox that they were expected to check before starting a shift so that they would be up to date on work-related information. All kinds of non-company material (e.g., notices for blood donor clinics, party invitations) were regularly left in the mailboxes. On at least two occasions during an organizing campaign, employees were forbidden to place union information in the mailboxes. The reasons given for this restriction were that, according to the company's written policies, the distribution of literature on company premises required company approval, and using company time for "purposes not directly related to company business" was prohibited.

After the organizing campaign started, the company's regional vice-president visited the centre and held what the company called "rap sessions." These were meetings that all employees were compelled to attend. During these sessions, management staff introduced themselves, talked about the company's business plans, and answered the employees' questions. The management staff made no specific statements about unionization, but if employees asked about the organizing campaign, they were told that they (the employees) had a choice whether or not to join a union.

The regional vice-president of the company claimed the employees were confused about the impact a union would have and sent all employees a letter that discussed the certification drive. The letter indicated that other companies in the same industry had reduced their workforce after their workplaces were unionized. The letter also stated, "We firmly believe the interest of both agent and clerical personnel and the company is best served by your remaining non-union." It went on to describe how the presence of a union would change seniority practices, reduce take-home pay because of union fees and dues, and possibly cause a strike if collective bargaining broke down. The letter concluded: "I hope you will think very seriously before you take any action that will make your job a Union job."

When an unfair labour practice complaint was brought to the labour relations board, it was apparent that the company and union disagreed on the intent and impact of the letter to the employees. The company's position was that the letter did not contain any direct threats or instructions not to join the union and that it was only a statement of the company's opinion. The union argued that the information presented in the letter was both coercive and threatening, since the wording of the letter implied that the negative consequences of unionization that occurred in other organizations would also occur in this organization if a union were formed.

After considering the arguments of both sides, the labour relations board ruled that the employer's right to manage efficiently included the right to communicate with employees, but that the employer must be sure that such communications were restricted to business considerations. The board noted that even statements that are not explicit threats can effectively be threats; that is, a statement clearly outlining the employer's position on an issue can intimidate employees who privately or publicly disagree with the employer. On those grounds, the labour relations board found that the letter constituted an unfair labour practice.

On the matter of union literature in the mailboxes, the labour relations board, again acknowledging the company's right to manage its business, recognized that the company had a written policy defining what material was acceptable for mailbox distribution. However, the board noted that the policy outlining appropriate mailbox materials had been in effect for several years and that the company had not enforced the policy when other non-company communications were regularly placed in the mailboxes. The board said that the company had not demonstrated that the presence of the union material in the mailboxes caused any disruption in operations. The labour relations board thus found that the ban on distribution of union material was an attempt to intimidate employees and constituted interference with the employees' right to representation by a union.

This example demonstrates that labour relations boards are very sensitive to the power imbalance between the employer and employees and to the great opportunity that exists for the employer, even unintentionally, to intimidate employees. In this example, the company held meetings and distributed materials to inform employees about its position on unionization. While the company may not have intended these actions to be intimidating, the labour relations board found that they were, since employees could have interpreted the information as threats about what would happen if the union were certified. The issue of access to the mailboxes also seemed to indicate that the company was interfering with the employees' right to organize. Even if the company had previously intended to enforce the regulations against non-company materials in the mailboxes, the fact that the company chose to enforce the policy after the organizing campaign had started made the enforcement appear to be an anti-union tactic. And, although the labour relations board did not specifically address the company's rap sessions in its ruling, these sessions could also have been interpreted as intimidation, since the employees' attendance was compulsory rather than optional.

Remedies for Unfair Labour Practices

A labour relations board that upholds a complaint of an unfair labour practice can take several courses of action. It will usually choose a remedy that will **make whole** the situation, meaning that the remedy will attempt to put the parties to the complaint in the same situation they were in before the unfair labour practice occurred. Examples of make-whole remedies include reimbursing a union for the cost of extra organizing expenses incurred in combating an employer's anti-union activity or reinstating employees who were disciplined because of anti-union animus. Make-whole remedies can also attempt to reverse any damage that an unfair labour practice has caused an organizing campaign. These kinds of remedies include allowing union organizers into the workplace, allowing employees or unions the use of company bulletin boards, or allowing the union to hold information meetings in the workplace during working hours.

Workers install a memorial to the men lost in the Westray Mine Disaster of 1992. Inquiry boards investigating disasters like this will often make recommendations to prevent a similar event, comparable to recommendations which a labour relations board makes.

However, it can be difficult to "make whole" the situation caused by an unfair labour practice for the simple reason that the unfair labour practice may already have had the effect of intimidating employees and any subsequent action may be ineffective in counteracting that intimidation. Because of this difficulty, labour relations boards have "wide powers to issue remedial orders" that are appropriate to the particular situation and the behaviour that is in dispute.[4] If the organizing campaign is still in progress when the board issues its ruling, the board can also issue a "cease and desist" order to direct that the unfair labour practice stop.

In most Canadian jurisdictions, labour relations boards can order that employees be compensated for any financial losses they sustained as a result of the employer's actions, such as lost earnings resulting from a demotion or dismissal. If there is concern that an unfair labour practice may not stop after an order is made, most Canadian labour codes allow a labour relations board to file an order in provincial or federal court, thus giving the order the same power as a judgement from that court. Violation of a court order can result in a finding of contempt of court and the imposition of associated penalties, which could include financial penalties or even jail time.

In extreme cases, employer or union actions may have so intimidated the employees that even pro-union employees would be afraid to vote in favour of certification or, alternatively, anti-union employees would be afraid to not vote for certification. In this situation, a labour relations board may order the remedy of a new representation vote, the results of which would override the results of any previous votes. Although this remedy may not completely solve the situation, since employees may still be intimidated during a new vote, it at least serves the important purpose of giving employees the chance to vote after having had the employer's or union's previous behaviour condemned. The labour relations board may, in some Canadian jurisdictions, even impose a certification order without there being the required percentage of support from employees or a clear majority in a new or existing representation vote.

What was the remedy in our case that demonstrated unfair labour practices? In that case, the labour relations board's remedy was to direct the regional vice-president to write a letter to all employees, on company letterhead, indicating that the earlier letter had been found to be an unfair labour practice. The regional vice-president was also directed to include with the letter a copy of the reasons for the labour relations board's decision. The company was also directed to allow distribution of union literature in the mailboxes as long as employees distributed the literature on their own time.

To conclude our discussion of unfair labour practices, we will note that although unfair labour practices often occur during the certification process, they are by no means restricted to the certification process. They can also occur after the issuance of the certification order and during the collective bargaining process. We will discuss unfair labour practices in those contexts in chapters 7 and 8.

SUMMARY

The certification process is the process through which unions are formally recognized as employee representatives in the workplace. After an application for certification is filed, a labour relations board will assess the application and determine whether to issue a certification order or not. The labour relations board has the ability to grant certification if there are exceptional circumstances surrounding the application, even if some of the conditions for certification are not met. Alternatively, the board can deny certification under special circumstances even if all of the conditions for certification are met. A certification order establishes the union as the employees' representative in the workplace and compels the union and the employer to commence bargaining in good faith to reach a collective agreement.

Certification can take place under a variety of different circumstances, and legislation governing certification acknowledges this by restricting when certification applications can be filed. The purpose of these restrictions is to reduce the possibility of workplace disruption from continuous certification campaigns. These restrictions also place some limits on when raids can occur. Raids—a controversial issue in the union movement—are attempts by one union to organize a group of workers who are already unionized.

Labour law has provisions that regulate employer and union behaviour during the organizing process that leads to a certification application. The unfair labour practices issue is particularly important during the certification process. An unfair labour practice is behaviour by either the union or the employer that unduly influences the employees' actions with respect to the union. Regulating workplace behaviour is difficult because the rights of employers and employees must both be balanced and protected. However, actions and statements can have a significant impact on the certification process, and thus labour relations boards are given a wide range of powers to counteract the negative effects of unfair labour practices.

KEY TERMS FOR CHAPTER 6

anti-union animus (p. 213)
application bar (p. 198)
balance of probabilities (p. 214)
certification order (p. 197)
make whole (p. 217)
open periods (p. 203)
raid (p. 201)

representation vote (p. 195)

reverse onus (p. 213)

terminal date (p. 194)

time bar (p. 198)

unfair labour practice (p. 210)

DISCUSSION QUESTIONS FOR CHAPTER 6

1. Under what circumstances might a representation vote not be required for certification?

2. How does labour legislation balance the employee's right to join a union with the employer's right to free speech during an organizing campaign?

3. Why does most Canadian labour law restrict the times when certification applications can be filed?

4. A maintenance and cleaning company employs many immigrants who are not fluent in English. After a certification application has been filed, the company manager calls each employee in for an individual meeting, with a translator present, to explain the implications of unionization. Would this be considered an unfair labour practice? Why or why not?

5. Why are some unions philosophically opposed to raiding?

6. Explain the difference between "balance of probabilities" and "beyond a reasonable doubt," and outline how these concepts are relevant to the issue of unfair labour practices.

7. What would be the advantages and disadvantages of being represented by a union whose primary membership was in an industry or occupation different than yours?

8. Why is it important to give labour relations boards a wide range of options in issuing remedies for unfair labour practices?

CASE *6-1*

ABSORBIT LTD. AND CLAY WORKERS UNION

(Based on *Western Industrial Clay Products and United Steelworkers of America Local No. 898*, 1999)

On March 11, 1999, the union applied for certification of a bargaining unit of employees at AbsorbIt's mine and processing plant. A representation vote was conducted March 22, 1999. The ballots from the vote were sealed until the outcome of the Labour Relations Board's decision.

The union and the employer settled several disputes regarding the conditions leading to the certification vote but still disagreed over one remaining issue: whether three employees—Smith, Jones, and Corbett—should be excluded from the bargaining unit and thus from the representation vote.

Background to the Case

AbsorbIt is a company that produces cat litter and industrial absorbent materials. It also mines and sells bulk bentonite, a material used as a bonder or sealer in many industrial processes. In early 1999, AbsorbIt's sales were down and the company lost a contract that accounted for 25 percent of its total sales revenue. On February 23, 1999, the senior management team met to discuss the decline in sales and decided to lay off five employees to reduce salary costs.

On February 24, 1999, the plant manager produced a list of five candidates for layoff. The plant supervisor and crew leaders discussed the list, which included the names of Smith and Jones. They agreed to lay off all of the employees on the list except for one, who the managers felt had a stronger work ethic than an employee named Corbett. Corbett, who had not been on the original layoff list, was added to the list in place of this employee.

Smith and Corbett were notified verbally on March 8, 1999, that they would be laid off on March 19, 1999. Jones was notified verbally on March 9, 1999, that he would be laid off on March 19, 1999. On March 12, 1999, Smith, Corbett, and Jones received identical letters confirming the verbal notice of layoff and reiterating that their last day of work would be March 19, 1999. The reason given for the layoffs was "slow sales." The letters did not state whether the layoffs were temporary or permanent and did not mention any potential for recall.

Smith and Corbett worked until their layoff date. Jones left work after the first half of his shift on March 15, 1999, complaining of illness. He advised the employer that he was going to the hospital. He never contacted the employer after that date and never returned to work.

The Employer's Position

Evidence submitted by the employer indicated that sales, income, and production at AbsorbIt were lower from January to April 1999 than during the same period in 1998. The only exception to this decline was in the bulk bentonite division, where a new contract with a major customer was signed in April 1999. The employees worked substantial overtime in April and May 1999 because plant modifications were needed to handle increased production for the new contract. The employer also indicated that a new employee was hired on May 18, 1999, to work in the newly expanded bentonite production operation. However, the new bulk bentonite contract was lost at the end of May. The new employee was kept on, but now this employee's main task was to put returned bentonite back into inventory.

The employer submitted documentation showing that 74 employees had been terminated from employment from 1995 to 1999. Thirty-eight of these employees were terminated due to "shortage of work." The employment records for 22 of the employees terminated for shortage of work show no expected date of recall; records for 11 of these employees have notations of "not returning"; and the records for four are blank in this regard. Eight of these 38 employees have been rehired after periods of layoff ranging up to six months.

The employer's "Employee Handbook" contains the following section:

It is the intention of [the company] to work at full capacity, subject, of course, to prices, markets and operational difficulties.

Should reductions in operating levels become unavoidable, your assistance in developing plans to minimize that disruption to you and your fellow employees will be solicited.

Where all other alternatives have been examined and layoffs become necessary, then those laid off will be entitled to preference on re-hiring and will be given credit for the length of service earned prior to layoff.

In determining those to be laid off, consideration will be given to:

- qualifications to perform the available work
- previous work record
- length of service
- attendance

The employer argued that Smith, Jones, and Corbett should not be included in the bargaining unit for purposes of membership support because they were laid off prior to the date when the representation vote was held. The employer contended that because there was no likelihood of recall for the three laid-off employees, these employees did not have "sufficient continuing interest" in the bargaining unit for their votes to be counted.

The Union's Position

The union did not dispute that Smith, Jones, and Corbett received layoff notices on March 8 or 9, 1999. The union also did not challenge the reasoning of the employer in issuing the layoff notices. The union and the employer agreed that the three employees were working on March 11, 1999, the date of the union's certification application.

The union argued, however, that while the layoff notice was given prior to the date of the certification application, the layoff actually occurred after the certification application had been filed. Thus, the employees should be counted as part of the bargaining unit. The union argued that the Labour Relations Board should only consider whether "sufficient continuing interest" existed at the time the certification application was filed and not whether "sufficient continuing interest" existed after the certification was filed.

The union contended that while there are reasons to exclude employees from a bargaining unit, allowing an exclusion in this case would lead to potential manipulation by employers. If the board established a precedent by excluding the votes of these three laid-off employees, employers might in the future be tempted to lay workers off as a means of reducing support for a union in a representation vote.

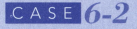 CASE 6-2

NEWSPAPER WORKERS ASSOCIATION AND *HIGHLAND DAILY STAR*

(Based on *Winnipeg Free Press and Media Union of Manitoba*, 1999)

This case involves two issues: (1) the question of whether contract workers can be considered employees for the purposes of organizing a bargaining unit; and (2) the question of what constitutes an unfair labour practice in an organizing situation. A certification vote was conducted in the proposed unit on June 30 and July 2, 1997, and the votes were sealed pending the resolution of the two issues.

Background to the Case

On June 20, 1997, the Newspaper Workers Association applied to certify a unit of employees at the *Highland Daily Star*. The proposed bargaining unit consisted of the newspaper carriers employed by the *Star*. The union held a planning meeting on June 26, 1997, and a certification vote was conducted in the proposed bargaining unit on June 30 and July 2, 1997.

On July 2, 1997, the *Star* filed an unfair labour practice complaint, alleging that the union had "persuade[d] and attempt[ed] to persuade" the carriers to sign applications for membership in the union. The *Star* alleged that the union representatives had conducted themselves in such a way that the carriers knew that their decision to join or not was being observed. The *Star* further alleged that this conduct constituted fraud, intimidation, coercion, and interference with individual rights, contrary to the

Labour Relations Act. On July 21, 1997, the *Star* filed an amended application to the complaint. The amendment alleged that from June 27 to June 29, 1997, 11 district managers (salaried employees of the *Star* who supervised the carriers) "directly and indirectly" told carriers that they should vote in favour of the union. The amendment also alleged that the carriers knew that their responses to such suggestions were "actually or likely" to be monitored by the district managers.

After some procedural clarification, including a request by the *Star* that the Labour Board release the names of those supporting the application for certification (a request that was denied), a hearing into the application was held in December 1997.

A lengthy statement of "agreed facts" (supported by both parties) was entered into the record at the hearing. This statement included descriptions of the disputed behaviour of the district managers. There was evidence that some district managers had allowed union recruitment to take place in parking lots adjacent to the distribution depots where carriers picked up their papers for delivery. Some district managers delivered union recruitment materials to carriers' homes at the carriers' request. Others, while working at the depots, allowed off-duty district managers to deliver recruitment materials directly to the depots.

It was noted that many of the carriers, particularly those who were adults, had other delivery contracts, usually with the *Star's* competitor or with advertising-flyer distribution companies. It was also not uncommon for an individual to hold the contract for a particular paper distribution route but to have someone else deliver the papers.

A copy of the standard agreement for carriers was also submitted into evidence. The agreement identified the carrier as an "independent representative/salesperson" and established a set of contractual conditions. These included rates of pay, expected times of paper pickup and delivery, the expectation that the carrier would provide a reliable vehicle and be responsible for costs associated with its operation, and the right of the *Star* to terminate the contract on two weeks' notice.

Both parties agreed that in recent years there had been several major changes in the *Star's* delivery operations. The paper had begun to publish seven days a week and had changed its publication time from afternoon to early morning. These changes, together with the recent construction of several very large apartment blocks in the city, meant that the paper now had to operate several hundred carrier routes. The length of the routes varied considerably depending on the type of building included in the route and the type of delivery permitted in larger buildings. (Some apartments required carriers to deliver papers directly to apartment doors, while others permitted carriers only to deposit papers in lobby mailboxes or with the building's caretaker.) In addition, payment methods for subscription had changed from door-to-door collection to pre-payment by credit card or cheque, which meant carriers no longer had to visit subscribers directly to collect payment.

The *Star's* response to these changing conditions had been to recruit adults as carriers, rather than continue to rely on the traditional teenage/young adult demographic. This change was made partly because of the change in delivery times. Many parents were nervous about the safety of children or teenagers delivering papers in the dark or extremely early in the morning. However, the change in recruitment was also undertaken because covering many of the new routes required an automobile, which younger teenagers would not have. Recruitment ads for carriers run by the *Star* in March 1997 were clearly directed at adults, with language referring to earning extra money for car or mortgage payments or starting a "family business."

Testimony from one adult carrier indicated that rates for delivery were fixed in the contract that carriers signed. The only room for negotiation was around the mileage allowance for covering a route. There was some variation in the so-called route allowance based on factors such as the amount of driving involved in covering a route and whether deliveries to an apartment building were to a lobby or caretaker or to each individual unit.

If carriers were unable to service their route (e.g., because of illness), they were expected to find a replacement. The district managers kept a list of possible replacements, but if individuals from this list were used to cover the route, the regular carrier's compensation would be reduced. Replacement carriers on the district manager's list received compensation for being on call, as well as a slightly higher rate for delivering the papers than the carrier would receive. Carriers were expected to find and sign up new customers, and they received some compensation for doing so. If a customer did not pay a subscription bill, carriers were expected to continue delivery for four weeks, after which the *Star* would reimburse the carrier for the unpaid invoices. The carriers were not compensated for extra time spent on the job, such as time spent waiting for a late delivery of papers to the distribution depot.

A district manager testified about recent changes in the carriers' and district managers' jobs. Under the previous distribution structure, when carriers had been mostly young people, the papers for delivery had been dropped at different designated places, usually close to the carriers' homes. Now all distribution was from centralized depots that the carriers reported to in order to collect their papers for delivery. Because of the new publishing schedule of seven days a week, a district manager now had to be present seven days a week at each depot.

The district managers had considerable discretion in the hiring and firing of carriers, as well as some discretion in determining the size and coverage of routes in their area. They also handled customer complaints about delivery. Complaints were given to the carrier via a standardized form containing a warning that continued complaints could lead to termination.

A city manager (the position that supervises district managers) testified that he had been told by the *Star* management to "go out and watch" the organizing campaign but not to interfere with what was going on. He testified that he had seen some activity at the depots that might have been related to organizing. He had noticed off-duty district managers at depots to which they were not usually assigned and had observed leaflets being distributed at depots, but he acknowledged that he had not seen any activity that would have interfered with the duties of district managers or carriers.

The Employer's Position

In regard to the question of which workers should be included in the application for certification, the lawyer representing the employer argued that having the same union represent both carriers and district managers would be inappropriate, since district managers would then no longer be able to discipline carriers. He pointed out that many of the carriers had contracts with other distribution services, and since employers generally do not permit their employees to work simultaneously for their competitors or businesses in the same industry, the carriers would not qualify as "employees" under employment and labour law. He also noted that a previous board decision in a different case had rejected a union membership card signed by a student on the grounds that the student had not understood the nature of joining a union. That ruling suggested that young people might not be considered eligible to join a union, and although the majority of newly recruited carriers were adults, several young carriers still worked for the *Star*.

The employer's lawyer then addressed the allegations of unfair labour practices. Citing the sections of the *Labour Relations Act* that prohibit an employer from asking an employee if he or she is a member of a union or not, the lawyer alleged that the union had violated these parts of the law by permitting district managers to ask carriers if they supported the union. The lawyer also cited prohibitions against organizing campaigns interfering with work and alleged that the unusual presence of district managers at particular distribution depots had the effect of disrupting work and intimidating carriers.

The Union's Position

In regard to the question of who should be included in the application for certification, the lawyer representing the union agreed that the majority of *Star* carriers were adults and that some young people still worked as carriers. He argued, however, that since labour and employment law did not explicitly prohibit youth from being represented by a union, potential bargaining unit members could not be excluded solely on the basis of their age.

The union's lawyer cited previous cases suggesting that the test of whether a worker was an employee or an independent contractor lay in identifying who in the contractual relationship had control, owned tools, and benefited from profit or carried the cost of loss. The distinction was important because independent contractors were not eligible for union membership. The union's lawyer pointed out that the carriers had signed a standardized contract and there was minimal room for negotiation on the terms of the contract. He reminded the Labour Relations Board that *Star* employees had testified that the district managers were expected to maintain conditions producing an average pay rate of $7 an hour for the carriers. Thus, any negotiations that took place were limited by this restriction, which effectively imposed a standard wage on the carriers. Additionally, the only "tool" the carriers provided for work was their cars. The *Star* provided the newspapers, determined the distribution routes, operated the distribution depot, and supplied other distribution materials, such as plastic bags to protect papers in bad weather. In this case, then, it was argued, most of the responsibility for control, tool ownership, and profit or loss lay with the *Star*. Thus, the carriers should be considered employees and eligible for union representation.

In regard to the allegation of unfair labour practices during the organizing campaign, the union's lawyer asserted that the *Star* had produced no factual evidence to show that the union had actually intimidated or coerced the carriers. The fact that off-duty district managers had been present at the distribution centres was not sufficient to establish that work had been disrupted or that individuals' intentions regarding union membership had been changed.

References

[1] Arrowsmith, D.L. (1992). *Canada's trade unions: an information manual*. Kingston, ON: Industrial Relations Centre, Queen's University.

[2] Carrothers, A.W.R., Palmer, E.E., and Rayner, W.B. (1986). *Collective bargaining law in Canada* (2nd edition). Toronto, ON: Butterworths.

[3] As described in Carrothers, Palmer, and Rayner, *op. cit.*

[4] Carrothers, Palmer, and Rayner, *op. cit.*

Rough ride for city:

Union: if brass have luxury cars,

then we want raise

TORONTO—If the city can find the money to lease luxury cars for its top bureaucrats, then there must be cash for almost 11,000 workers who haven't seen raises since 1991.

That's the message coming from the Toronto Civic Employees Union in the wake of revelations Toronto's paying $137,640 a year to keep its top 23 managers behind the wheels of luxury vehicles.

"If they can find the dollars for management, then they have to understand we'll be looking for some when it comes time to sit down and hammer out a collective agreement," said Brian Cochrane, president of Local 416.

Cochrane said the majority of his members haven't seen a wage increase for the past seven years, and won't until a new bargaining structure can be reached with the city at the Labour Relations Board.

Most of Local 416's members make between $30,000 and $60,000 a year—less than half of the average income drawn by the city's top executives who count a free car among their perks.

Yesterday, the *Toronto Sun* reported 23 of the city's top bureaucrats were given their pick of luxury cars for personal use, as long as they were North American-made.

Fifteen of 23 senior managers are already riding around in Buicks, Oldsmobiles, and Ford Explorers, while the rest finalize leases ranging from $470 to $650 a month.

City officials said the leasing allowances were approved by the Toronto Transition Team last year and are considered part of management's compensation.

(*Toronto Sun*, October 15, 1998)

chapter 7

DEFINING AND COMMENCING COLLECTIVE BARGAINING

objectives

One of the biggest tasks for unions and employers is negotiating a collective agreement. In this chapter, we will describe the effects of certification on the union-management relationship and the process of preparation for collective bargaining. We will examine the various structures within which collective bargaining can take place and describe how the participants begin the bargaining process. By the end of this chapter, you should be able to:

- describe how certification changes the relationship between employees and employers
- identify exemptions to the effects of certification
- name the participants on the union and management bargaining teams
- understand how bargaining structure is determined
- describe the process by which bargaining teams arrive at their list of desired outcomes
- identify practices that are considered bargaining in good faith

INTRODUCTION

In chapters 5 and 6, we described the process of certification through which a union becomes recognized as the legal representative of the employees in a workplace. One of the results of certification is that the union and the employer are compelled to commence collective bargaining, a process that will eventually produce a collective agreement that determines workplace rules and policies. In this chapter, we will start by describing how certification changes the relationship between the workers and the employer. We will then outline how both unions and employers prepare for collective bargaining. In Chapter 8, we will continue our discussion of collective bargaining by describing what actually happens in the bargaining process itself.

THE EFFECTS OF CERTIFICATION

When a certification order is issued, a number of changes occur in the relationship between employers and employees. One of the most immediate changes is the application of various sections of the labour code to ensure that the union has sufficient resources to represent all members of the bargaining unit effectively. These applications are usually reflected in contractual terms between the union and the employer, and are referred to as **union security** clauses. One typical clause requires that all union members pay union dues. Dues are usually calculated either as a standard flat fee or, on a sliding scale, as a percentage of the employee's monthly or annual pay. The percentage-based calculation is more common in Canada because it bases an employee's dues on what the employee actually earns, whereas a flat fee imposes a higher percentage rate of payment on lower-paid employees than on higher-paid employees.

All labour codes in Canada provide for the **dues check-off** as a form of union security. The dues check-off provision allows the union member to direct the employer to deduct union dues from his or her paycheque and to forward the deducted amount directly to the union. This provision exists so that the union does not have to go to the trouble of gathering money directly from every member after the paycheques are issued. It also ensures that the union receives its membership dues regularly and promptly.

There are, however, some generally permitted exceptions to the dues check-off provision. If employees object to belonging to a union for reasons associated with their religious affiliation, four provincial labour codes (those of British Columbia, Saskatchewan, Manitoba, and Ontario) and the *Canada Labour Code* permit a **religious exemption**. Employees can request that the amount they would have paid in union dues be directed to a registered charity mutually agreed upon by the employee and the union. In order to receive a religious exemption, employees must show that their religious beliefs conflict with the general idea of union membership. Employees cannot receive a religious exemption because they object to the particular union in their workplace or to specific actions undertaken by that union. Employees who receive a religious exemption are generally not eligible to participate in votes conducted by the union, although they are covered by the terms of the collective agreement.

Another union security provision is known as the **Rand formula**, whose origins were discussed in Chapter 3. The principle behind the Rand formula is that while not all employees may wish to be members of the union, all employees in a unionized workplace benefit from the contract terms the union negotiates, and therefore, all employees, whether union members or not, should financially support the work of the union. The Rand formula is often used to supplement or replace the religious exemption, especially in those provinces where there is no provision for religious exemption in the provincial labour code. Unlike the religious exemption, however, the Rand formula makes the payment of union dues compulsory while allowing employees the right to opt out of union membership.

After a certification order is issued, many unionized workplaces follow the **closed shop** or **union shop** model of employment. Under this union security provision, implemented through terms in the collective agreement, new employees, as a condition of employment, must agree to join the union and pay union dues. The closed shop or union shop model ensures that the employer will not be able to reduce union membership by hiring individuals into the bargaining unit who will not join the union.

A variation on the closed shop model occurs in the skilled trades and construction sectors. Here, prospective workers must already be union members before they are eligible for employment. The reasoning behind this requirement is that since workers in these occupations regularly move from employer to employer as each job or project is completed, allowing the union to control the supply of qualified labour ensures job security by restricting or eliminating non-union members' access to job openings.

In these same occupations, the matching of employees with employers occurs in a format known as the **hiring hall**. Employers wanting to hire tradespeople contact the appropriate union, which then posts the job opening at the hiring hall. The "hall" is sometimes a permanent posting site at the union offices that members can visit at their leisure to obtain information on available opportunities. Alternatively, a "hall" can be a scheduled meeting attended by all qualified members seeking employment during which the union posts hiring requests and attempts to match up potential employees and employers. Another hiring hall format is one in which the union maintains lists of qualified union members and will assign members, usually on the basis of seniority or specialized experience, to a potential employer when the employer submits a hiring request. All of these hiring hall formats maintain union security in occupations where employment relationships are flexible and frequently changing.

Another union security provision resulting from the contractual linking of union membership to employment compels an employer to discharge an individual from employment if he or she has been expelled from union membership. This provision strengthens union security by reinforcing the expectation that all workers in the bargaining unit be union members in good standing or pay union dues as a condition of employment. Expelling a member from a union is an extreme action, one that unions rarely undertake because of the impact that expulsion could have on the member's future employment. Expelled union members will generally not be hired at any other unionized workplace, and thus, in a highly unionized industry or occupation, an expelled member would have difficulty finding work. Unions usually expel members only as a last resort when other disciplinary measures have failed. Most union constitutions permit either the union executive or the membership (via a vote) to expel a member for such reasons as non-payment of dues or doing the work of another union member who is on strike or locked out. A number of cases before provincial labour relations boards[1] have established that if the union requests that an employer dismiss an employee because he or she has been expelled from the union, the employer is compelled to do so.

The most common union security provisions are outlined in Table 7-1.

TABLE 7-1	Union Security Provisions
Dues check-off	Employer deducts union dues for each employee and forwards money to union
Rand formula	Employees in bargaining unit pay union dues but choose whether or not to be union members
Closed shop/ Union shop	Employees must agree to join union as a condition of employment
Hiring hall	Unionized employees are supplied to employer by union
Union provisions to expel members	Employer may be compelled to dismiss employee if union expels employee from union membership

Finally, as we saw in previous chapters, one of the underlying principles of Canadian labour relations law is that once a certification order is issued, both the union and the employer are compelled to commence collective bargaining. At this point, neither party can refuse to acknowledge the other's role as a bargaining representative or refuse to participate in collective bargaining. It is also important to remember that as soon as a certification order is in place, individual employees become bargaining unit members and can no longer bargain individually with the employer to establish workplace conditions. Conversely, with the granting of the union's certification, the employer can no longer bargain individually with employees. An employer who attempts to bargain directly with individual employees, rather than with the union acting on behalf of the employees, may be breaching the expectation that the parties bargain in good faith. (This expectation will be discussed in detail later in this chapter.)

To introduce the topic of how collective bargaining commences, we will first outline the framework within which collective bargaining takes place.

THE FRAMEWORK FOR COLLECTIVE BARGAINING

The Structure of Collective Bargaining

The word "structure" as applied to collective bargaining has to do with the number of unions, employers, workplaces, or industries represented in a particular collective bargaining situation. Depending on the type of bargaining unit established by the certification order or by provisions in the relevant legislation, the structure of collective bargaining can be simple or complex. The degree of complexity depends on how many workplaces or business establishments, bargaining units or unions, and employers will be involved in bargaining.

The simplest and most common bargaining structure is "single unit–single employer," where one union negotiates with a single employer that operates a single location. However, more complex structures are also possible. Individual bargaining units can negotiate with a single employer who operates multiple locations; multiple units can negotiate with a single employer; and multiple units can negotiate with multiple employers. Table 7-2 outlines the different types of bargaining structures and gives examples of industries where each type of structure can be found.

TABLE 7-2 Bargaining Structures

Single Establishment

Single Union–Single Employer	Multiple Union–Single Employer
Most common bargaining structure in Canada. Individual unions bargain with employers operating at a single location.	Usually only found where multiple unions represent different groups of workers in a single workplace. Not common in Canada.
Single Union–Single Employer	**Multiple Union–Single Employer**
One collective agreement is negotiated and applies to all the employer's establishments where the union is certified. This is the model used in many Canadian public service bargaining structures.	Different unions representing different workers negotiate with one employer for contracts covering all locations. Used in the Canadian railway industry.

TABLE 7-2 Continued

Multiple Establishment

Single Union–Single Employer	Multiple Union–Single Employer
Different employers operating in different locations negotiate as a group with a single union. May require accreditation of employers as an employers' council. Used in several parts of the Canadian forest industry.	Highly centralized bargaining; usually only used where there are multiple unions and employers within a single industry that operates in multiple locations. Relatively rare in Canada.

The bargaining structure in a particular collective bargaining situation is usually determined by the certification order, which names the employer(s) and union(s) that will bargain with each other. The relevant labour legislation may also contain guidelines on how to determine the bargaining structure, especially with respect to the Canadian public sector. Legislation covering public sector bargaining outlines which part of government is considered the employer or the bargaining agent that will act on behalf of the employer in negotiations.

While most Canadian bargaining structures, as noted, involve a single employer and a single union, it is possible for groups of employers or groups of unions to bargain as a single entity. This situation most commonly arises when multiple employers in a single industry feel that their interests would be better served if they bargained as a group rather than individually. This structure helps employers in a single industry avoid the bargaining phenomenon of **pattern bargaining** or **whipsawing**, where an agreement reached by one union with one employer is used to pressure other employers in the same industry or that deal with the same union into agreeing to similar terms. Whipsawing was formerly very prevalent as a bargaining tactic in the American auto industry. The United Auto Workers union in the United States made no secret of its strategy of selecting a "target settlement" with one of the Big Three

Autoworkers' unions are famous for their use of whipsawing as a bargaining tactic.

automobile assembly companies (Ford, General Motors, and Chrysler) and then bargaining for the same settlement with the other companies.[2] Since the early 1980s, the effectiveness of whipsawing as a bargaining tactic in the auto industry and associated industries has declined, mostly because of changes in different companies' ability to pay the requested wages.[3] However, it is interesting to note that whipsawing has resurfaced as an employer (rather than union) tactic in the auto industry after the implementation of the *North American Free Trade Agreement*. Many companies in the auto industry have used the threat of transferring jobs to Mexico or other low-wage areas to resist organizing attempts and contract demands by American workers.[4]

When a number of unions represent different employees of a single employer, they may decide to bargain as a group. The unions may feel that they will thereby be able to exert more pressure on the employer. Unions that bargain as a group do exert greater pressure on the employer because of the increased impact of any job action they might take, such as a strike. Union members generally respect any job action taken by another union by refusing, for example, to cross the striking union's picket lines. Thus, in a multiple union–single employer relationship, it would be possible for employees belonging to one union to go on strike and shut down the entire operations of the employer.

The potential threat of a complete workplace shutdown as a result of the job action of relatively few employees would give unions a great deal of power over the employer during bargaining. In fact, labour relations boards are often reluctant to certify small bargaining units within large workplaces because of the power imbalance this bargaining structure might cause in negotiations. However, labour relations boards recognize that a multiple union–single employer bargaining structure has the advantage of efficiency. This is because issues common to all the unions can be addressed in one set of negotiations rather than in separate negotiations with each separate union.

Most Canadian labour codes specify that employers wishing to bargain as a group must apply to a labour relations board for certification as an **employers' council**. The process whereby this group of employers is recognized as a single unit for the purposes of bargaining is known as **accreditation**. Unlike unions applying for certification, employers applying for accreditation are not required to conduct a representation vote; the support of potential members is assumed on the basis of their participation in the application. However, members of an employers' council who decide that they no longer wish to bargain as a group and prefer to return to individual bargaining must apply to the labour relations board to have the accreditation cancelled before they can bargain individually.

Unions that bargain together as a group form an entity called a **bargaining council**; no formal recognition from a labour relations board is necessary for unions to adopt this bargaining structure.

The Participants in Collective Bargaining

Most collective bargaining is conducted by two teams of negotiators, one team representing the union and one team representing the employer. The size and composition of the teams are determined to a large extent by the size of the organizations, the number of issues to be resolved, and the resources each organization can draw upon to support the work of its team. However, there are particular individuals who are generally always included on each team. We will describe the composition of each team in turn.

The Union Team

The union negotiating team commonly includes a member or members of the union executive. These individuals are on the bargaining team because they have extensive knowledge of the union's operations and of the issues of concern to the union membership. Ordinary, or "rank and file," members of the union are also commonly included on the negotiating team. It is important for these individuals to be on the team because, as employees, they usually have a realistic perspective on how proposed contract terms will affect the day-to-day operations of the workplace. Having these individuals on the negotiating team, furthermore, gives the team greater credibility with the union membership, since with their presence the union executives will be less likely to be accused of dominating the bargaining process and addressing their own concerns instead of those of the union membership. Rank-and-file members of the union negotiating team are usually elected by the union membership.

If the bargaining unit is a local of a larger union, a regional or national representative may be present during negotiations either as a formal member of the union negotiation team or as an observer/advisor. This sort of representation is considered important for two reasons. First, the regional or national representative may be a very experienced negotiator and thus will be able to give strategic assistance to the local bargaining team; this is of particular value if the local members are inexperienced bargainers. Second, the regional or national representative will be aware of terms negotiated in other collective agreements involving the same union and will thus seek to ensure that the local team does not agree to terms inferior to those negotiated by other locals.

In large sets of negotiations involving national unions and/or large employers, the union negotiating team may include professional negotiators. These individuals are either union employees or persons hired on contract by the union to assist in developing bargaining strategies and tactics. Union negotiating teams may also include experts such as union researchers and economists. These individuals provide general information, such as trends in employment or inflation, as well as figures in support of the union's proposals, such as the impact a wage proposal will have on employees' take-home pay or earning potential.

The Management Team

The management negotiating team represents the employer and usually includes executives who deal with the union on a regular basis (e.g., the human resources director). These individuals are considered to have the knowledge of the workplace conditions and requirements necessary to bargain a collective agreement appropriate for the organization and its employees. Because these individuals are usually the ones who handle day-to-day problems arising from the terms of an existing collective agreement, they are also the ones most likely to have information about which terms of the existing collective agreement need to be altered or updated. The negotiating team may also include a financial officer, who will offer advice on the financial impacts of proposed settlements. This individual is aware of the resources the employer has to offer in bargaining and, ultimately, of what the employer is prepared to pay in total wage and salary costs. It is important for the employer's negotiating team to have this knowledge so that the team does not make financial offers that the employer cannot fulfill.

If the employer is a sub-unit of a larger organization (e.g., an individual store in a chain or franchise operation or an organization owned by a larger organization), the management negotiating team may also include representatives from the parent organization. These individuals play a role on the management negotiating team similar to the role that representatives from the regional or national union play on the union negotiating team. They are present to provide negotiating expertise and to ensure consistency in the collective agreements covering different parts of the parent organization's operations. Like the union negotiating team, the management negotiating team may also include professional negotiators, researchers, and/or other professionals who will supply negotiating assistance and information.

In negotiations involving a bargaining council or an employers' council, it is usual for the negotiating team to include at least one representative from each of the unions or employers participating in the council. Although the specific concerns of the individual unions or employers are usually incorporated into the council's overall bargaining strategy, it is still important that each participant in the council be represented in negotiations. This is because each participant's representative can inform the rest of the council how bargaining proposals would affect the representative's own workplace or membership. If the council has this information during negotiations, it can avoid the problem of the council agreeing to contract terms that are not appropriate for some or all of the participants.

A summary of the participants on each negotiating team is presented in Table 7-3.

TABLE 7-3 The Negotiating Teams

Union	Employer
Union executive members	Human resources director
Rank and file union members	Financial officer
Regional/national union representatives[i]	Parent organization representatives[ii]
Council member representatives[iii]	Council member representatives[iii]
Professional negotiators[iv]	Professional negotiators[iv]
Researchers[iv]	Researchers[iv]

[i] May or may not be included depending on union structure.
[ii] May or may not be included depending on employer's organizational structure.
[iii] May or may not be included depending on bargaining structure.
[iv] May or may not be included depending on team's or organization's resources.

What Can the Parties Bargain For?

Generally, the areas that collective bargaining will address are determined by the parties themselves. The issues most commonly addressed are wages, benefits, working hours, procedures for hiring and promotions, and working conditions. Theoretically, no issues are off limits in collective bargaining. We should note, however, that many collective agreements contain a so-called **management rights clause**. This clause states that management has the right to establish procedures or policies governing any issue not addressed in the collective agreement. Thus, while any issue is theoretically available for inclusion in collective bargaining, if a collective agreement contains a management rights clause, that agreement is not the absolute authority on how the workplace is to be operated.

Certain guidelines have been established in provincial and federal labour relations legislation that frame the terms that the parties can agree to in collective bargaining. Collective agreements in most jurisdictions, for example, must have a minimum term of one year. This stipulation is in place so that employers and unions do not have to commence bargaining for a new agreement immediately after concluding the previous agreement. Bargaining one contract immediately after concluding another would be very time-consuming for both employers and unions. Collective agreements also cannot contain terms that are inferior to the minimum conditions specified in the relevant employment standards act. For example, a collective agreement could not specify a wage rate lower than the applicable minimum wage or grant fewer holidays than the amounts specified in employment standards legislation. This restriction exists because an employment standards act is applicable to all workplaces in a jurisdiction, whether unionized or non-unionized.

As outlined in Chapter 1, collective agreements cannot contain any terms that discriminate against particular groups in the workplace. The definition of "discrimination" in this context is found in the provisions of the applicable provincial or federal *Human Rights Act*; it is considered to include both intentional and systemic discrimination. An example of discrimination in a collective agreement would be a clause giving white people priority in promotions. This would be an illegal contract clause because all Canadian human rights acts prohibit discrimination on the basis of race or ethnic origin.

Collective agreements are generally required to contain a grievance procedure so that disputes over interpretation or application of the agreement can be resolved once the agreement has been concluded and is in force in the workplace. Most Canadian labour relations legislation includes a grievance procedure that is considered applicable to any workplace without a grievance procedure in its collective agreement. The grievance procedure outlined in provincial labour legislation is similar to that in most collective agreements. While it is most uncommon for a grievance procedure to not be included in a collective agreement, the legislative provision is in place to ensure that there are grievance procedures available in all unionized workplaces. We will discuss the grievance procedure in greater detail in Chapter 11.

PREPARING TO COMMENCE BARGAINING

Once the bargaining structure is determined and the bargaining teams have been formed, the teams commence the process of preparing for collective bargaining. Through this process, both teams jointly determine how bargaining will proceed, and each team individually determines what outcomes it wants to achieve through bargaining. We will now describe how these two sets of decisions unfold.

Timelines for Bargaining

As we know, once a certification order is in place, the parties named in the order are compelled to begin bargaining. However, especially in situations where the certification order applies to a previously non-unionized group of workers, there can be reluctance on the part of one or both parties to start bargaining. Sometimes employers resent the union's formalized presence or are bitter about events during the certification process, and these feelings are manifested as an unwillingness to bargain. On the union side, the union members may be worn out from the effort of the certification campaign and do not feel ready to embark on another major process; there also may be concerns about having enough expertise to bargain effectively.

To ensure that the collective bargaining process is undertaken, most Canadian labour codes specify times by which collective bargaining must commence. There are also timelines to encourage the parties to begin bargaining when the term of an existing collective agreement is close to its end. In both situations, the bargaining process is initiated by one party issuing a **notice to bargain** to the other party. Most Canadian labour codes specify a deadline after the issuance of the notice by which bargaining is expected to begin. If bargaining does not begin by this deadline, the party that issued the notice can file a complaint of an unfair labour practice with the labour relations board. The other party may have reasons for not commencing bargaining that it considers valid—for example, the absence of a key member of the bargaining team. In such cases, the other party is not compelled to file an unfair labour practice complaint if it agrees that the reasons for the delay are valid and if the parties can mutually agree on an acceptable time to start bargaining. However, a party that is reluctant to bargain at all might manufacture numerous excuses to avoid starting bargaining; if the other party recognizes this pattern of behaviour, it can use an unfair labour practice complaint as a means to force the other party to the bargaining table.

At this point, we should mention briefly that if the union does not submit a notice to bargain to the employer or does not respond to an employer's notice to bargain within the specified time, it may be considered to have abandoned its bargaining rights. If a labour relations board determines that a union has indeed abandoned its bargaining rights, it may issue a decertification. We will discuss the issue of abandoned bargaining rights in more detail in Chapter 12.

The timelines in each Canadian jurisdiction for commencing bargaining are summarized in Table 7-4. Note that most of these legislative provisions permit the parties to set their own deadlines within the existing collective agreement for the commencement of collective bargaining toward a new agreement.

TABLE 7-4 Timelines for Commencing Collective Bargaining

	First Agreement	Prior to Expiry of Existing Agreement	Timeline for Commencing Bargaining
Federal	Upon notice issued by either party	Notice within 4 months preceding the date of expiry if no other agreement exists between the parties	Within 20 days of notice being given unless parties agree otherwise
Alberta	Upon notice issued by either party	No less than 60 days and no more than 120 days preceding the date of expiry if no other agreement exists between the parties	Within 30 days after notice is given unless parties agree otherwise; proposals must be exchanged within 15 days of first meeting unless parties agree otherwise
British Columbia	Upon notice issued by either party	Any time within 4 months preceding the date of expiry; if notice is not given 90 days or more prior to the expiry, the parties are deemed to have given notice 90 days prior to expiry	Within 10 days after the date of the notice
Manitoba	Upon notice issued by either party	No more than 90 days and no less than 30 days preceding the date of expiry if no other agreement exists between the parties	Within 10 clear days after the date of the notice or such further time as the parties may agree upon
New Brunswick	Upon notice issued by either party	Between the 90th and the 30th day preceding the date of expiry if no other agreement exists between the parties	Within 20 days after notice has been given or such further time as the parties may agree upon

TABLE 7-4 Continued

	First Agreement	Prior to Expiry of Existing Agreement	Timeline for Commencing Bargaining
Newfoundland	Upon notice issued by either party	No more than 60 days and no less than 30 days before the expiration or termination of the agreement, or within a period outlined in the collective agreement	Within 20 days after notice has been given or such further time as the parties agree upon
Nova Scotia	Upon notice issued by either party	Within 2 months preceding the expiry of the agreement	Within 20 days after notice has been given or such further time as the parties agree upon
Ontario	The trade union must give notice to commence bargaining	Within 90 days before the expiry of the agreement or in accordance with provisions in the collective agreement	The parties must meet within 15 days from the giving of the notice or within such further period as the parties agree upon
Prince Edward Island	Upon notice issued by either party	Within the time prescribed by the collective agreement or, if not specified, at least 2 months before the expiry date	Within 20 days after notice has been given or within such further period as the parties agree upon
Quebec	Either party must issue eight days' written notice to the other of the time and place its representatives will be ready to meet	Notice may be given by either party within 90 days preceding expiration unless another time is provided in the collective agreement	After a notice of meeting has been received, negotiations must begin and be carried on diligently and in good faith
Saskatchewan	None specified	Either party may give notice to bargain no less than 30 days and no more than 60 days preceding expiration	Where notice is given, parties must immediately bargain collectively in good faith

Source: Human Resources Development Canada, Labour Program, Summaries of General Private Sector Collective Bargaining Legislation (available at <http://www.hrdc-drhc.gc.ca>).

Setting Bargaining Priorities

One of the first actions that a well-prepared negotiating team will undertake is to decide what its priorities will be in bargaining. More specifically, the team will attempt to answer two questions: what outcomes does the team want to achieve, and which of these outcomes are the most or least important for it to achieve? This process of identifying and prioritizing outcomes is essential if the team is to bargain effectively. A comprehensive list of bargaining priorities ensures that all team members are directing their efforts in negotiation toward reaching agreed-upon outcomes. A prioritized list also allows a team to act strategically in assessing offers from the other team. The order of items on the list helps the team determine which of their bargaining outcomes they are prepared to concede or which they should maintain in response to the other side's proposals.

Job security has emerged as a union bargaining priority in many recent labour disputes as employers seek to farm out work to lower cost contract workers.

Agreeing on a set of goals and priorities can be a very challenging process for a negotiating team. For the union team, the challenge is to balance the different needs and wants of what is usually a diverse group of employees. Some employees may identify a pay increase as their desired outcome of bargaining; others may want changes in benefit packages or work schedules. Still other employees may have encountered ongoing problems in the workplace that they want resolved by new language in the collective agreement. Employees will expect all of these concerns to be addressed in bargaining, but this can be problematic if the union team considers other issues to have higher importance or believes there is little realistic chance of obtaining the members' desired outcomes.

For the management team, the challenge may be to balance the desires of various stakeholders inside and outside the organization. Some stakeholders may identify cost containment or cost reduction as a priority; others may want increases in pay so that the company can retain a skilled workforce; and others may want to invest in training programs to increase productivity. Some stakeholders may hope to improve workplace efficiency through the enforcement of standardized rules and regulations, while others may favour flexible rules that allow the organization to adapt quickly to changing business conditions. Like the union team, the management team may consider some desired outcomes more achievable than others, or it may disagree with individual stakeholders about the relative importance of some issues.

How, then, do the negotiating teams identify and prioritize these competing demands? On the union side, the process of identifying and prioritizing goals is accomplished through several means:

- *The union may conduct a survey of the membership to discover their concerns and their bargaining priorities.* This can be done by distributing a questionnaire and analysing the results or by holding votes at membership meetings. Since the union members must ultimately approve the negotiated agreement, it is important for the bargaining team to know what the membership wants so that the eventual agreement will not be rejected.

  In addition, some research shows that union leaders perceive bargaining effectiveness as one of the key determinants of how union members rate union effectiveness.[5] Incorporating the membership's wishes into bargaining priorities is therefore a way for union leaders to demonstrate their effectiveness to the membership. (However, other research indicates that bargaining effectiveness is not as important a determinant of union effectiveness for union members as union leaders think it is. Members may place a higher priority on effectiveness criteria such as quality of leadership, opportunity to participate in union activities, the degree of formalization and centralization in the union structure, and the willingness of the union to undertake innovative activities.)[6]

- *The union bargaining team may look at what was and was not accomplished in any previous negotiations.* This review provides two important kinds of information: how likely it is that current bargaining issues can be resolved satisfactorily, based on past experience, and whether goals that were not previously achieved are still important. For example, if in the past the union was reluctant to agree to work arrangements that could reduce work for union members, the management bargaining team will wonder whether it is worth the effort to introduce proposals similar to those the union previously rejected. If, however, management believes that these types of work arrangements are important because they would enable the organization to adapt to changing market conditions, it may reintroduce the proposals regardless of the previous rejection.

- *Both the union and the management negotiating teams may examine collective agreements in other locals of the union and/or in similar industries to see what has been agreed to elsewhere.* This source of information is particularly important if the union is a local of a larger union or if the organization has a "parent" organization, since neither team will want to unknowingly agree to contract terms inferior to what has been achieved elsewhere in the union or organization. Using this source of information can be equated to pattern bargaining or whipsawing, as previously discussed.

- *The union and management negotiating teams will examine the record of grievances filed since the last collective agreement went into effect.* If disputes have consistently arisen as a consequence of the application of a particular part of the agreement, that part of the agreement may need to be clarified or re-examined to determine whether it is accomplishing what it was intended to accomplish. The outcome of grievances, particularly resolutions where the complaint was found to be valid, may indicate to either the union or the management team how likely it is that certain bargaining objectives will be achieved. For example, if a grievance resulted in the ruling that management must consult with the union before substantially changing work schedules, the management negotiating team will probably not give a high priority in bargaining to any proposal suggesting that management should have the sole right to determine working hours. The management negotiating team would foresee that the union negotiating team would likely counter such a proposal in negotiations by citing the result of the grievance as evidence that management should not have that right.

- *The union and management negotiating teams will both look at environmental conditions outside the organization (e.g., inflation rates, labour market demographics, and economic indicators) to identify future trends that may affect the outcomes of bargaining.* A predicted increase in the inflation rate, for example, may affect whether or not the union bargaining team requests higher wages, since the employer's ability to pay may be reduced by increased costs. Environmental conditions also come into play when the union considers what priority it should give a pay increase for workers with a specialized skill. If labour market information indicates that there will soon be an oversupply of workers with this skill, it would be difficult for the union to achieve the outcome of a pay increase because the employer would not have to pay higher wages to attract and retain those particular workers.

A negotiating team's perception of what goals are realistic can also be influenced by the demographics of the team itself. This is particularly true with respect to the union negotiating team. While its priorities theoretically represent the concerns of all members of the bargaining unit, they may instead end up reflecting the priorities of the team members themselves. Some research has indicated that union members who are more dissatisfied than their co-workers with their job conditions tend to turn to union activism as a way to improve their own job conditions.[7] Since members who are active in the union are likely to be interested in participating in an important activity like collective bargaining, the issues that motivated them to become active in the union may thus assume greater importance in the prioritizing of bargaining demands.

Another study addressing how unions determine their bargaining priorities examined how the Canadian labour movement deals with issues of sexual orientation.[8] The results of this study indicated that issues of concern to minority groups in unions are usually only considered "important" once the minority group members form a significant part of the union membership or once they succeed in promoting their concerns within the union. If neither of these conditions is present, the concerns of demographic or numerical minorities within the union membership are not likely to be given priority in bargaining demands, even if the issue is significant or affects union members who are not part of the minority group. For example, extending spousal benefits to individuals who are not married would have the effect of benefiting heterosexual couples who are in a common-law relationship as well as same-sex couples. But if the issue of extended spousal benefits is being proposed as a bargaining concern by only a small number of minority group members, the bargaining team may consider the issue relatively unimportant and give it a low priority.

A further study indicates that decision making in local unions tends to be governed by explicit rules and policies, and that while this formalization does not appear to inhibit a local union's ability to innovate, those members unfamiliar with the formal regulations may be unable to participate effectively and make their particular issues visible.[9] Thus, newcomers to the union or members who do not regularly participate in union activities may not be able to influence the setting of bargaining priorities, since they do not know how to follow the formal procedures that help determine those priorities, such as the procedure for proposing motions at a membership meeting.

When they prioritize desired bargaining outcomes, however, union negotiating team members must remember that the collective agreement they negotiate will eventually have to be ratified by the entire membership. Therefore, they must be careful to ensure that the prioritized list of bargaining demands reflects the will of the membership and not their own personal preferences. If the eventual collective agreement does not at least appear to reflect the priorities of the membership, the membership may reject the agreement and send the bargaining team back to negotiate a more acceptable contract.

The process of identifying and prioritizing bargaining goals for the management negotiating team is somewhat more efficient and less formal than for the union team. This is because the management team is not usually formally accountable to its constituents in the sense that it would face, for example, a ratification vote on the negotiated contract. In creating its own set of bargaining goals and priorities, however, the management team will usually gather information on desired outcomes from the groups or individuals it represents, and will examine previous bargaining experiences or completed agreements in other organizations. Management may also acquire advance information on the union's bargaining intentions through discussions with supervisors and other non-union staff who interact with union members, and thereby be able to prioritize its bargaining demands accordingly.

There is one other source of information that both the union and management teams will draw on prior to bargaining. Court decisions and legislative changes may point to parts of the collective agreement that need re-examination. For example, if employment legislation changes the way certain benefits are provided or funded, or changes the eligibility requirements for certain benefits, the collective agreement language governing those benefits may have to be rewritten to reflect the new regulations.

Preparing for the Start of Bargaining

After bargaining issues have been identified and prioritized, both negotiating teams will develop a "laundry list" of proposals, usually ranked from the most to the least important and/or achievable. Each team will give a list of its proposals to the other team when negotiations actually start, but the exchanged versions do not indicate the priority of each individual item. In fact, the lists that are exchanged may include items that are considered to be low priority or unachievable.

While it may seem counterprodctive to present proposals that the team does not seriously intend to pursue, there are two strategic reasons for using this tactic. First, the tactic is useful because it allows the team to assure shareholders that "their" items were introduced in bargaining, even if these items were subsequently dropped from negotiations or were not resolved. This tactic is particularly important to union negotiators who have been chosen by a vote of the membership; to ensure continued membership support, they will want to be perceived as being responsive to members' concerns. The union negotiators can tell union members that the members' concerns were presented in bargaining but were not pursued when it became obvious that the management team would not agree to them, or they can justify their lack of action on some items on the grounds that their energy was better expended on bargaining for items that were achievable.

Second, the tactic of presenting a complete list of proposals, including unimportant items, allows the team to hide the true priority of individual items on the list and thus achieve its desired outcomes more easily. For example, the union might readily agree to a proposal that it considers minor but that, unknown to the union, management considers important; thus, one of the management team's desired bargaining outcomes would be achieved with minimal effort on the management team's part. If the union is aware that the issue is a high priority for management, it might not agree to it immediately; instead the union might offer to exchange the union's agreement on that item for management's agreement on an item of equal importance to the union.

The length of the list of proposals can also play a strategic role. A very lengthy list that shows the range of issues that one side is (theoretically) prepared to address may intimidate the other team. The grim prospect of interminable negotiations may encourage the other team to reduce the number of its demands or to rethink its priorities so that bargaining does not drag on for an excessively long time.

Bargaining in Good Faith

In commencing collective bargaining, the parties must be aware of the legal requirement that they **bargain in good faith**. A complaint about bargaining in bad faith can be made at any point in the collective bargaining process, but we will discuss the issue here, before outlining the actual bargaining process, because the first significant place where bargaining in bad faith can occur is before the bargaining process even begins. Specifically, if one party refuses to start negotiations or to meet at all, that party can be charged with bargaining in bad faith. The expectation that the parties will bargain in good faith underlies the entire bargaining process. This expectation should govern the parties in their preparations for bargaining, compelling them, for example, to ensure that they are making honest bargaining proposals.

Bargaining in good faith involves a commitment on both sides to an open and honest appraisal of the facts, with the intent of finalizing a contract which is agreeable to all.

Bargaining in good faith has two components. First, the parties are expected to enter into honest bargaining. In practice, this means that the parties must not, for example, make offers that they are not prepared to commit to, or withhold information that might affect how the other party responds to a proposal. Second, the parties are expected to bargain with the intent of reaching a collective agreement. This does not mean that one party must agree to every proposal from the other party or that there cannot be delays or breaks in the bargaining process. What it does mean is that the parties are expected to actively work toward achieving an agreement and should not jeopardize the process by, for example, making outlandish proposals that no reasonable negotiator would agree to or skipping scheduled negotiating meetings without good reason.

If one party believes that the other party is not bargaining in good faith, it can file a complaint of an unfair labour practice with a labour relations board. In seeking to determine whether bargaining in bad faith has taken place, the board will generally use both objective and subjective criteria. Examples of objective criteria are the definitions and language in the relevant labour legislation that determine whether illegal actions take place. An example of an illegal action would be one party's refusal to commence bargaining after the deadline for starting has passed if the other party has not consented to an alternative date for bargaining to begin. Subjective criteria involve ethical or moral issues. These criteria would be used to judge, for example, whether a party was justified in withholding confidential financial records from the other party.

In most Canadian jurisdictions, through legislation and case law, the following actions have been identified as bargaining in bad faith:

- outright refusal to bargain

- **surface bargaining** (i.e., participating in negotiations but having no intent of concluding a collective agreement)

- presenting an initial offer, possibly based on an employer survey of union members, as a final offer—without any justification or rationale—and refusing to negotiate further. This "take it or leave it" approach is known as **Boulwarism**, named for a vice-president of General Electric in the 1950s who used this bargaining tactic.

- firing or disciplining union members or negotiators for reasons unrelated to their performance at work, or for no reason, during the negotiation process

- the employer bargaining directly with employees rather than with the union (e.g., surveying bargaining unit members directly to identify their preferences and desired outcomes, and presenting proposals to the membership rather than to the union bargaining team)

- refusing to provide the rationale for a bargaining position

- attempting to reopen the negotiation of terms that have already been settled. (An exception would be if there has been some change in the workplace or external environment that requires that the terms be revisited.)

It should be noted that the expectation that the parties will bargain in good faith does not require that a collective agreement actually be reached. What is important is that the parties should be committed to concluding a collective agreement and should actively work toward that goal; not reaching an agreement is not in and of itself evidence of bargaining in bad faith. The expectation that the parties will bargain in good faith also does not mean that parties should "give in" or accept unsatisfactory terms for an item that is a bargaining priority just to conclude a collective agreement.

Most Canadian labour codes contain the provision that once collective bargaining begins, the workplace terms and conditions that were in place at the start of bargaining are under a **freeze**, or are "frozen," until a collective agreement is concluded. This means that the employer cannot unilaterally change contractual terms such as wage rates during the bargaining process. This provision applies even when a previous collective agreement has expired. The terms and conditions of the expired collective agreement are considered to be in effect as long as collective bargaining toward a new collective agreement is taking place. The terms and conditions cannot be changed until the new collective agreement is accepted or ratified by both parties and formally comes into effect.

A labour relations board faces a particular challenge in resolving unfair labour practice complaints related to bargaining in bad faith. For example, it is often difficult to distinguish between a hardline bargaining stance and surface bargaining. If one party consistently rejects the proposals of the other party, it may be because the party genuinely believes that the proposals are unreasonable. Alternatively, it could be that the party is attempting to prolong the bargaining process, making it so unpleasant and difficult that the other party, in order to end the process, will eventually concede to conditions it ordinarily would have rejected. The labour relations board must sort through evidence from both parties—evidence that can be quite contradictory—to determine what has actually happened or what has actually motivated the parties' actions.

Since the principles of collective bargaining suggest that the parties should, as much as possible, negotiate freely without the interference of third parties, it is often difficult for a labour relations board to prescribe an appropriate remedy when allegations of bargaining in bad faith have been made. The board does not want to have to actively manage the negotiations between the parties, since this would contradict the principle of allowing the parties to negotiate freely. However, the labour relations board is charged with the responsibility of repairing the damage to the relationship between the parties if bargaining in bad faith has occurred, and that repair can sometimes only be achieved by the board's directing or suggesting how the parties should act when negotiating.

If a labour relations board determines that a party to negotiations has not bargained in good faith, the usual remedy is for the board to state clearly what behaviour is and is not "bargaining in good faith." This declaration is intended to give the parties behavioural guidelines to follow in their subsequent bargaining sessions. These guidelines may be suggested to the parties even if the board does not uphold the complaint of bargaining in bad faith, since the board may feel that giving such guidance may avert future complaints or questionable behaviour. If necessary, or possible, the board will repair whatever substantive damage was caused by the unfair labour practice; it will restore wages to pre-negotiation levels if a freeze was broken, for example, or require that an unjustly fired union member be rehired.

A labour relations board must also come up with a remedy when a complaint of bargaining in bad faith is made while parties are negotiating their first collective agreement. Most Canadian labour legislation permits a labour relations board to impose a collective agreement if the parties are not able to settle a collective agreement themselves. As we will see in the discussion of third-party involvement in negotiations in Chapter 10, such a solution is not ideal, since it takes the responsibility for creating the agreement away from the parties that will administer the agreement in the workplace. If later on there are problems in applying or carrying out the imposed agreement, the parties may blame the third party that created the agreement rather than take a more proactive approach to resolving the disputes.

However, there is good reason to allow a labour relations board to impose a first agreement. The imposition of an agreement will end the bargaining disputes between the parties; it is sometimes the only solution, particularly if the parties are inexperienced negotiators who lack the skills needed to resolve disputes on their own. The parties may still have disagreements, but at least there will be a collective agreement in place so that the workplace can continue to function. A labour relations board may use an imposed collective agreement in order to bring into line an employer who is resisting a union's presence by being stubborn in contract negotiations. If a reluctant employer refuses to meet with a union or refuses to consider the union's proposals, the imposition of a collective agreement will bypass that resistance and ensure that a collective agreement is in place. An employer that does not like the terms of the imposed agreement will be motivated to participate more seriously in future negotiations so that subsequent contract terms will be more to its liking.

SUMMARY

When certification is granted, the parties are in a legal position to begin bargaining for a collective agreement. Union security provisions ensure that the union is able to effectively represent its members in bargaining. These provisions can include mandatory dues deductions, religious exemptions, the Rand formula, the closed shop, which requires union membership as a condition of employment, and the hiring hall, which gives the union some control over work assignments.

Several variables underpinning the bargaining process are established before the bargaining actually begins. The bargaining structure determines who will participate in bargaining; there can be different combinations of unions, employers, and workplaces, although the most common structure involves a single union and a single employer. The composition of union and management bargaining teams is also important in determining how the bargaining process unfolds. Each team has representatives who provide various kinds of expertise and guidance during bargaining.

The union and management bargaining teams prepare for bargaining by identifying and prioritizing their own desired bargaining outcomes. The union bargaining team collects various kinds of information to determine bargaining priorities; it will, for example, examine surveys of the membership, events in previous rounds of bargaining, disputes resulting from the application of the existing collective agreement, and external information such as inflation rates and labour market statistics. The union bargaining team must balance its own perceptions of reasonable outcomes against what the membership hopes to achieve through bargaining. The union bargaining team must, however, remember that the membership will eventually have to ratify any collective agreement achieved through bargaining. The management team is not as formally accountable to those it represents, but it will still have to satisfy the demands of various internal and external shareholders.

Before the parties commence collective bargaining, they must be aware of the legal provisions that ensure that bargaining actually begins and that the parties bargain in good faith. Most Canadian labour codes set deadlines by which collective bargaining must begin; the deadline is usually based on the date that one party issued a formal notice to bargain to the other party. Bargaining in good faith requires that the parties bargain honestly and with the intent of concluding a collective agreement. Bargaining in bad faith is sometimes responsible for the parties' inability to agree on a first collective agreement. In this situation, most Canadian jurisdictions permit the labour relations board to impose a collective agreement.

In Chapter 8, we will continue our discussion of collective bargaining by describing what actually happens in negotiations.

KEY TERMS FOR CHAPTER 7

accreditation (p. 238)

bargaining council (p. 239)

bargain in good faith (p. 252)

Boulwarism (p. 253)

closed shop (p. 233)

dues check-off (p. 232)

employers' council (p. 238)

freeze (p. 254)

hiring hall (p. 234)

management rights clause (p. 242)

notice to bargain (p. 244)

pattern bargaining (p. 237)

Rand formula (p. 233)

religious exemption (p. 233)

surface bargaining (p. 253)

union shop (p. 233)

union security (p. 232)

whipsawing (p. 237)

DISCUSSION QUESTIONS FOR CHAPTER 7

1. Most Canadian labour codes require that a collective agreement be a minimum of one year in length. Why do you think this provision exists?

2. Despite the fact that collective bargaining is one of the most important activities in labour relations, labour relations legislation concentrates mostly on establishing the conditions under which bargaining will proceed. Why do you think the legislation says relatively little about the bargaining process itself?

3. Identify the members of the union's and the employer's bargaining teams and discuss the reasons for each member's participation.

4. Why do labour codes generally require that wages and working conditions remain frozen during collective bargaining?

5. An employer presents an initial offer to a union and then makes minimal changes in response to the union's concerns. Is this bargaining in good faith? Why or why not?

6. Why is the issue of bargaining in good faith particularly important in negotiations for a first collective agreement?

CASE *7-1*

CEDAR BRANCH AND GOVERNMENT EMPLOYEES UNION

(Based on *Rok Tree [1999] Ltd. and N.B.G.E.U Local 27*, 2000)

The Government Employees Union has recently been certified as the bargaining agent for a local of workers at a city hotel. The union has now filed a complaint alleging bargaining in bad faith on the part of the hotel owner—specifically, that the owner had refused to make a reasonable effort to conclude a collective agreement and had refused to consider proposals by the union and to make any counter-proposals.

Background to the Case

Cedar Branch is an incorporated company that owns a hotel in eastern Canada. The owner of the company, Mr. Sing Yu, is from Asia and has lived in Canada for less than one year. By his own admission, Mr. Sing has considerable difficulty communicating in the English language.

On July 26, 1999, the Government Employees Union was certified as the bargaining agent for employees of the hotel. On August 18, 1999, the union, following the provisions of the provincial labour act, issued a "notice to bargain." The employer and the union agreed to meet on September 21, but on September 20, Mr. Sing requested that the meeting be rescheduled to October 15.

On October 15, the parties met at the hotel. Testimony by a union representative present at the meeting indicated that the meeting lasted no more than five minutes. The union presented Mr. Sing with a proposal that was based on the collective agreement the union had negotiated with another hotel in the same city. Mr. Sing did not have a proposal to present. He was asked if he would like the union representatives to review the proposal that was being presented, but he refused. He told the union representatives that if they wanted to negotiate they would have to give him a copy of the proposal translated into his native language. He then stated that he would not negotiate with the union representatives unless they gave him some money. The union representatives explained to Mr. Sing the ways that their negotiations could proceed, suggesting that the negotiations might eventually involve the use of a conciliator, and Mr. Sing stated that he was not going to negotiate.

On November 5, 1999, the union filed an unfair labour practice complaint with the labour relations board. Upon receiving notification of the complaint, Mr. Sing contacted the board's office and explained that he would have difficulty following proceedings conducted in English. The board attempted to find someone fluent both in English and in Mr. Sing's native language to act as a translator. Because of the difficulty in finding people in the area who spoke Mr. Sing's language fluently, the board's hearing of the case had to be postponed for two weeks. The board finally found a local university student whose family spoke Mr. Sing's language at home, and Mr. Sing acknowledged that with the student's help he would be able to understand the proceedings.

The Employer's Position

Mr. Sing testified at the hearing that he understood only basic English and could not understand the terminology in the proposal given to him by the union. He said that this was the reason he had asked the union to have the document translated into his native language; he would not sign any document that he did not understand. He said that the union was pressuring him to negotiate by suggesting that if the negotiations went to the labour board, things would be more "difficult." He said that he had asked the union to give him money because he could not afford to pay the wages the union was asking for and he would not be able to meet those demands unless the union helped him.

In response to questions by the union's lawyer, Mr. Sing acknowledged that the process of incorporating his company and the financial transactions relating to the hotel's purchase had all been conducted in English. However, Mr. Sing explained that he had relied upon his English-speaking lawyer to guide him through these procedures. He said that he could not afford a lawyer to assist him during the process of negotiating a collective agreement.

Mr. Sing also stated that the government had encouraged him to come and invest in Canada, but now was telling him that it was his own problem if he encountered difficulties because he could not speak fluent English. He suggested that it was a form of discrimination to present him with a proposal he could not understand and then to insist that he negotiate a collective agreement. He said that it was not possible for him to negotiate and that if there was no other recourse he would close the business.

The Union's Position

The union's lawyer argued that it was the employer's actions that had caused the negotiations to last just four or five minutes. The employer's demand that the proposal be translated into his native language had made a full discussion impossible, and thus, the lawyer stated, the employer had failed in his statutory obligation to "make every reasonable effort" to conclude a collective agreement. The union's lawyer suggested that if Mr. Sing had had problems with a non-translated document, he could have made an effort to obtain his own translation. The lawyer also stated that the union would be sympathetic to Mr. Sing's language difficulties if they felt he was acting in good faith, but their perception was that he was relying on his language difficulties to avoid bargaining in good faith.

CASE 7-2

FIBERGLASCO AND MANUFACTURING WORKERS OF AMERICA

(Based on *Plaza Fiberglas Manufacturing Ltd. and U.S.W.A*, 1990)

The union has filed a complaint with the labour relations board alleging that the employer has breached its duty to bargain in good faith. The union alleges that the employer has sent representatives to the bargaining table who were uninformed about the bargaining issues and who did not have the authority to conclude an agreement.

Background to the Case

The employer is a manufacturing plant that makes fibreglass parts used in automobile production. The company named as employer is one of three companies owned and operated by the same person, Mrs. Smith. The companies were founded by Mrs. Smith's late husband. Since his death, she has controlled all three companies and overseen their day-to-day operations.

The union filed an application for certification for all three companies in late 1985. At the same time as the union filed the certification application, it also filed an unfair labour practice complaint requesting that certification be granted without a representation vote because of alleged interference by the employer. The alleged interference was the employer's refusal to post the required notice informing employees that a certification application had been filed. The request for certification at one company was turned down because there were no employees at the address named. The other two companies were certified after the union and employer agreed to settle all the outstanding issues between them. The first collective agreement was negotiated and signed in late 1986.

The start of negotiations for the next collective agreement was delayed because the parties were unable to find meeting times when representatives of both the union and the employer could be present. Negotiations for the second collective agreement finally began in summer 1988, but they broke down not long after they started. Further talks were held with the assistance of a third party (a conciliator), but these sessions failed to help the parties reach agreement. The parties were in a legal strike/lockout position in mid-November 1988. A lockout eventually took place, but just before it began, the employer moved some of its production to a location not covered by the certification order.

During the negotiations and the conciliation sessions, the employer was represented by a three-member negotiating team: a lawyer (who was occasionally replaced by another lawyer from the same firm), the company's accountant, and the company's personnel manager. Mrs. Smith, the owner, attended the first negotiation session but did not attend any subsequent sessions. She was, however, present at some of the negotiation sessions which were held with the conciliator's assistance.

The Employer's Position

The lawyer on the employer's negotiating team testified that he had advised Mrs. Smith not to attend any negotiation meetings after the first session but to wait until the conciliator was present before attending negotiations again. He felt that there would be a better chance of reaching an agreement if a "low key" neutral third party were present.

Mrs. Smith testified that she had not attended any negotiation sessions after the first one because she "did not care for the attitude" of the union's chief negotiator and had felt that he had insulted her.

Testimony to the board indicated that Mrs. Smith had met with the employer's negotiating team at the start of negotiations to discuss the union's proposals. Mrs. Smith testified that each item in the proposals had been dealt with separately during these discussions and that there had been an understanding that "once it was decided whether an item was negotiable or non-negotiable," the team would have to act in accordance with that determination during the negotiations. At least one member of the team met with Mrs. Smith after each negotiation session, and she received the minutes of each meeting, prepared for her by the lawyer.

Mrs. Smith testified that she did not give the team the authority to reach an agreement because she felt the team members did not know enough about the plant's operations to agree to terms that would be suitable for the workplace.

The Union's Position

The union argued that the employer was bargaining in bad faith by sending a team to bargain that was uninformed about the company's plans. Other testimony to the board indicated that during negotiations the union specifically asked the employer's negotiating team whether the employer planned to relocate any of its production. The lawyer on the team testified that he had specifically asked Mrs. Smith this question and she had told him that there were no such plans. He had relayed this information to the union negotiators in response to their question. He testified that he subsequently did not become aware of any relocation plans. (Mrs. Smith testified that in mid-October she had instructed the lawyer that the company could no longer say it would not move production.)

The union also argued that the employer had breached its duty to bargain in good faith by sending negotiators to the bargaining table who did not have the authority to conclude or settle a collective agreement.

CASE 7-3

UNION OF MANUFACTURING WORKERS AND GENERAL STORE

(Based on *Raider Industries Inc. and Sask. Joint Board, R.W.D.S.U.*, 1997)

In this case, a newly certified union is engaged in collective bargaining with the employer for a first collective agreement. The company president has made comments regarding the progress of negotiations to shop stewards at two of the company's locations. Because of the nature of the comments, the union has made a complaint of bargaining in bad faith to the labour relations board. The union alleges that the president has used threats in an attempt to coerce the union into settling the agreement. The union has also asked that a third party be appointed to assist in the conclusion of the first collective agreement.

Background to the Case

The union was certified at one location of General Store in 1995. The union had alleged that the employer had engaged in unfair labour practices during the organizing campaign, but the board had dismissed the allegations. The certification has since been expanded to include employees at a General Store location in another community. The union made one previous complaint to the labour relations board about the employer failing to bargain collectively, alleging that the employer would not bargain over the creation of a particular job classification. The board upheld that complaint.

The current two complaints result from conversations that Mr. Williams, the president of the company, had with shop stewards at each of the two certified locations. The first conversation occurred in late June 1996. Williams approached Mr. Jones, a shop steward who was on the union negotiating team. Jones was engaged in his job duties at the time that Williams approached him in the workplace. According to Jones, Williams asked Jones why the union was threatening to apply to the labour relations board for the imposition of a first collective agreement. Jones responded by saying that the union was frustrated by the lack of progress in negotiations. Williams then told Jones that if the contract was decided by the labour relations board and he (Williams) did not like the contract, he would move the company to the United States. Jones testified to the board that he felt that these comments put the negotiating team in a position of having to decide the entire fate of the company. Jones also noted that Williams appeared to be upset, and Jones had encouraged him to speak to the union's staff representative.

Jones told the board that he is one of the most senior employees of General Store and had no union experience prior to the certification. He stated that his conversation with Williams lasted approximately 45 minutes and that it interrupted his work, which was a concern because he is paid on a piece-rate basis. He also told the board that the conversation took place the day after two bargaining sessions had concluded and that a conciliator had been present at every bargaining session except for one or two.

When queried about Williams's knowledge of the union's plans, Jones said that the union had told the conciliator of its intention to seek an imposed first collective agreement, but he did not think that any member of the union negotiating team had informed Williams directly of the union's plan. The employer's lawyer suggested that since the majority of General Store's shareholders lived in the United States, Williams was expressing a concern that the shareholders might decide to move the company to the United States if there were an unfavourable first agreement. Jones responded that he thought Williams was speaking of his own intentions as a shareholder and as president.

The second conversation took place at General Store's other certified location. Williams approached Mr. Jarvis to discuss Jarvis's return to work after an injury that had kept him off the job for several months. During the conversation, Williams asked another manager present to leave the meeting and, according to Jarvis, then told Jarvis that there was something he (Williams) "wanted to get off his chest." Williams told Jarvis that "they" (he and Jarvis) had to settle the contract because the American-based shareholders were tired of the lengthy contract talks. Williams also stated that the contract problems would not affect Williams or his family. However, he added, if there was a strike, the company, presumably including himself, would move across the border.

Jarvis testified that Williams said that the company could easily get out of the lease on the building it currently occupied at Jarvis's work location. Williams indicated that the only people who would "suffer" from the bargaining were the 150 members of the bargaining unit. Williams further stated that there were several items in the company's proposed contract that the company "needed," and if the company did not achieve these items, it would move to the United States. Williams added that no business plans would be put in place until the contract was resolved, including the opening of another retail outlet.

Jarvis told the board that he had worked for General Store for nearly 12 years and was chief shop steward in his work location in addition to being a member of the union negotiating team. He estimated that the parties had participated in 23 bargaining sessions and that only five or so of these had taken place without a conciliator present. He stated that it was the union that had applied for conciliation in late 1995, but acknowledged that the employer had agreed to participate in conciliation soon thereafter.

No one testified for the employer in relation to the allegation of unfair labour practices.

The Union's Position

The lawyer representing the union argued that Williams's conversations with the two employees were intended to intimidate and threaten them. He alleged that Williams's intent in making his statements was to have the union alter its bargaining positions or else take the responsibility for the company moving to the United States, with a loss of 150 jobs. The lawyer also stated that the relevant labour legislation clearly indicates that bargaining information from the employer is to be relayed directly to the union negotiating team and not to individual employees. He also alleged that the president's comments were intended to weaken the shop stewards' support for the positions taken by the union negotiating team, and thereby undermine the union in bargaining.

The Employer's Position

The lawyer representing the employer said that there was nothing in the labour relations legislation that restricted the bargaining process to "committee to committee" discussions. He characterized Williams's two conversations as "a legitimate part" of the bargaining process, where one party is conveying information to another through discussions with individual bargaining team members. In regard to Williams's conversation with Jones, the lawyer stated that Jones knew that Williams was referring to the views of the American-based shareholders and was simply expressing his concerns that these shareholders would move the company across the border if they did not like the contract. He characterized Williams's comments in the two conversations as attempts to influence the two employees, not to intimidate or coerce them.

The lawyer for the employer argued that there was no evidence indicating that the employer was dealing directly with employees or communicating inappropriately with employees. He noted that the company had not refused to meet with the union or to bargain with the union.

R e f e r e n c e s

[1] E.g., *British Columbia Hydro and Power Authority and Office and Technical Employees Union Local 378 and Tottle* (BCLRB No. 9/78).

[2] Budd, J.W. (1992). The determinants and extent of UAW pattern bargaining. *Industrial & Labor Relations Review, 45(3)*, 523–540.

[3] Budd, *op. cit.*

[4] Babson, S. (2000). Cross-border trade with Mexico and the prospect for worker solidarity: the case of Mexico. *Critical Sociology, 26(1/2)*, 13–36.

[5] Fiorito, J., and Stepina, L.P. (1997). Visions of success: national leaders' views on union effectiveness. *Labor Studies Journal, 22(1)*, 3–20.

[6] Hammer, T.H., and Wazeter, D.L. (1993). Dimensions of local union effectiveness. *Industrial & Labor Relations Review, 46(2)*, 302–320; Mellor, S., and Mathieu, J.E. (1999). A discriminant validity study of aggregate-level constructs and measures of local union formalization, centralization and innovation. *Journal of Psychology, 133(6)*, 669–684.

[7] McShane, S.L. (1986). The multidimensionality of union participation. *Journal of Occupational Psychology, 59(2)*, 177–187.

[8] Hunt, G. (1997). Sexual orientation and the Canadian labour movement. *Relations Industrielles, 52(4)*, 787–809.

[9] Mellor and Mathieu, *op. cit.*

Tenants face trashy time as talks collapse:

A long summer ahead

MONTREAL—Tenants of low-cost housing buildings across the city are staring at a summer without maintenance and repairs as talks have broken down again in the nine-month-old strike by 125 employees of the Office municipal d'habitation de Montréal who do those jobs.

The maintenance employees, who belong to the same union as City of Montreal and Montreal Urban Community blue-collar workers, earned an average $32,440 in 1997. Their principal demand is to reduce their schedule to a four-day 35-hour workweek.

The housing office has offered to pay a 2 percent wage increase on signing a deal and to add the equivalent of 6 percent by reducing the workweek to 37 1/2 hours from 40. That would mean an 8 percent increase for all the 125 employees, while 85 of them would also benefit from another 22 percent increase by getting parity with Quebec public service increases later on.

The offer would cost about $1 million, the housing office said.

Michel Perreault, director of building management services for the housing office, said the housing office is ready to consider reducing the workweek to 35 hours—but only if the union makes proposals first to increase worker productivity to cover the cost of reduced hours.

That's where talks ended three weeks ago, but the union hasn't come back with a response yet, he said.

For its part, the union accused the housing office of ending talks by changing its position on points that were already agreed to.

There's no deadline for the two sides to go back to the negotiating table.

(*Gazette* [Montreal], May 11, 1999)

chapter 8

THE COLLECTIVE BARGAINING PROCESS

objectives

After the union and management bargaining teams have determined their respective goals and priorities, they are ready to negotiate and make every reasonable effort to conclude a collective agreement. This chapter outlines the negotiation stages, negotiation sub-processes, and the strategies and tactics that each side uses to reach a collective agreement. We will also look at two alternatives to the traditional process of negotiation. At the end of this chapter, you should be able to:

- define the stages that negotiations go through
- describe the sub-processes that occur within negotiation stages
- understand how each side in negotiations acquires bargaining power
- outline an alternative model for union-management negotiations

INTRODUCTION

In Chapter 7, we described how unions and employers prepare for collective bargaining. As we noted in that chapter, union-management negotiations are regulated by legislation outlining how often negotiations must occur and requiring certain terms in the resulting collective agreement. Beyond the legislative framework, however, the "how" of negotiations is not easily captured. Union-management negotiations usually proceed through specific stages:

- the pre-negotiation stage
- the stage of establishing the negotiating range
- the stage of narrowing the negotiating range
- the crisis stage
- the ratification stage

After briefly outlining the basic process of negotiation, we will describe each of these stages in turn and the sub-processes that may occur in each stage.

HOW DO NEGOTIATIONS WORK?

As described in Chapter 7, the negotiation process begins when one side issues a formal notice to bargain to the other side. Legislation in most Canadian jurisdictions specifies a deadline by which negotiations must begin after the notice to bargain has been issued. The parties must then agree on when to have their first joint bargaining meeting.

At the initial meeting, each party introduces the members of its negotiating team. The teams exchange written proposals and demands, and decide when the next joint meeting will be. After the meeting adjourns, each negotiating team holds its own private meetings to discuss the other team's proposals and demands and to formulate a response.

At the second and subsequent joint meetings, each team makes counter-proposals and uses a variety of strategies and tactics to uncover the other team's real goals and priorities. These meetings continue until an agreement is reached or an impasse is declared.

When an agreement is reached, each team must go to its constituency or stakeholders and obtain their approval before the agreement can become official. If an impasse is declared (i.e., the parties do not believe they can settle on a mutually accept-able agreement), the parties may elect to take a short break from negotiating or to ask for the intervention of a third party to help them overcome the impasse. The union may choose to undertake a strike, or the employer may choose to undertake a lockout. The intent of each of these actions is to make the parties return to the bargaining table so that an agreement can be concluded.

STAGES OF UNION-MANAGEMENT NEGOTIATIONS

Although the process described in the previous section sounds relatively straightfor-ward, it can unfold over varied periods of time and with varying degrees of cooperation or hostile conflict. Despite this variability, however, studies of union-management nego-tiations have noted the remarkable similarity in the stages of negotiations in most cir-cumstances, despite the fact that every set of negotiations occurs in a different setting and involves distinct issues.[1] The process of union-management negotiations com-mences with the pre-negotiation stage, discussed in Chapter 7, in which each party pre-pares its priorities for negotiations. The actual negotiations proceed through three spe-cific stages: the stage of establishing the negotiating range, the stage of narrowing the bargaining range, and the crisis stage preceding the decision to settle or to invoke eco-nomic sanctions such as a strike or lockout.[2] It is not always possible to define clearly when one stage has ended and another has begun, but for the parties to reach an agree-ment, it is important that the negotiations progress through each of these three stages. Aborting or short-circuiting any stage in the negotiation process can cause the process to end abruptly or to fail to produce an agreement. To elaborate on these stages further, we will outline the events that occur in each of them.

Pre-negotiation Stage

In this stage, each side determines its priorities, goals, and ultimate proposals for the upcoming negotiations. As discussed in Chapter 7, the parties accomplish this by collect-ing information from a variety of sources and developing a laundry list of proposals. Some proposals are considered essential, while others—once negotiations have begun—may be traded or "dropped off the table" in exchange for agreement on more important proposals.

Still other proposals may be included to introduce the other side to issues that may become important in future bargaining. A long and inclusive list of proposals disguises real priorities and enhances each side's relationship with its own constituents by demonstrating to them that their negotiating team has heard and responded to their concerns.

It is common for the two sides to agree to meet jointly during the pre-negotiation stage to sound each other out informally on negotiating protocol and procedures. The purpose of these pre-negotiation informal meetings is to ensure that the negotiations themselves do not get bogged down in procedural wrangling. It is also a more efficient use of the parties' time to agree on procedural and protocol issues before negotiations begin, so that the time scheduled for negotiations can actually be spent in bargaining.

Establishing the Negotiating Range

This stage of bargaining typically begins at the first formal bargaining session where all the representatives of both parties are present. In this stage, both parties introduce their bargaining team members and present their proposals. Usually, the chief negotiator for each side orally presents the rationale for each proposal to the other side. These oral presentations are vigorous, spirited, and sometimes aggressive, because the negotiator is expressing the views of that side's members or constituencies. While the presentations are often characterized by emotional and even extreme rhetoric, the chief negotiators actually have a respectful and professional relationship with one another. The two negotiators may know each other from other negotiation scenarios and may perhaps have represented their respective parties in earlier negotiations within the same organization. Experienced negotiators know that bargaining will not proceed smoothly if the negotiators alienate each other at the first meeting. They also realize that a forceful presentation is expected of a chief negotiator, and they will thus not be personally offended by aggressive statements.

These oral presentations serve several purposes. One is to establish the bargaining range by identifying the issues of

Executives from General Motors Canada meet with CAW representatives as they prepare for the first bargaining session for a new contract.

importance to each side and stating what each side initially intends to achieve on these issues. The chief negotiator will typically outline the issue and attach an offer to the issue; for example, in presenting the issue of salaries, the chief negotiator will indicate the desired salary range. (Keep in mind that these are initial offers, and what the union or the employer is actually willing to settle for will likely not be fully revealed at this point.) Another purpose of these presentations is to demonstrate the degree of commitment each side has to its own positions. A spirited presentation indicates that the union or the employer is serious about its proposals and is willing to work to achieve the desired outcomes. Finally, these presentations provide an opportunity for each side to explain the reasoning behind its proposals and positions and thereby influence the perceptions and expectations of the other side. Giving some background on why a proposal is reasonable is a way to persuade the other side that the proposal should be adopted. This information also gives the other side some basis for its counter-proposals, for if counter-proposals are to be successful, they must address the reasoning used to support the original proposal.

Narrowing the Bargaining Range

The activities in the stage when the bargaining range is narrowed are perhaps best illustrated by the **zone of agreement** model.[3] Figure 8-1 gives an example of how the zone of agreement dictates each side's decisions in narrowing the bargaining range and, ultimately, whether the parties do or do not reach an agreement.

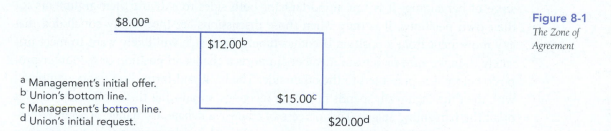

Figure 8-1
The Zone of Agreement

$8.00[a]

$12.00[b]

$15.00[c]

$20.00[d]

[a] Management's initial offer.
[b] Union's bottom line.
[c] Management's bottom line.
[d] Union's initial request.

Note: Management's initial offer is $8.00/hr. and its bottom line is $15/hr. The union's initial offer is $20/hr. and its bottom line is $12/hr. In this case, the zone of agreement is between $12/hr. and $15/hr.

Source: Adapted from R.E. Walton and R.B. McKersie, *A behavioral theory of labor negotiations: an analysis of a social interaction system.* (New York, NY: McGraw-Hill, 1963).

As Figure 8-1 demonstrates, each team enters negotiations (if it is well prepared) with an initial offer and a **bottom line** position for each proposed item. The initial offer is the first proposal given to the other side, and it is usually the team's most optimistic outcome for that item. Some initial offers may seem outlandish, but because there is always a chance that the other side will accept the initial proposal, it is common for an initial offer to represent the team's "dream" outcome for that item. In contrast, the bottom line position is the absolute minimum or maximum that the team would be willing to accept as a settlement for that item.

Figure 8-1 uses the wages issue to demonstrate how the zone of agreement affects bargaining behaviour. The initial offers of the two sides are far apart, which usually inspires the negotiators to consider offers that are more realistic and therefore possibly mutually acceptable. During the stage of narrowing the bargaining range, both sides start to retreat from their original positions in an attempt to find a point where a mutually satisfactory resolution can be reached. As Figure 8-1 shows, the terms of agreement on wages must not exceed the employer's or drop below the union's bottom line; terms that do will not be accepted, since the bargaining teams have not been authorized by their constituencies to agree to any term inferior to their agreed minimum. It is also apparent that for the zone of agreement to result in a settlement, there must be some overlap of both sides' positions. If there is no zone of agreement, either there will be no settlement or each team must adjust its bottom line, based on its perception of what the other side would be willing to agree to in order to achieve an agreement.

The timing of counter-proposals and **concessions** (i.e., deciding to agree to the other side's proposal or to adjust one's own position) is crucial during the narrowing stage of bargaining. It is first important for both sides to exhaust their arguments for their own positions. It is only when those discussions are thoroughly concluded that any movement from a position becomes timely. Each side will likely want to meet privately to make sure each team member supports a change in position or a counter-proposal before it is presented to the other side. The back-and-forth discussion, combined with the time each team spends in private meetings, means that this is often the longest of all the bargaining stages. This process of extensive debate, exchange of counter-proposals, concessions, and agreement on mutually acceptable positions continues, often issue by issue, until the crisis stage is reached.

The Crisis Stage

During the **crisis** stage of negotiations, one or both sides must decide whether to settle or whether to use economic sanctions such as a strike or lockout to pressure the other side into agreeing to its demands. The decision to settle or to invoke economic sanctions can be triggered by disputes over a single issue or disputes over a "package" deal involving several interrelated items.

By the time this stage of negotiations is reached, each side has argued extensively and tensions have increased. Hard and difficult decisions must now be made. Experienced negotiators view the noticeable rise in the tension level as confirmation that they have narrowed the bargaining range and are entering the crisis stage.

The process of invoking a strike or lockout is discussed in detail in Chapter 9. The purpose of one side undertaking such action as a negotiating tactic is to place such a heavy financial burden on the other side that the other side will eventually "give in" to bargaining demands. The use of these tactics can make the crisis stage short or lengthy, depending on the strength of the parties' resolve to resist pressure and the amount of resources they have to support their operations during a strike or lockout. However, once the desired concession occurs, both sides will settle on the terms and conditions of a collective agreement and recommend acceptance of the tentative agreement to their members or shareholders.

Ratification

Once mutually acceptable contract terms are agreed upon, both sides face the necessity of **ratification**. During ratification, the negotiating teams return to the constituencies they represent and present the negotiated contract terms for the constituencies' approval. Management negotiators have diverse stakeholders, such as the employer's finance, marketing, and production departments, and must satisfy the concerns of each in the ratification stage. As well, the management negotiator will want to have satisfied specific needs related to operational efficiency. The negotiated terms should not make the organization less efficient or less productive. The union faces similar challenges in presenting the negotiated terms to its membership. The union negotiators will want to have satisfied the legitimate and specific needs of bargaining unit members around issues such as job security and workplace equity, and they must assure members that the negotiated contract terms address these issues.

The actual process of ratification is under the control and direction of each side. Generally, the union will conduct a vote among its membership on whether or not to accept the negotiated agreement, and management will contact all relevant stakeholders to ensure that the terms of the negotiated agreement are acceptable. A major influence on the ratification process is the bargaining structure. For example, if a number of employers have bargained together, the ratification process would involve the acceptance of contract terms by all the employers represented in the negotiations. As well, if a number of unions representing different employees of a single employer have negotiated together, the ratification vote would include bargaining unit members from each of the unions. If one side rejects the negotiated agreement, the parties will have to return to the bargaining table and attempt to fashion an agreement that is acceptable to all constituencies. Once the ratification from each side has been completed, representatives from each side officially sign the collective agreement to bring it into legal effect.

A summary of the bargaining stages is presented in Table 8-1. Having outlined these stages, we will now discuss the sub-processes within each stage that influence how teams behave during that stage. We noted earlier that it is not always possible to determine when one bargaining stage concludes and another begins; likewise, within each stage, it is not always easy to identify which sub-processes are present. The sub-processes can occur independently of each other or simultaneously; in addition, not every sub-process is present in every bargaining situation.

TABLE 8-1 The Stages of Bargaining

Pre-negotiation	Parties determine and prioritize bargaining issues and determine desired outcomes.
	Informal meetings are held to determine bargaining procedure and protocol.
Establishing bargaining range	Parties meet and exchange initial offers.
	Parties adjust expectations based on other side's offers.
Narrowing the bargaining range	Parties discuss offers and develop and exchange counter-proposals.
Crisis	Parties disagree over items.
	One side may decide to start strike or lockout to pressure other side into agreeing to its terms.
	One side must agree to other side's proposal for crisis stage to be resolved, upon which parties settle an agreement.
Ratification	Parties take the agreement to their constituencies for approval.

NEGOTIATION STAGES AND NEGOTIATION SUB-PROCESSES

We have seen that union-management negotiations progress through a series of distinct stages. However, within each stage, we can also identify sub-processes that influence the parties' behaviour in that stage. R.E. Walton and R.B. McKersie[4] present a theoretical framework that is useful in helping us understand participants' behaviour during the negotiation process. Within this framework, four sets of activities are identified as negotiation sub-processes. After first exploring how these stages and sub-processes ebb and flow, merge and mesh, throughout the negotiation process, we will discuss each sub-process in detail.

The Sub-Processes within Each Bargaining Stage

In the pre-negotiation stage, several sub-processes can be identified. The first is **intra-organizational bargaining**, the sub-process in which each side's negotiators seek to achieve consensus within each bargaining team and within the organization each team represents. As we have seen, bargaining teams must first decide which of the various and often conflicting demands will be addressed in bargaining, and then assign the priority each demand should receive. This process often causes conflict within the bargaining team and the organization. Intra-organizational bargaining is the sub-process through which the bargaining team achieves its own consensus on bargaining priorities and obtains the support of the organization for the decisions it has made.

In their separate pre-negotiation meetings, each side also engages in the **attitudinal structuring** sub-process. This sub-process has to do with the formation of each side's attitude toward the other side and each side's attitude toward the relationship between the bargaining teams. Attitudinal structuring can result in positive attitudes if one side perceives that the other side will be relatively receptive to its proposals and that bargaining will be relatively speedy and cooperative. On the other hand, attitudinal structuring can have negative outcomes if one side perceives that the other side will be hostile and is likely to cause conflict in bargaining. Whether attitudinal structuring results in positive or negative attitudes depends on such factors as each team's knowledge of or experience with members of the other team, each team's perception of how difficult it will be to negotiate the identified issues, and any previous bargaining history shared by the two sides. The sub-process of attitudinal structuring also includes the adjustment of perceptions that have already been formed. For example, if one team member shares with his or her team previously unknown information about members of the other team, that information can alter the attitudes of all team members. The sub-process of attitudinal structuring affects the degree of trust each side feels toward the other side as well as the basic relationship between the teams; thus, its results can have a significant effect on the subsequent success of the bargaining process.

In the pre-negotiation stage, both sides also determine which items in their proposals are potentially suitable for the **integrative bargaining** sub-process. In integrative bargaining, the two sides try to resolve some of the issues by identifying common interests and thereby influencing the joint gain or "win-win" available to each side. In other words, during the integrative bargaining sub-process, the parties focus on what they have in common, rather than on where they differ, and try to develop solutions that benefit both sides, rather than having one party "win" and the other party "lose." Bargaining teams may attempt to identify items that would be appropriate for integrative bargaining, or they may seek to identify potential solutions to items that would result in gains for both sides. Making these identifications before the negotiations begin helps the parties go into bargaining with a cooperative rather than a conflictual attitude; this also gives the parties a proactive, problem-solving perspective on the entire bargaining process.

Finally, each side will identify bargaining items that are suitable for **distributive bargaining**. In the distributive bargaining sub-process, the two sides compete with one another over the division of limited resources. In this sub-process, when one side wins, the other side loses. When one negotiating team feels that it cannot compromise its desired outcomes for certain bargaining items, distributive bargaining may be the only way in which differences over desired outcomes can be resolved.

Different sub-processes become apparent during different stages of negotiations. The intra-organizational and attitudinal structuring sub-processes are most obvious during the negotiation stages of establishing and narrowing the bargaining range. The presentation and discussion of bargaining proposals during these stages affect each side's perceptions of, attitudes toward, and expectations of the other side. The integrative and distributive bargaining sub-processes, however, are more obvious during the narrowing of the bargaining range stage than during the establishing of the bargaining range stage, since the former involves determining which issues can be settled integratively and which must be settled distributively.

In the crisis stage, the distributive bargaining sub-process becomes more apparent as the parties move toward settlement of a collective agreement. The ratification stage is the closure stage for both sides, since this stage allows each side's members and constituents to have a say or vote on the resulting collective agreement.

Having identified the sub-processes and where they might occur during bargaining, we will now examine them in more detail, highlighting the strategies and tactics used while each sub-process is occurring.

The Intra-organizational Bargaining Sub-process

The intra-organizational bargaining sub-process involves the internal relationships that exist within each organization. It is thus distinct from the other three sub-processes, which involve external relationships between the union and management during negotiations.

It is through the intra-organizational bargaining sub-process that each bargaining team and the organization it represents reach internal agreement on bargaining priorities and strategies.[5] This process takes place prior to and sometimes during bargaining, although well-prepared bargaining teams attempt to reach internal agreement prior to the start of bargaining with the other side.

During the intra-organizational bargaining sub-process, two main types of internal conflict appear: role conflict and factional conflict. Role conflict occurs because there are conflicting expectations of each side's chief negotiator. There is an expectation that the negotiator will use all available strategies and tactics to secure the team's bargaining priorities, but there is also the expectation that the negotiator will respond to the other side's negotiator in a manner that does not jeopardize their professional relationship and hence the bargaining process itself. Thus, each side's negotiator has an internal leadership role within the organization he or she represents, as well as an external relationship role within the context of the negotiations. There may be conflict between these two roles because the behaviour and attitudes demanded by each of them may not be easy to reconcile. For example, if the chief negotiator acts respectfully toward the other side's chief negotiator when presenting important proposals, the members of his or her bargaining team may be upset because they would feel that the chief negotiator should be aggressive and forceful in this situation.

The second kind of conflict, factional conflict, develops within an organization when different groups have conflicting demands. As we have seen, different constituencies within the union or the employer may have different ideas about which issues should receive priority in bargaining. The result of these different ideas is disagreement within the organization over bargaining goals and priorities.

Negotiators can use a variety of strategies and tactics to manage role and factional conflict during intra-organizational bargaining.[6] These are outlined in Table 8-2. Although the intra-organizational bargaining sub-process primarily occurs during the pre-negotiation stage, role or factional conflict can arise at any time during the bargaining process, and the strategies and tactics outlined in Table 8-2 can be used during or after the pre-negotiation stage. These strategies and tactics are designed to facilitate the desired outcome of the intra-organizational bargaining sub-process: that is, to bring the expectations of the organization's members into alignment with the achievements of their negotiators.

TABLE 8-2 Strategies and Tactics for Resolving Role and Factional Conflict in the Intra-organizational Bargaining Sub-process

Avoiding incompatible expectations

- keeping the expectations of the organization's members vague and conservative
- focusing the members on specific objectives
- limiting the participation of members in union-management negotiations

Revising expectations

- ensuring that the organization's members are informed of the other side's counter-arguments
- using the negotiator's personal leadership power and prestige to generate support for bargaining strategies or priorities
- considering the impact of taking a strike or lockout vote

Rationalizing the result

- maintaining a laundry list of goals or priorities as camouflage for true intentions
- utilizing mediators, fact finders, or conciliators to save face by shifting accountability for decisions to a third party
- providing substitutes for any unmet expectations, goals, or priorities

Obscuring the result

- limiting participation in decision making to key members of the organization
- controlling communications during the final stage of negotiations
- emphasizing the importance of gains in negotiations

The Attitudinal Structuring Sub-process

One of the defining characteristics of the union-management negotiation process is the long-term relationship between the two parties. This relationship likely predates the bargaining process, and it continues to exist after the negotiations conclude, because the parties not only participate in collective bargaining, but also interact daily in the workplace and engage in other processes together, such as grievance resolution. Therefore, the quality of existing interpersonal relations affects how each side approaches the negotiation process as well as how the resulting collective agreement is administered. The attitudinal structuring sub-process is one part of the larger process that establishes the relationship patterns that define and shape each side's negotiation behaviour.

Prior to the start of negotiations, the relationship between the parties includes the following characteristics: [7]

- each side's motivation to be competitive or cooperative with the other side

- each side's attitudes and beliefs about the legitimacy of the other side's organization and leadership

- the level of trust each side has in the other side

- each side's feelings of friendliness or hostility toward the other side

Ideally, union-management negotiations should be conducted in an atmosphere of trust, respect, and openness, and this positive atmosphere should be maintained during the administration of the resulting collective agreement. The attitudinal structuring sub-process can assist in creating this atmosphere by confirming, or if necessary changing, each side's beliefs and perceptions of the other side.

The Integrative Bargaining Sub-process

In integrative bargaining, a gain for one side is also a gain for the other side and the resolution of goals, priorities, and demands results in a joint advantage for both sides. The integrative bargaining sub-process is different from the distributive bargaining sub-process in that the former deals with mutual problems, while the latter deals with more contentious issues.[8] Other major differences between these two sub-processes are outlined in Table 8-3.

TABLE 8-3 Differences Between the Distributive and Integrative Bargaining Sub-processes

	Distributive Bargaining	Integrative Bargaining
Type of item being negotiated	Issue	Problem
Focus of each party's strategy	Maximizing own gains	Mutual interests
Use of information bargaining	Use of selective disclosure to maintain own power	Sharing information to motivate resolution of problem
Spokesperson	Single spokesperson for each side to control disclosure and disguise bottom line	Committees have informal, exploratory discussions
Trust	Low level of trust because of adversarial positions	Higher level of trust because of shared interest and greater disclosure

When problems are under negotiation, the use of the integrative bargaining sub-process potentially permits both sides to win, since both sides are concerned with finding solutions to the problems. Integrative bargaining is often one of the elements of a "fostering strategy"[9] that is used to develop cooperation between the parties and that ultimately may create a better overall relationship and facilitate other parts of the bargaining process. Because integrative bargaining creates a cooperative atmosphere through its emphasis on the parties' shared interest in reaching a resolution to problems, those problems that can be solved through integrative bargaining are often addressed before the distributive issues are negotiated. This is done in the hope that the cooperative atmosphere will carry over into the discussion of the more contentious issues.

However, despite its cooperative nature, integrative bargaining can be a difficult sub-process in union-management negotiations.[10] This is because, in order for each side to realize its gain, the two sides must jointly decide how to divide the overall gain equitably. In this way, integrative bargaining becomes "distributive" in nature. The parties must address issues like equity in sorting out how gains are to be shared, and they may have different ideas about what makes an "equitable" division. Thus, the success of an integrative bargaining sub-process in solving problems can be blocked by either side's inability or unwillingness to agree to distributive solutions.

The strategies and tactics that are used to resolve disputes during integrative bargaining[11] are outlined in Table 8-4. The success of the integrative bargaining sub-process often depends on how well each side's chief negotiator handles the distinct and concurrent requirements of integrative bargaining and distributive bargaining.

TABLE 8-4 Strategies and Tactics for Resolving Disputes in the Integrative Bargaining Sub-process

---

Identifying the problem

- convening frequent negotiation sessions at the request of either side
- developing agenda items that have the potential for joint problem-solving, rather than presenting items in a format that requires resolution by individual parties
- formulating negotiation subjects as specific problems rather than as general, undefined concerns

---

Searching for alternative solutions

- giving advance notice of negotiation times
- using informal and exploratory discussions prior to exchanging formal proposals or formally bargaining
- sequencing agenda items with easily resolved items first to create a pattern of early success

---

Systematically comparing alternatives

- accurate reporting by each side of their preferences
- combining or dividing proposals to make patterns of agreement or disagreement more apparent
- considering remedial actions as part of a general solution in order to improve the relationship between the parties as well as to solve the problem

---

The Distributive Bargaining Sub-process

The most highly visible negotiation sub-process and the one most often associated with union-management negotiations is the distributive bargaining sub-process. In distributive bargaining, both sides are involved in a fundamental conflict over the allocation of a fixed amount of resources.[12] As a result, distributive bargaining is essentially adversarial in nature, since each side is committed to achieving maximum gain for itself. One of the parties may use distributive bargaining as part of a "forcing strategy" to achieve a desired change.[13] Distributive bargaining strategies are commonly used when wage and benefit issues are being negotiated. Unions are usually concerned with maximizing wages and benefits for their members, and management is usually concerned with minimizing costs. These are opposing goals, and therefore, a gain for one party means a loss for the other.

During the distributive bargaining sub-process, each side strives to collect and exchange whatever information might persuade the other side to agree to its demands. Each party will seek to collect and distribute this information in a manner that benefits its own side without unduly empowering the other side. A variety of strategies and tactics can be used in doing this, some of these are presented in Table 8-5.[14]

TABLE 8-5 Strategies and Tactics for Collecting and Controlling Information during the Distributive Bargaining Sub-process

Discovering the other side's bottom line

- observing non-verbal behavioural cues, such as facial expressions, to discern the other side's true intentions
- using probing and clarifying questions to elicit reactions to proposals
- using open-ended questions to determine the other side's interests

Disguising your own side's bottom line

- having a single spokesperson in order to present a unified front and to control the amount and kind of information that is revealed
- submitting a laundry list of proposals or demands to obscure actual priorities
- safeguarding all written material

TABLE 8-4 Continued

Persuading or pressuring the other side to move its bottom line

- making public pleas for support
- negotiating for long periods of time, exhausting the other side
- discussing cost implications

Emphasizing your commitment to a position

- repeating your demands
- invoking the reputation of your side to reinforce the legitimacy of your position
- raising the expectations of your side's membership to create support for your position

Blocking the other side's commitment to a position

- limiting opportunities for public commitment to a position
- minimizing opportunities for the other side to repeat its position
- ignoring any public commitments

The goals, priorities, and demands that are the basis of the distributive bargaining sub-process are considered central issues in most labour-management negotiations and in the ongoing relationship between the parties. Ultimately, the determination of these distributive issues—that is, who ends up winning—involves the use of bargaining power. We will now discuss the role of power in determining the outcomes of the bargaining process as a whole.

THE ROLE OF BARGAINING POWER IN UNION-MANAGEMENT NEGOTIATIONS

Distributive bargaining implicitly involves the use, implied use, or potential use of power.[15] The classic definition of **bargaining power**, in the context of the union-management negotiation process, is the measure of the ability of one side to secure the other side's agreement to its own terms.[16] The amount of bargaining power that each side holds in negotiations cannot be precisely measured, and the amount will vary depending on a number of factors, some of which may be unique to the particular set of issues being negotiated or to the specific parties involved in the negotiations.

Environmental, socio-demographic, and organizational factors, for example, can affect both parties' bargaining power.[17] Environmental factors affecting the amount of power held by each side include public opinion, legislation, and the economy. These can either decrease or increase each side's bargaining power, depending on whether they support or undermine a side's position or demands. For example, the public perception that a union is being greedy in its bargaining demands reduces the union's bargaining power because it gives the employer a reason to disagree with the union's proposals. The socio-demographic factors affecting bargaining power include the diversity of bargaining priorities among negotiators and their constituencies. When negotiators and their constituencies have the same bargaining priorities, their unity can increase the negotiators' bargaining power, particularly if the other party is aware of this unity and feels there is less unity on its own side. The organizational factors affecting bargaining power include the intra-organizational dynamics of both the union and management. Because unions and management interact daily in the workplace, each party is usually well aware of the internal disputes or conflicts within the other party and can exploit these problems to gain power in negotiations.

The sight and stench of garbage piled in Toronto streets in July 2002 caused many residents to insist that the provincial government force striking city workers back to work.

Other factors affecting bargaining power can be more specifically associated with either the employer's or the union's bargaining power.[18] Factors affecting the employer's bargaining power include the size of its inventory, the structure of its operation, its competitiveness, whether the business is seasonal, whether the business can operate during a strike, and the business's labour costs. For example, a large inventory would increase the employer's bargaining power because having a large stock of raw material available would allow a company to continue production during a strike or lockout during which regular deliveries of materials might be cut off.

Factors affecting the union's bargaining power include the strength of the union's commitment to specific issues, the union's access to funds for supporting strike activity, and the timing and effectiveness of a possible strike. For example, having access to extra funds for supporting locked-out union members would increase the union's bargaining power, since the funds would enable the union to resist the pressure of a lockout used by the employer as a bargaining tactic.

However, despite the role that bargaining power plays in determining bargaining outcomes, union-management negotiations involve much more than a clash of differing amounts of bargaining power. Integrative bargaining, as we have seen, is an important part of the negotiation process, and because it emphasizes mutually developed and mutually beneficial solutions to problems, it does not require one side or the other to exercise its bargaining power to achieve desired outcomes. However, as mentioned above, distributive bargaining requires the use of bargaining power to achieve outcomes, and it is the more common and more visible form of bargaining in most negotiations.

Although distributive bargaining is the sub-process most commonly used to achieve the eventual outcome of a completed collective agreement, its use can have damaging long-term effects on the relationship between the parties because of its competitive nature. In distributive bargaining, one party ends up failing to achieve its desired outcome; the resentment that may result may spill over into the parties' relationship long after negotiations have concluded. Thus, while distributive bargaining is commonly used, it is not the most positive (nor necessarily always the most effective) means of resolving bargaining disputes.

Because of the potentially harmful effects of distributive bargaining, a number of authors and researchers have proposed alternative models of negotiation that focus on building productive long-term relationships between unions and management, as well as on achieving the short-term goal of settling a collective agreement.

TWO ALTERNATIVE MODELS OF UNION-MANAGEMENT NEGOTIATIONS

In examining how the distributive and integrative bargaining sub-processes affect the parties' behaviour in negotiations, it becomes clear that the strategies and tactics used in these sub-processes are not always conducive to building a positive relationship between the parties involved. This shortcoming is significant because it may spell eventual disharmony in the workplace. The negotiation process is essentially a process of introducing changes to the workplace through revisions to the collective agreement. Most attempts to introduce change generate conflict—not only in the short term around specific proposals but also, potentially, in the long term. Conflict generated in negotiations can spill over into the workplace and generate further conflict there.

Ideally, the goal of maintaining a positive relationship between the parties should be emphasized through the negotiation process, but a number of historical, institutional, and economic realities work against the achievement of this goal. Union-management relationships are usually adversarial in nature because of the inherently different interests of the parties. As discussed in previous chapters, unions are concerned with protecting or improving their members' working conditions, while management is concerned with operating the workplace in an economically efficient manner. There is also a general acceptance of conflict as a way to obtain desired outcomes. This acceptance exists not only in the context of negotiations but also in society at large. In fact, a lack of conflict during negotiations may be perceived by either party, or by their constituencies, as an indication that bargaining is not being pursued with adequate commitment.

These realities must be acknowledged in the union-management negotiation process, a process that is generally emotional, hard fought, and characterized by distrust between the parties. However, negotiations often address mutual problems that are easily resolved in a "win-win" or cooperative manner and whose resolution does not require adversarial interactions. We will examine two alternative models of bargaining that attempt to emphasize cooperation, rather than confrontation, between the parties.

The Cost of Disputes Model

The "costs of disputes" model of union-management negotiations focuses on the interaction among the bargaining power, the interests, and the rights of each side, and how this interaction affects the costs associated with negotiating disputes.[19] **Interests** are the needs, wants, fears, concerns, desires, or other motivators that underlie a **position**, or the preferred outcome, of one side in negotiations. **Rights** are formal powers that are granted to the parties in a number of ways. Rights may be defined in the legislation governing collective bargaining, in any existing collective agreement, in other legislation (e.g., employment standards acts), or in **arbitral jurisprudence**, which is a body of decisions on legal cases dealing with the interpretation and/or application of collective agreement language.

The cost of disputes model outlines how interests, rights, and power interrelate during the bargaining process. The parties' differing interests are reconciled within the context of each side's rights and bargaining power; for example, while interest-based negotiations focus on mutual problem-solving, the party with more rights may be able to dominate the process and choice of outcome. The determination of each side's rights, also, takes place within the context of each side's bargaining power; the authority associated with one party's rights may be overshadowed by the bargaining power of a stronger party. As well, at any given stage in union-management negotiations, the context of negotiations may change, shifting to interests, rights, or bargaining power, depending on the issues being discussed and the power of each party to promote its interests or positions.

The cost of disputes model proposes that to assess the degree to which the interrelationship among rights, interests, and power has influenced the outcome of a bargaining dispute, we should analyse bargaining in terms of the costs incurred by the parties involved in the process. There are four criteria to consider in determining the amount of these costs: transaction costs, satisfaction with the outcome, the effect on relationships, and whether there has been a recurrence of a problem.

Transaction costs associated with negotiations include expenditures of time, money, resources, and emotional energy; they include as well the value of opportunities lost because of disagreement. In the specific context of union-management negotiations, transaction costs include the costs of striking, locking out, or attempting to operate during a strike.

The second criterion in evaluating the cost of bargaining, the level of satisfaction with the result of bargaining, depends upon how well the ultimate resolution fulfills each side's underlying interests. An unsatisfactory resolution will incur costs because it will be an inefficient resolution to disputed issues and will also cause frustration to the parties.

The third criterion for determining costs, the long-term effect of bargaining on the union-management relationship, is similar to the effect that the attitudinal structuring sub-process has on the union-management relationship. A poor relationship will be costly because it will lead to disputes between the parties; disputes are sometimes based more on the parties' dislike of each other than on any substantive problem.

The last criterion for determining costs, recurrence, relates to whether the negotiations produced an agreement that resolved the issues between the parties, or whether the problems recurred after ratification and during the administration of the new collective agreement. Recurring issues will be costly because of the expenses associated with their further resolution.

An evaluation of a bargaining process on the basis of these four criteria will indicate the overall costs incurred by the two parties in bargaining the disputes between them.[20]

The cost of disputes model suggests that, in general, the cost of disputing will be less when interests are reconciled within the context of rights and bargaining power.[21] In other words, the costs of disputes can be reduced if, in bargaining, the parties focus on interests rather than on issues that can only be resolved if they exercise their rights or bargaining power. Because interests involve common problems and mutually acceptable solutions, it will be ultimately less costly to deal with interest-based issues because better-quality solutions will be produced.

This model does not suggest that negotiations should ignore distributive issues or should persist in using interest-based bargaining techniques when it is apparent that no solution can be generated. The exercise of rights and bargaining power can sometimes bring about resolutions to disputes when interest-based negotiations cannot. But, ideally, a focus on interests, rather than on rights or power, in bargaining results in lower transaction costs, greater satisfaction with the resulting agreement, less strain on the ongoing relationship between the parties, and a lower recurrence of disputes.

The Mutual Gains Model of Bargaining

Over the last 20 years, both unions and employers have been actively searching for alternative models of negotiation—or solutions to bargaining issues—that would incorporate changing economic realities. While union-management negotiations are traditionally adversarial, many leaders on both sides are interested in collaborative arrangements that respect differences but search for common ground and win-win resolutions.[22]

A model of negotiations that is widely used to change both the focus of bargaining and its adversarial approach is the one proposed by R.E. Fisher and W.L. Ury.[23] Their model is referred to by several different names: principled negotiations, negotiation on the merits, mutual gains, or interest-based negotiations. In the context of union-management negotiations, it is most often called "mutual gains bargaining." The process of bargaining outlined by this model is similar to the distributive bargaining sub-process described earlier in this chapter.

The traditionally adversarial relationship between employer and employee is not the only model for collective bargaining. The mutual gains model focuses on cooperation and collaboration.

The mutual gains model of bargaining is founded on four principles that define a straightforward method of negotiations. These principles, with their corresponding actions, are as follows:

1. People: Separate the people from the problem.

2. Interests: Focus on interests, not positions.

3. Options: Generate a variety of possibilities before deciding what to do.

4. Criteria: Insist that the result of negotiations be based or evaluated on some objective standard.

There have been a number of attempts to change the adversarial model of union-management negotiations to a mutual gains model of bargaining.[24] Improving the collective bargaining relationship and the resulting collective agreement requires joint union-management training.[25] Joint union-management training has produced positive effects. Some participants say that their training in mutual gains bargaining has helped them to listen better, has helped them to avoid unproductive arguments, and has strengthened their trust in the other side by allowing them to gain a perspective on the other side's interests and positions.[26]

However, the results of various studies have indicated that there is, at best, an imperfect fit between mutual gains bargaining techniques in general and the specific demands of union-management negotiations.[27] Often, there is an inherent power imbalance between the parties and different perspectives on what constitutes an acceptable solution to an issue. These conditions can make it difficult to use the mutual gains model of bargaining, since the model emphasizes equality and commonality between the parties. Suggestions for improving the applicability of mutual gains bargaining to union-management negotiations include increasing the trust between the union and management sides, reshaping the roles and responsibilities of individuals on both negotiation teams, and changing the power balance (or imbalance) between the sides.

It has also been noted that adversarial conflicts in bargaining can be caused by the traditional bargaining model's division of issues into integrative bargaining and distributive bargaining. Three different approaches have been proposed to resolve the adversarial conflicts caused by having to deal with the differences between the distributive bargaining and integrative bargaining sub-processes.[28] First, each side should strive to establish a minimum degree of trust in and level of communication with the other side. Second, each side should determine a minimum level of acceptance of the other side.

Third, both sides should recognize the level of common dependency they share. These suggestions are intended to help the parties maintain a positive relationship, regardless of whether integrative or distributive bargaining is taking place.

The studies that have investigated mutual gains bargaining conclude that this bargaining method can lead to improvements in the attitudes generated by attitudinal structuring. As well, it can result in more innovative solutions during the integrative bargaining sub-process. However, a major transformation of the traditional structures of both unions and management will be required for a wider acceptance of mutual gains bargaining. Improved methods of implementation and practical suggestions for action are also needed to complement the mostly theoretical discussions of mutual gains bargaining. Without these changes, it will be difficult to institutionalize mutual gains bargaining techniques, even in circumstances where using these techniques would be potentially beneficial to both sides.

SUMMARY

In this chapter, we have attempted to describe what actually goes on in collective bargaining by outlining the basic process of bargaining and then identifying the sub-processes that take place during the various bargaining stages. Most negotiations begin with a pre-negotiation stage, during which the parties prepare their bargaining priorities. During the first few formal meetings of the negotiating teams, the parties enter the stage of establishing the bargaining range; here the parties determine the range of acceptable outcomes for each item presented at the bargaining table. The parties then narrow the bargaining range by exchanging proposals and counter-proposals on each item. Agreement on an item can only be reached if there is a zone of agreement or a set of possible solutions that would be acceptable to both sides. During the crisis stage, each party must decide whether to settle or whether to exert pressure on the other party to accept its demands. Finally, when a settlement is reached, the parties enter the ratification stage, where the negotiated agreement is presented to stakeholders for acceptance or rejection.

Within each of the bargaining stages, various sub-processes can be observed. In the pre-negotiation stage, intra-organizational bargaining shapes the parties' bargaining priorities and attitudinal structuring influences both the parties' attitude toward each other and their mutual relationship. During this stage, the parties may also identify which bargaining items are suitable for integrative and distributive bargaining. Intra-organizational bargaining and attitudinal sub-processes are also evident in the stages of establishing and narrowing the bargaining range, during which the parties exchange information and modify their expectations on the basis of solutions suggested by the other side. In the crisis stage, distributive bargaining ideally results in a satisfactory agreement and movement into the ratification stage.

The role of bargaining power is also important in determining bargaining outcomes. The amount of power that each party has and is able to use in negotiations can vary depending on a number of factors. Environmental conditions, socio-demographic factors, organizational factors, and the different kinds of resources available to both unions and management can affect how much power each party has and how much effect that power has on the outcome of negotiations.

Finally, because there are deficiencies in the way that collective bargaining is usually conducted, researchers have created alternative models of bargaining that encourage more positive relationships between the parties and better-quality solutions. The cost of disputes model identifies the effect on negotiations of interactions between bargaining power, interests, and rights. This model encourages negotiators to look at various financial and non-monetary costs incurred in bargaining and afterwards, and suggests that a focus on interests in bargaining will reduce those costs. The mutual gains model of bargaining uses four criteria and suggestions for action to encourage negotiations that concentrate on producing results that are satisfactory for both parties.

Our discussion of bargaining continues in Chapter 9, where we will describe strikes and lockouts in the context of the bargaining process.

KEY TERMS FOR CHAPTER 8

arbitral jurisprudence (p. 289)

attitudinal structuring (p. 278)

bargaining power (p. 286)

bottom line (p. 274)

concessions (p. 274)

crisis (p. 275)
distributive bargaining (p. 279)
integrative bargaining (p. 278)
interests (p. 289)
intra-organizational bargaining (p. 278)
position (p. 289)
ratification (p. 275)
rights (p. 289)
zone of agreement (p. 273)

DISCUSSION QUESTIONS FOR CHAPTER 8

1. Outline the stages of union-management negotiations.

2. What are the four sub-processes identified by Walton and McKersie?

3. Explain the link between bargaining stages and bargaining sub-processes.

4. Why is the zone of agreement important in negotiations?

5. The bargaining power of both sides is affected by a number of factors. Identify the factors that affect management's and the union's bargaining power.

6. Mutual gains bargaining is based on four principles. Identify these principles and explain what difference they make in the way a negotiation process is conducted.

7. What criteria can be used to assess the cost of disputes in negotiations?

CASE *8-1*

EUROAIR AND ASSOCIATION OF FLIGHT WORKERS

(Based on *Iberia Airlines of Spain and Canadian Union of Public Employees [airline division]*, 1990)

This case involves allegations by the union that the employer is violating the duty to bargain in good faith by practicing "surface bargaining" and refusing to bargain unless the union withdraws an unfair labour practice complaint.

Background to the Case

The Association of Flight Workers was certified in 1987 to represent approximately 30 EuroAir employees who work as ticketing and reservation agents in one of the company's three Canadian offices. The ticketing and reservation agents in EuroAir's two other Canadian offices, located in different cities, are not unionized. However, the work done in all three offices is very similar, and in many instances, unionized and non-unionized employees are in the same job classification. The parties are currently bargaining for their first collective agreement.

The bargaining has not proceeded smoothly. The labour relations board was asked to intervene to resolve two issues that arose at the initial meetings in 1987. Bargaining broke off at the start of 1988 because of disputes over the language used in meetings and documents; a board-appointed conciliator managed to reconcile the parties so that bargaining could recommence. Bargaining continued without much success until mid-December 1988, when the employer submitted an offer it described as "final." The union membership voted on this offer and rejected it on the recommendation of the union bargaining team.

A conciliator was again called in to assist in bargaining, and the parties met in the conciliator's presence in April 1989. Issues surrounding salaries and several standard clauses in the agreement were still to be settled. The parties were finally able to agree on the language in the standard clauses, but the issue of salaries was not resolved.

In May 1988, non-unionized staff had received an annual 5 percent pay increase, but unionized staff did not receive this increase. The employer's "final" offer of December

1988 included a series of pay raises over three years. In the opinion of the union, the proposed increases were "ridiculous," since the total of all three raises would still amount to less than the 5 percent increase received by the non-unionized staff in May of that year. At the bargaining sessions in April 1989, the employer offered a larger increase along with a lump-sum payment. The union negotiators were reluctant to accept this proposal because in May 1989 the non-unionized staff were scheduled to again receive a 5 percent pay increase and thus the overall outcome of the employer's new proposal would be that the unionized staff would still be paid less than the non-unionized staff. The negotiating team took the newest salary offer and the agreement on the language of the standard clauses to a vote of the bargaining unit. Both the salary offer and the agreed-upon language were rejected by the union membership.

In July 1989, the employer gave its non-unionized staff both a 5 percent increase, retroactive to May 1989, and a $500 bonus. The employer also increased vacation allocations, meal allowances, sick-leave reimbursements, and paid-leave provisions for non-unionized staff.

The union filed its first unfair labour practice complaint in August 1989. It alleged that the employer had refused to give the unionized employees the same salary increase awarded to non-unionized employees doing the same work. After the complaint had been filed, a union representative contacted the employer and suggested that bargaining should resume, since the increases in benefits the employer had given non-unionized employees were very similar to those offered to the union in the April bargaining sessions. The employer refused to resume bargaining.

A date for a hearing on this complaint had already been set when, in late 1989, the union filed a second unfair labour practice complaint. The union alleged that in August 1989 the employer had refused to continue collective bargaining if the first complaint was not withdrawn. The labour relations board decided to hold one hearing to address both complaints.

The Employer's Position

In response to the first unfair labour practice complaint, which involved pay increases given to non-unionized staff but not to unionized staff, the employer pointed to a clause in the relevant labour relations code. This clause states that complaints of unfair labour practices must be made no later than 90 days after the date on which the complainant knew, or in the opinion of the board ought to have known, of the action or circumstances giving rise to the complaint. The employer argued that it had given its last offer to the union on April 13, 1989, and the union had filed the unfair labour practice complaint on August 28, 1989. The time between these dates was more than 90 days, and thus, the employer argued, the complaint should be dismissed because it did not meet the deadline stated in the labour relations code.

In response to the second complaint, which alleged a refusal to bargain, the employer stated that it did not want to resume bargaining under the "pressure" of an unfair labour practice complaint. It also stated that there was no point in resuming bargaining, since the employer did not intend to create wage parity between unionized and non-unionized staff. The employer argued that it was not illegal to make proposals that maintained this distinction between these groups. The leader of the employer's negotiating team, the director of international labour relations for EuroAir, stated that the employer's goal in bargaining was to find a "point of equilibrium" between unionized and non-unionized wages, where the psychological impact of the differences between the two groups would be minimized.

The employer pointed out that it had agreed to some of the union's proposals, such as language providing for automatic promotion between job classifications upon the attainment of certain levels of experience, and thus it could not be accused of being unwilling to bargain. It claimed that the impasse in bargaining was because of the union's insistence on wage parity between unionized and non-unionized employees. It also noted that if the union wanted to press its demands, it could do so by other means (e.g., a strike), instead of by asking a third party to intervene to "solve [its] problem of its weakness at the bargaining table."

The Union's Position

The union alleged that the employer's insistence on maintaining a distinction between union and non-union wages resulted in "surface bargaining." In other words, although the employer attended the bargaining sessions, the manner in which it bargained and the offers it presented "could only result in an impasse." This, argued the union, could not be considered a reasonable attempt to conclude a collective agreement.

The union also argued that the board should consider the previous complaints made to the board about the employer's conduct in bargaining as "significant and exacerbating factors."

CASE *8-2*

COFFEE CUP LTD. AND RESTAURANT WORKERS' UNION

(Based on *Starbucks Corporation and National Automobile, Aerospace and Agricultural Implement Workers Union of Canada [CAW-Canada] Local 3000*, 1997)

The parties in this case are engaged in bargaining for a first collective agreement. The employer has announced plans to close a regional distribution centre that is part of its operations and part of the bargaining unit. The union has filed a complaint with the labour relations board alleging that the planned closure is an unfair labour practice.

Background to the Case

Coffee Cup is an international company that operates coffee shops. It has more than 90 locations in this region. The union was initially certified to represent employees in three of those locations in late 1996. In February 1997, the certification was expanded to cover a total of eight locations as well as the distribution centre that supplies pastries to the majority of the region's locations. (The locations that do not use the distribution centre obtain their pastries directly from bakeries or from independent wholesalers.) The union now represents 110 of approximately 1,400 employees in the region.

Collective bargaining for a first collective agreement began in October 1996. In the first bargaining session, the union presented its initial offer and indicated that its key issues were wages, seniority, and shift scheduling. The employer indicated that it preferred to discuss non-monetary items before monetary items. In the next session, in early November, the employer presented information on how it currently manages and compensates employees. In late November, the employer presented a written offer, and the parties were able to agree on approximately 50 "administrative" items.

The union attempted to arrange bargaining sessions in early December, but the employer indicated that this was the start of its busy season and requested that bargaining not take place during this period. The parties agreed on one meeting in mid-December and several meetings in early January 1997. When the parties met in mid-December, several more items were resolved, but over 80 remained outstanding. After holding a caucus, the union negotiators informed the employer that it would be applying to the labour relations board for the assistance of a mediator. The employer was surprised by this action, feeling that it was premature to bring in a mediator when there were so many items left outstanding. Nevertheless, a mediator was appointed, and several bargaining sessions were scheduled in late January. These sessions were to replace the early January sessions previously agreed upon.

When the parties met with the mediator, the employer's negotiators indicated to the mediator that they felt that mediation was premature after only six bargaining sessions. The mediator suggested that the parties attempt to reach a settlement on the issue of shift scheduling; the union agreed to discuss the issue, but the employer refused on the grounds that the issue was too closely linked to other unresolved items for it to be considered separately. However, the parties did agree on a common list of issues that they could work on. Another bargaining session was scheduled for early February.

At the end of January 1997, the union sent a fax to the employer with the demand that the employer state its position on all existing proposals. The union stated in its fax that the employer had not addressed the issues that the union had identified as its priorities and that the employer had been unavailable for bargaining for all but three weeks since the certification. The employer responded in a letter two days later, stating that the union had agreed in October to discuss non-monetary issues first and that it (the employer) had responded to all the union's non-monetary demands. The employer also asserted that the union had not responded to the employer's counter-proposal and had varied little from its original offer; it further stated that it had no intention of tabling a monetary offer on six days' notice. Two days later, the union announced its intention to hold a strike vote.

Because of a death in one union negotiator's family, the parties and the mediator did not meet again until early March. At this meeting, the union submitted a written counter-proposal that included terms for the employees added to the bargaining unit after the expanded certification was granted in February. This counter-proposal involved the reintroduction of some earlier proposals, including language to prohibit the employer from contracting work out. The union felt that these terms were necessary to protect the interests of the employees in the distribution center, which was now part of the bargaining unit. The union specified that the "contracting out" language was only intended to apply to the distribution centre employees.

On March 18, 1997, the strike vote was held and a majority of employees voted in favour of strike action. Several other meetings with the mediator occurred in March, with little progress in bargaining. Another mediation session was scheduled for April 7, but a separate session to discuss the distribution centre issues was arranged for April 1. The employer advised the mediator that in the meantime the employer's negotiating team would meet with officials at Coffee Cup's head office to obtain financial information for use in formulating a response to the union proposals.

On March 24, 1997, Coffee Cup's chief negotiator learned that Coffee Cup was planning to close the distribution centre. He thus postponed the April 1 meeting. On April 2, the union wrote to Coffee Cup saying that it had not agreed, as the employer had previously asserted, to settle non-monetary issues prior to discussing monetary issues. The union also stated that since over two months had passed since its request for the employer's full proposal, it expected a full response to all the union proposals from the employer at the next scheduled meeting.

On April 4, the employer's negotiators were authorized to reveal the decision to close the distribution centre. The leader of the union's negotiating team was out of town on this date. He stated that he had heard that the employer planned a press conference for April 4 but he had been unable to confirm this information and had thought the event had been cancelled.

Immediately prior to the scheduled April 7 meeting, the employer's chief negotiator told the mediator that the company planned to close the distribution centre; he also provided the mediator with the Coffee Cup financial statements that the negotiating team wanted to discuss. The mediator advised the negotiator to deal with the issue of the closure first. At 10:10 a.m., the employer's chief negotiator spoke privately with the union's chief negotiator and informed him of the planned closure, which was to take place between June 11, 1997, and the end of July 1997, when the centre's property lease expired. The employer's negotiator indicated that the employer would be willing to negotiate a severance package for the distribution centre employees and would assist the employees in finding employment opportunities elsewhere in the company at pay rates equivalent to their current pay.

The issue of the announcement's timing became significant when the union's chief negotiator indicated that he had received phone calls prior to 10 a.m. that day (April 7) from the media requesting comment on the closure. He had also received a company fax, time-stamped at 9:57 a.m., containing the news of the closure. The company's explanation for this discrepancy (it seemed that others had been informed of the closure before the union's chief negotiator) was that April 7 was the first day of daylight savings time and the fax clocks at the company's office had not been reset to reflect the changed time.

At approximately 12 p.m., the employer's negotiating team and the director of the distribution centre met with the union's negotiating team. The director explained that the distribution centre was an experiment for the company, and its closure had been under discussion since 1994. He stated that the closure was now occurring for "business reasons." The union representatives said that in early 1997 the director had indicated to the distribution centre employees that the centre was the best in the entire Coffee Cup operation and was making a profit. The union also alleged that the notice of the closure had been released to the media before it had been released to the union. Mediation broke off that day.

On April 10, the union filed an unfair labour practice complaint against the employer. The parties met on April 21 to discuss the complaint, but no resolution was reached and the union filed a strike notice on April 23. The parties met again on May 7, and the union presented a new proposal. On May 12, the employer indicated in a letter to the union that it saw no substantive change in the union's position and therefore interpreted the purpose of the May 7 meeting as having been to lend support to the unfair labour practice complaint and to provoke a strike. The strike began on May 16.

Testimony to the labour board provided additional background to the history of the distribution centre. In 1994, after experiencing problems with the bakery that supplied pastries to Coffee Cup locations in the region, Coffee Cup began investigating the possibility of opening its own distribution centre. The centre was established in June 1994 and operated in a facility with a three-year, non-renewable lease. At that point, the centre was something of a test project, since all of Coffee Cup's other North American outlets had their pastries directly supplied by local bakeries. Initially, the distribution centre ran into problems. It had been anticipated that the prices of goods supplied by the bakeries would drop because the bakeries no longer had to bear the costs of distribution and delivery to the stores, but when the expected price reductions did not occur, the anticipated cost savings from the operation of the distribution centre did not materialize. The Coffee Cup manager who established the centre ended up leaving the company out of frustration over how the project was handled. However, in late 1994, a centre modelled on this first one was established in the eastern United States, and this second centre was very successful and profitable.

Several managers whose responsibilities included the distribution centre passed through the company between 1994 and 1997. All of these managers dealt with various phases of a plan to contract out pastry distribution to a third party. The manager who initiated the contracting-out plan believed that Coffee Cup's expertise lay in the coffee business and that parties more experienced in baked-goods distribution should handle that part of the operation. The contracting-out plan was developed throughout 1995, and bids on the pastry distribution contract were accepted in late 1995. At that point, there was another change in management personnel, and it was not until the spring of 1996 that a new Coffee Cup manager approached a firm that had expressed interest in the contract. The contract terms discussed with that firm, however, identified several other cities on the U.S. West Coast as the first areas where third-party distribution would be adopted. The region served by the current distribution centre was last on the list of the regions identified for contracting out because the centre was seen as being relatively problem-free and because it was assumed that its operations would continue until its lease ran out, in 1997.

The formal contract for third-party pastry distribution was signed in July 1996, and the firm started its pastry distribution service in the first West Coast region in August. Despite the certification of the distribution centre in February 1997, Coffee Cup continued with its plans to close the centre and contract out the centre's work in the summer of 1997.

The Union's Position

The union argued that the employer was unwilling to conclude a collective agreement, and it pointed to several pieces of evidence in support of this argument. It stated that the employer had not yet responded to the union's request that it provide a position on several key issues, including wages and seniority. The employer's only response to the union's key issue of scheduling was to insist on keeping the current system, in which seniority plays a very minimal role.

The union accused the employer of "circular bargaining"—that is, the employer would refuse to consider one issue on the grounds that it was related to another issue and then refuse to consider the other issue on the grounds that it was related to the first issue. The union identified issues for which the employer had provided a "first" position but had not provided any subsequent positions.

The union indicated that the employer had been asked to supply wage and bargaining unit information in September of 1996 but had not done so until after the unfair labour practice complaint had been filed.

In addressing the distribution centre issue, the union stated that the employer's chief negotiator had not been informed of the pending closure until March 21, 1997, although the human resources director at Coffee Cup had known of a possible closure at the time the centre was included in the expanded bargaining unit. The union also stated that the employer's negotiator had known of the closure plans when he had attended bargaining meetings on March 24 and 25, but had not revealed the closure to the union until April 7.

The union also provided evidence, mostly involving the leasing of resources needed to operate the distribution centre and the dates in the contract with the third-party distribution firm, that the company could continue operating the distribution centre in another location if it chose to do so. The union argued that the decision to close the distribution centre was motivated by anti-union animus.

The Employer's Position

The employer noted that the bargaining process had been conducted under the terms of the relevant labour legislation until the union had chosen to abandon that process. The employer also noted that it had issued a notice of closure of the distribution center but had not actually closed the location yet.

The employer pointed to a section in the labour legislation that permits parties to ask for recommendations from a mediator if there are problems with one party's actions. The employer stated that the union had had the option to take this course of action rather than to file an unfair labour practice complaint.

The employer's assessment of the evidence presented was that the evidence did not indicate a refusal to bargain. Bargaining was proceeding with the assistance of mediation. Fifty items had already been settled, and the employer, at the request of the mediator, had presented a proposal. The employer had also had information it had been prepared to give to the mediator, but had been unable to do so because of the breakdown of negotiations.

On the issue of the distribution centre, the employer said that the fate of the distribution centre had been clear in 1995 when the initial plans had been developed for third-party distribution of baked goods. The employer contended that the initial projections of profitability for the centre were flawed because the costs of overhead had not been included in the calculations. When questioned about the statements made to the distribution centre employees regarding the success and profitability of the centre, the distribution centre manager stated that these statements had been true at the time they were made. At that point, the contract with the third-party distributor had not been finalized, and it would have been "irresponsible" to disclose the intention to close the centre before the final arrangements had been made.

The employer cited several previous cases that suggested that holding a firm position in bargaining did not in and of itself constitute bargaining in bad faith.

COLLECTIVE BARGAINING SIMULATION EXERCISE

Newtown School Dispute

Introduction

In this bargaining simulation, you will play a member of either a school board's or a teacher association's bargaining team. You, the other members of your team, and the members of the other team are negotiators representing specific constituencies. You will deal with a complex mix of bargaining issues, and you will be subjected to a variety of pressures during the negotiations.

Advance Preparation

Before the bargaining session, you should read two sets of information:

- the "Background Information" presented below. This is information that both teams have.

- the "Team Information" (either Board of Education or Teacher Association) for your team in the negotiations. This information will be provided by your instructor. You should not permit any members of the other side's bargaining team to have access to this information.

Based on this information, you and your team should prepare a written proposal to present to the other side at the start of negotiations. This proposal should outline your opening position on each of the bargaining issues. Your team should also be prepared with alternate positions and a bottom line for each bargaining issue. This information will guide your strategies in the actual bargaining.

Bargaining Procedure

Your instructor will announce the team assignments and time schedules for bargaining; he or she will also designate locations for negotiations and private team meetings.

At the start of the negotiations, your instructor will provide each set of negotiators with a "Final Settlement" form. This form should be used to record agreements on each item, and it must be signed by all participants at the conclusion of the bargaining period. If the agreement is incomplete, each party's final bargaining positions on those items still in dispute should be recorded.

Teams may negotiate as a group or through spokespersons. Who makes the first offer, how the time for negotiations is used, how time is used for private meetings, and other rules for conducting bargaining are all controlled by the teams themselves.

When the bargaining process has been completed, the instructor will provide a summary of the final settlement(s) to all the participants.

Background Information

It is now September 10, the opening day of the school year in Newtown. The contract between Newtown School District and the Newtown Teacher Association expired on June 30. Since then, the Board of Education and representatives of the Teacher Association have met on several occasions in an attempt to finalize the contract, but these attempts have not been successful.

Prior to June 30 and during the summer months, there was increasing talk among the membership of the Teacher Association of the possibility of calling a strike if the contract was not finalized by the start of the school year. However, the executive of the Teacher Association agreed that, for the benefit of the community, the teachers would resume normal operations on opening day throughout the system, without a contract, on a day-to-day basis. This was in response to parent pressure to resume normal operations. Parents have been placing pressure on both teachers and the board to keep schools operating, but they have twice defeated referenda on increased taxes to cover budgetary increases over and above those of the previous year. Owing to decreased enrolments, fixed income from local taxes and from provincial and federal grants, and increased costs, maintaining of the school budget at a level consistent with the previous year would produce a 4.98 percent budget shortfall. The board believes that allocations for budget items would begin to be exhausted in April of the coming school year. Therefore, the board feels that if the system is to function effectively within its budgetary constraints to the end of the current fiscal year (June 30), programs and personnel must be cut and teachers' productivity (workload) must be increased. In this regard, the school district must provide 190 instructional days, as mandated by provincial law.

The Board of Education is caught between the Teacher Association and community pressure groups. The board believes that it must satisfy the pressure groups and at the same time keep the teachers on the job with a contract that is acceptable to the bargaining unit's membership. The board is concerned that if it fails to respond appropriately to community pressures for cost reductions, the board members may be removed. The board's primary objective, therefore, is to cut costs while retaining as many programs as possible. It hopes to accomplish this through cutbacks in the number of teaching personnel and increases in teacher workload. The board also wishes to eliminate certain existing agreements in order to increase productivity. To achieve this objective, the board wants to negotiate a three-year contract that will stabilize the situation by creating orderly and predictable budgetary needs that will be seen to be less excessive by various community groups. The Teacher Association, on the other hand, wants a one-year contract in order to maintain flexibility.

The Teacher Association also feels caught between community pressure groups, who hope that a strike can be averted, and the board's apparent unwillingness to fight for increased budgetary allocations to run the system. The teachers feel that the board has not confronted the community over its unwillingness to accept increased taxation in order to pay for education, and that its response to this community unwillingness is simply to pass the burden along to teachers.

Newtown is a relatively settled and stable upper-middle-income community with a strong interest in quality education. However, as mentioned, the residents are reluctant to increase the community's already burdensome tax rate. The Newtown School District consists of 12 schools: nine elementary schools (kindergarten–Grade 8) and three senior high schools. The student population is 12,000, divided into 8,000 elementary and 4,000 high school students. The bargaining unit represents 95 percent of all teachers and consists of 250 elementary teachers in all categories and 125 high school teachers in all categories.

Both sides wish to conclude an agreement to avert a strike. However, the Teacher Association's bargaining team is adamantly committed to improving the conditions of its membership, and the board is just as committed to keeping its costs as low as possible. Nevertheless, each side feels it has some room to move on certain issues.

Newtown School District Teachers' Salary Schedule ————————————

S*	Amount	Last Year's Number of Teachers	Cost	Current Year's Number of Teachers	Cost
0	12,000	20	240,000	0	0
1	13,500	20	270,000	20	270,000
2	14,000	28	392,000	20	280,000
3	15,000	31	465,000	26	390,000
4	16,000	30	480,000	28	448,000
5	17,500	23	402,500	26	455,000
6	18,500	24	444,000	23	425,500
7	19,500	15	292,500	22	429,000
8	21,000	16	336,000	15	315,000
9	22,000	13	286,000	16	352,000
10	23,000	180	4,140,000	179	4,117,000
TOTALS		400	7,748,000	375	7,481,500

(*S=steps on salary scale; 0=entry level.)

Current School Year, July 1-June 30: Projected Budget

1.   INCOME

   1.1 Local tax (same rate as last year, $4.86 per $1,000
         of property value. No significant increase in property
         values expected.) $12,151,000

   1.2 Provincial funding (formula per pupil will remain the
         same. Legislature may possibly raise formula next year.)   4,916,880

   1.3 Federal funding   750,000

   TOTAL INCOME $17,817,880

Note: this is a decrease of $380,517 (-2.09%) from the previous year's income.

2   EXPENDITURES
      2.1 Administration
            2.1.1 Professional salaries $1,137,500
            2.1.2 Clerical/secretarial salaries   281,250
            2.1.3 Other   250,000
      Subtotal   1,668,750

      2.2 Instruction
            2.2.1 Teachers[i]
                   Salaries $7,481,500
                   Other benefits   1,420,000
            2.2.2 Aides   1,187,600
            2.2.3 Materials/supplies[ii]   943,750
      Subtotal   11,032,850

---

[i] Twenty-five teachers did not return to the system owing to retirement or other reasons.
[ii] Costs of materials and supplies will be up 12 percent over last year based on currently known price increases.

2.3 Plant operation/maintenance
    2.3.1 Salaries $1,266,250
    2.3.2 Utilities[iii]   975,000
    2.3.3 Other[iv]   258,750
Subtotal   2,500,000

2.4 Fixed charges
    2.4.1 Retirement[v] $1,176,450
    2.4.2 Other[vi]   425,700
Subtotal   1,602,150

2.5 Debt servicing[vii]   1,026,000

2.6 Transportation
    2.6.1 Salaries $ 400,000
    2.6.2 Other[vii]   395,000
Subtotal   795,000

TOTAL EXPENDITURES $18,624,750

BUDGET SURPLUS (SHORTFALL)   (1,806,870)

Total number of pupils: 12,000
Total number of teachers: 375
Per pupil expenditure: $1,552

[iii] Cost of utilities is expected to increase by more than 20 percent over the current year's costs.

[iv] Cost projections indicate a 15 percent increase in this category.

[v] The cost of teacher retirements is up by 5 percent owing to increases in the cost of benefits mandated by the provincial legislature.

[vi] Other fixed charges have increased 32 percent for this current year.

[vii] The cost of debt servicing has increased 14 percent owing to difficulty in floating bonds.

[viii] Transportation costs have increased 31 percent owing to increases in operating and maintenance costs.

Last School Year, July 1–June 30: Audited Budget ————————————————

1.   INCOME

    1.1 Local tax ($4.86 per $1,000
        of property value) $12,204,444

    1.2 Provincial funding (based on an equalization
        formula, improved during the last sitting of
        the legislature. Yielded $409.74 per pupil in
        administration last year)   5,244,709

    1.3 Federal funding   749,244

TOTAL INCOME $18,198,397

2   EXPENDITURES

2.1 Administration		
2.1.1 Professional salaries	$1,137,248	
2.1.2 Clerical/secretarial salaries	281,067	
2.1.3 Other	261,129	
Subtotal		$1,679,444
2.2 Instruction		
2.2.1 Teachers		
Salaries	$7,748,000	
Other benefits	1,394,643	
2.2.2 Aides	1,183,275	
2.2.3 Materials/supplies	842,633	
Subtotal		$11,168,551

2.3	Plant operation/maintenance		
	2.3.1 Salaries	$1,266,250	
	2.3.2 Utilities	812,268	
	2.3.3 Other	225,198	
	Subtotal		$ 2,303,716
2.4	Fixed charges		
	2.4.1 Retirement	$1,120,428	
	2.4.2 Other	324,773	
	Subtotal		$ 1,445,201
2.5	Debt servicing		$ 900,260
2.6	Transportation		
	2.6.1 Salaries	$ 399,698	
	2.6.2 Other	301,527	
	Subtotal		$ 701,225
	TOTAL EXPENDITURES		$18,198,397
	BUDGET SURPLUS (SHORTFALL)		0

Total number of pupils: 12,800
Total number of teachers: 400
Per pupil expenditure: $1,421

References

[1] Downie, B.M. (1990). The negotiation process. In J.A. Willes (Ed.), *Labour relations in Canada: readings and cases*. Scarborough, ON: Prentice-Hall.

[2] Downie, *op. cit.*

[3] Walton, R.E., and McKersie, R.B. (1963). *A behavioral theory of labor negotiations: an analysis of a social interaction system*. New York, NY: McGraw-Hill.

[4] Walton and McKersie, *op. cit.*

[5] Peach, D.A., and Bergman, P. (1991). *The practice of labour relations* (3rd edition). Toronto, ON: McGraw-Hill Ryerson.

[6] Education Relations Commission of Ontario (1983). *The bargaining process and mediation.* Toronto, ON: Education Relations Commission of Ontario.

[7] Walton and McKersie, *op. cit.*

[8] Walton and McKersie, *op. cit.*

[9] Walton, R.E., Cutcher-Gershenfeld, J.E., and McKersie, R.B. (1994). *Strategic negotiations: a theory of change in labor-management relations.* Boston, MA: Harvard Business School Press.

[10] Katz, H.C., and Kochan, T.A. (1992). *An introduction to collective bargaining and industrial relations.* New York, NY: McGraw-Hill.

[11] Education Relations Commission of Ontario, *op. cit.*

[12] Peach and Bergman, *op. cit.*

[13] Walton, Cutcher-Gershenfeld, and McKersie, *op. cit.*

[14] Education Relations Commission of Ontario, *op. cit.*

[15] Peach and Bergman, *op. cit.*

[16] Chamberlain, N.W., and Kuhn, J.M. (1986). *Collective bargaining* (3rd edition). New York, NY: McGraw-Hill.

[17] Chaykowski, R.P. (2001). Collective bargaining: structure, process and innovation. In M. Gunderson, A. Ponak, and D. Taras (Eds.), *Union-management relations in Canada* (4th edition). Don Mills, ON: Addison-Wesley.

[18] Craig, A.W.J., and Solomon, N.A. (1993). *The system of industrial relations in Canada* (4th edition). Scarborough, ON: Prentice-Hall.

[19] Ury, W.L., Brett, J.M., and Goldberg, S.B. (1988). *Getting disputes resolved: designing systems to cut the cost of conflict.* San Francisco, CA: Jossey-Bass.

[20] Ury, Brett, and Goldberg, *op. cit.*

[21] Ury, Brett, and Goldberg, *op. cit.*

[22] Fisher, R.E., and Ury, W.L. (1991). *Getting to yes: negotiating agreement without giving in* (2nd edition). Boston, MA: Houghton-Mifflin.

[23] Fisher and Ury, *op. cit.*

[24] Susskind, L.E. and Landry, E.M. (1991). Implementing a mutual gains approach to collective bargaining. *Negotiation Journal*, January 1991, 5–10.

[25] Hunter, L.W., and McKersie, R.B. (1992). Can 'mutual gains' training change labor-management relationships? *Negotiation Journal*, October 1992, 319–330.

[26] Walton and McKersie, *op. cit.*

[27] Heckscher, C., and Hall, L. (1994). Mutual gains and beyond: two levels of intervention. *Negotiation Journal*, July 1994, 235–248.

[28] Hunter and McKersie, *op. cit.*

Prison strike in Newfoundland off—again.

Government lockout ends.

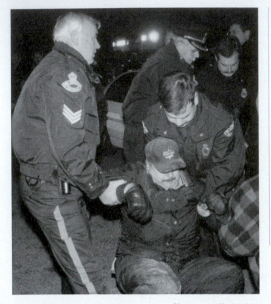

ST. JOHN'S—An on-again, off-again illegal strike by Newfoundland jail guards finally ended Saturday after the province lifted a lockout order against the workers.

Roughly 220 corrections officers returned to work after the union assured the province the guards would not walk out for a third time.

The announcement came after two days of confusion on the picket line in which strikers initially defied a court injunction imposed Tuesday to return to work.

The guards, who work at seven Newfoundland jails, ended a four-day walkout late Thursday after the province appointed a mediator in the dispute.

But they walked out again early Friday over the temporary hiring of a guard at a Labrador jail.

They agreed to return to work Friday night after hearing that the guard in question had resigned. But when they showed up they found they were locked out by the government.

Union negotiator Leo Puddister said Saturday the government allowed workers back in only after the union pointed out that the lockout violated the court injunction.

"That's why [government] changed their mind," he said. "They don't understand what court orders mean. They interfered with a court order since [midnight Friday] and they're going to have to pay for it."

Premier Brian Tobin said Saturday that the government wanted to make sure workers would not walk off the job again. "You can't have a situation where people return to work, stay for a few hours, walk out again and start making demands," he said. "We've always said the walkout is illegal, it is a defiance of a court of law, and when the workers return to work they must do so unconditionally."

Justice Minister Paul Dicks said Saturday that members of the union will be suspended without pay for the illegal job action.

(*Edmonton Journal*, November 7, 1999)

STRIKES AND LOCKOUTS

objectives

In this chapter, we will discuss how strikes and lockouts take place, why and when they are used in the collective bargaining process, and how legislation controls their use. By the end of this chapter, you should be able to:

- define a strike and a lockout
- explain why a strike or lockout would be used as a bargaining tactic
- outline the legislative guidelines for the use of a strike or lockout in bargaining
- describe an essential service
- outline legislative guidelines on picketing
- explain what replacement workers are and when and how they might be used in strikes
- assess the impact of strikes in Canada

INTRODUCTION

The strike and the lockout are the two most public events in the entire industrial relations process. Because strikes and lockouts are visible actions—deliberately so, since one of their purposes is to draw public attention to a dispute—they are often perceived as being regular, inevitable events. In fact, when viewed in the context of the amount of collective agreements annually negotiated in Canada, strikes and lockouts are unusual events. In 1998, approximately 87 percent of private sector collective agreements in Canada were settled without a strike or lockout taking place.[1]

Even though strikes and lockouts are relatively uncommon, they can have a widespread impact and long-lasting effects. Therefore, it is important to understand what strikes and lockouts are and how they are conducted. We will begin our discussion by explaining what strikes and lockouts are and describing why and when they are used as part of the bargaining process. We will then outline the restrictions and conditions that labour legislation places on activities related to strikes and lockouts, such as picketing and using replacement workers. We will conclude by describing how a strike or lockout ends and by analysing the overall impact of strikes and lockouts in Canada.

DEFINING STRIKES AND LOCKOUTS

A **strike** occurs when union members in a bargaining unit withdraw their labour—that is, they refuse to perform part or all of their regular duties or refuse to come to work. A **lockout** occurs when the employer closes all or part of the workplace so that the workers cannot enter the premises and perform their jobs. The terms **industrial action** and **industrial conflict** are also used to describe either strikes or lockouts.

As we know from previous chapters, strikes were often used in the early days of Canadian unionism as a way to pressure an employer into recognizing a union as the representative of employees in a workplace. A strike undertaken for this purpose was known as a **recognition strike**. The need for recognition strikes disappeared when Canadian labour legislation formalized the process of certification and gave employers the legal responsibility of accepting their employees' chosen workplace representative.

While recognition strikes are no longer necessary (and in fact are banned in every Canadian jurisdiction), there are still legal restrictions on the use of strikes or lockouts in every Canadian jurisdiction. A legal strike or lockout can only take place while collective bargaining is in progress. It is important to note, though, that negotiation sessions do not actually have to be taking place; in fact, most strikes or lockouts occur as a consequence of collective bargaining breaking down. However, for a strike or lockout to be legal, the parties must be in the process of bargaining and a collective agreement must not have been settled. Additionally, in most Canadian jurisdictions, the employer is prohibited from dismissing striking employees while a strike is taking place, and striking employees are entitled to return to their jobs after the strike is over.

It is also important to note that work does not have to stop completely for a legal strike to occur. Several provincial labour codes as well as the *Canada Labour Code* state that a work "slowdown" can be considered a strike. A number of activities fall into this category, including union-imposed overtime bans and **rotating strikes**, where workers at one location of a business stop their work but workers at other locations continue working. **Work-to-rule campaigns**, where union members interpret the terms of the collective agreement very narrowly and follow them very closely in order to slow down production, have also been determined to constitute strike action.[2]

WHY STRIKES OR LOCKOUTS HAPPEN

The basic purpose of a strike or lockout is to inflict "economic pain" on the other side in a bargaining situation in order to force acceptance of one's bargaining demands. If a strike takes place, the employer is hurt financially by losing revenue as a consequence of being unable to produce or sell products or services. The striking union members are also hurt financially, since they do not receive their regular pay. Similarly, if a lockout takes place, the union members must go without their wages because they are not able to work and the employer loses money because production is halted. While both parties suffer economic pain during a strike or lockout, the goal of the party undertaking the action is to make the other party suffer more and thus be motivated to accept the first party's bargaining demands. Thus, the successful party in a strike or lockout (i.e., the party that achieves the outcome it desires) is, in many cases, the party with enough resources or determination to withstand the economic pain inflicted by the action. A strike or lockout is not always won by the party with the more reasonable, ethical, or equitable proposals; in fact, it is more often won by the party with more resources, regardless of the merit of that party's position.

Several factors affect a union's or employer's decision to commence a strike or lockout. Much research has been conducted to identify these factors and to determine when they may or may not be important in the strike or lockout decision. A thoroughly comprehensive review of this research is beyond the scope of this discussion, but we will briefly examine some of the major strike determinants that have been identified.

Motivations for Striking or Locking Out

One way to understand why a strike or lockout occurs is to look at the motivations of the parties undertaking the action. We already know that the party instigating a strike or lockout intends to inflict economic suffering on the other party. However, some research suggests more complex motivations. The results of this research have been classified into two categories: "strikes as mistakes" and "strikes as collective voice."[3]

The strikes-as-mistakes perspective suggests that strikes or lockouts occur as a result of mistaken perceptions developed during bargaining. One party may misunderstand the position of the other and thus erroneously believe there is no common ground for settlement. This party then undertakes a strike or lockout to force an agreement. In this scenario, the strike or lockout is a mistake because the parties actually could have agreed on the issues without the pressure of industrial action to motivate them into settling.

Why do parties develop inaccurate perceptions of each other's positions? The strikes-as-mistakes perspective proposes several reasons why inaccurate perceptions develop. They may result from a lack of experience on the part of the bargainers, limited disclosures of information during bargaining, the complexity of the issues being negotiated, miscalculations of the other side's position, or changes in the parties' expectations during bargaining.[4]

If the parties are not experienced bargainers, they may not know how to elicit or interpret information during bargaining. Less-experienced bargainers may also misinterpret how much the other party is willing to concede or compromise on bargaining items. Misunderstandings may also occur when complex issues like downsizing or new job classifications are being bargained and one or both of the parties do not fully understand the issue or the related proposals. In other situations, one party may choose to withhold information that could affect the other side's perceptions. For example, if management negotiators are proposing a wage freeze, they might withhold from the union negotiators the information that the company made a large profit in the last financial quarter in order to strengthen the credibility of their position. And finally, as outlined in previous chapters, the parties' expectations may change during bargaining because of input from their constituencies or changes in the external environment, such as new legislation. All of these errors in perception can cause a strike or lockout when there is no actual reason for one.

The strikes-as-mistakes perspective acknowledges that there are financial burdens on both sides during a strike or lockout. Striking or locking out is often not the ideal choice of action to support a bargaining demand, particularly when the financial burdens implicit in such an action are such that the resources of one or both parties might become seriously depleted.

The second perspective, strikes as collective voice, suggests that strikes and lockouts are likely to occur because there is always an element of mistrust in the union-management relationship. Because unions and management represent different interests and have different philosophies on how the workplace should be governed, the two parties have fundamental reasons to distrust each other, even if a particular relationship is relatively cordial. What, then, determines whether this basic distrust will be manifested in a strike or lockout?

According to the strikes-as-collective-voice perspective, the occurrence of a strike or lockout depends on several factors.[5] The first is the amount of worker discontent. Obviously, dissatisfied workers are more likely to strike than relatively satisfied workers. The second factor is the extent of management's willingness or ability to address discontent, since reducing discontent or dissatisfaction will also likely reduce the possibility of a strike. The third factor is the existence or non-existence of other means to express discontent. Formal or informal means of employee-management communication, such as the grievance procedure or "open door" management policies, may provide an alternative to strikes as an expression of unhappiness. The ability of union leaders to mobilize discontent is the fourth factor. Union leaders must be able to present a strike as a reasonable and productive expression of discontent if union members are going to commit themselves to that means of expression. The fifth and final factor is the social legitimacy of strikes. If society in general does not see strikes as legitimate means to express discontent, a strike will not gain public support and thus may not be successful in pressuring management to accept union demands.

The strikes-as-collective-voice perspective suggests that although strikes and lockouts are considered to be a means of inflicting economic pain, they may also be used for non-economic purposes, such as expressing worker discontent. Non-economic motivations for strikes and lockouts sometimes dominate over economic motivations, causing a strike or lockout even if the parties recognize that such action is not economically rational or viable. The opportunity for a party to have a "voice" to express its concerns visibly and to release tension or high emotions that have built up during the bargaining process may be considered more valuable than the economic impact of the action.

Bargaining Structure

The size of the bargaining unit has been identified as another factor that affects the incidence of strikes. In the United States, larger bargaining units have been found to be more likely to go on strike than smaller bargaining units.[6] This finding is attributed in part to the perception that larger bargaining units will have a greater economic impact on the employer by striking than smaller bargaining units will, simply because more workers are involved in a larger bargaining unit and thus more labour is withdrawn with greater impact.

Ascertaining whether this tendency also exists in Canada is somewhat difficult, since national strike statistics in the past have only been consistently collected for bargaining units of more than 500 members. This cut-off point excludes smaller bargaining units and makes a comparison of strike rates in different-sized bargaining units somewhat skewed. However, a study conducted in Ontario, using nine years of data from all public and private sector certifications in the province, found that strikes were most frequent in bargaining units of 150 to 300 members, least common in units with less than 21 members, but almost even in frequency in units of 50 to 149 members and units of 300 to 499 members.[7] These findings indicate, at least, that very small bargaining units in Canada are less likely to strike but that the tendency to strike varies among larger-sized units. We should also keep in mind that workers' ability to strike may be more restricted in the Canadian public sector than in the private sector, so the lack of a strike may not always indicate an unwillingness to strike. There may instead be a legislative barrier that prevents a strike from happening.

Individual Factors

Another important factor in whether a strike occurs is how willing the union members are to undertake strike action, given that they will individually bear a large part of the economic pain inflicted by a strike. One study involving a survey of 44 workers in a single bargaining unit indicated that higher loyalty to the union results in a higher propensity to support strike action.[8]

While the results of this study are obviously limited by the small number of workers surveyed, it is not illogical to deduce that employees who are loyal to the union will be more likely to support actions proposed by the union than are less loyal union members. Furthermore, as we will see, it is the union members, not only the union executive, who give the mandate for strike action, and thus the support of the union members is essential for a strike to take place.

Another individual factor that may be relevant in determining whether a strike or lockout occurs is the history and quality of the relationship between the parties. If the parties have a history of using strikes or lockouts against each other in past bargaining disputes, they may be more likely to do so in subsequent disputes. If the parties have experienced strikes or lockouts in the past and thus are knowledgeable about how these actions are conducted, they may be less fearful to undertake these actions than parties that are unfamiliar with the strategic use of these actions. In addition, if the parties had a hostile relationship prior to the start of bargaining or if their relationship became contentious as bargaining progressed, they might be willing to consider more confrontational bargaining tactics than they would have been otherwise.

Economic Conditions

The general economic conditions in which the bargaining takes place also have an effect on whether a strike or lockout occurs. Such factors as unemployment rates, the financial position of the employer, the general profit picture in the industry, and the current stage in the employer's "business cycle" all affect strike or lockout propensity.[9]

High unemployment rates negatively affect union members' willingness to strike if the members perceive that other work opportunities are not readily available; this factor is particularly important if union members perceive that a strike will be lengthy rather than brief.

The financial position of the employer or the industry affects the union's perceptions of the employer's ability to pay. Such perceptions are then balanced against the perceived likelihood of obtaining desired financial goals through strike action. A union may want a large wage increase, but if the employer is perceived as being unable to afford that increase and a strike is not perceived as a means of changing that situation, it is unlikely that a strike will be perceived as the most productive action to gain a wage increase. A strike in such a situation has a negative economic impact on individual union members if the amounts gained through a negotiated wage increase do not equal or exceed the amount of wages they lost during the strike.

The stage of the employer's business cycle is influential in that strikes will not have a particularly large financial impact on the employer during slow times in the employer's business. For example, a strike by employees of a ski resort would not have much impact during the summer, since the resort might be closed or might be operating on a very limited basis. However, a strike by the same employees would have a very large impact in January or February when the resort is operating in peak season. An employer, particularly one in a seasonal business, cannot afford to be closed for a long period during the time when most of its revenue is generated. When planning strike action, unions might also take into consideration any major events the employer is planning. For example, hotel employees could threaten to go on strike when a large convention is scheduled for the hotel facility. The employer would not want to lose the revenue (or suffer the damage to its reputation) that a cancellation would likely cause and thus might be more willing than at other times to accede to the union's bargaining demands.

Legislative Restrictions

As we will see in the next section, federal and provincial labour laws require that several conditions be met for a legal strike or lockout to take place. While these laws have a direct bearing on whether a legal strike or lockout is possible, they do not always completely discourage a strike or lockout from happening when the requirements are not met. Despite the bans in most Canadian labour codes on strikes during the term of a collective agreement, Canada has a long history of these types of strikes. Such strikes may occur spontaneously as an expression of dissatisfaction, or they may be planned and facilitated by union leaders, despite the fact that they are technically illegal.

Additionally, in many jurisdictions in Canada, the ability of public sector workers to strike is severely restricted or banned outright. Nevertheless, public sector strikes represent between 20 and 30 percent of annual strike activity in Canada.[10] It has been argued that the restrictions on striking in the public sector are themselves a major cause of public sector strikes.[11] It has been proposed that the "no-strike laws" restrict the ability of public sector union negotiators to press their demands to the limit; this is because the negotiating team representing the government knows that the union cannot threaten to strike if the union negotiators' demands are not met. No-strike laws can also cause dangerously high levels of conflict to build up between the parties, since a strike cannot be used as a means of expressing discontent or resolving bargaining disputes.

Bargaining Process Factors

Strikes and lockouts are sometimes resorted to as a means of providing a break from bargaining and an emotional release for the bargainers and the parties they represent. If tensions are running high at the bargaining table, a strike or lockout may be perceived as a way to give the parties time away from bargaining so that they might return with new energy and ideas. Moreover, the union members represented in bargaining will have an opportunity to express their feelings through picketing and other forms of public action. While it is highly unlikely that a potentially costly or lengthy strike or lockout would occur for the sole reason of releasing emotional tension, a beneficial side effect of a strike or lockout may be that the bargainers will return to the negotiating table in a better frame of mind.

We should also remember that a party can be pressured into accepting the other party's demands without a strike or lockout actually occurring. The mere threat of strike or lockout action may be enough to gain bargaining concessions, especially if one party knows that the other party does not have the resources to endure even a minor work stoppage. One party can therefore use the possibility of a strike or a lockout as a bargaining tactic to make gains in bargaining without a strike or lockout actually taking place.

The factors affecting the likelihood of a strike or lockout taking place are summarized in Table 9-1. We will now go on to discuss how a strike or lockout actually occurs.

TABLE 9-1 Factors Affecting the Likelihood of a Strike or Lockout	
Motivations for striking or locking out	– strikes as mistakes – strikes as collective voice
Bargaining structure	– size of bargaining unit
Individual factors	– willingness of union members to support or authorize strike – history or quality of previous relationship between the parties
Economic conditions	– unemployment rate – employer's business cycle – employer's financial position
Legislative restrictions	– conditions that must be met for strike or lockout to be legal – ability to strike, especially in public sector
Bargaining process factors	– level of tension at bargaining table – strike or lockout as a break from bargaining – strike or lockout as form of emotional release – effectiveness of threat of strike or lockout, not actual event

HOW DOES A STRIKE OR LOCKOUT BEGIN?

Provincial and federal labour laws in Canada specify several conditions that must be in place for a strike or lockout to occur. Preconditions to the specific federal and provincial jurisdictions are outlined in Table 9-2; there are, however, several general preconditions that are fairly consistent across jurisdictions, and we will now turn our attention to these.

TABLE 9-2 Preconditions for a Legal Strike or Lockout

	Strike Vote	Third-Party Intervention	Notice
Federal	Compulsory vote by secret ballot; results valid for 60 days or agreed-upon period. Results determined by majority of those voting. No vote required if lockout has occurred	Notification must be issued of failure to settle dispute before strike or lockout permitted, unless minister responsible for labour has already assisted	At least 72 hours notice to other party with a copy to minister of labour. Notice not required if legal strike/lockout by other party has already occurred
Alberta	Compulsory supervised secret-ballot vote; results valid for 120 days. Results determined by majority of those voting	No strike or lockout until formal appointment of a mediator. A party accepting mediator's recommendations may request a vote on them by other party	At least 72 hours notice to other party, with a similar notice to appointed mediator
British Columbia	Compulsory secret-ballot vote unless lockout has lasted more than 72 hours. Results valid for 3 months or agreed-upon period. Results determined by majority of those voting	Not required	At least 72 hours notice to other party and labour relations board. Board may order a longer notice period for protection of property or persons
Manitoba	Compulsory secret-ballot vote. Results determined by majority of those voting	Not required	Not required
New Brunswick	Compulsory secret-ballot vote; results valid for one year. Results determined by majority of employees in bargaining unit who vote	No strike or lockout can occur until one party has requested the appointment of a conciliator	24 hours notice to other party

TABLE 9-2 Continued

	Strike Vote	Third-Party Intervention	Notice
Newfoundland	Compulsory secret-ballot vote. Results determined by majority of those voting	No strike or lockout permitted until a party has requested a conciliation board hearing	Not required
Nova Scotia	Compulsory secret-ballot vote. Results determined by majority of those voting	No strike or lockout permitted until appointment of a conciliation board and until minister of labour has received 48-hour strike/lockout notice	48 hours notice to minister of labour
Ontario	Compulsory secret-ballot vote taken at earliest 30 days before collective agreement expires or, if no agreement, from date of conciliator's appointment. Results determined by majority of employees in unit who vote	Not required	Not required
Prince Edward Island	Compulsory secret-ballot vote. Results determined by majority of employees in unit who vote	No strike or lockout permitted until appointment of a mediator, conciliator, or conciliation board	Not required
Quebec	Compulsory secret-ballot vote. Results determined by majority of union members in unit who vote	Not required	Not required
Saskatchewan	Compulsory secret-ballot vote unless unit is 1 or 2 employees. Labour relations board may supervise vote upon application for supervision by either party. Results determined by majority of unit members who vote	Not required, although 48 hours notice of strike/lockout must be given to other party and to minister of labour	At least 48 hours notice to other party and to minister of labour

Source: Human Resources Development Canada, Labour Program, Synoptic Charts on Legislation Pertaining to Certain Major Collective Bargaining Issues: Strike Vote, Strike/Lockout Notice, Check-off of Union Dues and Ratification Vote (available at <http://www.hrdc-drhc.gc.ca>).

The first general precondition is that a legal strike or lockout can only occur while collective bargaining is taking place and when an existing collective agreement has expired. Occasionally, a strike will take place during the term of the collective agreement, usually in reaction to a controversial workplace event or series of events. This type of illegal strike is called a **wildcat strike**. In a wildcat strike, employees will usually walk off the job or not show up for work, even if directed to do otherwise by their union executive. When a wildcat strike occurs, the employer usually applies to a labour relations board for a declaration that the strike is illegal and an order for the strikers to return to work. The employer usually obtains the declaration within a few hours so that the impact of the strike can be kept to a minimum and the workers return to work as soon as possible.

The second precondition for a legal strike is that it must be authorized by a vote of the bargaining unit. This precondition is in place to ensure that strike action truly reflects the will of the union membership and is not just an idea of the union executive or bargaining team. The vote authorizing strike action, known as the **strike vote**, is conducted by secret ballot. The vote consists of a simple yes/no response to the question of whether the voter supports the union's undertaking strike action.

In most provinces, a majority (usually defined as 50% + 1) of voters in favour of a strike is required for a **strike mandate**, that is, for the union to be authorized to begin a legal strike. As shown in Table 9-2, some provincial labour codes have specific provisions for who may participate in a strike vote and how a majority in a strike vote is to be calculated. In some provinces, there must be a majority of support among all members of the bargaining unit; this is a slightly stricter standard than in other jurisdictions, which simply require a majority among those voting. The reasoning behind the stricter standard is to ensure that majority support for the strike exists in the

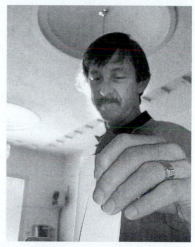

Bernie Young of Steelworkers Local 6500 casts his strike vote in a contract dispute with INCO. Most agreements are reached without the need for a strike or lockout.

entire bargaining unit and not just among those who took the time to participate in the strike vote. However, the reasoning for using the simple majority of voters as the determinant of strike support is that since unions are democratic organizations, every member of the bargaining unit has the opportunity to participate in the strike vote, but if individuals choose not to use that opportunity, that choice should not affect the outcome of the vote of those who did participate.

A vote in support of a strike does not guarantee that a strike will occur immediately or even that it will occur at all. Often, a vote to strike is used to support the union's bargaining demands, since it shows the employer that the bargaining unit members are prepared to withdraw their labour to achieve their demands. It is not uncommon that the bargaining following a successful strike vote results in a collective agreement without a strike ever happening. However, in some provinces (Alberta, British Columbia, and New Brunswick), there is a time limit on the validity of a strike vote. If this time limit passes and the union wishes to have a valid strike mandate, the union must conduct another strike vote and again receive the required level of support.

The third precondition for a legal strike or lockout in several (but not all) Canadian jurisdictions is that the parties make use of third-party intervention before the strike or lockout. Depending on the jurisdiction, this intervention can take the form of a conciliator who reports on the bargaining situation to the relevant minister of labour, or a mediator who actually participates in the bargaining process to help the parties reach an agreement. Third-party intervention will be discussed in more detail in Chapter 10, but we will briefly comment at this point on its role in the strike/lockout process.

The philosophy behind the requirement of third-party intervention in collective bargaining is that since a strike or lockout has a potentially widespread damaging effect, the parties should explore every possible opportunity for resolution before a strike or lockout occurs. The role of the third party is to assist in identifying such opportunities and to help bring the parties to an agreement. The participation of a neutral third party may help the parties recognize common ground on contentious issues and shift their focus from perceived differences and conflicts that obscure potential mutually acceptable solutions. However, there are those who believe that if the parties are committed strongly enough to their bargaining positions to consider a strike or lockout, it is unlikely that a third party will be able to overcome such major differences and the intervention of the third party will be resented and ineffectual.[12] Third-party intervention, furthermore, can have the opposite effect than intended if the parties are forced to sit through a process they are not committed to and did not request; in such situations, their differences and resentments may be heightened rather than reduced.

The fourth precondition for a legal strike or lockout in several jurisdictions is that the party initiating a strike or lockout must give notice to the other party of when the strike or lockout will begin. There may be arrangements that must be made in the workplace to accommodate the effects of a strike or lockout, since there will be limited or blocked access to the workplace while the strike or lockout is in progress. For example, the employer may have cash, business documents, or other valuables in the workplace that need to be secured or moved to a more accessible location. In some workplaces, there are perishable goods that must be removed and stored elsewhere. As well, employees may have personal belongings that they would like to remove from the workplace. A strike or lockout notice gives time for all these activities to occur.

Most jurisdictions in Canada also have legislation that restricts or forbids workers in certain occupations from striking. These occupations are referred to as **essential services**. The criteria used to designate these occupations vary, and the occupations are not always specifically named in the labour legislation. However, the general principle is that workers are considered to be providing an essential service if their absence from the workplace would cause a threat to public safety or health. Therefore, occupations such as police officer, correctional officer, medical doctor, and firefighter are usually considered essential services. An example of legislation defining essential services is section 41(5) of the *Labour Act* of Prince Edward Island, which states: "No member of the police force, employed in any city, town or incorporated community, nor any person being a full-time employee of any fire department, nor any person employed by a hospital as defined in the *Hospitals Act* nor any employee of a nursing home or community care facility nor non-instructional personnel as defined in the *School Act* has the right to strike, or to engage in any stoppage of work."

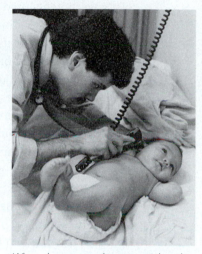

When doctors or other essential workers go on strike, provisions are made to ensure their absence does not compromise public health and safety.

When a breakdown or dispute in collective bargaining involves an occupation designated as an essential service, there is usually provision in the relevant collective agreement or labour legislation for resolution through some form of third-party intervention rather than by a strike or lockout. Similarly, in any public sector bargaining situation where strikes are restricted or not permitted, disputes are resolved through some form of third-party intervention. However, if a legal or illegal public sector strike occurs, governments can use **back-to-work legislation**, a dispute-resolution method that is not available to employers in the private sector. Provincial or federal legislatures can pass a law ordering the strike to end and the public sector workers to return to work, usually with a provision that some form of third-party intervention be employed to resolve the disputes that caused the strike. Governments and private sector employers can also use the courts to order an end to a strike that is deemed illegal. An example of a government using a court order to end a public sector strike is described in the vignette that opens this chapter.

According to a study covering the years 1965 to 1993, Canadian federal and provincial governments used back-to-work legislation 62 times as a method of resolving public sector strikes.[13] This figure indicates that Canadian governments are not reluctant to use back-to-work legislation as a method of resolving bargaining disputes. However, passing such legislation can be a tricky political matter for governments. While the passage of such legislation has the immediate desired effect of ending the strike, this method of dispute resolution can make the government appear heavy-handed, especially if public support is on the side of the strikers. Government use of back-to-work legislation can also cause long-term problems in the bargaining relationship between the government and its employees, as the employees may resent the government's exercising this exceptional power rather than constructively addressing the disputes that caused the strike.

In several Canadian jurisdictions, workers in some parts of the public sector, such as health care, must provide a designated minimum level of service during a strike in order for the strike to be designated as legal. The numbers and types of employees that must be working to maintain this level of service are determined either by legislation, by negotiation, or by third-party intervention, depending on the jurisdiction or what the parties themselves can agree to.

Now that we have outlined the conditions that must be met for a legal strike or lockout to take place, we will turn to describing what actually happens during a strike or lockout.

WHAT HAPPENS WHEN A STRIKE OR LOCKOUT TAKES PLACE

During a strike or lockout, as previously described, the workplace is usually inaccessible, the workers do not perform their regular jobs, and the employer is generally unable to continue with regular business activities. It is not illegal for workers on strike to seek employment elsewhere, and many do so in order to supplement **strike pay**, which is payment issued by the union to its striking members to partially compensate for the loss of regular employment income.

Collective bargaining may or may not resume while a strike or lockout is in progress. Once the strike or lockout starts having a noticeable economic impact, one or both of the affected parties may be sufficiently motivated to return to the bargaining table. On the other hand, one party may refuse to return to the bargaining table simply because of the pressure of a strike or lockout and may instead demand that the strike or lockout end as a condition of resuming bargaining.

Two major factors affect how a strike or lockout proceeds once it begins: picketing and the use of replacement workers. We will discuss each of these factors in turn.

Picketing

Picketing is probably the most visible indication of a strike or lockout. Picketing union members walk around the perimeter of the employer's premises on a **picket line**, usually wearing or carrying signs to indicate that a strike or lockout is in progress. Picketers may hand out information pamphlets to passers-by or engage interested members of the public in discussions about their dispute with the employer.

Picketing serves two major functions. First, it attempts to help the strikers gain the support of the public by physically demonstrating the workers' lack of access to their workplace and publicizing their dispute with the employer. Second, it discourages individuals from attempting to enter the premises. Although the workplace is closed to the union members, management employees may be expected to attend work regardless of the strike or lockout. In addition, suppliers may bring materials to the workplace, and workers associated with the maintenance of the premises may be expected to provide their usual services. Customers, clients, or service users may also attempt to continue business transactions with the employer. The presence of a picket line is intended to hamper physical access to the entrances and thus discourage these parties from entering the premises.

While picketing itself is a fairly straightforward activity, attempting to regulate it can be quite complex. As discussed in Chapter 1, the Supreme Court of Canada has dealt with cases dealing with the issue of whether the right to picket is addressed by the provisions in the Canadian *Charter of Rights and Freedoms* guaranteeing freedom of association and freedom of expression. The Supreme Court's rulings indicate that the definition of "picketing" and any associated restrictions on picketing activity must be carefully applied so as not to restrict the picketers' freedom of expression. However, the Supreme Court has determined that picketing is not an inherent right under the Charter provisions and thus reasonable limitations can be placed on picketing activity.[14]

Another consideration in regulating picketing is the need to balance the rights of the various parties involved or affected. A labour relations board must ensure that workers have the opportunity to promote their cause through picketing; at the same time, other individuals, such as non-union staff or suppliers, should not be unduly constrained from conducting their regular business. Because of the many unique factors in each strike or lockout and the differing natures of the parties involved or affected, labour relations board or court rulings in many picketing cases are fairly situation-specific. However, a few general guidelines can be presented.

Cases of Shared Premises   If the employer shares premises with businesses or organizations that are not directly involved with the strike or lockout, the picketers must not interfere with the legitimate business activities of these tenants. For example, the picketers should not picket in front of a doorway that is the primary business entrance for other tenants, and they should picket only the employer's premises in an industrial park and not the common gateway shared by all tenants. A labour relations board may restrict picketing to specific times of day or limit the number of picketers in order to reduce the amount of disruption that a picket line may cause to other tenants' activities.

Secondary Picketing   To interfere with the employer's business, picketers often appear at the "non-struck" premises of suppliers that are doing business with the employer or at other locations or separate businesses operated by the employer where workers are not on strike. This type of picketing is called **secondary picketing**. The main purpose of secondary picketing is to restrict or curtail the possibility of the employer's using a secondary location to carry out work that would usually be conducted at the struck or locked-out location. Secondary picketing is also intended to hamper the employer's ability to generate revenue by making it difficult for the employer to conduct its usual business with suppliers or in other locations.

Secondary picketing of the employer's other business locations is usually permitted without much dispute. However, for secondary picketing of the employer's suppliers or other business associates to be considered legal, the union usually must prove that the supplier or other business associate is doing business only or primarily with the "struck" employer. Irregular transactions (such as a pickup or drop-off once a day) are rarely sufficient to justify legal secondary picketing. Some form of dependency or ongoing regular business relationship with the struck employer must be shown for legal secondary picketing to be permitted at the locations of businesses not operated by the employer.

Compliance with the Law   The picketers, their supporters, the employer, and anyone else involved in the strike or lockout must conduct themselves according to the law. Destruction of property, physical violence, or intimidation of individuals entering or leaving the employer's premises are not legal, just as they would not be legal in any other setting. If such events occur, the individuals involved could face charges under civil or criminal law, as well as penalties from a labour relations board. However, it is often difficult to determine when picket line behaviour becomes unacceptable, since what is intimidating to one person may not be to another. The struck employer or inconvenienced customers may complain about behaviour that in other contexts might be considered simply forceful or rude. In such situations, it may be up to the authorities present at the event (if there are any), such as police officers, to determine whether the behaviour should cease and to take appropriate action. Alternatively, a labour relations board may have to assess the evidence of the participants in or witnesses to the event and decide whether permanent intervention (such as a "cease and desist" order) is warranted.

Adherence to the Facts   Picket signs and information leaflets distributed by picketers must contain factual statements and must not be libellous. Libel is broadly defined as a statement of something untrue that would damage an individual's reputation. For example, it would probably be considered libellous to say that the employer is a liar or is corrupt; if such a statement is made, the employer could sue the union for compensation to repair its damaged reputation or make up for lost business. To avoid such legal entanglements, picket signs usually contain the simple statement "On Strike" and the name of the union or unions involved. Information leaflets generally describe the bargaining situation as factually as possible: for example, "On [date] the union proposed a wage of $15. On [date] the employer responded by offering a wage of $10. The union considered this unacceptable and went on strike." Information leaflets may contain a request for public support and, possibly, contact information for the employer so that members of the public can contact the employer directly and encourage the employer to address the union's concerns.

Although, as we have mentioned, the purpose of a picket line is to discourage individuals from entering the employer's premises, some union members choose to cross their own union's picket line or the picket line of another striking union. Generally, they do this because they do not agree with the rationale behind the strike. However, most unions consider it a serious offence for a unionized worker to cross a picket line, particularly a picket line maintained by his or her own union. The slang term for a person who crosses a picket line is a **scab**; this term is also used to refer to replacement workers, who will be discussed in the next section. Although replacement workers are usually not union members, they cross picket lines to enter the employer's premises.

It is considered a serious offence for a unionized worker to cross another union's picket line or to perform work that would ordinarily be done by a worker who is on strike or locked out. Both of these actions have the effect of undermining the unity of the striking workers, and a unified front for unions is important in maintaining a strong position at the bargaining table. The action of crossing a picket line could result in the offending individual being penalized by his or her own union; in extreme cases, the individual could be expelled from the union, which, as discussed in Chapter 7, would severely hamper his or her ability to find work at other unionized workplaces.

Two other forms of pressure that can be brought to bear on the employer during a strike are the **boycott** and the **hot declaration**. If a union is on strike and the employer is still able to produce and sell goods, whether directly to the consumer or through secondary sources such as distributors, the union will often contact other unions or labour federations to request a boycott declaration. This declaration encourages other union members not to purchase the employer's products while the strike or lockout is in progress, the boycott's intent being to further reduce the employer's revenue.

A hot declaration is somewhat more direct in its impact than a boycott. If a union or labour federation issues a hot declaration with respect to a struck company's goods or services, other union members may have the right to refuse to handle those goods or services in the course of their work. For example, if a company whose workers are on strike attempts to place an advertisement in a newspaper with unionized production staff, a hot declaration might mean that the production staff will refuse to accept the advertisement, create the advertisement's layout, or print the section of the paper with the advertisement in it. Where it exists, the right of union members to honour a hot declaration is usually outlined in a provision in the collective agreement.

The success of a boycott depends on the union's ability to generate publicity and make other union members aware of the strike or lockout and the request not to buy the employer's products. Members of other unions also must be informed about what the employer's products are—a tricky undertaking if the employer sells its goods or services under a variety of brand names. And, of course, the boycott will only be successful if union members actually refuse to purchase the boycotted products. Most labour federations strongly encourage their members to honour boycotts as a means of building unity within the entire labour movement. In fact, the websites of most large unions and labour federations list boycotts that are currently in effect.

Usually, a boycott ends when the strike or lockout ends. If an employer has a history of poor labour relations, however, an ongoing boycott may be imposed to discourage individuals from seeking work there. Two examples of ongoing boycotts are the Canadian Association of University Teachers' and the American Association of University Professors' lists of censured administrations. The employers on these lists are universities or colleges that, in the associations' opinion, have violated principles of academic freedom. While members of unions belonging to these associations are not formally forbidden from taking employment with an employer on these lists, they are encouraged to educate themselves on the employer's past actions before they do so. In the words of the American Association of University Professors, "The association leaves it to the discretion of the individual, possessed of the facts, to make the proper decision."[15]

Replacement Workers

As we have seen, the intent of a strike is to interfere with the employer's ability to continue business through the use of a variety of tactics, including removing the workers that carry out the business's operations. Thus, one of the more controversial areas in Canadian labour law is whether the employer should be permitted to use or hire **replacement workers**, workers who carry out tasks usually performed by workers who are currently on strike.

The theoretical argument in favour of permitting replacement workers is that the employer's business should not be affected by the decision of the workers to withdraw their labour and

Striking *Calgary Herald* workers yell at a replacement worker as he tries to cross the picket line. The use of replacement workers remains a controversial issue in Canadian industrial relations.

that a prolonged shutdown or reduction in production could cause the business lasting harm. It is also argued that if striking workers are not banned from earning money through other sources of employment, it is unfair to ban the employer from earning money from its business operations while a strike is taking place.

The theoretical argument against permitting replacement workers is that giving the employer the ability to use replacement workers creates a severe imbalance in bargaining power. A withdrawal of labour will have virtually no economic impact on the employer if the employer can easily replace the striking workers and continue operating as usual. Thus, the argument proceeds, the balance of power in bargaining is clearly weighted in the employer's favour if replacement workers are permitted. The ability to replace striking workers removes any economic incentive the employer might have had to concede to the union's demands. There is also a great potential for conflict and violence on the picket line if replacement workers are regularly confronting picketing union members when entering or leaving the employer's premises.

Both of these philosophical positions are apparent in the different ways that the use

TABLE 9-3 Regulations on the Use of Replacement Workers during a Strike or Lockout

	Who Can Work during a Strike or Lockout	Other Conditions	Returning to Work after a Strike or Lockout
Federal	Employers or their agents are prohibited from using "for the demonstrated purpose of undermining a trade union's represented capacity, rather than the pursuit of legitimate bargaining objectives" the services of persons not in the bargaining unit on the date notice to bargain was given and hired or assigned after that date to perform duties of striking or locked-out employees	Certain activities must be maintained to the extent necessary to prevent an immediate and serious danger to public health or safety The board may issue orders to ensure maintenance of activities	Employees in the bargaining unit who were on strike or locked out have the right to be reinstated in preference to any persons not in the bargaining unit on the date notice to bargain was given and hired or assigned after that date to perform duties of striking or locked-out employees

TABLE 9-3 Continued

	Who Can Work during a Strike or Lockout	Other Conditions	Returning to Work after a Strike or Lockout
Alberta	No specific prohibitions	No specific prohibitions	When a strike or lockout ends through a settlement or the cancellation of bargaining rights or two years after the strike or lockout began, any employee whose employment relationship has not been legally terminated can apply to return to work in preference to any employee hired as a replacement worker
British Columbia	Employers are prohibited from using the paid or unpaid service of anyone transferred, hired, or engaged after notice to bargain was issued; anyone who ordinarily works at another of the employer's operations; or anyone employed, engaged, or supplied to the employer by another person. These individuals cannot be used to perform the work of striking or locked-out workers or the work ordinarily done by personnel permitted to perform replacement work (i.e., managers or members of the bargaining unit who consent to do such work)	The board chair or either party in bargaining may request an investigation into whether a dispute poses a significant threat to public health, safety, or welfare. The minister, upon receiving the board's report, may direct the board to designate an essential service in case of a danger of this nature that is immediate and serious	No specifications

TABLE 9-3 Continued

	Who Can Work during a Strike or Lockout	Other Conditions	Returning to Work after a Strike or Lockout
Manitoba	Employers cannot hire, offer to hire, or threaten to hire replacement workers prior to or during a work stoppage for any period of time longer than the duration of the work stoppage	Employers cannot take action against an employee who refuses to perform the work of a striking or locked-out worker Employers cannot take action against an employee covered by a collective agreement who refuses to do work that would directly facilitate the business of another employer whose employees within Canada are on strike or locked out	When an application is made by either party to settle a collective agreement, the strike or lockout must be terminated and employees reinstated in the jobs they had at the time the work stoppage began
New Brunswick	No specific prohibitions	No specifications	No specifications
Newfoundland	No specific prohibitions	No specifications	No specifications
Nova Scotia	No specific prohibitions	Employers are prohibited from refusing to employ or discriminating against anyone who has participated in a legal strike Employers are prohibited from penalizing an employee who refuses to perform the work of another employee participating in a legal strike	No specifications

TABLE 9-3 Continued

	Who Can Work during a Strike or Lockout	Other Conditions	Returning to Work after a Strike or Lockout
Ontario	No specific prohibitions	Employers are not permitted to employ professional strike-breakers, and no one is permitted to act as one	Within 6 months of the start of a legal strike, an employee can apply to the employer to return to work. The employer is then obliged to reinstate the employee unless the work formerly done by the employee no longer exists
Prince Edward Island	No specific prohibitions, although the employment of replacement workers is considered terminated at the end of a strike or lockout	No specifications	When a legal strike or lockout ends, affected employees are to be reinstated unless operations have been discontinued or suspended. If operations resume, the striking or locked-out employees must be reinstated first
Quebec	Employers are prohibited from using replacement employees, defined as: – those hired between the start of negotiations and the end of a strike/lockout – employees of other employers or sub-contractors – members of the bargaining unit involved, unless the work is a designated essential service – persons employed in the employer's other establishments	Employers are prohibited from using the services of striking or locked-out employees in any of their other establishments The government, on the recommendation of the minister, may require essential services to be maintained. This order may be issued any time prior	At the end of a strike or lockout, any affected employee is entitled to return to his/her employment in priority over any other person, unless the employer can produce a "good and sufficient reason" for not recalling the employee

TABLE 9-3 Continued

	Who Can Work during a Strike or Lockout	Other Conditions	Returning to Work after a Strike or Lockout
Quebec	– managers employed by the employer in other establishments – employees who do not belong to the bargaining unit on strike or locked out	to the filing of a completed collective agreement	
Saskatchewan	No specific prohibitions	No specifications	At the conclusion of a strike or lockout, if the parties have not reached an agreement on reinstatement, the employer must reinstate employees to their original positions. An employee who is not reinstated due to lack of work is entitled to layoff notice or pay in lieu of notice. Striking or locked-out employees are entitled to displace any persons hired to perform their work during a work stoppage

Source: Human Resources Development Canada, Labour Program, Summaries of General Private Sector Collective Bargaining Legislation (available at <http://www.hrdc-drhc.gc.ca>).

of replacement workers is addressed in labour legislation across Canada. This legislation is summarized in Table 9-3.

As we can see from Table 9-3, restrictions on the use of replacement workers range from being non-existent in some jurisdictions to being very strict in others. British Columbia and Quebec have the strongest restrictions on replacement workers. Legislation in both of these jurisdictions defines replacement workers not only as those brought in to perform work once a strike or lockout begins, but also as any workers hired after collective bargaining begins. Legislation containing these terms attempts to prevent the employer from pre-empting the effects of a strike or lockout by hiring employees prior to a strike or lockout. The concern is that the employer could hire people at this time as a means of acquiring workers to replace unionized workers who would not be present in the workplace once a strike or lockout started.

The *Canada Labour Code* restricts the employer's ability to "stack" the workplace with additional workers prior to a strike or lockout. However, the federal code stipulates that workers brought in after collective bargaining begins are only considered replacement workers if they are hired or assigned to do the work of striking or locked-out employees. Manitoba legislation does not allow replacement workers to be hired during a strike or lockout. British Columbia forbids the use of **professional strike-breakers**: individuals whose sole source of employment is replacing workers on strike. Usually, these individuals can be supplied through an employment agency that specializes in providing such workers to employers undergoing a strike or lockout. Some of these agencies specialize in providing workers with skills in particular occupations or industries, so the employer can resume production with minimal disruption or time lost in training the workers.

However, most jurisdictions in Canada do not explicitly forbid managers from doing the work of union members during a strike or lockout. As we know, managers are usually excluded from union membership and are usually employed in the workplace on an ongoing basis. Thus, managers who continue to work during a strike or lockout are not generally considered to be replacement workers, even if they do tasks that would usually be done by union members. Some jurisdictions specify that managers can only legally work in a struck or locked-out location if they were managers at that location prior to the commencement of the strike or lockout. This provision prevents employers from stacking the workplace with managers in the event of a strike or lockout; this provision has the same intention as those that restrict the hiring of non-managerial employees prior to a strike or lockout.

We should note that in the jurisdictions that restrict the use of replacement workers, there are provisions for the maintenance of essential services, as mentioned above. Replacement workers might be needed to keep essential services functioning if a strike or lockout occurs. Thus, the legislation in these jurisdictions usually makes some distinction between work that takes place during a strike or lockout to generate revenue for the employer and work that contributes to maintaining required levels of essential services.

Jurisdictions that allow the use of replacement workers during a strike or lockout generally specify in their legislation what will happen to replacement workers when the strike or lockout ends. Without such legislation, it would be unclear whether the replacement worker or the worker on strike has the right to continue in a job when regular work resumes. Most jurisdictions indicate that the worker on strike must be given priority over a replacement worker for the job when the strike ends, or that the striking worker must be reinstated in his or her previous position after the strike or lockout ends. Alberta and Ontario both allow striking workers to apply to the employer for reinstatement and to return to work after a strike has continued for a certain length of time. These provisions are intended to allow workers who so choose to resume their regular jobs and not suffer the financial consequences of a lengthy strike. We should, however, note that unions on strike do not encourage their members to exercise this option. The return of union members to their jobs while the strike is still in progress would considerably weaken the united support behind the strike and increase the employer's ability to withstand the impact of the strike action.

Having outlined some of the events and conditions that happen while a strike or lockout is in progress, we will now describe why and how a strike or lockout ends.

ENDING A STRIKE OR LOCKOUT

A strike or lockout ends in one of two ways: (1) the bargaining parties reach a collective agreement or (2) one party chooses to cease its actions and, usually, return to bargaining. The length of time it takes to reach either of these forms of resolution depends on a number of factors, the most important being the ability of the parties involved to endure the economic impact of a strike or lockout.

As mentioned, unions are usually able to replace at least some of their members' lost wages with strike pay while a strike or lockout is in progress. The funding for strike pay comes from the union's own financial resources. Many unions have funds banked specifically for this purpose, set aside from the regular revenues generated by union dues. The union's ability to continue paying strike pay is clearly an important determinant of how long a strike lasts. If the strike is longer than the union has budgeted for, union members may be dissatisfied with reduced or non-existent strike pay. If the union is a local of a larger national or international union, the parent union might provide additional funds for strike pay, allowing the union to prolong the strike action beyond what it could afford on its own. However, strike pay is rarely the same as the amount that workers earn from their regular job, and poorer unions may not be able to offer any strike pay at all. Therefore, the individual financial situations of the members and the amount of financial support the union is able to offer can strongly influence a strike's duration.

If the local unemployment rate is low and union members are easily able to find alternative work during a strike, the strike may be longer than it would otherwise be. The loss of income for individual members might not be as dramatic as it would be with a shorter strike since they can make money at other jobs while the strike is in progress. However, the relevance of this factor is somewhat dependent on the individual union members and the type of alternative work available. If, for example, union members are older clerical workers and the only type of short-term employment available involves hard physical labour, the availability of alternative employment is not as relevant, as the striking workers may not want to, or cannot, take the jobs that are available.

The employer's ability to endure the economic pain of a strike or lockout is also affected by a variety of factors. The employer, like the union, may have funding set aside to offset the impact of a shutdown, perhaps a contingency fund established for exactly this purpose. The employer may also have sufficient inventory on hand, or enough alternative sources of income, to allow it to continue production or operations. And though a business may suffer loss of income from reduced sales during a shutdown, it also saves money by not having to pay many of its normal operating expenses, including wages and benefits, which are a significant portion of most employers' budgets. And, like the local union, if the employer is a branch or subsidiary of a larger company, there may be funds available from the parent organization to offset losses from a work shutdown. Whether the employer can hire replacement workers or not also affects its ability to withstand a strike. A study of Canadian strike data from 1966 to 1985 indicated that strikes were significantly longer in jurisdictions that banned the use of replacement workers. This finding suggests that an employer that can use replacement workers has a much greater ability to compel the union to settle a collective agreement quickly.[16]

An American study recently identified the amount of media attention a strike receives as a factor affecting the length of a strike.[17] Although this study only analysed

90 American strikes, each involving more than 10,000 workers, the results indicated that pre-strike media attention significantly increased strike duration. The author of the study speculates that such attention causes the negotiators to increase their commitment to their publicized bargaining positions and thus become less willing to make compromises. There is also the possibility that the parties use media attention to increase their own power in bargaining and to generate public sympathy for their cause; such efforts can be expected to intensify conflict at the bargaining table.

When a strike ends because the negotiating teams have settled on a collective agreement, the union members must vote on whether to accept the terms of the proposed collective agreement. This vote is known as a **ratification vote**, as described in Chapter 8. If the majority of bargaining unit members vote to accept the terms that have been negotiated, the terms are incorporated into a collective agreement that is signed by union and management representatives. Once the collective agreement has been signed, the strike formally ends.

The union and the employer will usually also agree on conditions governing the employees' return to work. For example, it is common to set a deadline by which employees must report to work, allowing employees who have undertaken other commitments during the strike (such as jobs elsewhere) sufficient time to satisfy those commitments. Other issues that might need to be negotiated at the end of a strike include how to deal with disputes related to incidents on the picket line (e.g., how or whether employees involved in unlawful or disruptive activities will be disciplined by the employer).

If the ratification vote fails, the terms of the agreement are returned to the bargaining table and the union negotiating team must continue negotiating for an agreement more acceptable to the union membership. As Chapter 8 describes, the management negotiating team will also ensure that the terms of the agreement are acceptable to the stakeholders they represent; if the stakeholders are not satisfied with the agreed-upon terms, the team will have to return to the table and reopen negotiations.

We should note, however, that the effects of a strike or lockout may last far beyond its formal ending. Since strikes and lockouts are clearly hostile events that generate strong emotional reactions, the resentments and conflicts fuelled by a strike or lockout may, directly or indirectly, cause further conflict after the parties return to work. The attitudes toward the "other side" created by a strike or lockout, particularly a lengthy one, may influence how union members and management treat each other on a daily basis in the workplace. Residual hostility between union and management can also have a negative effect on future interactions, such as grievance resolution or bargaining for subsequent collective agreements.

Having outlined the process of strikes and lockouts, we will now attempt to put those processes in context by discussing some data that attempt to measure the impact of strikes in Canada.

PUTTING CANADA'S STRIKE RECORD IN CONTEXT

To attempt to understand the impact that strikes have in Canada, we will examine two kinds of data relating to Canadian strike activity. The first is data that relates to Canada's strike record over several decades. The second is data that compares Canada's strike record to that of other industrialized countries.

Measuring the impact of strikes is a challenging task because of the many different measures that can be used and the difficulty of accurately capturing some data. Counting the frequency or duration of strikes is relatively straightforward, since it is easy to maintain actual records of strikes and their length. However, these measures in isolation do not always fully reflect a strike's impact. The average length of a strike may be skewed upwards by a few very long strikes, and a simple count of how many strikes occur during a given period will not reflect such important information as the number of workers involved and the length of time they were affected. Other potential measures, such as financial impact, are also difficult to estimate accurately. Determining the value of lost sales or production during a strike or lockout is not easy because it is not always apparent what sales or production levels would have been if the strike or lockout had not occurred. It is also difficult to assign a dollar value to potentially affected intangibles such as customer goodwill and relationships with suppliers.

The measure of strike and lockout activity that has been used most often in Canadian strike records is **lost person-days**, that is, the number of days of labour that were lost in a year because of industrial disputes. Lost person-days in a given year are calculated by multiplying the number of disputes by the total duration of the disputes (in days) by the total number of workers who were involved in all the strikes or lockouts. In order to put the number of lost person-days into context, it is useful to compare the number of lost person-days to the total number of person-days worked during the same period. Table 9-4 presents this data for the 1976–99 period in Canada.

TABLE 9-4	Work Stoppages in Canada, 1976–1999			
Year	Total Stoppages during Year[i]	Number of Workers	Lost Person-Days	% of Estimated Working Time[ii]
1976	1,040	1,584,721	11,544,170	.53
1977	806	217,647	3,320,050	.15
1978	1,057	400,622	7,357,180	.32
1979	1,049	462,386	7,819,350	.33
1980	1,028	439,003	9,129,960	.37
1981	1,049	341,331	8,850,040	.35
1982	679	464,128	5,702,370	.23
1983	645	329,472	4,440,900	.18
1984	716	186,916	3,883,400	.15
1985	829	162,333	3,125,560	.12
1986	748	484,255	7,151,470	.27
1987	668	581,882	3,810,170	.14
1988	548	206,796	4,901,260	.17
1989	627	444,747	3,701,360	.13
1990	579	270,471	5,079,190	.17
1991	463	253,334	2,516,090	.09
1992	404	149,940	2,110,180	.07
1993	381	101,784	1,516,640	.05
1994	374	80,856	1,606,580	.06
1995	328	149,159	1,583,061	.05
1996	330	281,816	3,351,820	.11
1997	284	257,664	3,610,206	.12
1998	381	244,402	2,443,876	.08
1999	413	158,612	2,445,770	.08

Source: Human Resources Development Canada, Labour Program, Workplace Information Directorate (available at <http://www.hrdc-drhc.gc.ca>).
[i] Includes work stoppages in progress at the start of the year and strikes that began during the year.
[ii] Lost person-days divided by the estimated total person-days worked during the year.

In assessing the data in Table 9-4, we must keep several historical facts in mind. Unionization levels in Canada have increased steadily since strike and lockout data have been collected, so increases in strike and lockout levels will in part reflect the increase in the number of unionized workers. The size of the Canadian workforce has also increased, so the greater number of workers involved in industrial disputes may in part reflect this growth in the workforce. Furthermore, some of the figures relating to lost person-days in Table 9-4 have been inflated because of unusually long disputes or short disputes involving unusually large numbers of workers. In 1976, there was a one-day, Canada-wide strike (the "Day of Protest") against the federal government's wage and price controls. In 1981, there was a lengthy strike involving Canada Post, a large national employer.[18] Clearly, these strikes contributed significantly to the amount of strike activity in those two years, but the overall figure of lost person-days probably does not reflect the impact of the average strike or lockout during those periods.

Despite these constraints, we can see that strikes and lockouts in Canada have not represented a significant loss of working time in any recent period. The rate in any given year has never exceeded six-tenths of 1 percent. We can also see that time lost owing to industrial disputes appears to be declining. This trend has been noted in other analyses of more detailed data, which have indicated that both the average annual number of work stoppages and the lost person-days in the 1990s were half of what they were in the 1980s.[19]

Given this information, however, it is also worth remembering that Canada has traditionally been reputed to be more strike-prone than other industrialized nations.[20] To see whether this reputation is justified, we can compare recent industrial dispute rates in Canada with those in other North American countries and other industrialized nations. Table 9-5 shows some comparative data, but before assessing this, we should be aware that, as the table footnotes indicate, the different countries included in the table have different criteria for defining strikes and collecting strike data. Many countries rely on voluntary, rather than mandatory, reporting of industrial disputes to a national or local government agency.[21] Also, some countries include in their count of lost person-days workers who are not themselves on strike but who cannot work because, for example, the supplier of

"Gosh, everyone seems to be out celebrating Labour Day..."

TABLE 9-5 Canadian Work Stoppage Activity in Comparison with Other Countries

	Canada[i]	United States[ii]	Japan[iii]	United Kingdom[iv]	Spain	Denmark[v]	Australia[vi]	Mexico[vii]
1991								
Number of strikes and lockouts	463	40	310	369	1,645	203	1,036	136
Workers involved (thousands)	253.4	392.0	52.8	176.0	1,983.8	37.9	1,181.6	64.9
Workdays not worked (thousands)	2,516.0	4,583.6	96.4	761.0	1,983.8	70.0	1,160.6	1,619.5
1992								
Number of strikes and lockouts	404	35	263	253	1,360	151	728	156
Workers involved (thousands)	149.9	363.8	109.3	148.0	5,192.1	32.9	871.5	91.4
Workdays not worked (thousands)	2,110.2	3,988.6	231.4	528.0	6,332.6	62.8	941.2	1,601.9
1993								
Number of strikes and lockouts	381	35	252	211	1,209	218	610	155
Workers involved (thousands)	101.8	181.9	64.0	385.0	1,076.8	58.7	489.6	31.7
Workdays not worked (thousands)	1,516.7	3,981.2	116.0	649.0	2,141.3	113.7	635.8	1,843.0
1994								
Number of strikes and lockouts	374	45	230	205	908	240	560	116
Workers involved (thousands)	80.9	322.0	49.0	107.0	5,437.4	36.8	265.1	27.1
Workdays not worked (thousands)	1,606.9	5,021.5	85.4	278.0	6,276.7	75.0	501.0	1,370.4

| TABLE 9-5 | Continued | | | | | | | |

	Canada[i]	United States[ii]	Japan[iii]	United Kingdom[iv]	Spain	Denmark[v]	Australia[vi]	Mexico[vii]
1995								
Number of strikes and lockouts	328	31	209	23.5	883	424	643	96
Workers involved (thousands)	149.2	191.5	37.5	174.0	573.5	124.5	344.3	12.2
Workdays not worked (thousands)	1,516.6	5,771.2	77.0	415.0	1,457.0	197.3	547.6	1,304.4
1996								
Number of strikes and lockouts	328	37	193	244	830	930	543	51
Workers involved (thousands)	281.7	272.2	23.2	364.3	1,087.8	65.7	577.7	10.5
Workdays not worked (thousands)	3,342.2	4,888.6	42.8	1,303.3	1,579.7	75.7	928.5	701.8
1997								
Number of strikes and lockouts	279	29	x	216	744	1,008	447	39
Workers involved (thousands)	253.6	338.6	x	130.0	650.6	73.7	315.4	9.4
Workdays not worked (thousands)	3,568.8	4,497.1	x	234.7	1,836.8	99.2	534.2	500.4

Source: International Labour Office (1998), *Yearbook of Labour Statistics.*
[i] Excludes work stoppages involving less than 10 workdays.
[ii] Excludes work stoppages involving less than 1,000 workers and lasting less than a full day or shift.
[iii] Excludes work stoppages lasting less than half a day; x=data unavailable.
[iv] Includes work stoppages lasting less than one day and including less than 10 workers only if more than 100 workdays not worked.
[v] Excludes stoppages in which less than 100 workdays were missed.
[vi] Excludes work stoppages involving less than 10 workdays.
[vii] Strikes only. Excludes enterprises covered by local jurisdiction. Only union members are included in "workers involved."

their raw materials is involved in a work stoppage. Canada does not count these workers, but the United States, the United Kingdom, and Australia do. This makes comparisons of the impact of work stoppages in different countries difficult. We should also keep in mind that the labour legislation governing strikes may differ from jurisdiction to jurisdiction, so that the conditions under which strikes can occur may also not be comparable.

Nevertheless, we can see that even with these methodological limitations Canada does not seem to have an excessively high number of strikes in comparison to other countries. It does, however, tend to have a comparatively high rate of workdays not worked because of strikes or lockouts, even though the numbers of workers involved are not large in comparison to other countries and workers who are only indirectly affected are not included in this count. In sum, the data indicates that while Canada has fewer strikes than other industrialized nations, Canadian strikes tend to be longer than strikes in other countries, which accounts for the relatively high number of lost workdays.

SUMMARY

The strike or lockout is used by one party as a tactic in bargaining to pressure the other party into conceding to its bargaining demands. This is achieved through closing down the employer's operations or withdrawing the labour of union members so that revenue cannot be generated or wages cannot be earned. A strike or lockout is intended to cause enough economic pain to the other party to convince it that settling a collective agreement is preferable to bearing the cost of a continued workplace shutdown.

Labour legislation establishes several preconditions that must be met for a strike or lockout to be legal. A legal strike or lockout can only occur once a collective agreement has expired and bargaining is in progress. A strike vote must be taken among union members to ensure that there is majority support for strike action. In some Canadian jurisdictions, the party intending to commence a strike or lockout must give notice to the other party. As well, in some Canadian jurisdictions, a third party must be brought in to assist the parties in reaching an agreement before a strike or lockout can commence.

Once a strike or lockout occurs, legislation that governs the ability of the union to picket and of the employer to use replacement workers comes into effect. Picketers must not interfere with the activities of other tenants that share premises with the employer, and they can only engage in picketing at other, non-struck locations under certain circumstances.

Picketers and other individuals involved in a strike or lockout must not commit illegal acts on the picket lines. The legislation governing the use of replacement workers varies across Canada; replacement workers are permitted in some jurisdictions but not in others, and the definition of who qualifies as a replacement worker also varies.

The length of a strike or lockout is dependent on the ability of the parties to withstand the economic pain inflicted. This ability may be affected by a number of specific and general factors, such as the financial resources available to the parties and the unemployment rate in the area where the strike or lockout occurs. A strike or lockout concludes when the parties return to bargaining or when a collective agreement is reached.

Finally, data on Canadian work stoppages indicate that the rate of strikes and lockouts in Canada is declining, but in comparison to other industrialized countries, Canada may still have a relatively high number of workdays lost to industrial disputes.

KEY TERMS FOR CHAPTER 9

back-to-work legislation (p. 331)
boycott (p. 336)
essential service (p. 331)
hot declaration (p. 336)
industrial action (p. 318)
industrial conflict (p. 318)
lockout (p. 318)
lost person-days (p. 347)
picket line (p. 333)
professional strikebreakers (p. 343)
ratification vote (p. 346)
recognition strike (p. 318)
replacement workers (p. 337)
rotating strikes (p. 319)
scab (p. 336)
secondary picketing (p. 334)
strike (p. 318)
strike mandate (p. 329)
strike pay (p. 332)

strike vote (p. 329)
wildcat strike (p. 329)
work-to-rule campaigns (p. 319)

DISCUSSION QUESTIONS FOR CHAPTER 9

1. Why would a union choose to engage in a work-to-rule campaign or a rotating strike rather than a full-scale strike?

2. Identify some of the individual and situational factors that might determine whether a strike or lockout happens or not.

3. Different provinces have different rules on whose votes will count when a strike vote is taken. What effects might these differences have on the outcome of a strike vote?

4. Explain why a union would take a strike vote when it had no immediate intention of actually going on strike.

5. What purposes are served by the requirement of advance notice of a strike or lockout?

6. Labour codes have general rules on picketing. Explain why labour boards often have to make situation-specific rulings on picketing activity.

7. Outline the arguments for and against the use of replacement workers.

8. Is Canada's reputation as a strike-prone country a deserved reputation? Discuss.

CASE 9-1

SUPER FOOD STORES AND COMMERCIAL WORKERS UNION

(Based on *The Great Atlantic & Pacific Company of Canada Limited and United Food and Commercial Workers International Union Locals 175 and 633 et al.*, 1994)

A strike is taking place at some Super Food locations, and picketers have attempted to restrict the delivery of inventory to the stores that are not on strike. Super Food has applied to the labour relations board to have picketing restricted at the non-struck stores.

Background to the Case

The Commercial Workers Union started a legal strike at several locations of the Super Food chain in mid-November. In early December, the union started secondary picketing at a store whose employees were not on strike. This store is located at one end of a mall and is surrounded by a parking lot. The picketers blocked Super Food trucks at the entrance to the mall, which meant that the trucks could not enter the parking lot and unload and deliver goods to the store.

In mid-December, the Super Food store ran out of produce and many popular items, so the employer applied to the courts for an order that the picketers not obstruct the trucks from entering the mall parking lot. This order was granted. However, the next day, when the trucks entered the lot, there were some incidents of scuffling and punching between the truck drivers and the picketers. Police attended the scene of the dispute and ended up acting as mediators between the representatives of the employer and the union. The police at the scene indicated to the employer's representative that they were not prepared to remove picketers from the trucks' path as long as the picketers were peaceful. Both representatives eventually agreed that the trucks would not be allowed into the store's loading dock and that instead the truck drivers would unload goods in the parking lot and transport them to the store.

This arrangement continued until late January. On January 25, the employer's lawyers went to the parking lot for what was, in their words, a "planned attempt to get a truck to the loading dock." A truck carrying only a few cases of soft drinks arrived at the mall, and picketers directed it to the usual unloading spot. The truck did not stop to unload its contents, but instead turned and moved toward the loading dock. When it arrived there, its path was blocked by picketers. The truck remained at the dock for approximately seven minutes, after which Super Food representatives ordered the driver to leave. The Super Food managers at the store did not try to unload the truck or attempt to persuade the picketers to let the truck through their picket line. Super Food employees videotaped the entire incident.

The next day, angry picketers permitted Super Food trucks into the parking lot but imposed a two-hour interval between the unloading of each truck. The picket leaders met with Super Food management and stated their position: either unloading would continue with the two-hour delay or the trucks would be blocked from entering the parking lot as they had been when picketing began. The manager of the Super Food store decided to "do what was necessary" to get stock into the store, and the two-hour delay continued. Two days later, the employer filed the current complaint with the labour relations board.

The Employer's Position

The employer made it clear to the board that it was not disputing the union's right to undertake secondary picketing and that it did not dispute that the picketing in this case was legitimate secondary picketing. It argued, however, that the picketing should be restricted because it was obstructing access to the employer's premises. The employer pointed to the section of the relevant labour code that states: "The Board shall impose such restrictions ... as it considers appropriate in order to prevent the undue disruption of the operations of the applicant." The employer argued that "undue" should be interpreted as "unlawful" and indicated that a court order had already imposed restrictions on the picketers that the picketers were not obeying. Hence, in the employer's opinion, the picketers' actions were unlawful. The employer suggested that the labour relations board should follow the practice of the courts and limit the picketers in order to allow access to the loading dock.

The Union's Position

The union acknowledged that delivery of goods to the store had been disrupted. It argued, however, that the primary business purpose of the store was the sale of goods to the public and this part of the operations had not been disrupted. Access to the store by the public and the store employees had been maintained, and the employer had not presented any evidence to show that the picketing had any effect on the store's overall operations or on the regular operations of the Super Food chain at large.

The union stated that the disruption in the delivery of goods was "well within the expected realm of events" during an industrial relations dispute. The union also pointed out that it had agreed with the employer and with the police to an arrangement that allowed Super Food trucks into the mall parking lot. This arrangement had been satisfactory to all concerned until the employer's lawyers had made a deliberate attempt to challenge the terms of the arrangement.

CASE 9-2

SILVER SCREEN THEATRES AND THEATRE WORKERS UNION

(Based on *Famous Players Inc. and International Alliance of Theatrical Stage Employees, Moving Picture Technicians, Artists and Allied Crafts, Local 348*, 1999)

The union representing projectionists at a chain of movie theatres is engaged in a legal strike. One location in the chain hosted the Reel Fun Film Festival, and the union has filed a complaint with the labour relations board alleging that the employer used replacement workers—employees from other locations of the chain—as projectionists during the festival. The relevant labour code prohibits the use of replacement workers, including employees who ordinarily work at the employer's other places of operation.

Background to the Case

Silver Screen Theatres is a chain of 18 movie theatres located in a major Canadian city and its suburbs. The Theatre Workers Union represents projectionists working at all 18 locations of the chain. The union has been involved in a legal strike for one year.

The union filed a complaint six months ago alleging that the employer was using replacement workers. In resolving that complaint, the board determined that although

Silver Screen operates 18 theatres, its organizational structure is such that groups of those theatres, known as "clusters," are treated as a single place of operation. Managers and assistant managers are regularly rotated between the theatres within a cluster. Floor staff, such as ushers and concession workers, are limited in their ability to rotate. Many of them are young people who do not have access to a car and cannot attend locations other than the one they were hired to work at. However, a floor staff member can be rotated within the theatres in the cluster if the staff member is able to attend work at more than one location. At the time of this earlier complaint, two downtown theatres were operated as a single cluster. Three months after the settlement of this complaint, the two downtown theatres and two suburban theatres were reorganized into a new four-theatre cluster.

Two months after the reorganization of the clusters, Silver Screen hosted the annual Reel Fun Film Festival at one of the downtown theatres. Two employees—Angle and Snow—acted as projectionists during the festival. A third employee—Morley—also worked during the festival, but there was some question whether or not he had worked as a projectionist.

Prior to the reorganization, Angle had worked as a manager and a projectionist at two suburban theatres, one of which was now in the cluster. Since the reorganization, he has worked at all four theatres in the cluster and at one location in another cluster. Before the reorganization, Angle had never worked at the downtown theatres.

Prior to the reorganization, Snow had also worked as a manager and projectionist at two suburban theatres, one of which Angle had also worked in (the location that was now in the relevant cluster). Since the reorganization, he too has worked at all four theatres in the cluster. The general manager of the cluster testified that he thought that Snow had worked as a projectionist after the film festival had ended, but he was not positive that this was so.

The same general manager testified that he had assigned Morley to supervise the projectionists at the film festival. Usually, the projectionists work on their own without a supervisor present, but there had been problems with the quality of the projection at the previous year's festival. The festival organizers had issued a public apology for the problems and were concerned that future festivals might be jeopardized if the problems continued into another year. The manager testified that this year the organizers of the festival wanted assurances that there would not be a recurrence of the projection problems, and thus the employer had decided to assign a supervisor to the projection booth. This individual was to supervise the projectionists and act as a liaison between the employer and the film festival personnel.

At the downtown theatre, there is only one entrance to the projection booth. The entrance is located in the lobby and is visible from the plaza outside the theatre doors. A number of union witnesses testified that they saw Morley regularly enter the booth during the film festival and spend a considerable amount of time there before leaving. Other evidence led the union to believe that Morley was in fact acting as a projectionist during the film festival. Morley himself testified that he had not done any projectionist work.

The Employer's Position

The employer argued that the issue in this case was not whether the employer had used replacement workers during a strike, but whether the employer had the right to reconfigure its places of operation. The employer argued that it did have this right. The employer pointed out that since the strike began, it had opened and staffed several new theatres, and that if it was allowed to do that, it should also be allowed to change the structure of its existing locations (i.e., the composition of the theatre clusters).

In respect to the cases of Angle and Snow, the employer claimed that it did not violate the prohibition on replacement workers by using them as projectionists at the downtown theatres. Angle and Snow were already working at one theatre in the relevant cluster, and their work at the downtown theatre was simply added to their pre-existing duties at the other theatre. Thus, they had not been "transferred" to the downtown theatre, which would have been in violation of the labour legislation.

The employer added that it believed it was acting within the law as defined by the labour relations board in its ruling on the earlier union complaint. The employer suggested that if it were found in breach of the legislation on the current complaint, it should only be declared as breaching the law and should not be assessed a penalty. The employer claimed that it was being "up front" in its actions and was not deliberately flouting the terms of the legislation.

The employer argued that Morley was not a replacement worker because he had not done any of the work (projection) usually done by the striking workers. He had been present in the booth for legitimate business reasons: to supervise the projectionists and interact with the film festival staff. The employer also stated that if Snow and Angle had not been used as film festival projectionists, it would have called on other eligible replacement workers and not on projectionists from the union local that was on strike.

The Union's Position

The union made minimal arguments in the case of Morley and instead focused on the cases of Angle and Snow. The union noted that both parties agreed Angle and Snow had previously worked as projectionists, and thus they did not qualify as illegal replacement workers doing work they had not performed before the strike. In the union's opinion, the question to be resolved was whether Angle and Snow's assignment to the downtown theatre qualified as a transfer to perform work ordinarily done by striking employees.

The union argued that if each theatre in the Silver Screen chain were considered a single unit, then Silver Screen would have acted illegally by using Angle and Snow. Neither Angle nor Snow had worked at the downtown theatre prior to the strike, and neither had any previously established work attachment to that theatre. The union then argued that if the new cluster were considered a single unit, then Angle and Snow had been transferred into it with the reorganization of the clusters, since they had been part of a different cluster prior to the reorganization. Since they were transferred after the strike began, they were illegally being used as replacement workers when they worked at the downtown theatre.

The union requested that the employer be found in breach of the legislation and that the board issue a cease-and-desist order to stop the employer from using replacement workers. The union also requested financial damages equal to the value of the work done by the replacement workers. The union noted that the employer had previously been found in breach of the same part of the legislation, and requested that an official of the board be appointed to investigate the situation if the employer was found to have again violated the legislation.

References

[1] Gunderson, M., Hyatt, D., & Ponak, A. (2000). Strikes and dispute resolution. In Gunderson, M., Ponak, A., & Taras, D.G. (Eds.), *Union-Management Relations in Canada* (4th edition). Toronto, ON: Pearson Education.

[2] Snyder, R. (1995). *The Annotated Canada Labour Code*. Scarborough, ON: Carswell.

[3] Godard, J. (1994). *Industrial Relations, the Economy and Society*. Toronto, ON: McGraw-Hill Ryerson.

[4] Godard, *op. cit.*

[5] Godard, *op. cit.*

[6] Card, D. (1990). Strikes and bargaining: a survey of the recent empirical literature. *American Economic Review, Papers and Proceedings*, May 1990, 410–415.

[7] Hebdon, R., Hyatt, D., & Mazerolle, M. (1999). Implications of small bargaining units and enterprise unions on bargaining disputes. *Relations Industrielles/Industrial Relations, 54(3)*, 503–525.

[8] Barling, J., Fullagar, C., Kelloway, E.K., & McElvie, L. (1992). Union loyalty and strike propensity. *Journal of Social Psychology, 132(5)*, 581–590.

[9] Gunderson, Hyatt, & Ponak, *op. cit.*

[10] Gunderson, Hyatt, & Ponak, *op. cit.*

[11] Hebdon, R. (1998). Behavioural determinants of public sector illegal strikes: cases from Canada and the U.S. *Relations Industrielles/Industrial Relations, 53(4)*, 667–689.

[12] Godard, *op. cit.*

[13] Ponak, A., & Thompson, M. (1995). Public sector collective bargaining. In Gunderson, M., & Ponak, A. (Eds.), *Union-Management Relations in Canada* (3rd edition). Toronto, ON: Addison Wesley Longman.

[14] Jackson, R. (2000). Collective bargaining legislation in Canada. In Gunderson, Ponak, & Taras, *op. cit*; Dessler, G., Cole, N., & Sutherland, V.L. (1999). *Human Resources Management in Canada* (7th Canadian edition). Scarborough, ON: Prentice-Hall.

[15] "List of Censured Administrations" (2001). American Association of University Professors. Available at <http://www.aaup.org/Censure.htm>.

[16] Budd, J.W. (1996). Canadian strike replacement legislation and collective bargaining: lessons for the United States. *Industrial Relations*, *35(2)*, 245–260.

[17] Flynn, F.J. (2000). No news is good news: the relationship between media attention and strike duration. *Industrial Relations*, *39(1)*, 139–160.

[18] Peirce, J. (2000). *Canadian Industrial Relations*. Scarborough, ON: Prentice-Hall.

[19] Akyeampong, E. (2001). Time lost to industrial disputes. *Canadian Economic Observer* (Statistics Canada Catalogue No. 11-010-XPB), September 2001, 3.1–3.4.

[20] Gunderson, Hyatt & Ponak, *op. cit.*

[21] Akyeampong, *op. cit.*

War of words heats up between RC board, teachers:

Who's avoiding who?

HAMILTON—Halton's Catholic school board has accused its high school teachers' union of dodging a review of board finances requested by a mediator last week, unleashing a war of words in the already bitter labour dispute.

In a news release entitled "Union appears to evade mediator's request—stalls progress of negotiations," the board charges the union is misleading parents about what the board can afford in its contract negotiations.

"The Halton OECTA Secondary Unit has not contacted the board's superintendent of business services to arrange a meeting to begin a review and discussion of the board's current financial situation," wrote board chairman Jim Sherlock. "The board can only assume that its secondary teachers' bargaining team prefers to continue to misrepresent the board's budget to the public and to their membership."

The release is another example of accusations flung back and forth in the labour dispute between the board and union, now in the fifth month of job action. Teachers are refusing all voluntary activities. Sherlock did not return calls yesterday. But the local union president denied the charges.

"They don't call me for a meeting, yet they automatically assume we're not interested," said Joe Pece, Halton secondary president of the Ontario English Catholic Teachers' Association. He said messages left with the school board have not been returned.

"For them to say we don't want to meet at this point is utterly ridiculous," Pece said yesterday. "I would be ready to meet with them tonight."

The press release comes one day after the school board sent a written offer by courier to the teachers' union, which the union turned down in a letter faxed to the board office last night.

Though details of the latest offer have not been made public, major issues in the dispute include salary and teachers' workload. The union has stuck to its original position of six classes each year, while the board has continued to ask for some increase.

Pece said he believes the offer, and the press release that followed it, are a cover for the absence of a key member of the board's negotiating team.

(*Hamilton Spectator*, January 29, 1999)

chapter 10

THIRD-PARTY INTERVENTION DURING NEGOTIATIONS

objectives

Collective bargaining is usually an adversarial process. Strikes and lockouts happen because the parties are unable to reach an agreement. When it appears that a strike or lockout may occur, certain individuals enter the process either to prevent the action or to help the parties resolve the underlying disputes. These neutral third parties—mediators, conciliators, special officers, fact finders, and industrial inquiry commissioners—assist the union and management in finding a solution to the immediate dispute. At the same time, they encourage the parties to create harmonious relations in the future. By the end of this chapter, you should be able to:

- explain why a third party would be used to help negotiators reach a collective agreement

- understand the difference between conciliation, mediation, and arbitration

- outline the conciliation process

- define interest arbitration and understand how it is used

- explain the role of mediators

- discuss industrial inquiry commissions

- understand the purpose of a disputes inquiry board

INTRODUCTION

As we saw in Chapter 9, strikes and lockouts have the potential to be damaging and lengthy. Because of this possibility, labour legislation in most Canadian jurisdictions provides for various forms of third-party intervention in collective bargaining. The intent of bringing a third party into the bargaining process when disputes occur is to help the parties resolve their differences without using a strike or lockout as a bargaining tactic.

Ideally, a third party is perceived as neutral by both negotiating teams, so he, she, or they can provide suggestions to one side in bargaining without being perceived as promoting the interests of the other side. Since the third party has not been involved in the bargaining process from the beginning, it is possible that they can identify solutions or outcomes that the parties may have missed because of their focus on their own bargaining positions. As we will see, third parties are also occasionally introduced to the bargaining process by the government; in such cases, the government uses the third party as a direct or indirect messenger to convey its interest in seeing a speedy resolution to the disagreement.

The main types of third-party intervention used in Canadian jurisdictions are conciliation, mediation, and arbitration. Depending on the circumstances of the bargaining situation and the relevant legislation, the use of these types of third-party intervention may be voluntary or mandatory. There are also less common forms of third-party intervention: mediation-arbitration, industrial inquiry commissions, and dispute-resolution boards. We will describe each of these types of third-party intervention and explain when and how they are used.

CONCILIATION

In all Canadian jurisdictions except British Columbia and Alberta, **conciliation** is the first step in attempting to resolve an impasse in negotiations. The conciliator's role is to assess the positions of the parties and the reasons for their inability to reach agreement. The conciliator will then submit a report of his or her findings to the provincial or federal minister of labour, the parties, or both. Table 10-1 outlines the legislation governing the use of conciliation.

TABLE 10-1 Conciliation Legislation in Canada

	Type	Appointed By	Are Recommendations Binding?
Federal	Conciliation officer	Minister of labour on own initiative	No
	Conciliation commissioner/ Conciliation board	Minister of labour on own initiative	Yes, if parties agree in advance
Manitoba	Conciliation officer	Request of parties or minister of labour on own initiative	Yes, if parties agree
New Brunswick	Conciliation officer	Either party or minister of labour	No
	Conciliation board	Either party or minister of labour	Yes, if parties agree
Newfoundland	Conciliator	Either party or minister of labour on own initiative	No
	Conciliation board	Either party or minister of labour on own initiative	If parties agree in writing
Nova Scotia	Conciliator	Either party or minister of labour on own initiative	No
	Conciliation board	Either party	Yes, if parties agree
Ontario	Conciliator	Either party	No
	Conciliation board	Minister of labour, if conciliator unsuccessful	No

TABLE 10-1 Continued

	Type	Appointed By	Are Recommendations Binding?
Prince Edward Island	Conciliator	Either party or minister of labour on own initiative	No
	Conciliation board	Minister of labour	Yes, if parties agree
Quebec	Conciliator	Either party or minister of labour on own initiative	No
Saskatchewan	Conciliation board	Either party or minister of labour on own initiative	Yes, if parties agree in writing

Source: Human Resources Development Canada, Labour Program, Summaries of General Private Sector Collective Bargaining Legislation (available at <http://www.hrdc-drhc.gc.ca>).

The conciliator does not participate in bargaining sessions or impose an agreement on the parties. Therefore, conciliation is preferred as the initial form of third-party intervention because it allows the bargaining parties to retain a greater amount of control over the process and outcomes of bargaining.

In some jurisdictions, conciliation is required as a precondition to the use of a strike or lockout; that is, the conciliator's report must be completed and submitted before a strike or lockout can occur. However, even in jurisdictions where conciliation is voluntary, the parties can undertake conciliation on their own initiative to see if their differences can be resolved by this means. The parties may prefer to take this voluntary step before using (or being forced to use) other forms of third-party intervention that give the third party more control over bargaining outcomes.

The conciliator can be a conciliation officer (a single individual) or, in the federal jurisdiction, a conciliation commission. Saskatchewan provides for the appointment of a three-member conciliation board rather than an individual officer. A conciliation officer or conciliation commissioner is usually a government employee, appointed at either the request of the parties or on the initiative of the minister of labour. Conciliation officers usually have experience in collective bargaining or in dispute resolution that they can draw on when assessing a specific collective bargaining process and the issues causing conflict between the parties.

The actual process of conciliation begins with the conciliation officer meeting with the parties and investigating the issues in dispute. The officer will take note of the bargaining items that have already been settled, look at the issues still being negotiated, and see what the parties' current positions are on unresolved items. The officer will also ascertain what factors, in his or her opinion, are preventing the parties from reaching an agreement. These factors could include the quality of the parties' bargaining relationship, the amount of difference between the parties' offers on bargaining items, or the degree of the parties' willingness to make concessions. If conciliation was not undertaken voluntarily by the parties, all of this information will then be compiled in a report and submitted to the minister of labour. If conciliation was voluntarily undertaken by the parties and was not ordered by the minister of labour, the report of the conciliation board or officer will be given directly to the parties themselves.

A minister of labour may use conciliation not only as a means of assisting the parties to reach an agreement, but also as a means of utilizing public opinion to resolve the dispute. If the conciliation order is made public or becomes the subject of media attention, the parties may settle their dispute because of the threat of further embarrassment or damage to their public image. When an order for conciliation is made with the intent of creating this kind of pressure, the minister will likely specify that the recommendations of the conciliation officer will be made public. This directive lets the parties know that the details of their dispute will be publicized if they are not able to come to an agreement prior to the submission of the conciliation officer's report. If the parties do not reach an agreement and the conciliation officer's recommendations are made public, the parties may experience a negative public reaction that could have a long-term effect. The parties may agree to accept the recommendations, even if they do not completely agree with them, in order to preserve their reputations.

In most Canadian jurisdictions, if the report of the conciliation officer fails to resolve the dispute by bringing the parties to an agreement, legislation provides for a further step in the conciliation process. This is the appointment by the minister of labour of a tripartite conciliation board. This board is made up of an individual appointed by the employer, an individual appointed by the union, and a neutral third party, hence the name "tripartite" (which means "three-member"). The neutral third party can be appointed either jointly by the union and employer representatives or by an external authority such as the minister of labour.

The conciliation board carries out the same basic process of investigation and reporting as does the conciliation officer or commission, with one major difference in the method of collecting information on the dispute. The conciliation board will hold a formal hearing at which both parties will present their respective positions on the bargaining issues in dispute. Shortly thereafter, the conciliation board will make recommendations to the minister of labour. If the parties agree in advance, the recommendations of the conciliation board can be **binding**—that is, the parties will accept the board's recommendations as the resolution of their dispute.

The conciliation process is used in federal disputes, as well as in most provincial and municipal public service disputes, because these disputes often involve essential services. The use of conciliation can delay a strike or lockout or, if the conciliation is binding, can allow the parties to avoid a strike or lockout entirely, an important consideration in negotiations involving essential services. For example, conciliation was recently used in a negotiating dispute between the federal government and 8,500 technical workers in the public sector.[1] Bargaining broke down over the issue of wages when the Treasury Board, which negotiates on behalf of the federal government, offered a pay increase of 2 to 2.5 percent per year over three years, and the union requested a pay increase of 5 percent a year over the same period. A conciliation board was appointed to investigate the dispute and recommended a settlement of 3.5 percent in the first year, 4 percent in the second, and 4 percent in the third. This recommendation was sufficiently satisfactory to bring the parties back to the bargaining table and to temporarily prevent a full-scale strike.

As this example demonstrates, conciliation can help the parties settle their bargaining disputes by recommending potential solutions the parties may have overlooked. As we know from our discussion of bargaining in Chapter 8, parties are sometimes so committed to a particular desired outcome that they overlook other solutions that could actually satisfy the concerns of both sides. Conciliation is one way in which the parties can be made aware of solutions that they might not recognize on their own. It can also be used as a means to help the parties overcome differences, whether great or small, between their positions. One recent example of this function of conciliation occurred when a conciliator was appointed to investigate a bargaining dispute between NAV Canada, the company that provides air traffic control services at Canadian airports, and the union representing the workers who install and repair electronic systems at those airports.[2] The union wanted a 60 percent increase in wages over three years, basing its demands on what its members could earn in the private sector or in similar jobs in other industrialized countries. The leader of the union negotiating team acknowledged that the employer's negotiators "almost died" when they were presented with the wage demand. In a situation like this, a conciliator could investigate whether the evidence supporting the demand was valid, and consider whether the employer would be able to meet such a demand. Presenting such information to the negotiators on both sides might cause them to consider whether the demand should be seriously entertained, and move them toward a mutually acceptable solution.

Despite its extensive use in the public sector, however, the conciliation process rarely resolves disputes. Rather than giving it their full support, the two parties may perceive conciliation only as a first step that they must take before they can use more intensive means to pressure for acceptance of their demands, such as a strike or lockout, or before they can use more directly interventionist forms of third-party involvement. Additionally, because conciliation usually happens relatively early in the bargaining process, the parties are seldom prepared to compromise at this early stage.

One study of bargaining-related legislation governing the Canadian private sector investigated whether the use of conciliation reduced the likelihood of strikes

Miners from Thompson, Manitoba burn a conciliation board report in 1964 before calling a strike.

or their cost, calculated by estimating the amount of wages lost during the strike and the costs incurred by employers.[3] This study looked at data on strike activity and wage settlements in Canada between 1967 and 1993. The analysis of the data indicated that the use of conciliation did not significantly reduce strike activity, either in reducing the number or the length of strikes. More detailed analysis of the data suggested that the two-stage conciliation process (a conciliation officer and then a conciliation board) was somewhat more effective in reducing strike activity when a two-week "cooling-off" period was part of the conciliation process. (This cooling-off period took place between the date that the final conciliation report was submitted and the date that a legal strike could begin; legislation incorporating this requirement existed in some Canadian jurisdictions during the period for which data was collected.) With respect to conciliation's impact on the cost of strikes, the study indicated that because of conciliation's general ineffectiveness in reducing strike activity, conciliation was not significantly effective in reducing the cost of strikes; during the period studied, it was estimated that strikes cost each striking worker approximately $100 per day and employers approximately $900 per day.

The features of conciliation are summarized in Table 10-2. If conciliation is unsuccessful, the next kind of third-party intervention that may be used is mediation. However, particularly in the public sector, interest arbitration may directly follow a failed conciliation attempt. We will first turn our attention to mediation.

TABLE 10-2   Features of Conciliation

Conducted by	– Conciliation officer – Conciliation board (second step, some jurisdictions)
When it is used	– By order of minister of labour – May be voluntarily chosen by parties – Report of conciliation officer must be submitted prior to legal strike or lockout starting (in some jurisdictions)
What happens	– Officer is appointed – Officer meets with parties and investigates disputed issues – Officer writes report with recommendations – Report is submitted to minister of labour or to parties (or to both) – Minister may publicize recommendations – Recommendations are not binding unless parties agree to this in advance – In some jurisdictions, if report does not resolve dispute, minister of labour appoints conciliation board – Conciliation board holds hearing and submits report and recommendations to minister of labour

MEDIATION

When union and management negotiators are unable to resolve their differences during collective bargaining, an application may be made for the assistance of a mediator. **Mediation** is a more intensive form of third-party intervention than conciliation because the mediator, unlike a conciliator, usually participates in the actual bargaining process, meeting jointly and separately with the parties during bargaining sessions.

The legislation in each Canadian jurisdiction governing the use of mediation is outlined in Table 10-3. In most Canadian jurisdictions, a mediator is appointed at the request of one or both parties, or at the initiative of the minister of labour. In addition, in all jurisdictions except Prince Edward Island, the mediator's recommendations are not binding; in Prince Edward Island, the mediator's recommendations can be binding if both parties in the negotiations agree to this condition prior to the start of mediation.

TABLE 10-3 Mediation Legislation

	Type	Appointed By	Are Recommendations Binding?
Federal	Mediator	Request of parties or minister of labour on own initiative	No
Alberta	Mediator	Either or both parties	No
British Columbia	Mediation officer	Request of parties	No
	Special mediator	Minister of labour	No
Manitoba	Mediator	Request of either or both parties	No
New Brunswick	Mediator	Either party or minister of labour	No

TABLE 10-3 Continued

	Type	Appointed By	Are Recommendations Binding?
Newfoundland	Mediator	Either party or minister of labour	No
Nova Scotia	Mediator	Minister of labour	No
Ontario	Mediator	Joint request of parties	No
Prince Edward Island	Mediator	Minister of labour	Yes, if parties agree
Quebec	Special mediator	Minister of labour	No
Saskatchewan	Special mediator	Either party or minister of labour on own initiative	No

Source: Human Resources Development Canada, Labour Program, Summaries of General Private Sector Collective Bargaining Legislation (available at <http://www.hrdc-drhc.gc.ca>).

Generally, either the labour relations board or the ministry of labour is the authority responsible for appointing mediators. However, the person appointed as a mediator does not need to be an employee of the labour relations board or of the government. Those appointed as mediators often have experience as labour or management negotiators, or they are lawyers, university professors, or other suitable individuals who have earned the parties' trust and confidence. The cost of using a government-appointed mediator is usually borne by the government agency that makes the appointment.

When a mediator becomes involved in negotiations, he or she investigates the dispute in a slightly more proactive way than does a conciliator. The mediator will attend bargaining sessions and observe the negotiating teams in action to see if there are factors in the negotiation process, such as the parties' attitudes or behaviour toward each other, that could be blocking a potential settlement. The mediator will also listen to each party's position to determine where differences on bargaining items exist. He or she will then suggest to the parties, either privately or jointly, possible resolutions for the issues under dispute. Since the suggestions are not binding, the parties are under no obligation to accept them.

At the conclusion of the mediation process, at the request of either party, the mediator will provide a report that may include recommended terms of settlement. These recommendations are often persuasive and of real use in helping the parties reach a collective agreement. The mediator's recommendations tend to be more persuasive than the conciliator's because the mediator has been more closely involved in the bargaining process. The mediator's recommendations are generally more realistic or practical than the conciliator's, since he or she has a greater familiarity with the parties and the issues. Similarly, the parties may treat the mediator's recommendations more seriously than the conciliator's because of the parties' close contact with the mediator during the bargaining process.

The lengthy Vancouver transit strike in 2001 is a good example of how a mediator's recommendations can be used to create pressure for a settlement, even though these recommendations are not binding. Two months into the strike, when negotiations were clearly becoming unproductive, the British Columbia minister of labour appointed a mediator to assist in finding a resolution to the dispute. The mediator investigated the dispute and offered a proposal for settlement to the parties; the parties then shared the proposal with the constituencies they represented.[4] The mediator's report also noted that there was an important public interest issue involved in settling the strike: 37 percent of the bus company's customers did not have access to a car, and thus, the longer the strike went on, the more these individuals would be inconvenienced.

The bus drivers' union, a local of the Canadian Auto Workers, conducted a membership vote to assess the level of support for the mediator's proposed settlement. The union membership voted overwhelmingly in favour of accepting the terms of the proposal, and the union negotiating team subsequently indicated that it was willing to settle for the contract terms recommended by the mediator. The employer, however, claiming that implementing the recommendations would be too expensive, rejected the mediator's recommendations. This decision was highly unpopular with the bus-riding public, many of whom were encountering significant difficulties because of the lack of public transit. At the same time that the employer announced its decision to reject the mediator's recommendations, the Vancouver media carried numerous stories about senior citizens who could not go shopping or visit doctors and individuals who had lost their jobs because they did not have reliable transportation. The employer's decision to reject the mediator's recommendations became even more unpopular when the transit shutdown lasted another two months. The strike only ended after back-to-work legislation was imposed by the provincial government. The legislation contained contract terms substantially similar to those recommended by the mediator.[5]

As we know from Chapter 9, in some Canadian jurisdictions (Alberta and Prince Edward Island), a mediator or conciliator must be appointed prior to the start of a legal strike or lockout. In other jurisdictions (New Brunswick, Newfoundland, and Nova Scotia), a conciliator or conciliation board must be appointed before a legal strike or lockout can happen. Although mediators or conciliators are not required to complete their work before a strike or lockout begins, the usual practice is that they will book out of the negotiations before the strike or lockout occurs. **Booking out** means that the mediator stops trying to help the parties overcome their differences and formally leaves the proceedings. This occurs either at the request of the parties or on the initiative of the mediator, on the basis either that the mediator is unable to help the parties resolve their disputes or that the parties have no common ground on which to reach an agreement.

The basic features of mediation are outlined in Table 10-4. To conclude our discussion of mediation, we will briefly describe two specific forms of mediation that occur in some Canadian jurisdictions: special mediation and fact finding.

TABLE 10-4   Features of Mediation

Conducted by	Mediator
When it is used	– By order of minister of labour – May be requested by parties – Mediator must be appointed prior to start of legal strike or lockout (in some jurisdictions)
What happens	– Mediator is appointed – Mediator observes bargaining sessions

TABLE 10-4	Continued

> – Mediator meets with parties and investigates disputed issues
> – Mediator proposes solutions
> – Recommendations are not binding: in some jurisdictions they can be if parties agree to this in advance or if mediation has been privately requested with this condition
> – Mediator usually books out before strike or lockout starts

Special Mediation

British Columbia, Saskatchewan, and Quebec have a provision in their labour relations legislation for the minister of labour to appoint a **special mediator** at any time during collective bargaining. A similar provision exists in Nova Scotia, although the process is called "preventive mediation" in that jurisdiction. The special mediator often has expanded protection, privileges, and powers conveyed by legislation, and is usually directed to keep the minister informed on the progress of the mediation process. One of the distinctions between special mediation and the usual forms of mediation is that much of the special mediator's authority is determined by the terms of each individual appointment. However, the main distinction between special mediation and the usual forms of mediation is that a special mediator can be appointed at any time during the bargaining process, not only after a dispute or disagreement has arisen. Therefore, a minister of labour may choose to appoint a special mediator to participate in a bargaining process from the very beginning if, in the minister's opinion, the bargaining is likely to be difficult or if the minister believes that a strike or lockout would have an unusually negative impact.

In special or preventive mediation, the mediator may be requested to submit a report to the minister of labour, to the parties involved, or to both. If the minister so chooses, this report can be considered to have the same status as a report from a conciliation officer and thus be treated accordingly.

Fact Finding

In British Columbia, the associate chair of the mediation division of the labour relations board can appoint a fact finder to meet with parties engaged in bargaining. The **fact finder** is responsible for inquiring into the issues between the parties and submitting a report to the associate chair. The fact finder's report sets out the issues already agreed upon as well as those issues remaining in dispute. The fact finder's report may also include "any findings in respect of a matter considered relevant to the making of a collective agreement between the parties." Upon receipt of the fact finder's report, the associate chair provides the parties with a copy and may also make the report public. Thus, the fact finder, although technically a mediator, serves a function similar to that of a conciliator.

Having outlined the first two forms of third-party intervention, we will now turn to describing the third form—interest arbitration.

INTEREST ARBITRATION

Interest arbitration is considered the most intensive and invasive form of third-party intervention in the bargaining process. This is because in interest arbitration the arbitrator establishes some or all of the terms of the collective agreement between the parties. If the parties are unable to agree on mutually acceptable solutions to bargaining disputes, the arbitrator will create a solution that then becomes part of the collective agreement.

Interest arbitration is distinct from grievance arbitration, which will be discussed in Chapter 11. In grievance arbitration, a third party determines the application or interpretation of the terms and conditions of the collective agreement. In other words, interest arbitration takes place while the collective agreement is being negotiated, and grievance arbitration is used to settle disputes that arise once the collective agreement is in place. The Canadian legislation governing interest arbitration is summarized in Table 10-5. As the table shows, not all Canadian jurisdictions make formal provision for interest arbitration as a method of dispute resolution during bargaining, although all Canadian jurisdictions specify procedures for the use of grievance arbitration after the collective agreement is in effect. However, in jurisdictions with no legislation to govern it, interest arbitration can still be used during collective bargaining if both parties agree to its use and can settle on a mutually satisfactory arbitrator or arbitration board. And, as noted in Chapter 7, in most Canadian jurisdictions, an arbitrator can be appointed to create a collective agreement in first-contract situations where the parties have been unsuccessful in concluding an agreement. This particular use of arbitration is specified in most Canadian legislation to motivate employers and newly certified unions to commence negotiations and reach a mutually satisfactory first collective agreement, rather than have a third party create a possibly unsatisfactory collective agreement for them.

An important feature of interest arbitration as a method of dispute resolution is that, unlike the conciliator's or mediator's decision, the arbitrator's decision is binding. In other words, the arbitrator's decision settles the disputes and the parties cannot appeal the arbitrator's decision. (There are some rare and exceptional circumstances under which interest-arbitration and grievance-arbitration decisions can be appealed; these are described in Chapter 11.)

TABLE 10-5 Interest Arbitration Legislation

	Type	Appointed By	Are Recommendations Binding?
Alberta	Arbitration board	Parties	Yes
New Brunswick	Arbitration	Parties	Yes
Ontario	Arbitration	Parties	Yes, if parties agree in writing
Quebec	Arbitration	Minister of labour on written request of both parties	Yes, but parties may agree to amend award
Saskatchewan	Labour relations board (acting as arbitrator)	Parties	Yes

Source: Human Resources Development Canada, Labour Program, Summaries of General Private Sector Collective Bargaining Legislation (available at <http://www.hrdc-drhc.gc.ca>).

In jurisdictions where legislation provides for the use of interest arbitration, the process commences when one or both of the parties request that the minister of labour appoint an arbitrator. The minister of labour then appoints either an individual or a tripartite panel to act as an interest arbitrator or interest arbitration panel. Arbitrators or members of an arbitration panel usually have experience similar to those of mediators, either as negotiators or as labour lawyers. An exception to this process occurs in Saskatchewan, where members of the Labour Relations Board serve as arbitrators.

Once an interest arbitrator or arbitration panel has been appointed, a formal hearing is held. The purpose of the hearing is to give the arbitrator or the arbitration panel the opportunity to investigate the parties' positions and gather information on the dispute. The hearing is conducted very much like a court session. The arbitrator or the panel will call witnesses for each side who will present oral and documentary evidence to persuade the arbitrator of the correctness of their position. The arbitrator or the panel will ask questions of the witnesses to clarify the presentations and the evidence. Once the hearing is completed, the arbitrator or panel will then consider the evidence and create a binding decision.

In some Canadian jurisdictions, legislation provides criteria that guide interest arbitrators in their decision making. However, in the majority of Canadian jurisdictions, where criteria are not mandated, interest arbitrators traditionally use a form of arbitration known as **final offer selection**. If the parties agree, the arbitrator is free to create contract terms based on his or her own judgement rather than on the final offers submitted by the parties, but final offer selection is the more common form of interest arbitration in Canadian jurisdictions. There are two types of final offer selection used by Canadian interest arbitrators: total-package final offer selection and item-by-item final offer selection. We will briefly outline each of these.

Total-Package Final Offer Selection

When **total-package final offer selection** is used as a method of determining arbitration outcomes, each party presents the interest arbitrator with a total package of offers covering all the outstanding issues. The package includes the party's desired solutions to the issues and suggested terms for the collective agreement. During the hearing, each party will present evidence to convince the arbitrator of the superiority of its package. The interest arbitrator then selects one party's total package, and the selected package forms part or all of the terms of the collective agreement. If the parties have previously been able to agree on resolutions for some issues, those agreements will remain, and the total-package selection will create terms and conditions only for the unresolved issues. If the parties have not agreed on any issues, the total package will create all the terms and conditions of the collective agreement. The suggestions made in the package that is not selected will not be incorporated into the collective agreement.

To illustrate how total-package final offer selection works, we present here a simple fictional example involving two disputed issues. (In real-life arbitrations, an arbitrator may have to deal with many difficult issues and examine extensive and complex evidence supporting the validity of each party's position on each issue.) In our example, negotiations have broken down and the parties have been asked to submit proposals on two issues, wages and the number of hours in a workweek. The union has proposed a wage of $20 an hour and a workweek of 37 hours. The employer has proposed a wage of $15 an hour and a workweek of 40 hours. Under total-package final offer selection, the arbitrator's decision will be either $20 a week and a 37-hour week or $15 an hour and a 40-hour week.

The advantage of using total-package final offer selection to resolve bargaining disputes is that it encourages the parties to submit realistic suggestions, since they know that if the arbitrator finds them more acceptable than the other party's, their suggestions may end up being part of the collective agreement. However, the parties will not, or should not, suggest contract terms that they would not be willing to work with, since the arbitrator will not alter the terms of the package that is selected. The disadvantage of using total-package final offer selection is that it establishes a win-lose scenario. The party whose package is not chosen by the arbitrator will end up having its suggestions completely absent from most or all of the collective agreement. This party will likely be irritated and resentful; worse, since the "losing" party has not had any direct input into the agreement, that party may not be fully committed to making the collective agreement work.

Total-package final offer selection was recently used in the arbitration that settled the high-profile Nova Scotia nurses' strike in the summer of 2001.[6] Among other issues, the nurses' union and the government disagreed on the wage increases and how they would be paid. The union wanted an 18 percent increase compounded over three years; the government offered 12.87 percent compounded over three years in addition to a

$3,000 lump-sum payment. The actual difference in payment between the two final offers was only $121 per worker over the life of the contract, but the nurses' union argued that its proposal was superior because it would be more effective in attracting nurses to the province and helping reduce the province's nursing shortage. The arbitrator, Susan Ashley, agreed and selected the nurses' proposal, but she also outlined in her report what she perceived as the deficiencies in the total-package solution in this case. She noted, among other things, that there was the possibility that the employer would attempt to compensate for the nurses' higher wage costs by giving nursing duties to lower-paid health-care staff. Ashley commented, "The [final offer arbitration] process has not operated to bring the parties closer together. The unions would never have accepted the employer's final offer if it had been presented in free collective bargaining."[7]

Item-by-Item Final Offer Selection

As the name suggests, when **item-by-item final offer selection** is used to determine interest-arbitration outcomes, the interest arbitrator can select specific items from either side's proposals. In item-by-item final offer selection, each party submits its package of proposals and the arbitrator selects from one or the other package a proposal for each outstanding item. Therefore, the resulting collective agreement could contain all, some, or none of the proposals made by a particular party. As with total-package final offer arbitration, the parties' offers should be realistic to enhance their chance of being incorporated into the collective agreement.

Whatever combination of the items the arbitrator selects forms some or all of the terms of the collective agreement. Whether the arbitrator's decision forms some or all of the agreement depends, as noted before, on whether or not the parties have previously reached agreement on any items. Any previously agreed-upon terms will be incorporated into the collective agreement along with the arbitrator's choices.

Our fictional example from the previous section can also be used to illustrate the process of item-by-item final offer selection. Recall that the union's proposal was a wage of $20 an hour and a workweek of 37 hours, while the employer's proposal was $15 an hour and a 40-hour week. If item-by-item final offer selection is used, the arbitrator has several potential choices:

- $20 an hour and a 37-hour week

- $15 an hour and a 40-hour week

- $20 an hour and a 40-hour week

- $15 an hour and a 37-hour week

"So that's collective bargaining."

The advantage of using item-by-item final offer selection to resolve bargaining disputes is that the arbitrator's choice can incorporate items from each side's package of proposals. Thus, the arbitrator lessens the possibility that one side or the other will have its suggestions ignored and thereby become resentful. The collective agreement will, ideally, include terms proposed by both parties, and thus both will be committed to supporting the agreement and making it work. The disadvantage of using item-by-item final offer selection is that the resulting collective agreement does not integrate both sides' suggestions in a way that could satisfy both parties; instead, it is simply an arbitrary collection of choices between the positions of both parties. Thus, neither party is likely to be completely satisfied with the agreement.

In several Canadian jurisdictions, interest arbitration is used as a compulsory method of solving bargaining disputes. If the parties cannot agree on a solution to a bargaining issue, they must use interest arbitration rather than undertake other actions such as strikes or lockouts. Interest arbitration is also used as a "last resort" form of third-party intervention when neither conciliation nor mediation has been successful. Both these situations may result in the regular use of interest arbitration to settle bargaining disputes, especially if the parties have historically had very different interests that are not easily reconciled. This is often the case in the public sector. The employer in the public sector (government) has a limited ability to pay large wage increases because revenues can only be gained through changes in taxation, and taxpayers usually resent increases in taxes. However, public sector unions want their members to have reasonable wage parity with the private sector, and thus expect their members' wages to increase to keep pace with private sector wages.

The regular use of interest arbitration to resolve bargaining disputes, despite the disadvantages mentioned above, does result in a completed collective agreement and ensures some degree of workplace stability for the term of that agreement. However, two significant problems have been identified with the use of interest arbitration (or of binding conciliation, which produces similar results) on a continuing basis as a means of resolving bargaining disputes. The first problem is that the availability of these compulsory and binding processes results in a reduction of the parties' desire to resolve outstanding issues on their own. The parties may not be seriously committed to bargaining because they know that if they reach an impasse, a third party will resolve the impasse for them. This phenomenon is called the **chilling effect**. The second problem is that the parties can become addicted to the habitual use of compulsory conciliation or interest arbitration and may lose the ability to resolve disputes on their own. If the responsibility for resolving disputes is consistently taken away from the parties and given to a third party, the parties will not develop effective conflict-resolution skills of their own and over time they will become progressively less skilled at bargaining successfully. This phenomenon is called the **narcotic effect**.[8]

One Canadian study attempted to determine if the narcotic effect actually existed. The author of the study examined the use of interest arbitration in one public sector setting: 35 years' worth of contract settlements involving British Columbia teachers.[9] During this period, one province-wide teachers' union negotiated on an individual local level with district school boards. This study looked at the factors that had influenced the parties in these negotiations to pursue a bargaining dispute to the point of arbitration. These included whether the most recent set of negotiations had been settled through interest arbitration and the number of times each set of parties (the teachers' union and each district school board in the province) had used interest arbitration over the entire length of the bargaining relationship. The study also analysed whether the overall level of interest-arbitration usage in the province as a whole had affected whether the individual school boards and the teachers' union had used interest arbitration.

The results of the analysis indicated general support for the existence of the narcotic effect. When interest arbitration was used in one set of negotiations, there was a greater possibility that the next set of negotiations would end through the use of interest arbitration. Also, the more times an individual set of parties used interest arbitration, the more likely it was to use interest arbitration in subsequent negotiations. The author of the study suggests that these findings support the existence of the narcotic effect, since they appear to indicate that the parties increasingly rely on interest arbitration to reduce the perceived uncertainty of reaching settlements through negotiations. However, the analysis included one contradictory finding: following periods of increasing rates of interest-arbitration use across the entire province, there was a slight decrease in the likelihood of interest arbitration being used in an individual set of negotiations. This finding contradicts the existence of the narcotic effect, since it seems to indicate that having previous general examples of successfully concluded arbitrations does not always predispose individual parties to use arbitration themselves.

The general features of arbitration are summarized in Table 10-6. Before concluding our discussion of arbitration, we will discuss one other form of arbitration that is available in some Canadian jurisdictions.

TABLE 10-6   Features of Interest Arbitration

Conducted by	– Arbitrator or arbitration board. – Labour relations board (in Saskatchewan).
When it is used	– By request of parties to labour relations board. – May be voluntarily chosen by parties if they can mutually agree on acceptable arbitrator.
What happens	– Arbitrator or board is appointed. – Arbitrator or board holds hearing. – Each party presents proposals and evidence supporting validity of proposals. – Arbitrator considers proposals and evidence and then creates award. – Award can be based on total-package final offer selection, item-by-item final offer selection, or arbitrator's own solution. – Award is binding and forms part or all of collective agreement.

Mediation/Arbitration

In some Canadian jurisdictions, there is a provision for parties involved in bargaining to use another form of interest arbitration. This type of arbitration is called **mediation-arbitration**, or med-arb. Med-arb has occasionally been used to resolve bargaining disputes in the Canadian public sector. In this form of third-party intervention, the third party initially enters the bargaining process in the role of a mediator and attempts to resolve the bargaining disputes in the same fashion that a "regular" mediator would. However, if the issues in dispute cannot be resolved through mediation, then the third party changes its role to become an arbitrator and, in that capacity, chooses the terms and conditions of the collective agreement.

Med-arb is an attractive form of third-party intervention because it guarantees that a solution to bargaining disputes will be reached. Furthermore, with med-arb, the parties can avoid some of the time delays that may occur if mediation is unsuccessful and arbitration is implemented only after that point. Because the mediator and the arbitrator are the same person or persons, there is a minimal turnaround time between the two steps. Also, less time is required for the further collection of evidence and subsequent decision making that arbitration requires, as the mediator is already familiar with the situation. Using the same individual or panel as both mediator and arbitrator may also promote higher-quality solutions in arbitration, since the individual or panel is more closely acquainted with the parties and the situations in dispute.

However, notwithstanding these advantages, med-arb is not widely used as a form of third-party intervention. This is because the parties may not respond as cooperatively to the third party acting as mediator when they know that if the third party later becomes an arbitrator, he or she will ultimately determine the content of the collective agreement.[10] Thus, since the mediation part of med-arb tends to be ineffectual, med-arb essentially functions as an extra-lengthy form of arbitration. Additionally, an arbitrator who enters into a dispute as an arbitrator may be more objective about the bargaining situation than an arbitrator who has previously served as a mediator in the same dispute. Even if the mediator-arbitrator does his or her best to be neutral in the arbitration phase of the process, the parties may distrust the final result if they suspect that the arbitrator's objectivity has been clouded by his or her experience with the parties as a mediator.

Having outlined the three main kinds of third-party intervention in bargaining disputes, we will now discuss in greater detail the conditions under which the parties in negotiations may choose to use one or the other of these forms of intervention.

USING CONCILIATION, MEDIATION, OR ARBITRATION

We have presented the three main types of third-party intervention in the order of conciliation, mediation, and arbitration for two reasons. First, this ordering arranges the forms of third-party intervention from the one that is least intrusive on the bargaining process (i.e., conciliation, where the third party observes or investigates and makes recommendations) to the one that is most intrusive (i.e., arbitration, where the third party actually formulates part or all of the collective agreement). Second, as we have seen, several jurisdictions in Canada require third-party intervention to proceed in this order. Initially, the parties must submit to conciliation if they are unable to reach an agreement; if that effort fails, mediation takes place; and if mediation does not succeed, then arbitration is used to resolve disputes. The structure of this process clearly encourages the parties to resolve their disputes themselves. They know that if they do not do so, they may end up having the terms of the collective agreement imposed on them, having lost the freedom to fashion their own terms.

However, in some Canadian jurisdictions, the parties have a greater degree of freedom to choose the form of third-party intervention they see as appropriate to their own situation. In this section, we will briefly discuss the requirements or options for choosing third-party intervention in Canadian bargaining disputes. Because the public and private sectors differ in the kinds of third-party intervention they use, our discussion will focus on the two sectors separately.

Third-Party Intervention in Private Sector Bargaining Disputes

Management and unions operating in the private sector in Canada prefer the mediation process to either conciliation or arbitration. As we know, conciliation is not always effective in resolving private sector bargaining disputes and arbitration reduces the bargainers' control over the final outcome. As a result, conciliation and arbitration are seldom used in private sector disputes, except where required by legislation. Mediation is preferred because it gives the parties some practical assistance in solving their disagreements while allowing them to retain control over the contents of the eventual collective agreement.

We should note that bargainers involved in private sector negotiations can either use a mediator supplied by the labour relations board or ministry of labour, or privately choose their own mediator. A privately chosen mediator can have any combination of skills and experience, as long as both parties agree on the choice. In some private sector bargaining scenarios, the parties agree in advance on the mediator who will be brought into the process if a dispute arises. The parties may even agree to include in their collective agreement the names of potential mediators who will be called upon to resolve disputes during the term of the collective agreement or during negotiations for a subsequent agreement. If a privately chosen mediator is used, the parties usually share the cost of the mediator's services equally.

Third-Party Intervention in Public Sector Bargaining Disputes

As we have seen, because of the potential impact of work stoppages in the public sector, most Canadian jurisdictions require that public sector bargaining disputes be subject to some form of third-party intervention. These requirements are in place to avoid the use of strikes or lockouts in the bargaining process. Such job actions are particularly damaging or dangerous if they result in an essential service becoming unavailable.

Canadian jurisdictions have different requirements about which form of third-party intervention will be used at which point in the public sector bargaining process. In some jurisdictions, because of the negative impact that might result from a protracted dispute or the lack of a completed collective agreement, the parties are required to proceed immediately to arbitration if a dispute arises. In other jurisdictions, the parties follow the progression of interventions previously described, with arbitration being used only if conciliation and mediation have been unsuccessful in resolving disputes.

British Columbia is the only jurisdiction in Canada that does not require binding conciliation or arbitration in the public sector if regular conciliation does not succeed. The sentiment underlying the British Columbia legislation is that employers and unions, even those in the public sector, should be free to agree—or not to agree—to arbitration to resolve their disputes and that they should not have arbitration forced upon them if they do not see that process as appropriate for their situation. Consequently, public sector arbitration is voluntary in British Columbia. Furthermore, if public sector employers and unions choose to use arbitration to settle bargaining disputes, they are free to fashion their own decision criteria for the arbitrator to follow, including whether the arbitrator will use total-package or item-by-item final offer selection.

We will now conclude our discussion of third-party intervention in bargaining by describing other, less common forms of intervention that are available in some Canadian jurisdictions.

OTHER FORMS OF INTERVENTION IN THE BARGAINING PROCESS

Up to this point, we have reviewed methods of resolving bargaining disputes that involve a third party. There are, however, three methods of resolving bargaining disputes that do not always actively involve a third party in the bargaining process: final offer votes, industrial inquiry commissions, and disputes inquiry boards. We will outline each of these methods in turn.

Final Offer Votes

Most Canadian labour relations legislation provides for a **final offer vote** to be taken during a strike or lockout. The minister of labour is permitted to order that the bargaining unit members or the employers in an employers' organization be given an opportunity to accept or reject the last offer made by the other party. A secret-ballot vote is conducted to determine whether the party's constituents accept or reject the other party's position on all matters that remain in dispute between the parties. The voters are presented with the terms of the other party's final offer and asked whether they would accept or reject the offer. If the majority of the employees in the bargaining unit or the majority of the employers in the employers' organization accept the last offer received, then the parties must conclude a collective agreement incorporating the terms of that final offer.

The purpose of making a final offer vote available is twofold. First, a final offer vote determines whether a party's offer is actually acceptable to the constituents represented by the other party's negotiating team, even if the offer has been rejected by the negotiating team itself. In essence, a final offer vote circumvents the possibility that the negotiating team is not fully communicating the other party's offer to its constituents, either intentionally or unintentionally. Second, a final offer vote provides another opportunity for bargaining disputes to be resolved before a strike or lockout takes place (or before a third party is brought into the process).

Industrial Inquiry Commission

All Canadian jurisdictions expect New Brunswick and Saskatchewan make provision for the appointment of an **industrial inquiry commission** to investigate a bargaining dispute. In most jurisdictions, the minister of labour appoints the commission on his or her own initiative, but in British Columbia and Newfoundland, there is also the opportunity for the negotiating parties to request that an industrial inquiry commission be appointed. While the appointment of an industrial inquiry commission is a relatively rare event, it is still important to understand what the commission is and under what circumstances it might be used.

When an industrial inquiry commission is created, the minister of labour provides it with a statement of the matters in dispute that are to be investigated. The commission then commences its investigation of the identified matters. If the parties do not settle the matters in dispute within a short time (usually 14 days) after the commission's appointment, the commission must report the results of its investigation, along with recommendations for resolving the dispute, to the minister of labour. Thus, the appointment of an industrial inquiry commission is a clear sign to the parties that the minister of labour will be informed of the dispute and will possibly get involved in its resolution if they do not quickly act to resolve the dispute on their own. The terms of appointment for most industrial inquiry commissions also provide another method of dispute resolution. The parties will be bound by the recommendations contained in the commission's report submitted to the minister of labour if they agree in writing to this condition prior to the commission commencing its work.

A recent human rights hearing dealt with the issue of obesity as a disability. An industrial inquiry commission would follow a similar process as a human rights commission in addressing bargaining-related conflicts.

It is important to note that while industrial inquiry commissions are usually appointed in relation to a bargaining dispute, a strike, or a lockout, most legislation permits commissions to be appointed for any situation that the minister of labour or the parties consider appropriate. An industrial inquiry commission can be empowered to promote conditions favourable to the settlement of disputes as well as to do whatever is necessary to maintain or secure labour relations stability. For example, in British Columbia, an industrial inquiry commission can be appointed if a dispute in an industry is likely to arise; there is no need to wait until a dispute actually exists.

Disputes Inquiry Board

In Alberta and Ontario, the minister of labour can establish a **disputes inquiry board** after a legal strike or lockout commences. A disputes inquiry board is usually composed of three individuals who are charged with the responsibility of gathering evidence about a dispute that has led to a strike or lockout. Like industrial inquiry commissions, disputes inquiry boards are appointed on a relatively infrequent basis.

The board usually carries out its mandate by holding a formal hearing at which the employer and the union each present oral and written evidence. At the conclusion of the hearing, the board presents recommendations for the resolution of all outstanding issues in dispute to the minister of labour. In Ontario, the minister of labour is then free to act on the recommendations as she or he sees fit. In Alberta, if the recommendations of the disputes inquiry board are not accepted by the representatives of one side in the bargaining dispute, that side's members are given the opportunity to vote on whether to accept or reject the recommendations. In other words, the recommendations are subjected to a process very similar to that of a final offer vote. If a majority of those voting agree to accept the recommendations of the disputes inquiry board, the recommendations are then considered binding and are incorporated into the terms of the collective agreement.

The purpose of a disputes inquiry board is similar to that of an industrial inquiry commission. However, the major difference between the two is that a disputes inquiry board is specifically charged with investigating disputes that have led to a strike or lockout, while an industrial inquiry commission can be appointed at any time to investigate any issue the minister or the parties feel is appropriate. In addition, the recommendations of a disputes inquiry board have more formal weight than the recommendations of an industrial inquiry commission. The recommendations of a disputes inquiry board may result in a vote to accept or reject the recommendations or informal action on the recommendations by the minister of labour. The recommendations of an industrial inquiry commission may also be acted upon by the minister of labour, but the power of an industrial inquiry commission to resolve disputes is more dependent on the power of persuasion.

SUMMARY

Third-party intervention in collective bargaining is available in a variety of forms in Canada, and it is voluntary or mandatory depending on the type of negotiations. Mandatory third-party intervention is more common in the public sector as a means of delaying or replacing a strike or lockout. Third-party intervention is intended to introduce a party into the bargaining process who either helps the parties reach agreement on their own or who recommends or imposes solutions to bargaining disputes.

The most common forms of third-party intervention are conciliation, mediation, and arbitration. Conciliation is a form of investigation in which an individual or board investigates bargaining disputes and makes recommendations for solutions to the parties or to the minister of labour. In mediation, the mediator actually becomes involved in the negotiations and encourages or assists the parties to find their own solutions to disputes. In arbitration, the arbitrator creates a solution that becomes part of the collective agreement; he or she does this either by fashioning a solution or by choosing final offers made by the parties. In some jurisdictions, parties can choose the form of third-party intervention they prefer; in others, they are required to try each form in turn as long as the disputes remain unsettled.

In some Canadian jurisdictions, other forms of intervention are available, such as mediation-arbitration, special mediation, fact finding, industrial inquiry commissions, final offer votes, and disputes inquiry boards. All of these are intended to assist the negotiating parties in resolving bargaining disputes and completing a collective agreement or, if the parties are unable to overcome their differences, to ensure that a solution is put into place and a collective agreement is reached.

KEY TERMS FOR CHAPTER 10

binding (p. 370)
booking out (p. 376)
chilling effect (p. 384)
conciliation (p. 366)
disputes inquiry board (p. 391)
fact finder (p. 378)
final offer selection (p. 380)
final offer vote (p. 389)
industrial inquiry commission (p. 390)
interest arbitration (p. 378)
item-by-item final offer selection (p. 382)
mediation (p. 373)
mediation-arbitration (p. 386)
narcotic effect (p. 384)
special mediator (p. 377)
total-package final offer selection (p. 380)

DISCUSSION QUESTIONS FOR CHAPTER 10

1. Explain the rationale for using the conciliation process.

2. What is interest arbitration and when might it be used?

3. Explain how interest arbitration differs from rights arbitration.

4. Outline how the mediation process works.

5. Distinguish between a mediator and a fact finder.

6. When would a final offer vote be ordered?

7. Explain the advantages and disadvantages of using total-package final offer selection and item-by-item final offer selection.

8. When do parties have the option of choosing conciliation, mediation, or arbitration?

9. Why would either an industrial inquiry commission or a disputes inquiry board be established? When might one be used in preference to the other?

C A S E *10-1*

INDUSTRIAL WORKERS OF CANADA AND FLEXIBLE PLASTICS LTD.

(Based on *Royalguard Vinyl Co. and United Steelworkers of America*, 1995)

In this case, the parties agreed to submit their disputes over the terms of a first collective agreement to a board of arbitration. Once the board had been appointed and had commenced its work, the employer requested that the minister of labour conduct a final offer vote. The union has objected to the request, saying that the labour legislation governing final offer votes only allows such votes once a strike or lockout has commenced and that allowing a vote would undermine the purpose of the arbitration.

Background to the Case

The union was certified as the bargaining agent for the employees in early 1994. The union and the employer have been engaged in collective bargaining for some time but have not been able to agree on terms for a first collective agreement. On December 6, 1994, the union contacted the provincial minister of labour and requested that an arbitration board be appointed to settle the bargaining issues that the parties had not resolved. The minister granted the request, and both parties appointed nominees for the board. Two nominees were chosen, and both parties then mutually selected the third nominee, who would act as chair of the board. The board scheduled its first two meetings for February 6 and February 20, 1995.

Both parties in the negotiations attended the first scheduled meeting on February 6 and made submissions outlining their positions on the unresolved issues. The hearing was then adjourned to the next scheduled meeting date of February 20. However, on February 17, the employer sent a letter to the minister of labour requesting a final offer vote. The relevant labour legislation states that the minister is required to order a final offer vote if one of the parties requests it, so the minister directed the labour relations board to begin planning a final offer vote. A meeting was scheduled for February 27 to select a date when the vote would take place.

On February 22, the union sent a letter to the minister of labour objecting to the scheduling of the vote. The union argued that the employer could not request a final offer vote once arbitration had been initiated because the relevant labour legislation also stated that a final offer vote had to be initiated "before or after the commencement of a strike or lockout." Since arbitration had started, the union argued, neither party could legally commence a strike or lockout, and thus the conditions necessary to order a final offer vote did not exist.

After receiving the union's letter, the minister decided to postpone the vote and asked the labour relations board to settle the dispute over whether the vote should be held or not. The minister also requested that the board deal with the dispute as quickly as possible. On March 8, 1995, the labour relations board held a hearing and received the parties' submissions on whether the final offer vote should be held or not.

The relevant terms of the labour legislation state:

> Where, at any time, after the commencement of a strike or lockout, the Minister is of the opinion that it is in the public interest that the employees in the affected bargaining unit be given the opportunity to accept or reject the offer of the employer last received by the trade union in respect of all matters remaining in dispute between the parties, the Minister may ... direct that a vote of the employees in the bargaining unit to accept or reject the offer be held forthwith....
>
> Before or after the commencement of a strike or lockout, the employer of the employees in the affected bargaining unit may request that a vote of the employees be taken as to the acceptance or rejection of the offer of the employer last received by the trade union in respect of all matters remaining in dispute between the parties, and the Minister shall ... direct that a vote of the employees to accept or reject the offer be held and thereafter no further request shall be made.

The Union's Position

The union argued that the phrase "before or after the commencement of a strike or lockout" meant that a final offer vote could not be held after arbitration for the terms of a first collective agreement had begun. To support this argument, the union cited another part of the labour legislation that stated: "If first agreement arbitration is initiated, the employees in the bargaining unit shall not strike and the employer shall not lock out the employees." The union stated that the language permitting a final offer vote implied a "precondition" that a strike or a lockout was an option. The union's interpretation of the legislation was that a strike or a lockout was not an option when first-agreement arbitration was taking place. Thus, the precondition for a final offer vote could not be met, and a final offer vote should not be permitted to proceed.

The union stated that allowing a final offer vote to proceed would disrupt the process of arbitration and that the results of the vote "could only serve to improperly influence" the members of the arbitration board.

The Employer's Position

The employer agreed with the union that the section of the labour legislation stating when a final offer vote could be conducted was "clear and unambiguous." However, the employer stated that the effect of the words "before or after the commencement of a strike or lockout" was to authorize final offer votes at any time in the bargaining process. The employer argued that these words did not constitute a precondition but were instead a clarification intended to distinguish a final offer vote ordered by the minister of labour from a final offer vote requested by one of the parties.

The employer also contended that the two sections of the legislation that the union claimed were interrelated were in fact enacted at different times and thus could not be interpreted as dependent on each other.

The employer further argued that the provisions in the legislation for a final offer vote and first-contract arbitration were both intended as "tools for resolving [a] bargaining impasse" and that there was nothing inconsistent in using both simultaneously. A final offer vote might have the effect of resolving a collective agreement more quickly than would the process of arbitration. The employer's interpretation of the legislation was that the only time a final offer vote could not be held was after a first agreement had been settled by the arbitration board.

References

[1] Mofina, R., & May, R. (2001). PS workers, government closer to settlement: conciliation report viewed as a basis for renewed negotiations. *The Ottawa Citizen*, August 25, 2001, A3.

[2] Guy, D. (2001). Conciliator to resolve NAV Canada dispute: workers demand 60% wage increase. *The Ottawa Citizen*, July 7, 2001, A7.

[3] Cramton, P., & Gunderson, M. (1999). The effect of collective bargaining legislation on strikes and wages. *Review of Economics and Statistics, 81(3)*, 475–490.

[4] Bohn, G. (2001). Mediator's report fails to solve transit strike: union urges acceptance, but company says: 'We don't have the funds.' *The Vancouver Sun*, June 16, 2001, A1.

[5] McInnes, C., & Nuttall-Smith, C. (2001). Three days of free rides when buses return on Tuesday: back-to-work bill sends part-time issue to committee. *The Vancouver Sun*, August 2, 2001, A1.

[6] Flinn, B. (2001). Unions win some, lose some: arbitrator picks nurses' proposal over government's, but other health workers disappointed. *The Daily News* (Halifax), August 14, 2001, 4.

[7] Quoted in Flinn, *op. cit.*

[8] Godard, J. (1994). *Industrial relations, the economy and society.* Toronto, ON: McGraw-Hill Ryerson.

[9] Currie, J. (1989). Who uses interest arbitration? The case of British Columbia's teachers, 1947–1981. *Industrial and Labour Relations Review, 42(3)*, 363–379.

[10] Craig, A.W., & Solomon, N. (1996). *The system of industrial relations in Canada* (5th edition). Scarborough, ON: Prentice-Hall.

Breastfeeding ruling gives mom her job back:

Arbitrator rules in favour of breastfeeding mother

CALGARY—A woman fired when her employer wouldn't let her breast-feed at work has won a 16-month fight to get her job back.

An arbitrator has ruled Carewest Cross Bow, a continuing care facility, engaged in a form of sex discrimination when it fired Doris DeGagne. The company fired her after refusing to make accommodations for DeGagne, then 32, to breast-feed on the job, or, alternatively, to extend her maternity leave by six months.

"Breast-feeding in my view is as intimately connected to childbirth as pregnancy is to childbirth and should be safeguarded in the same way," arbitrator John Moreau wrote in his decision. "I agree ... that discrimination on the basis that a woman is breast-feeding is a form of sex discrimination."

He ordered Carewest to immediately reinstate DeGagne without loss of seniority and issue back pay and benefits back to September 22, 1999, the date her additional six-month leave of absence would have expired.

DeGagne, now 34, lost her job as a part-time recreational therapist at Carewest Cross Bow after failing to return from a nine-month-long maternity leave in April 1999. DeGagne argued her newborn daughter Danna would benefit from breast-feeding beyond DeGagne's maternity leave, and hoped to extend the leave by an additional six months or make special arrangements to breast-feed at work. One option was to have her baby brought to the centre for feeding.

DeGagne had worked at Carewest for 10 years and claimed she was wrongfully dismissed based on gender.

Carewest executive director Nora Kirkham defended the facility's actions. "Carewest wholeheartedly endorses and supports breast-feeding," she said in a statement. "Without question it benefits both infant and mother. The issue at hand is not about breast-feeding itself but accommodating individual needs and the ability to care for residents."

She further pointed to the challenges of understanding how the collective agreement language works when taking into consideration human rights legislation. In this case, said Kirkham, "there may be extenuating circumstances that go beyond collective agreements." In mutual agreement with the union, Carewest has since extended maternity leave to one year from nine months.

The arbitrator was hired by both parties to handle the grievance. The union and Carewest both agreed beforehand to abide by his ruling.

DeGagne, pregnant with her second child which is due at the end of May, said she hopes to return to work soon. "It's great. It's been a roller-coaster ride for sure."

(*Calgary Herald*, January 19, 2001)

chapter 11

THE GRIEVANCE ARBITRATION PROCESS

objectives

Once collective bargaining has concluded, a collective agreement is settled and put into effect. During the time the collective agreement is in effect, there may be disputes about the interpretation or application of the terms of the collective agreement. These disputes are resolved through a process known as grievance arbitration. By the end of this chapter, you should be able to:

- discuss and give examples of different types of grievances
- describe the grievance procedure
- define the duty of fair representation
- distinguish between different standards of proof in arbitration
- describe the purpose and role of an arbitrator
- explain alternatives to the arbitration process

INTRODUCTION

After studying the process of negotiation that leads to a collective agreement, we know that the document resulting from those negotiations contains terms and conditions that govern the operations of the workplace. However, we also know that the parties represented in negotiations have different concerns that may or may not be addressed either in bargaining or in the final version of the collective agreement. We also know that the collective agreement may not completely represent the desired outcomes of one or both of the parties, but may instead be the most satisfactory settlement that both parties feel they can live with. In addition, it is possible that conditions in the workplace or the external environment will change during the time the collective agreement is in effect, which can make applying the collective agreement difficult if the changes relate to conditions the agreement was intended to address. Given all these possibilities, even the best-intentioned and most-skilled negotiators find it difficult to create a collective agreement that will suit the workplace perfectly for its full duration.

How, then, are disputes over the collective agreement resolved while the collective agreement is in effect? As we know from Chapter 9, strikes and lockouts are prohibited during the term of the collective agreement. If a strike or a lockout were used as a means of settling a dispute every time there were problems in applying the collective agreement, these actions would be not only illegal but also very disruptive to the efficient functioning of the organization. Thus, it is obvious that there needs to be an another way to settle disagreements about the interpretation, application, or administration of the terms of the collective agreement. Disagreements of this kind are known as **grievances**, and Canadian labour legislation provides for a process called **grievance arbitration** to settle them.

It is important to understand the grievance arbitration system because this system is one of the major mechanisms that facilitate the development of the relationship—whether positive or negative—between the union and the employer. Since grievances arise from the application of the collective agreement to the day-to-day events in the workplace, dealing with grievances requires the union and the employer to interact on a regular basis. If the parties are able to work together constructively and productively, and both parties feel satisfied with the outcomes of the grievance procedure, that positive relationship can affect how the parties interact in other ways, including during collective bargaining. A positive relationship developed through interactions over grievances can lead to more positive interactions in bargaining, and thus to a more satisfactory collective agreement. On the other hand, if the union and the employer experience conflict in dealing with grievances and come to distrust or dislike each other, that negative relationship can make other forms of interaction more adversarial and less productive.

Grievance arbitration is also referred to as **rights arbitration** to distinguish it from interest arbitration. As we discussed in Chapter 10, interest arbitration determines the terms and conditions of the collective agreement itself. In contrast, rights arbitration is concerned with the rights of the employer, the individual, and the union that arise from the interpretation, application, or administration of the collective agreement. These rights include the right of the employee to be treated fairly by the employer, the right of the employer to exercise control over its operations, and the right of the union to act as the representative of the employees. Frequently, the central issue in resolving grievances is determining which of these rights is most important in specific workplace situations.

As noted in Chapter 7, Canadian legislation establishes that each collective agreement must outline a grievance resolution procedure; moreover, Canadian labour law in every jurisdiction contains a grievance procedure that is considered to apply if a collective agreement does not include its own procedure. Thus, there is a grievance procedure present in every unionized workplace, either explicitly in the collective agreement or implicitly in the legislation governing the workplace. We should note, in addition, that grievance resolution procedures are not limited to unionized workplaces. Although non-unionized workplaces do not have collective agreements containing grievance procedures, many have disciplinary or "fair treatment" procedures in place to deal with disagreements between workers and managers or the employer.[1] These procedures are very similar in intent and structure to the grievance procedures found in unionized workplaces. In addition, the *Canada Labour Code* and the Nova Scotia and Quebec labour codes permit non-unionized workers to file appeals similar to grievances in cases of dismissal and discipline.[2] Therefore, although this chapter will describe grievance procedures that deal with disagreements related to collective agreements, the general process that we will outline is also present in many non-unionized workplaces.

Since a collective agreement is a legal contract, disagreements over its interpretation, application, or administration are legal disputes over rights, and these disputes can be resolved by the adjudicative process of grievance arbitration. Grievances are initially addressed within the workplace, and it is only when a resolution cannot be reached there that grievances are taken to grievance arbitration. We will first examine the grievance process within the workplace, a process that involves the union, the employee, and the employer. We will then describe the grievance arbitration process, which involves a third party as a decision maker. Lastly, we will discuss some alternatives to the traditional grievance arbitration process.

THE GRIEVANCE IN THE WORKPLACE

In order for a grievance to be addressed through arbitration, it must first be determined whether or not grounds for a grievance actually exist. What one person perceives as a misinterpretation or misapplication of the collective agreement may be different from what another person perceives. Therefore, we will start our discussion of the grievance arbitration procedure by outlining what constitutes a grievance. We will then describe how the procedure unfolds once it has been established that grounds for a grievance exist.

Definition of a Grievance

The term "grievance" is used to describe an alleged violation of one or more of the terms of the collective agreement. Not every complaint arising in an employment relationship meets the test of being a grievance. From a union's perspective, a grievance occurs when the employer violates the collective agreement by either taking or failing to take a specific action.[3] For example, there would be grounds for a grievance if the collective agreement states that work schedules must be posted two weeks in advance of the scheduled shifts but the employer posts the schedule only one week in advance; the late posting would violate the terms of the collective agreement. Employers and employees should be aware that when they act or fail to act and such action or non-action violates the collective agreement, a grievance may arise; in other words, any violation of the collective agreement has the potential to generate a grievance.

Under most grievance procedures, both the union and the employer can file grievances against the other party. However, it is far more common for the union to file grievances against the employer, for the simple reason that it is the employer that is responsible for controlling the day-to-day operations in the workplace. The employer has the greater amount of responsibility for carrying out the terms of the collective agreement as they relate to the workplace's functioning, and thus there is more opportunity for the employer to be perceived as violating the collective agreement. Most grievances filed by employers against unions are the result of union actions arising from work stoppages during the term of a collective agreement.

We should also note that in some provincial labour codes, there are specific definitions that make distinctions between different kinds of disagreements in the workplace. The *Quebec Labour Code* specifies that a "grievance" is any disagreement respecting the interpretation or application of a collective agreement and that a "dispute" is a disagreement respecting the negotiation or renewal of a collective agreement. The *Alberta Labour Relations Code's* definition of "dispute" is similar to that in the Quebec legislation. The *New Brunswick Labour Act*, the *British Columbia Labour Relations Code*, the *Ontario Labour Relations Act*, the *Newfoundland Labour Relations Act*, and the *Nova Scotia Trade Union Act* all define a "dispute" as relating "to any manner or thing affecting or relating to terms or conditions of employment of work done or to be done," but none of them define "grievance." Thus, in order for a disagreement to be handled under a grievance procedure, it must meet the definition of a grievance or a dispute that can be settled in this manner, as specified in the relevant labour legislation. To accommodate the variations in terminology among the different Canadian labour laws, we will use the term "disagreement" to describe the differences between employers, employees, and unions that may lead to grievances.

Types of Grievances

While each individual grievance relates to the specific terms and conditions of a particular collective agreement, there are four general types of workplace grievances. We will outline each of these types.

Individual Grievance   If an action taken or not taken by the employer specifically affects an individual employee, the resulting grievance is called an **individual grievance**. Discipline is a common cause of individual grievances. An example of an individual grievance involving discipline is a situation where an employer suspends an employee the first time that the employee is late for work. If the collective agreement states that suspension can only be used as a form of discipline after other disciplinary actions such as warning letters have been used, the suspended employee could file an individual grievance. The newspaper story at the beginning of this chapter discusses an example of an individual grievance.

Group Grievance   If the action of the employer affects a number of employees in the same manner, then a **group grievance** may be filed. For example, suppose an employer has decided that it must undertake layoffs and tells all the employees in a particular department that they will be laid off. If the collective agreement states that any layoffs must be conducted on a company-wide basis and must be determined on the basis of employee seniority, then the employer's action has apparently violated this part of the collective agreement. The employees who have received the layoff notices could file a group grievance.

Continuing Grievance   Grievances can also be recurring; they may not involve a single incident but instead involve an ongoing practice. Grievances of this kind are called **continuing grievances**. An example of a continuing grievance would be one involving the employer's refusal to consider seniority in scheduling shifts within a particular division of the company. If the union or an employee disagrees with the employer's interpretation of the contract terms defining how seniority is to be used in determining shift assignments in this part of the organization, a continuing grievance could be filed.

Policy Grievance   The fourth type of grievance is called a **policy grievance**. The union files this kind of grievance on behalf of all employees, alleging that an employer's action or lack of action is a violation of the collective agreement that affects all employees. A policy grievance could occur over an issue such as the employer's interpretation of contract provisions for payment of holiday pay, since under employment standards law all employees are entitled to holiday pay. Thus, all employees of the organization would be affected by the employer's interpretation of holiday pay provisions. A policy grievance can be filed regardless of whether the contract interpretation or application has actually affected all employees or not; the feature that distinguishes policy grievances from continuing grievances or group grievances is the potential of the issue in dispute to affect all employees. If the issue could potentially affect all employees, the grievance is a policy grievance.

A recent example of a policy grievance occurred in Newfoundland when the Newfoundland and Labrador Nurses' Union filed a grievance against the Health Care Corporation of St. John's.[4] The employer imposed a policy that stated that any staff members unable to come to work because of bad weather conditions would have to take time from their annual leave allocation to compensate for the missed work time. The union filed a policy grievance because of evidence that employees in some departments were told that they did not have to report to work when the weather was bad. The union argued that the employer's policy potentially affected all employees and was not fairly applied, since employees who were told to report for work should not have to take time from their leave allocation.

We should also note that grievances can be classified according to which part of the collective agreement was allegedly violated; for example, there are job classification grievances, work-scheduling grievances, compensation grievances, and discharge and discipline grievances, to name a few. As we can see, these groups of grievances are defined by the type of contract term involved in the disagreement, not by the number of employees affected or by the manner in which the contract was allegedly violated.

Having established what a grievance consists of and what types of grievances might occur in a workplace, we will now discuss the importance of timing in filing a grievance.

Timeliness of a Grievance

A grievance commences when the affected individual or group knows, or ought to reasonably know, that an action (or lack of action) violates the collective agreement. It is impossible for a union to constantly police the application, administration, and interpretation of the collective agreement in every part of a workplace. It therefore falls to the employees to notify the union immediately when they believe that the collective agreement has been violated. It is also important to note the provision that a violation of the collective agreement can be said to have occurred if an individual or group "ought to reasonably know" that an action contravenes the collective agreement. This expectation implies that the employer and the union should be familiar with the contractual terms of the collective agreement and be aware of what actions, or lack of actions, might be considered grounds for a grievance. It also implies that the parties affected by the alleged violation of the collective agreement have a responsibility to make their concerns known as soon as possible.

If the party filing a grievance has failed to complain when an alleged grievance first occurred, two problems can arise. First, the employer may dismiss the grievance out of hand, taking the position that since the practice has been ongoing and no previous complaint has been filed, then, even if the action is clearly in contravention of the collective agreement, the employees have, in effect, accepted the practice and have no grounds to complain. This principle is sometimes referred to as the principle of **past practice**. The principle of past practice does not mean that employees have no right to complain about an alleged violation of the collective agreement if they have not done so on previous occurrences of the violation, but their ability to make an effective complaint (and to receive a remedy) is reduced. However, when a complaint is not made in a timely manner, the union retains the right to proceed with the grievance procedure even if the employer dismisses the grievance, but the union's chances of being successful in an arbitration may be reduced.

The second problem associated with a failure to file a timely grievance is that even if the grievance is considered, the lack of timeliness in alerting the employer to the error of its ways can affect the eventual remedy granted. For example, an arbitrator might make a monetary award based on payments that employees lost because of the employer's misinterpretation of the collective agreement. However, if the affected employees did not complain as soon as the first miscalculated payment was made, allowing the employer to keep making incorrect payments for a period of time, the monetary award to the employees might reflect only those payments lost after the grievance was filed, not all of the incorrect payments.

We will now look at how the grievance procedure is initiated in the workplace.

The Steps In The Grievance Procedure

As previously noted, Canadian labour legislation does not require any specific process or procedure for handling grievances between the union and the employer. Rather, the legislation leaves it to the individual union and employer to develop their own internal process, although the legislation provides a standard procedure that is considered to apply if the parties have neglected to include a grievance procedure in their collective agreement. An example of a standardized grievance procedure outlined in labour law is presented in Table 11-1.

Having a grievance procedure available to resolve disagreements is very important in ensuring that the collective agreement is correctly and effectively applied in the workplace. Therefore, the grievance procedure is usually negotiated into the collective agreement, and

TABLE 11-1 An Example of A Legislated Grievance Procedure

Provision for final settlement

78(1) Every collective agreement shall contain a provision for final settlement without stoppage of work, by arbitration or otherwise, of all differences between the parties thereto, or persons bound by the agreement or on whose behalf it was entered into, concerning its meaning, application, or alleged violation.

Deemed arbitration procedures

78(2) Where a collective agreement does not contain a provision as required under subsection (1), it shall be deemed to contain the following provisions, which shall be numbered or lettered as may be required in the collective agreement:

(a)   Where a violation of this agreement is alleged, or a difference arises between the parties to this agreement relating to the discipline or dismissal of an employee, or to the meaning, interpretation, application or operation of this agreement (including a difference as to whether or not a matter is arbitrable), either party, without stoppage of work and after exhausting any grievance procedure established by this agreement, may notify the other party in writing of its desire to submit the alleged violation or difference to arbitration; and thereafter the parties shall, subject to clause (b), agree on an arbitrator to hear and determine the matter and issue a decision, which decision is final and binding on the parties and any person affected thereby.

(b)   Where the parties agree that an arbitration board rather than an arbitrator should determine a matter, the parties shall appoint an arbitration board to hear and determine the matter and issue a decision, which decision is final and binding on the parties and any person affected thereby.

(c)   The provisions of *The Labour Relations Act* respecting the appointment, powers, duties and decisions of arbitrators and arbitration boards apply hereto.

Source: *Manitoba Labour Relations Act*, R.S.M. 1987, c. L10.

the process of negotiating this procedure can provide an opportunity for the employer and union to develop a unique and personalized dispute resolution process. While unions and employers naturally make an effort to shape the grievance procedure to suit their own organizations and workplaces, grievance procedures in general share a number of characteristics. We will now outline these common features. The steps in the grievance process—before arbitration—are summarized in Table 11-2.

TABLE 11-2 Steps in the Grievance Procedure

Step	Who Is Involved	Process
Step 1	Individual employee with or without a shop steward or grievance committee member	Normally an oral presentation by employee to immediate supervisor with or without representation by the union
	Foreman, section head, supervisor, or other employer representative	Immediate supervisor has time limits (usually 14 days) within which to resolve or reject the grievance
Step 2	Grievance committee member(s) or shop steward	Grievance is presented in written format to next level of management
	Union business agent may accompany committee or steward	If not resolved, the grievance advances to next step within the time limits (usually 14 days)
	Department head, superintendent, or intermediate management	Time limits may be extended or waived (in writing) by mutual agreement
		If the grievance is not advanced within time limits or time limits are not jointly waived, grievance can be deemed abandoned
Step 3	Local union executive member, usually with business agent	Senior levels of union and employer discuss grievance
	Senior management with human resource/industrial relations officer	Usually all outstanding grievances are discussed as part of regularly scheduled labour-management meetings
		If the grievance is not resolved, the union may refer it to arbitration within the time limits (usually 14 days)

Filing the Grievance: Step One

The first step of the grievance process is the filing of a complaint about a violation of the collective agreement. As outlined, an individual, a group of employees, or the union on behalf of all employees can file a complaint. The person or party initiating the grievance is referred to as the **grievor**. The grievance itself is usually submitted, orally or in writing, either to the immediate supervisor of the area where the violation is alleged to have occurred or to the human resources department. Most grievances are filed in response to specific actions, such as decisions or orders, by supervisors.[5]

In some workplaces, the first step of the grievance procedure, in practice, actually contains two parts. In the first part, the grievance is brought to the attention of the employer through an oral complaint and there is an initial attempt to resolve the grievance through informal discussion between the parties. Several studies of grievance arbitration processes have indicated that a significant percentage of grievances are settled through informal discussion before more formal steps in the grievance procedure are taken.[6] If the grievance is not successfully resolved through this relatively informal method, it may proceed to the second part, which involves submitting a written complaint.

At the first step in the grievance procedure, the parties involved are usually the individual employee, with or without a shop steward to assist him or her, and the employee's immediate supervisor. Although the collective agreement does not always require that a shop steward be involved in this stage of the grievance procedure, some employees choose to have a shop steward assist them to ensure that the procedure is correctly followed. Similarly, although the human resources department of the organization is not usually formally involved at this stage of the grievance procedure, the supervisor may consult this department for advice or direction prior to dealing with the grievance.

In some workplaces, a grievance committee member may fill the role of a shop steward in assisting the employee. Grievance committee members

An employee meets with his union representative from the Halifax Longshoremen's union. Every grievance procedure starts with a face-to-face meeting like this.

are elected by union members, ideally on a departmental or other basis to ensure representation of the diversity among employees. Shop stewards and/or grievance committee members may also be useful participants at this stage of the procedure because of their expertise in assessing the validity of a grievance (and, hence, how much attention should be given to resolving it). Shop stewards and grievance committee members may also be able to promote an informal resolution so that the grievance does not unnecessarily proceed to more formalized steps in the grievance procedure.[7]

An issue that often arises with the filing of a grievance is whether the employee should continue working under the disputed conditions or withhold his or her labour until the grievance is resolved. The general principle governing this situation is "grieve, then work"—that is, in most situations, the employee is expected to continue his or her regular work. If the grievance is supported, the expectation is that any material harm the employee suffered as a result of the collective agreement's violation, such as lost wages or working time, will be reversed or compensated as part of the grievance resolution. The only generally recognized exceptions to the "grieve, then work" rule are cases where the alleged violation of the collective agreement puts the employee in a physically dangerous situation. For example, if the collective agreement sets out safety rules for performing particular jobs and a supervisor orders the employee to ignore those rules, the employee is generally entitled to refuse to perform the dangerous work and may also file a grievance.

For the individual worker, step one is the most important in the grievance procedure. It is the only step in which the individual, with or without the steward or grievance committee member, has control over the grievance and its outcome. Occasionally, an employee may bring a complaint to the union's attention that the union feels is not substantial enough to warrant filing a grievance. In this situation, the grievance will not likely proceed beyond the first step in the grievance procedure. If the employee feels that the union has unjustly refused to consider the complaint, the employee has the option of filing a complaint against the union for not fulfilling its duty of fair representation. This type of complaint will be discussed later in the chapter.

To conclude our discussion of the first step in the grievance procedure, we will note that most grievance procedures include time limits governing how long each step in the procedure must take. Each step of the grievance procedure has its own time limit, which usually ranges from 10 to 14 days. If the matter is not resolved during the time limit, the grievance automatically proceeds to the next step. The purpose of these time limits is to ensure that, when grievances are filed, they are promptly addressed and not ignored in the hope that the grievors will abandon their complaints. However, time limits can be waived by mutual consent. For example, if a particular employee was needed to provide evidence relating to another employee's grievance and this employee was on vacation, the employer and the union or employee could agree to waive the time limit for that stage of the grievance procedure until the needed employee was available. We should note, though, that failure to obtain an agreement to waive a time limit can result in a grievance being deemed abandoned and not being pursued any further.

Formal Complaint and Investigation: Step Two

If a grievance is not satisfactorily resolved by the individual employee and the employer within the time limit established for step one of the grievance procedure, the grievance will proceed to the next step, the written complaint. As noted, in some organizations, steps one and two are combined.

At step two the individual grievor (or group of grievors) is not extensively involved, even though he or she may have initiated the grievance. This is because the union, on behalf of its members, is the party that signed the collective agreement and is therefore also the party that would allege a violation of the collective agreement.

In most cases, the grievance is formally put into writing at step two of the grievance procedure. Most unions have a grievance form that is filled out by the grievor with the assistance of the steward or grievance committee member. This form usually contains the following:

- the name of the grievor

- the date, time, and specifics of the alleged violation

- the provisions of the collective agreement that are affected

- the identification of witnesses (if any) to the violation

- the immediate supervisor involved

- the requested remedy for the damage caused by the alleged violation

The grievance form is signed by the grievor and the shop steward or grievance committee member, as well as by the immediate supervisor, whose signature indicates that he or she is aware that the grievance has been filed. The grievance form is then given to the employer. The union and grievor each retain a copy.

After the formal written grievance has been submitted, the union and employer each commence their own investigation of the facts surrounding the grievance. This investigation usually entails interviewing the grievor, interviewing the manager or employer representative alleged to be responsible for the violation of the collective agreement, interviewing any witnesses, and collecting any physical evidence (such as payroll records or work schedules) that may support or disprove the allegations. Once the investigations are complete, the shop steward or the grievance committee will meet with management. Typically, middle-level managers such as senior supervisors represent management at this meeting; the union's business agent may also attend.

Since the union and the employer have independently investigated the allegations, both sides come to the meeting prepared to argue their position. Each side presents its evidence and position, and the parties attempt to determine whether a mutually satisfactory resolution is possible. A resolution at this stage of the grievance procedure is desirable because it allows both management and grievance committee members to retain control of the issue and its solution; it also reduces the likelihood of interference from higher levels of the union or management. If, however, the grievance is not resolved at this step within the time limit specified, the grievance will advance to step three.

The Final Attempt Before Arbitration: Step Three

At the third step of the grievance procedure, the union business agent, along with a representative of the local union, meets with senior management representatives. In most organizations, these parties meet regularly to discuss larger matters requiring input from both sides; grievances that have proceeded to step three are usually considered important enough to be discussed at these high-level meetings. As in the first two steps of the grievance procedure, both sides present their evidence related to the grievance, along with information on what happened in the first two steps of the procedure. After discussing the evidence, the parties attempt to reach a mutually satisfactory solution.

The third step of the grievance procedure is the last opportunity for the union and management to resolve the issue between them and control the outcome without the input of a third party. The amount of control that the parties perceive they have over the grievance procedure affects their level of satisfaction with the results; the more control the parties perceive they have over the procedure, the more satisfied they will likely be with the outcome.[8] Failure to reach a satisfactory settlement at this step leads to the option of undertaking an arbitration to resolve the grievance. As mentioned previously, the union may have to decide whether the grievance justifies proceeding to arbitration. However, if the union chooses not to proceed to arbitration and decides to abandon the grievance, it may be subject to a complaint from one or more of its members that it has abandoned its duty of fair representation. Before describing the process of grievance arbitration, we will discuss the issue of fair representation.

Duty of Fair Representation

The union, as the exclusive bargaining agent for the employees, is obligated by Canadian labour legislation to fairly represent its members. The **duty of fair representation** means that a union (as well as an employers' association) must not act toward its members in a manner that is arbitrary, discriminatory, or in bad faith.

When deciding whether or how to settle a grievance, to withdraw a grievance at a particular step in the grievance procedure, or to proceed to arbitration with a grievance, the union must make its decision in a manner that does not contradict its duty of fair representation. To fulfill the obligation that its conduct not be arbitrary, the union must fully investigate the grievance and make a reasonable determination based on a consideration of all the facts. Arbitrary conduct by a union has been described as conduct that is superficial, capricious, indifferent, or reckless with regard to the members' interests.[9] For example, a union would be acting arbitrarily if it assembled evidence that clearly indicated a violation of the collective agreement and then refused to pursue the grievance for the reason that the grievance was unjustified.

For a union to fulfill its obligation to fairly represent its membership without discrimination, it is important that it not be influenced in its handling of the grievance by factors such as race, religion, gender, and age. As noted in previous chapters, the various forms of "discrimination" are defined in the provisions in the relevant human rights codes. A union would be discriminatory if, for example, it refused to pursue a grievance only because the grievor was female or of Asian descent.

Finally, a union acts in bad faith if its decision respecting the grievance is influenced by dishonesty, personal hostility, or revenge. It can be difficult to determine whether a union has acted in bad faith in situations where there is a history between the union and the grievor that might have influenced the union's decision. For example, after a grievor has filed several grievances on the same issue that were not upheld by the employer, the union might refuse to pursue any further similar grievances on the grounds that the grievance would probably not be successful. The grievor, however, may believe that the union, in its refusal, is seeking to discourage a "troublemaker" and has ignored an injustice that the grievor genuinely believes he or she has suffered.

Sometimes, the duty of fair representation may appear to conflict with the union's willingness or ability to pursue a grievance to the point of arbitration. As we will see later in this chapter, grievance arbitration can be very expensive and time-consuming for all of the parties involved. In deciding whether to take a grievance to arbitration, unions sometimes weigh the likelihood of winning the grievance against the cost of the grievance arbitration. In other words, does the financial investment in the case justify the value of the outcome? "Value" could be determined either by the potential financial award the arbitrator could give to the winning party or by the usefulness of the precedent the arbitrator's decision could establish. While an arbitration award might not completely reimburse the parties' cost of going to arbitration, the union might still decide to go ahead with an arbitration because the arbitrator's decision could establish an important precedent affecting future workplace policies or practices.

In other situations, there may be sufficient evidence to support the union's position on the grievance, but the union may feel that the chances of winning are not good enough to warrant the cost of pursuing the grievance. The union might also feel that any precedent set by an arbitrator's decision would not be significant enough to justify the cost of an arbitration. However, the grievor may disagree with the union's assessment of these possible outcomes, and interpret the abandonment of the grievance as the union's failure to fulfill its duty of fair representation.

If a union member decides to file a complaint against a union for failing to fairly represent that member, the procedure usually commences with the member completing a standardized form and submitting it to a labour relations board. The board will then decide whether to accept or reject the member's complaint. If it accepts the complaint, the board will commence an investigation and, if warranted, hold a hearing to determine whether the complaint is justified.

It is important to note that even if the labour relations board accepts a complaint regarding a union's duty of fair representation, the board will not investigate the actual grievance. In other words, the labour relations board is not concerned with whether the grievance itself was justified; rather, the board will attempt to determine whether the union acted in a manner that was arbitrary or discriminatory or in bad faith in representing the union member, both in the grievance procedure and in the union's decision on whether to pursue the grievance.

If the labour relations board finds that the complaint is justified and that the union did not fairly represent the member, it can choose from a number of potential remedies. If the union member has suffered in some way because of the union's lack of representation, the board may attempt to remedy the damage. For example, a union member might file a grievance if she or he was demoted to a position that paid less than his or her original job. If the union refused to pursue the grievance, the board could order the union to compensate the member for the difference between the salary in the original position and the salary in the position that the member was demoted to, for as long as the member is in the lower-paying job.

If the failure to fairly represent involved a decision not to take a grievance to arbitration, a common remedy is for the board to rule that the union must continue to represent the member in the grievance and that the grievance must proceed to arbitration. We will now describe how the process of grievance arbitration works.

THE GRIEVANCE ARBITRATION PROCESS

Preparing for a Grievance Arbitration

If a grievance is not settled by the end of step three of the grievance procedure, it may proceed to arbitration. Grievance arbitration, as the final step in the grievance procedure, is designed to bring a final and conclusive resolution to the disagreement. Arbitration is also the only step in the entire grievance procedure where both the union and the employer can have a decision imposed on them by a neutral third party.

Shiv Chopra leaves a hearing in Ottawa after filing a grievance alleging management was pressuring him and other Health Canada scientists to approve questionable drugs.

Appointment of an Arbitrator

All Canadian jurisdictions leave the initial selection of a single **arbitrator** or an arbitration panel to the mutual agreement of the parties. This agreement is usually reached during the collective bargaining process. The parties will have to live with any decision imposed on them by an arbitrator, and it is therefore important that they agree on the persons who will make the final and binding decisions on grievances that may arise during the term of the collective agreement. Because of the importance of mutual agreement in this context, grievance arbitration is sometimes referred to as **consensual adjudication** to distinguish it from other types of adjudication imposed by legislation. Accordingly, grievance arbitrators are also referred to as "adjudicators."

A collective agreement may contain a list of names of individuals who are acceptable to the parties as adjudicators during the term of the agreement. The parties usually rotate through the names on the list to determine which adjudicator will arbitrate a particular grievance. Individuals named in collective agreements as potential arbitrators generally have a background in industrial relations or law. They usually have experience as advocates for either a union or an employer in grievance arbitrations, but most of them also have some experience as a neutral third-party decision maker.

In the event that the parties are unable to agree on a mutually acceptable arbitrator or list of arbitrators, all jurisdictions make some provision for the appointment of an adjudicator, usually by the labour relations board on the request of the parties. Labour relations boards usually maintain a list of active arbitrators and either name one who is acceptable to both parties or select an arbitrator on the basis of a simple rotation through the list.

If the parties so choose, they may appoint a tripartite arbitration board, rather than an individual arbitrator, to arbitrate the grievance. The composition of a board for a grievance arbitration is similar to that used in an interest arbitration: each party chooses one member and then both parties mutually choose a third member who will act as chair of the board. An alternative method of appointing a tripartite board is for each party to select one member and then for those two members to select the third member. Some unions and employers prefer a tripartite board over an individual arbitrator because of the way the board members are appointed. Since each party is allowed to choose one member of the board, they may feel that at least one board member is "on their side." There may be a perception that a single arbitrator, although theoretically neutral, will not thoroughly consider all aspects of each party's case, whereas the union or employer appointees to a tripartite board can advocate for having "their" side's evidence taken into account. Also, members of a board who are familiar with an industry or occupation can provide information that would result in a more informed decision than that of a single arbitrator without a similar range of experience to draw on.[10] However, because of the extra costs involved in having three arbitrators and the extra time it takes for three individuals to arrive at a decision, it is not common to see tripartite boards in grievance arbitrations.

The role of the arbitrator in the grievance arbitration process is to investigate the grievance and to render a decision. The primary method of investigating the grievance is through a hearing, which the arbitrator presides over much like a judge in a court case. As in interest arbitration, which was discussed in Chapter 10, the decision of an arbitrator in a grievance procedure is binding. There are, however, limited circumstances under which an arbitrator's award can be appealed. These circumstances will be outlined later in the chapter.

Arranging an Arbitration Hearing

Once the parties have agreed upon an arbitrator, they notify the arbitrator in writing of the appointment. The letter of appointment typically indicates how long the parties anticipate the hearing will take and whether the parties have a preferred location for the hearing. Most arbitration hearings are held near the location of the employer in a neutral facility, such as a hotel meeting room. It is important to the smooth functioning of the arbitration that the location be perceived as neutral; there could be concerns about undue influence on the arbitrator if, for example, the employer allocated a meeting room at the workplace for the arbitrator's use.

At this stage in the process, the arbitrator also responds to requests from either party to issue subpoenas to ensure that the appropriate witnesses and documentation are available for the hearing. A **subpoena** is a legal order that compels a witness to attend and testify at a hearing. The employer or the union may want particular individuals to testify at the hearing or want certain pieces of evidence to be presented for the arbitrator's information. If so, they will ask the arbitrator to inform the desired individuals—or those in possession of the evidence—of the date and location of the hearing. The arbitrator will then issue subpoenas to request that those individuals be present at the hearing with any relevant evidence.

Costs of an Arbitration Hearing

There are many expenses involved in an arbitration hearing, including the rental of the space where the hearing is held, the arbitrator's fees and expenses, the cost of recording and transcribing the proceedings, and any legal assistance the parties decide to retain. The union and employer each pay their own costs for the hearing. These costs include legal fees if a lawyer is retained, lost time and wages for the participants representing that party (such as the grievor and union or management representatives), and one-half of the arbitrator's costs. The arbitrator's costs include a fee for conducting the hearing, a writing fee for time spent considering and rendering an award, and travel and per diem expenses. The average cost per side for a one-day hearing has been estimated at $15,000.[11]

Having discussed the preparation for the arbitration hearing, we will now outline what happens at the hearing itself.

The Arbitration Hearing

Preliminary Issues

At the start of the hearing, the arbitrator confirms that both parties agree that he or she has jurisdiction under the collective agreement to hear the issue in dispute and determine an award. This confirmation is necessary in order to establish that both parties accept the arbitrator's jurisdiction and authority. The question of the arbitrator's jurisdiction is crucial, for under Canadian labour law the arbitrator is empowered to rule only on whether an interpretation, application, or administration of the collective agreement is correct; the arbitrator is not empowered to change the terms of the collective agreement. For the success of the arbitration, it is important that the question of jurisdiction be resolved at the outset of the hearing so that one or both of the parties do not later attempt to overturn the arbitrator's decision on the grounds that he or she exceeded his or her jurisdiction.

It is at this stage of the hearing that any objections concerning the timeliness of the grievance or whether the issue in question constitutes a grievance are raised before the arbitrator. This is also the stage of the hearing where any other procedural objections are presented to the arbitrator. When an objection is raised, the party making the objection usually asks the arbitrator to adjourn the hearing until the objection can be resolved. The arbitrator then has the choice of acceding to this request and adjourning the hearing, ruling against the objection and proceeding with the hearing, or reserving judgement on the objection and proceeding with the hearing. Usually, the arbitrator will choose one of the latter two courses of action. This is because considerable time, effort, and cost have already been expended in preparing for the hearing, and it may be very difficult or expensive for the parties to reconvene at a later date. Thus, it makes more sense for the arbitrator to deal with the objection in a way that will allow the hearing to proceed as scheduled.

In dealing with any of these preliminary objections, arbitrators refer to the relevant labour legislation; this legislation gives them the necessary authority to provide a final and conclusive settlement of the disagreement. Arbitrators appointed under a collective agreement are granted a wide range of powers under Canadian labour legislation. These include, for example, the ability to hear a grievance even if the time limits were exceeded in the previous steps in the grievance procedure, a situation that theoretically should disqualify the grievance from proceeding any further. The arbitrator is allowed to **relieve** against breaches of time limits or other procedural requirements in the collective agreement and to hear the grievance regardless of these breaches if he or she believes that there are just and reasonable grounds for doing so.[12]

Procedural Onus

Also determined at the start of the hearing is the issue of which party bears the **procedural onus**: that is, which party bears the responsibility for proving their case in the proceedings, rather than simply responding to allegations. As in all proceedings of this type, "he who alleges must go first and prove." Since it is usually the union that files a grievance, it is usually the union that proceeds first in the hearing and that bears the onus of proving that its allegation of violation of the collective agreement is justified. The major exception to this rule is a grievance arbitration that involves the discipline or discharge of an employee. In arbitrations involving these issues, the onus is on the employer to prove that the discipline or discharge was justifiable. The onus is reversed in these types of cases because it is the employer who is best able to explain the reasoning behind the decision to discipline or discharge an employee.[13] It would be difficult for the discharged or disciplined employee to explain the employer's reasons for taking the action or to produce evidence that is generally only held by the employer, such as personnel records.

Standard of Proof

The final procedural issue that is dealt with before the hearing commences is the establishment of a **standard of proof** to determine whether a party has sufficiently proved its case. The standard of proof used in arbitrations is the **balance of probabilities**, which is the same standard used in other civil proceedings. In an arbitration hearing, the party alleging a violation must prove "on balance" that its version of the facts or events is true. The arbitrator may not be satisfied that either party's case is completely accurate or reasonable, but the standard of the balance of probabilities requires the arbitrator to accept the case that is more likely to be accurate than the other, even if the case is not complete in and of itself. The standard of the balance of probabilities is more liberal than the standard of **beyond a reasonable doubt** used in criminal proceedings, as the latter requires the party making the allegation to present enough evidence to remove any doubt about the justification of the allegation.

Certain employment offences that lead to discipline or dismissal, such as theft of company property, theft of company time, or other forms of dishonesty, demand a standard of proof higher than the balance-of-probabilities standard and yet not as high as the criminal standard of beyond a reasonable doubt. The concern here is whether or not someone who is alleged to have committed such a serious offence should be reinstated or compensated simply because one party's weak case is comparatively better than the other party's weak case. Thus, in arbitrations involving serious employment offences, most arbitrators use the standard of proof of **clear and cogent evidence**. This standard of proof requires that there be sufficient relevant evidence to convince the arbitrator that the grievance is or is not justified.

Order of Proceeding

Once any preliminary issues are resolved, the actual hearing of the grievance begins. The party proceeding first makes an opening statement. This statement is designed to tell the arbitrator about the issue in dispute and the elements of the alleged violation of the collective agreement.

The statement will also include a summary of the evidence that the party will present and the case law (if any) that the party will rely upon to support its position. The other party also has an opportunity to make a similar opening statement to the arbitrator. After both opening statements have been made, the party proceeding first calls its witnesses. Witnesses participating in an arbitration hearing may include the actual grievor, any other employees affected by the alleged violation of the collective agreement, supervisors or managers involved in the alleged violation, and any workers or managers who observed events related to the alleged violation.

The party calling a witness to the stand has the first opportunity to ask questions of the witness. This process, called **direct examination**, is intended to allow the party to present its case through the witness's statements. When direct examination has concluded, the witness is then cross-examined by the other party. The intent of **cross-examination** is to clarify statements that the witness made in direct examination and, through questioning, to reveal inconsistencies or flaws in the witness's statements or to provide evidence that strengthens the other party's position. When cross-examination has concluded, the party that originally called the witness then has a limited right of re-examination. During **re-examination**, the party is allowed to ask its witness further questions to clarify any point raised during cross-examination or any information not addressed during direct examination.

This procedure of direct examination, cross-examination, and re-examination is repeated for each witness. In addition to the parties' examinations of the witnesses, the arbitrator may also ask questions of the witnesses. During examinations, the witnesses may be asked to present physical evidence such as letters, memos, or personnel records. If such evidence is presented, copies are given to the arbitrator and to the other party. The arbitrator is entitled to rule on the admissibility of evidence or on any other procedural issues that may arise while the hearing is being conducted.

Once all the evidence has been presented and all the witnesses have testified, the first party makes a closing argument. This argument follows the elements of the opening statement. It states the issues from the perspective of the first party, summarizes how the evidence of its witnesses supports the elements of the alleged violation of the collective agreement, and, if necessary, quotes other arbitration cases in support of its perspective. The second party then makes its closing argument. The first party has a limited right of reply to make a brief response to the second party's closing argument. The arbitrator then formally adjourns the hearing.

Creating the Arbitration Award

After the hearing is adjourned, the arbitrator retires to write the arbitration award. Some collective agreements prescribe time limits within which the arbitration award must be written after the hearing ends. The award will usually contain the following elements:

- a summary of the evidence presented by each party

- the arbitrator's assessment of the evidence (which party's case is more convincing and why)

- the arbitrator's verdict on the grievance, along with an explanation of the reasoning leading to the verdict

- the arbitrator's prescribed remedy if the grievance is found to be justified

- any direction for the implementation of the remedy (e.g., a deadline by which the remedy must be carried out)

When the arbitration award is completed, it is sent to the union and the employer. The receipt of the award by the union and the employer formally concludes the grievance arbitration process.

Arbitration awards are designed to be final and binding on the union, its members, and the employer. It is possible to appeal an arbitration award, but if an appeal is permitted, it is heard in civil court. Canadian labour legislation restricts the use of this process so as to reinforce the provision that the arbitration award is the final resolution of the grievance. Most jurisdictions make limited provisions for a judicial appeal based on a matter of general law. Appeals may be permitted if one or both of the parties can show that any of the following conditions existed:

- the arbitrator was biased in some fashion (e.g., the arbitrator's conduct or ruling was unduly influenced by some connection with one of the parties)

- the arbitrator did not follow correct procedure in conducting the hearing (e.g., the arbitrator did not allow a witness to testify or refused to let a witness present his or her evidence)

- the arbitrator ruled on matters outside his or her jurisdiction or on matters not related to the issue he or she was asked to arbitrate

- the arbitrator fundamentally misunderstood or misinterpreted the collective agreement language involved in the grievance

We should emphasize that a successful appeal of an arbitrator's award is very rare. Most experienced arbitrators are careful not to put themselves in any situation that might be subsequently interpreted as grounds for an appeal of their award. For example, experienced arbitrators will excuse themselves from an arbitration where their neutrality might be questioned (e.g., where there is a professional or personal relationship between the arbitrator and one of the witnesses). If the parties disagree with the arbitrator's award, that in and of itself is not grounds for appeal, as the parties enter into arbitration knowing that the arbitrator's award is binding. By agreeing to the arbitration process, the parties are implicitly expressing trust in the arbitrator's skills and decision-making ability; notwithstanding that trust, there is always the possibility that the arbitrator's decision may contradict one or both parties' expectations. This is simply one of the inherent risks of engaging in the arbitration process. The potential for disappointment is countered by the fact that arbitration at least ends in a resolution of the grievance, an outcome that the parties have been unable to achieve by themselves.

When parties disagree with the arbitrator's award, they will sometimes attempt to appeal the award by alleging that the arbitrator committed one of the errors noted above and claiming that this led to an incorrect ruling. For example, one party might claim that the arbitrator did not allow a witness to finish giving his or her evidence at the hearing and that had the arbitrator heard all the evidence, his or her perspective on the case would have been different and the award would consequently have been different. However, for an appeal of this sort to be successful, the party making the allegation must produce fairly substantial and convincing evidence both of the alleged error and of the alleged error's effect on the arbitrator's award.

Since the arbitrator's award is binding, the parties are expected to abide by the terms of the award and to carry out any ordered actions, such as making a payment or reinstating a dismissed or demoted employee. If a party does not comply with the terms or direction of an arbitration award, the award may be filed in the relevant provincial court registry and enforced as if it were a decision of that court.

Having concluded our outline of how the traditional grievance arbitration process operates, we will now turn our attention to some alternatives to this process. We will first identify some problems that sometimes occur when the traditional grievance arbitration process is used and will then show how some alternative forms of arbitration can help the parties avoid those problems.

PROBLEMS WITH THE TRADITIONAL GRIEVANCE ARBITRATION PROCESS

The purpose of the grievance arbitration process is to provide a method of resolving grievances that arise under the terms of the collective agreement without having the parties resort to work stoppages to force a resolution. As mentioned earlier, this process is presumed to be fast, cost-effective, and informal. In reality, the grievance arbitration process can be slow, costly, formal, and legalistic.[14]

Speed of the Process

The intent of the grievance arbitration process is to resolve workplace issues in a timely manner. In reality, grievances filed in Canadian jurisdictions can take up to one year to be resolved, from the time a grievance is first filed until an arbitration award is finally issued.[15] There are a number of factors behind the delays in the arbitration process.

In all Canadian jurisdictions, a few well-known and busy arbitrators conduct the majority of arbitration cases. Once an arbitrator has been appointed, it is often difficult to find hearing dates that are convenient for all the participants—the arbitrator, counsel for the parties, representatives of the parties, and all the individual witnesses. When the parties finally agree on acceptable dates and the hearing begins, complex issues can be raised that may require scheduling additional hearing days. Finally, the arbitrator must spend considerable time writing the arbitration award or decision if he or she is to produce a document of a high quality.

The amount of delay at different stages of the arbitration process are related to different factors that may or may not be relevant in individual cases.[16] Highly complex and legalistic issues can increase the time that passes between the filing of the initial grievance and a referral to arbitration. The selection of an arbitrator may be a lengthy process when legal counsel are involved in the selection and when an arbitration board, rather than a single arbitrator, must be selected. The time to write a decision may also be extended if an arbitration board must collectively reach a verdict or if the case is complex.

Formality and Legality of the Process

The grievance arbitration process was initially designed to be an informal proceeding conducted by the union and the employer representatives. Since the union and the employer negotiated the terms and conditions of the collective agreement, it was assumed that these parties, or their representatives, would be comfortable enforcing the administration of the agreement they negotiated.

In reality, the grievance procedure is usually an adversarial process, because unions and employers have different and conflicting interests in the workplace. The adversarial nature of the process commonly results in both parties retaining legal counsel either to advise them prior to the arbitration hearing or to represent them during the hearing. The involvement of lawyers, coupled with the fact that most arbitrators are also lawyers, introduces a level of formality and legalism into the arbitration process that was not intended in the initial design.

On the one hand, formalizing the arbitration process to the degree that arbitration hearings resemble court proceedings gives some consistency and rigour to the process. The relatively standardized hearing procedure ensures that all parties in the case receive a fair hearing. On the other hand, this degree of formalization may negatively affect the quality of the process and outcome by unduly intimidating witnesses who are not comfortable testifying in a court-like atmosphere. It may also bring further conflict into the process in the form of arguments over procedure.

It is questionable whether the involvement of legal counsel in arbitration makes a difference to whether a party is effectively represented in the proceedings. One recent study addressing this question examined the outcome of 272 Canadian arbitration and labour relations board cases involving disciplinary issues. The study attempted to determine whether the involvement of lawyers as advocates made a difference in the direction of the decision.[17] The results of the study indicated that legal representation for employees makes it more likely that employees will win the arbitration, whereas there is no such advantage to legal representation for employers. However, if both sides use lawyers to represent them in the proceedings, neither side increases its chances of obtaining its desired outcome.

Another consideration in the formality and legalism of the traditional arbitration process is the nature of the arbitration award itself. The arbitration award is often lengthy and written with a view to furthering labour relations policy. Consequently, the award is legalistic in form and results in one party winning and the other party losing. Arbitration decisions in this form can have a negative impact on the labour-management relationship, since the parties may not understand the discussion in the award or agree with the legalistic reasoning that led to the award.

Cost-Effectiveness of the Process

Another result of the involvement of lawyers in the arbitration process is an increase in the cost of the process. As noted earlier, each party is responsible for its own legal fees as well as for one-half of the arbitrator's fees and one-half of other expenses associated with conducting a hearing. These other expenses can include the cost of a neutral hearing room (usually in a hotel), the travel expenses, if any, for the arbitrator, and other miscellaneous costs. Less direct costs associated with the arbitration process include production and labour lost because of the time spent by the parties preparing for and attending the arbitration hearing. As well, there are the hidden or indirect costs that are generated by the impact that an adversarial adjudication process has on the parties' relationship and the workplace.

The cumulative impact of these costs can discourage parties from pursuing valid grievances that could be resolved through arbitration. As mentioned earlier, unions and employers both have to decide whether the value of an arbitration award is worth the cost of participating in an arbitration. Furthermore, because of the impact of costs associated with arbitration, one party might use the grievance process as a way to damage the other party, not as a way to resolve significant issues related to the collective agreement. If one party knows that dealing with a grievance will negatively affect the other party financially, that party may be tempted to file as many grievances as possible, regardless of their merit, simply to drain the other party's finances or resources. The grievance procedure is sometimes misused when one party has much greater resources than the other party. The richer party may be tempted to engage in behaviour that clearly violates the collective agreement in order to provoke the other party into filing a grievance and then having to bear the costs associated with pursuing that grievance.

Despite these problems with the grievance arbitration process, the process continues to play a major role in the Canadian labour relations system. However, some jurisdictions are attempting to develop alternative processes that complement or replace the traditional grievance arbitration process. These alternative

NBA union organizer Billy Hunter filed a grievance asking for payment of $700 million in salaries during a management lockout. Cost increases like this are making alternatives to traditional grievance arbitration more attractive.

processes can be either imposed by legislation or mutually agreed to by the parties in their negotiations. We will now examine a few of these alternatives.

ALTERNATIVES TO THE TRADITIONAL GRIEVANCE ARBITRATION PROCESS

Expedited Arbitration

Expedited arbitration is designed to be faster, less expensive, less formal, and less legalistic than the traditional arbitration process. The Canadian jurisdictions that provide the option of expedited arbitration are described in Table 11-3. Expedited arbitration processes created by legislation are known as statutory expedited arbitration processes. In jurisdictions where expedited arbitration is not provided by legislation, the parties to a grievance can use expedited arbitration to resolve the grievance if they both accept its use. Expedited arbitration processes that are voluntarily adopted by the parties are known as consensual expedited arbitration processes.

TABLE 11-3 Expedited Arbitration

	Preconditions	How Process Is Started	Settlement Officer	Hearing Timelines	Decision Timelines
Alberta	Not specified	Not specified	Not specified	Not specified	In any arbitration, if one of the parties complains that an award has not been rendered within a reasonable time, the board may issue a directive to ensure an award is rendered or may appoint a new arbitrator or arbitration board

TABLE 11-3 Continued

	Preconditions	How Process Is Started	Settlement Officer	Hearing Timelines	Decision Timelines
British Columbia	The matter must not have already been referred to arbitration and must not exceed any time limits in the collective agreement for referral to arbitration	One of the parties submits a request to director of the Collective Agreement Arbitration Bureau	Single arbitrator appointed by director of the Collective Agreement Arbitration Bureau	Not specified, but if settlement officer attempts mediation and fails, expedited arbitration must proceed as soon as officer reports to director	Within 21 days after conclusion of hearing
Manitoba	Not specified	Not specified	Not specified	Not specified	In all arbitrations, a single arbitrator must issue a decision within 30 days of hearing conclusion and an arbitrtion board must issue a decision within 60 days of hearing conclusion
Ontario	Not stated	If there is a failure to appoint an arbitrator under a collective agreement, the minister may appoint one on the request of either party. The minister may also, on the request of	Single arbitrator, board, or settlement officer; arbitrator or arbitration board appointed through terms in collective agreement or by minister; settlement officer appointed by minister	None specified, other than that settlement officer must endeavour to effect a settlement before the start of any hearing by arbitrator or arbitration board	Arbitrator must give decision within 30 days after hearings conclude; arbitration board must give decision within 60 days after hearings conclude. These times may be extended with the consent of the parties or in

TABLE 11-3 Continued

	Preconditions	How Process Is Started	Settlement Officer	Hearing Timelines	Decision Timelines
		either party, appoint a settlement officer to effect a settlement before an arbitrator begins to hear the matter; however, no appointment will be made if the other party objects			the discretion of the arbitrator or arbitration board as long as reasons are stated. Arbitrator or arbitration board may give oral decisions (in which case, they must be given promptly after hearings are concluded) and shall give writ-ten decisions promptly or written deci-sions with re-sons within a reasonable peri-od of time, on the request of either party
Saskatchewan	The matter must not have been already referred to arbitration and must not exceed any time limits in the collective agreement for arbitration	Both parties apply to the minister of labour	Single arbitrator appointed by minister of labour. If one party requests and the other agrees, a grievance mediator may be appointed prior to a hear-ing to assist parties in reach-ing resolution	Date for hearing must be set within 28 days of date of application to minister of labour	Decision must be issued within 21 days after conclusion of hearing

In most Canadian jurisdictions, either the union or management can refer a grievance to expedited arbitration. Where the parties have mutually agreed to establish an expedited arbitration process, the process usually includes a clear definition of which types of grievances will be handled in this manner. Some expedited arbitration processes are only used to resolve minor discipline grievances, such as those involving a penalty of less than 30 days' suspension or lost pay. Others are used to resolve all discipline grievances, including discharge grievances, but not to resolve policy grievances or grievances involving interpretation of the collective agreement.

A distinctive characteristic of expedited arbitration is its reliance on specified timelines for holding the arbitration hearing and issuing the arbitration award. These timelines work because most expedited arbitration processes involve a roster system for appointing arbitrators. In statutory processes, the arbitrators on the roster report their availability weekly or monthly to an administrator, who then assigns the arbitrators as needed, knowing the length of time the arbitrators are available and the timelines within which the cases must be resolved. In consensual processes, if an arbitrator on the roster is not available to conduct the hearing within the specified time, he or she is passed over in favour of the next available arbitrator.

Arbitration awards issued in expedited arbitrations are usually not considered to be precedent setting. This means that the parties will not quote the award to support their arguments in other grievances or otherwise attempt to use the award to set a precedent for future grievances. In many expedited arbitration procedures, the parties do not quote other arbitration awards in their presentation or argument. As a result, awards in expedited arbitrations are shorter, more fact based, and less legalistic than traditional arbitration awards.

Finally, in most expedited arbitrations, the parties are encouraged to represent themselves before the arbitrator, without the assistance of legal counsel. By presenting their own case, the parties reduce the costs of the arbitration.

In summary, both statutory and consensual expedited arbitration processes reduce the cost of participating in an arbitration, lessen the time within which the grievance must be heard and a decision must be given to the parties, and provide awards that are shorter, less legalistic, and non-precedent setting. Any solution to the problem of the time involved in arbitrations must address factors such as the presence of legal counsel, the method of selecting an arbitrator, and the arbitrator's workload, and must focus on the impact that these factors have on the different stages of the arbitration process.[18] We can see that the intent of the expedited arbitration process is to minimize the delays associated with these factors throughout the arbitration process, and for this reason the expedited process has several advantages over the traditional arbitration system. However, as noted, expedited arbitration is sometimes only considered appropriate for smaller or less complicated grievances, and traditional grievance arbitration is relied upon to resolve complex or lengthy grievances.

Grievance Mediation

Another alternative to the traditional grievance arbitration process is **grievance mediation**. The provisions for grievance mediation in the Canadian jusrisdictions that allow it are described in Table 11-4.

TABLE 11-4   Grievance Mediation

	How Mediator Is Appointed	Time Frame	Mediator's Mandate	Person or Body to Whom Mediator Reports
British Columbia	On request of one of the parties, the director of the Collective Agreement Arbitration Bureau appoints a settlement officer. The officer may be appointed prior to expedited arbitration hearing taking place	Must commence proceedings within 5 days of officer's appointment	Inquire into differences between parties; assist in settling differences; report to director on results of inquiry and success of settlement effort	Director of the Collective Agreement Arbitration Bureau

TABLE 11-4 Continued

	How Mediator Is Appointed	Time Frame	Mediator's Mandate	Person or Body to Whom Mediator Reports
Manitoba	On request of both parties, the minister of labour appoints grievance mediator. If collective agreement names grievance mediator, minister of labour may pay 1/3 of cost of mediator's expenses. Grievance mediator may be appointed prior to arbitration hearing taking place	Must commence proceedings within 7 days of appointment or as minister of labour specifies	Inquire into grievance; assist in settling grievance; report to minister of labour and labour board on result of inquiry and success of effort	Minister of labour and Manitoba Labour Board
New Brunswick	Appointed by the minister of labour at the request of either party. Grievance mediator may be appointed prior to arbitration hearing taking place	Must commence proceedings within 10 days after mediator's appointment or as minister of labour specifies	Inquire into differences; assist the parties in settling differences; report to minister of labour on results of inquiry and success of effort	Minister of labour
Nova Scotia	The minister of labour may appoint a mediation officer at any time to bring about settlement of an industrial dispute or to prevent an industrial dispute	Not specified	Investigate causes of dispute; attempt to bring about settlement or prevent a dispute; assist in development of effective labour-management relations; make a report to minister of labour	Minister of labour

TABLE 11-4 Continued				
	How Mediator Is Appointed	**Time Frame**	**Mediator's Mandate**	**Person or Body to Whom Mediator Reports**
Ontario	The minister of labour may appoint a settlement officer prior to an arbitration hearing. An arbitrator may also act as a mediator at any stage in the proceedings with both parties' approval	Not specified	To effect a settlement between the parties	Minister of labour
Saskatchewan	Joint request by parties. Grievance mediation may occur prior to hearing in expedited arbitration	Must begin proceedings within 10 days of being appointed	Assist parties to settle grievance by mediation; if unsuccessful, assist parties to agree on material facts, after which parties may take matter to grievance arbitration	Minister of labour

In grievance mediation, the mediator is often an industrial relations officer or settlement officer employed by a labour relations board. These highly trained individuals meet with the parties within 5 or 10 days of their appointment to inquire into the grievance and assist the parties in settling their differences.

Grievance mediation is timely, cost-efficient, informal, and non-adversarial. A further advantage of grievance mediation, as noted in the wording of the Nova Scotia legislation, is its ability to assist the parties in developing effective long-term labour-management relations by emphasizing mutual problem solving. It may seem that mediation is not totally suitable as a mechanism to resolve disputes over contractual rights, since mediation does not determine whose rights take precedence. However, as one researcher states, "The focus of mediation is reaching a mutually acceptable agreement, rather than winning a rights dispute."[19] Clearly, then, for grievance mediation to be successful, the employer and the union must be willing to work actively toward a mutually beneficial solution, and not be primarily concerned with which party is declared a winner and which party becomes a loser.

As in other forms of mediation, the grievance mediator assists the parties in reaching their own mutually satisfactory solution to the grievance. Most jurisdictions permitting grievance mediation also establish the rule that information disclosed to a mediator is considered confidential and cannot be disclosed in any subsequent arbitration hearing (i.e., if the grievance is not resolved through mediation and proceeds to a formal arbitration).[20] This rule is intended to encourage the parties to share information freely with the mediator, without fearing that such information could be used to their disadvantage in any subsequent proceedings. Because the mediator does not act as an arbitrator and thus does not make a formal decision on the grievance, grievance mediation does not require a written award.

Different mediators bring different philosophical approaches to grievance mediation.[21] One approach, referred to as the **settlement orientation**, is often found in situations where grievance mediation is imposed by legislation. In these situations, where mediation is not voluntary, there is increased pressure on the parties to agree on a resolution, and thus many parties feel unsatisfied with the resulting agreement. However, the advantage of the settlement orientation is that the parties are eventually persuaded or influenced to reach a resolution without having to resort to the arbitration process.

Another approach to grievance mediation is referred to as the **transformative orientation**. This approach focuses on teaching the parties to resolve their own disagreements and to understand each other's point of view, information, and interests. This approach enhances communication between the parties, assists in fostering their ongoing relationship, and results in higher satisfaction with the mediated result. However, the transformative orientation often results in a more time-consuming process than does the settlement orientation.

Mediation-Arbitration

Another alternative to the traditional grievance arbitration process is a combination of the mediation and arbitration processes known as **mediation-arbitration** or med-arb. Med-arb was described in Chapter 10 as a method for resolving disputes during collective bargaining, but it can also be used for resolving disputes related to the application or interpretation of the collective agreement. The provisions for med-arb in the Canadian jurisdictions that allow it are described in Table 11-5.

TABLE 11-5 Mediation-Arbitration

	Preconditions	How Process Is Started	Timelines for Proceedings	Mediator's Mandate	Timeline for Arbitration Decision
Federal	Not specified	Not specified	Not specified	Arbitrator may assist in resolving differences; issues not settled in mediation may continue without prejudice to arbitration	Not specified
British Columbia	The parties must agree on the nature of any issues in dispute	Both parties agree to refer issues to mediation-arbitration; parties may choose own single mediator-arbitrator or may ask director of the Collective Agreement Arbitration Bureau for appointment if unable to agree	Proceedings must begin within 28 days of mediator-arbitrator's appointment	Mediator-arbitrator assists parties to settle grievance by mediation; if mediation is unsuccessful, mediator-arbitrator must assist parties to reach agreement on material facts in dispute and then determine outcome by arbitration	Within 21 days of completion of proceedings

TABLE 11-5 Continued

	Preconditions	How Process Is Started	Timelines for Proceedings	Mediator's Mandate	Timeline for Arbitration Decision
Ontario	The parties must agree on the nature of any issues in dispute. An arbitrator may mediate at any stage with the consent of both parties	The parties may choose own single mediator-arbitrator or may ask minister of labour for appointment if unable to agree	Within 30 days of mediator-arbitrator's appointment	Mediator-arbitrator assists parties to settle grievance by mediation; if unsuccessful, mediator-arbitrator must assist parties to reach agreement on material facts in dispute and then determine outcome by arbitration	Within 5 days of completion of proceedings

Med-arb processes in most jurisdictions utilize arbitrators skilled in dispute resolution techniques. The med-arb process used in grievance resolution is very similar to the med-arb process used in resolving collective-bargaining disputes. The third party first acts as mediator and, in an informal setting, attempts to assist the parties in resolving their differences. As with other expedited arbitration processes, there are specific time frames (usually less than 30 days) within which all the parties must meet and attempt to resolve the grievance. If the third party is successful in helping the parties reach settlement on some but not all of the grievance's issues, the third party then arbitrates the outstanding issues and writes an arbitration award.

Med-arb attempts to combine the advantages of the grievance mediation and the grievance arbitration systems. It is initially an informal process that facilitates the relationship between the parties and helps them develop problem-solving skills through the use of mediation. If mediation is not successful in resolving all the disputed issues, the parties have a timely and cost-effective method of reaching a final and binding resolution in the form of an arbitration award.

SUMMARY

Because it is not possible to create a collective agreement that will apply perfectly to all parts of a workplace over the agreement's entire term, it is necessary to have a process by which disagreements over the application, interpretation, or administration of the collective agreement can be resolved. The grievance arbitration process fills this role. Grievance arbitration is also known as rights arbitration and consensual adjudication.

There are four generally recognized types of grievances. An individual grievance is a single employee's complaint about an employer action that allegedly violates the collective agreement. If the employer's alleged violation affects several employees, then any resulting grievance is referred to as a group grievance. A continuing grievance involves a series of ongoing actions that allegedly violate the collective agreement. And, finally, a policy grievance is filed by the union on behalf of all employees and usually concerns the employer's interpretation or application of the collective agreement.

The grievance procedure has several steps. The usual first step is an informal meeting between the complainant and his or her immediate supervisor. If the disagreement cannot be resolved at this point, the grievance is usually recorded in writing and brought to the attention of union and management representatives. These parties then meet and attempt to reach a mutually satisfactory solution to the disagreement. If they are unsuccessful, the disagreement is generally brought to higher authorities within the union and management in a final attempt to resolve the disagreement internally.

If the parties cannot agree on a solution to the grievance on their own, a third party—the grievance arbitrator—becomes involved in the process. In most situations, the arbitrator holds a hearing to investigate the evidence for and against each party's position and then issues a decision that is binding on both parties. However, the traditional grievance arbitration process can be rendered less than effective because of factors like time, cost, and excessive formality.

Several alternative forms of grievance arbitration are characterized by a faster, less legalistic process and solutions that attempt to build positive long-term relationships between the parties. Expedited arbitration only deals with particular types of grievances and has predetermined timelines to ensure a solution is reached within a certain period. Grievance mediation attempts to resolve grievances by informally assisting the parties to reach their own solution. Mediation-arbitration is a two-step process in which a third party first acts as a mediator and then, if necessary, acts as an arbitrator to resolve any problems that have not been settled through mediation.

KEY TERMS FOR CHAPTER 11

arbitrator (p. 416)
balance of probabilities (p. 420)
beyond a reasonable doubt (p. 420)
clear and cogent evidence (p. 420)
consensual adjudication (p. 416)
continuing grievances (p. 404)
cross-examination (p. 421)
direct examination (p. 421)
duty of fair representation (p. 413)
expedited arbitration (p. 427)
grievances (p. 400)
grievance arbitration (p. 400)
grievance mediation (p. 431)
grievor (p. 409)
group grievance (p. 404)
individual grievance (p. 403)
mediation-arbitration (p. 434)
past practice (p. 406)
policy grievance (p. 404)
procedural onus (p. 419)
re-examination (p. 421)
relieve (p. 419)
rights arbitration (p. 401)

settlement orientation (p. 434)
standard of proof (p. 420)
subpoena (p. 417)
transformative orientation (p. 434)

DISCUSSION QUESTIONS FOR CHAPTER 11

1. Define and give examples of the different types of grievances.
2. Outline and explain the steps in a typical grievance procedure.
3. Why would the employer or the union raise preliminary objections at an arbitration hearing?
4. What does it mean to have the "procedural onus" in an arbitration case?
5. What are the different "standards of proof" used in an arbitration, and when would each apply?
6. Describe how an arbitration hearing is conducted.
7. Explain the disadvantages of the traditional grievance arbitration process.
8. What is meant by "expedited arbitration"?
9. Discuss the advantages and disadvantages of grievance mediation.
10. What is "med-arb"?

CASE 11-1

MILL WORKERS UNION AND LARRY LEVY AND WOOD PRODUCTS INC.

(Based on *MacMillan Bathurst and IWA-Canada Local 1-830*, 1999)

In this case, the employer has disciplined an employee, Larry Levy, for actions he undertook as a shop steward. Levy, in his role as shop steward, was present at a disciplinary interview for another employee who the employer alleged was working a second job while on disability leave. Levy was aware of the other employee's actions because he had been working on the second job with the other employee. However, he did not disclose this information during the disciplinary interview. The company has issued a written reprimand to him, and he has filed a grievance against the reprimand.

Background to the Case

Larry Levy has been working for Wood Products Inc. for 19 years and has been a shop steward for the Mill Workers Union for five years. He has also had a home renovation business on the side and has occasionally employed another Wood Products Inc. employee, Sean Mason, to assist him.

In early 1998, Mason went on disability leave and was receiving weekly disability payments as outlined in the collective agreement. Levy was apparently aware that Mason was on disability leave. In May 1998, the insurance company that funded the company's disability plan became suspicious of Mason's disability claim and decided to conduct surveillance on him. A private investigator hired by the company followed Mason and videotaped several instances of Mason and Levy renovating a house. On June 11, 1998, the private investigator showed the videotape to Jim Paterson, Wood Products Inc.'s personnel supervisor, and George James, the company's production manager. Paterson and James arranged a meeting with Levy and Mason for the next day.

The next day, Paterson and James met with Levy, Mason, and Bill Ritter, the union's secretary/treasurer. (There was some dispute between the parties as to why Levy was at the meeting; the reasons for the dispute will be outlined in the description of each party's position.) Paterson asked Mason if he was doing renovation work on the side while on disability, and Mason said, "No." Paterson then named one of the dates and locations where Mason had been seen doing the work, and Mason continued to deny his involvement. The following dialogue then took place:

Paterson: Did you pick up supplies at Home Depot that day?
Mason: I get supplies for Larry.
Paterson: But you do not help him do work?
Mason: No.
Paterson: We do have a real problem here. I had to confront you with the information we had received. We'll need to seek further advice and will get back to you. Does anyone have anything to add? [No one responded to this question.]

Paterson then asked Mason a few questions about his scheduled knee surgery and ended the meeting after that. Levy said nothing during the meeting and no specific questions were directed at him. Later that day, Ritter was shown the video of Mason and Levy doing renovation work. A few days later, three other union executive members also saw the video.

The company felt that Levy should be disciplined and asked the union "what they were going to do about him." The chief shop steward claimed that he had told Paterson that the union would deal with the issue at its September meeting, but James said he did not recall this statement being made. However, the company had the impression that the union had committed to "doing something about it."

Having heard nothing back from the union concerning the case, Paterson and Ritter called a meeting on June 24, 1998, with Levy and the chief shop steward. At the meeting, Paterson told Levy that he would be given a written reprimand for "knowingly misleading the company" while representing Mason at the June 12 meeting. Levy responded, "As a union representative, I wasn't to volunteer information." The reprimand given to Levy stated:

> This letter serves as a Written Reprimand to you for knowingly allowing an Employee to mislead the Company during an interview with that Employee.

> We feel that it was your duty as a representative of the Union to intervene and not permit these circumstances to occur.
>
> The Company finds this totally unacceptable and any further occurrence in a similar situation will result in further disciplinary action—not excluding the possibility of a dismissal.

On July 7, 1998, Levy filed a grievance against the reprimand. The grievance proceeded through the initial steps of the grievance procedure, and early in September, the union advised the company that it wished to proceed to arbitration. However, the union then advised the employer that it intended to ask the labour relations board to hear the case and would withdraw the request for arbitration if the board accepted the case. The employer's lawyer then wrote to the labour relations board asking it to hear the case because of the unusual circumstances.

The board scheduled a hearing to deal with the case, and at the start of the hearing, the board raised the preliminary issue of jurisdiction. The board felt that the grievance was a disciplinary case and that since arbitration would be available to settle the grievance, the board would not have jurisdiction to hear the case. However, both parties argued that the issues raised in this case—namely, shop steward conduct and the ability of union officers to properly represent employees—were matters of general importance to labour relations and thus should be discussed by the board. The union's lawyer also pointed out that an arbitrator would not have the ability to award the remedies the union was seeking. The union wanted both a declaration of an unfair labour practice against the employer for its alleged interference with the right of the shop steward to participate in the activities of the union and a penalty assessed against the employer for its actions, but an arbitrator would not have the power to declare an unfair labour practice or assess a penalty if an unfair labour practice had been committed. The board accepted both sides' arguments and agreed to hear the case and render a decision.

The Union's Position

The union argued that there is no general duty of disclosure compelling employees to disclose information to the employer about improper conduct of other employees. The union also argued that even if employees did have such a duty, the duty would not extend to employees who are officers of the union.

The union also addressed the question of why Levy was present at the June 12 meeting. Normally, two union representatives attend disciplinary meetings, and these two representatives are the local president and the chief shop steward. George James, the company's personnel manager, contacted the chief shop steward on the morning of the meeting, but the chief shop steward was off work that day. The local president was also off work, but he did meet with James early that day about another matter. The local president said that at their meeting James had not mentioned the Levy/Mason case to him or the meeting about it. James subsequently contacted Bill Ritter, the union's secretary/treasurer, who in turn asked Levy to attend the meeting. Ritter testified that James had asked him to bring Levy to the meeting and had only told him that the meeting was about Mason.

The union pointed out that the written reprimand given to Levy identified him as having attended the meeting as a "representative of the Union" and that the minutes of the meeting, taken by James, identified both Ritter and Levy as union representatives. However, the union argued that the employer put Levy in an "impossible position" by not informing him or the union of his possible conflict of interest in acting as a union representative at the meetings.

The Employer's Position

The employer argued that "as a matter of policy" employees acting as union representatives had a duty to disclose relevant information to the employer, including information about the misconduct of other employees.

The employer also disputed that Levy was present at the June 12 meeting as a union representative. James, the personnel manager, testified that he had met with the local president early in the morning of the meeting day, but had not asked him to attend the meeting. James said that he had thought the local president had been taking a training course that day and would not have been available. James also said that at the time he had met with the local president he had been waiting for a call from senior management with instructions about how to handle the Mason case and had not wanted to proceed with planning the meeting until he had those instructions. (The local president testified that his meeting with James had been later in the day, rather than early in the morning, and that he could have attended the Mason meeting if asked.) James also testified that he had not asked Ritter to bring Levy to the meeting.

CASE *11-2*

ARNOLD THOMPSON AND BARTENDERS UNION AND THOROUGHBRED ASSOCIATION

(Based on *Hotel Restaurant & Culinary Employees & Bartenders Union, Local 40, and Pacific Racing Association*, 2000)

In this case, a union member has filed a "duty of fair representation" complaint against the union. The union refused to proceed with the member's grievance when the member's employment was terminated, and the member is alleging that the union's decision was based on "arbitrary and discriminatory reasons." The member is asking the labour relations board to waive the time limit under the collective agreement for referring a grievance to arbitration and to require the union to arbitrate the grievance and provide the member with independent legal counsel.

Since the union is the party accused of failing to fulfill its duty of fair representation, the onus is on the union to prove that its actions are justified.

Background to the Case

Arnold Thompson works as a bartender at the Oakwood Racecourse. Thompson has been employed at the racecourse since 1978 and has been a bartender since August 1986. The Bartenders Union has represented restaurant employees at the racecourse since 1980, and the Thoroughbred Association has operated the food and beverage services at the racecourse since 1998. The union's current business agent is Steven Muir, who has held that position since 1987.

In March 1995, Thompson received a written reprimand for failing to count cash accurately. Bartenders at the racecourse are responsible for accepting payments from customers when customers purchase beverages. After that incident, Thompson's disciplinary record remained clean until May 1997. From that date onward, he was disciplined several times for not balancing his cash and receipts at the end of a shift. He was also disciplined for his personal appearance, for failure to maintain an accurate inventory, and for failure to properly secure the bar at the end of his shift.

On August 20, 1998, Thompson was suspended for five days for twice handing in unreceipted cash and for failing to remit a signed credit charge. At the end of August, the suspension was grieved. In early November, Thompson was given a 10-day suspension for seven alleged incidents of unsatisfactory performance between August 8 and October 24, 1998. The alleged incidents related to forgetfulness and/or cash discrepancies. This suspension was grieved on November 12, 1998.

In mid-December 1998, the union and the employer settled the two grievances by mutual agreement. Thompson was to serve a six-day suspension, withdraw an accusatory letter he had written to the employer, receive retraining in bartending duties, and, upon his return to work after retraining, be given a probationary period during which he would not be suspended. Thompson attended the meeting at which this settlement was reached, as did Muir. At one point during the meeting, Thompson was asked if he could suggest any reason for his problems. He said that his mother had told him he had dyslexia.

That night, after returning home from the meeting, Muir consulted a book about dyslexia and concluded that it was a learning disability that affects an individual's ability to read and write. Muir has since stated that he did not believe dyslexia could account for Thompson's performance difficulties. In an earlier discussion with Thompson, Muir suggested that a checklist would help Thompson ensure that he followed correct procedures when closing the bar. A shop steward subsequently helped Thompson prepare such a checklist.

On January 10, 1999, Claude Lewis, the racetrack's food and beverage director, wrote a letter to Thompson stating that his probationary period was over and that "any further misconduct" would result in Thompson's termination. On January 24, 1999, Thompson was given a written warning for failing to lock a dispenser at the end of his January 15 shift. This warning also informed Thompson that his probation had ended on January 16.

On February 4, Thompson was called to a meeting with the racetrack's human resources director and a shop steward. Thompson understood that he was being terminated for failing to lock a beer cooler on January 31. Thompson told the human resources director that he had locked the cooler. He was discharged and given a termination letter written by Lewis. The letter stated that Thompson had been "witnessed" failing to lock the cooler; it continued: "Regrettably, after many warnings, letters, and suspensions, you continue to fail in your job as bartender. You leave us with no alternative but to terminate your employment effective immediately."

Thompson met with Muir on February 10 and told him that on January 31 he had consulted his checklist and locked the beer cooler. Muir completed a grievance form and faxed it to the racecourse, and Thompson then took Muir to the racecourse to meet with Lewis and the human resource manager. In the 20-minute meeting that took place, Muir asked Lewis who the person was who had witnessed Thompson failing to lock the beer cooler. Lewis said that the supervisor on duty at the time, Jerome Kahn, had discovered that the cooler was unlocked after Thompson had closed the bar. In relating these events to the board, Muir told the board that he had not had much time to prepare for the meeting and just wanted to deal with the grievance quickly.

Sometime after that meeting, Thompson told Muir that after he had closed the bar on January 31, another shift supervisor had gone to the bar to borrow a liqueur bottle. Thompson said that a bar in a different location at the racecourse had run out of this particular beverage and that the supervisor at that bar had gone to Thompson's bar to obtain another bottle. Muir, knowing that this beverage could be either stored in a cooler or kept behind the bar, asked Thompson where the bottle was kept at his bar. Thompson replied that it was kept behind the bar. Muir told Thompson that if the beverage was kept in the bar's beer cooler, they could "pull a rabbit out of a hat" and get Thompson back to work. But, Muir said, they could not do this because the beverage was not stored in the beer cooler at Thompson's bar. Muir then told Thompson that his statement about having left the beer cooler locked was not credible given his record of forgetfulness.

Muir told the board that after this conversation he contacted the shop steward who had helped Thompson write the checklist and the shop steward who had attended the meeting at which Thompson had been terminated. Muir said that he had told both men what Thompson had said about the other shift supervisor's visit to the bar and had indicated to the men that Thompson could get his job back if it could be proved that the other shift supervisor had been in the cooler. Muir said that he had understood that the first shop steward would investigate the issue. Unfortunately, this man passed away prior to the hearing, and there was no record of any response to Muir's request. The second shop steward said that he had no recollection of this conversation with Muir and no knowledge of the fact that the union was seeking more information on Thompson's case.

Subsequent to the conversation with the two shop stewards, Muir received a written statement from Kahn, the supervisor who had been identified as the witness to Thompson's leaving the cooler unlocked. In his statement, Kahn indicated that the lock for the cooler door had been found hanging on a bracket next to the door at nine in the morning on February 1, 1999. After receiving this information, Muir did not tell the employer that the other shift supervisor might have entered the cooler. He also did not attempt to interview that supervisor or any other employees on shift at the time. Muir told the board that he had not known if the supervisor would be truthful and that he had relied on the two shop stewards to provide any information that might assist Thompson.

On February 16, Muir wrote a letter to Thompson stating that after the February 10 meeting with the employer,

> I [Muir] have had an opportunity to review your issues with the union's director of legal services. Due to your extensive disciplinary record, the union would not be successful in proceeding any further with your grievance. If you have evidence that would allow the union to be successful in proceeding with your grievance, please provide same by March 3, 1999. If we have not received any new evidence from you by that date ... the union will withdraw the grievance.

Thompson and Muir met again on March 3. Thompson asked Muir to consider three points: that the retraining he received was inadequate; that "anyone" could have access to the keys to the racecourse's food and beverage operations; and that the keys were kept in an unlocked box and "on many occasions" had disappeared for several days. Muir responded in a letter dated March 5, stating that "only one [item] is relevant to your termination and that is the access to the keys." Muir's letter also stated that the argument about the keys had already been raised as a defence in the grievance involving the September 1998 events, and noted that the employer had warned Thompson on January 24 that any further violations would result in termination. The letter continued: "You [Thompson] agreed with your [disciplinary] letter, with no argument about the access to keys. With your previous history, which includes not locking up your department/bar in a proper manner, an arbitrator would be inclined to dismiss the argument about the access of keys. The information that you have provided is insufficient for the union to be successful in proceeding any further with the grievance, [and] the union therefore withdraws the grievance."

The Union's Position

Muir told the board that several factors had affected his decision to withdraw Thompson's grievance. He believed that Thompson was "a bit slow" but not disabled, and did not think that a disability might have caused Thompson's failure to lock the cooler. He did consider the possibility that the other shift supervisor had unlocked the cooler, but did not believe that this was the case because the lock was left hanging beside the door. Muir stated that a person making only one trip in and out of the cooler would likely have carried the lock in his or her hand. The fact that the lock was found hanging next to the door, he said, indicated that the person who opened the cooler was intending to visit it more than once.

Muir also told the board that he was "kept busy" at the racecourse with many different issues and many grievances. He stated that "every time [he] solved one of [Thompson's] problems, another one arose."

EXERCISE

The "Wally Worker" Grievance Arbitration Simulation

(Reproduced with the permission of the Canadian Labour Congress)

In this exercise, you and your classmates will participate in a simulation of a grievance arbitration hearing. Each simulation will have eight participants:

- the arbitrator
- Wally Worker, the grievor
- Bobby Boss, Wally's supervisor
- Tanker Treadmill, the union business agent
- John Demanding, the company personnel manager
- Sidney Steward, the shop steward
- the union's lawyer
- the company's lawyer

The arbitrator will preside over an arbitration hearing, after which the arbitrator will make his or her decision and report his or her award to the participants.

Your instructor will give you the information you need to prepare for the simulation as well as the times and locations for the hearings.

References

[1] Dessler, G., Cole, N.D., & Sutherland, V.L. (1999). *Human resources management in Canada* (7th Canadian edition). Scarborough, ON: Prentice-Hall.

[2] Craig, A.W.J., & Solomon, N.A. (1996). *The system of industrial relations in Canada* (5th edition). Scarborough, ON: Prentice-Hall.

[3] Trower, C. (1974). *Arbitration at a glance*. Labour Research Institute, 9–14.

[4] Barron, T. (1999). Union files grievance: memo says nurses have to use leave if work missed due to storm. *The Telegram* (St. John's), April 14, 1999, 3.

[5] Bemmels, B. (1994). The determinants of grievance initiation. *Industrial & Labor Relations Review, 47(2)*, 285–302.

[6] Thornicroft, K.W. (2000). The grievance arbitration process: theory and ..practice. In Gunderson, M., Ponak, A., & Taras, D.G. (Eds.), *Union-management relations in Canada* (4th edition). Toronto, ON: Addison Wesley Longman.

[7] Bemmels, B., & Lau, D. (2001). Local union leaders' satisfaction with grievance procedures. *Journal of Labor Research, 22(3)*, 653-668; Bemmels, B. (1995). Shop stewards' satisfaction with grievance procedures. *Industrial Relations, 34(4)*, 578–592.

[8] Bemmels & Lau, *op. cit.*

[9] B.C. Labour Relations Board, Practice Guideline No. ADJ-3, 3–6.

[10] Craig & Solomon, *op. cit.*

[11] Elliott, D.C., & Goss, J.H. (1994). *Grievance mediation: why and how it works.* Toronto, ON: Canada Law Book.

[12] See, for example, *B.C. Labour Relations Code*, sections 82 and 89.

[13] Thornicroft, *op. cit.*

[14] Elliott & Goss, *op. cit.*, 7–14.

[15] Olson, C., & Ponak, A. (1990). Time delays in grievance arbitration in Alberta. Presented at 8th Annual Arbitration Conference, Calgary, AB; Weatherill, J.F.W. (1980). *The grievance arbitration process: problems and perspectives.* Edmonton, AB: Alberta Labour Preventive Mediation Services.

[16] Ponak, A., & Zerbe, W. (1996). Using event history analysis to model delay in grievance arbitration. *Industrial & Labor Relations Review, 50(1)*, 105–122.

[17] Harcourt, M. (2000). How attorney representation and adjudication affect Canadian arbitration and labour relations board decisions. *Journal of Labor Research, 21(1)*, 149–159.

[18] Ponak & Zerbe, *op. cit.*

[19] Thornicroft, *op. cit.*, 377.

20 Thornicroft, *op. cit.*

21 Beattie, S. (1997). *Grievance mediation*. Vancouver, BC: British Columbia Continuing Legal Education Labour Arbitration, 5–6.

Airline unions in bitter clash over seniority:

Canadian employees angry over Air Canada stance

TORONTO—Unionized workers at Canadian Airlines Corp. are consulting lawyers and threatening to involve an arbitrator in a bitter clash over seniority with their counterparts at Air Canada.

Union sources say Canadian Airlines employees are angry over a united stand by Air Canada unions, which are insisting Canadian staff be pushed to the bottom of Air Canada's seniority lists when the workforces of the two carriers are integrated. Calgary-based Canadian, with 16,000 employees, was acquired in January by Montreal-based Air Canada, which has 24,000 employees.

"The Air Canada unions are screwing the Canadian Airlines unions, yet they are all in the same brotherhood," one unidentified union leader stated in a news article published Friday. He said even intimidation tactics have been used. "Their attitude is that Canadian was almost bankrupt, and so…they should be at the bottom," said the source, who requested anonymity.

Except for pilots, unionized workers in both airlines are represented by different locals of the same national unions. "Both sides are very bitter," said Denise Hill, president of the airline division of the Canadian Union of Public Employees, which represents flight attendants at both carriers.

Since Air Canada did more hiring than Canadian over the past 10 years, the members of Air Canada's unions are concerned that 60 per cent of their membership will end up at the bottom of the seniority list if the two workforces are merged on the basis of date of hire, Hill said. For example, Air Canada has hired 2,500 flight attendants over the last five years, while Canadian only hired 300 in the last 10.

"They [the Air Canada employees] feel they won," Hill said. "They are the surviving carrier, they are taking over Canadian Airlines, so why should they be disadvantaged?" She said her union will try to resolve the issue internally before considering arbitration.

If Air Canada unions get their way, a Canadian Airlines employee with 30 years of experience would have less seniority than a new hire at Air Canada, making the Canadian Airlines worker more vulnerable to being laid off and disadvantaged in bidding for shifts and vacations.

The merger of the two labour groups is seen as a key step in finalizing the integration of Canadian into Air Canada and realizing the full benefits of the merger, which Air Canada president Robert Milton said could amount to $800 million a year. But until the two labour groups come to an agreement, Canadian will be run as a separate brand, despite significant progress in merging many operational areas, said a Canadian spokesperson.

(*National Post*, *Financial Post*, March 17, 2000)

chapter 12

CHANGES TO THE UNION OR THE EMPLOYER

objectives

In this chapter, we will discuss how labour legislation accommodates changes that occur in the union or the company while a collective agreement or certification is in effect. By the end of this chapter, you should be able to:

- define successorship and understand what criteria are used to assess whether successorship has occurred or not

- describe the process of decertification

- understand what happens to certifications and collective agreements when unions or companies merge

- explain some of the ways that technological change and restructuring affect union-employer relationships

INTRODUCTION

In previous chapters we have described the process of certification, through which a union becomes the legal workplace representative of a group of employees, and the process of collective bargaining, through which a collective agreement is reached. The outputs of both of these processes—certifications and collective agreements—have temporal elements. A certification is considered to be in effect indefinitely, while a collective agreement lasts for a predetermined period, after which a new collective agreement is negotiated.

That both these documents have a life over time—whether for a fixed or an indefinite period—presents a problem, since both reflect the status of the union and the employer only at the time when these documents were completed. What happens if something changes after a certification begins or a collective agreement goes into effect? What if the workplace conditions change or there is a change in the status of the parties named in the certification or collective agreement?

Workers strike against Falconbridge Ltd., in Sudbury, 2001. Although an acceptable agreement was finally reached, many predicted "critical issues" ahead that would impact both workers and shareholders.

This chapter will address how labour legislation deals with changes that occur in the parties or the workplace conditions during the life of a collective agreement or a certification. We will start by discussing the issue of successorship and move on to explain what happens when the union or the employer experiences a merger or some other change. Our discussion will conclude with an overview of how changes in the actual work itself, such as technological change, are accommodated.

SUCCESSORSHIP

The term **successorship**, as used in labour legislation, relates to the status of a certification order after some material change in a business or employer occurs, given that the certification order was already in place before the change. If a labour relations board determines that past and present forms of the business are sufficiently similar, then successorship is declared to exist. The employer is then bound by the terms of any certification or collective agreements—or other formal relationships with a union—that existed in the earlier form of the business.

The question of successorship can arise in a number of different situations. One has to do with a change in location, such as when an employer moves the place of business or when a business expands to new locations or closes existing locations. Another successorship situation is when the business itself is sold or transferred to a new owner or when the purpose of the business changes or broadens (e.g., the business moves into new types of services or products not necessarily related to the original business). And another is when the employer transfers work to other locations or to other workers or organizations through subcontracting.

In situations like these, it is sometimes unclear whether the existing certification and collective agreement should continue to apply. The terms of both documents may refer to an entity that no longer exists if the business has changed its name or location, or they may refer to a workplace that is substantially different if the types or numbers of workers have changed because of changes in the purpose or type of business. As we know, a certification order is very specific in naming the parties to the certification and the locations and positions that the certification covers, and we also know that certifications and collective agreements are legally binding documents. Any change to the parties may or may not make a certification or collective agreement invalid. Whether the certification or collective agreement is still valid after a change in the workplace is a fairly significant question for the business and for the employees, because the presence or absence of a collective agreement and union representation has major implications for how the workplace functions.

If a change occurs, one of the parties to the certification or the collective agreement will apply to a labour relations board to determine whether a declaration of successorship should be issued. If a declaration of successorship is issued, it has the effect of applying the existing certification or collective agreement to the new form of the business. Thus, a declaration of successorship ensures that the new employer is bound by the same obligations to bargain and to recognize the union as the previous employer. It is important to note that Canadian labour legislation clearly states that the new employer is automatically bound by the certification or collective agreement covering the previous employer unless the change in the business entailed exceptional circumstances. The *New Brunswick Industrial Relations Act*'s language is a good example of the wording that most Canadian labour codes contain to make this relationship explicit:

> Where an employer who is bound by or is a party to a collective agreement with a trade union or council of trade unions sells his business, the person to whom the business has been sold is, until the Board otherwise declares, bound by the collective agreement as if he had been a party thereto. (Section 60[2])

When the change in the business involves an expansion, a spinoff of part of the business, or a merger, a declaration of successorship serves to clarify the extent of the employer's new obligations, especially if different unions or collective agreements are involved. A declaration of successorship clarifies which employees are in the new bargaining unit, which union is the new bargaining agent for the employees, and which collective agreement is now in force.

We should note that a declaration of successorship can also apply to situations where the employer is involved in some union-related process that has not yet been completed. These processes could include a certification campaign, a notice to commence collective bargaining, an application for decertification, or a complaint or case involving the employer that is before a labour relations board. According to Canadian labour codes, if the employer sells or changes the business while any of these processes are unfolding and not yet complete, the altered employer is still considered the employer and is bound by the obligations required by these processes unless a labour relations board declares otherwise. The purpose of this legislation is to discourage employers from attempting to avoid dealing with a union by selling or changing the business during processes that might alter the union-employer relationship. Were it not for such legislation, an employer could, for example, avoid entering into collective bargaining by changing the form or ownership of the business and then claiming that a notice to commence bargaining was not valid because it was issued to a form of the business that no longer existed.

Determining whether successorship exists or not can be quite complicated. Labour relations boards recognize that changes in a business can occur for legitimate business reasons—that is, the changes would have taken place regardless of whether the certification existed or not. Labour relations boards also recognize that changes in a business may be as simple as a name change or as complex as a total reorganization and that change in one area of a business may not be representative of the direction of the organ-ization as a whole. Thus, a change in how a business operates may not be intentionally undertaken to disrupt the union-employer relationship. It is even possible that the employer has not considered how changes in the business may affect the ability of the union to represent its membership.

However, labour relations boards must balance these realities against the possibility that an employer has undertaken change for no other reason than to weaken the power of the union or to avoid the obligations associated with unionization of the workforce. For example, if a business is certified and then expands its operations to multiple locations that are not certified, the employer would gain a distinct advantage in collective bargaining. The workers at the certified location would be disadvantaged in bargaining because they would be representing the interests of only a small part of the employer's total workforce. The employer could easily transfer business to the non-certified locations during bargain-ing disputes, thus lessening the impact of any industrial action. The advantages associat-ed with this shift of power in favour of the employer might entice an employer to expand locations simply to weaken the union. Alternatively, an employer could sell or transfer the ownership of the business, but retain control over its operations, and then claim that a cer-tification should no longer apply because the business would not be the same business that existed at the time the certification was issued. The employer could then continue to run the business, which would not have changed at all except for the legal ownership, without having to deal with the presence of a union.

Because of these possibilities, labour relations boards, in assessing whether succes-sorship exists or not, look for evidence that employer actions are not motivated by anti-union animus. As previous chapters have noted, while employees may be enthusiastic about joining a union, employers are not always as enthusiastic about having a union in their workplace. Employers may see the presence of a union as a threat to their ability to operate the organization efficiently or effectively, and they may fear that a union will inflate labour costs to the extent that the business will cease to be profitable. Some employers are opposed to unions on general principle because they perceive that unions interfere with management's right to control the workplace.

We have previously discussed employers' anti-union attitudes in the context of the certification process, but it is important to know that these anti-union attitudes do not always disappear after certification. If the employer feels that its concerns were not fairly or completely addressed during the certification process, its anti-union attitudes may become even more intense after a certification declaration. Therefore, labour legislation usually contains language to deal with employer actions that may be motivated by a desire to evade responsibilities after certification; such language would include, for example, timelines outlining when collective bargaining must commence and provisions for arbitration to resolve disagreements over the application of the collective agreement. The sections of labour law dealing with successorship are also part of the legislation intended to ensure that employers, as well as unions and employees, fulfill the obligations that certification and collective agreements place upon them.

Because the circumstances of successorship may vary considerably from case to case, depending on the structure of the business and the events that have occurred, there are no hard and fast rules that determine when successorship has occurred and when it has not. The legislation summarized in Table 12-1 gives some guidance, but it is only a starting point, as it deals just with successorships involving changes to a business. As we know, successorship issues also arise when a union merges or changes (these issues will be discussed separately at a later point in the chapter). Since employers who are vehemently opposed to unionization can be quite creative, labour relations boards regularly find themselves having to evaluate and pass judgement on new situations. Thus, many of the criteria used to determine whether successorship has occurred or not have developed through case law. Judgements from previous cases may or may not be relevant to a current case, depending on the amount of similarity between the cases.

TABLE 12-1 Legislation Governing Successorship

	Who Can Apply for Declaration of Successorship	Situations That May Be Considered Successorship [i]	Actions Labour Relations Board Can Take If Successorship Exists
Federal	Any employer or trade union affected	Sale, transfer, lease, or other disposition of a business; sale, transfer, lease, or other disposition of a provincial business so that it falls under federal regulation, or an employer under federal regulation	Determine appropriate bargaining unit; determine any questions arising
Alberta	Any employer, trade union, or person affected	Sale, transfer, lease, merger, or other disposition of a business; an undertaking, or part of it, so that control, management, or supervision of business passes to purchaser, lessee, transferee, or person acquiring it	Make any inquiries and direct the taking of any votes considered necessary; decide any questions arising; declare which union shall be bargaining agent; amend certification(s); cancel or amend collective agreement(s) in force; determine whether results of ongoing proceedings are binding
British Columbia	Any person	Sale, lease, transfer or other disposition of a business or part of it	Determine what rights, privileges, or duties have been acquired or retained; make enquiries or direct votes as necessary or advisable; determine appropriate bargaining unit; determine bargaining agent; amend certification(s); modify collective agreement(s) to define seniority rights; give direction

TABLE 12-1 Continued

	Who Can Apply for Declaration of Successorship	Situations That May Be Considered Successorship [i]	Actions Labour Relations Board Can Take If Successorship Exists
Manitoba	Any bargaining agent affected, or by labour relations board's own motion	Where an employer sells the employer's business to another person, or where two or more businesses are amalgamated or merged	Determine appropriate bargaining unit; determine bargaining agent and order vote if necessary or advisable; amend certifications(s); amend collective agreement(s); give any further direction; declare timelines for applicability of any determination or declaration
New Brunswick	Any person, trade union, or council of trade unions concerned	Sale of a business or part thereof to a person, including leases, transfers, and any other manner of disposition	Determine bargaining unit; amend certification(s); declare which collective agreement shall continue in force
Newfoundland	An employer, purchaser, lessee, transferee, person otherwise acquiring the business, bargaining agent, trade union, council of trade unions	Sale, lease, transfer, or other disposition of business, its operations, or a part of either of them, or agreement to sell, lease, transfer, or otherwise dispose of business, its operations, or a part of either of them	Amend or rescind existing collective agreement(s); revoke or amend certification(s); modify or restrict the operation of any notice; determine appropriate bargaining unit; designate employees to be covered by continuing collective agreements; define the rights of employees covered by collective agreement; declare which trade union will be bargaining agent; interpret any collective agreement provision

TABLE 12-1 Continued

	Who Can Apply for Declaration of Successorship	Situations That May Be Considered Successorship [i]	Actions Labour Relations Board Can Take If Successorship Exists
Nova Scotia	Any employer. purchaser, lessee, transferee, bargaining agent, or trade union	Sale, lease, transfer, of business, operations thereof, or any part of either, or agreement to sell, lease, or transfer business, operations thereof, or any part of either. Successorship legislation may also apply if board determines that employer has contracted out work to avoid obligations under *Trade Union Act*	Modify or rescind any collective agreement(s); amend or revoke any certification(s); modify any notice or entitlement to give notice; determine appropriate bargaining unit; determine coverage of collective agreements if more than one is to remain in force; declare bargaining agent; interpret any provision of any collective agreement
Ontario	Any person, trade, union, or council of trade unions concerned	Sale of business to a person, including lease, transfer, and any other manner of disposition of a business	Determine appropriate bargaining unit; amend certification(s); declare bargaining agent
Prince Edward Island	Any employer, purchaser, lessee, transferee, bargaining agent, or trade union	When an employer sells, transfers, or leases or has agreed to sell, lease, or transfer a business, the operations thereof, or any part of them	Amend or rescind existing collective agreement(s); revoke or amend certification(s); modify or restrict the operation of any notice; determine appropriate bargaining unit; designate employees to be covered by continuing collective agreements; define the rights of employees covered by collective agreement; declare which trade union will be bargaining agent; interpret any collective agreement provision

TABLE 12-1 Continued

	Who Can Apply for Declaration of Successorship	Situations That May Be Considered Successorship [i]	Actions Labour Relations Board Can Take If Successorship Exists
Quebec	Not specified	Alienation or operation by another in whole or in part of an undertaking, otherwise than by judicial sale	Labour commissioner can rule on any matter arising; can determine applicability of legislation; can issue any order deemed necessary; can settle any difficulty arising out of application of legislation
Saskatchewan	Any employer, employee, or trade union directly affected	Sale, lease, transfer, or other disposition of a business or part thereof	Determine whether disposition relates to a business or part of it; determine appropriate bargaining unit; determine what trade union represents majority of employees in new unit; direct a representation vote; amend description of unit in collective agreement; give any direction board considers necessary

Source: Human Resources Development Canada, Labour Program, Summaries of General Private Sector Collective Bargaining Legislation (available at <http://www.hrdc-drhc.gc.ca>).

i All of the legislation in this table states or implies that at least some of the employees in the affected business must be represented by a certified bargaining agent and/or have a collective agreement currently in place in order for successorship to be declared.

If there is any general guideline underlying decisions on successorship cases, it is whether or not there is any evidence of **continuity** or **control** between the previous and the present form of the business. "Continuity" refers to any form of connection between the two forms of the business. Continuity could be indicated by evidence as substantial as financial records showing that two supposedly separate businesses are actually incorporated as a single entity, or as minor as a new business honouring coupons or discounts issued by the previous form of the business. The amount of evidence of continuity that is required to prove successorship is dependent on the facts of the individual situation; however, some evidence of continuity, no matter how small, would usually be expected to form at least the basis of an argument that successorship exists.

The question of control is usually considered in determining successorship if it appears that an employer has established a new business entity for the purposes of avoiding the obligations that come with certification. "Control" refers to how much direction the management or owners of the previous business give to the new business. For example, the owner of a unionized business might set up a separate non-unionized business with different management but still give direction and orders to that management and that business. A labour relations board might find that there was successorship in this situation because the owner of the first business retained control over the second business.

We should note that it is not necessary to prove both continuity and control for a declaration of successorship to be issued. The issue of continuity is more important in situations involving a sale, lease, or transfer of a business; the issue of control is more important when a new business is established or part of an existing business's operations is assigned to another employer or another business entity.

There are often other criteria that labour relations boards will consider when determining if successorship should be declared or not.[1] We will briefly describe each of these.

Direct Contact   Successorship may be declared if there had been direct contact between the owner or manager of the previous form of the business and the owner or manager of the new form of the business. Sometimes direct contact is very easy to prove because the previous owner or manager and the current one are the same person. In situations where these individuals are not the same person, determining whether direct contact existed would include such considerations as:

- whether the individuals previously knew each other

- whether they had any previous business relationships

- whether one of the individuals had previously been an employee of another of the individuals

Transfer of Assets   A labour relations board would also consider whether there has been any transfer of assets between the two forms of the business. If a new business uses assets previously owned by the former business, the board will usually consider this as evidence of continuity. The board might also be concerned with the price associated with a transfer of assets and would likely be suspicious if the selling price of the assets is considerably below what the assets would be expected to sell for in other situations. The reason that a labour relations board would be suspicious of such a transaction is because an employer trying to avoid dealing with a union might sell assets at an artificially low price to a business run by a sympathetic associate. The employer might then attempt to have the certification cancelled on the grounds that the business has ceased to exist and, if successful, repurchase the assets at the same low price and resume operations as a non-unionized company. The board would also examine the disposition of goodwill and other intangible assets in determining whether a transfer of assets took place.

Identification   If there was a transfer of a logo, trademark, or some other distinctive identification from the previous business to the new business, this action would likely be considered evidence of continuity. A logo or trademark is generally the legal possession of a business and thus its transfer could be considered a transfer of assets. Moreover, a logo or trademark is a strong public indicator of a business's identity, and a transfer of such identification to another business would give a public impression of continuity.

Transfer of Customer Lists   A present business having the same customer base as the former business is not, in and of itself, an indication that successorship exists. However, the transfer of customer lists from one business to another would indicate continuity, since most businesses that maintain such lists rarely share them with other companies, particularly those in the same industry or serving the same customer market.

Transfer of Accounts Receivable, Existing Contracts, and/or Inventory   Accounts receivable and inventory are both assets that generate revenue for the company. Contracts are assets that will produce future revenue, so they are not likely to be transferred from one business to another except under exceptional circumstances.

Pledges by the Successor to Maintain the Good Name of the Predecessor or Pledges by the Predecessor Not to Compete with the Successor If these sorts of promises exist between the owners or managers of the old and new businesses, they are evidence of continuity because they determine the terms under which the business transition will occur.

Whether the Same Employees Perform the Same Work If the new business uses the same employees carrying out the same tasks that they did in the old business, a continuity between the two businesses would be indicated. Another staff-related criterion for determining successorship is the key person doctrine, discussed below.

Whether There Was a Hiatus in Business between the Two Companies This criterion may or may not assist in determining whether successorship exists. Business owners quite commonly close one business and after a period of time open another without ever having intended to avoid the obligations associated with certification or a collective agreement. However, an employer attempting to avoid those obligations may try to disguise intent by closing the unionized business, waiting for a while, and then opening a non-unionized business, claiming that there is no continuity because the second business did not immediately replace the first business. An employer might also use a hiatus in business to attempt to avoid certain obligations; for example, a collective agreement might expire during a hiatus (this would not, however, relieve the employer of the responsibility to participate in collective bargaining for a new collective agreement).

Whether the Customers of the Predecessor Are Now Serviced by the Successor This criterion is distinct from the criterion involving customer lists. Instead, it looks at whether a new business is serving the same geographic or demographic market or in some other way serves the same customer base as the previous business. This in and of itself is not an indication that successorship should be declared, but it could be significant in combination with other criteria.

Another criterion that is used in some successorship cases is the **key person doctrine**. Successorship may exist if the successor business includes individuals from the previous business whose knowledge or skills were essential for the operation of the business. For example, if the previous business used a specialized piece of equipment and only a few employees knew how to operate and service that equipment, successorship might exist if those individuals performed the same work at the new business. The key person doctrine can also apply to individuals with specialized contacts or customer lists, such as salespeople whose rosters of regular customers cannot easily be duplicated.

In addition to evidence of continuity, as mentioned, a labour relations board also looks at the actions that caused the transformation of the business and tries to determine whether these actions were motivated by legitimate business reasons or by anti-union animus. In successorship cases, as in complaints alleging unfair labour practices by the employer, the onus is on the employer to prove that there were legitimate business reasons for its actions. In the words of the Ontario Labour Relations Board, "the applicant has the onus to prove that the sale of a business took place. However, when the union is the applicant, the employer has an obligation to present all of the relevant facts of which it has knowledge."[2]

If a labour relations board decides that sufficient evidence exists to establish that there was continuity or control within the two forms of the business or that changes in the business were motivated by the intent to avoid the obligations associated with certification, a declaration of successorship is issued. As Table 12-1 indicates, there are a variety of other actions that a labour relations board can take to clarify the successorship, including altering the scope of certifications and the application of collective agreements, or redefining the bargaining unit to reflect the new form of the business. In most provinces, a labour relations board also has the ability to order representation votes if the new bargaining unit includes employees from two or more unions and there is a question of which union should represent the employees in the newly defined bargaining unit.

If the successorship situation involves a unionized business expanding to non-unionized locations or the creation of a completely separate business entity owned by the employer, the board may issue a **common employer declaration** in addition to a declaration of successorship. A common employer declaration states that all the employer's businesses are considered to be a single business for the purposes of certification and the collective agreement. A labour relations board usually issues this declaration where it has been shown that the employer attempted to avoid obligations by moving some or all of the unionized parts of the business to a non-unionized business or part of the business.

If the application for a declaration of successorship is denied, the original certification order continues to exist without any changes. However, in cases where the business has changed substantially, a labour relations board's failure to declare successorship may substantially impair the union's ability to function effectively as the workers' representative. This is especially true if the union represents workers in what is now a small part of an expanded business or if the certification now applies to a business that has effectively ceased to function, such as a location that has closed or downsized. In such cases, the union members may choose to apply for decertification. (We will discuss decertification in the next section of this chapter.) On the other hand, if the change in the business involves expansion or the creation of new business entities, workers at the new non-unionized business or at the new parts of the unionized business may apply for a separate certification as a new bargaining unit if successorship is not declared.

DECERTIFICATION

During the term of a collective agreement, union members may decide that they no longer wish to have the certified union as their representative in the workplace. This situation can occur either because the members are dissatisfied with the performance of their particular union in representing their concerns or because they no longer wish to have any union represent them. In order for any change to be made to the designated bargaining agent, the existing certification must be nullified. The process that is used to cancel the certification is called **decertification**.

The process of decertification is an important part of labour relations legislation because it provides a way for union members to hold their unions accountable for performance. Having decertification available as an option allows employees to remove "weak, indifferent, or ineffective unions"[3] or union representation of any type if they feel that union representation no longer serves their interests in the workplace. If workers are to have the unrestricted ability to choose how they want to be represented in the workplace, providing them with a method of removing a union is as important as providing them with a method of joining a union.

Inter-Canadian airline employees had to decide if they wished to retain their union status after the Quebec Federation of Labour solidarity fund decided not to invest in the ailing airline.

Table 12-2 outlines the specific provisions for decertification in each Canadian jurisdiction. We can see from this table that, as with certification, specific timelines restrict when applications for decertification can be made. The timelines serve two main purposes. First, they give newly certified unions a chance to establish themselves as credible worker representatives. As discussed in Chapter 5, new unions often have difficulty in obtaining certification, and members or executives of a newly certified union may be relatively inexperienced. The timelines restricting when decertification applications can be made are intended to give new unions and new union members a reasonable chance to establish themselves in the workplace and gain some experience in union operations. The second purpose of these timelines is to minimize the possibility that decertification applications will be made during times when feelings about the union might be particularly heated, such as during collective agreement negotiations. Banning applications entirely during these times would be an unfair restriction on the employees' right to freely choose their representation in the workplace. Nevertheless, the legislation recognizes that employees can be dissatisfied with their union's performance under certain circumstances but generally satisfied with its performance otherwise. Negotiations, for example, can cause heightened conflict and strong emotions because of the significance of the matters being bargained, and at times like these, employees might be tempted to apply for decertification, even though they would not have considered doing so in less extreme situations. It is also important to note that several jurisdictions ban decertification applications outright during strikes or lockouts.

TABLE 12-2 Decertification Legislation

	Timelines	Criteria	Other Conditions
Federal	If a collective agreement exists, the timelines are the same as for certification; if no collective agreement exists, applications can be made after 12 months from the date of certification; no application can be made during a strike or lockout.	A majority of employees in the unit must support application. A vote may be held if the board deems it appropriate. If no collective agreement exists, the board must be satisfied that reasonable effort was made to obtain one.	If certification was obtained by fraud, an application can be made at any time by a concerned employee, employer, or union.

TABLE 12-2 Continued

	Timelines	Criteria	Other Conditions
Alberta	If no collective agreement is in force, application may be made at any time by the union. Employees may apply under the same timelines as for certification. An employer may only apply when it has not bargained collectively for at least 3 years after the end of the first collective agreement.	At least 40% of employees in the unit must indicate in writing their support for the application. A representation vote will be conducted and results must indicate that a majority of employees voting support decertification. If an employer applies, they must show there have been no employees in the unit for at least 3 years or that the bargaining agent has abandoned its bargaining rights.	The board may decertify if it is satisfied that the bargaining rights of the union should be revoked. The board may at any time give notice of intent to decertify and may do so if it receives no objection within 60 days of notice. If an application for decertification is withdrawn or abandoned, no similar or substantially similar application can be made for 90 days without board consent.
British Columbia	There may be no applications during the 10 months after certification, during the 10 months following a refusal to decertify because of interference or unfair labour practices, and during a period (minimum 90 days) prescribed by the board following a refusal to decertify if a majority of votes are in favour of the union.	At least 45% of employees in the unit must sign an application to cancel the certification. The vote must be held within 10 days after the application or a longer period as ordered by the board if conducted by mail. The board may order another vote if participation by eligible employees is less than 55%. The board may refuse to cancel certification, regardless of vote results, if employees are affected by an order pertaining to a prohibited act or if employer interference is likely to make a vote not reflect the true wishes of the employees.	The board may cancel certification if it is satisfied the union has ceased to be a union or that the employer has ceased to employ the employees in the unit, or if it is satisfied that the trade union has abandoned its bargaining rights.

TABLE 12-2 Continued

	Timelines	Criteria	Other Conditions
Manitoba	The same timelines apply as for certification. An application may be made at any time with the consent of the board.	An employee may apply if he or she claims to represent a majority of the unit. If the board is satisfied that fewer than 50% of employees in a unit support the application, it may dismiss the application. The board conducts a vote if support is greater than 50%. A majority of employees in the unit who participate in the vote must support the decertification.	If certification was obtained by fraud, an employee, employer, or union may apply. The board may dispense with a vote if the union does not oppose the application. The board may dismiss an application, even with sufficient support, if it believes employer failure to bargain in good faith resulted in the bargaining process being frustrated.
New Brunswick	The timelines are the same as for certification. The board may allow earlier applications in certain circumstances. An application is subject to delays related to concilation, mediation, strike, or lockout. Decertification may take place at any time when there have been no employees in the bargaining unit for 2 years or where certification was obtained fraudulently.	At least 40% of employees must support the application. A representation vote is taken. At least 50% of all those eligible to vote must support decertification. Employees absent from work during voting hours and who do not cast their ballots are not counted as eligible. Decertification may take place without a vote if there is failure to give notice to bargain, to commence bargaining, or to seek to bargain within the specified time limits.	The board may refuse to accept new applications from an unsuccesful applicant for a period not exceeding 10 months. An application may be made by any employee, another trade union, or the employer if the board is satisfied that there is a question over whether a majority of employees support an application.

TABLE 12-2 Continued

	Timelines	Criteria	Other Conditions
Newfoundland	Application may be made 12 months after certification, 6 months after an application for decertification was dismissed, 12 months after the union gave notice to bargain, or earlier at the board's discretion.	Application must be supported by at least 40% of employees in a bargaining unit. The board will take a vote which must be taken no later than 5 working days after receipt of application. A majority of the unit must vote in favour, or 70% of the unit must vote and a majority of those must vote in favour. The board is bound by the outcome of a vote unless it determines the results have been influenced by intimidation, threat, or coercion.	Following investigation and a hearing if necessary, the board may revoke certification, on application or on its own initiative, if it determines that a bargaining agent no longer represents the majority of employees in a bargaining unit.
Nova Scotia	If no agreement is in force, application can be made at least 12 months after certification; if an agreement is in force, the timelines are the same as for certification.	A significant number of members of the union must indicate that the union is not fulfilling its responsibilities or that it no longer represents a majority of employees in the unit. The board may order the taking of a vote and may revoke or confirm the certification in accordance with the result.	None specified

TABLE 12-2 Continued

	Timelines	Criteria	Other Conditions
Ontario	The same timelines as for certification. Upon application by the employer or any employees in the bargaining unit, decertification may take place with or without a vote if there is failure to give notice to bargain, to commence bargaining, or to seek to bargain within the timelines prescribed in legislation. If the board has ordered the settlement of a first collective agreement by arbitration, no application can be considered until after the agreement is settled.	Applications must include a list of the names of employees in the bargaining unit who express a desire not to be represented by the union, along with evidence of those wishes. If no less than 40% of employees in the bargaining unit express such wishes, the board must order a secret-ballot vote within 5 working days of the application's filing. More than 50% of ballots must be in opposition to the union for decertification to occur.	The board may bar a new application by any employee affected by an unsuccessful application for no longer than one year. The board may not consider any challenge to the information supporting the application. An application may be dismissed if the employer or its representative engaged in threats, coercion, or intimidation.
Prince Edward Island	The timelines are the same as for certification. An employer, the trade union, or a majority of employees in the bargaining unit may make an application.	If the majority of the employees desire decertification, the board will decertify the union. If an employer applies, the board can only revoke certification if it is satisfied that the union has abandoned its bargaining rights.	The board will take a decertification vote whenever it deems necessary.

TABLE 12-2 Continued

	Timelines	Criteria	Other Conditions
Quebec	The timelines are the same as for certification.	A labour commissioner may cancel the certification if the association has ceased to exist or if it no longer comprises a majority of employees in the unit.	The labour court may order an association to be dissolved if it is proven that the association is dominated or financed by the employer or its representative. The association has the opportunity to be heard and to attempt to prove that it is blameless.
Saskatchewan	If an agreement exists, applications can be made no less than 30 days or more than 60 days before the anniversary of the effective date. If no agreement exists, applications can be made no less than 30 days or more than 60 days before the anniversary date of the certification order.	If the board finds that the union or an employee has committed an unfair labour practice or other illegal act and there is no evidence of majority support for an application that otherwise would have been obtained, it must order a representation vote.	If the board is satisfied that a certification order was obtained by fraud, it may rescind the order.

Source: Human Resources Development Canada, Labour Program, Summaries of General Private Sector Collective Bargaining Legislation (available at <http://www.hrdc-drhc.gc.ca>).

As Table 12-2 indicates, some jurisdictions in Canada allow employers, as well as employees or unions, to make applications for decertification. This provision may seem somewhat contrary to one of the primary purposes of certification, which is to allow the "true wishes" of the employees to be expressed without interference from the employer. To some degree, allowing employers to apply for decertification gives them another way to resist unionization. When employers object to having to deal with the presence of a union or to abide by the conditions of a collective agreement, for example, they might be tempted to apply for decertification. This phenomenon has been observed in the United States, where the number of applications for decertification has increased along with the use of other employer anti-union tactics such as shutdowns, relocations, and the hiring of non-union employees.[4] In Canada, the successful use of decertification as an employer tactic to avoid union influence is much less common.

Prior to describing how the process of decertification actually works, we will point out two other features of the relevant Canadian legislation. The first is that most jurisdictions have some provision in place that permits a labour relations board, on its own initiative, to declare a decertification if there is evidence that fraud took place during the certification process. Fraud of this kind most often involves falsified evidence on the application for certification, such as forged signatures. Usually, such evidence is uncovered relatively soon after the original certification is issued, but most legislation places no time restriction on when a decertification can be declared owing to fraud. In a case in British Columbia in 2001, a decertification was declared four years after the original certification was issued when evidence was produced to show that four signatures on the initial certification application were false.[5]

The second feature in most Canadian labour codes is a provision that permits an employer to make an application for decertification, or a labour relations board to issue a decertification on its own initiative, if there is an **abandonment of bargaining rights** by the union. As we know, a certification order places an obligation on the union, as well as on the employer, to commence collective bargaining. If a union has not issued a notice to bargain to the employer or has not commenced bargaining, it may be considered to have abandoned its bargaining rights. Thus, it is no longer fulfilling its obligation to represent the employees as their bargaining agent and may consequently be decertified.

However, we should also note that it is fairly unusual for a decertification to be granted on the basis of abandonment of bargaining rights. Special circumstances may account for a union's failure to issue a notice to bargain after a certification is granted; such failure could indicate, for example, that union members are unwilling or unable to participate on the bargaining team, not that the union itself has no intention of bargaining. As one decision in an abandonment case stated, "A certification order is ... proof that employees have chosen to bargain collectively through the union designated in the order. The onus of proving that this right has been lost through abandonment ... is on the party alleging it, and is a heavy one.... A clear repudiation of bargaining rights [is] needed to support a finding of abandonment."[6] Labour relations boards have even refused to declare an abandonment of bargaining rights in situations where an employer has terminated its employees and closed its place of business and the union no longer has had a group of employees to represent.

The usual reason for such decisions is that the union has expressed an intention to continue representing the employees if the employer resumes operations at some point in the future.[7]

The actual process of decertification is similar in structure to the process of certification. An application for decertification must be made to a labour relations board, showing a sufficient level of support for the decertification among the bargaining unit members. In most Canadian jurisdictions, the level of support required for a decertification application is identical to the level of support required for a certification application. A labour relations board will also usually conduct the same verification of signatures and employment status that it would conduct in assessing an application for certification. This task is somewhat easier in an application for decertification because the composition of the bargaining unit has already been established. Thus, in a decertification application, the question of whether an individual signing the application is or is not in the bargaining unit is much more straightforward than in a certification application, where the bargaining unit may not yet be definitively determined.

Many jurisdictions in Canada require a vote to be taken among the members of the bargaining unit after the application for decertification has been received. The purpose of this vote is to determine the actual level of support for the decertification attempt. As we know, in certification applications a vote may or may not be required, depending on the circumstances of the application and the level of support for the application. However, a vote on a decertification application is mandatory in most Canadian jurisdictions to ensure that the majority of employees truly support the cancellation of the certification and that the decertification application is not simply the work of a dissatisfied minority.

The decertification vote is a secret-ballot vote conducted in the workplace by a labour relations board. As in a certification vote, the ballot in a decertification vote contains a simple yes/no question asking if the voter wishes the union to continue as the bargaining agent for the employees in the bargaining unit. The vote is successful if a majority (50% + 1 of eligible voters, as defined in the relevant labour relations legislation) indicate that they do not want to be represented by the union. The labour relations board will then issue an order of decertification, after which the union ceases to legally represent the employees in the workplace and any current collective agreement is no longer in force.

When an application for decertification has been submitted by an employer, most labour relations boards will scrutinize it quite carefully to ensure that the application is not motivated by anti-union animus. Successful applications for decertification made by employers are likely to involve situations where the employer has ceased to do business and the decertification is simply part of the task of concluding the employer's existing business relationships.

Another circumstance in which a decertification application might be submitted to a labour relations board is when a raid is taking place. **Raiding** was described in Chapter 6 as an attempt by one union to certify a group of workers already represented by another union. When a raiding attempt takes place, a decertification application may be filed for the current union prior to or at the same time as the raiding union makes an application for certification. As also noted in Chapter 6, there are time bars in place to restrict when applications for certification can be made for a group of workers already in a certified bargaining unit. These time bars are outlined in Table 6-3 on page 204.

If the raiding union is successful in the decertification vote, the previous union is decertified and a new certification order is issued with the newly certified union identified as the legal representative of the employees in the bargaining unit.

Another situation where decertification—and even successorship—issues might become relevant is when there are changes in the union itself, rather than changes in the employer or in the union's status as employee representative. We will now turn our attention to a description of what happens in this situation.

The Canadian Congress of Labour was formed by a merger of two earlier union federations, and it later merged with the Trade and Labour Congress to form the CLC.

UNION MERGERS

The merging of existing unions is a relatively recent trend in Canadian industrial relations. This action has become more common for a number of reasons. A merger can serve as a means to ensure the continued viability of unions, particularly smaller unions. As we know, the larger the membership a union has, the more impact it can have in the workplace and the more "economic pain" it can inflict on the employer in bargaining disputes. Smaller unions may have particular difficulty dealing with the employer if they do not represent enough workers in a business or industry to be able to exert a significant influence on the employer; merging with a larger union is one way to counteract this problem.

Larger unions, too, may find a benefit in merging. If they see that their historical membership base is diminishing (e.g., if there is downsizing or closures in the relevant industry), they may feel that a merger with other unions offers them a way to maintain their existence. A union can also enjoy the benefits of increased size without undertaking the effort of recruiting unorganized workers by merging with one or more existing unions to form a single union. Such a merger usually takes place among unions that have a common interest, either through representing the same kind of workers at different employers or through representing workers in related industries. An example of this kind of merger occurred recently in the Canadian newspaper industry when several bargaining units of workers formerly represented by The Newspaper Guild joined the Communications, Energy and Paperworkers Union (CEP). The CEP was itself the product of a merger of unions representing electrical, chemical, and pulp and paper industry workers. Its merger with The Newspaper Guild was based on the recognition that newspapers are one of the primary consumers of a major forestry product (newsprint) and thus there would likely be common concerns among workers in these industries.

Union mergers are also a response to the general trend in business toward larger organizations. Globalization and increased ease of communication, among other factors, have encouraged organizations to grow through mergers or acquisitions. In order to match the bargaining power of these larger organizations, unions themselves may also need to be larger, and mergers are one way to accomplish this. Larger unions have greater power than smaller ones because of their strength in numbers and also because of the increased financial resources that a larger membership provides.

Finally, as the newspaper story that opens this chapter shows, union mergers may also be forced by company mergers. If workers at two different companies are represented by different unions and those companies merge, the unions are usually also forced to merge, unless there is some exceptional reason for maintaining two separate bargaining units with separate union representation within the new company. As the newspaper story also demonstrates, these types of union mergers raise complicated issues, such as how to determine criteria for seniority among the newly merged workforce and how to combine two different organizational cultures.

Table 12-3 outlines the legislation in Canadian jurisdictions that regulates changes in certified unions. As we can see, this legislation is quite similar to successorship legislation, with the major difference being, of course, that it is the union that is changing rather than the employer. The legislation governing these changes is intended to ensure, as is legislation governing successorship, that there is continuity in representation for the union members after the change takes place.

TABLE 12-3 Legislation Governing Changes in Certified Unions

	Situations Where Legislation Applies	Effect of Change
Federal	Merger of amalgamation of trade unions or transfer of jurisdiciton among trade unions. Successor union must be certified as a bargaining agent.	Successor union is deemed to have acquired rights, privileges, and duties of predecessor; board may resolve any question arising and may order a representation vote if necessary.
Alberta	Merger or amalgamation of trade unions or transfer of jurisdiction. Successor union must be a bargaining agent for a unit of employees of an employer.	On application by union or any person concerned or through a hearing, board may declare that successor union has acquired predecessor's rights, privileges, and duties; board may examine evidence or order representation vote.
British Columbia	Merger or amalgamation of trade unions or transfer of jurisdiction. Successor union must be certified or voluntarily recognized as a bargaining agent.	On application by union or through a hearing, board may either declare that successor union has acquired predecessor's rights, privileges, and duties or dismiss application; board may also order representation vote or examine evidence.
Manitoba	Merger, amalgamation, or transfer of jurisdiction. Successor union must be a bargaining agent.	Board may declare that successor has or has not acquired rights, privileges, and obligations of predecessor or may dismiss application.

TABLE 12-3 Continued

	Situations Where Legislation Applies	Effect of Change
New Brunswick	Merger, amalgamation, or transfer of jurisdiction between unions or councils of trade unions. Successor union or council must be the certified bargaining agent of a unit of employees of an employer.	On application of any person or trade union concerned or in a board hearing, board may declare that successor has or has not acquired rights, privileges, and duties of predecessor; board may also examine evidence, order evidence to be produced, or conduct representation vote.
Newfoundland	Merger, amalgamation, or transfer of jurisdiction between trade union(s) or councils of trade union(s). Successor union or council must be bargaining agent of a unit of employees of an employer.	On application of person, trade union, or council of trade unions affected, board may declare that successor has or has not acquired rights, privileges, and duties of predecessor; board may also examine evidence or order votes as necessary. If union changes name, board will order certification order to be amended.
Nova Scotia	Merger, amalgamation, or transfer of jurisdiction. Successor union must be a bargaining agent of a unit of employees of an employer.	On application of any person or trade union affected, board may declare that successor has acquired rights, privileges, and duties of predecessor; board may examine evidence or order representation vote.
Ontario	Merger, amalgamation, or transfer of jurisdiction. Successor union must be a bargaining agent of a unit of employees of an employer.	Board may declare that successor has or has not acquired rights, privileges, and obligations of predecessor or may dismiss application; board may examine evidence or order representation vote.

TABLE 12-3 Continued		
	Situations Where Legislation Applies	**Effect of Change**
Prince Edward Island	Merger or amalgamation of trade union or transfer of jurisdiction. Successor union must be certified as bargaining agent of a unit of employees of an employer.	On application of any person or union affected or in a board hearing, board may declare that successor has or has not acquired the rights, privileges, and duties of predecessor; board may examine evidence, order evidence to be produced, or order representation vote.
Quebec	No specifications	No specifications
Saskatchewan	Merger, amalgamation, or affiliation of one trade union with another.	All existing orders, assignments, and proceedings relating to the predecessor apply to successor; board orders collective agreements or proceedings are not voided, terminated, abrogated, or curtailed by reason of a name change; by amalgamation, merger, or affiliation of union or part of a union; or by transfer or assignment by one union of its rights to another union.

Union mergers have different effects on an existing certification, depending on the reason for the merger. If one union merges with another or if locals merge within a single union, the affected locals usually apply to a labour relations board for a change in the existing certification order to reflect the status of the newly merged union. These types of changes do not usually require a labour relations board to conduct a vote among the affected employees, although in most Canadian jurisdictions a labour relations board would be able to order such a vote if it was considered necessary.

If a business merger results in two unions now representing the employees of a single company, the employees are usually asked to vote on which union they wish to represent them; the result of this vote would determine which collective agreement would be in effect. The vote itself is a secret ballot similar to a representation vote, and a majority of employees in the new bargaining unit must vote in favour of a union for it to be certified as the representative of the new company's employees. If a sufficient level of support for one union is indicated by the vote, the certification of that union is changed to reflect its representation of the new bargaining unit. The collective agreement negotiated by that union is considered to regulate the newly formed workplace until it expires and a new collective agreement is negotiated. The certification of the other union is cancelled, and its collective agreement is no longer in effect.

TECHNOLOGICAL CHANGE

Change during the lifetime of a collective agreement may come about because of changes in the workplace itself. Work restructuring can occur when **technological change** alters the content of jobs or how work is conducted. Although technological change is usually described in terms of computerization or mechanization, it encompasses any change in the tools used to perform a job that leads to a change in the way the job itself is done. For example, many jobs in banking have been affected by technological change. The introduction of automatic teller machines has allowed bank customers to perform many functions (e.g., cash withdrawals and bill payments) that were formerly handled by bank employees. While technological change does not always cause a substantive change in working conditions, in the composition of the bargaining unit, or in the structure of the employer, it may create new situations that are not adequately addressed by the existing collective agreement.

When technological change occurs, its effects may be addressed through collective bargaining if the timing in the bargaining cycle is such that the issue can be dealt with relatively quickly—for example, if an existing collective agreement is close to its expiry date. However, if a collective agreement is in place and will be for some time, there may be the need to find an alternative way to address the effects of technological change—especially since technological change can occur at a rapid pace.

Gertrude Lee received training in information technology after working for 20 years in the Newfoundland cod fishery.

There are two methods available under Canadian labour legislation to address workplace changes caused by technological change. First, the legislation in some jurisdictions contains language dealing specifically with how the impact of technological change is to be handled. Second, some legislation permits collective agreements to contain a **reopener clause**. A reopener clause in a collective agreement allows the union and employer to renegotiate terms of the collective agreement while it is still in effect, rather than observing the legislated timelines for renegotiating the entire agreement. The availability of these two methods in different Canadian jurisdictions is outlined in Table 12-4.

TABLE 12-4 Provisions for Technological Change and Reopener Clauses

	Definition of Technological Change	Provisions for Technological Change	Provisions for Reopener Clauses
Federal	The introduction by an employer into his or her work, undertaking, or business of equipment or material of a different nature or kind than that previously utilized by the employer in the operation of the work, undertaking, or business; and a change in the manner in which the employer carries on the work, undertaking, or business that is directly related to the introduction of that equipment or material.	Employer must give at least 120 days' written notice of proposed change to bargaining agent; notice must state the nature of the change, the proposed date of the change, the approximate number and type of employees affected, and the effect that the change is likely to have. The bargaining agent may apply to the board for an order permitting the bargaining agent to serve a notice to commence collective bargaining to revise or replace terms of existing collective agreement. The change may not take place until the board rejects the bargaining agent's request or the collective agreement has been revised.	The parties can agree to revise any provision of a collective agreement other than the term of the agreement itself.

TABLE 12-4 Continued

	Definition of Technological Change	Provisions for Technological Change	Provisions for Reopener Clauses
Alberta	None specified	None specified	None specified
British Columbia	None specified, but legislation provides for adjustment if employer introduces or intends to introduce a measure, policy, practice, or change that affects the terms, conditions, or security of employment of a significant number of employees to whom a collective agreement applies.	Employer must give 60 days notice to relevant trade union before date on which measure, policy, practice, or change is to be effected; after notice is given, employer and union must meet to develop an adjustment plan, which is then enforceable as if it were part of the collective agreement.	None specified
Manitoba	A technological change that is likely to affect the terms or conditions, or the security of employment of a significant number of employees in the unit or to alter significantly the basis upon which the collective agreement was negotiated.	Employer must give bargaining agent at least 90 days' notice in writing of the nature of the change, the date on which the change is proposed to take effect, the approximate number of employees affected, and the effect that the change is likely to have. Bargaining agent may then give notice to negotiate a new collective agreementor to negotiate revisions to the present agreement. Arbitration may be used to settle questions over the change or its effects.	Parties can agree to amend a provision of the collective agreement during the term of that agreement.

TABLE 12-4 Continued

	Definition of Technological Change	Provisions for Technological Change	Provisions for Reopener Clauses
New Brunswick	None stated in legislation, but every collective agreement must contain a definition of technological change.	None stated in legislation, but every collective agreement must contain terms requiring employer to give reasonable advance notice of technological change to the bargaining agent and specifying the content of such notice.	If the parties consent, any provision of a collective agreement can be revised at any time except for provisions relating to the term of the agreement.
Newfoundland	None specified	None specified	None specified
Nova Scotia	None specified	None specified	Collective agreements may provide for the revision of any part of the collective agreement during the term of that agreement, with the exception of parts relating to the term itself.
Ontario	None specified	None specified	If the parties mutually agree, they may revise any part of a collective agreement at any time other than the term of the agreement itself.
Prince Edward Island	None specified	None specified	The parties may by mutual consent revise any provisions of a collective agreement.

TABLE 12-4	Continued		
	Definition of Technological Change	**Provisions for Technological Change**	**Provisions for Reopener Clauses**
Quebec	None specified	None specified	None specified
Saskatchewan	The introduction by an employer into the employer's work, undertaking, or business of equipment or material of a different nature or kind than previously utilized by the employer in the operation of the work, undertaking, or business and a change in the manner in which the employer carries on the work, undertaking, or business that is directly related to the introduction of that equipment or material; or the removal or relocation outside of the appropriate unit by an employer of any part of the employer's work, undertaking, or business.	The employer must give bargaining agent and minister of labour at least 90 days' written notice of change, specifying the nature of the change, the proposed date of the change, the number and type of employees affected, the effect that the change may have, and any other information requested by the minister. Within 30 days of receipt of the notice, the bargaining unit may serve notice on the employer to commence bargaining for the development of a workplace adjustment plan. A conciliator may be appointed to assist in the process at the request of either party. The change may not be implemented until a plan has been developed or the minister has been informed that the parties have bargained but failed to develop a plan.	None specified

With respect to the first method, in five Canadian jurisdictions (federal, British Columbia, Manitoba, New Brunswick, and Saskatchewan), labour legislation requires employers to give notice of intended technological changes. As Table 12-4 shows, this notice usually must specify the intended date for the change's implementation, identify which employees will be affected, and describe what the effect of the change will be. After this notice has been issued, the parties will either reopen collective bargaining to alter the collective agreement or develop a mutually acceptable plan to facilitate the implementation of the proposed change. While these requirements do not protect unionized employees against substantive changes in working conditions caused by technological change, they do at least provide for advance notice of such change so that employers and unions can make adjustments and perhaps attempt to negotiate the impact of the change.

Of course, in dealing with technological change, the parties to a collective agreement can always negotiate appropriate language in the collective agreement itself, language that recognizes the possibility of such change occurring and creates conditions whereby such changes can be addressed during the term of the collective agreement. A study in 1987 examined the language dealing with technological change in a selection of Canadian collective agreements covering more than 500 workers.[8] This study found that slightly over half of the agreements had some technological change provision, although most required only advance notice of such change. Less than half of the agreements addressed change-related issues such as retraining, employment security, relocation, joint consultation, and layoff notices. Other studies have indicated that even where such provisions exist in collective agreements, labour relations boards have been reluctant to enforce them, and even when applied, these provisions appear to provide little real protection for workers in the change process, which employers continue to control.[9]

The second method of dealing with technological change, or indeed with any change that may arise during the term of the collective agreement, is for the parties to make use of the reopener clause included in the agreement itself. As Table 12-4 shows, this provision is available in several Canadian jurisdictions. A reopener clause in a collective agreement allows the parties, by mutual consent, to revise any part of the collective agreement during its term without having to renegotiate the entire collective agreement. Thus, if technological change occurs, the parties can immediately negotiate new collective agreement terms to address the change; they do not have to postpone dealing with the change until negotiations for a completely new collective agreement can begin. We should note that some

Canadian jurisdictions specify that the term of the collective agreement itself is one part that cannot be revised while the agreement is in effect. This provision exists to prevent the parties from avoiding negotiations for a new collective agreement by simply extending the term of the existing agreement.

WORKPLACE RESTRUCTURING

Changing economic conditions have led to another type of change during the life of the collective agreement: **workplace restructuring**. This rather wide-ranging term encompasses such events as downsizing in the workforce; work being partially or completely shifted to other locations, companies, or countries; and increased industry competitiveness leading to changes in working conditions or redesigned work.

Most collective agreements have language in place to deal with such events as layoffs or termination. This language usually outlines the procedure for making such changes and the criteria that should be used in determining which employees will be affected. The collective agreement generally specifies, for example, how much notice must be given to employees who will be laid off or terminated; whether financial compensation above the legal minimum will be provided for laid-off or terminated employees; whether the employer will provide employees with services such as retraining or assistance in finding new employment; and how factors such as seniority, experience, and current employment status will be applied in identifying candidates for layoff or termination.

However, a larger issue that to date has not been widely addressed by Canadian labour relations boards involves the role a union can or should play in any decision-making process leading to restructuring and the part it should have in managing the layoffs or terminations that may result. On one hand, most collective agreements in Canada explicitly or implicitly give management the ultimate right to manage the workplace, including the right to make decisions about areas not addressed in the collective agreement.[10] The principle expressed in these collective agreements is known as the doctrine of **management rights** (also called **residual rights**). According to the doctrine of management rights, management has the unchallenged right to decide on whatever workplace changes it deems appropriate—unless the collective agreement specifically states that the union must be consulted or must share in such decisions. Applying this doctrine to workplace restructuring would mean that management has the right to make its own decisions on when restructuring is necessary, how it will be carried out, and what the results will be, as long as the collective agreement does not address these questions.

On the other hand, collective agreements also implicitly contain a competing principle, usually called the doctrine of **implied obligations**. This principle suggests that when a union is certified as the bargaining agent for employees and engages in collective bargaining with the employer, a relationship is established whereby the union and the employer share the responsibility for the regulation and administration of the workplace.[11] According to this principle, once such a relationship is established, it is unreasonable for arbitrary limits to be set that allow some aspects of the workplace to be jointly governed by the union and the employer but other aspects of the workplace to be left solely under the employer's control. Thus, this principle implies that if restructuring occurs, the union, as the designated representative of employees in the workplace, should be involved in the planning of workplace restructuring because of the large impact it could have on the employees the union represents. The union may have information or expertise that could result in a more effective restructuring process, and its involvement might facilitate employee acceptance of a change that might otherwise be perceived as a unilateral or insensitive management action.

To date, only a few cases before Canadian labour relations boards have attempted to define whether unions have a right to participate in restructuring and, if so, what part unions should play in that process. In one case, an employer had established a process to solicit employee input on proposed workplace changes; the employer believed this workplace restructuring was necessary because imminent technological and funding changes were about to significantly affect how the employer conducted its business.[12] The union contended before the labour relations board that it had been excluded from participating in the planning and implementation of the process to solicit employee input, and the board agreed that this exclusion had undermined the union's position as bargaining representative for the employees. In another case, an employee who had been demoted from his first-level managerial position claimed that his removal was due to anti-union animus. However, the employer claimed that the demotion was justified because of workplace restructuring and that the management rights clause in the collective agreement gave the company the unilateral right to make such changes.[13] The arbitrator hearing this case ruled that the restructuring undertaken by the employer had created the necessity for changes in the management structure of the organization, but that there was insufficient evidence to find that the change in this particular employee's work was due to anti-union animus. However, the arbitrator also found that the restructuring had the effect of shifting job duties formerly performed by bargaining unit members to non-union positions in the organization and that this change violated the collective agreement.

While these cases are far from definitive, simply because to date there are so few of them, they do suggest some concerns that need to be addressed when workplace restructuring is undertaken. While it is not clear whether the employer is legally compelled to include the union in planning or carrying out restructuring efforts, the employer must be careful to ensure that restructuring does not undermine or bypass the union's legal role as representative of the bargaining unit membership. As we know, once a certification is in place, the employer is prohibited from bargaining directly with employees, and employer actions such as requesting employee input on organizational structure or operations could be interpreted as bypassing the union on potential bargaining issues. As we also know, employers must be careful that their actions are not perceived as being motivated by anti-union animus, and if restructuring involves changes to job descriptions or workplace structure, employers must ensure that there are legitimate business reasons for those changes. Employers and unions should also ensure that changes do not contravene any terms of the applicable collective agreement. Language that defines the ability of non-union personnel to carry out work usually done by bargaining unit members or that determines the role of seniority or relevant experience in reassigning workers to new positions may suggest some guidelines for how restructuring can be designed or implemented.

In studies of restructuring efforts in Canadian workplaces that have involved union participation, researchers have attempted to identify factors that affect whether unions can or cannot effectively participate in restructuring. One recent study contrasted the restructuring processes at four different steelmaking sites where all of the workers were represented by different locals of the same union.[14] There was particular value in studying these processes, as the union took similar approaches to restructuring issues at all four workplaces. Thus, any differences in the success of the union's participation in restructuring would be more directly attributable to factors specific to the individual union local and/or the workplace, since the actions of the union as a whole were consistent regardless of the workplace setting.

The results of this study indicated that two of the union locals were successful in participating in restructuring and in obtaining their desired outcomes and two were not. The following four factors were identified as contributing to whether the union local was successful in its participation in restructuring:

- the local's ability to access and transmit internal and external information among its membership

- the local's ability to convey the union's vision to the membership and mobilize the membership in support of that vision

- the local's ability to participate in decision making at multiple rather than single points in the restructuring process

- the local's ability to cooperate with management while retaining its independence as the workers' representative

These findings suggest that strong internal and external relationships established prior to restructuring may strengthen a union's ability to represent its membership effectively in a restructuring process. In other words, a union's ongoing activities in representing its membership serve to support its effectiveness if or when restructuring occurs; unions are less effective in dealing with restructuring when they do not already have internal and external resources to draw on.

Another study examined how a union's response to workplace restructuring affects different types of employees.[15] This study is valuable in that it recognizes that union membership is not homogeneous; rather, it is made up of workers with different personal attributes and different status and responsibilities within the workplace. This diversity means that the same restructuring plan may affect different union members in different ways. The study focused on the Ontario supermarket industry at a time when the number of competitors was increasing and there was downward pressure on wages because of the entrance into the market of several large non-union employers. There was a general desire on the part of management for greater flexibility in the workforce.

The unions in this industry chose to respond to the employers' requests for restructuring by negotiating new collective agreements with two-tier wage systems (different pay rates for current employees and those hired later on), buyouts for existing employees, and wage cuts. The results of the study indicate that this method of dealing with employer restructuring affected the workforce in several ways. The employers, for example, increased the numbers of new part-time employees, who under the new collective agreement occupied the lowest-paid job classification. There was also increased management pressure on part-time workers to work full-time hours even though these workers were still classified and paid as part-time workers. Also, the newly negotiated terms of the collective agreement had much more impact on female than on male workers, since female workers dominated the occupational categories that were most severely affected by the restructuring.

The results of this study suggest that unions involved in restructuring efforts must be conscious of the overall effect of restructuring proposals and should attempt to ensure that the interests of all members are equally represented and defended. In the restructuring process examined in this study, the employers' arguments in support of restructuring was that the existing collective agreement, if continued, would lead to job loss. The employers argued that the cost of wages (and the consequent cost of goods) would make the companies incapable of competing in a price-sensitive market. A union faced with this argument has to make a difficult choice: should it protect the status of some existing jobs and lose others, or should it retain the majority of jobs but with a general reduction in working standards? (This assumes, of course, that the union accepts the employer's reasoning and/or is unable to suggest an alternative that the employer would accept.) However, the union's duty of fair representation would suggest that in restructuring, as in other situations, the union should be motivated to ensure that any change does not unduly harm one group of bargaining unit members while protecting or benefiting other groups.

SUMMARY

Because workplace conditions change over time, both certifications and collective agreements must have some flexibility to allow the parties to adapt to these changes. In this chapter, we have outlined some of the mechanisms that facilitate this flexibility. Successorship legislation ensures that certifications and collective agreements remain in effect if there are changes in the employer's business; it also serves as an attempt to discourage employers from avoiding interaction with the union by moving or changing their businesses. Decertification allows employees to remove union representation or to change union representation if they feel that the current union is not doing an adequate job of protecting their interests. Technological change, addressed either in legislation or in collective agreements, can affect job content and organizational structure; legislation and collective agreements can ensure that unions have the opportunity to be involved in how technological change is planned or implemented. Reopener clauses in collective agreements permit the renegotiation of agreements so that the parties can deal with technological change or other kinds of change within the life of a contract. And finally, unions have a role to play in representing the interests of the workers when workplace restructuring takes place, although to date there are relatively few situations in Canada where unions have played this role.

KEY TERMS FOR CHAPTER 12

abandonment of bargaining rights (p. 474)

common employer declaration (p. 466)

continuity (p. 462)

control (p. 462)

decertification (p. 467)

implied obligations (p. 488)

key person doctrine (p. 465)

management rights (p. 487)

raiding (p. 476)

reopener clause (p. 482)

residual rights (p. 487)
successorship (p. 454)
technological change (p. 481)
workplace restructuring (p. 487)

DISCUSSION QUESTIONS FOR CHAPTER 12

1. Why might employers be tempted to use expansion or relocation as a tactic to avoid the effects of unionization?

2. Name and describe some of the criteria that labour relations boards might use in determining whether successorship should apply or not.

3. Why is it important to have both certification and decertification processes available to workers?

4. Why might an employer apply for decertification?

5. Explain why it is difficult for collective agreements to include exact language dealing with technological change.

6. What sorts of issues do you think would be important for a union to negotiate in managing technological change?

7. Outline the reasons for and against union participation in the planning of workplace restructuring.

8. What factors might affect whether a union is successful in achieving its desired outcomes in workplace restructuring?

CASE 12-1

PUBLIC SECTOR EMPLOYEES AND NORTHERN UNIVERSITY

(Based on *Canadian Union of Public Employees Local 2424 and Carleton University,* 1998)

In this case, the employer has initiated a restructuring exercise that includes identifying areas of its operations where changes could be made. The employer has sent a questionnaire to employees asking them, among other things, where they obtain services for their "unit." The questionnaire also asks whether their services could be obtained from other sources or whether their unit could provide some services for other units. The union has filed an unfair labour practices complaint alleging that the employer's questionnaire bypassed the union as the employees' representative and thus the employer is engaging in direct bargaining with the employees.

Background to the Case

Northern University has approximately 600 employees at its central campus. These employees are represented by seven different locals of the Public Sector Employees. Recently, owing to anticipated funding reductions, the university has undertaken a restructuring exercise. The stated purposes of the exercise are to reduce costs, improve service levels, and improve working conditions. The restructuring exercise is taking place simultaneously in several different areas of the university.

This case arises from the part of the restructuring effort that focuses on the administrative structure of the university. The university's new president, Dr. McMahon, initiated this part of the restructuring exercise. Dr. McMahon was hired after the overall restructuring exercise had commenced.

Dr. Regal, the administrator appointed to oversee the administrative restructuring process, testified to the labour relations board that he and six other members of a committee prepared terms of reference for the administrative review. Senior management approved these terms of reference in August 1996. Dr. Regal said that no specific attention was given to how the review would be conducted or to whether the union would play a role in the process. The union was not mentioned in the approved terms of reference.

The union president, Ms. Gould, testified that although she had heard rumours about the administrative review taking place, her first formal notification of the review occurred in late October 1996, when the university invited her to a meeting and presented her with the approved terms of reference. Because of an earlier union complaint about exclusion from the overall restructuring exercise, Gould anticipated that the union would be invited to participate in the administrative review. Instead, the university presented the review as an approved document for her information only.

The university representatives who met with Gould explained to her that employees would be invited to make submissions to the review committee, that particular individuals would be invited to meet with the committee, and that a questionnaire related to the review would be distributed to employees. Gould was not provided with a copy of the questionnaire or with a draft of the call for submissions. She testified that at the end of the meeting she expressed her concerns about the university having direct contact with bargaining unit members on these issues, when it should have used the union to address the bargaining unit members. She told the labour relations board that she understood from the responses of the university representatives that the committee would deal with her concerns before any action was taken. Dr. Regal testified that he did not recall giving such an undertaking.

A few days after Gould's meeting with the university representatives, Dr. Regal sent Gould a draft of the call for submissions to the review committee. Regal asked for Gould's comments within two days, since the call for submissions was scheduled for publication in the university newspaper that week, but Gould indicated that she could not reply that quickly. The call for submissions was published three days later without the union's input.

Around the same time as the call for submissions was published, the university sent out approximately 100 questionnaires to bargaining unit members. The university also scheduled two information sessions for those receiving questionnaires. Gould testified that a number of bargaining unit members contacted her with concerns about the questionnaire; specifically, the members felt that some of the questions addressed matters that could be viewed as collective bargaining issues. Because of these concerns, Gould requested permission to attend the information sessions. Dr. Regal felt that her presence would be "inappropriate" and refused to give her permission to attend. At the two information sessions, some of those present told Dr. Regal that they were uncomfortable with the review process and with Gould's exclusion from the sessions.

Dr. Regal indicated at one meeting that while the questionnaire itself was not intended to identify areas where layoffs could occur, the recommendations based on the questionnaire results could result in layoffs.

As a consequence of Gould's exclusion from the university's information sessions, the union scheduled its own information sessions in early November. The union contacted the university to inform them of these meetings and to request that the questionnaires not be dealt with until after the union's meetings. At the union's meetings, the union informed those present that they could respond to the disputed questions on the questionnaire by indicating that the questions be referred to the bargaining agent (i.e., the union). In early December, the union made a formal submission to the review committee in which it again indicated its discomfort with some of the questionnaire's questions. The questions of particular concern to the union and its members were the following:

- a question asking what services were obtained from external suppliers, the nature and cost of these services, and how the services' effectiveness was determined

- a question asking whether the unit's ability to provide service was hindered by "institutional impediments" and if there were suggestions for improvement

- a question asking whether the unit provided services that "could or should" be located in other units

- a question asking whether there were services in other units that "should be done or located" within this unit

- a question asking whether there were any "practices, policies, procedures, or organizational structures" in the university that the review committee should examine

Dr. Regal acknowledged in his testimony to the labour relations board that at the time the questionnaire was distributed, bargaining unit members were concerned about job loss as a result of restructuring. He acknowledged that restructuring could indeed result in job loss. He also observed that ongoing funding pressures could lead to reduced student enrolment at the university and that decreases in enrolment could also cause further restructuring.

One of the recipients of the questionnaire testified that it was sent out with a cover letter signed by Dr. McMahon. The recipient stated that he had understood that completion of the questionnaire was a work assignment and was not voluntary. The recipient stated that when he had filled out the questionnaire, he had replied to the disputed questions by saying that these matters should be referred to the bargaining agent.

The Union's Position

The union argued that the manner in which the administrative review was conducted prohibited the union from fulfilling its role as representative of the bargaining unit members. It argued that this exclusion, in the eyes of the members, eroded the ability of the union to properly represent the membership.

The union stated that the distribution of the questionnaire initiated a discussion of issues—such as workplace structure and job descriptions—that would be more properly addressed through collective bargaining. Thus, the employer was engaging in direct bargaining with employees, which contravened the relevant labour legislation.

The Employer's Position

The employer argued that its actions in the review process were legitimate information-gathering activities intended to support important long-term decisions. The employer stated that it was acting responsibly by making sure that the information collected "truly reflected" the views of the employees who would be most affected by the restructuring process.

CASE *12-2*

PRINTING TRADES UNION AND GUTENBERG INC.

(Based on *Graphic Communications International Union, Local 500M, and H & S Reliance Limited et al. 1998*)

In this case, a business has gone into receivership and the union representing employees of the business has requested that the labour relations board issue a declaration of successorship declaring the receiver as the successor employer. Although the business has ceased to operate, the union wants the declaration of successorship because it intends to pursue arbitration. It hopes that an arbitrator will rule that the receiver, as the "agent" or legal representative of the business, must make pension contributions for the period during which the receiver operated the business.

Background to the Case

Gutenberg Inc. is a company that produces pre-press materials for a variety of clients. The work done at Gutenberg is taken to a print shop where it is used to create the final printed product. The Printing Trades Union is the certified bargaining agent for all of Gutenberg's employees.

Gutenberg has two general security agreements with a local bank that are secured by the assets of the company. In early 1997, Gutenberg defaulted on the security agreements. On June 16, 1997, the bank appointed a local accounting firm as the receiver and manager of Gutenberg. The accounting firm commenced its duties as receiver on June 17, 1997.

On the day the accounting firm commenced its duties as receiver, its representatives held a meeting at Gutenberg involving employees from two of the three scheduled work shifts. At the meeting, the representatives explained to the employees that the accounting firm was now the receiver and manager of Gutenberg and that the business would be sold as a going concern. The representatives stated that the accounting firm was not a party to the existing collective agreement. The employees were told that they would be paid on a "go forward" basis; that is, salary and vacation pay would only be paid for days worked from that point on and no salary or vacation pay that was currently owing would be paid. The employees were also told that employment was now on a day-to-day basis and that they would be paid at the existing rates in the collective agreement. At a meeting the next day for the employees on the third shift, the same information was communicated.

On June 18, all employees received a letter from the accounting firm confirming the information from the meeting. The letter made it clear that the accounting firm considered that it had no obligations with regard to termination notice or pay and/or severance pay; it also stated that no additional benefits would be provided with respect to employment. The letter asked employees to sign and return a copy of the letter to acknowledge that they recognized and accepted these terms of employment as being different from their terms of employment with Gutenberg. No signed copies of the letter were returned.

On July 4, the accounting firm informed the employees that the company would not be sold as a going concern; the firm instead proceeded to liquidate the company's assets.

The union advised the accounting firm that the general security agreement originally signed by Gutenberg contained a section entitled "Remedies" that indicated that the receiver was considered to be an agent of the debtor and not of the bank holding the agreement. This meant, in the union's opinion, that the accounting firm was liable for all the obligations that Gutenberg had assumed as the employer and co-signer of the collective agreement. The union also noted that a letter sent by the accounting firm to Gutenberg's clients indicated an intention to continue the business with "no interruption in service" and with only the management team changing.

The Employer's Position

As Gutenberg did not make a formal submission to the labour relations board in response to the union's complaint, the accounting firm acted as the respondent to the complaint. The accounting firm argued that it did not have control over either the assets of the business or the employment relationship between the employer and the employees. Control over the assets and the employment relationship, the accounting firm stated, would be expected to be present in a successorship situation. The accounting firm argued that the labour relations board would set a dangerous precedent by naming a receivership firm as a successor employer; in the future, firms would be discouraged from acting as receivers if they thought they might be liable for the employer's former obligations to its employees. The accounting firm accused the union of using labour legislation in an attempt to bypass other claimants in the bankruptcy process.

In its response to the union's argument regarding the application of the "Remedies" section of the general security agreement, the firm stated that being declared an agent of the debtor is not the same as being declared a successor, since the agent only acts on behalf of the debtor and does not formally replace the debtor. The firm also responded to the union's interpretation of the statements made in the firm's letter to Gutenberg's clients upon its appointment as receiver. The firm noted that it had been appointed privately as the agent, rather than through the courts, and that this distinction meant that it was an agent rather than a court-appointed receiver. The firm stated that in the past the board had acknowledged that firms in these different positions had different levels of control over the companies they were appointed to manage and that an agent had less control than a receiver.

The firm also noted that although none of Gutenberg's employees had signed and returned the letter concerning their employment status, the employees had continued working, which was evidence that they accepted the new terms of employment.

The Union's Position

The union stated that it was not trying to bypass other claimants in the bankruptcy proceedings, as the accounting firm claimed, but was instead trying to protect the bargaining rights of the employees it represented. The union affirmed that it was not attempting to make the accounting firm liable for all outstanding obligations of the employer, but only to make it fulfill its obligations to the employees during the period it was the successor employer.

In response to the accounting firm's arguments about the level of control it exercised over Gutenberg after its appointment, the union argued that the accounting firm had effective control over the business, as indicated by the letters to clients and employees. This, in the union's opinion, was the test that should determine whether successorship existed or not, and it was the union's contention that the accounting firm was in effect responsible for Gutenberg's operations, regardless of the formalities associated with how that appointment was made.

The union also argued that the accounting firm was acting as an agent of the bank that held Gutenberg's general security agreement and was not acting as an agent of Gutenberg itself as debtor. The union noted that the "Remedies" section of the agreement described the receiver as "deemed" to be the agent of the debtor. It argued that if the receiver is "deemed" to be the agent, then it is not really the agent. The union also stated that the general security agreement was a commercial law document that should not be accepted for labour relations purposes. However, the union also noted that the general security agreement grants a great deal of authority to the receiver, even to the point of allowing the receiver to refuse the debtor entry to the workplace.

CASE 12-3

CONSTRUCTION WORKERS' UNION AND CHOICE FLOORS

(Based on *Precision Floor & Roof Truss and C.J.A. Local 2004*, 1998)

In this case, some but not all of the parts of one business have been sold to another business. A collective agreement is in effect at the first business, but the second business is not unionized. The union is seeking a declaration of successorship on the basis that the sale creates continuity between the two businesses. The employer argues that there is minimal connection between the two businesses and that there are justifiable reasons for the connections that do exist.

Background to the Case

The Construction Workers' Union was certified as the bargaining agent for the employees of Loren Floors in late 1992. A collective agreement was signed in early 1993, and it expired in early 1995. At that time, George Robin was the owner of Loren. He attempted to sell the entire business in early 1997 but was unsuccessful. Instead, in August 1997, he sold the inventory of Loren to Choice Floors. Some manufacturing equipment still remains in Loren's plant, but Robin claims that the business is no longer operating.

Choice Floors was incorporated in June 1997. The principal of the company named on the incorporation documents is Bill Stein. At the time Choice began operating in August 1997, some staff were transferred from Loren to Choice, and Choice purchased Loren's inventory. Choice is located in a building that previously housed Knox Floors, another company that was operated by Robin. Choice shares the building with EZ Garage Overhead Doors, another business that Robin owns. EZ only has one employee, and this employee can have access to Choice's plant and equipment without having to obtain prior authorization.

Testimony at the board hearing revealed that Knox Floors' plant and equipment had been sold at a tax auction several years previously, after Knox Floors ceased to operate. The purchaser was an individual who had "apparently" had other business dealings with Robin in the past. Choice Floors now leases its space in the building from this purchaser. Robin testified that at the tax auction he purchased some of the equipment that was previously owned by Knox Floors; in other words, he purchased some of the assets of a company that he had owned before the assets were seized for non-payment of taxes. David Rigg, Choice's production manager, testified that when he started work at Choice he assumed the equipment in the plant was the same equipment that had been there when Knox Floors occupied the space.

Other testimony at the hearing indicated that equipment owned by Loren Floors, such as computers, office furnishings, microwaves, saws, and vehicles, was transferred to the building occupied by Choice Floors. Some work in progress was also transferred from Loren's building to Choice's building. However, a significant amount of equipment remains in the Loren Floors plant. Robin told the hearing that he had attempted to sell all of the equipment belonging to EZ Garage Overhead Doors and Loren Floors, but he had been unsuccessful because there were still questions about who actually owned the equipment. Robin testified that he was expected to remove all of Loren Floors' equipment from its location by the end of the year and that he was considering having the equipment put into storage, as there was apparently no other appropriate plant location available. Robin said that one of the officers of Choice Floors had offered to have the equipment stored.

There are 14 plant employees at Choice Floors, 12 of whom were previously employed by Loren Floors. One is Robin's brother. Rigg, the Choice production manager, stated that the company advertised for employees in April 1997, when the creation of the company was being formulated. He testified that the company received a large number of replies to its advertisements, but only a few applicants had the skills required to work in the business. One of the applicants was employed at Loren Floors at the time he submitted his application to Choice. This individual testified to the board that he had submitted his application after seeing the advertisement in April and had heard nothing further from the company until September, when Rigg hired him at Choice Floors. Rigg stated that he had called Robin for references for the applicants who were employed at Loren Floors, and Robin told him that these applicants were probably leaving because they were not getting enough work hours at Loren Floors.

Both Loren and Choice produce floor and roof trusses, and they occasionally produce wall panels if a customer requests them. Most orders are obtained by salespeople who have contacts with dealers and contractors. Representatives of both companies admitted at the hearing that the companies have very similar customer lists, but stated that this is not unusual in an industry where there is a fairly limited customer base. All of the salespeople at Choice were previously employed at Loren; one of them owned shares in Loren, and another was employed at Loren under a government-sponsored training program that continued while he was employed at Choice.

There was some confusion in testimony about the status of Martin Haskell, who is listed as the controller and agent of both Loren Floors and EZ Garage Overhead Doors. Robin stated that Haskell works for him. Rigg, however, stated that Haskell works for Choice, organizing payroll and doing the company accounting. Rigg also claimed that Haskell has an office at Choice and regularly reports to that office.

The Union's Position

The union argued that there is sufficient continuity between Loren Floors and Choice Floors to establish successorship, even if both companies still exist and there was no complete transfer of assets between the two companies. The union pointed to evidence of continuity such as the shared customer lists, the number of employees who had worked at both companies without a significant break in employment in between, and the connection between the physical locations and equipment of the two businesses.

The union also pointed out other evidence connecting Loren Floors to Choice Floors. When work in progress was transferred from Loren to Choice, the work was completed without any notification to customers of the change in the companies carrying out the work. There was no advertising to indicate that Loren would no longer be operating. Loren's phone line was call-forwarded to Choice's line. Choice buys some raw materials using an account with a major supplier that was originally opened by Loren, but Choice repays Loren for any charges made to the account. Choice also uses Loren's corporate credit card for gas purchases.

The union also produced business cards used by Robin that identify him as chief executive officer of "Choice-Loren Floor and Roof Truss."

The Employer's Position

Robin pointed out that Loren and Choice still have separate physical plants and that he still owns a significant portion of Loren's equipment. He also noted that the power supply and phone lines at the Loren plant have not been cancelled. He stated that the location of the manufacturing plant is not important because instead of having customers come to the plant to examine or purchase the goods, the business delivers most of the finished products to the customers.

In response to the evidence produced by the union concerning Robin's business cards, Robin stated that he had had the cards made up for a promotional trip to Germany during which he would promote both companies in the international export market. He said that the cards had been created with the approval of Mr. Stein, the owner of Choice named on the incorporation documents.

Robin also countered the evidence presented by the union indicating that Choice used Loren's accounts and gas credit cards. He stated that he had authorized such usage as a way to assist a new company that had not yet established its own credit.

References

[1] These criteria were originally established in *Expert Floors* (British Columbia Labour Relations Board, Case No. B279/93) and were restated in *Cineplex Odeon & Bollywood Cinemas* (British Columbia Labour Relations Board, Case No. B490/00).

[2] Ontario Labour Relations Board (2000). *A guide to the Labour Relations Act, 1995, and other statutes administered by the Ontario Labour Relations Board.* Toronto, ON: Ontario Labour Relations Board.

[3] Craig, A.W.J., & Solomon, N. (1996). *The system of industrial relations in Canada* (4th edition). Scarborough, ON: Prentice-Hall, 149.

[4] Godard, J. (1996). *Industrial relations: the economy and society.* Toronto, ON: McGraw-Hill Ryerson.

[5] *Certain employees of R.C. Purdy Chocolates Ltd. and Communications, Energy and Paperworkers Union of Canada, Local 2000.* British Columbia Labour Relations Board, Case No. B376/2001; decision issued October 15, 2001.

[6] *Federated Co-operative Ltd., Saskatoon, and R.W.D.S.U., Locals 539 & 540.* Saskatchewan Labour Relations Board, file no. 256–88; decision issued July 14, 1989.

[7] For example, *R.P. Scherer Canada Inc. and CAW-Canada and Local 195.* Ontario Labour Relations Board, Case No. 3825–97–R; decision issued September 17, 1998.

[8] Peirce, J. (1987). Collective bargaining over technological change in Canada: a quantitative and historical analysis. Ottawa, ON: Economic Council of Canada, Discussion Paper No. 338.

[9] Peirce, *op. cit.*; Giles, A., & Starkman, A. (1995). The collective agreement. In Gunderson, M., & Ponak, A. (Eds.), *Union-management relations in Canada* (3rd edition). Toronto, ON: Addison Wesley Longman.

[10] Giles, A., & Starkman, A. (2000). The collective agreement. In Gunderson, M., Ponak, A., & Taras, D.G. (Eds.), *Union-management relations in Canada* (4th edition). Toronto, ON: Addison Wesley Longman.

[11] Godard, *op. cit.*

12 *Canadian Union of Public Employees, Broadcast Division, and Canadian Broadcasting Corporation*. Canada Labour Relations Board, file no. 745–4575, decision no. 1102; decision issued December 23, 1994.

13 *United Food and Commercial Workers International Union, Local 175, v. Canadian Waste Services Inc*. Ontario Labour Arbitration, Case Nos. A/Y001600, A/Y001601, A/Y001602; decision issued October 28, 2000.

14 Frost, A.C. (2000). Explaining variation in workplace restructuring: the role of local union capabilities. *Industrial & Labor Relations Review*, 53(4), 559–578.

15 Kainer, J. (1998). Gender, corporate restructuring, and concession bargaining in Ontario's retail food sector. *Relations Industrielles/Industrial Relations*, 53(1), 183–205.

Workload a major issue survey finds:

Finding ways to ease pressures on the job is becoming a high priority for unions

TORONTO—Workload is emerging as a key collective bargaining issue as time-squeezed employees demand their unions do something to ease the pressure.

A poll by Ottawa-based Ekos Research Associates Inc. found that 71 percent of unionized workers want organized labour to give high priority to workload issues and work-family balance.

Suggested remedies, the polling company said, include: more negotiated paid time off; more family-friendly work schedules; caps on workload; child and elder care assistance; greater pay to reflect heavier job responsibilities; and more vigorous resistance to workplace "speedup."

The poll, commissioned by the Canadian Union of Public Employees, found that full-time employees, on average, are putting in an extra 5.5 hours a week on top of their regularly scheduled hours. Ekos surveyed 1,213 private- and public-sector employees in early January.

Half of those surveyed acknowledged that their employers have tried to address workload concerns by introducing better tools, technology and training, increasing staff levels, organizing work more efficiently, and establishing more flexible work arrangements. But burnout can occur even within the standard 40-hour week as employees strain to

pick up the slack after a decade of downsizing, CUPE president Judy Darcy said in an interview.

For CUPE, Canada's largest union with 485,000 members, workload has emerged "as the number 1 issue," Darcy said. It is landing on the bargaining table in the private sector.

As CUPE prepared to release its poll findings, the Saskatchewan Federation of Labour was wrapping up a three-day "Get a Life Conference" in Saskatoon, co-sponsored by Status of Women Canada. Participants discussed strategies to continue to push for shorter work weeks, paid family and parental leaves, alternate work arrangements such as job sharing and flextime, and an end to overtime.

Unions have had mixed success in winning contract language to help employees balance work and family obligations, Saskatchewan Federation of Labour researcher Cara Banks said in a policy paper. "Lack of money in the public sector, most evidently in health care, has made it very difficult to make gains…. In the private sector, layoffs and skeleton staffing are often more pressing problems." Flextime has successfully been negotiated for office workers, Banks wrote, but "a good deal of skepticism exists around how flextime could be implemented in other sectors, particularly where operations run on a 24-hour clock."

Darcy said balancing work and family life is the dominant theme in the current round of negotiations for 12,000 Saskatchewan health-care workers, and "case load" was the issue that drove 250 employees of the Catholic Children's Aid Society of Toronto to strike for six and a half weeks last summer.

(Globe and Mail, February 8, 2001)

FUTURE ISSUES FOR WORKERS, WORK ARRANGEMENTS, ORGANIZATIONS, AND THE INDUSTRIAL RELATIONS SYSTEM

objectives

In the last few decades, there have been significant changes in the Canadian workplace. The demographics of the workforce have altered, along with changes in work arrangements and organizational structures. These changes have posed considerable challenges for unions, forcing them to redefine their relevance in this new reality. In this chapter, we will describe some of the ways in which Canadian unions are adapting to the changing workplace. We will also discuss some of the environmental factors that may affect Canadian industrial relations in the future. By the end of this chapter, you should be able to:

- describe the demographic changes occurring in the Canadian workplace

- identify some of the union strategies that address demographic change

- understand the different forms of work arrangements

- explain how unions have responded to new work arrangements

- discuss new forms of organizational structure

- identify factors that may influence Canadian industrial relations in the future

INTRODUCTION

As we have seen in previous chapters, the period of the greatest growth in Canadian union membership occurred in the mid-1960s, mostly as a result of organizing in the public sector. Since then, the Canadian workplace and workforce have both changed significantly. Employment in traditionally strong areas of the workforce, such as the public sector and primary industries, has stabilized or shrunk, and employment has grown in the private sector and in service industries. New types of workers and new forms of work arrangements have also emerged.

These changes have posed challenges to the survival and vitality of Canadian unions. Many unions were originally structured to function as employee representatives in industries or occupations with a relatively stable workforce and traditional hierarchical relationships between workers and management. Unions are now facing the necessity of having to adapt to new realities of work and proving their relevance to a new generation of workers in a variety of workplaces.

Both unions and employers must also consider factors that will affect the Canadian industrial relations system in the future. Declining union membership in the United States has raised the question of whether a similar trend will occur in Canada. The Canadian union movement has a stable, but not expanding, membership and is not immediately threatened by the same decline that has occurred in the United States. However, other factors, such as legislative changes and new organizing strategies, will perhaps determine whether Canadian union membership stays the same, grows, or follows the same path as American union membership.

In this chapter, we will describe some of the issues that unions face in adapting to a changing workforce, a changing work environment, and changing types of work. We will outline the challenges related to these changes and then describe specific initiatives that Canadian unions are undertaking to address these challenges. We will conclude the chapter by discussing what the future may hold for industrial relations in Canada.

CHANGES IN WORKFORCE DEMOGRAPHICS

The composition of the Canadian workforce is changing in many ways. There is a wider age range among workers than in the past, since more young people are entering the workforce and older workers are not retiring as early as in previous decades. There are more women in the workforce, owing to fewer barriers to women working outside the home and the frequent need for a family to have two incomes if a certain standard of living is to be maintained. And there is also more ethnic and racial diversity in the work-force because of changing trends in Canadian immigration and stronger legislative pro-hibitions against discrimination in hiring. Each of these trends poses a different chal-lenge to unions.

Young Workers

Approximately 2 million Canadians aged 15–24 hold some sort of paid job.[1] Nearly 1.2 million workers in this age group hold full-time employment, while about 950,000 hold part-time jobs. Part-time employment is more prevalent among this age group than among any other age group in the Canadian workforce.[2]

There are varied opinions on whether the dominance of part-time work among young workers is beneficial or not. Some researchers argue that the high incidence of part-time jobs among workers in this age group is not a problem, since many attend high school or university and part-time work is the only option available to them because of these other commitments.[3] Others, however, contend that we gain a more accurate picture of youth employment by examining the category of **non-standard work**, which includes—in addition to part-time work—temporary work, multiple job-holding, and self-employment.[4] Sixty-one percent of workers aged 15–24 fall into this broader category of employment, and the predominance of work of this kind among young people may be a concern because of the non-permanence and insecurity of the employment relationship.

These conflicting perspectives on youth employment, although differing in their analysis, both acknowledge that younger workers' jobs are concentrated in the more unstable segments of the labour market. In the past, this concentration was not seen as a concern, because it was assumed that younger workers would gain their initial work experience in the unstable, lower-paying parts of the labour market and then move into more permanent and stable employment with higher pay. However, it appears that younger workers are not, as expected, finding permanent and better-paying work as they gain experience. Young workers continue to be concentrated in lower-paying occupations such as retail sales, service work, and clerical jobs.[5] This is partly because employment in these segments of the labour market has grown, while employment in more stable segments, such as primary industry, has declined,[6] but also because part-time work is more common in these segments.

Twelve-point-six percent of workers between the ages of 15 and 24 belong to a union, a significantly lower percentage than for any other age group in the Canadian workforce. By contrast, 30.7 percent of workers aged 25–44 are union members; 42.1 percent of workers aged 45–54 are union members; and 33.9 percent of workers aged 55 and older are unionized.[7] Several characteristics of younger workers' employment make union organizing among this age group particularly challenging. Historically, the types of work and work arrangements most prevalent among young workers have not been conducive to successful organizing. There is a high turnover rate in the occupations and sectors where young workers are commonly employed. Thus, workers who promote unionization may suddenly leave the workplace to pursue other opportunities, and once they are no longer present, support for a union among the remaining workers may quickly dissipate.

Furthermore, workers in these occupations and sectors tend to be more vulnerable to employer retaliation against organizing attempts. Because the level of skill in many jobs in the service and retail sectors is relatively low, workers can easily be replaced; the knowledge that they are easily replaceable can increase workers' fear of employer retaliation against pro-union members. If employers can change workers with little disruption to the workplace or to productivity, they may be tempted to resist unionization by firing or reassigning union supporters—even though such actions are illegal.

Moreover, employers in the industries employing non-standard workers traditionally display higher resistance to unionization than employers in industries where more stable employment relationships are the norm. Employers in retail and service industries generally operate with small profit margins in highly price-sensitive markets. They may therefore resist unionization because of their perception that union demands for higher wages would lead to reduced profits.

Organizing campaigns targeting young workers must also confront the reality that young workers are often unfamiliar with unions or have an unfavourable perception of them. A survey of young workers conducted by the Australian Council of Trade Unions indicated that young people are generally not aware of unions, that the information they do have tends to be negative, and that they do not see unions as being useful in helping them enter or stay in the workforce.[8] The results of this survey also showed that while young workers felt that unions protected workers in general from exploitation, they themselves did not see any personal value in union membership. The attitudes of parents toward unions has also been shown to influence their children's attitudes significantly; if parents express negative attitudes toward unions it is likely that their children will express similar attitudes.[9] Other research has suggested that negative images of unions in popular culture—for example, movies showing union corruption or connections between unions and organized crime—may also support young people's negative attitudes toward unions.[10]

However, the problems associated with unionizing young workers cannot always be attributed to the actions or opinions of workers or their employers. There can also be opposition within the union movement to organizing the industries or sectors where young workers are usually employed. Some unions oppose the organization of part-time and temporary workers because of the perceived threat these forms of work pose to the job security of the full-time workers who dominate union membership. Unions supporting this position argue that organizing part-time and temporary workers (and thus giving them the same protection under the collective agreement as full-time workers) encourages employers to create part-time or temporary jobs rather than full-time permanent jobs. Thus, the argument proceeds, organizing part-time and temporary workers indirectly promotes work arrangements that counteract unions' goals of improving employment security and working conditions. Unions may also be reluctant to organize in less stable parts of the labour market because of the cost of potentially challenging and lengthy organizing campaigns. They may not anticipate a sufficient financial benefit from entering sectors of the labour market that are historically difficult to organize—

particularly if there is a perception that an organizing campaign has a low chance of success—and they may prefer to concentrate their efforts and resources in areas where organizing campaigns are more likely to succeed.

Female Workers

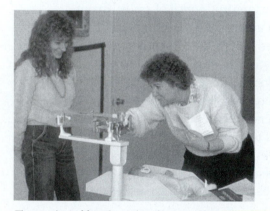

The number of female workers has steadily increased in the past few decades, creating new challenges and opportunities as unions respond to their needs.

The current size of the Canadian workforce is over 12 million workers, and nearly 6 million of those workers are female.[11] The number of Canadian women in the workforce has increased steadily over the past few decades, rising from 37.1 percent of the total workforce in 1976 to 45.9 percent in 1999.[12] The majority of Canadian women who work outside the home work in full-time jobs, although the proportion of part-time to full-time workers is higher for women than for men.[13] The number of women in managerial and professional jobs is steadily increasing, but the majority of women still work in occupations that are traditionally regarded as female, such as clerical and administrative jobs, nursing, and teaching.[14]

As the number of women in the Canadian workforce has risen, so has the number of Canadian women who belong to unions. This number has risen to a point where both the percentage (women as a percentage of total union membership) and density (female union members as a percentage of all working women) are comparable to those of male workers. This increase has been attributed both to the larger numbers of women in the workforce and to the unionization of the Canadian public sector, which has a large number of female workers.[15] In 2000, the most recent year for which data is available, union density for female workers was 29.6 percent, while density for male workers was 31.1 percent.[16] It should be noted, however, that density patterns change somewhat when union membership totals are subdivided into public and private sector segments. Approximately 60 percent of public sector union members are female, while only 22 percent of private sector union members are women.[17]

The relatively comparable levels of female and male representation in unions is not an indication that unions have been targeting female workers as a source of membership. A recent study analysed union organizing attempts in Ontario from 1985 to 1999 to determine whether the gender of workers made a difference in the success of an organizing campaign (i.e., whether gender had a bearing on whether certification was achieved or not).[18] Female-dominated workplaces (defined either as those with a simple majority of female workers or as workplaces where more than 60 percent of the workforce was female) were much more likely to vote in favour of certification than male-dominated workplaces, but 62 percent of the organizing attempts counted in the study were conducted in male-dominated workplaces (36 percent were conducted in workplaces with no female employees at all). Only 38 percent took place in female-dominated workplaces, where women constituted between 51 percent and 80 percent of the workforce.

The results of this analysis suggest that while female workers may be more likely than male workers to support unionization, unions may not always recognize this tendency when they seek to identify workplaces suitable for organizing campaigns. The author of the study attributes this oversight to unions' "internal inertia": that is, unions have focused more on consolidation than on expansion, and union members may fear that there will be a reduction in existing services if resources are diverted into organizing or addressing diverse populations.[19]

Unions' ability to represent their female members effectively has also been hampered by the frequent inability or unwillingness of female workers to participate in union activities. Because many female workers have commitments outside of work such as family, they tend to have less time than male workers for non-work activities like union participation. Studies examining gender differences in union participation have indicated that while men and women may not differ significantly in their attitudinal commitment to their union, men are more likely to participate in union activities (e.g., they are more likely to serve as elected officers and attend membership meetings).[20] This gender imbalance in union participation, even when men and women are equally represented in a union's membership, may mean that issues of concern to female union members, such as wage disparities between female- and male-dominated occupations, are not adequately addressed. If there are not enough women actively involved in the union to advocate for these issues, the importance of the issues may not be recognized (this point was made in our discussion in chapters 7 and 8 about how issues for collective bargaining are identified and prioritized). It has also been argued that gender imbalances in union participation may result in some "traditional" union goals being mistakenly conceptualized as gender-neutral since there are not enough "non-traditional" participants to point out instances when traditional goals do not serve diverse populations. Such misconceptions about the neutrality or universality of some issues may lead to women's issues being marginalized as "special interest" issues and consequently not being given a high priority.[21]

One further challenge that unions face in organizing and representing women is that women enter and leave the labour force or change their employment status more often than men do. This is primarily due to women having the primary responsibility for childcare and domestic duties in most Canadian households. Women leave the workforce to care for children more often than men do (although 93 percent of Canadian women who take maternity leave return to employment within two years of the birth of their child).[22] Furthermore, more women than men engage in temporary work, part-time work, self-employment, or multiple jobs as ways of balancing family responsibilities with work commitments, and 41 percent of Canadian women, as opposed to 29 percent of Canadian men, are involved in non-standard work arrangements.[23] It is difficult for unions to organize women workers, or to represent them effectively, when women's patterns of participation in the workforce are not consistent and linear over time.

Older Workers

For the past decade, over 90 percent of Canadian men and over 70 percent of Canadian women held paid employment outside the home by the time they have reached the age of 25.[24] However, it is surprising to see how many older workers continue to participate in the labour force beyond the standard ages for retirement. In 2000, the **participation rate** (the percentage of individuals in a given demographic group who hold paid employment outside the home) for men aged 55–59 was 72.9 percent; for men aged 60–64, the rate was 46.1 percent; for men aged 65–69, the rate was 16.1 percent; and for men aged 70 and older, the rate was 6.1 percent. For women, the participation rates for the same age groups were 53.4 percent, 27.2 percent, 7.3 percent, and 1.8 percent respectively.[25]

These numbers indicate that, echoing the gender-based patterns found in younger age groups, there are fewer older female workers than older male workers. But we should also be aware that the participation rate for older female workers, with the exception of the 70-

plus age group, has been increasing over the past 10 years, while the participation rate for older male workers has been decreasing. The largest increases in labour force participation for older female workers have occurred in the 50–54 and 55–59 age groups.[26]

Several different reasons have been cited for the changes in participation rates among older Canadian workers. The median age of retirement for both men and women has declined since the 1970s, partly owing to changes in pension administration that allowed individuals to begin drawing federal pensions at younger ages. In addition, many organizations started using early retirement as a means of downsizing their work-forces, and the recession of the 1980s caused a general reduction in employment oppor-tunities, which affected older workers as much as younger ones.[27]

However, there also exist trends that have encouraged older workers to stay in the workforce. As a result of Canada's system of social security programs, many jobs offer ben-efits—subsidized medical and dental care, for example—that would be very expensive on an individual basis. Older workers may be tempted to stay in the workforce longer to take advantage of employer support for these benefits. Researchers have also speculated that women just entering the older age groups will stay in the workforce longer than their pred-ecessors because they have a greater commitment and attachment to work outside the home.[28] Older workers are also staying in the workforce in part-time work and in self-employment; the percentage of older workers in these types of work rises steadily as the age of the workers increase. It has been suggested that workers choose these forms of employment as a means of delaying retirement—that is, as an alternative to simply leav-ing the workforce when full-time work is no longer appealing or feasible.[29]

Just as we saw in the data presented in the discussion of younger workers, union-ization rates for older workers aged 55 and up are comparable to the overall average rate of unionization in the Canadian workforce. Therefore, Canadian unions have not felt the need to increase unionization among older workers. It is also possible that unions pre-fer to direct their organizing efforts toward workers who have most of their working lives (and potential union membership) before them, rather than trying to attract work-ers who are closer to departing from the workforce. However, if older workers are a minority within a union, they may have difficulty promoting their issues, just as any other minority group would. Older workers may have trouble demonstrating the bene-fits of "their" issues to younger workers. For example, in Canada, workers between the ages of 45 and 54 are the ones most likely to contribute to registered retirement savings plans (RRSPs).[30] RRSPs can be opened as soon as a worker enters the workforce, and many financial planners recommend that workers start RRSPs as soon as possible so that they can build up enough funds to support a decent lifestyle after retirement. Thus, RRSPs can benefit younger workers as much as they do older workers, and may even benefit them more, since younger workers have a longer earning period during which to make RRSP contributions. However, older workers who want their union to negotiate for contract terms such as employer contributions to RRSPs may have trouble achieving this goal if younger workers dominate the union. Younger union members may not see the value in having employer-supported retirement benefits, since retirement security is not as immediately important for the younger worker.

Ethnic and Racial Diversity in the Workforce

Another major change in the Canadian workforce has been an increase in the number of workers belonging to visible minority groups. The Canadian census defines visible minority groups as Blacks, Chinese, Filipinos, Japanese, Koreans, Latin Americans, Pacific Islanders (other than white Australians, white New Zealanders, and white Hawaiians), South Asians, South East Asians, West Asians, and Arabs.[31] About 10 percent of the Canadian population over the age of 15 can be classified as belonging to one of these groups, and it is projected that this percentage will increase to nearly 20 percent by 2006.[32] Approximately 53 percent of visible minority women and 65 percent of visible minority men hold paid employment. These rates are slightly lower than the participation rates for non-minority women and men, which are 63 percent and 74 percent respectively.[33] However, the occupational patterns for visible minority men and women are very similar to those of non-minority men and women, with women most often employed in administrative, clerical, sales, or service work and men in managerial or professional work.

It is interesting to note, however, that more visible minority than non-minority women work in jobs involving manual labour, and that more visible minority than non-minority men work in sales and service jobs.[34] Employment data also show that adults who belong to a visible minority are more likely to have university degrees than adults who do not belong to a visible minority, but visible minority members with university degrees "are not as likely as others with the same level of education to be employed in the higher-paying professional or managerial occupations."[35] This mismatch between education level and occupational level is referred to as **underemployment**.

The increase in ethnic and racial diversity in the Canadian workforce can be attributed to several interrelated causes. One is higher rates of immigration to Canada, especially among members of visible minorities. Since the mid-1980s, immigration has been the largest source of growth in the Canadian population.[36] The patterns of immigration to Canada have also changed. The number of immigrants from Western Europe, the United Kingdom, and the United States, formerly the major sources of immigration to Canada, has dropped since the late 1960s. The majority of immigrants to Canada now come from Asia, the Middle East, Eastern Europe, and Central and South America.[37] Obviously, many of these immigrants belong to the visible minority groups identified in the Canadian census.

Another reason for increased workforce diversity in Canada is legislation such as federal and provincial employment equity laws. Most of these laws identify demographic groups that have historically been under-represented in employment in relation to the proportion they make up of the population as a whole. The federal *Employment Equity Act* identifies four of these groups: women, visible minorities, First Nations people, and people with disabilities. Employment equity law encourages organizations to develop plans to increase representation of these groups in the workforce to match their representation in the population or workforce. For example, if women make up 40 percent of the labour force in a particular region, employers should strive to have a workforce that is 40 percent female. There are many debates over whether these laws are effective or whether they cause **reverse discrimination**, where individuals not belonging to designated groups are unjustly excluded from hiring or promotion opportunities. Assessing these arguments is beyond the scope of this discussion, but we will simply note that the presence of employment equity law may encourage employers to consider members of visible minorities for employment opportunities in situations where these individuals might otherwise be ignored.

Statistics Canada currently does not collect data on union membership or density among workers who belong to visible minorities, so it is difficult to estimate how extensive union membership is among visible minorities. However, it is not unreasonable to assume that problems of racial and ethnic inclusion in unions would be similar to the previously identified problems regarding the inclusion of working women. Members of racial or ethnic minorities may not be willing or able to be active participants in union governance, or they may be actively discouraged from doing so. Exclusion may result from intentional discrimination (e.g., individuals may not be informed of meeting times and places) or from less explicit forms of discrimination (e.g., individuals may lack the linguistic or cultural skills to participate in union activities successfully). Either form of discrimination can lead to the neglect of concerns to visible minorities. We should also note that members of visible minorities in Canada are more likely than non-minority workers to be employed in occupations that have traditionally been difficult to organize, for the reasons discussed earlier.

An additional concern in unionizing members of visible minorities is that immigrants may come from cultures or countries where unions are perceived as corrupt or as an unwarranted challenge to management's right to manage. In some countries or cultures, moreover, union members are the target of violence because of unions' social activism or opposition to the government. Individuals with these sorts of attitudes or experiences may not wish to support unions in Canada, even though the union experience in this country is considerably different.

UNION STRATEGIES FOR DEALING WITH THE CHANGING WORKFORCE

It is generally acknowledged that if unions are to survive and provide effective representation for their membership, some of the characteristics of traditional unionism, including those based on the assumption that workers are "masculine, white, heterosexual, [and] full-time," need to change.[38] As one writer notes, "As [unions'] traditional manufacturing base wanes, they are being forced to look elsewhere for membership."[39] To achieve this membership expansion, unions need to recognize the characteristics of diverse sectors of the labour market and develop strategies to address those characteristics or to promote the value of unions in addressing the problems experienced by workers in those sectors.

Some Canadian researchers have attempted to determine whether unions are actually attempting to attract a wider range of potential members, and if so, whether those unions undertaking such attempts are attaining their desired outcomes. The results of these studies are mixed. On the positive side, most national unions in Canada now have policy statements on issues like workplace equality, affirmative action, harassment, and violence.[40] The fact that these statements exist shows, at least at a strategic level, that these issues are acknowledged as being important to a diverse workforce and are worthy of attention. However, policy statements at the national level do not always translate into action at the local level. There appears to be "entrenched resistance" at some local levels either to adopting these policies or to taking such actions as creating bargaining initiatives that address the concerns of diverse segments of the union membership.[41] This resistance is attributed to lack of support from elected union officials, to the influence of individuals with attitudes or values that contradict the policies, to insufficient resources to support every single issue that is presented, and to inadequate education on the issues and on the reasoning behind them.

Some unions have gone beyond simply formulating policy statements and have undertaken more substantive actions to address increased workforce diversity and to make unions more relevant to diverse groups of workers. For example, the Canadian Union of Public Employees (CUPE) has created two "diversity vice-president" positions on its national executive. One of these vice-presidents represents First Nations workers and the other represents workers from ethnic or racial minorities. The existence of these positions ensures the formal presence on the national union executive of members of demographic groups that otherwise might not be represented. CUPE has also attempted to increase the visibility of traditionally marginalized groups of union members, sponsoring a national conference for gay, lesbian, and bisexual union members, for example, and conducting a publicity campaign to raise the visibility of this segment of its membership.

Union activities targeting young workers are somewhat less prevalent. Some researchers have suggested that the lack of interest in unionization among younger workers may not be a problem. Issues traditionally addressed by unionization, such as long-term employment and economic security, are more important to older workers than to high school students who are only working part time, and unionization likely becomes more important to young workers as they move into more substantive and permanent employment.[42] However, some Canadian unions have taken the position that young workers can benefit from unions even when they are starting their careers in non-permanent positions. Also, young workers are the potential union supporters of the future, so some unions anticipate long-term benefits from recruiting or educating young workers.

The Canadian Labour Congress has attempted to reach young workers by adding a "YouthNet" section to its website.[43] "YouthNet" offers information on unions, presenting

CLC President Bob White welcomes Craig Kielburger and Asmita Satyarthi to the CLC convention in 1996, highlighting the CLC's focus on young workers' concerns.

them as a solution to the problems experienced by young workers and providing hints for conducting successful organizing campaigns. This strategy is particularly appropriate with respect to young workers because it recognizes the importance of the Internet as a source of information for young people (as opposed to older people who may be less comfortable using computers). The dissemination of information through websites rather than through more traditional means of contact, such as telephone calls, printed literature, or workplace visits, also allows young workers to investigate unionization without the fear of employer discovery and possible retaliation. The Confédération des syndicats nationaux (Quebec Federation of Labour) has embarked on a similar venture by creating a Youth Committee and having a separate section for this committee on its website.[44]

Other unions have initiated education programs for young people as a means of reaching potential young union members. The North Okanagan Labour Council in British Columbia has developed a course called "Job Smart." Presented by union members in local schools, Job Smart teaches young adults about employment and labour law and gives them information about their rights and responsibilities in the workplace.[45]

As most of these initiatives are relatively recent, their long-term success remains to be determined. They do, however, follow the direction taken by the successful organizing strategies identified in the previously cited study of union organizing in Ontario.[46] This study indicated that at least some unions were recognizing the changes in the labour market by concentrating their organizing efforts on growing rather than declining employment sectors. In the 1980s, approximately 17 percent of certification applications in Ontario were for private sector employers, but by the mid-1990s, this figure had risen to 48 percent, indicating that unions were acknowledging increased employment activity in this sector and adjusting their organizing efforts accordingly.

Internal problems in union administration can sometimes inhibit organizing activity, however. Declining union membership results in reduced revenues from membership dues, and that reduced revenue has, in some cases, led to union staff cutbacks and difficulties with burnout among remaining staff.[47] Such a situation may then result in fewer union resources to support organizing, potentially leading to a downward spiral, as reduced organizing results in fewer new members and even less financial support for further organizing efforts.

It should be noted that the most successful organizing campaigns do not rely only on the participation of paid union staff. One of the most effective organizing tactics is the technique of "salting"—using workers already employed in the potential bargaining unit as the "inside" primary organizers, rather than having a paid union staffer direct the organizing campaign externally. Salting is especially effective in workplaces with diverse groups of workers because inside organizers will, or should be, aware of the particular issues and problems facing different types of workers. The union and the organizers can then conduct an organizing campaign that addresses concerns specific to the workplace and the workers. Moreover, the message of unionization may have more impact coming from a co-worker than from an external and possibly less credible source. The salting technique has been used in organizing campaigns for taxi drivers[48] and fast food workers.[49]

Having described the changes in the composition of the Canadian workforce and their implications for unions, we will now turn our attention to changes in the workplace itself, beginning with changes in work arrangements.

CHANGING WORK ARRANGEMENTS

Unionism first evolved, as outlined in Chapter 2, according to an "industrial" model, which means that unions were developed in workplaces where workers attended work regularly and worked shifts determined by the employer. Partly because of advances in technology that allow more flexibility in how work is carried out and partly through the recognition that not all workers work efficiently or productively in rigidly structured settings, many workplaces have moved away from the industrial model and are exploring alternative ways of structuring work. While these new work arrangements may offer advantages to workers and employers, they have also posed challenges for unions, which now have to develop new ways to organize and represent workers employed in these new work arrangements

Scheduling

Alternate forms of work scheduling include **flextime** (workers are allowed to partially or completely determine their own work hours), **compressed workweeks** (workers are allowed to work longer shifts in exchange for more days off), and **job sharing** (two employees share one full-time job). Work arrangements like these are becoming more common in organizations where job tasks can accommodate this sort of flexibility. A 1997 survey of 345 Canadian organizations indicated that over 50 percent of the organizations surveyed offered at least one of these forms of work scheduling.[50] Employees tend to favour flexible scheduling because it allows them to adjust their work arrangements to accommodate non-work commitments such as child care or education. However, there are concerns that the option of flexible work arrangements might give the employer the power to impose work hours that meet the employer's rather then the employees' needs. Flexible work arrangements may also lead to a lack of clarity about work expectations, which can then cause conflict between employers and employees.

Unions attempting to organize workers on flexible work schedules are often challenged by very practical matters, such as how they contact an employee whose hours or days of work are continually changing. Most labour codes specify that organizing campaigns must be conducted outside working hours, but determining when working hours start and end can be problematic when flexible work arrangements are in place. Organizers run the risk of contacting employees during working hours and of thus committing an unfair labour practice. Unions may also have a hard time making a case for their usefulness if the employer has already responded to worker needs for flexibility without being motivated by the pressure of a union. However, as the newspaper story that opened this chapter indicates, employees may perceive that unions will help them achieve a lighter workload in situations where the availability of flexible work arrangements is not considered a sufficient recompense for excessive workloads or overtime.

Telecommuting

Another type of flexible work arrangement is **telecommuting**. An employee in this arrangement works partially or fully at home and communicates with the workplace through computers, faxes, and telephones. Like flexible work schedules, telecommuting allows the employee some degree of freedom in determining how and when the work will be done. In telecommuting arrangements, the employer usually specifies the nature of the work and the time by which it must be completed and lets the employee determine how these conditions will be met.

Despite the advantages that telecommuting offers, concerns have been voiced about it and other forms of flexible work that parallel some of the original reasons for unionization: namely, the arrangements allow for the possibility of abuse or exploitation by the employer. In telecommuting, for example, workers may find that the cost of upgrading their computer equipment or remodelling a work space at home exceeds any savings they realize by not working outside the home. In addition, telecommuters may have anticipated that they could both work at home and meet other commitments, such as care for their children, but instead find that they are working extended or unreasonable hours to meet the demands of both employer and family.

Telecommuting arrangements are challenges for unions because these arrangements contradict one of the most basic implicit assumptions in labour and employment standards legislation: namely that employees work at a centralized workplace where the employer dictates the conditions and content

Contract workers and telecommuters provide another challenge for union organizers who seek to provide a collective voice for a decentralized workforce.

of work. If employees are not working at the employer's workplace, and their communication with the workplace is solely through a supervisor or other manager and not through peers or co-workers, such basic union organizing activities as distributing information to potential union members suddenly becomes very difficult. And, as with workers in other forms of flexible work arrangements, selling the benefits of union membership to telecommuters may be difficult, since the employer has already permitted non-traditional work arrangements without having been pressured to do so by a union.

Different Employment Relationships

Unlike the traditional employment relationship, some alternative work arrangements do not presume an ongoing connection between the employer and the employee, or assume that an employee will pursue the same occupation or progress within the same industry throughout his or her working life. Frequent changes in employment used to be considered a sign of a worker's instability or unwillingness to commit to serious employment. Now workers may have multiple employers, multiple occupations, or even multiple careers during their lifetime.[51]

One major change in the workplace is the increasing availability of **non-permanent employment relationships** such as contract, term, or temporary work. Employment relationships such as these are no longer seen as inferior or supplemental to full-time permanent work. In fact, some career theorists have suggested that future career patterns will resemble the career patterns that already exist in industries such as filmmaking. In these industries, employees engage in temporary work arrangements for a series of employers; they focus on developing a range of different skills through their varied experiences rather than on having a permanent employment relationship as their ultimate goal.[52]

Non-permanent employment relationships may allow greater opportunities for workers to gain a variety of skills and to change occupations or employers to match their own interests. However, the downside of these non-permanent relationships is that they offer employers more extensive power to terminate workers, sometimes for unjustified reasons, because there is no expectation of an ongoing relationship between employer and employee. Employers may also engage in such employment practices as continually renewing a temporary contract with the same employee. These practices give the employer the productivity equivalent of full-time employment but do not give the employee the benefits usually associated with a permanent job.

UNION RESPONSES TO CHANGING WORK ARRANGEMENTS

Some of Canada's largest unions, such as the Canadian Auto Workers (CAW) and the United Steelworkers of America, have addressed changing work arrangements by negotiating collective agreements that validate these arrangements but establish rules to regulate their use. To guard against employer exploitation, unions have often insisted that their acceptance of these arrangements be tied to the adoption of other conditions. For example, one CAW agreement accepted a reduction in work hours only if the employer promised a reduction in overtime and the retention of jobs that were targeted for elimination. However, one recent survey of Canadian collective agreements found that 70 percent of those analysed contained no provisions for flexible work arrangements.[53] This rather significant omission suggests either that many Canadian unions do not yet perceive flexible work arrangements as a bargaining priority or that employers are not willing to negotiate the control or regulation of these arrangements.

The relatively low level of unionization in the types of organizations where telecommuting is often found—high-tech companies, for example—suggests that Canadian unions and legislators have not yet developed the means to facilitate effective union representation in non-traditional forms of work. Most Canadian collective agreements contain language restricting the excessive use of overtime or reliance on temporary workers, but beyond those basic provisions they do not contain language relating to non-permanent work, even in those industries where such work is the norm rather than the exception.

An example of collective agreements that actively address issues related to non-traditional forms of work can be found in the British Columbia film industry. Unions representing workers in this industry have negotiated contract terms that attempt to balance flexibility in employment and alternative employment relationships with protection of their members' working conditions. One provision in these contracts allows members to accept wage and benefit reductions when working on productions that offer opportunities for skill development. Another provision allows members to take equity (a share in the eventual earnings of the production) rather than immediate wage payments when working on locally made films with small commercial potential. This provision increases union members' opportunities to work on productions that would not otherwise be able to afford to hire unionized workers. Another provision requires certain levels of Canadian staffing on productions funded by American-based companies; this ensures that Canadian union members have equal or preferred access to job opportunities generated by foreign productions.[54]

Generally, however, unions are reluctant even to suggest any form of non-traditional work arrangements, preferring to place a higher priority on maintaining the standards associated with full-time permanent employment and its attendant benefits. They fear that agreeing to any form of flexible work arrangements or non-traditional employment relationships in one collective agreement will weaken the union's ability to protect full-time permanent work in subsequent rounds of bargaining.

Having outlined some of the implications of new forms of work arrangements, we will now turn our attention to changes in the structure of the organization itself. This form of change can cause changes in the relationships between employees and managers.

CHANGES IN ORGANIZATIONAL STRUCTURES

As we have learned, unions evolved within the context of traditionally structured industrial organizations which have several distinctive levels of hierarchy, each of which has different amounts of power and decision-making authority. Authority and power increase at higher levels of the hierarchy, with the most power and responsibility concentrated at the top. Non-managerial workers are usually at the bottom of the hierarchy, which means that they have the smallest amount of power and responsibility in the organization. Figure 13-1 shows two examples of traditional organizational structures.

Figure 13-1
Traditional Organizational Structures

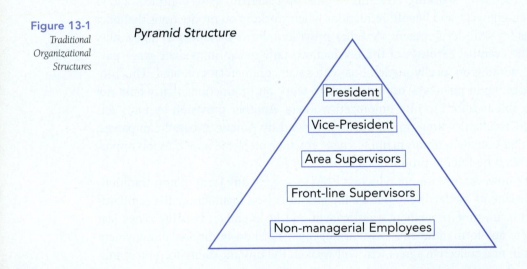

Pyramid Structure

President
Vice-President
Area Supervisors
Front-line Supervisors
Non-managerial Employees

Divisional Structure

Figure 13-1
*Traditional
Organizational
Structures*

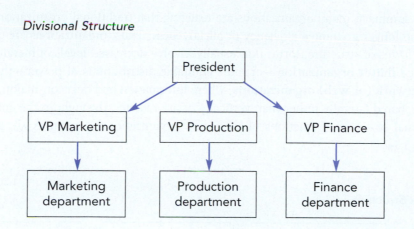

One of the motivations behind the formation of unions was dissatisfaction with the distribution of power and authority in traditionally structured organizations. Employees at the bottom of the hierarchy had little opportunity to participate in any decisions within the organization, even those that affected them. Unions became a means through which employees could be represented in the decision-making process for some issues (e.g., wages, overtime). Previously, the formal organizational structure had excluded their representation in such decisions.

A number of environmental changes beyond the emergence of unions have revealed the limitations of traditional organizational structures. Changes in markets, such as globalization, have necessitated the creation of new forms of organization to accommodate companies that conduct business in multiple locations or cultures. Changes in the purpose of organizations, such as broadened product or service offerings, have forced organizations to alter their structures so that new goals can be more easily achieved. As the rate of change increases in many industries and markets, the need for increased information flow and faster decision-making capability highlights the limitations of traditional structures, in which information flows from the top down and takes a considerable amount of time to disseminate throughout the entire organization.

In summary, many organizations are realizing that traditional organizational structures no longer guarantee efficiency or effectiveness. Thus, organizations are exploring newer forms of structure, forms that usually involve decreased levels of hierarchy—the so-called **flatter organization**—or more equitable distributions of power—the **matrix** and **network (or web) organizations**, where information and decision-making authority are shared laterally rather than vertically or are radiated throughout the entire organizational structure. Depictions of these new organizational structures are shown in Figure 13-2.

Figure 13-2
New Organizational Structures

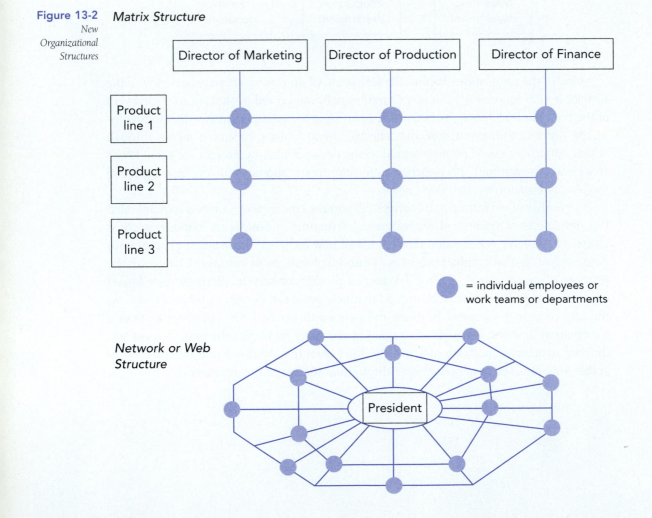

Matrix Structure

Network or Web Structure

The emergence of new forms of organizational structures may be beneficial for employers, but these structures are problematic for unions because they reduce or eliminate the traditional hierarchical distinctions between managers and employees. As we know from previous chapters, labour law makes clear distinctions between managerial and non-managerial employees and usually excludes managers or individuals with managerial duties from membership in a bargaining unit. These distinctions may make it difficult to unionize within an organizational structure where there are few or no clearly defined boundaries between management and employees.

One often-cited advantage of new forms of organizational structures is that the historically adversarial relationship between employees and employers is somewhat diffused, as managers may no longer have the sole authority to direct workers and workers are given much more autonomy in determining how their work will be conducted. However, this advantage can be problematic for unions. The union's function of representing workers' interests may be undermined if workers are allowed to have more formal input into decision making or are able to work more cooperatively with other parts of the organization, including managers.

Unions may also have to deal with practical problems associated with structural change, such as **downsizing** (the elimination of jobs or the reduction of work through such methods as changing full-time work to part-time), or changes in job content that reflect the new interrelationships in the organization. These problems may be difficult to address effectively within the context of labour law or collective agreements that implicitly assume traditional organizational structures or traditional manager-employee relationships.

More direct threats to the ability of unions to represent their members may be posed by changes associated with the forces of globalization. Globalization may mean that many jobs are moved from Canada to other countries where labour costs are lower, thus reducing the size and influence of the union as its membership base is eroded. Alternatively, globalization may mean that international companies entering Canada can change the practices of domestic industries, possibly causing reduced employment. For example, the Japanese automobile industry's entry into North America meant that many North American auto assembly plants, attempting to match the high-speed parts delivery of Japanese manufacturers, outsourced many component production processes that were formerly operated "in-house." Because of these changes, some Canadian firms moved parts of their operations to the United States, where workers were better trained and there was greater financial investment to ensure technology was the most current.[55]

UNION RESPONSES TO CHANGING ORGANIZATIONAL STRUCTURES

Dealing with new forms of organization and new manager-employee relationships is a balancing act for unions. On the one hand, the structure of the organization is sometimes changed to a form that encourages more cooperative worker-employer relationships. In such situations, the control and direction of the organization still remains with the employer, even with the most progressive forms of organizational structure, and thus unions still have a role to play in ensuring that workers' issues are addressed. Many unions fear that their compromise on structural issues will lead employers to expect similar compromises on more significant issues and that unions will eventually become ineffective as employees' advocates. Some unions thus feel compelled to resist structural change; such change does not represent any fundamental alteration to the allocation of power and control within the organization, and if they agree to structural changes, their ability to influence the employer in the future may be diminished.

On the other hand, structural changes are often undertaken to ensure an organization's continued vitality. In these situations, a union's adversarial opposition to change may impair the organization's chances for long-term survival. The union also has an interest in seeing the company succeed, because success and survival mean that the union maintains its membership base and its revenues. Therefore, even within a traditionally adversarial relationship, the parties do have at least one long-term common goal, and a union's willingness to support structural change may facilitate the achievement of that goal.

Two brief examples will demonstrate some of the ways in which Canadian unions have attempted to balance these competing positions when faced with organizational restructuring. The Canadian Auto Workers, while formally rejecting the idea of "employee partnership" or other forms of employer-employee cooperation, have undertaken certain cooperative initiatives, participating, for example, in a General Motors Quality Council headed by the president of GM Canada. The CAW has encouraged its locals to emphasize issues like quality control, training, and safe work practices on the shop floor as a means of discouraging restructuring that could lead to job loss. It was anticipated that the Canadian automobile industry would suffer greatly in the 1990s because of increased competition and jobs moving to the United States or Mexico as a consequence of the

North American Free Trade Agreement. However, independent research has indicated that Canadian automobile plants are now more productive and generate higher-quality output than plants in other North American locations, partly as a result of these initiatives.[56]

The Communications, Energy and Paperworkers Union (CEP) took a different direction in agreeing to a labour-management partnership at Saskatoon Chemicals. Historically, the CEP and plant management had had an acrimonious relationship, but changes in plant management and a recognition on the part of the union executive that strategic change was necessary for the company's continued profitability led to a re-examination of the relationship. The parties agreed to negotiate a significant work redesign involving joint union-management planning and "continuous bargaining," a change to a skill- and knowledge-based pay system, and "gain sharing" (sharing of profits among all employees). Some significant conflict involving this approach arose within the union membership, primarily with respect to how the redesign was to be implemented without the workers losing the gains that had been achieved in the past. However, the membership ratified the eventual agreement, and the new partnership has proved successful in developing and maintaining a high-performance work system and generating benefits for both parties.[57]

WHAT HAPPENS NEXT? FACTORS INFLUENCING THE FUTURE OF INDUSTRIAL RELATIONS IN CANADA

In the preceding section, we described some of the ways in which unions and employers have adapted to changes in the workforce, work arrangements, and organizations. However, as we have seen, many of these changes are not widespread, and it would appear that the majority of Canadian unions and employers are still following the more traditional models of union-management relationships. This resistance to change, whether intentional or unintentional, generates questions about what the future holds for industrial relations in Canada.

The Canadian industrial relations system has certainly been successful in maintaining and improving working conditions for unionized workers in Canada as well as for many non-unionized workers, thanks to the influence unions have had on overall wage rates and employment standards legislation. However, the context within which this system has been evolving is changing, and some researchers question whether a system based on an industrial and hierarchical model of organization can continue to be effective if that model is no longer dominant or practical. Other researchers point to the troubles faced by unions in the United States, which as we know has experienced a steep decline in unionization rates, and suggest that Canadian unions will soon encounter the same troubles. Still other researchers argue that the Canadian industrial relations system is healthy and will continue to be so in the future. We will conclude our discussion of future issues by outlining the factors that these researchers identify as being significant to the future of the Canadian industrial relations system, and speculating about the projected impact that these factors will have.

Legislation

As we know, one significant difference between the Canadian and American industrial relations systems is the allocation of jurisdiction over industrial relations and the effects of that allocation. In the United States, industrial relations legislation is the responsibility of the federal government, whereas in Canada there is a division of jurisdiction between the federal and provincial governments, with the primary responsibility for labour relations legislation assigned to the provinces. There is little consensus on whether the decentralization of Canadian labour legislation will help or hinder Canadian industrial relations in the future. Some researchers argue that decentralization is appropriate in Canada because the wide variations in labour markets and types of employment across the country make it more fitting to have different jurisdictions, each with the ability to create legislation appropriate for conditions in its area.[58] It has also been suggested that the centralized system of legislation in the United States has hindered the growth of unions in that country because centralized legislation cannot adequately address regional variations.[59] However, decentralization has also been characterized as hindering the growth of Canadian unions because of the need to change organizing, certification, and collective-bargaining strategies to accommodate variations in legislation across jurisdictions. While decentralized legislation is not a significant problem for employers or unions that work within a single jurisdiction in Canada, decentralization can become a major difficulty for employers or unions that operate in multiple jurisdictions, a situation that may become more common as businesses expand or merge to keep pace with regional, national, or international competition.

A more significant factor than jurisdiction over labour law, however, is the content of the laws themselves. The content of labour law is one area where American and Canadian industrial relations systems are very different, and this is one factor that is consistently identified as a reason why American union density rates have been lower than Canadian rates for the past four decades.[60] Canadian labour law is generally perceived as being more pro-union than American labour law because of differences in such areas as certification procedures, remedies available to labour relations boards in resolving disputes, protections for newly certified bargaining units, and the protection of striking workers.[61] Researchers have questioned whether Canadian legislators will come to perceive American laws as the more appropriate model to follow and whether Canadian legislation will be modified to give employers more power than they have in the current Canadian industrial relations system.

In the past decade, two provincial governments in Canada have made alterations to labour legislation which suggest that at least some Canadian legislators believe that the current Canadian industrial relations system does not "create an environment for employees, employers and trade unions to build healthy enterprises that can compete on a world scale."[62] The Conservative government of former premier Mike Harris altered the *Labour Relations Act* in Ontario in several significant ways during the 1990s. For example, the legislation governing certification had previously only required that the application demonstrate support from a majority of workers in the proposed bargaining unit, but the Harris government's amendment introduced a mandatory certification vote, regardless of the level of support demonstrated in the certification application. The result was an immediate decline in the number of certification applications and in the number of successful union organizing campaigns.[63]

More recently, in May 2002, the Liberal government of Premier Gordon Campbell made several major revisions to British Columbia's *Labour Relations Code*. The option of automatic certification has been removed, as discussed in Chapter 5, and the code has also been modified to give the British Columbia Labour Relations Board eight specific duties that it must consider in its interpretation and application of the code. (The previous version of the code established five criteria as "purposes of the Code" and only stated that the board must exercise its powers "having regard to [these] purposes".) These duties are:

- to recognize the rights and obligations of employees, employers, and trade unions under the Code

- to foster the employment of workers in economically viable businesses

- to encourage the practice and procedures of collective bargaining between employers and trade unions as the freely chosen representatives of employees

- to encourage cooperative participation between employers and trade unions in resolving workplace issues, adapting to changes in the economy, developing workforce skills, and developing a workforce and a workplace that promotes productivity

- to promote conditions favourable to the orderly, constructive, and expeditious settlement of disputes

- to minimize the effects of labour disputes on persons who are not involved in those disputes

- to ensure that the public interest is protected during labour disputes

- to encourage the use of mediation as a dispute-resolution mechanism[64]

The British Columbia *Labour Relations Code* was also altered so that the language governing communication during an organizing campaign permits "a person [to have] the freedom to express his or her views on any matter, including matters relating to an employer, a trade union or the representation of employees by a trade union, provided that the person does not use intimidation or coercion."[65] This language is considerably broader than the previous language in the Code, which stated, "Nothing in this Code deprives a person of the freedom to communicate to an employee a statement of fact or opinion reasonably held with respect to the employer's business."[66]

Changes in labour legislation are certainly not uncommon in Canada. However, their effect may be reduced by changes favouring a different policy direction. As one study of changes in Canadian employment legislation observes, "[A]djustments have usually been marginal, and they have often been offsetting, with reforms made by pro-labour governments subsequently offset by reforms from pro-business governments, and so forth."[67] Furthermore, changes to a single part of labour legislation may have a minimal effect if similar changes are not enacted in other parts of the legislation. For example, a change in the level of support required for certification applications may not have a major impact unless changes are also made in other regulations governing the certification process, such as regulations restricting employer or union conduct during the organizing campaign.

However, these changes in the British Columbia *Labour Relations Code* are considerably more extensive than any recent changes in other jurisdictions. In addition, the changes in the B.C. code were accompanied by extensive revisions of the British Columbia *Employment Standards Act*. These revisions include the following: a "training wage" of $6 (less than the existing minimum wage) has been established for employees with less than 500 hours of work; employers are now allowed to call employees in for a two-hour shift (the former minimum was a four-hour shift); and employers are now required to keep employee records for only two years. The revisions also changed how work hours are allocated by permitting the standard 40-hour workweek to be averaged across two, three, or four weeks; for example, employees could work 60 hours in one week and 20 hours in the next week without the employer being required to pay overtime for the 60-hour week. Taken together, these changes to British Columbia labour and employment law represent a significant shift in public policy—one that will likely be closely observed by other provinces.

It is obviously too soon to predict what effect these changes will have and whether they will be copied in other jurisdictions. Reaction to the changes in British Columbia has been mixed. The B.C. Federation of Labour has argued that the provincial economy is too unstable for changes of this sort to be introduced and that stability and cooperation are more important in ensuring competitiveness than are "minimal public protections of employee rights and interests with little enforcement, and a weakened ability for workers to organize to improve conditions through collective bargaining."[68] On the other hand, some businesspeople in British Columbia have argued that the changes do not go far enough and should have included such changes as greater freedom for employers to decertify inactive or bankrupt companies.[69]

Another factor affecting the impact of the British Columbia changes may be the way that the new legislation is being applied or interpreted, particularly in conjunction with the application or interpretation of existing legislation or case law. After the Ontario government imposed the requirement for certification votes, the Ontario Labour Relations Board continued to enforce the existing sanctions against employer interference in organizing campaigns and promptly held certification votes in situations where employer interference might have affected employees' voting intentions.[70] These actions may have somewhat offset the impact of the legislative changes. However, unlike the Ontario Labour Relations Board, the B.C. Labour Relations Board has been given legislated criteria to guide its decision making. The presence of such criteria may or may not change the outcome of such matters as disputed certification applications and grievance arbitrations. The B.C. Federation of Labour contends that legislating the use of these criteria "[will] reduce the flexibility of the Labour Relations Board and arbitrators in an attempt to tightly bind them to a 'checklist' approach, limiting their ability to give proper weight to other factors or fashion compromises that may be essential to a fair result."[71] It remains to be seen whether this prediction proves to be true and whether other Canadian jurisdictions will follow the precedent set by the British Columbia legislative changes.

Political Influence

Another factor that may affect the future of industrial relations in Canada is the amount of political power held or exercised by Canadian unions. As outlined in Chapter 3, the Canadian labour movement does not have a close formal relationship with a political party, as is the case in some countries. However, the Canadian labour movement has a historical affiliation with the New Democratic Party (NDP), and it is the declining political fortunes of this party that have led some observers to question whether this affiliation threatens to damage the future of the Canadian labour movement. Only 8.5 percent of voters supported the NDP in the 2000 federal election, and it is at present the governing party in only two Canadian provinces (Manitoba and Saskatchewan). In addition, the NDP governments in those provinces have been accused of abandoning the party's basic social democratic principles in favour of more centrist policies that emphasize themes of fiscal prudence.[72]

The low level of electoral support for the NDP and the apparent movement of the party away from its founding principles are not positive trends for the political influence of Canadian unions. In order to have a meaningful voice in shaping public policy, the Canadian labour movement needs to be aligned with a political party that has sufficient representation or support to achieve labour-friendly goals. It appears that the NDP is no longer able or willing to fulfill that role, even in those provinces where the party forms the government. No national political party has emerged as an adequate replacement for the NDP, and thus, unless the labour movement and the NDP are able to rebuild their formerly productive relationship, the labour movement must seek other allies through which to generate political influence.

For examples of these new kinds of alliances, we can look at the experience of unions in the United States. The American labour movement has historically lacked a significant alliance with a major political party. The Democratic Party is the national party whose philosophy most closely matches that of the labour movement, but even when the Democratic Party has been in control of the American government, the labour movement has found it difficult to promote labour law reform. Former president Bill Clinton was elected with the help of funding from American unions, and in return Clinton convened a commission to review possibilities for labour-business compromises on new labour legislation. However, the commission's work failed because unions could not agree on appropriate strategies for compromise and few employers were interested in participating.[73] The American union movement has also had to contend with nearly two decades of so-called neo-liberal monetary and investment policies; these policies are based on the assumptions that competitive markets are the most efficient form of economic regulation and that maximizing economic growth should be a primary goal of economic policy. Neo-liberalism, in the opinion of some researchers, has weakened union power by increasing unemployment and exacerbating income and wealth inequalities by reducing wages for low-skill workers.[74]

American unions have responded to their lack of political influence in several innovative ways. The American Federation of Labour-Council of Industrial Organizations (AFL-CIO), the American counterpart of the Canadian Labour Congress, has explicitly changed its strategic focus to include international issues such as global protectionism and international monetary policy. Rather than focusing on "narrow features," such as changes in labour law or the actions of a specific company, the AFL-CIO attempts to identify "systemic features" that affect all workers. This strategic direction acknowledges that the globalization of markets means that there will be competition between workers in all countries; hence, labour organizations should attempt to counteract this by promoting policies that benefit all workers rather than policies that foster competition.[75] The AFL-CIO has also formed alliances with groups that share its concerns about international policies; such groups include students, clergy, and social movement organizations. In general, the American labour movement can be seen as having recognized the limitations of the traditional model of business unionism and to be moving instead toward a model of social unionism that addresses the concerns of all workers, unionized or not.[76]

The Canadian union movement has also taken steps in this direction, even though Canadian unions have arguably not faced as extensive and systematic an opposition to their goals as American unions have. As described in Chapter 4, Canadian unions at the local, national, and international levels have formed alliances with other social activist groups. These alliances were most recently and visibly demonstrated through the participation of labour groups in the protests at recent G8 (Group of Eight) and WTO (World Trade Organization) meetings in Seattle, Quebec City, and Kananaskis. Many Canadian unions and labour federations have adopted policies similar to the AFL-CIO policies that address global and national trends affecting workers. Canadian unions have also been involved in mobilizing protests against perceived anti-labour and anti-worker policies at the federal and provincial levels (e.g., the B.C. Federation of Labour was a key player in organizing protests against the provincial government's cutbacks in social programs).

It is debatable whether these sorts of alliances will create the degree of influence necessary to significantly affect government policy and legislation. In the words of one author who examined the experience of American unions, "Refusal to rely exclusively on conventional political channels often provokes hostility on the part of economic and political elites."[77] In other words, alliances that attempt to exert influence in ways that do not follow the established processes for legislative or policy reform are often disregarded or marginalized, and they never succeed in achieving their goals. Canadian unions thus find themselves in a difficult situation; their existing political alliance is proving to be ineffective as the influence of the political party declines, yet alliances with other organizations may not generate sufficient influence to achieve desired outcomes.

Some Canadian unions have investigated another possible solution to this dilemma— "strategic voting," an option that uses the ability of unions to mobilize voters at election time.[78] The results of several studies of union influence on election outcomes have indicated that union members are more likely to participate in elections than non-union members. This phenomenon has been observed in most industrial democracies, including Canada and the United States.[79] A coalition of unions attempted to build on this tendency in the 1999 Ontario provincial election by encouraging union members in key constituencies to vote for the opposition (non-Conservative Party) candidate with the best chance of winning. This strategy represented a major shift from the traditional union election strategy of automatically supporting the NDP candidate, and it was therefore criticized for weakening support for the already struggling NDP. While the strategy did not succeed in ousting the Conservative government, it did achieve some success in the targeted constituencies.[80] If the Canadian labour movement wishes to achieve legislative and policy changes through established political processes, it may have to choose between attempting to rebuild the NDP as a political entity and actively supporting labour-friendly candidates who may or may not represent the NDP.

Union Organizing

The future of Canadian industrial relations will also be affected by whether Canadian unions are able to maintain or increase their current membership levels. If union density significantly increases or decreases, the Canadian industrial relations system will have to adjust to the reality of more or less union membership.

As discussed in previous chapters, Canadian union density has remained at approximately 30 percent of the overall workforce for the past decade. In contrast, union density in the United States has sharply declined from 25 percent in the late 1970s to less than 14 percent in 1999.[81] A variety of reasons have been cited for this difference, including Canadian legislation that offers better protection to organizing campaigns, the inability of American unions to resist concession bargaining and the associated erosion of previously achieved standards, and stronger affiliations

Though global, societal, and technological changes provide new challenges, the strength and vitality of unions in the future still rests with the individual member.

between unions and organized political parties in Canada than in the United States.[82] Better union security provisions in Canada, such as the Rand formula (discussed in Chapter 7) which requires all workers to pay union dues regardless of whether they actually join the union or not, have also been identified as a reason why Canadian union membership has not experienced the same drop as American union membership.[83]

However, Canadian unions cannot afford to become complacent simply because union membership in Canada did not decline during the period when American union membership was dramatically reduced. Canadian union density has not decreased, but neither has it shown any significant increase for some time. This plateauing has been attributed to a number of factors, some of which have been described in detail in earlier chapters. The Canadian public sector is highly unionized, but this sector of the labour market is not growing and has in fact been reduced in many areas because of downsizing and privatization. Unions have also not succeeded in creating a noticeable presence in the sectors of the labour market that have been showing growth: retail, sales, and service occupations, and part-time, temporary, and other forms of non-permanent jobs. In addition, Canadian law, unlike American law, permits workplaces to operate non-union representation plans in which workers are elected by their peers to meet with management and mutually solve problems that in a unionized workplace would usually be addressed through collective bargaining. These plans are guided by a formal worker-management agreement that parallels a collective agreement in structure and function. While their use is not widespread in Canada, these plans do offer an alternative to unionization that may be attractive to workers who do not want to join a union but still wish to have a formal voice in workplace operations.[84]

Clearly, membership growth rather than membership maintenance is a preferable strategy for unions because of the increased power associated with larger membership and the increased revenues from union dues. But will Canadian unions be able to pursue a strategy of growth given the stagnation of the past two decades? Opinions on this issue are mixed. On the negative side, it is argued that unions have only achieved very modest increases in density rates over the past 20 years for part-time workers and, in the same period, have made almost no improvement in density rates for major parts of the private sector labour market, such as financial industries, accommodation, food services, and professional occupations. This suggests either that unions are not successful when they do attempt to organize these types of workers or that their organizing attempts are minimal. Evidence suggests that the second scenario is the more accurate one. It appears that Canadian unions prefer to protect their bargaining successes rather than undertake organizing campaigns, and that they also prefer to organize in their traditional jurisdictions rather than venture into other industries and occupations.[85] This analysis suggests that a significant increase in union membership hinges on four conditions: unions should increase their commitment to the NDP; reciprocally, the NDP must make a commitment to support progressive labour laws; unions will have to commit considerable amounts of resources to organizing; and unions will have to "sell [their] attractiveness" to non-unionized workers.[86]

On the positive side, the major differences between American and Canadian labour law may at least ensure that Canadian union membership remains steady and that Canadian unions will therefore not have to direct their resources to addressing decreases in membership. Canadian labour law is much stricter than American labour law in restricting or outlawing the use of replacement workers during strikes, a characteristic that strengthens the ability of Canadian unions to gain desired outcomes in collective bargaining. Additionally, the process of certification is much easier in Canada because of the provisions in nearly every jurisdiction that certifications can be granted if sufficient membership support is demonstrated (American law requires a representation vote regardless of levels of support for the certification application) and because of strong sanctions against employers who interfere in organizing campaigns. These two forms of legislation have been cited as reasons why Canadian union membership has managed to remain consistent while American union membership has declined.[87]

In addition, while Canadian unions have not been completely successful in organizing some sectors of the Canadian labour market, there is evidence that Canadian unions are making attempts to adapt to changing workplace realities, as discussed earlier in this chapter. If unions are able to adapt their organizing, bargaining, and representation strategies to the needs of particular workers and workplaces, then it is entirely possible that union membership levels in Canada will grow. An example of this sort of adaptive strategy can be found, ironically, in the United States, in the case of unions in the entertainment industry. Work in this industry is characterized by many of the features cited as typical of modern employment practices: frequent changes of employer, non-permanent work arrangements, and job selection based on the opportunity to develop one's skills rather than on the hope of ongoing job security. Workers in these sorts of work arrangements are often considered too challenging for unions to organize successfully. Nevertheless, the entertainment industry is one of the most heavily unionized industries in the United States, and it has remained so over the past 70 years in the face of opposition from powerful and wealthy employers, legislation that is unfavourable to unions, and changes in technology that have affected methods of film production and distribution.[88]

How have the American unions in the entertainment industry maintained their status despite such formidable challenges? Three major strategies have been used to adapt to these different forms of opposition. First, the entertainment unions do not focus on bargaining individualized agreements for each workplace or project, aiming instead to achieve standard or national agreements with major employers. This bargaining structure forces unions to address major issues affecting overall employment rather than specific issues pertaining to individual jobs. Second, entertainment unions have bargained not only for wages, but for mechanisms that will protect their members' employment prospects and skill development. An example of these mechanisms is the system of residual payments that provides compensation each time a production is presented or reissued in a new medium. Residual payments allow union members to receive a share of all profits from productions they have participated in, and also provide income for members during periods of unemployment. Third, the entertainment unions place a high priority on providing services to members: for example, they notify them about auditions, give assistance in filing tax returns, provide systems for resolving disputes over production credits, and promote members' skills and experience to producers seeking workers with particular abilities.[89]

While this example is American based, it holds important lessons for Canadian unions facing organizing difficulties. It is apparent that if unions take a long-term rather than a short-term perspective in bargaining, do not focus solely on wage issues, actively adapt to changes in workplace conditions in ways that benefit the membership, and serve the specific needs of the membership, they can survive and even expand in an unfavourable environment. As mentioned earlier in this chapter, Canadian unions in the film industry have followed the lead of their American counterparts in negotiating contract terms that facilitate members' skill development without compromising standards that have already been achieved. Other Canadian unions may benefit from considering similar initiatives in their own negotiations or planning.

Finally, a recent Supreme Court of Canada decision has raised the possibility that unions may be able to increase membership by organizing workers previously excluded from unionization. In the case of *Dunmore v. Ontario (Attorney General)*, which was discussed in Chapter 1, the Supreme Court reversed the Ontario government's decision to exclude farmworkers from the coverage of the Ontario Labour Code. As mentioned in Chapter 1, it has been suggested that this decision may set a precedent that will permit unions to organize not only farmworkers but also other groups of workers who have generally been excluded from labour code coverage, such as professionals, domestic workers, and some types of public servants. The applicability of the precedent established by this case will only become apparent if organizing campaigns are undertaken for these groups of workers, but even now the decision does appear to offer another option to increase union density in Canada.

SUMMARY

Several significant changes have been occurring in Canadian workplaces and within the Canadian workforce. These changes pose a number of different challenges for Canadian unions. Young workers, female workers, and workers from visible minorities have special workplace concerns that Canadian unions have not always addressed; in addition, the employment patterns of these groups of workers make them difficult to organize. New forms of work and employer-employee relationships are not always accommodated by traditional union-employer relationships, and unions face problems in organizing workers who are in these forms of work, both in actually conducting organizing campaigns and in proving the value or relevance of union representation. Finally, changing organizational structures reduce power and authority distances between employees and employers, which makes the traditional adversarial relationship between unions and employers less applicable. Canadian unions have responded in different ways to these multiple challenges, but it is not yet apparent how successful these responses will be in the long term. The future of the Canadian industrial relations system will be affected by trends in legislation, political influence, and union organizing, but it is unclear what the directions of these trends are or what impact they will have.

KEY TERMS FOR CHAPTER 13

compressed workweeks (p. 524)
downsizing (p. 531)
flatter organization (p. 530)
flextime (p. 524)
job sharing (p. 524)

matrix organizations (p. 530)
network (or web) organizations (p. 530)
non-permanent employment relationship (p. 526)
non-standard work (p. 511)
participation rate (p. 516)
reverse discrimination (p. 519)
telecommuting (p. 524)
underemployment (p. 518)

DISCUSSION QUESTIONS FOR CHAPTER 13

1. Why are some unions opposed to part-time, temporary, contract, and other forms of non-traditional work?

2. What difficulties do unions face in organizing workers in service occupations?

3. What difficulties do unions face in organizing female workers, young workers, and visible minority workers?

4. This chapter identifies some of the techniques that unions have used in organizing diverse workforces and occupations that have historically had low rates of unionization. Can you think of other techniques that could be used to organize these workers and occupations?

5. Explain some of the difficulties in applying traditional labour relations processes to telecommuting.

6. How do traditional forms of organizational structure distribute power and authority?

7. Why are newer forms of organizational structure a challenge to traditional union-employer relationships?

8. After reading the discussion of the future of Canadian industrial relations, what do you think will happen to the Canadian industrial relations system and why? Can you identify other factors that may affect the Canadian industrial relations system in the years to come?

CASE *13-1*

JIM TURNER AND SUPERMARKET WORKERS' UNION AND MEGAMART STORES

(Based on *Robson and U.F.C.W., Local 1518*, 1999)

In this case, seven part-time student employees are alleging that the collective agreement negotiated by their union effectively gives part-time workers a lower rate of vacation pay than that mandated by the relevant employment standards act. They also allege that when they brought this matter to the union's attention, they were treated rudely by the union representative. They have filed a complaint with the labour relations board alleging that the union has discriminated against them and has not fulfilled its duty of fair representation.

Background to the Case

The Supermarket Workers' Union represents employees at several locations of Megamart Stores. In May 1997, seven part-time student employees at one Megamart location, led by Jim Turner, filed a complaint with the labour relations board. They stated that one clause in the collective agreement allowed 4 percent of total pay as vacation pay to employees who worked less than 1,700 hours during a calendar year, but the relevant employment standards act establishes a minimum of 6 percent vacation pay after five consecutive years of employment. The students said that the collective agreement restricts the number of hours that student or part-time employees are allowed to work each week and thus there was no way they would ever be able to achieve 1,700 hours of work in a calendar year. Therefore, they alleged, the collective agreement effectively restricted them to a 4 percent rate of vacation pay, which contradicts the employment standards legislation.

The students further alleged that when they called the union's head office in late February 1997 to bring this matter to the union's attention, they were "stonewalled and insulted" by Tom Lacey, a business agent for the union. In early March, the students sent a letter to the union president in which they claimed that Lacey "blam[ed] his inability to cooperate with us on everything from last summer's job action to the fact that he considered us 'cherry pickers' of the Labour Standards Act." They requested in the letter, a copy of which was submitted with the complaint, that Lacey formally apologize to them within the next two weeks.

Although the students stated that the union did not respond to their letter, the union provided the board with a letter dated April 2, 1997, and addressed to the students. The letter stated that the issue raised by the students was currently the subject of another grievance and that a copy of the arbitrator's decision in that case would be provided to the students when the case was complete. It is unclear whether this letter reached the students or not. The arbitrator had rendered a decision in this case in June 1996, and the union was in the process of appealing for a review of the arbitrator's award.

In their complaint to the board, the students asked that all holiday pay owed to employees affected by this clause in the collective agreement be paid, along with interest on that pay.

In the previous arbitration referred to in the union's letter, an employee at another Megamart location had 18 years' service but had received 4 percent vacation pay and two weeks' vacation in her most recent year of employment. The union argued in the arbitration case that the employment standards act established minimum standards of 6 percent vacation pay and three weeks' vacation and that the minimum requirements of the act should apply to every individual employee. The employer argued that the employment standards act should not override the collective agreement if the majority of employees effectively received the level of coverage stated in the act. The arbitrator decided that the legislation "requires [the arbitrator] to compare a group of statutory rights with a group of collective bargaining rights, [but] it does not require [comparison of] particular collective bargaining rights currently applying to a particular employee with a particular minimum requirement." Thus, the arbitrator dismissed the union's grievance. The union appealed the arbitrator's decision.

The Union's Position

The union stated that in its most recent round of bargaining, it had been faced with some "hard decisions" regarding contract provisions for vacation and vacation pay. It claimed that it had agreed to the current terms only after considering the options, ramifications, and legal implications of its choice. It also argued that it was not insensitive to the problems created by the new contract, as evidenced by its support of the grievance of the other Megamart employee and its willingness to appeal the arbitrator's award in that case.

   The union argued that it was not able to deal with the students' complaints until the appeal on the previous similar grievance was resolved. The union also stated that Lacey had explained this to the students when they contacted the union's head office, and if he had been "unhelpful and uncooperative," it was only to the extent that he had refused to put his answers to the students in writing at that time. However, the union stated, a letter with the same information given by Lacey had been sent to the students.

The Employer's Position

The employer argued that the matter of variations in vacation pay had already been addressed in the previous similar grievance and thus there was no merit to the current grievance.

The Complainants' Position

In responding to the union's and employer's position, the students argued that there were enough differences between their complaint and the previous grievance to warrant a "fresh interpretation of the facts." They also stated that the arbitrator's award contained "seriously flawed logic." They alleged that the union was discriminating against junior and part-time employees by negotiating contract terms, including job classifications, which placed those employees at a disadvantage in relation to other employees and to the conditions established in the employment standards act. They alleged that the union had violated its duty of fair representation by negotiating these contract terms.

CASE 13-2

TELEVISION ARTISTS UNION AND BROADCASTERS UNION AND NATIONWIDE NETWORKS

(Based on *Société Radio-Canada and Association des réalisateurs de Radio-Canada*, 2000)

In this case, the employer has undergone a major restructuring that involved the creation of new bargaining units and "cross-unit" job descriptions that fall into more than one bargaining unit. Two separate unions represent the different bargaining units of the employer. The union filing the complaint is alleging that in the most recent round of contract negotiations, the employer negotiated contract terms for the cross-unit jobs with the other union but not with the union filing the complaint. The union is thus asking the labour relations board to declare some of the terms of the resulting collective agreement null and void.

Background to the Case

Nationwide Networks operates two national television channels, Network One and Network Two. There are several kinds of employees at each channel: on-air personnel, production personnel, technical personnel, and office personnel. In 1997, Nationwide was faced with severe funding shortages and realized that it had to restructure its operations and create more flexibility in staffing at each network. Each network underwent a major reorganization, which resulted in changes to the composition of bargaining units. At both networks, there is one bargaining unit for technical workers and one bargaining unit for office workers. At Network One, there is now also a bargaining unit for production personnel and another bargaining unit for on-air personnel. However, at Network Two, production and on-air personnel are now in a single bargaining unit. Thus, Network One has four bargaining units and Network Two has three bargaining units. There is a separate collective agreement for each bargaining unit.

After the restructuring was completed, Nationwide decided that it could achieve flexibility in staffing by creating so-called cross-unit jobs. These are positions that are assigned tasks from the work of more than one bargaining unit. Nationwide felt that creating these cross-unit positions would give it more flexibility in assigning work. Bargaining for a new collective agreement began in mid-1997, and Nationwide was able to persuade all seven bargaining units to agree to language that created cross-unit jobs within each network. The unions and the employer agreed in principle that a job would become a cross-unit job when more than 40 percent of a worker's time was spent performing tasks outside of his or her basic duties.

Because of the re-certification that was required as a result of the restructuring, Nationwide was not able to negotiate new collective agreements simultaneously with all seven bargaining units, since not all of the new bargaining units had been formally created by the time negotiations commenced. At Network One, this meant that Nationwide commenced bargaining with the Broadcasters Union, one of the bargaining units for which the re-certification had been completed. The Broadcasters Union agreed to accept the "in principle" definition for the cross-unit jobs, but with one addition: that "cross-unit" jobs would also be created for any tasks done by both journalists and producers. However, the Television Artists Union objected to this part of the Broadcasters Union's agreement. The Television Artists Union represented the journalists at Network One and had not agreed to this much wider definition of cross-unit jobs than had been originally agreed to in principle. Thus, the Television Artists Union filed a complaint with the labour relations board alleging that Nationwide had not respected the union's jurisdiction as exclusive bargaining agent for the Network One journalists when it had negotiated contract terms with another union that affected the Television Artists Union's members.

The Employer's Position

The employer argued that it had not violated the union's jurisdiction as exclusive bargaining agent since its negotiations with each union had only involved the work that would be performed by that union's members. It also stated that all the unions had agreed to an "opening up" of jurisdictions that would result in job classifications' incorporating duties from more than one bargaining unit, and thus the union was aware that cross-unit positions would be negotiated and created.

The employer further argued that the collective agreement of one bargaining agent is not binding on another bargaining agent and thus the union could not claim that it had lost work from its bargaining unit. If there were any problems involving work assignment, the union had the option of pursuing a complaint through the grievance procedure.

The Union's Position

The union stated that its objection was not to the cross-unit job classifications, but to the fact that the cross-unit job classifications were defined differently in separate collective agreements. It also objected to the widening of the definition of these job classifications beyond what had been originally agreed to in principle, and it objected to the widened definition's including job tasks that were done by members of the bargaining unit represented by the union. The union argued that negotiating this broader definition amounted to breaching its jurisdiction without its consent and that the employer had bargained with another union for contract terms affecting the union's members.

CASE *13-3*

SUPPORT STAFF UNION AND CONSOLIDATED SCHOOL BOARD

(Based on *Cape Breton Victoria Regional School Board and C.U.P.E., Local 5050*, 1999)

In this case, two school districts have amalgamated, and the certification for the union representing support staff in both districts has been amended to reflect the employer's new structure. The union has now asked the labour relations board to further amend the certification to include a group of employees classified as "casual" workers. The union claims that these workers are in fact regular part-time workers and should be part of the bargaining unit.

Background to the Case

In early 1997, two school districts merged to form the Consolidated School District. The Support Staff Union was certified as the bargaining agent for support staff in each of the original districts. The union applied to the labour relations board to have the certifications amended so that one local would be formed from the two existing locals. The union also specified that the local should be an all-employee local and should exclude managerial staff, teaching staff, and any other workers excluded under the relevant labour legislation.

The board granted the union's request but noted that it would retain jurisdiction to make further rulings on the definition of an "all-employee" unit. The board was concerned about the status of employees who were classified as "casual" and "regular part-time" workers, especially since the two collective agreements governing the previous locals had different contract terms defining "regular part-time employee," "casual employee," and "temporary employee." Both collective agreements defined "regular part-time employee" similarly, but one collective agreement defined "casual employee" (and not "temporary") and the other defined "temporary employee" (and not "casual"). In both collective agreements, the difference between regular part-time employees and casual/temporary employees was that regular part-time employees worked scheduled shifts and casual/temporary employees did not.

The board asked the union and the employer to supply lists of casual or temporary employees in both of the former bargaining units. The lists that were provided contained approximately 350 names. The parties were able to agree that 174 of the employees on the lists were clearly casual or temporary workers. This left 176 workers whose status was unclear. The employer partially solved the problem of status by hiring 100 of these workers as regular part-time workers. However, this still left the status of 76 workers in dispute. These are the workers that the union is asking the labour relations board to include in the new bargaining unit.

Representatives of the school district told the board that the district utilizes a pool of approximately 150 to 225 casual workers and employs approximately 800 regular workers. The casual workers are called in to replace regular employees as needed; usually they are called in on the day they are needed or on the day before. They have the option of refusing work assignments if they are not available (e.g., if they are ill or are having difficulty obtaining reliable transportation to the work site), and are not penalized if they refuse an assignment. The casual workers can work for as little as a day, or they can work for up to six months in the place of workers who are on maternity or disability leave. Casual workers are also used for special projects of limited length—for example, as bus drivers for a designated extra trip.

Neither of the former collective agreements specifies any point at which a casual or temporary worker becomes a regular part-time worker, and neither sets any maximum time for which a casual employee can be used in a work assignment. One agreement states that after 10 continuous working days, casual employees must start paying union dues and that after 20 continuous working days in the same position, the casual employee must be paid the same wage as the employee regularly occupying the position. The other agreement states that temporary employees must pay union dues after 20 continuous working days.

The Employer's Position

The employer argued that the casual workers should be excluded from the bargaining unit because of the flexibility they offer to the employer in staffing and because of the cost savings associated with their use. The school district's representatives told the board that the board's ability to use casual workers has resulted in the board not having to lay off any regular full-time workers for the past 16 years. The availability of casual workers has allowed the school district the flexibility to quickly fill positions that might become vacant on very short notice (e.g., because of illness).

The Union's Position

The union argued that the casual employees should be included in the bargaining unit because these employees have an ongoing relationship with the employer. Although their hours of work might not be consistent and their work assignments vary, they still have a "continuity of employment" because they can be called on to work at very short notice.

The union also argued that employees who fill long-term positions—for example, those who are replacing employees on maternity or disability leave—cannot reasonably be considered casual workers. These work arrangements are not unpredictable and the length of the work assignment is known when the casual worker is offered the opportunity.

References

[1] Akyeampong, E. (2001). Fact-sheet on unionization. *Perspectives on Labour and Income* (Statistics Canada, catalogue no. 75-001-XPE), Autumn 2001, 46–54.

[2] Statistics Canada, CANSIM II data.

[3] For example, Gallagher, D.G. (1998). Youth and labor representation. In Barling, J., & Kelloway, E.K. (Eds.), *Young workers: varieties of experience*. Washington, D.C.: American Psychological Association.

[4] Lowe, G. S. (1998). The future of work. *Relations Industrielles*, 53(2), 235–257.

[5] Statistics Canada, 1996 census data; Canadian Council on Social Development (1999). *Youth at work in Canada: a research report*. Ottawa, ON: Canadian Council on Social Development.

[6] Statistics Canada, 1996 census data, available at <http://www.statscan.ca/english/Pgdb/People/Labour/labor46.htm>.

[7] Akyeampong, *op. cit.*

[8] Cited in Gallagher, *op. cit.*

[9] Barling, J., Kelloway, E.K., & Bremermann, E.H. (1991). Pre-employment predictors of union attitudes: the role of family socialization and work beliefs. *Journal of Applied Psychology*, 76, 725–731.

[10] Puette, W.J. (1992). *Through jaundiced eyes: how the media view organized labor*. New York, NY: St. Martin's Press.

[11] Akyeampong, *op. cit.*

[12] Statistics Canada Labour Force Survey data, cited in Zukewich, N. (2000). Paid and unpaid work. In Statistics Canada, *Women in Canada 2000* (Statistics Canada, catalogue no. 89-503-XPE). Ottawa, ON: Statistics Canada.

[13] Statistics Canada, CANSIM II data.

[14] Statistics Canada Labour Force Survey data, cited in Zukewich, *op. cit.*

[15] Swimmer, G., & Thompson, M. (1995). Collective bargaining in the public sector: an introduction. In Swimmer, G., & Thompson, M. (Eds.), *Public sector collective bargaining in Canada*. Kingston, ON: Queen's IRC Press.

[16] Akyeampong, *op. cit.*

[17] Swimmer & Thompson, *op. cit.*

[18] Yates, C.A.B. (2000). Staying the decline in union membership: union organizing in Ontario, 1985–1999. *Relations Industrielles*, 55(4), 640–671.

[19] Yates, *op. cit.*

[20] For example, Gordon, M.E., Philpot, J.W., Burt, R.E., Thompson, C.A., & Spiller, W.E. (1980). Commitment to the union: development of a measure and an examination of its correlates. *Journal of Applied Psychology Monograph*, 65(4), 479–499.

[21] Creese, G. (1995). Gender equity or masculine privilege? Union strategies and economic restructuring in a white collar union. *Canadian Journal of Sociology*, 20(2), 143–165.

[22] Zukewich, *op. cit.*

[23] Zukewich, *op. cit.*

[24] Sunter, D. (2001). *Demography and the labour market. Perspectives on Labour and Income* (Statistics Canada, catalogue no. 75-001-XPE), Spring 2001, 28–39.

[25] Sunter, *op. cit.*

[26] Sunter, *op. cit.*

[27] Sunter, *op. cit.*

[28] Dugan, B., & Robidoux, B. (1999). Demographic shifts and labour force participation rates in Canada. *Canadian Business Economist*, 7(2), 42–56. Cited in Sunter, *op. cit.*

[29] Sunter, *op. cit.*

[30] Palameta, B. (2001). Who contributes to RRSPs? A re-examination. *Perspectives on Labour and Income* (Statistics Canada, catalogue no. 75-001-XPE), Autumn 2001, 7–11.

[31] Kelly, K. (1995). Visible minorities: a diverse group. *Canadian Social Trends* (Statistics Canada, catalogue no. 11-008-XPE), Summer 1995, 4–14.

[32] Taylor, C. (1995). Building a case for business diversity. *Canadian Business Review* 22(1), 12–15. Cited in Dessler, G., Cole, N., & Sutherland, V. (1997), *Human resources management in Canada* (7th Canadian edition). Scarborough, ON: Prentice-Hall.

[33] Statistics Canada, 1996 census data. Cited in Statistics Canada, *Women in Canada 2000*, *op. cit.*

[34] Statistics Canada, 1996 census data. Cited in Statistics Canada, *Women in Canada 2000*, *op. cit.*

[35] Kelly, *op. cit.*, 9.

[36] Data from Statistics Canada, Demography Division, available at <http://www.statscan.ca/english/Pgdb/People/Population/demo03.htm>.

[37] Statistics Canada, 1996 census data, available at <http://www.statscan.ca:80/english/Pgdb/People/Population/demo25a.htm>.

[38] Creese, *op. cit.*, 144.

[39] Bourette, S. (1997). Organized labour lures growing number of youth. *The Globe and Mail*, July 4, 1997, B1.

[40] Hunt, G. (1995). Sexual orientation and the Canadian labour movement. *Relations Industrielles*, 52(4), 787–809.

[41] Hunt, *op. cit.*, 788.

[42] Gallagher, *op. cit.*

[43] Available at <http://www.clc-ctc.ca/youth/index.html>.

[44] Available at <http://www.csn.qc.ca/Jeunes/JeunesAcc.html>.

[45] Bulmer, P. (2001). Working locally: local labour councils bring the issues home. *CEP Insider*, 2(2), 6–7.

[46] Yates, *op. cit.*

[47] Lowe, *op. cit.*; Yates, *op. cit.*

[48] Galt, V. (1994). Reinventing the labour movement. *The Globe and Mail*, June 6, 1994. Cited in Craig & Solomon, *op. cit.*

[49] Kidd, K. (1994). Big Mac meets the McUnion Kid. *Report on Business Magazine*, June 1994, 46–50.

[50] Carlyle, N.B. (1997). *Compensation planning outlook 1997*, Conference Board of Canada. Cited in Dessler, Cole, & Sutherland, *op. cit.*

[51] Sullivan, S.E. (1999). The changing nature of careers: a review and research agenda. *Journal of Management*, 25(3), 457–484.

[52] Jones, C., & DeFillippi, R.J. (1996). Back to the future in film: combining industry and self-knowledge to meet the career challenges of the 21st century. *Academy of Management Executive*, 10, 89–103.

[53] Giles, A., & Starkman, A. (2000). The collective agreement. In Gunderson, M., Ponak, A., and Taras, D.G. (Eds.), *Union-management relations in Canada* (4th edition). Toronto: Addison Wesley Longman.

[54] Murphy, D.G. (1997). The entrepreneurial role of organized labour in the British Columbia motion picture industry. *Relations Industrielles*, 52(3), 531–553.

[55] Rutherford, T. (2000). Re-embedding, Japanese investment, and the restructuring buyer-supplier relations in the Canadian automotive components industry during the 1990s. *Regional Studies*, 34(8), 739–751.

[56] Frost, A.C. (2000). Union involvement in workplace decision making: implications for workplace democracy. *Journal of Labor Research*, 21(2), 265–286.

[57] Clarke, L., & Haiven, L. (1999). Workplace change and continuous bargaining. *Relations Industrielles*, 54(1), 168–191.

[58] Weiler, P. (1993). Promises to keep: securing workers' rights to self-organization under the NLRA. *Harvard Law Review*, *96*, 1769–1827. Quoted in Troy, L. (2000), U.S. and Canadian industrial relations: convergent or divergent? *Industrial Relations*, *39(4)*, 695–713.

[59] Lipset, S. (1989). *Continental divide: the values and institutions of the United States and Canada.* New York, NY: Routledge.

[60] Logan, J. (2002). How "anti-union" laws saved Canadian labour: certification and striker replacements in post-war industrial relations. *Relations Industrielles*, *57(1)*, 129–158.

[61] Taras, D.G., & Ponak, A. (2001). Mandatory agency shop laws as an explanation of Canada-U.S. union density divergence. *Journal of Labor Research*, *22(3)*, 541–568.

[62] British Columbia Ministry of Skills Development and Labour (2002). Backgrounder to the Labour Relations Code Amendment Act 2002. Document no. 2002-006. Available at <http://www.labour.gov.bc.ca/news/2002/2002-006.htm>.

[63] Martinello, F. (2000). Mr. Harris, Mr. Rae, and union activity in Ontario. *Canadian Public Policy*, *26(1)*, 17–33.

[64] Section 1, Bill 42 (2002), *Labour Relations Code Amendment Act*. Victoria, BC: Crown Publications.

[65] Section 3, Bill 42, *op. cit.*

[66] Section 8, *British Columbia Labour Relations Code*, 1997. Victoria, BC: Crown Publications.

[67] Gunderson, M., & Riddell, W.C. (1999). The changing nature of work: implications for public policy. Paper prepared for the Institute for Public Policy.

[68] British Columbia Federation of Labour (2002). Assessing the employers' wish list: comments on 'A Review of Labour Relations in British Columbia.' Submission to the British Columbia Minister of Labour. Available at <http://www.bcfed.com/news/media/extra/codebrief.htm>.

[69] Penner, D. (2002). B.C. reaction mixed to code changes. *Vancouver Sun*, May 14, 2002, A2.

[70] Logan, *op. cit.*

[71] British Columbia Federation of Labour, Assessing the employers' wish list, *op. cit.*, 10.

[72] Rose, J.B., & Chaison, G.N. (2001). Unionism in Canada and the United States in the 21st century: the prospects for revival. *Relations Industrielles*, *56(1)*, 34–65.

[73] Robinson, I. (2000). Neoliberal restructuring and U.S. unions: toward social movement unionism? *Critical Sociology*, *26(1/2)*, 109–139.

[74] Robinson, *op. cit.*

[75] Robinson, *op. cit.*

[76] Robinson, *op. cit.*

[77] Robinson, *op. cit.*, p. 112.

[78] Rose & Chaison, *op. cit.*

[79] Radcliff, B., & Davis, P. (2000). Labor organization and electoral participation in industrial democracies. *American Journal of Political Science*, *44(1)*, 132–142.

[80] Rose & Chaison, *op. cit.*

[81] Rose & Chaison, *op. cit.*

[82] Rose & Chaison, *op. cit.*; Logan, *op. cit.*

[83] Taras & Ponak, *op. cit.*

[84] Taras, D.G. (1998). Contemporary experience with the outlawed Rockefeller Plan. In Estreicher, S. (Ed.), *Employee representation in the emerging workplace: alternatives/supplements to collective bargaining*. Boston, MA: Kluwer Law International.

[85] Rose & Chaison, *op. cit.*

[86] Rose & Chaison, *op. cit.*

[87] Logan, *op. cit.*

[88] Gray, L., & Seeber, R. (1996). The industry and the unions: an overview. In Gray, L., & Seeber, R. (Eds.), *Under the stars: essays on labor relations in arts and entertainment*. Ithaca, NY: IRL Press/Cornell University Press.

[89] Watanabe, R. (1996). The fat lady can't get a gig: the union movement is alive and well in show biz. In Estreicher, *op. cit.*

GLOSSARY

(NOTE: THE NUMBER AFTER EACH ENTRY INDICATES THE CHAPTER IN WHICH THE TERM IS FIRST DISCUSSED.)

Abandonment of bargaining rights   A reason for **decertification** based on a union's failure to commence bargaining for a first collective agreement. (12)

Accreditation   The legal process by which a group of employers (employers' council) is certified as a single entity for bargaining purposes. (7)

Adjudicator   An alternate term for **arbitrator**. (11)

Affiliates   A term used by the Canadian Labour Congress to describe its member organizations. (4)

Anti-union animus   The motivation to undertake an action solely to weaken or attack a union or its members. (6)

Application bar   Timelines in labour legislation that specify certain times when applications for certification can be filed with a labour relations board if a previous certification attempt has failed. (6)

Application for Certification   The application submitted to a labour relations board by a union wanting to represent a designated group of employees. (5)

Arbitral jurisprudence   Decisions in previous cases that deal with interpretation and/or applications of collective agreement language. (8)

Arbitration process   In **grievance arbitration**, a series of steps through which a resolution to an employer-union dispute is achieved. (11)

Arbitrator   An individual who makes a final and **binding** resolution to an employer-union dispute. (11)

Attitudinal bargaining   A sub-process in bargaining that affects the parties' attitudes toward each other and toward their mutual relationship. (8)

Automatic certification   A process available in some Canadian jurisdictions allowing unions to be certified without a representation vote if a specified percentage of support is obtained from the members of the proposed bargaining unit. (5)

Back-to-work legislation   Legislation passed by a provincial or federal government to end a legal or illegal strike or lockout. (9)

Balance of probabilities   The standard of proof used in cases involving alleged unfair labour practices. (6)

Bargaining agent   After certification, the union's role as its members' representative in collective bargaining with the employer. (5)

Bargaining council   A group of unions who bargain as a single unit. (7)

Bargaining in good faith   The expectation that during collective bargaining, parties will bargain honestly and with the intention of concluding a collective agreement. (7)

Bargaining power   The ability of one side in bargaining to secure the other side's agreement to its terms. (8)

Bargaining unit   The group of workers represented by a union in collective bargaining. (5)

Beyond a reasonable doubt   The standard of proof used in criminal court cases. (11)

Binding   In the context of arbitration, an agreement by the parties that the arbitrator's decision will be final. (10)

Booking out   A mediator removing him or herself from the mediation process when he or she feels that his or her presence will no longer assist in solving the dispute. (10)

Bottom line   The absolute minimum that a negotiating team is prepared to accept as a settlement for a bargaining item. (8)

Boulwarism   The bargaining tactic of presenting a single offer, sometimes based on an employers' survey of union members' preferences, and refusing to negotiate any further. (7)

Boycott   A union request that its members not buy or use products or services from an employer whose employees are on strike or locked out. (9)

Business agent   A staff member of a union who administers the union's affairs. (4)

Business unionism   A type of unionism that focuses on protecting workers in a particular industry or occupation, or under a specific employer. (2)

Canadian Congress of Labour (CCL)   Founded in 1940 from a merger of the All-Canadian Congress of Labour and the American-based Council of Industrial Organizations, the second Canadian national labour federation after the Trades and Labour Congress. (3)

Canadian Labour Congress (CLC)   The largest national labour federation in Canada. (3)

Centrale des syndicats du Québec (CSQ)   A Quebec labour federation with membership primarily in the public sector. (4)

Certification order   An order issued by a labour relations board that names a union as the exclusive representative of the employees in a workplace and creates a collective bargaining relationship between the union and the employer. (6)

Charter of Rights and Freedoms   A part of Canada's constitution that guarantees certain basic rights to all Canadians. (3)

Chilling effect   In negotiations, the inability of parties to settle an agreement on their own because of continued reliance on third-party intervention. (10)

Clear and cogent evidence   The standard of proof used in grievance arbitrations involving serious employment offences. (11)

Closed shop   A union security provision requiring union membership as a condition of employment. Also known as a **union shop**. (7)

Common employer declaration   A declaration by a labour relations board that two separate businesses are a single entity. (12)

Commonwealth Trade Union Council   An international labour organization representing unions and federations in the Commonwealth countries. (4)

Community of interest   Some form of commonality among workers in a proposed bargaining unit that must be present for a labour relations board to grant certification to the unit. (5)

Company union   A union controlled by the employer. (5)

Compressed workweek   A form of work scheduling in which longer hours are worked over fewer days than in a normal work schedule. (13)

Concessions   A party's willingness to agree to the other side's proposal in negotiations or to adjust their own bargaining position. (8)

Conciliation   A form of third-party intervention in which the third party investigates a bargaining dispute and makes a report on its findings. (10)

Conciliation Act   An act passed in 1900 that created a federal department of labour and gave the department the ability to appoint third-party intervenors or commissions of inquiry to assist in resolving labour disputes. (3)

Confédération des syndicats nationaux (CSN)   A Quebec labour federation with over 2,000 member locals in various industries. (4)

Confederation of Canadian Unions (CCU)   A national federation formed in 1973 for Canadian-based and controlled unions. (3)

Confederation of National Trade Unions (CNTU)   A Quebec-based labour federation formed in 1961. (3)

Congress of Industrial Organizations (CIO)   An American labour federation that affiliated with several unions and labour federations in Canada. (3)

Consensual adjudication   An alternate term for grievance arbitration. (11)

Continental movement   A movement of American-based international unions who solicited membership in Canada during the mid-1800s. (3)

Continuing grievance   A grievance involving an ongoing practice rather than a single incident. (11)

Continuity   In the context of successorship, the criterion deciding whether there is evidence indicating linkages between a former and current business. (12)

Control   (1) In the context of reasons for unionization, the ability of a union to allow workers some degree of control over their workplaces or jobs; (2) in the context of successorship, the criterion deciding whether two businesses are owned and/or operated by the same party. (12)

Convention (or **congress**)   Regular meetings of union members or delegates where policies or a direction for the union are set through votes on motions. (4)

Craft union   A union that represents workers in a specific occupation, trade, or craft. (3)

Creature comforts   The ability of a union to improve its members' standards of living. (2)

Crisis   A bargaining stage in which parties decide whether to settle or to use economic sanctions to pressure an agreement. (8)

Cross-examination   An examination of one party's witnesses conducted by the other party during an arbitration hearing. (11)

Decertification   The process through which a union is removed as the legal representative of a group of employees. (12)

Deskilling   Management decisions that focus on designing a job to minimize the skills needed to perform it successfully. (2)

Device of restriction of numbers   Union structures such as apprenticeship that restrict the number of individuals employed in a craft or trade and control entrance to that craft or trade. (2)

Device of the common rule   Union structures that ensure the union's activities are guided by democratic principles and the vote of the membership. (2)

Direct examination   An examination of one party's witnesses by a representative of the same party during an arbitration hearing. (11)

Disputes inquiry board   A form of third-party intervention similar to conciliation that is available in some Canadian jurisdictions. (10)

Distributive bargaining   A sub-process in bargaining that consists of competitive behaviours intended to influence the distribution of limited resources. (8)

Downsizing   A temporary or permanent reduction in the size of a company's workforce. (13)

Dues check-off   A union security provision permitting union members to request that the employer automatically deduct union dues from their pay and forward the dues to the union. (7)

Duty of fair representation   The legal duty of a union to represent all its members fairly and without bias. (11)

Employer   An individual or organization that employs one or more individuals to carry out specified tasks, usually for pay. (1)

Employers' council   A group of employers who bargain as a single unit. *See also* **accreditation**. (7)

Essential service   A service whose provision is determined to be necessary to ensure public safety or health. (9)

Exempt employees   Non-management employees who may be excluded from a bargaining unit, usually because of access to confidential information. (5)

Expedited arbitration   An arbitration process which operates within predetermined timelines and which has the parties represent themselves in hearings. (11)

Fact finder   A form of third-party intervention similar to conciliation available in some Canadian jurisdictions. (10)

Fédération des travailleurs et travailleuses du Québec (FTQ)   The Quebec Federation of Labour who is affiliated with the Canadian Labour Congress. (4)

Final offer selection   A method of fashioning arbitration awards in which each party submits its final offer on each outstanding item and the arbitrator chooses some or all of the offer to create the award. *See also* **total-package final offer selection** and **item-by-item final offer selection**. (10)

Final offer vote   A method of resolving bargaining disputes in which members of one party vote on whether to accept the other party's final bargaining offer. (10)

Flatter organization   A redesigned organizational structure that has fewer hierarchical levels. (13)

Flextime   A form of work scheduling that allows employees to set their own working hours. (13)

Freeze   The requirement that working conditions established by a collective agreement remain in effect until a new collective agreement is completed. (7)

Friendly or uplifting unionism   A form of unionism that emphasizes the creation of social connections among the membership. (2)

Grievance   A dispute between the union and the employer over the interpretation, application, or administration of the collective agreement language. (11)

Grievance arbitration   The process through which employer-union disputes during the term of the collective agreement are settled. (11)

Grievance mediation   A process of grievance resolution in which a third party assists the parties in reaching their own resolution to a dispute. (11)

Grievor   An individual or party alleging that misinterpretation, misapplication, or improper administration of the collective agreement language has occurred. (11)

Group grievance   A **grievance** alleging that actions have affected a group of employees rather than a single employee. (11)

Hiring hall   A union security provision in which the employer contacts the union with job opportunities and the union provides qualified union members as job candidates. (7)

Hot declaration   A declaration by a union that its members will refuse to work with any product or service from a company whose employees are on strike or locked out. (9)

Implied obligations   The philosophy that if a union and employer collectively bargain to determine workplace conditions, any workplace issues not addressed by the collective agreement should also be resolved by mutual negotiation. (12)

Individual grievance   A grievance submitted by an individual union member regarding an alleged violation of the collective agreement affecting that member. (11)

In good standing   A requirement for officers of most labour councils; officers must be full members of their own union and follow the union's rules and policies. (4)

Industrial action   *See* **strike**. (9)

Industrial conflict   *See* **strike**. (9)

Industrial Disputes Investigation Act Federal legislation passed in 1907 requiring industrial disputes to be submitted to a third party for resolution. (3)

Industrial inquiry commission   A form of third-party intervention similar to conciliation

that is available in some Canadian jurisdictions. (10)

Industrial union   A union that represents workers regardless of their occupation or employer. (3)

Industrial Workers of the World (IWW) Also known as "Wobblies," an industrial union with socialist philosophies that recruited extensively in Canada during the early 1900s. (3)

Information   The ability of a union to improve its members' working lives by supplying information they would not otherwise receive. (2)

Instrumentality   The perception that a union will be able to help workers achieve desired outcomes in the workplace. (5)

Integrative bargaining   A sub-process in bargaining that consists of problem-solving behaviour focusing on common interests and joint gains. (8)

Integrity   The ability of a union to enhance its members' feelings of self-respect and fairness. (2)

Intentional discrimination   An action deliberately undertaken to deny opportunity to an individual on the basis of his or her personal characteristics. (1)

Interest arbitration   Arbitration that settles disputes during collective bargaining. (10)

Interests   The needs, wants, fears, concerns, desires, or other motivators of the parties in bargaining. (8)

International Confederation of Free Trade Unions (ICFTU) An international organization representing unions and federations throughout the world. (4)

International Labour Organization (ILO) A labour organization based in Switzerland that provides research and information about unions and working conditions worldwide. (4)

International union A union with membership in more than one country. (3)

Interprovincial component The part of a business's operations that cross provincial boundaries; it is used to determine whether federal or provincial labour law applies to the employees of the business.

Intra-organizational bargaining A subprocess in bargaining during which negotiators for each side attempt to achieve consensus within the bargaining team on goals and objectives. (8)

Iron law of oligarchy A principle suggesting that leadership of any organization will eventually be controlled by an elite whose actions are intended to maintain that control. (4)

Item-by-item final offer selection A form of interest arbitration in which the arbitrator creates a collective agreement by selecting one party's final offer on each individual bargaining item. (10)

Job sharing A work arrangement in which two workers share one full-time job. (13)

Jurisdiction The legal responsibility for governance of an issue or area. (1)

Justification In the terminology of the Canadian Labour Congress, a claim made by a member union to support its actions in attempting to certify another union's members. (4)

Key person doctrine A criterion used in **successorship** that examines whether employees with highly specialized or difficult to replace skills or knowledge who were employed by the former employer are now employed by the current employer. (12)

Knights of Labor An industrial union that recruited in Canada in the early 1900s. It distinguished itself by recruiting among previously unorganized workers and industries. (3)

Labour councils Organizations composed of union representatives from unions in a specific geographic area. (4)

Labour relations board A body established by a government to administer labour relations law. (1)

Local union (or **local**) The "smallest" unit of a union, representing workers in a particular industry or workplace. (4)

Lockout An action by an employer barring employees' physical access to the workplace. (9)

Lost person-days A calculation used to estimate the amount of working time lost because of strikes or lockouts. (9)

Make whole   The guideline used by labour relations boards in making decisions or remedies for unfair labour practices. It attempts to put the parties in the situation they were in before the unfair practices occurred. (6)

Management rights   The philosophy, often expressed in a clause in collective agreements, that management has the exclusive right to make decisions on workplace issues not addressed by the collective agreement. Also called the philosophy of **residual rights**. (12)

Management rights clause   A clause in a collective agreement giving management authority over any matters not specifically outlined in the agreement. (7)

Matrix organization   A form of organizational structure in which functional and productive departments are linked by sharing employees. (13)

Mediation   A form of third-party intervention in which the third party participates in bargaining and helps negotiators reach a solution on their own. (10)

Mediation-arbitration   A form of third-party intervention in which the third party acts first as a mediator, and, if negotiators are still unable to agree, then becomes an arbitrator who determines solutions to bargaining disputes. (10)

Method of collective bargaining   The method of achieving a union's goals through negotiating with the employer. (2)

Method of legal enactment   The method of achieving a union's goals by pressuring a government to pass legislation supporting unionism and workers' rights. (2)

Method of mutual insurance   The method of achieving a union's goals by using part of the union dues to support workers who are injured or sick. (2)

Monopoly laws   British laws passed during the late 1800s that were intended to counteract restraints of trade but were instead used to restrict the growth of unions. (3)

Narcotic effect   In negotiations, the parties' unwillingness or reluctance to settle disputes on their own because third-party intervention is available. (10)

Network (or web) organization   A form of organizational structure in which individuals or departments are linked by connections and not by hierarchical levels. (13)

Nine-Hour Movement   A movement in Central Canada during the late 1800s that lobbied for legislation to restrict the working day to nine hours. (3)

Non-permanent employment relationship   Any form of employer-employee relationship where the employee is not indefinitely employed by the employer (e.g., contract work or temporary work). (13)

Non-standard work   Any work relationship other than full-time permanent employment. (13)

North American Free Trade Act (NAFTA)   Legislation that reduces or removes trade barriers among North American countries. (3)

Notice to bargain   A formal notice issued by one party to the other after which collective bargaining must usually commence. (7)

One Big Union (OBU)   An American-based international union that recruited extensively in Western Canada during the early 1900s. (3)

Open periods   Times during which an application for certification can be filed with a labour relations board. (6)

Organizing campaign   The campaign undertaken by a union to persuade workers to express support for the union as their representative. (5)

Outsourcing   Removing jobs or tasks from an organization and contracting other organizations or individuals to perform those jobs or tasks. (5)

P.C. 1003   A Canadian order-in-council passed during World War II. It was the first piece of Canadian legislation to contain the principles of the American *Wagner Act*. (3)

Para-public/quasi-public sector   The labour market sector consisting of organizations funded by the government but not directly operated by the government (e.g., schools and hospitals). (1)

Parent union   A regional, national, or international union composed of locals. (4)

Participation rate   The number or percentage of individuals in a demographic group who are employed or otherwise in the labour market. (13)

Past practice   In the context of grievance arbitration, the acceptance of a previous or consistent violation of the collective agreement when a current occurrence of the same violation is now the subject of a grievance. (11)

Pattern bargaining   A bargaining strategy used when there are multiple employers in a single industry; the contract negotiated with one employer is used as a pattern for contract demands in negotiations with the other employers. Also known as **whipsawing**. (7)

Picket line   A demonstration outside the employer's place of business by employees on strike or locked out. *See also* **secondary picketing**. (9)

Policy grievance   A **grievance** filed by a union alleging that an employer's incorrect action has affected all employees. (11)

Position   The preferred outcome of one side in negotiations. (8)

Predatory unionism   A form of unionism in which unions are primarily concerned with increasing their power by any means possible. (2)

Primary industry   A resource-based industry such as mining or forestry. (3)

Procedural onus   In the context of an arbitration hearing, the expectation that one party to the alleged offence bears the responsibility of proving its actions were justified. (11)

Professional strikebreaker   An individual hired specifically to do the work of an employee on strike. The use of these individuals is illegal in some Canadian jurisdictions. (9)

Protected grounds   Personal characteristics (e.g., gender or ethnic background) defined in provincial and federal human rights legislation as factors which are forbidden from being used as the basis of discrimination. (1)

Provincial labour federation   A federation representing unions and labour councils in a specific Canadian province or territory. (4)

Psychology of the labourer   The principle underlying the idea that unions should be controlled by workers rather than intellectuals because workers are better able to understand the working-class experience. (2)

Public sector   The labour market sector consisting of municipal, regional, provincial, and federal government employment. (1)

Quasi-judicial   Having regulatory, enforcing, or interpretive powers similar to those of a civil or criminal court, but not operating in exactly the same manner. (1)

Quebec Federation of Labour (FTQ)   A Canadian Labour Congress-affiliated federation of Quebec unions. (4)

Raid   An attempt by a union to certify workers already belonging to another union. (6)

Rand formula   A collective agreement provision that permits workers to choose whether or not to join a union, but requires all workers in a unionized workplace to pay union dues regardless. (3)

Ratification   The bargaining stage in which the parties present the negotiated agreement to the constituencies they represent for approval. (8)

Ratification vote   A vote conducted by a union at the end of collective bargaining to determine whether bargaining unit members accept the negotiated agreement. (9)

Recognition strike   A strike intended to pressure an employer into recognizing a union as the legal representative of the employees. (9)

Re-examination   In a grievance hearing, the process in which one party's advocate can ask further questions of a witness supporting that party after the witness has been cross-examined. (11)

Relieve   In the context of grievance arbitration, the ability of the arbitrator to hear complaints that might otherwise be disqualified on procedural grounds (e.g., a complaint filed after a predetermined deadline). (11)

Religious exemption   A union security provision that allows workers whose religious beliefs discourage union membership to pay a sum equal to union dues to a mutually agreed upon charity. (7)

Reopener clause   A clause in a collective agreement permitting the union and management to renegotiate terms of the agreement before its expiry date without renegotiating the entire agreement. (12)

Replacement workers   Workers who carry out work usually done by union members who are on strike or locked out. (9)

Representation vote   A vote conducted by a labour relations board to determine whether employees wish to be represented by a union or not. (6)

Residual rights   *See* **management rights**. (12)

Reverse discrimination   When preference in access to services or employment is given to a designated demographic group, the discrimination that may result against individuals who do not belong to that group. (13)

Reverse onus   In unfair labour practice complaints against the employer, the expectation that the employer must prove its actions were not motivated by anti-union animus. (6)

Revolutionary unionism   A form of unionism in which unions are primarily agents for large-scale social change. (2)

Rights   The formalized powers of the parties in a negotiation. (8)

Rights arbitration   An alternative term to **grievance arbitration**, referring to the fact that grievance arbitration may deal with whether the employer or the union has the right to determine outcomes for matters not addressed in the collective agreement. (11)

Rotating strike   A strike action where different units of an employer's operation go on strike at different times. (9)

Scab   A slang term for an individual who does the work of employees on strike. (9)

Secondary industry   Industries such as manufacturing that process the products of resource industries. (3)

Secondary picketing   Picketing at a location of the employer which is not on strike, or picketing business associates of a struck or locked-out employer. (9)

Settlement orientation   An approach to **grievance mediation** in which grievance mediation is imposed by legislation and the parties are pressured to reach an agreement. (11)

Shop steward   A union member who acts as the union representative in the workplace. (4)

Single employer (common employer)   A declaration issued by a labour relations board when multiple businesses are under common control. The effect of the declaration is to treat all the businesses as a single employer for the purposes of certification. (5)

Social status   The ability of unions to improve their members' status in the community or workplace or within the union itself. (2)

Special mediator   A mediator appointed at any time during collective bargaining, generally with a wider range of powers than "regular" mediators. (10)

Standard of proof   Guidelines to assist arbitrators in determining which party's case should be upheld or accepted. *See also* **reasonable doubt**, **clear and cogent evidence**, and **balance of probabilities**. (11)

Strike   An action where bargaining unit members withdraw their labour. (9)

Strike mandate   An indication by bargaining unit members that they are willing to undertake strike action. *See also* **strike vote**. (9)

Strike pay   Payments given by the union to workers on strike to offset their loss of employment income. (9)

Strike vote   A vote by bargaining unit members to authorize strike action by the union. It is required in most Canadian jurisdictions prior to a strike for the strike to be legal. (9)

Subpoena   A legal order issued by an arbitrator for a party to testify or to provide evidence at an arbitration hearing. (11)

Successorship   The legal obligation of an employer to continue its relationship with a union if the company undergoes changes. (12)

Surface bargaining   Engaging in collective bargaining without any intention of concluding a collective agreement. (7)

Sweetheart agreement   A collective agreement that unduly favours the employer's interests. (5)

Systemic discrimination   Discrimination caused by policies or practices which have the effect of excluding particular individuals or groups, even if the policies or practices were not established with the intent to create discrimination. (1)

Technological change   A change to the technology used to perform a job that may entail changes in the structure or content of the job itself. (12)

Telecommuting   A work arrangement involving computers, fax, telephone, or any technology permitting a worker to work from someplace other than the employer's premises. (13)

Terminal date   In some Canadian jurisdictions, the date by which all submissions related to an application for certification must be received by a labour relations board. (6)

Tertiary industry   Service industries and other non-resource related industries. (3)

Time bar   Restrictions in Canadian labour law that specify times when organizing campaigns can take place in a workplace. (6)

Total-package final offer selection   A form of interest arbitration in which the arbitrator creates a collective agreement by accepting the entire final offer of one party. (10)

Trades and Labour Congress (TLC)
Formed in 1883, the first truly representative national labour federation in Canada. (3)

Trades Union Advisory Committee of the Organization for Economic Co-Operation and Development (TUAC-OECD)   An international committee of labour unions which provides information on labour-related issues to OECD members. (4)

Transaction costs   Costs incurred in negotiations through expenditure of time, money, resources, and emotional energy. It also includes the cost of opportunities lost because of disagreement between the parties. (8)

Transformative orientation   An approach to **grievance mediation** in which the parties to the dispute are educated to resolve their own disagreements. (11)

Underemployment   When an individual is employed in a job requiring a lower level of training, experience, or education than that he or she possesses. (13)

Unfair labour practice   Any activity or behaviour by a union or employer that has the effect of unduly influencing employees. (5)

Union   A group established by and for workers to represent them in the workplace. (1)

Union dues   Membership fees paid to the union by its members. (5)

Union executive   A group elected by union members to run a local union. (4)

Union security   Structures and processes put into place after certification that assist the union in its ability to fully represent its members. (7)

Union shop   *See* **closed shop**. (7)

Voluntary recognition   When an employer accepts a union as the employees' representative in the workplace without the union having to go through the process of certification. (5)

Wagner Act   Federal legislation passed in the United States in 1935 that gave workers the right to unionize and legally strike, and compelled employers to bargain with unions. It was the basis for P.C. 1003 and subsequent labour legislation in Canada. (3)

Whipsawing   *See* **pattern bargaining**. (7)

Wildcat strike   A strike that occurs spontaneously without a strike vote or strike mandate. (9)

Winnipeg General Strike   A strike that occurred in 1919 and was the first long, large-scale general strike in Canadian history. (3)

Workplace restructuring   Changes to jobs or to an entire workplace or workforce (e.g., downsizing, relocation, or job redesign). (12)

Work-to-rule campaign   A form of industrial action in which bargaining union members rigidly adhere to collective agreement terms. (9)

Zone of agreement   A range of potential solutions to bargaining issues which are acceptable to both parties. (8)

PHOTO CREDITS

CALM=Canadian Association of Labour Media
CP=Canadian Press Archive
NAC=National Archives of Canada
TVO=TV Ontario, Visual Research Department.

2: PhotoDisc/Getty Images Ltd. 5: (left) De Havilland Aircraft; (right)British Columbia Ministry of Energy, Mines and Petroleum Resources. 12: Gerry Richard/CN Images of Canada Gallery. 19: Robert Cooper/NAC/PA-140705. 21: Canadian Tourism Commission. 34: PhotoDisc/Getty Images Ltd. 36: TVO. 39: Metro Toronto Library Board. 43: NAC/C-30945. 56: W. Harland/Mail & Empire. 66: B.C. Archives/E-01194. 75: NAC/PA-103086. 82: Provincial Archives of Manitoba/Foote 1696(N2762). 86: TVO. 95: NAC/PA-163000. 112: Bryan Schlosser/CP. 119: Randy Quan/CP. 124: Steve McKinley/CP. 139: CALM. 145: Derek Oliver/Photo Features. 152: McDonald's Restaurants of Canada Ltd. 156: Dave Chidley/CP. 165: Saskatchewan Federation of Labour/CALM. 169: Michael Stuparyk/CP. 176: Ryan Remiorz/CP. 192: PhotoDisc/Getty Images Ltd. 197: Len Norris/Simon Fraser University. 202: Health Canada. 211: B.C. Archives/G-05174. 217: Andrew Vaughan/CP. 230: Steve Russell/CP. 237: General Motors of Canada. 247: Canadian Union of Public Employees, Local 43. 252: Don Tremain/PhotoDisc/Getty Images Ltd. 268: Robert Skinner/CP. 272: Aaron Harris/CP. 287: Kevin Frayer/CP. 291: Eric Parker. 316: Bob Leonard/CP. 329: John E. Lightfoot Jr./CP. 331: Toronto General Hospital, Media Support. 337: Jeff McIntosh/CP. 349: Len Norris/Simon Fraser University. 364: PhotoDisc/Getty Images Ltd. 371: NAC/PA-120633. 383: Len Norris/Simon Fraser University. 390: Larry MacDougal/CP. 398: Colleen Kidd/CP. 409: NAC/PA-115252. 415: Tom Hanson/CP. 426:Suzanne Plunkett/CP. 452: Marcos Townsend/CP. 454: Avard Productions Inc./CAW. 467:Joe Gibbons/CP. 476: Eric Parker. 481: Randy Turner/CP. 508: CP. 514: Health Canada. 522: Chuck Stoody/CP. 525: Keith Brofsky/ PhotoDisc/ Getty Images Ltd. 541: CALM.

INDEX